COMPUTER SECURITY
AND CRYPTOGRAPHY

THE WILEY BICENTENNIAL—KNOWLEDGE FOR GENERATIONS

$\mathcal{E}$ach generation has its unique needs and aspirations. When Charles Wiley first opened his small printing shop in lower Manhattan in 1807, it was a generation of boundless potential searching for an identity. And we were there, helping to define a new American literary tradition. Over half a century later, in the midst of the Second Industrial Revolution, it was a generation focused on building the future. Once again, we were there, supplying the critical scientific, technical, and engineering knowledge that helped frame the world. Throughout the 20th Century, and into the new millennium, nations began to reach out beyond their own borders and a new international community was born. Wiley was there, expanding its operations around the world to enable a global exchange of ideas, opinions, and know-how.

For 200 years, Wiley has been an integral part of each generation's journey, enabling the flow of information and understanding necessary to meet their needs and fulfill their aspirations. Today, bold new technologies are changing the way we live and learn. Wiley will be there, providing you the must-have knowledge you need to imagine new worlds, new possibilities, and new opportunities.

Generations come and go, but you can always count on Wiley to provide you the knowledge you need, when and where you need it!

WILLIAM J. PESCE
PRESIDENT AND CHIEF EXECUTIVE OFFICER

PETER BOOTH WILEY
CHAIRMAN OF THE BOARD

COMPUTER SECURITY AND CRYPTOGRAPHY

ALAN G. KONHEIM

WILEY-INTERSCIENCE
A JOHN WILEY & SONS, INC., PUBLICATION

About the Cover: The term *cipher alphabet* is used when referring to a *monoalphabetic* substitution. When text is written using the letters A, B, ..., Z, a cipher alphabet is a permutation or rearrangement of the 26 letters. In the fifteenth century, cryptography became more sophisticated and cryptographers proposed using multiple cipher alphabets, a process referred to as *polyalphabetic* substitution. Blaise de Vigenère's book *A Treatise on Secret Writing* published in the sixteenth century contains the basic *Vigenère tableux*, specifying the ciphertext in polyalphabetic substitution. Rotor machines introduced in the 20*th*-century provided mechanical means for implementing and speeding up polyalphabetic substitution.

The cover is a *modified* set of 17 cipher alphabets; the black background color is symbolic of the U.S. State Department's *Black Chamber* in which American cryptanalysis originated in the early part of the 20*th*-century. It is technically defective in several aspects (*i*) fewer than 26 letters in each row are displayed and (*ii*) repeated letters occur in the rows containing the word CRYPTOGRAPHY and my name.

Nevertheless, the cover hopefully projects the message to read *Computer Security and Cryptography*.

Copyright © 2007 by John Wiley & Sons, Inc. All rights reserved

Published by John Wiley & Sons, Inc., Hoboken, New Jersey
Published simultaneously in Canada

For general information on our other products and services or for technical support, please contact our Customer Care Department within the United States at (800) 762-2974, outside the United States at (317) 572-3993 or fax (317) 572-4002.

Wiley also publishes its books in a variety of electronic formats. Some content that appears in print may not be available in electronic formats. For more information about Wiley products, visit our web site at www.wiley.com.

Library of Congress Cataloging-in-Publication Data:

Konheim, Alan G., 1934–
    Computer security & cryptography / by Alan G. Konheim.
       p. cm.
    Includes bibliographical references and index.
    ISBN-13: 978-0-471-94783-7
    ISBN-10: 0-471-94783-0
1. Computer security. 2. Cryptography. I. Title.
    QA76.9.A25K638 2007
    005.8--dc22   2006049338
Printed in the United States of America

10 9 8 7 6 5 4 3 2 1

CONTENTS

CHAPTER 7   THE JAPANESE CIPHER MACHINES

CHAPTER 8   STREAM CIPHERS

CHAPTER 9   BLOCK-CIPHERS: LUCIFER, DES, AND AES

CHAPTER 10   THE PARADIGM OF PUBLIC KEY CRYPTOGRAPHY

CHAPTER 11   THE KNAPSACK CRYPTOSYSTEM

CHAPTER 12   THE RSA CRYPTOSYSTEM

FOREWORD

It's not easy being a writer on cryptology. Actually, it's not easy being a writer. You have to think about what subjects you want to cover. Then you have to decide in what order you want to put them—not so simple, because the most logical progression isn't always the best for teaching. Then comes the worst part: You actually have to cover a blank screen or sheet of paper with letters and figures that make sense.

Alan Konheim has sweated through it many times. He has written a number of technical articles, which demonstrates that he has mastered the technicalities of his subject. And he has passed through the fire of book authorship once before, in his acclaimed *Cryptography: A Primer*. In the years that followed, he has learned what worked in that book and what didn't, and has applied those lessons in the present work. The result is a fine amalgam of scholarship and pedagogy.

But if the elements of writing—clarity and concision—have remained the same, cryptology has not. For centuries, it was axiomatic that both en- and decipherer had to have the same key, though used inversely. The invention of public-key cryptography abolished that axiom. It has transformed and energized the practical applications of cryptography. Many of these remain grounded in the classical, or symmetric, systems of cryptography. And the enormous expansion of communications has driven its child, secret communications, into vast new fields. Once the exclusive domain of soldiers and diplomats and spies, cryptology has become almost ubiquitous. People use it without knowing that they are doing so. Every time a person uses an automatic teller machine, his or her transaction is encrypted. So are online bank transactions. Whenever anyone sends his or her credit card number securely to, say, E-bay or Amazon, he or she is using cryptography.

And the field has emerged from the shadows, The National Security Agency, once so secret that it was referred to as "No Such Agency," is now mentioned in movies and on the evening news almost without any identification, just as the CIA and FBI are. The post-9/11 flap over the Bush administration's warrantless wiretapping has further brought cryptology, the NSA, and privacy into the open. The International Association for Cryptologic Research publishes its *Journal of Cryptology* four times a year. The aura of mysticism that long enshrouded it has been dispelled by the cold logic of mathematics that now dominates it.

Alan Konheim knows all about this because he worked for IBM when it was a leader in the field of cryptology and because he has kept up with new developments, as his many technical articles demonstrate. His experience in teaching tells him what questions students are likely to ask and what problems in understanding they are likely to encounter. His previous book has taught him how to explain complicated matters effectively. The result is this excellent book, which joins the permanent qualities of its writing to the immediacy of its coverage. Cryptologists—beginners and veterans alike—will welcome it. As do I.

Long Island, New York   DAVID KAHN
October 2006

ix

PREFACE

NATIONAL SECURITY AND COMPUTER SECURITY

On September 11, 2001, the word *security* moved into the foreground of our national consciousness, where it continues to reside today. The presidential election in 2004 was largely decided on the basis of which candidate was perceived to best manage security for the American people. Americans are puzzled about the hatred expressed by certain ideologies and foreign governments about our way of life and culture. The missions of the National Security Agency/Central Security Service (CSS) include both the protection of U.S. communications and the production of foreign intelligence. Although cryptography plays a role in both of these areas, this book is not about either.

This book is about the role of cryptography in our day-to-day lives. Today, there is no activity that does not depend on computers. When there is a power outage in Santa Barbara, I often cannot buy *Twinkies* at the supermarket, to my dismay and that of the merchant, but to the delight of my endocrinologist. The use of traveler's checks has declined because of the convenience and availability of ATM machines. Vast amounts of data are maintained by banks and credit card companies. Stories of their mismanaging customer data appear regularly in the news. Identity theft is well on its way to becoming a flourishing industry. Credit card companies now have the nerve to advertise identity theft insurance to protect the information that they are legally obliged to guard, but fail to do so.

Cryptography has a role to play in many areas. Like seat belts, it will not completely protect us. In the chapters that follow, I will develop the basic ideas about cryptography and then illustrate some of the ways it interacts with and protects us.

WHY STUDY CRYPTOGRAPHY?

There is a symbiotic relationship between cryptography and the development of high-performance computing systems. Modern-day computers were created at the behest of twentieth-century cryptanalysts. As the complexity of cryptographic systems progressed from mechanical to electronic systems, so did the need to develop more efficient methods to cryptanalyze them.

Every cryptosystem, which has a finite number of keys, can usually be analyzed by *key trial*, deciphering the ciphertext with all possible keys until some recognizable text appears. In many "classical" cryptographic systems, the testing of keys could be performed by hand. The stimulus for the development of computers was the need to be able to test large sets of possible keys to decipher coded traffic. Modern cryptosystems are such that the number of possible keys is generally so large as to make exhaustive key trial infeasible. Even computers are limited, and some analysis must precede key testing for the process to be successful.

The marriage of computing and cryptography provides a marvelous real-life application of mathematics, and develops the inference skills that are fundamental to engineering and science. When a student first views the ciphertext

```
To-drijohrunurmanpmlgchd-ehapuotp,te-nmabsno-nitioippmbo-a-a
sTasm-h-op-ms-vye-m.ikndu-n-atscegnetoin-l-rs-v-e-u-ta-olati
s-t-sccw——eorrgdhgngP.r-stenvercenhnerhchoie-nun-sr-tois-rma
eaeeadadrssou-o-etat-iefeotifc-m-a——ergua-eiuo-oixeordalmyes
```

there may be confusion. Word fragments may be detected, but how can the text be recovered? After students learn to critically examine the ciphertext, they are often capable of deciphering it. Cryptography teaches students how clever they can be. Of course, instructors should caution their students as the television commercials for ED advise; to wit, if their efforts in cryptanalyzing some ciphertext "last more than four hours, they should seek tutorial assistance."

Although computer security is certainly a hot topic today, its public discussion is often accompanied by a great deal of hype. People are impressed by cryptosystems with large key spaces and the press releases make liberal use of the term *unbreakable*. The Kryha machine, a mechanical ciphering machine invented in 1924, had more than 4.57×10^{50} keys, but it did not offer much secrecy protection. Invoking the lore of large numbers to "prove" the strength of an encipherment scheme often fails to measure the real strength.

This book will provide the tools for understanding the central issues in data security. It will provide an instructor with a wide range of topics to train students to evaluate critically the factors that affect the effectiveness of secrecy, authentication, and digital signature schema, sensitize a student to some of the factors that determine the strength of an algorithm and its protocol implementations, and provide hands-on experience to the student with cryptanalysis.

The book's goal is to explain the nature of secrecy and the "practical" limitations of cryptography in providing secrecy and its derivatives (authentication and digital signatures).

MY PRIOR ART

Parts of *Computer Security and Cryptography* have served as the text for CMPSC 178 (Introduction to Cryptography) at UCSB. It is an upper-division elective in the undergraduate program of the Computer Science Department of the University of California (Santa Barbara) from 1983 to 2005. CMPSC 178 is ten-week four-unit course, meeting 75 minutes twice weekly. Class lectures are supplemented by a Discussion Section conducted by a Teaching Assistant. CMPSC 178 is usually taken in the Junior or Senior year by students from the Departments of Computer Science, Electrical and Computer Engineering, and Mathematics. The prerequisites are CMPSC 10 (a Java programming language course), and PSTAT 120A or 121A (an entry-level course in probability and statistics).

Eight or nine homework assignments require students to write programs to carry out the cryptanalysis of various cryptosystems and various exercises related to other cryptologic topics. Although in class I hand out a hard copy of the assignments containing the ciphertext, the nature of ciphertext requires the students to copy the ciphertext files from my Web page. The same procedure will be followed with *Computer Security and Cryptography*; the ciphertext for the exercises may be downloaded from Wiley's ftp-site at ftp://ftp.wiley.com/public/sci_tech_med/computer_security.

CMPSC 178
Introduction to Cryptography
Spring 2002

I think it's secure, Chief!

A replica of the cover page of my CMPSC 178 *Reader* appears above. One of my colleagues claimed that my New York humor would not be understood by California students. They would fail to grasp the cryptographic significance of the inverted cone. Perhaps, but many apparently watched television late at night and understood.

I dispensed with both an in-class Midterm and Final Examination in 1997 as there is no subject matter that can realistically be tested in class. In its place, I require a Term Paper; the topic is selected by the student and approved by me. The Term Paper is a short report (under 10 pages) on some cryptologic topic, based on related material from at least two related papers. The Term Paper need not contain a single equation nor deal only with theoretical issues. In fact, I encourage students to look for topics that are historical in nature, relate to applications or social issues. The Term Paper must include a summary of the Paper and the student's evaluation of the Paper's contributions. The Term Paper is due at the last class session. I provide a list of reference material, but the Web provides a more extensive source of topics and material.

Except for the introductory material, a solid mathematical background is needed, including probability theory and statistics. Much of modern cryptography depends on the fundamentals of number theory, but most engineering and computer science students do not enter with such preparation. If this material was imposed as a prerequisite, the potential audience would be reduced, so I develop the relevant mathematical topics in the course.

The *Course Syllabus*, distributed in class at the first lecture, is perhaps an exaggeration of the course's scope.

1. Aperitifs – Overview of Cryptography
2. Columnar Transposition
3. Monoalphabetic Substitution
4. Polyalphabetic Substitution
5. Statistical Tests
6. Rotor Encipherment
7. The World War II Cipher Machines
8. Stream Ciphers (LFSR, Cellphone)
9. The NIST Encryption Standards
10. The Paradigm of Public Key Cryptography
11. The Knapsack Cryptosystem
12. The RSA Cryptosystem
13. Primality and Factorization
14. The Discrete Logarithm Problem
15. Elliptic Curve Cryptography
16. Key Exchange in a Network
17. Digital Signatures & Authentication
18. Applications (ATM, Access Control, the Web)
19. Patents in Cryptography

Computer Security and Cryptography is an expanded version of the CMPSC 178 *Reader*, modified to make it appropriate for a wider audience. The Instructor should choose the topics that match his/her interests and those of the class.

ORGANIZATION OF THE BOOK

There are three types of chapters in this book:

1. Those that develop technical details;
2. Those that describe a cryptosystem and possibly indicate method(s) of analysis; and
3. Those that describe a cryptosystem, indicate method(s) of analysis, and provide problems to test the students understanding; these are signalled with ◇.

Classical Cryptography

1. Aperitifs
2. Columnar Transposition ◇
3. Monoalphabetic Substitution
    (a) Cribbing and Scoring a Monoalphabetic Substitution ◇
    (b) Hill Substitution ◇
    (c) The Hidden Markov Model
4. Polyalphabetic Substitution ◇
5. Statistical Tests ◇

World War II Cryptography

6. Emergence of the Cipher Machine
    (a) The German Enigma Machine
    (b) The Lorenz Schlusselzusatz
7. The Japanese Cipher Machines
    (a) The Japanese RED Machine
    (b) The Japanese PURPLE Machine

Modern Cryptography

8. Stream Ciphers ◇
9. The NIST Encryption Standards
    (a) LUCIFER
    (b) DES
    (c) Rijndael (AES)
    (d) Design of Block Ciphers
10. The Paradigm of Public Key Cryptography
11. The Knapsack Cryptosystem ◇
12. The RSA Cryptosystem

ACKNOWLEDGMENTS

I am in debt to many people, who have helped and encouraged me in the writing of this book:

- My colleague and friend of 46 years, Dr. Roy L. Adler, recently retired from the Mathematical Sciences Department of the IBM Thomas J. Watson Research Center (Yorktown Heights, New York), who read chapters and provided me with considerable material on the cryptographic work at IBM.

- My colleague and friend of 36 years, Dr. Raymond Pickholtz, Professor Emeritus at George Washington University, who visited UCSB several times, read all of the chapters and provided advice.

- Mr. I. Benjamin Blady and Mrs. Sara Beth Mitchell, who were kind enough to edit Chapter 19 on Patents in Cryptography.

- My son Keith, who helped me with graphics; together with my son Jay, he simplified my transition from MAC to PC; and my son Seth, who read early chapters and wisely urged me to moderate my wit.

and

- Carol, my wife of nearly 50 years, who continues to amaze me by her wide-ranging talents. I could not have undertaken this book without her encouragement, assistance, and advice.

I have offered CMPSC 178 twenty-one times at UCSB and once each in Australia, Israel, and Hawaii. One benefits from the questions, advice, and criticisms of students. In *Penses, Essais, Maximes et Correspondanee de J. Joubert*, in 1842, the French philosopher Joseph Joubert wrote

To teach is to learn twice.

Santa Barbara, California   ALAN G. KONHEIM
April 2006

ABOUT THE AUTHOR

After completing graduate study in 1960, I became a Research Staff Member at the IBM Thomas J. Watson Research Center (Yorktown Heights, New York). During my 22 years in the Department of Mathematical Sciences at IBM, I researched the applications of mathematics in computer science problems.

Starting in the mid-1960s, I became the Manager of the Mathematical Sciences' cryptography program; in particular, the evaluation of the Data Encryption Standard (DES).

Yearning for the sun, along with my wife Carol, I left IBM Research in 1982 and accepted a position as a professor in the Computer Science Department at the University of California (Santa Barbara). In my 24 years at UCSB, I taught courses in Assembly Language, Performance Evaluation, Computer Networks and Cryptography. I developed CMPSC 178 (Introduction to Cryptography) and offered this course 21 times at UCSB and three times at the Technion (Haifa, Israel), LaTrobe University (Melbourne, Australia) and at the University of Hawaii (Honolulu).

I retired from UCSB on July 1, 2005 to pursue a life of indolence.

Cryptography: A Primer was published by John Wiley & Sons Inc., in 1981. It might yet be made into a movie.

I spent the summer of 1984 at the National Security Agency (Fort George G. Meade, Maryland), the following three summers at Communications Research Division at the Institute for Defense Analysis (Princeton, New Jersey) and was a consultant at the National Security Agency during the summers 1997–1999.

CHAPTER 1

APERITIFS

"Yet it may be roundly asserted that human ingenuity cannot concoct a cipher that human ingenuity cannot resolve"
— *The Gold Bug* (Edgar Allan Poe)

"It Ain't Necessarily So"
— Song from *Porgy and Bess* (George and Ira Gershwin)[1]

"Skipper" the sailor said to his captain as he saluted,
"*A special message just came in for you from the admiral. I have it right here.*"
 "*Read it to me,*" the captain ordered.
The sailor began reading nervously, "You are without a doubt the most idiotic,
  lame-brained officer ever to command a ship in the United States Navy."
  "Have that communication decoded at once!," The skipper responded
— Pastor Tim's Clean Laugh List

1.1 THE LEXICON OF CRYPTOGRAPHY

The word "cryptography" is derived from the Greek words *kryptos*, meaning hidden, and *graphien*, meaning to write. Historians believe Egyptian hieroglyphics, which began about 1900 B.C.E., to be an early instance of encipherment. The key that unlocked the hieroglyphic secrets was the *Rosetta Stone*, discovered in 1799 in lower Egypt and now located in the *British Museum* in London. François Champollion, using the Rosetta Stone, deciphered the hieroglyphics in 1822. The books by David Kahn [1967, 1983] and Simon Singh [1999] provide extensive accounts of cryptography and its influence on history.

Every scientific discipline develops its own *lexicon*, and cryptography is no exception. We begin with a brief summary of the principal terms used in cryptography.

An *alphabet* $\mathcal{A} = \{a_0, a_1, \ldots, a_{m-1}\}$ is a finite set of *letters*; examples include

1. $m = 2^r$: (0,1)-sequences of fixed length r
   $Z_{r,2} = \{\underline{x} = (x_0, x_1, \ldots, x_{r-1}): x_i = 0, 1, 0 \leq i < r\}$;

2. $m = 2^7$: the ASCII character alphabet;

3. $m = 26$: the alphabet consisting of upper-case Latin letters: $\{A, B, \ldots, Z\}$

Text is formed by concatenating letters of $\mathcal{A}$; an *n-gram* $(a_0, a_1, \ldots, a_{n-1})$ is the concatenation of n letters. We do not require that the text be *understandable* nor that it be grammatically correct relative to a *natural language*; thus

$$\text{Good\_Morning} \quad \text{and} \quad \text{vUI*\_9Uiing8}$$

are both examples of ASCII text.

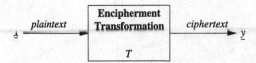

Figure 1.1 The encipherment transformation.

Encipherment or *encryption* is a transformation process (Fig. 1.1), T enciphering the *plaintext* $\underline{x} = (x_0, x_1, \ldots, x_{n-1})$ to the *ciphertext* $\underline{y} = (y_0, y_1, \ldots, y_{m-1})$, where

$$\underline{T}: \texttt{Good\_Morning} \rightarrow \texttt{Kssh\_Qsvrmrk}$$

is an example of encipherment introduced nearly 2000 years ago by Julius Caesar during the Gallic Wars in order to communicate with his friend and lawyer Marcus Tullius Cicero. It is not necessary that

1. The plaintext and ciphertext alphabets be identical; nor that
2. Encipherment leaves the number of letters unchanged.

The only requirement on T is the obvious one; it must be possible to reverse the process of encipherment.

Decipherment, or *decryption*, is also a transformation, T^{-1} (Fig. 1.2), which recovers the plaintext $\underline{x}$ from the ciphertext $\underline{y}$.

$$T^{-1}: \texttt{Kssh\_Qsvrmrk} \rightarrow \texttt{Good\_Morning}.$$

Additional properties are sometimes imposed on T, for example, that encipherment does not change the number of letters.

The three principal applications of cryptography are *secrecy*, *authentication*, and *access control*. Secrecy intends to deny information contained in text by disguising its form, for example,

1. In order to prevent an *eavesdropper* from learning the content of the communication when two users communicate over an open or *insecure* network; and
2. To hide information stored in a file system.

When two parties communicate over an open or insecure network, each needs to be certain of the identity of the other. Webster's dictionary defines authentication as "a process by which each party to a communication verifies the identity of the other." The term IFF, for *identification, friend or foe*, was an authentication protocol introduced during World War II to protect U.S. airspace from intrusion by enemy aircraft. The identity of a plane entering U.S. airspace was authenticated using a challenge–response pair; the correct response is determined by a cryptographic function of the challenge.

Access to files and other facilities in an information processing system is still another area in which cryptographic ideas have found application. In Chapter 18, we

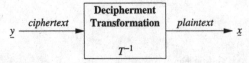

Figure 1.2 The decipherment transformation.

describe the authentication process when a customer engages in an ATM (automated teller machine) transaction. Authentication requires the customer to have

1. Possession of a valid ATM card; and
2. Knowledge of the corresponding personal identification number (PIN).

A new class of security problems in the twentieth century arose from communication over public networks. The ubiquitous nature of computer networks has given rise to *e-commerce*, and in the process has enlarged the area in which cryptography is needed. Transactions over the *Web* have changed the scale and environment in which the problems of secrecy and authentication exist. As discussed in Chapter 18, the principal security issues are:

1. *Privacy.*   Users may insist that their data transmitted on the Web be hidden from any parties who monitor communications and the contents of their records in a file system be hidden.
2. *Authentication: User Identity.*   As users communicating data over a network are not in physical proximity – for example, do not see or talk to one another – both need to be confident of the identity of the other.
3. *Authentication: Message Integrity.*   When users communicate over a network, each wants to be certain that not other party has maliciously modified the transmitted data. Although it is not possible to *prevent* transaction data from being altered a scheme must be implemented that will be *likely* to detect changes.

A transaction between two users involves one or more exchanges of data. Each transmission of *transaction data* is suffixed by a message authentication code (MAC) or *digital signature* (SIG); the MAC/SIG authenticates both the (sender, receiver) pair and the content of the communication (Fig. 1.3). The MAC is a sequence of 0's and 1's functionally dependent on the transaction data and the identities of the corresponding parties.

1. If privacy is required, the concatenated Transaction Data and MAC must be enciphered.
2. The authenticity of participants in a transaction must be established.
3. To insure the integrity of the exchange of information, the MAC must depend on the transaction data in such a way that
   (a) MAC-1, a *secret* element is involved in the construction of the MAC;
   (b) MAC-2, *no* user can *expect* to construct a valid MAC for the transaction data without knowledge of the secret element;
   (c) MAC-3, *any* change in the transaction data will *likely* change the MAC.

Web-based electronic transactions (Chapter 18) require a framework in which the purchaser and seller can be confident of the integrity of their transactions.
    We shall show that each of these different applications of cryptography involves the same principles.

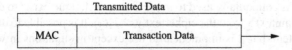

Figure 1.3   The message authentication MAC appended to transaction data.

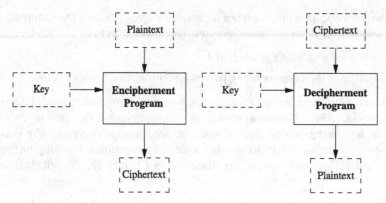

Figure 1.4 The software encipherment/decipherment processes.

1.2 CRYPTOGRAPHIC SYSTEMS

When a pair of users encipher the data they exchange over a network, the cryptographic transformation they use must be specific to the users. A *cryptographic system* is a family $\mathcal{T} = \{T_k : k \in \mathcal{K}\}$ of cryptographic transformations. A *key k* is an identifier specifying a transformation T_k in the family $\mathcal{T}$. The *key space* $\mathcal{K}$ is the totality of all key values. In some way the sender and receiver agree on a particular k and encipher their data with the enciphering transformation T_k.

Encipherment originally involved pen-and-pencil calculations. Mechanical devices were introduced to speed up encipherment in the eighteenth century, and they in turn were replaced by electromechanical devices a century later. Encipherment today is often implemented in software (Fig. 1.4); T_k is an algorithm whose input consists of plaintext $\underline{x}$ and key k and with ciphertext $\underline{y}$ as output.

1.3 CRYPTANALYSIS

Will encipherment provide secrecy? Cryptography is a contest between two adversaries:

- The *designer* of the system (algorithm, key space, protocol implementation), and
- The *opponent*, who attempts to circumvent the effect of encipherment.

Can an opponent recover all or part of the plaintext $\underline{x}$ from the ciphertext $\underline{y} = T_{k_0}(\underline{x})$ and knowledge of the cryptographic system $\mathcal{T}$ but without the key k_0. Cryptanalysis encompasses all of the techniques to recover the plaintext and/or key from the ciphertext.

The ground rules of this contest were set forth in the nineteenth century by Kerckhoffs[1] in his book "La Cryptographie militare." Kerckhoffs formulated six attributes that a cryptographic system should enjoy in order for the designer to triumph in the struggle.

K1. The System Should be, if not Theoretically Unbreakable, Unbreakable in Practice.

The term *unbreakable* is colloquially used to mean that *no* technique exists to determine the key k or plaintext $\underline{x}$ from the ciphertext $\underline{y} = T_k(\underline{x})$. It is possible to design an unbreakable system, but it is impractical to use except in situations in which

---

[1]Jean-Guiullaume-Hubert-Victor-Francois-Alexandre-Auguste-Kerckhoffs von Niuewenof, born in 1835 in Nuth (Netherlands), was a professor of German in Paris. The Kerckhoffs must have had spectacular towels!

only a modest amount of traffic is exchanged and an alternative secure path for exchanging the key is available.

More relevant is the amount of computational effort – measured by time and memory – needed to produce k and/or $\underline{x}$. Claude Shannon's paper [Shannon, 1949] developed a theory of *secrecy systems* and defined the *work function*, a quantitative measure (computational time/memory) of the strength of encipherment. The larger the work function, the more secrecy that results from encipherment. The minimum work function required is application-dependent. A patient's medical records may require protection for years, military plans, a shorter time.

Alas, the work function is not generally computable. It may be possible to bound the work function *from above* and thereby to often show that secrecy is not achieved. It is much more difficult to obtain a lower bound needed to conclude that *no* methods exist that will *break* the system with an effort less than the lower bound.

K2. *Compromise of the System Should not Inconvenience the Correspondents.*

A cryptographic system T has two types of information:

(a) The *public information*, a description of the algorithms $\{T_k : k \in \mathcal{K}\}$ and the key space $\mathcal{K}$.

(b) The *private information*, the particular key k chosen by the correspondents.

If a cryptographic system T is commercially available, manuals need to exist to describe the encipherment algorithmn. Whatever secrecy results from encipherment must depend on *keeping the key secret*. By *compromise*, Kerckhoff meant that knowledge of the public information should not adversely affect the secrecy achieved.

K3. *The Method for Choosing the Particular Member (Key) of the Cryptographic System to be Used Should be Easy to Memorize and Change.*

It is common for users to select names `Alan G. Konheim`, dates `11/26/37` or phrases `Now is the time`... to serve as a key. In some applications, part of the key will be recorded magnetically on a card and part will be memorized. Databases now exist containing phrases and names, so computer searches today make these choices risky. Although a key should ideally be selected randomly, users always balance the tradeoff between the danger of someone guessing their key and the perceived risk of forgetting the key.

K4. *Ciphertext Should be Transmittable by Telegraph*

Telegraphy was the dominant communication technology in the nineteenth century; this requirement is interpreted today to mean that text can be coded into a sequence as 0's and 1's suitable for transmission and storage. Excluded are the methods of *steganography*, which hide the very existence of text using invisible inks or by using a microdot.

K5. *The Apparatus Should be Portable*

The relatively bulky equipment of World War II has been replaced by microprocessors, which fulfill Kerckhoffs' requirement.

K6. *Use of the System Should not Require a Long List of Rules or Mental Strain.*

The ease, cost, and performance impact (speed) on encipherment continue to be dominant issues today.

Figure 1.5 Side information: Where's the *Toyota* and *Honda*?

In assessing the strength of encipherment, it must be assumed that the cryptographic system $T = \{T_k : k \in \mathcal{K}\}$ is known, but that the key k_0 producing the ciphertext $T_{k0} : \underline{x} \to$ is not. Three environments in which cryptanalysis may be attempted are:

1. *Ciphertext Only.* The ciphertext $\underline{y} = T_{k_0}(\underline{x})$ is known by the opponent; $\underline{x}$ and k_0 are unknown.

2. *Corresponding Plain- and Ciphertext.* The plaintext $\underline{x}$ and ciphertext $\underline{y} = T_{k_0}(\underline{x})$ are both known by the opponent; k_0 is unknown.

3. *Chosen Plaintext and the Corresponding Plain- and Ciphertext.* The plaintext $\underline{x}$ and ciphertext $\underline{y} = T_{k_0}(\underline{x})$ are both known for some set of *chosen* plaintext $\{\underline{x}_i\}$; k_0 is unknown.

1.4 SIDE INFORMATION

Side information about ciphertext is any information relating to the content of the plaintext. The following puzzle asks you to unravel each of the words, where the letters have been rearranged.

DFOR	KIBUC	TECRELOHV	DONSHU
KADCRAP	GEDOD	LADCLIAC	NOCILLN

A solution to the puzzle is easy using the side information provided (Fig. 1.5), that *the words are names of automobiles*! Has anyone seen a *Hudson* SUV lately?

1.5 THOMAS JEFFERSON AND THE M-94

The M-94, (Fig. 1.6) was adopted by the U.S. Army after World War I; the same device, now designated as the CSP-488, was adopted by the Navy. This encryption device was invented by Alberti in the fifteenth century; subsequently, Thomas Jefferson invented his *Wheel Cipher*, using the same idea. A good idea is not readily abandoned and the wheel cipher continued to be reinvented, in 1901 by the French Major Etienne Bazeries

Figure 1.6 The Thomas Jefferson/M-94 Wheel Cipher (Courtesy, NSA).

and in 1914 by Colonel Parker Hitt, who was a member of the Army Signal Service and the author of the *Manual for the Solution of Military Ciphers* (1915).

The M-94 had 25 wheels numbered 1, 2, . . . , 25; a different permutation of the letters A, B, . . . , Z is written around the circumference of each wheel. To encipher, the order of the wheels on the spindle is determined by sorting a repeated key word alphabetically. For example, the key CHINESEFOOD is repeated to obtain 25 characters, which are numbered in sorted order. In the following array, the first row lists the wheel identifiers (numbers), the last row specifies the wheel positions on the spindle:

$$
\begin{vmatrix}
1 & 2 & 3 & 4 & 5 & 6 & 7 & 8 & 9 & 10 & 11 & 12 & 13 & 14 & 15 & 16 & 17 & 18 & 19 & 20 & 21 & 22 & 23 & 24 & 25 \\
C & H & I & N & E & S & E & F & O & O & D & C & H & I & N & E & S & E & F & O & O & D & C & H & I \\
1 & 12 & 15 & 18 & 6 & 24 & 7 & 10 & 20 & 21 & 4 & 2 & 13 & 16 & 19 & 8 & 25 & 9 & 11 & 22 & 23 & 5 & 3 & 14 & 17
\end{vmatrix}
$$

Wheel no. 1 is placed on the leftmost position of the spindle, wheel no. 12 next, wheel no. 23 next and finally wheel no. 17 on the right. Having placed the 25 disks on the common spindle in this order, the wheels are rotated so that the letters of the plaintext message are aligned with the top bar and the ciphertext read out from some specified adjacent row.

1.6 CRYPTOGRAPHY AND HISTORY

David Kahn's recent biography [Kahn, 2004] about Herbert O. Yardley relates the beginning of American cryptologic activities. Although Secretary of State Henry Stimson's famous statement "Gentlemen do not read other people's mail" marked a temporary end of *official* U.S. codebreaking activities in 1929, the intelligence needs of America, however, led to the establishment of a nongovernmental cryptanalysis effort.

Cryptography has played a significant role in the history of the United States, often providing our country with crucial information.

1. The *Zimmerman telegram* in January 1917, from the German Foreign Minister Zimmerman to the German Minister von Eckhardt in Mexico, offered to return territory to Mexico – perhaps Arizona and California – in exchange for Mexico's support against the United States. Even better than a California driver's license! Mexico declined!! British cryptanalysts deciphered the telegram, revealing the perfidy of the Germans. The impact on the American public was immense, causing the United States Congress to declare war on Germany in 1917.

2. The cryptanalysis of the German *Enigma* machine allowed the United States and Great Britain to read enciphered messages; the ability to read known messages led to victory in the Battle of the Atlantic against German U-boats.

3. The cryptanalysis of the Japanese PURPLE machine and its related "color" machines allowed the United States to prevail in the Battles of the Carol Sea and Midway. Deciphered Japanese messages gave the United States the route to be followed by Admiral Yamamoto Isoruku – the architect of the Japanese attack on Pearl Harbor – on a visit to his troops in the Pacific, leading to his death.

4. The cryptanalysis of the KGB *one-time* system, which provided the United States with insights into the espionage activities of the Soviet Union, revealed the Rosenbergs and Alger Hiss to be traitors.

1.7   CRYPTOGRAPHY AND COMPUTERS

There has been a symbiotic relationship between cryptography and the development of high-performance computing systems. As cryptographic systems increased in their sophistication, the need to develop more efficient methods to cryptanalyze them became the stimulus for the development of computers.

Chapter 6 describes two of the three cryptographic systems used by Germany during World War II.

1. Military communications by radio were enciphered by the *Enigma* rotor system.
2. The *Geheimfernschreiber*[2] or T52e manufactured by Siemens and Halske was a binary device in which plaintext was first converted into the 5-bit *Baudot code*.
3. The Lorenz *Schlusselzusatz*[3] or SZ40/SZ42 also performed encipherment on plaintext converted into binary data.

The T52e and SZ40 devices were on-line devices connected to a teletypewriter. They were both used to protect high-level communications.

The Polish Cipher Bureau started to develop methods to analyze Enigma-enciphered traffic in 1932. The task was given to three recent university graduates – Marian Rejewski, Jerzy Różycki, and Henryk Zygalski, who developed the bombe,[4] a mechanical computer. When Poland was invaded by Germany, the Polish cipher bureau fled to southern France and then England. Their contributions were great, and although they shared their analysis with the British, they were not permitted to work on the *Ultra* project – the name of the Allied effort in cryptanalysis.

An excellent narrative of the breaking of the naval Enigma is given in David Kahn's book *Seizing the Enigma* [Kahn, 1991].

The United Kingdom's cryptanalytic effort during World War II was located at the General Communications Headquarters (GCHQ) in Bletchley Park, a suburb of London. Alan Turing, regarded as the inventor of the stored program concept and the universal automation or Turing machine [Turing, 1936] participated in the Bletchley Park cryptanalysis effort. His achievements are described in the work of Hodges [1983] and Cave Brown [1975]. Turing, together with a group of engineers including Tommy Flowers, designed the machines to crytanalyze German ciphertext, first the primitive electromechanical bombes and later their successors (the *Colossi*), the first programmable processors.

Different operational procedures were used with the Enigma machine during World War II and when they were changed, the Polish bombe was no longer effective. Turing developed a new bombe to search the ciphertext for *isomorphs* of plaintext believed to occur in the message.

The development of the *Colossus* machine [Lavington, 1980; Randall, 1982] illustrates the interplay of computers and cryptography. The need for testing many possible key settings to decipher ciphertext led to the invention of the computer. *Heath Robinson*, named after a famous British cartoonist, was the name of the first machine; it had teleprinter tape input and was used to attack the Schusselzusatz ciphertext. Professor

---

[2]*Geheim* is the German root for secret, *schreiben*, the verb to write, and *fern* indicates distance; that is, the Geheim fernschreiber was used to communicate secretly between parties separated from one another.

[3]*Schlussel* for key and *zusatz* for attachment; that is, the Schlusselzusatz was an attachment to a teletypewriter.

[4]*Bombe* is the French word for *bomb*. There are two explanations for the term. Some authors claim the "ticking" sound of the bomb's mechanical components is the source of the name. Other sources report that the moment of discovery of the bombe's concept came to the inventors in a restaurant when a *bombe* – a pastry with a hemispherical shape – was delivered to the patrons at an adjacent table.

M. H. A. Newman and a team of engineers headed by Tom Flowers worked at the Post Office Research Station for the Government Code and Cipher School at Dollis Hill (London). It contained 15900 *thermionic valves* (electronic tubes); each character was coded with the 5-bit Baudot teleprinter code, read by an optical character reader and punched on a paper moving at a rate of 5000 characters per second. It began analyzing ciphertext at Bletchley Park in December 1943. Its successor, *Colossus Mark II* (1944), contained 2500 valves and allowed conditional branching but did not implement the internal program store central to the concept of a computer.

1.8   THE NATIONAL SECURITY AGENCY

The development of the computer in the United States was fostered in part by the National Security Agency (Fig. 1.7) [Bramford, 1982], which merged several separate cryptologic organizations when it came into being on November 4, 1952. The National Security Agency/Central Security Service (CSS) is responsible for the protection of U.S. communications and the production of foreign intelligence. The Director of NSA (DIRNSA) is a military officer, currently Lieutenant General Keith B. Alexander, USA. The Deputy Dirrector of NSA (D/DIRNSA) is normally someone from within the organization, and is currently, Mr William B. Black Jr.

The NSA distinguishes between various types of communication intelligence activities:

- *COMSEC* (*Communications Security*). The protection resulting from any measures taken to deny unauthorized persons information derived from the national-security-related telecommunications of the United States, or from any measure taken to ensure the authenticity of such telecommunications. (*National Intelligence Reorganization and Reform Act of 1978.*)

- *COMINT* (*Communications Intelligence*). The interception and processing of foreign communications passed by radio, wire, or other electromagnetic means, and the processing of foreign encrypted communications, however transmitted. Interception comprises search, intercept, operator identification, signal analysis, traffic analysis, cryptanalysis, decryption, study of plaintext, the fusion of these processes, and the reporting of results. Excluded from this definition are the unencrypted written communications, press and propaganda broadcasts. (*National Security Council Intelligence Directive (NSCID) Number 6.*)

- *SIGINT* (*Signals Intelligence*). Comprises communications intelligence (COMINT), electronic intelligence (ELINT), foreign instrumentation signals

Figure 1.7   The NSA seal and a variant.

intelligence (technical and intelligence information derived from the collection and processing of foreign telemetry, beaconry, and associated signals), and information derived from the collection and processing of nonimagery, infrared, and coherent light signals. (*National Intelligence Reorganization and Reform Act of 1978.*)

Further information on NSA can be found at www.nsa.gov.

The role of NSA in computer development can be traced to the *Electronic Numerical Integrator and Calculator* (ENIAC) built in 1943–44 at the University of Pennsylvania's Moore School of Electrical Engineering under the supervison of Drs J. W. Mauchly and J. P. Eckert. ENIAC was built for the U.S. Army's Aberdeen proving ground and was intended to make artillery calculations. It contained 25,000 relays and 13,000 thermionic valves and occupied an area of 20 × 30 ft. In spite of this size, it held only 20 numbers. ENIAC incorporated the concept of a stored program due to John von Neumann, although the idea is also implicit in Turing's paper [Turing, 1936].

Once ENIAC was operational, its designers began to proselytize, to lecture about the great potential of computers. Attending one of the lectures was Lieutenant Commander James T. Prendergrass of the Naval Security Group (NSG), a part of the CSS that recognized the potential speedup in cryptanalysis. This led to the support provided by the cryptologic community in the advancement of the design of information processing technology. Some of the benchmarks are as follows.

- Engineering Research Associates (ERA), formed at the end of World War II, participated with NSA in the development of leading-edge computer technology. Among the machines developed was *Atlas* (1950), which had a memory of 16,384 words, a parallel architecture, and incorporated drum storage.
- *Abner* was developed by the Army Security Agency in 1952 and used a key-punch, paper tape, magnetic tape input/output, parallel printer, typewriter, and console.
- In response to the need for bigger and faster processors, Harvest (Project Lightning) was started in June 1957. IBM developed two *Stretch* machines which incorporated the "*tractor*," a mechanical device capable of locating cartridges from a tape library.
- Seymour Cray, an alumnus of ERA, founded Cray Research. Cray designed and produced *Loadstone* and the *Cray-1* (1976).

A history of the role played by the cryptologic organizations on the development of computers is contained in a paper by Snyder [Snyder, 1979].

1.9   THE GIANTS

William Friedman (Fig. 1.8), who was born September 24, 1891, in Russia, emigrated to the United States in 1892 when his parents settled in Pittsburgh. Friedman studied farming at

Figure 1.8   William Friedman (Courtesy of NSA).

the Michigan Agricultural College, because this program was tuition-free. When Friedman discovered that he was more interested in science, he enrolled in the genetics program at Cornell, which was also free as a land-grant college. While in Graduate School, Friedman met George Fabyan, who established the Riverbank Laboratories in Geneva, Illinois.

Fabyan, known as the "Colonel," was interested in acoustics, chemistry, genetics, and cryptography. Friedman began to work at Riverbank in 1915. Fabyan had been convinced by Ms Elizabeth Wells Gallup, a librarian at the Riverbank Laboratories, that there existed a cipher embedded in the first editions of the works of Shakespeare and that it would prove Bacon wrote some of the works attributed to the bard of Stratford-upon-Avon.

Friedman became head of the Department of Codes and Ciphers at Riverbank and actively began the study of cryptography. Friedman developed the first true cryptographic competence in the United States, developing methods for the analysis of polyalphabetic systems (Chapter 4). They were published originally in a series of Riverbank Monographs and our now reprinted by Aegean Park Press.

Actually, Friedman became interested in both cryptology and Miss Smith, an assistant to Ms Gallup. Love and cryptography – an unbeatable combination. Friedman and Miss Smith were married in 1917.

Although Henry L. Stimson ended the official United States codebreaking activities in 1929, there remained a need to monitor foreign communications. George Fabyan offered the services of the Department of Codes and Ciphers to the U.S. Government with the start of World War I. The Congress of the United States declared war against Germany on April 6, 1917. At that time, a group of 125 Hindus operating in the United States were working for the independence of India; they were seeking to purchase arms on the West Coast. This group was supported by Germany, which believed their activities would distract the British.

Friedman was presented with intercepted ciphertext messages. The encipherment method used a book cipher; some plaintext letters were enciphered by a triple of numbers a-b-c; a gave the page number, b the line, and c the position of the letter on the line. Although Friedman did not know at the time, the book was Price Collier's "Germany and the Germans"; he guessed some words – Sucio, revolution – and used the high-frequency letters in these words to guess others. Friedman submitted his solution and testified at the trials of this group, at which they were convicted.

Friedman's greatest genius was assembling the nucleus of what has become the National Security Agency. In 1930, as a civilian employee in the Signals Intelligence Service, Friedman hired three mathematicians: Frank B. Rowlett, Dr Abraham Sinkov, and Dr Solomon Kullback.

Frank B. Rowlett (1908–1998) (Fig. 1.9), born in Virginia, was hired as a junior cryptanalyst. He studied mathematics and chemistry. A lengthy period of training under Friedman followed his appointment at the SIS. Rowlett worked in both the design and cryptanalysis of cryptosystems. Together with Friedman, he designed the SIGABA

Figure 1.9 Frank B. Rowlett (Courtesy of NSA).

Figure 1.10   Dr Abraham Sinkov (Courtesy of NSA).

Figure 1.11   Dr Solomon Kullback (Courtesy of NSA).

(Chapter 6), the most secure U.S. cryptosystem used during World War II. Congress awarded Rowlett $100,000 in 1964 for his work on the SIGABA.

Dr Abraham Sinkov (1907–1998) (Fig. 1.10), born in Philadelphia, was the son of immigrants and was a mathematics teacher in New York City. He studied mathematics at CCNY and received his Ph.D. (Mathematics) at George Washington University in 1933. Sinkov took the Civil Service Examination in 1930 and obtained a job with Friedman. After his retirement in 1962 from NSA, Sinkov moved to Arizona and began a second career as a Professor of Mathematics at the Arizona State University.

Dr Solomon Kullback (1903–1994) (Fig. 1.11) attended high school in Brooklyn, New York. He intended to teach at Boys High, but met his CCNY classmate Abraham Sinkov, from whom he learned about jobs as a "junior mathematician" at $2000/year. Along with Sinkov, he took the Civil Service Examination and was hired by Friedman. Kullback and Rowlett worked on the cryptanalysis of the Japanese RED messages, the predecessor of the PURPLE system used at the start of World War II. After his retirement in 1962 from NSA, he began a second career as a Professor at the George Washington University.

1.10   NO SEX, MONEY, CRIME OR … LOVE

Cryptanalysis refers to the methods for the analysis of cryptographic systems, and in particular, to recover the plaintext and/or key from ciphertext. Cryptanalysis makes use of

1. Knowledge of the structure of the cryptographic system $\mathcal{T}$,
2. Cribs – information believed to be contained in the plaintext, and
3. Characteristics of the underlying language of the plaintext.

The frequencies of occurrence of letters constitute an elementary characteristic of a natural language. In English, the most frequent letters are E, T, A, O, N, R, I, S, and H. Roughly 13% of the letters in a large sample of English text should be E's.

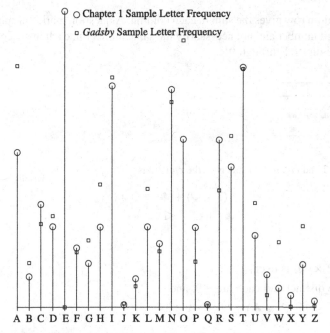

Figure 1.12   Letter frequencies in English and *Gadsby*.

In 1937, Ernest Vincent Wright published the novel *Gadsby* [Wright, 1931] in which the most frequent letter in English, E, did not appear. It could not have been a very big seller – it could not mention sex, money, murder, greed, or tenure, but it is remarkably coherent. Gadsby begins

Youth, throughout all history, had had a champion to stand up
for it; to show a doubting world that a child can think; and,
possibly, do it practically; you would constantly run across
folks today who claim that 'a child don't know anything'.

Figure 1.12 compares the letter frequencies of A, B, ..., Z (upper and lower case) in an early version of this chapter with standard letter probabilities in English and those in Wright's *Gadsby*. The success of cryptanalysis cannot depend on the striking agreement between the ciphertext statistics and the frequencies of the underlying language, as the above graph illustrates. On the other hand, it is unreasonable to assume that plaintext has been artificially created to mask the letter frequencies.

1.11   AN EXAMPLE OF THE INFERENCE PROCESS IN CRYPTANALYSIS

Although statistical characteristics provide information to aid in cryptanalysis, more often internal constraints in the cryptographic system provide a great deal of information. We give an example in this section of the *inference* process.

A PUZZLE

Each of the nine symbols △ ◁ ▷ ◯ ♡ ♠ ◇ ♣ • appearing in the array below stands for a *unique* encoding of one of the digits 1 through 9. The rightmost column gives the sum in each row; the bottom row gives the sum in each column. A question mark can stand for any one- or two-digit number and not necessarily the same number in each instance. Find the encoding of the digits 1 through 9!

1	2	3	4	
△	△	◁	○	?
♡	♡	♠	♡	◇◇
?	?	◁	♣	••
?	♡	♠	♡	•▷
•♡	◇◇	••	•◇	

Solution The *row 2* and *column 3* sums give the equations

$$(3 \times \heartsuit) + \spadesuit = \Diamond\Diamond \tag{1.1}$$

$$(2 \times \spadesuit) + (2 \times \triangleleft) = \bullet\bullet \tag{1.2}$$

As

$(2 \times \spadesuit) + (2 \times \triangleleft)$ is even,

$\heartsuit$, $\spadesuit$, $\triangleleft$, are distinct and each are ≤ 9, and

$(3 \times \heartsuit) + \spadesuit \leq 35$, $(2 \times \spadesuit) + (2 \times \triangleleft) \leq 34$,

it follows that $\bullet\bullet = 22$ and $\Diamond\Diamond = 11$ or 33.

The only integer (diophantine) solution of Equations (1.1) and (1.2) consistent with the uniqueness of the symbols is $\bullet = 2$ and $\Diamond = 3$ and

◇	•	♡	♠	△
3	2	9	6	5

The *column 4* sum provides the equation

$$\bigcirc + (2 \times \heartsuit) + \clubsuit = \bullet\Diamond$$

which requires

$$\bigcirc + \clubsuit = 5 \Longrightarrow \bigcirc, \clubsuit \in \{(1,4), (2,3), (3,2), (1,4)\} \tag{1.3}$$

As $\Diamond = 3$, it follows that

$$\bigcirc, \clubsuit \in \{(1,4), (4,1)\}$$

are the only possible consistent values satisfying Equation (1.3). It follows therefore that $\triangle, \triangleright \in \{7,8\}$ by the uniqueness constraints.

We now test an assumption on the value of $\triangleright$ when we impose the constraints on some of the remaining row and column sums and draw the consequences of the assumption:

A1. $\triangleright = 7$

A1(a) $\triangle = 8$;

A1(b) *Row 4* sum: $?_{4,1} + 9 + 6 + 9 = 27 \Longrightarrow ?_{4,1} = 3$;

A1(c) *Column 1* sum: $8 + 9 + ?_{3,1} + ?_{4,1} = 29 \Longrightarrow ?_{3,1} = 9$ from A1(b);

A1(d) *Column 2* sum: $8 + 9 + ?_{3,2} + 9 = 33 \Longrightarrow ?_{3,2} = 7$;

A1(e) *Row 3* sum: $?_{3,1} + ?_{3,2} + 5 + \clubsuit = 22 \Longrightarrow \clubsuit = 1$.

A2. $\triangleright = 8$

A2(a) $\Delta = 7$;

A2(b) *Row 4* sum: $?_{4,1} + 24 = 28 \Longrightarrow ?_{4,1} = 4$;

A2(c) *Column 1* sum: $7 + 9 + ?_{3,1} + ?_{4,1} = 29 \Longrightarrow ?_{3,1} = 9$ from A2(b);

A2(d) *Column 2* sum: $7 + 9 + ?_{3,2} + 9 = 33 \Longrightarrow ?_{3,2} = 5$;

A2(e) *Row 3* sum: $?_{3,1} + ?_{3,2} + 5 + \clubsuit = 22 \Longrightarrow \clubsuit = 3$, a contradiction!

The complete solution is

8	8	5	4	25
9	9	6	9	33
9	7	5	1	22
3	9	6	9	27
29	33	22	23	

'Elementary, my dear Watson!'

1.12 WARNING!

The Surgeon General has determined that *large* key spaces may not truly protect you data!

Several examples may illustrate this point.

1. The mechanical ciphering machine invented by Alexander von Kryha in 1924 received the Prize of the Prussian Ministry of the Interior at the 1926 Police Fair and a Diploma from the famous postwar Chancellor of Germany, Konrad Adenauer, at the International Press Exhibition in Cologne two year later. Von Kryha was not only an inventor, but also an astute entrepreneur. To promote his commercial venture Internationale Kryha Machinen Gesellschaft of Hamburg, Kryha turned to the famous mathematician Georg Hamel for an endorsement. Hamel calculated the size of the key space to be 4.57×10^{50} and concluded that only immortals could cryptanalyze Kryha ciphertext. Not withstanding Hamel's estimate, a cryptanalysis of the Kryha machine by Friedman did not require as much time and is described in the *"2 Hours, 41 Minutes,"* a chapter in *Machine Cryptography and Modern Cryptanalysis* [Devoirs and Ruth, 1985].

2. A U.S. patent [Merkle and Hellman, 1980] accompanied the publication Deavours and Kruh [1985] of the paper by Merkle and Hellman [1978] announcing the first public key cryptosystem (Chapter 10). The inventors wrote in the description of the preferred embodiment of the '582 patent

   But, the eavesdropper trapdoor knapsack problem can be made computationally infeasible to solve, thereby preventing the eavesdropper from recovering the plain-text message X.

   In spite of this pronouncement, Adi Shamir electrified the attendees at 'CRYPTO' 82 meetings[5] with an analysis of the Merkle–Hellman cryptosystem [Shamir,

[5] 'CRYPTO'N is an annual workshop on Cryptography held each August since 1981 at UCSB.

1984] (Chapter 11). A program running on an Apple during his lecture illustrated the solution technique.

3. Martin Gardner's article [Gardner, 1979] appeared a year before the publication of the paper that defined the RSA cryptosystem [Rivest et al., 1998] (Chapter 12). Gardner's article contained the first of many factoring challenges; RSA-129 is a 129-digit integer, which is the product of two primes. RSA-129 was factored in eight months (April 1991) and did not, as Gardner's article suggests, "... take millions of years ... ," to factor, claiming the prize of $100 for the first solution.

4. Finally, Certicom markets products using an elliptic curve cryptosystem (Chaper 15). It is stated in one of Certicom's whitepapers that

> *A comparison of the three hard mathematical problems on which the well-known public-key cryptosystems are based clearly highlights the fact that none of these are provably intractable. Years of intensive study has resulted in a widely held view that the ECDLP[6] is significantly more difficult than either the IFP[7] or the DLP.[8] The general conclusion of leading cryptographers is that the ECDLP in fact requires the full exponential time to solve. Based on this research and their own cryptographic expertise, industry leaders have accepted the Elliptic Curve Cryptosystem as a mature technology and are now implementing it for widespread deployment.*

The point of these examples is not to ridicule the judgment of their makers, but to emphasize that

---

1. Weakness in a cryptosystem is demonstrated by providing a feasible cryptanalytic technique.
2. Proving the strength of a cryptosystem is generally more difficult to effect.

The history of cryptography is littered with encipherment systems thought to offer security, but which on careful reflection and study have failed to provide the advertised protection. Only *one* cryptographic system offers absolute security and when it was improperly used during World War II (Chapter 4), it failed to secret the transmitted messages.

Claude Shannon's paper [1948] on the mathematical theory of communication gave birth to *information theory*. In the sequel [Shannon, 1949], he pointed out the common features of two problems:

- Recovering data transmitted over a *noisy* channel, and
- Secreting of transmitted information.

Shannon's model relating communication and secrecy is formulated within a statistical model as follows:

1. The *initial* statistical information of plaintext is represented by the *a priori* probability of plaintext $\underline{x}$ notationally $\Pr_{\text{PLAIN}}\{\underline{x}\}$.

2. When the ciphertext $\underline{y}$ of $\underline{x}$ is observed, the statistical information about the plaintext *changes* to the *a posteriori* probability of plaintext $\underline{x}$ given that encipherment has resulted in ciphertext $\underline{y}$, notationally $\Pr_{\text{PLAIN/CIPHER}}\{\underline{x}/\underline{y}\}$.

---

[6]ECDLP elliptic curve discrete logarithm problem.

[7]IFP, integer factorization problem.

[8]DLP, discrete logarithm problem in $\mathcal{Z}_p^+$.

Shannon defined an encipherment system as providing *absolute secrecy* if knowledge of the ciphertext did not give any additional statistical information about the plaintext than was known before the ciphertext was observed; namely,

$$Pr_{\text{PLAIN/CIPHER}}\{\underline{x}/\underline{y}\} = Pr_{\text{PLAIN}}\{\underline{x}\}$$

whenever $Pr_{\text{PLAIN}}\{\underline{x}\} > 0$ and $Pr_{\text{CIPHER}}\{\underline{y}\} > 0$. Shannon further proved that absolute secrecy for all n-grams requires that there be as many keys as there are plaintext n-grams of positive probability. If the plaintext and ciphertext consist of all n-grams formed from the alphabet $\{0, 1\}$, to guarantee the absolute secrecy of plaintext requires one bit of key per plaintext bit. The one-time tape (or pad), a cryptographic system discussed in Chapter 4, is based upon this result from Shannon.

REFERENCES

J. BRAMFORD, *The Puzzle Palace*, Houghton Mifflin, Boston, Massachusetts, 1982.

A. CAVE BROWN, *Bodyguard of Lies*, Harper & Row, New York, NY, 1975.

A. HODGES, *Alan Turing*, Simon & Schuster, New York, NY, 1983.

D. KAHN, *The Codebreakers*, MacMillan, New York, NY, 1967.

D. KAHN, *Kahn on Codes: Secrets of the New Cryptography*, MacMillan, New York, NY, 1983.

D. KAHN, *The Reader of Gentlemen's Mail: Herbert O. Yardley and the Birth of American Codebreaking*, Yale University Press, New Haven, Connecticut, 2004.

D. KAHN, *'Seizing the Enigma': Race to Break the German U-Boat Codes, 1939–43*, Houghton Mifflin, Boston, Massachusetts, 1991.

S. LAVINGTON, *Early British Computers*, Digital Press, Bedford, Massachusetts, 1980.

R. MERKLE AND M. HELLMAN, "Hiding Information and Signatures in Trapdoor Knapsacks," *IEEE Transactions on Information Theory*, **IT-24**, 525–530, (1948).

B. RANDALL, *The Origins of Digital Computers*, Brian Randall, (ed.), 3rd edn, Springer-Verlag, New York, 1982.

R. L. RIVEST, A. SHAMIR, AND L. ADELMAN, "A Method for Obtaining Digital Signatures and Public-Key Cryptosystems," *Communications of the ACM*, **21**, 120–126, (1978).

C. E. SHANNON, "Communication Theory of Secrecy Systems," *Bell Systems Technical Journal*, **28**, 656–715, (1949).

C. E. SHANNON, "A Mathematical Theory of Communication," *Bell Systems Technical Journal*, 27, 379–423, (1948).

S. S. SNYDER, "Influence of U.S. Cryptologic Organizations on the Digital Computer Industry," *The Journal of Systems and Software*, **1**, 87–102, (1979).

S. SINGH, *The Code Book: The Science of Secrecy from Ancient Egypt to Quantum Cryptography*, Anchor Books, New York, 1999.

A. M. TURING, "On Computable Numbers with an Application to the Entscheidungsprobem, Decision Problem," *Proceedings of the London Mathematical Society*, **42**, 230–267, (1936).

E. V. WRIGHT, *Gadsby*, Wetzel Publishing Company, Los Angeles, 1931.

R. MERKLE AND M. HELLMAN, "Public Key Cryptographic Apparatus and Method," U.S. Patent #4,218,582, filed October 6, 1977, granted August 19, 1980.

C. A. DEAVOURS AND L. KRUH, *Machine Cryptography and Modern Cryptanalysis*, Artech House, 1985.

A. SHAMIR, "A Polynomial Time Algorithm for Breaking the Basic Merkle-Hellman Cryptosystem," *IEEE Transactions on Information Theory*, **IT-30**, Number 5, September, 699–704, (1984).

M. GARDNER, "A New Kind of Cipher That Would Take Millions of Years to Break," *Scientific American*, **237**, 120–124, August 1979.

CHAPTER 2

COLUMNAR TRANSPOSITION

THIS CHAPTER defines columnar transposition encipherment. Searching for a fragment of text (cribbing) and using the statistical characteristics of the language to recover the plaintext and key will be explained. Problems to test your skills follow the text.

2.1 SHANNON'S CLASSIFICATION OF SECRECY TRANSFORMATIONS

Two building-blocks were identified in Claude Shannon's [1949] formulation of the design principles for secrecy systems:

- *Substitution.* Ciphertext results when the letters in the plaintext $\underline{x} = (x_0, x_1, \ldots, x_{n-1})$ are substituted by the letters in a ciphertext alphabet $(x_0, x_1, \ldots, x_{n-1}) \rightarrow (y_0, y_1, \ldots, y_{n-1})$.
- *Transposition.* Ciphertext results when the positions of letters in the plaintext $\underline{x} = (x_0, x_1, \ldots, x_{n-1})$ are rearranged $(x_0, x_1, \ldots, x_{n-1}) \rightarrow (x_{\pi_0}, x_{\pi_1}, \ldots, x_{\pi_{n-1}})$ according to a permutation $\underline{\pi} = (\pi_0, \pi_1, \ldots, \pi_{n-1})$.

Shannon proposed that an effective encipherment system might be built by iterating the two operations substitution (*confusion*) and transposition (*diffusion*).

Giovanni Battista della Porta (1535–1615) was born into a wealthy Naples family. He made contributions to astrology, optics, meteorology, magic, and cryptography. Porta's four-volume work "Magia Naturalis" was first published in 1555 and later expanded to twenty volumes. His place in cryptography is due to his book "De Furtivis Literarum Notis," published in 1563, which described digraphic substitution and transposition and is considered the first serious work in cryptography.

This chapter defines columnar transposition and illustrates two techniques for its cryptanalysis.

2.2 THE RULES OF COLUMNAR TRANSPOSITION ENCIPHERMENT

Columnar transposition (CT) uses a key consisting of

K1. A (columnar) *width N*, and

K2. A *transposition* $\tau = (\tau_0, \tau_1, \ldots, \tau_{N-1})$, a permutation of the integers $0, 1, \ldots, N - 1$.

Computer Security and Cryptography. By Alan G. Konheim
Copyright © 2007 John Wiley & Sons, Inc.

The encipherment of the plaintext $\underline{x} = (x_0, x_1, \ldots, x_{n-1})$ of *length* $n = (r - 1)N + \ell \geq N$ $(0 < \ell \leq N)$ proceeds in two steps:

CT1. The plaintext $\underline{x} = (x_0, x_1, \ldots, x_{n-1})$ is read by rows into an array X of width N.

$$X = \begin{vmatrix} x_0 & x_1 & \cdots & x_{\ell-1} & x_\ell & \cdots & x_{N-1} \\ x_N & x_{N+1} & \cdots & x_{N+\ell-1} & x_{N+\ell} & \cdots & x_{2N-1} \\ \vdots & \vdots & \ddots & \vdots & \vdots & \ddots & \vdots \\ x_{(r-2)N} & x_{(r-2)N+1} & \cdots & x_{(r-2)N+\ell-1} & x_{(r-2)N+\ell} & \cdots & x_{(r-1)N-1} \\ x_{(r-1)N} & x_{(r-1)N+1} & \cdots & x_{(r-1)N+\ell-1} \end{vmatrix}$$

CT2. The ciphertext $\underline{y}$ results when X is read out by columns, the order in which the columns are read out being specified by the transposition $\underline{\tau}$.

The ciphertext is the concatenation of segments corresponding to the columns of X

$$\underline{y} = (\underbrace{x_{\tau_0}, x_{\tau_0+N}, \ldots}_{\text{column } \tau_0}, \underbrace{x_{\tau_1}, x_{\tau_1+N}, \ldots}_{\text{column } \tau_1}, \ldots, \underbrace{x_{\tau_{N-1}}, x_{\tau_{N-1}+N}, \ldots}_{\text{column } \tau_{N-1}})$$

We use the notation $\underline{y} = T_{N,\underline{\tau}}(\underline{x})$ to denote that the plaintext $\underline{x}$ has been enciphered to the ciphertext $\underline{y}$ by the columnar transposition $T_{N,\underline{\tau}}$ with key $(N,\underline{\tau})$.

2.2.1 The Shape of X

If $n = (r - 1)N + \ell$ with $0 < \ell \leq N$, then X is a possibly *ragged* array, where X has[1]

1. $\begin{cases} \lfloor \frac{n}{N} \rfloor & \textit{full} \text{ rows, each containing } N \text{ letters if } 0 < \ell < N \\ \lceil \frac{n}{N} \rceil & \textit{full} \text{ rows, each containing } N \text{ letters if } \ell = N; \end{cases}$
2. A final partial row of ℓ letters, if $0 < \ell \leq N$;
3. ℓ *long* columns, each containing $L = \lceil \frac{n}{N} \rceil$ letters; and
4. $c = N - \ell$ *short* columns, each containing $S = \lfloor \frac{n}{N} \rfloor$ letters.

We write $L(j)$ for the length of the jth column of X.

The *inverse* of the transposition $\underline{\tau}$ is $\underline{\tau}^{-1} \equiv (\tau_0^{-1}, \tau_1^{-1}, \ldots, \tau_{N-1}^{-1})$ defined by $i = \tau_{\tau_i^{-1}} = \tau_{\tau_i}^{-1}$ for $0 \leq i < N$, where

- τ_i identifies the ith columns *read from* X, and
- τ_i^{-1} identifies the column of X corresponding to the ith segment.

2.2.2 Invertibility of CT

The following argument shows columnar transposition $T_{N,\tau}$ is invertible:

1. The transposition width N and ciphertext length n together determine the number of the *long* and *short* columns (ℓ, c) and their respective lengths (L, S);
2. (ℓ, c, L, S) and $\underline{\tau} = (\tau_0, \tau_1, \ldots, \tau_{N-1})$ permit the parsing of segments of the ciphertext $\underline{y}$;
3. $\underline{\tau}^{-1} = (\tau_0^{-1}, \tau_1^{-1}, \ldots, \tau_{N-1}^{-1})$ determines the column of X into which the segments of $\underline{y}$ are located.

---

[1]The *floor of x*, denoted by $\lfloor x \rfloor$, is the largest integer *not greater* than x; and the *ceiling of x*, denoted by $\lceil x \rceil$ is the smallest integer *not less* than x.

The program

```
ColTranInv
```

Input:	y, N, τ
Output:	x

reverses the steps in the encipherment process and produces the plaintext x:

1. The length n of the ciphertext y and N determine the parameters (ℓ, c, L, S);
2. (ℓ, c, L, S) and τ determine the segments of the ciphertext y;
3. (ℓ, c, L, S) and τ^{-1} determine which columns of X correspond to the segments of the ciphertext y;
4. The plaintext x is obtained by reading out X by rows.

2.2.3   The Size of the Columnar Transposition Key Space

Stirling's formula $N! \approx \sqrt{2\pi} N^{N+\frac{1}{2}} e^{-N}$ shows the key space grows faster than an exponential with N. Conclusion: Key trial is not feasible for $N \approx 32$.

2.2.4   Convention on the Display of Plain- and Ciphertext

Plaintext and ciphertext in this chapter will be written using either the ASCII alphabet or the alphabet $\mathcal{U}_{26} = \{\, A, B, \ldots, \; Z\}$ of 26 upper-case Latin letters. A letter will usually be displayed by its Latin symbol, for example T (in the typewriter font). In some instances, a letter might be referred by its *ordinal* position in the alphabet; for example, T as 84 (in the ASCII alphabet) and 19 (in $\mathcal{U}_{26}$).

Example 2.1

The columnar transposition encipherment of Good morning. How are you today? is produced by first reading the plaintext x of length $n = 32$ into the array X of $N = 6$ columns by *rows*:

$$
X = \begin{vmatrix}
\text{G} & \text{o} & \text{o} & \text{d} & & \text{m} \\
\text{o} & \text{r} & \text{n} & \text{i} & \text{n} & \text{g} \\
\text{.} & & \text{H} & \text{o} & \text{w} & \text{.} \\
\text{a} & \text{r} & \text{e} & & \text{y} & \text{o} \\
\text{u} & & \text{t} & \text{o} & \text{d} & \text{a} \\
\text{y} & \text{?} & & & &
\end{vmatrix}.
$$

X is a ragged array containing

- $\lfloor \frac{32}{6} \rfloor = 5$ full rows of 6 letters each, and a final partial row of 2 letters;
- $\ell = 2$ long columns each of length $L = 6$ letters and $c = 4$ short columns, each of length $S = 5$ letters.

The ciphertext results when the columns of X are read out in the order determined by the transposition $\tau = (1, 4, 0, 3, 5, 2)$:

$$y = (\text{or r ? nwydGo.auydio o mg oaonHet}).$$

The shape of the ragged array X and $\tau = (1, 4, 0, 3, 5, 2)$ infer that the column boundaries in the ciphertext (denoted by |) are

$$\underline{y} = \begin{matrix} (\text{or r ?|} & \text{nwyd|} & \text{Go.auy |} & \text{dio o |} & \text{mg oa|} & \text{onHet)} \\ \text{L} & \text{S} & \text{L} & \text{S} & \text{S} & \text{S} \end{matrix}$$

$\underline{\tau} = (1, 4, 0, 3, 5, 2)$	$\underline{\tau}^{-1} = (2, 0, 5, 3, 1, 4)$
The segment or r ? is the $\tau_0 = $ 1st column in X	Column 0 in X is the $\tau_0^{-1} = $ 2nd segment Go.auy
The segment nwyd is the $\tau_1 = $ 4th column in X	Column 1 in X is the $\tau_1^{-1} = $ 0th segment or r ?
The segment Go.auy is the $\tau_2 = $ 0th column in X	Column 2 in X is the $\tau_2^{-1} = $ 5th segment onHet
The segment dio o is the $\tau_3 = $ 3rd column in X	Column 3 in X is the $\tau_3^{-1} = $ 3rd segment dio o
The segment mg oa is the $\tau_4 = $ 5th column in X	Column 4 in X is the $\tau_4^{-1} = $ 1st segment nwyd
The segment onHet is the $\tau_5 = $ 2nd column in X	Column 5 in X is the $\tau_5^{-1} = $ 4th segment mg oa

The cryptanalysis of columnar transposition,

- *Given*: ciphertext $\underline{y}$
- *Find*: plaintext $\underline{x}$ and key $(N, \underline{\tau})$

requires solving two problems; determining

P1. Possible columnar widths N, and

P2. possible transpositions $\underline{\tau}$.

Two methods for the cryptanalysis of columnar transposition will be illustrated.

2.3 CRIBBING

The *Oxford Dictionary of English Etymology* gives *to steal* and *to pilfer* as definitions of the Shakespearian verb *to crib*. The term *cribbing* in cryptography refers to the process of inferring key and plaintext from ciphertext based on partial knowledge of the plaintext. A *crib* is a word or phrase $\underline{w} = (w_0, w_1, \ldots, w_{M-1})$ known (or assumed) to appear in the plaintext. Partial knowledge of the plaintext is a reasonable assumption:

- Letters usually contain stereotyped beginnings and/or endings: Dear..., Sincerely yours, Att:, Senator...;
- Message transmitted over a network have special formats; and
- Files are often highly structured, records divided into fields containing data with known characteristics.

When the crib $\underline{w} = (w_0, w_1, \ldots, w_{M-1})$ occurs in the plaintext $\underline{x}$, certain strings of letters derived from $\underline{w}$ will also occur in the ciphertext $\underline{y} = T_{N,\tau}(\underline{x})$.

If $N \geq \overline{M}$, then $\underline{w}$ determines N *subcribs*, which are all the *maximal length* strings $\mathcal{S} \equiv \{S_0, S_1, \ldots, S_{N-1}\}$ formed by the letters in $\underline{w}$, which are pairwise-separated by exactly N positions.

$$S_0 = (w_0, w_N, \ldots, w_{(s_0-1)N})$$
$$S_1 = (w_1, w_{1+N}, \ldots, w_{1+(s_1-1)N})$$

$$\vdots$$

$$S_{N-1} = (w_{N-1}, w_{N-1+N}, \ldots, w_{N-1+(s_{N-1}-1)N})$$

where s_i will denote the length of S_i.

The cryptanalysis of columnar transposition by cribbing is based on the following result.

Proposition 2.1: If $\underline{x} \to \underline{y} = T_{N,\tau}(\underline{x})$, then

2.1a Pairs of letters (x_t, x_{t+N}) in the plaintext separated by N places are *adjacent* in the ciphertext. In particular, the s_i letters in the ith subcrib S_i are adjacent in the ciphertext for $0 \le i < N$.

2.1b If $\tau_r = j$, $\tau_{r+1} = k$, the distance in the ciphertext

- $D(x_{j+iN}, x_{k+iN})$ from the letter x_{j+iN} in the ith row, jth column of X to the letter x_{k+iN} in the ith row, kth column of X is $L(j)$;

- $D(x_{j+iN}, x_{k+(i-1)N})$ from the letter x_{j+iN} in the ith row, jth column of X to the letter $x_{k+(i-1)N}$ in the $(i-1)$st row, kth column of X is $L(j) - 1$;

- $D(x_{j+(i-1)N}, x_{k+iN})$ from the letter $x_{j+(i-1)N}$ in the $(i-1)$st row, jth column of to the letter x_{k+iN} in the ith row, kth column is $L(j) + 1$.

The possible values of $L(j)$, $L(j) \pm 1$ are $\{S-1, S, S+1, S+2\}$.

Proof: As the letter x_t is directly above x_{t+N} in X, they are adjacent in the ciphertext, proving Proposition 2.1a.

To prove the first assertion made in Proposition 2.1b, consider the entries in the jth and kth columns in X as shown within brackets in Figure 2.1. There are

- $L(j) - i$ entries in the jth column of X in rows that are at or below the ith row entry x_{j+iN} and

- $(i + 1)$ entries in the kth column of X in rows that are at or above the ith row entry x_{k+iN}

When the kth column of X is read out by $\underline{\tau}$ immediately following the jth column of X, the distance $D(x_{j+iN}, x_{k+iN})$ from x_{j+iN} to x_{k+iN} is $L(j) = L(j) - i + (i + 1) - 1$.

The proofs of the remaining assertions in Proposition 2.1b are left to the reader.

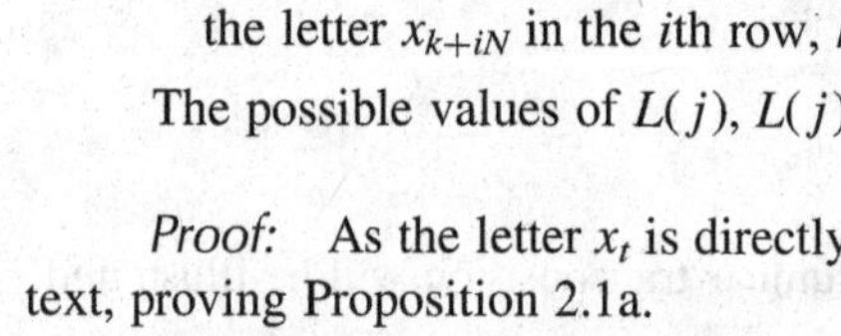

Figure 2.1 The ith and jth columns in X.

TABLE 2.1 A Complete Set of Width 6 Subcribs of Good Morning

or		n		Go		di		mg		on
0		6		11		17		22		27
	6		5		6		5		5	

TABLE 2.2 The Columns Containing the Complete Set of Width 6 Subcribs of Good Morning

The subcrib or is in column τ_0 of X

The subcrib n is in column τ_1 of X

The subcrib Go is in column τ_2 of X

The subcrib di is in column τ_3 of X

The subcrib mg is in column τ_4 of X

The subcrib on is in column τ_5 of X

Example 2.1 (continued)

The $N = 6$ subcribs of Good morning are $S = \{ \text{Go or on di n mg} \}$. Table 2.1 lists the subcribs and their positions sorted in the order of their occurrence in the ciphertext and the differences between these positions. The entries imply the relationships shown in Table 2.2, involving $\underline{\tau} = (\tau_0, \tau_1, \ldots, \tau_5)$. If $\tau_0 = k$ with $0 \leq k < 6$, the values of τ_i for $i \neq 0$ are determined from Table 2.3.

Tables 2.4–2.9 examine the consequences of placing G in each of the six columns, using the separations between the subcribs contained in Table 2.1. For each choice of column, the resulting transposition $\underline{\tau}$ is given as well as a contradiction, if any, of a subcrib separation listed in Table 2.1. For example, Table 2.5 lists $D(\text{or}, \text{n}) = S \neq 6$, which violates the data in Table 2.1.

From Tables 2.4–2.9 we conclude that

1. The G of the subcrib Go is located in column 0 of X and
2. $\underline{\tau} = (1, 4, 0, 3, 5, 2)$.

Furthermore, only a single m appears in the ciphertext; if we assume that the crib Good morning occurs in the plaintext, this implies that $N = 6$.

The analysis given in Example 2.1 is easy to generalize. Assume the crib $\underline{w} = (w_0, w_1, \ldots, w_{M-1})$ appears in the plaintext $\underline{x}$. Let $\underline{P} = (P_0, P_1, \ldots, P_{N-1})$ denote the positions in the ciphertext $\underline{y} = T_{N,i}(\underline{x})$ at which the subcribs of $\underline{w} = (w_0, w_1, \ldots, w_{M-1})$ occur

$$(y_{P_i}, y_{P_{i+1}}, \ldots, y_{P_i+s_i-1}) = (w_{iN}, w_{(i+1)N}, \ldots, w_{(i+s_i-1)N})$$

and let ν be the permutation of $0, 1, 2, \ldots, N-1$ that sorts the positions in $\underline{P}$:

$$P_{\nu(0)} < P_{\nu(1)} < \cdots < P_{\nu(N-1)}.$$

TABLE 2.3 The Transpositions Determined by Table 2.2

$\tau_2 = k$	$\tau_0 = (k + 1)$ (modulo 6)	$\tau_5 = (k + 2)$ (modulo 6)
$\tau_3 = (k + 3)$ (modulo 6)	$\tau_1 = (k + 4)$ (modulo 6)	$\tau_4 = (k + 5)$ (modulo 6)

TABLE 2.4

		Column 0			
		$\underline{\tau} = (1, 4, 0, 3, 5, 2)$			
0	**1**	**2**	**3**	**4**	**5**
G	o	o	d		m
o	r	n	i	n	g
L	L	S	S	S	S
		No contradictions			

TABLE 2.5

		Column 1			
		$\underline{\tau} = (2, 5, 1, 4, 0, 3)$			
0	**1**	**2**	**3**	**4**	**5**
	G	o	o	d	
m	o	r	n	i	n
g					
L	L	S	S	S	S
		$D(or, n) = S \neq 6$			

TABLE 2.6

		Column 2			
		$\underline{\tau} = (3, 0, 2, 5, 1, 4)$			
0	**1**	**2**	**3**	**4**	**5**
		G	o	o	d
	m	o	r	n	i
n	g				
L	L	S	S	S	S
		$D(n, Go) = L - 1 \neq 6$			

TABLE 2.7

		Column 3			
		$\underline{\tau} = (4, 1, 3, 0, 2, 5)$			
0	**1**	**2**	**3**	**4**	**5**
		G	o		o
d		m	o	r	n
i	n	g			
L	L	S	S	S	S
		$D(di, mg) = L \neq 5$			

TABLE 2.8

		Column 4			
		$\underline{\tau} = (5, 2, 4, 1, 3, 0)$			
0	**1**	**2**	**3**	**4**	**5**
			G	o	
o	d		m	o	r
n	i	n	g		
L	L	S	S	S	S
		$D(di, mg) = L \neq 5$			

TABLE 2.9

		Column 5			
		$\underline{\tau} = (0, 3, 5, 2, 4, 1)$			
0	**1**	**2**	**3**	**4**	**5**
					G
o	o	d		m	o
r	n	i	n	g	
L	L	S	S	S	S
		$D(n, Go) = S \neq 5$			

The pair$(\mathcal{S}, \underline{P})$ forms a *complete set of the subcribs* of $\underline{w}$ if

$$P_{v(r)} - P_{v(r-1)} \in \{S - 1, S, S + 1, S + 2\} \quad 0 < r < N,$$

The cryptanalysis of columnar transposition by cribbing tests a possible width N by searching for a complete set of subcribs. If the width is correct and the crib in the plaintext, the process will produce *at least* one complete set of subcribs and lead to a partial determination of a transposition. However,

1. The crib may occur several times in the plaintext;
2. More than one transposition may be consistent with a specific complete set of subcribs;
3. A complete set of subcribs may appear in $\underline{y}$ *without* N being the correct width;
4. If the crib $M \geq N$ length is only slightly larger than N, many of the subcribs may consist of a single letter, making an identification of a complete set of subcribs somewhat tedious.

On the other hand, if the length of the crib $M \geq N$ is $\sim 2N$, it is unlikely that *all* subcribs will be detected with an incorrect width and cribbing is likely to be successful.

2.4 EXAMPLES OF CRIBBING

Example 2.2
The ciphertext is of length $n = 446$:

---

cipherEx2.2

```
m c g trfttsaocehyhrsayohalolcintTm cgt s ilcdlCtf aunods ng
c ea  e ts enuuc nnrcog e eam otsliy, ukrsima meuc aUotxgits
nmotr tad inw  e wafscfuus ttihdea dri d.yptlo in  2rtsatmts
s tipmCvhc  ecepnhors  oldlwc iin  iids,irornsraaeow acT tcg
cuemar blte nos ornoaBrstua p eosrsiro skdins eerfn ,nad.Cee
ae mp onle ,ueouov wf4 e teuiy.ceer Seiimfdi.1 ige bbfl ehau
ndgaoecyi nypseuodii hhtddorn e  nsmone locsehpser c enteiio
i pml aykaoehbd roasitbsds
```

We assume it is known that `plainEx2.2` is from a 1982 UCSB Computer Science Department brochure. It is therefore reasonable to assume `computer science`, `Computer science`, or `Computer Science` as possible cribs.

2.4.1 Testing Possible Widths

Table 2.10 lists the subcribs of `computer science` for widths $5 \leq N \leq 9$.

Table 2.11 contains the output of the program `Search1`, which lists all subcribs of `computer science` that do *not* occur in $\underline{y}$:

`Search1`

Input:	Interval of widths $N_0 \leq N \leq N_1$, $(\underline{w}, \underline{y})$
Output:	All subcribs of $\underline{w}$ which do *not* occur in y

---

TABLE 2.10   The Subcribs of `computer science` for $5 \leq N \leq 9$

N	$\lfloor \frac{n}{N} \rfloor$	Subcribs
5	89	ctce oei mre p n usc
6	74	cee orn m c pse uc ti
7	63	crc o e ms pc ui te en
8	55	c os mc pi ue tn ec re
9	49	cs oc mi pe un tc ee r

TABLE 2.11   Output of `Search1` for `computer science` width $5 \leq N \leq 9$

N	Subcribs not found
5	ctce oei mre p n usc
6	
7	crc o e ms pc
8	mc pi tn re
9	mi pe

Table 2.12 is the output of the program Search2, which lists the positions in $\underline{y}$ of all subcribs of computer science for $N = 6$:

Search2

Input:	$(N, \underline{w}, y)$
Output:	Subcribs of $\underline{w}$ and their positions in y

Tables 2.11 and 2.12 shows that X has $c = 4$ short columns, each of length $S = \lfloor \frac{n}{N} \rfloor = \lfloor \frac{446}{6} \rfloor = 74$ letters, and $\ell = 2$ long columns, each of length $L = S + 1 = 75$ letters.

Table 2.13 lists the positions and separations of the single complete set of subcribs for the width $N = 6$. The entries in Table 2.13 imply the relationships shown in Table 2.14 involving the components of $\underline{\tau}$. If $\tau_4 = k$ with $0 \le k < 6$, the values of τ_i for $i \ne 4$ are determined from Table 2.14 as shown in Table 2.15.

TABLE 2.12 Output of Search2 for computer science and $N = 6$

cee	331
orn	222 256 386
m c	0 34
pse	372 406
uc	74 108
ti	148 182

TABLE 2.13 The Complete Set of Width 6 Subcribs of computer science

m c	uc	ti	orn	cee	pse
34	108	182	256	331	406
	74	74	74	75	75

TABLE 2.14 The Columns Containing the Complete Set of Width 6 Subcribs of computer science

The subcrib cee is in column τ_4 of X
The subcrib orn is in column τ_3 of X
The subcrib m c is in column τ_0 of X
The subcrib pse is in column τ_5 of X
The subcrib uc is in column τ_1 of X
The subcrib ti is in column τ_2 of X

TABLE 2.15 The Transpositions Determined by Table 2.14

$\tau_4 = k$	$\tau_3 = (k + 1)$ (modulo 6)	$\tau_0 = (k + 2)$ (modulo 6)
$\tau_5 = (k + 3)$ (modulo 6)	$\tau_1 = (k + 4)$ (modulo 6)	$\tau_0 = (k + 5)$ (modulo 6)

TABLE 2.16

	Column 0				
	$\tau = (2, 4, 5, 1, 0, 3)$				
0	**1**	**2**	**3**	**4**	**5**
c	o	m	p	u	t
e	r	s	c	i	
e	n	c	e		
L	*L*	*S*	*S*	*S*	*S*
	No contradictions				

TABLE 2.17

	Column 1				
	$\tau = (3, 5, 0, 2, 1, 4)$				
0	**1**	**2**	**3**	**4**	**5**
	c	o	m	p	u
t	e	r		s	c
i	e	n	c	e	
L	*L*	*S*	*S*	*S*	*S*
$D(\text{uc},\text{ti}) = S + 1 \neq 74$					

TABLE 2.18

	Column 2				
	$\tau = (4, 0, 1, 3, 2, 5)$				
0	**1**	**2**	**3**	**4**	**5**
		c	o	m	p
u	t	e	r		s
c	i	e	n	c	e
L	*L*	*S*	*S*	*S*	*S*
$D(\text{m c},\text{uc}) = S + 1 \neq 74$					

TABLE 2.19

	Column 3				
	$\tau = (5, 1, 2, 4, 3, 0)$				
0	**1**	**2**	**3**	**4**	**5**
			c	o	m
p	u	t	e	r	
s	c	i	e	n	c
e					
L	*L*	*S*	*S*	*S*	*S*
$D(\text{m c},\text{uc}) = S + 1 \neq 74$					

TABLE 2.20

	Column 4				
	$\tau = (0, 2, 3, 5, 4, 1)$				
0	**1**	**2**	**3**	**4**	**5**
				c	o
m	p	u	t	e	r
	s	c	i	e	n
c	e				
L	*L*	*S*	*S*	*S*	*S*
$D(\text{m c},\text{uc}) = L \neq 74$					

TABLE 2.21

	Column 5				
	$\tau = (1, 3, 4, 0, 5, 2)$				
0	**1**	**2**	**3**	**4**	**5**
					c
o	m	p	u	t	e
r		s	c	i	e
n	c	e			
L	*L*	*S*	*S*	*S*	*S*
$D(\text{m c},\text{uc}) = S + 1 \neq 74$					

2.4.2 Finding the Transposition

To find the column k containing the subcrib cee, we use the separations between the subcribs contained in Table 2.13. Locating cee in X for each of the six values of k is carried out in Tables 2.16 to 2.21; in each instance, the tables lists the implied transposition τ. The final row of each table gives *any* contradiction; for example, Table 2.17 lists $D(\text{uc},\text{ti}) = S + 1 \neq 74$, which violates the observed distance in Table 2.13.

Tables 2.16 to 2.21 enable us to conclude that $\underline{\tau} = (2, 4, 5, 1, 0, 3)$.

ColTranInv produces the plaintext:

---

plainEx2.2

Computer science has undergone a dramatic period of growth in
the last decade. Today, computer technology touches our lives
in many ways, from 4 hour banktellers to satellite
communications systems. The computer science program at UCSB
covers this exciting multi faceted discipline. Completion of
this program results in a broad body of skills and knowledge
which can be used in a wide range of areas of scientific study,
business, and industry.

Example 2.3
The ciphertext is of length $n = 240$:

---

cipherEx2.3

---

g eunatii0ea.Plusman ala A ,pn acgN m r mhnn0mn rys olgu enl
SP ode heogepepmet 0bgWi emrl shvgiIaIs nga.hvmetonMsCayayae
ic nhnglae cs: oolieoahggah6s g?rcthcgagh g oau dydensrsar c
8sle ia' hin leBrlpao nti l ri oM luhmb ueetiieukCs eIjol

It is assumed that `plainEx2.3` describes some aspect of the MC68000 assembly language programming. It is therefore reasonable to search for the crib `language` that *might* occur

- Within the plaintext followed by a blank space or comma,
- As the last word in a sentence, in which case the blank space should be replaced by a period, or
- At the start of a sentence `Language`.

We will search for the crib `language`.

2.4.3 Testing a Possible Width

Table 2.22 lists the subscribs determined by `language` for widths $5 \leq N \leq 8$. *Only for* $N = 7$ does `Search1` find occurrences of all 7 subcribs of `language`. The output of `Search2` listing the subscribs and their positions in `cipherEx2.3` is given in Table 2.23. X has $c = 5$ short columns, each of length $S = \left[\frac{n}{N}\right] = \left[\frac{240}{7}\right] = 34$ letters, and $\ell = 2$ long columns, each of length $L = S + 1 = 35$ letters.

TABLE 2.22   The Subscribs of `language` for Widths $5 \leq N \leq 8$

N	$\left[\frac{n}{N}\right]$	Subcribs
5	47	la ag ne g u
6	39	lg ae n g u a
7	24	le a n g u a g
8	39	l a n g u a g e

TABLE 2.23   Locations of the $N = 7$ Subcribs of `language`

Block	Positions
le	183 195
a	23
n	4 19 29 42 43 46 58 100 110 123 125 172 192 205
g	0 33 54 70 81 93 101 126 143 144 150 157 159 162
u	3 15 55 166 218 223 230
a	5 11 18 21 23 31 96 102 114 116 118 128 141 145 158 165 176 187 201

TABLE 2.24   A Complete Set of Width 7 Subscribs of `language`

a		n		g		a		g		le		u
23		58		93		128		162		195		230
	35		35		35		34		33		35	

TABLE 2.25   The Columns Containing the Complete Set of Width 7 Subcribs of language

The subcrib le is in column τ_5 of X
The subcrib a is in column τ_0 of X
The subcrib n is in column τ_1 of X
The subcrib g is in column τ_2 or τ_4 of X
The subcrib u is in column τ_6 of X
The subcrib a is in column τ_3 of X

TABLE 2.26   The Transpositions Determined Using Table 2.24

$\tau_5 = k$ $\qquad\qquad$ $\tau_0 = (k+1)$ (modulo 7)
$\tau_1 = (k+2)$ (modulo 7) $\qquad$ $\tau_6 = (k+4)$ (modulo 7)
$\tau_3 = (k+6)$ (modulo 7) $\qquad$ $\begin{cases} \tau_2 \\ \tau_4 \end{cases} = \begin{cases} (k+3) \text{ (modulo 7)} \\ (k+5) \text{ (modulo 7)} \end{cases}$

As there is only one occurrence of a in `cipherEx2.3`, the entries of Table 2.23 yield a complete set of subcribs displayed in Table 2.24. The entries in Table 2.24 imply the relationships in Table 2.25 involving $\underline{\tau} = (\tau_0, \tau_1, \ldots, \tau_6)$. If $\tau_5 = k$ with $0 \le k < 7$, the values of τ_i for $i \ne 5$ are partially determined from Table 2.25 (Table 2.26).

2.4.4   Finding the Transposition

To find the column k, containing the subcrib le, we use the observed separations between the subscribs contained in Table 2.24. Locating le in each of the seven values of k is carried out in Tables 2.27 to 2.33; in each instance, the table lists the implied transposition $\underline{\tau}$. The final row of each table gives *any* contradiction; for example, Table 2.27 lists $D(n, g) = S \ne 35$, which violates the observed distance in Table 2.24. The letter g is a width $N = 7$ subscrib of `language` twice in Example 2.3 and it is necessary to consider both of the positions of g. Table 2.32 shows that $D(g, a) = 35$, which gives $\underline{\tau} = (6, 0, 1, 3, 4, 5, 2)$.

TABLE 2.27

Column 0
$\underline{\tau} = (1, 2, 3, 5, 6, 0, 4)$
$\underline{\tau} = (1, 2, 6, 5, 3, 0, 4)$

0	1	2	3	4	5	6
l	a	n	g	u	á	g
e						
L	L	S	S	S	S	S

$D(n, g) = S \ne 35$

TABLE 2.28

Column 1
$\underline{\tau} = (2, 3, 4, 6, 0, 1, 5)$
$\underline{\tau} = (2, 3, 0, 6, 4, 1, 5)$

0	1	2	3	4	5	6
	l	a	n	g	u	a
g	e					
L	L	S	S	S	S	S

$D(a , n) = S \ne 35$

TABLE 2.29

Column 2
$\underline{\tau} = (3, 4, 5, 0, 1, 2, 6)$
$\underline{\tau} = (3, 4, 1, 0, 5, 2, 6)$

0	1	2	3	4	5	6
		l	a	n	g	u
a	g	e				
L	L	S	S	S	S	S

$D(a , n) = S \ne 35$

TABLE 2.30

Column 3						
$\tau = (4, 5, 6, 1, 2, 3, 0)$						
$\tau = (4, 5, 2, 1, 6, 3, 0)$						
0	1	2	3	4	5	6
		l	a	n	g	
u	a	g	e			
L	L	S	S	S	S	S
D(a, n) = ≠ 35						

TABLE 2.31

Column 4						
$\tau = (5, 6, 0, 2, 3, 4, 1)$						
$\tau = (5, 6, 3, 2, 0, 4, 1)$						
0	1	2	3	4	5	6
			l	a	n	
g	u	a	g	e		
L	L	S	S	S	S	S
D(a, n) = S ≠ 35						

TABLE 2.32

Column 5						
$\tau = (6, 0, 1, 3, 4, 5, 2)$						
$\tau = (6, 0, 4, 3, 1, 5, 2)$						
0	1	2	3	4	5	6
				l	a	
n	g	u	a	g	e	
L	L	S	S	S	S	S
D(g, a) = S ≠ 35						

TABLE 2.33

Column 6						
$\tau = (0, 1, 2, 4, 5, 6, 3)$						
$\tau = (0, 1, 5, 4, 2, 6, 3)$						
0	1	2	3	4	5	6
						l
a	n	g	u	a	g	e
L	L	S	S	S	S	S
D(g, a) = S ≠ 35						

`ColTranInv` gives the plaintext

> `plainEx2.3`

```
Nothing gives me more pleasure than programming the Macintosh
in MC68000 assembly language. Why? Primarily
because it's much more challenging than using a high level
language like BASIC or Pascal, I suppose: and I do enjoy
and good challenge.
```

2.5 PLAINTEXT LANGUAGE MODELS

Natural languages have statistical characteristics that are generally reflected in the ciphertext. We will show how these characteristics may be recognized and used to recover the plaintext and key from columnar transposition ciphertext.

We assume a language model in which plaintext, with letters in a generic alphabet $\mathcal{Z}_m = \{0, 1, \ldots, m - 1\}$, is generated by a statistical *source* (Fig. 2.2). The *iid source* is

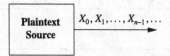

$X_0, X_1, \ldots, X_{n-1}, \ldots$

Figure 2.2 Generic statistical plaintext source.

the simplest example of a language model; it generates plaintext as a result of independent and identically distributed trails of a *chance experiment*. The iid source generates the plaintext n-gram $\underline{X} = (X_0, X_1, \ldots, X_{n-1})$ with probability

$$\Pr\{\underline{X} = (x_0, x_1, \ldots, x_{n-1})\} = \prod_{t=0}^{n-1} \pi_t(x_t)$$

$$\pi(i) = \Pr\{X_t = i\}, \quad 0 \le i < m, \ 0 \le t < n.$$

For example, the probability of the ASCII plaintext `Good morning` is

$$\pi(\text{G})\pi(\text{o})\pi(\text{o})\pi(\text{d})\pi(\ )\pi(\text{m})\pi(\text{o})\pi(\text{r})\pi(\text{n})\pi(\text{i})\pi(\text{n})\pi(\text{g}),$$

where π is a probability distribution on the plaintext letters. As the iid source generates letters independently, plaintexts that differ only by the arrangement of their letters are assigned the same probability; that is, $\Pr\{\text{Good morning}\} = \Pr\{\text{Gd moogninr}\}$.

Because columnar transposition enciphers plaintext by rearranging the positions of letters, the iid source is not appropriate for analyzing columnar transposition ciphertext. It is necessary to use a source that assigns probabilities depending on the order in which letters occur.

2.5.1 The Homogeneous Markov Source

A *Markov*[1] source that generates plaintext is determined by two parameters:

1. A probability distribution $\pi(i)$ on 1-grams

$$\Pr\{X_t = i\} = \pi(i) \ge 0, \quad 0 \le i < m \tag{2.1}$$

$$1 = \sum_{i=0}^{m-1} \pi(i)$$

2. A *transition function*, $P(j/i)$ for pairs of 2-grams

$$\Pr\{X_t = j/X_{t-1} = i\} = P(j/i) \ge 0, \quad 0 \le i, j < m \tag{2.2}$$

$$1 = \sum_{j=0}^{m-1} P(j/i), \quad 0 \le i < m.$$

An additional homogeneity condition is imposed requiring $\pi(i)$ and $P(j/i)$ to satisfy

$$\pi(j) = \sum_{i=0}^{m-1} \pi(i) P(j/i), \quad 0 \le i < m. \tag{2.3}$$

The probability that the source generates the n-gram of plaintext $(x_0, x_1, \ldots, x_{n-1})$ is given by

$$\Pr\{(X_0, X_1, \ldots, X_{n-1}) = (x_0, x_1, \ldots, x_{n-1})\} = \pi_0(x_0) \prod_{t=1}^{n-1} P(x_t/x_{t-1}). \tag{2.4}$$

Equation (2.4) implies the probability $\Pr\{(X_s, X_{s+1}, \ldots, X_{s+n-1}) = (x_0, x_1, \ldots, x_{n-1})\}$ is the same for each position s in the plaintext. In particular,

---

[1]For a good source of material on Markov chains, see Grimmett and Stirzaker, 1992.

- The probability of observing $\{X_t = i\}$ in the plaintext is $\pi(i)$ for each position t in the plaintext, and
- The probability of observing $\{X_t = i, X_{t+1} = j\}$ in the plaintext is $\pi(i)P(j/i)$ for each position t in the plaintext.

2.5.2 Letter Counts and Probabilities

The most immediately observable statistical characteristics of natural languages are the frequency of occurrence of k-grams. The number of times the 1-gram i occurs in the plaintext $\underline{x}$ of length n is the random variable

$$N_n(i) = \sum_{t=0}^{n-1} \chi\{X_t = i\} \tag{2.5}$$

where $\chi\{\ldots\}$ in Equation (2.5) is the *indicator function*:

$$\chi\{\cdots\} = \begin{cases} 1 & \text{if } \{\cdots\} \text{ is true} \\ 0 & \text{otherwise} \end{cases}.$$

The expectation and frequency of occurrence of 1-grams are

$$E\{N_n(i)\} = \sum_{t=0}^{n-1} \Pr\{X_t = i\} = n\pi(i) \tag{2.6}$$

and

$$f_n(i) = \frac{E\{N_n(i)\}}{n} = \pi(i). \tag{2.7}$$

Similarly, the number of times the 2-gram (i, j) occurs in adjacent letters in the plaintext $\underline{X}$ is the random variable

$$N_n(i, j) = \sum_{t=0}^{n-2} \chi_{\{X_t=i, X_{t+1}=j\}}. \tag{2.8}$$

The expectation and frequency of occurrence of 2-grams are

$$E\{N_n(i, j)\} = \sum_{t=0}^{n-2} \Pr\{X_t = i, X_{t+1} = j\} = (n-1)\pi(i)P(j/i) \tag{2.9}$$

and

$$f_n(i, j) = \frac{E\{N_n(i, j)\}}{n - 1} = \pi(i)P(j/i) \tag{2.10}$$

Equations (2.5)–(2.10) relate the observable statistical characteristics of language to the parameters of the Markov source. Conversely, if we start with the frequencies of 1- and 2-grams, the parameters of a Markov source may be determined so that plaintext generated by the source exhibits these 1- and 2-gram frequencies.

2.6   COUNTING k-GRAMS

The plan is simple – start with a large sample of plaintext and count

- The number of times, $N(i)$, the 1-gram i occurs in the text, and
- The number of times, $N(i, j)$, the 2-gram (i, j) occurs in the text,

and use the sample to construct the parameters of a Markov source. This process has been used by several authors.

- Kullback's early monograph [Kullback, 1938] on statistical methods in cryptanalysis includes tables of k-gram counts derived from government plaintext telegrams.
- Appendix A in Seberry and Pierprzyck's [1989] book includes frequency tables of 1-gram and 2-grams in several languages.

It is easy to derive Markov source parameters from a text downloaded from *The Project Gutenberg Free eBook Library* on the Web site www.gutenberg.com. The text of over 16,000 famous books, including William Shakespeare, H. G. Wells, and Jack London is available for downloading. There are two methods to determine frequencies from downloaded texts: Sliding window counts and jumping window counts.

2.6.1   Sliding Window Counts

Initialization: $N(i) = N(i, j) = N(i, j, k) = 0$ for $0 \le i, j, k < m$;

for t := 0 to n − 1 do

$N(x_t) = N(x_t) + 1$;

for t := 0 to n − 2 do

$N(x_t, x_{t+1}) = N(x_t, x_{t+1}) + 1$;

for t := 0 to n−3 do

$N(x_t, x_{t+1}, x_{t+2}) = N(x_t, x_{t+1}, x_{t+2}) + 1$;

The resulting sliding window counts satisfy

$$\left| \sum_{\ell} N(i, \ell) - \sum_{\ell} N(\ell, i) \right| \le 1, \qquad 0 \le i < m \tag{2.11}$$

$$\left| \sum_{\ell} N(i, j, \ell) - \sum_{\ell} N(\ell, i, j) \right| \le 1, \qquad 0 \le i, j < m. \tag{2.12}$$

2.6.2   Jumping Window Counts

Initialization: $N(i) = N(i, j) = 0$ for $0 \le i, j, k < m$;

for t := 0 to n := 1 do

$N(x_t) = N(x_t) + 1$;

for t := 0 to $\left[\frac{n-2}{2}\right]$ do

$N(x_{2t}, x_{2t+1}) = N(x_{2t}, x_{2t+1}) + 1$;

The resulting jumping window counts generally do *not* satisfy the conditions in Equations (2.11) and (2.12).

2.7 DERIVING THE PARAMETERS OF A MARKOV MODEL FROM SLIDING WINDOW COUNTS

The Markov model parameters are defined from the sliding window counts of 2-grams $\{N(i,j)\}$ derived from a *large* sample $\underline{x} = (x_0, x_1, \ldots, x_{n-1})$ of text as follows:

$$\hat{\pi}_1(i) \equiv \frac{\sum_\ell N(i, \ell)}{n - 1}, \quad 0 \le i < m \tag{2.13}$$

$$\hat{\pi}_2(i) = \frac{\sum_\ell N(\ell, i)}{n - 1}, \quad 0 \le i < m \tag{2.14}$$

$$P(j/i) \equiv \frac{N(i, j)}{\sum_\ell N(i, \ell)}, \quad 0 \le i, j < m. \tag{2.15}$$

We assume the sample size n is large enough so that $\hat{\pi}_1(i) = \hat{\pi}(i) = \pi(i)$ for $0 \le i < m$ and that π satisfies

$$\pi(j) = \sum_{i=0}^{m-1} \pi(i)P(j/i), \quad 0 \le j < m. \tag{2.16}$$

To prove Equation (2.16), we start with Equations (2.13) to (2.15), writing

$$\sum_{i=0}^{m-1} P(j/i)\hat{\pi}_1(i) = \sum_{i=0}^{m-1} \left\{ \frac{N(i, j)}{\sum_{\ell=0}^{m-1} N(i, \ell)} \times \frac{\sum_{\ell=0}^{m-1} N(i, \ell)}{n - 1} \right\} = \frac{1}{n - 1} \sum_{i=0}^{m-1} N(i, j) = \hat{\pi}_2(j)$$

This book provides three sets of Markov source parameters:

- Smarkov1 and Smarkov2:   These Markov source parameters were derived from a *non*sliding window count of 67,320 2-grams in the alphabet {A, B, ..., Z} appearing in Abraham Sinkov's book [Sinkov, 1968]. $P(j/i)$ was derived using Equation (2.15) from Sinkov's 2-gram counts and written to Smarkov2; thereafter, $\pi(i)$ was calculated to satisfy Equation (2.3) and written to Smarkov1.

- Gmarkov1 and Gmarkov2:   These Markov source parameters were derived from a table containing a sliding window count of 10,000 2-grams in the alphabet {A, B, ..., Z} contained in Helen Fouché Gaines's book [Gaines, 1939].

- Hmarkov1 and Hmarkov2:   These Markov source parameters were derived from a sliding window sample of 280,810 2-grams in the alphabet {A, B, ..., Z} contained in *War And The Future: Italy France and Britain at War* by H. G. Wells.

The files *markov1 and *markov2* = S, G and H may be downloaded from the following ftp address: ftp://ftp.wiley.com/public/sci_tech_med/computer_security.[3]

2.8 MARKOV SCORING

Given: columnar transposition ciphertext $\underline{y}$;

Find: the transposition width N and transposition τ.

---

[3]The file *markov1 contains a vector of length 26; the file *markov2 is a matrix of dimension 26×26.

Our plan is to test N as a possible width by computing a *Marko score* for the adjacency of columns in the ciphertext, assuming each of the $N!$ transpositions of width N are equally likely to have been used.

Testing a width N is formulated as a hypotheses *testing* problem; for each pair (i, j) with $i \neq j$, decide which of the two hypotheses is the most likely to be true.

$\text{ADJ}(i, j) \Leftrightarrow \tau_j = 1 + \tau_i,$ jth column is read from X immediately after the ith column is read from X.

$\overline{\text{ADJ}}(i, j) \Leftrightarrow \tau_j \neq 1 + \tau_i,$ jth column is *not* from X immediately after the ith column is read from X.

When $\text{ADJ}(i, j)$ is true, the ith and jth columns must be columns $(k, k+1)$ in X for *some* k with $0 \leq k < N - 1$. As the $N!$ transpositions τ have been chosen with equal probability, the *a priori*[4] probabilities of the hypotheses $\text{ADJ}(i, j)$ and $\overline{\text{ADJ}}(i, j)$ are

$$\Pr{}_{a \ priori}\{\text{ADJ}(i, j)\} = \frac{N - 1}{N(N - 1)}$$

and

$$\Pr{}_{a \ priori}\{\overline{\text{ADJ}}(i, j)\} = \frac{N - 1}{N}$$

The ratio of these probabilities is the *a priori odds* of $\text{ADJ}(i, j)$ over $\overline{\text{ADJ}}(i, j)$

$$\text{ODDS}_{a \ priori}(i, j) \equiv \frac{\Pr_{a \ priori}\{\text{ADJ}(i, j)\}}{\Pr_{a \ priori}\{\overline{\text{ADJ}}(i, j)\}} = \frac{1}{N - 1} \tag{2.17}$$

The term ODDS has the same interpretation as in gambling; namely the bet of $1 that $\text{ADJ}(i, j)$ is true

- Pays $$\text{ODDS}_{a \ priori}(i, j)$ when $\text{ADJ}(i, j)$ is the correct outcome, and
- Loses $1 if $\overline{\text{ADJ}}(i, j)$ is not the correct outcome of the array X.

These odds constitute a *fair* wager with 0 expected gain.

Next, we assume the plaintext $\underline{X}$ has been generated by a Markov source and $\underline{Y} = T_{N,\tau}(\underline{X})$. The parameters $(\pi(i), P(j/i))$ of the Markov source reflect characteristics of the language; for example, in English

- $P(u/q) \sim 1$ – the letter q is invariably followed by the letter u;
- $P(h/t) > P(r/t)$ – it is more likely that the letter t will be followed by the letter h than by the letter r.

The *a posteriori*[5] odds of the hypotheses $\text{ADJ}(i, j)$ and $\overline{\text{ADJ}}(i, j)$ is the ratio of these hypotheses using information contained in a ciphertext sample $\underline{y} = T_{N,\tau}(\underline{x})$.

As N is unknown, the exact parsing of the segments

$$\underline{y} = (\underline{y}^{(0)}, \underline{y}^{(1)}, \ldots, \underline{y}^{(N-1)})$$

is not possible except in one case.

---

[4]The term *a priori* refers to statistical inferences without knowledge of the ciphertext.
[5]The term *a posteriori* refers to inferences with knowledge of the ciphertext.

Case 1

$n - LN$, the length n of $\underline{y}$ is a multiple of the width N. As the column boundaries in the ciphertext are determined, the *a posterior odds* are

$$\text{ODDS}_{a\,posteriori}(i, j/\underline{y}^{(i)}, \underline{y}^{(j)}) = \frac{\Pr_{a\,posteriori}\{\text{ADJ}(i, j)/\underline{y}^{(i)}, \underline{y}^{(j)}\}}{\Pr_{a\,posteriori}\{\overline{\text{ADJ}}(i, j)/\underline{y}^{(i)}, \underline{y}^{(j)}\}}$$

can be calculated. Using the formula

$$\Pr\{A/B\} = \frac{\Pr\{A \cap B\}}{\Pr\{B\}}, \quad \text{if } \Pr\{B\} > 0$$

we obtain

$$\text{ODDS}_{a\,posteriori}(i, j/\underline{y}^{(i)}, \underline{y}^{(j)}) = \frac{\Pr_{a\,posteriori}\{\underline{y}^{(i)}, \underline{y}^{(j)}/\text{ADJ}(i, j)\} \Pr_{a\,priori}\{\text{ADJ}(i, j)\}}{\Pr_{a\,posteriori}\{\underline{y}^{(i)}, \underline{y}^{(j)}/\overline{\text{ADJ}}(i, j)\} \Pr_{a\,priori}\{\overline{\text{ADJ}}(i, j)\}}$$

$$= \frac{1}{N - 1} \frac{\Pr_{a\,posteriori}\{\underline{y}^{(i)}, \underline{y}^{(j)}/\text{ADJ}(i, j)\}}{\Pr_{a\,posteriori}\{\underline{y}^{(i)}, \underline{y}^{(j)}/\overline{\text{ADJ}}(i, j)\}}. \tag{2.18}$$

The plan is to accept the hypothesis $\text{ADJ}(i, j)$ if

$$\text{ODDS}_{a\,posteriori}(i, j/\underline{y}^{(i)}, \underline{y}^{(j)}) = \max_{\ell \neq j} \text{ODDS}_{a\,posteriori}(i, \ell/\underline{y}^{(i)}, \underline{y}^{(\ell)}).$$

Example 2.4

($N = 6$, $n = 336$, $L = 56$)

The ciphertext $\underline{y}$ written in rows of 60 letters is

---

```
                        cipherEx2.4
```

```
dhuledhvyeoetiedmeinghuor ec e,he m r,s reh i.rmta a  nio tb
na rc,med rilesb gtbeyClnei  eflnetrhptselB aeshitnvyHnFy  tU
se enacanlm,lereet hldin n idnhoars roetr  eoadee a Ga nin n
tyet o iaa etao  v pcfe delte o mfhefo nt  rltcCrntittcc  le
scnencdtghnrretreasfs l s rdaoe lfn,eUs elue ee rmmosb area a
eb eac esoiai ctenihp e hgttsait
```

As the length $n = 336$ of the ciphertext is a multiple of the width $N = 6$, $\underline{y}$ can be parsed into six segments, each containing 56 characters

---

$\underline{y}^{(0)} = $ (dhuledhvyeoetiedmeinghuor ec e,he m r,s reh i.rmta a ni)
$\underline{y}^{(1)} = $ (o tbna rC, med rilesb gtbeyClnei eflnetrhptselB aeshitnvy)
$\underline{y}^{(2)} = $ (HnFy tUse enacanlm,lereet hldin n idnhoars roetr eoade)
$\underline{y}^{(3)} = $ (e a Ga nin ntyet o iaa etao v pcfe delte o mfhefo nt r)
$\underline{y}^{(4)} = $ (ltcCrntittcc lescnencdtghnrretreasfs l s rdaoe lfn,eUs)
$\underline{y}^{(5)} = $ (elue ee rmmosb area a eb eac esoiai ctenihp e hgttsait)

It remains to determine the columns of X into which the segments $\{\underline{y}_{(i)}\}$ are to be placed.

If $\text{ADJ}(0, 1)$ is true, then Table 2.34 applies. The ciphertext $\underline{y}$ in Example 2.4 contains $N - 2$ intervening letters between the letters in successive rows as shown in Table 2.34:

$$\underline{y}^{(0)}, \underline{y}^{(1)} = (\text{do} \underbrace{\dots}_{N-2} \text{h} \underbrace{\dots}_{N-2} \text{ut} \underbrace{\dots}_{N-2} \text{iy}).$$

TABLE 2.34   The Relationship of $\underline{y}^{(0)}$, $\underline{y}^{(1)}$ when ADJ(0,1) is True

	0th 1st ← Columns		
$X =$	... d o ... ... h ... ... u t ... ⋱ ⋮ ⋮ ⋱ ... i y ...	d immediately precedes o in the plaintext; h immediately precedes in the plaintext; u immediately precedes t in the plaintext; ⋮ i immediately precedes y in the plaintext;	$\pi(\text{d})\,P(\text{o}/\text{d})$ $\pi(\text{h})\,P(\ /\text{h})$ $\pi(\text{u})\,P(\text{t}/\text{u})$ $\pi(\text{i})P(\text{y}/\text{i})$

If the events in different rows of Table 2.34 were *independent*,

$$\Pr\{\underline{y}^{(0)}, \underline{y}^{(1)}/\text{ADJ}(0, 1)\} = \Pr\{\text{do} \underbrace{\ldots}_{N-2} \text{h} \underbrace{\ldots}_{N-2} \text{ut} \underbrace{\ldots}_{N-2} \text{iy}/\text{ADJ}(0, 1)\}$$

$$= \Pr\{\text{do}\}\ \Pr\{\text{h}\}\ \Pr\{\text{ut}\}\cdots\Pr\{\text{iy}\}$$

$$= \pi(\text{d})P(\text{o}/\text{d})\pi(\text{h})P(\ /\text{d})\pi(\text{u})P(\text{t}/\text{u})\cdots\pi(\text{i})P(\text{y}/\text{i}).$$

The events in Table 2.34 are not independent; for example, as the 2-grams do and h are separated by four positions, we have

$$\Pr\{\text{do} \underbrace{\ldots}_{N-2} \text{h} \underbrace{\ldots}_{N-2}\} \neq \Pr\{\text{do}\}\Pr\{\text{h}\}.$$

However, as the separations between these 2-grams in the plaintext increase, meaning as $N \uparrow$, the dependency of the 2-grams in $(\underline{y}^{(0)}, \underline{y}^{(1)})$ lessens.

We will compute $\Pr_{a\ posteriori}\{\underline{y}^{(i)}, \underline{y}^{(j)}/\text{ADJ}(i, j)\}$ as if the adjacent 2-grams were independent. If $\overline{\text{ADJ}(0, 1)}$ is true, the letters in the 2-grams of the segments $\underline{y}^{(0)}$ and $\underline{y}^{(1)}$ contain intervening letters as follows:

$$\underbrace{\text{d}\cdots\text{o}}_{M} \underbrace{\ldots}_{N-(M+2)} \underbrace{\text{h}\cdots}_{M} \underbrace{\ldots}_{N-(M+2)} \underbrace{\text{u}\cdots\text{t}}_{M} \underbrace{\ldots}_{N-(M+2)} \underbrace{\text{i}\cdots\text{y}}_{M}$$

As M and $N - (M + 2)$ both increase, the dependence lessens and

$$\lim_{\substack{M\to\infty \\ N-M\to\infty}} \Pr_{a\ posteriori}\{\underbrace{\text{d}\cdots\text{o}}_{M} \underbrace{\ldots}_{N-(M+2)} \underbrace{\text{h}\cdots}_{M} \underbrace{\ldots}_{N-(M+2)} \underbrace{\text{u}\cdots\text{t}}_{M} \underbrace{\ldots}_{N-(M+2)} \underbrace{\text{i}\cdots\text{y}}_{M}/\overline{\text{ADJ}(0, 1)}\}$$

$$= \pi(\text{d})\pi(\text{o}) \times \pi(\text{h})\pi(\ ) \times \pi(\text{u})\pi(\text{t}) \times \cdots \times \pi(\text{i})\pi(\text{y})$$

We ignore the dependence and use the formula

$$\text{ODDS}_{a\ posteriori}(0, 1)/\underline{y}^{(0)}, \underline{y}^{(1)}$$

$$= \frac{1}{5}\frac{\pi(\text{d})P(\text{o}/\text{d}) \times \pi(\text{h})P(\ /\text{h}) \times \pi(\text{u})P(\text{t}/\text{u}) \times \cdots \times \pi(\text{i})P(\text{y}/\text{i})}{\pi(\text{d})\pi(\text{o}) \times \pi(\text{h})\pi(\ ) \times \pi(\text{u})\pi(\text{t}) \times \cdots \times \pi(\text{i})\pi(\text{y})}$$

$$= \frac{1}{5}\frac{P(\text{o}/\text{d}) \times P(\ /\text{h}) \times P(\text{t}/\text{u}) \times \cdots \times P(\text{y}/\text{i})}{\pi(\text{o}) \times \pi(\ ) \times \pi(\text{t}) \times \cdots \times \pi(\text{y})}.$$

The computation of the odds score requires several additional modifications:

1. Multiplying a large number of probabilities or ratios of probabilities is likely to cause underflow, leading to errors in the scoring. To avoid underflow, the Markov

odds score will be replaced by the Markov *log-odds score*.

$$\text{Log} - \text{ODDS}_{a\ posteriori}(0,1)/(\underline{y}^{(0)}, \underline{y}^{(1)})$$

$$= \log_2 \text{ODDS}_{a\ posteriori}(0,1)/(\underline{y}^{(0)}, \underline{y}^{(1)})$$

$$= \log_2 P(\text{o}/\text{d}) + \log_2 P(/\text{h}) + \log_2 P(\text{t}/\text{u}) + \cdots + \log_2 P(\text{y}/\text{i})$$
$$- [\log_2 \pi(\text{o}) + \log_2 \pi(\ ) + \log_2 \pi(t) + \cdots + \log_2 \pi(\text{y}) + \log_2 5].$$

2. A computation of the Markov log-odds score in Example 2.4 requires the values of $\pi(i)$ and $P(j/i)$ for letters in the ASCII alphabet. Instead of scoring ASCII text, we will use the files `Smarkov1` and `Smarkov2`, which contain Markov source parameters for text written in the alphabet $\mathcal{U}_{26} = \{A, B, \ldots, Z\}$.

$$\underline{y} = (y_0, y_1, \ldots, y_{n-1}) \qquad \underline{y}^{(i)} = (y_{iL}, y_{iL+1}, \ldots, y_{(i+1)L-1}),$$

then only the pairs (y_{iL+k}, y_{jL+k}) in the kth row of X, which are both letters in $\mathcal{U}_{26} = \{A, B, \ldots, Z\}$, and for which $P(y_{jL+k}/y_{iL+k}) > 0$ are counted in the Markov log-odds score.

If $ADJ(i, j)$ is *not* true or there is a data entry error, then $P(y_{jL+k}/y_{iL+k})$ may equal 0.0; for example, if $y_{iL+k} = \text{q}$ and $y_{jL+k} = \text{u}$. This will result in a log-odds score of $-\infty$.

An *impossible* pair is a pair of letters (y_{iL+k}, y_{jL+k}) in $\mathcal{U}_{26} = \{A, B, \ldots, Z\}$ for which $P(y_{jL+k}/y_{iL+k}) = 0.0$.

As the number of pairs involved in scoring may varying with i and j, the Markov log-odds score must be normalized by the number of terms $L(i, j)$ included. We define

$$d(i,j) = \frac{1}{L(i,j)} \log\text{-ODDS}_{a\ posteriori}(i,j)/(\underline{y}^{(i)}, \underline{y}^{(j)})$$

$$\log\text{-ODDS}_{a\ posteriori}(i,j)/(\underline{y}^{(i)}, \underline{y}^{(j)}) = \sum_{\substack{k \\ y_{iL+k}, y_{jL+k} \in \mathcal{U}_{26} \\ P(y_{jL+k}/y_{iL+k}) > 0}} [\log_2 P(y_{jL+k}/y_{iL+k})$$

$$- \log_2 \pi(y_{iL+k})] - \log_2 5$$

Table 2.35 contains the Markov log-odds score $d(i, j)$ and the number of impossible pairs $IMP(i, j)$ for $0 \leq i, j < 6$ and $i \neq j$. The largest column in *each* row in Table 2.35 is underlined. This permits the adjacency of columns to be inferred; for example, $\underline{y}^{(0)} \prec \underline{y}^{(5)}$, where we write $\underline{y}^{(i)} \prec \underline{y}^{(j)}$ – read *column j stands to the right of column i* when $\bar{d}(i, j) > 0$. The Markov scores in Table 2.35 allow us to conclude that

$$\underline{y}^{(0)} \prec \underline{y}^{(5)} \qquad \underline{y}^{(2)} \prec \underline{y}^{(3)} \qquad \underline{y}^{(3)} \prec \underline{y}^{(4)} \qquad \underline{y}^{(4)} \prec \underline{y}^{(0)} \qquad \underline{y}^{(5)} \prec \underline{y}^{(1)}$$

TABLE 2.35 Markov Log-Odds Scores for Example 2.4

	0	1	2	3	4	5
0	*	−1.1539(2)	−1.3812(0)	−0.9549(2)	−0.6275(0)	0.6101(0)
1	−0.3844(2)	*	−1.5023(1)	−1.3333(1)	−1.5110(2)	−0.4915(1)
2	−1.2013(0)	−0.7991(0)	*	0.8334(0)	−1.7384(1)	−1.1583(1)
3	−1.3124(0)	−1.3680(2)	−1.0595(0)	*	0.9011(0)	−1.2790(1)
4	0.9127(0)	−1.0359(4)	−2.0056(3)	−0.5005(0)	*	−0.9906(1)
5	−0.4844(0)	0.8314(0)	−0.9219(0)	−1.1889(1)	−1.8481(1)	*

where $\prec$ is a linear order and gives

$$\underline{y}^{(2)} \prec \underline{y}^{(3)} \prec \underline{y}^{(4)} \prec \underline{y}^{(0)} \prec \underline{y}^{(5)} \prec \underline{y}^{(1)}.$$

Note that $d(1, j) < 0.0$ for $j \neq 1$, which is consistent with $\underline{y}^{(1)}$ being the rightmost column in X. We conclude that $\underline{\tau} = (2, 3, 4; 0, 5, 1)$.

We will now explain why the Markov scoring *might* reveal the adjacency of columns in the rectangular array X. The starting point is

$$Pr_{a\ posteriori}\{\underline{Y}^{(i)}, \underline{Y}^{(j)}/\mathrm{ADJ}(i, j)\} \simeq \prod_{k=0}^{L-1} \pi(Y_{kL+ik}) P(Y_{kL+j}/Y_{kL+ik}) \qquad (2.19)$$

$$Pr_{a\ posteriori}\{\underline{Y}^{(i)}, \underline{Y}^{(j)}/\overline{\mathrm{ADJ}}(i, j)\} \simeq \prod_{k=0}^{L-1} \pi(Y_{kL+ik}) \pi(Y_{kL+j}) \qquad (2.20)$$

where $\underline{Y}^{(i)}$ and $\underline{Y}^{(j)}$ are the random ith and jth segments of the random ciphertext $\underline{Y}$. The right-hand sides in Equations (2.19) and (2.20) are also random variables interpreted as follows:

- $\pi(Y_{iL+k}) P(Y_{jL+k}/Y_{iL+k})$ is the probability of the Markov source generating letter Y_{iL+k} (row k and column i) and letter Y_{jL+k} (row k and column j) if $\mathrm{ADJ}(i, j)$ is true.
- $\pi(Y_{iL+k}) \pi(Y_{jL+k})$ is the probability of the Markov source generating letter Y_{iL+k} (row k and column i) and letter Y_{jL+k} (row k and column j) if $\overline{\mathrm{ADJ}}(i, j)$ is true.

The *a posteriori* log-odds scores are

$$\text{log-ODDS}_{a\ posteriori}(i, j/\underline{Y}^{(i)}, \underline{Y}^{(j)})$$

$$\simeq \log_2\left[\frac{1}{N-1} \times \frac{Pr_{a\ posteriori}\{\underline{Y}^{(i)}, \underline{Y}^{(j)}/\mathrm{ADJ}(i, j)\}}{Pr_{a\ posteriori}\{\underline{Y}^{(i)}, \underline{Y}^{(j)}/\overline{\mathrm{ADJ}}(i, j)\}}\right] \qquad (2.21)$$

$$\frac{1}{L}\text{log-ODDS}_{a\ posteriori}(i, j/\underline{Y}^{(i)}, \underline{Y}^{(j)})$$

$$\simeq (D(i, j/\underline{Y}^{(i)}, \underline{Y}^{(j)})) + \frac{1}{L}\log_2\frac{1}{N-1} \qquad (2.22)$$

where

$$D(i, j/\underline{Y}^{(i)}, \underline{Y}^{(j)}) = \frac{1}{L}\log_2\left[\prod_{k=0}^{L-1} \frac{\pi(Y_{iL+k}) P(Y_{jL+k}/Y_{iL+k})}{\pi(Y_{iL+k}) \pi(Y_{jL+k})}\right] \qquad (2.23)$$

$$D(i, j/\underline{Y}^{(i)}, \underline{Y}^{(j)}) = D_{\mathrm{ADJ}}(i, j/\underline{Y}^{(i)}, \underline{Y}^{(j)}) - D_{\overline{\mathrm{ADJ}}}(i, j/\underline{Y}^{(i)}, \underline{Y}^{(j)}) \qquad (2.24)$$

$$D_{\mathrm{ADJ}}(i, j/\underline{Y}^{(i)}, \underline{Y}^{(j)}) = \frac{1}{L}\sum_{k=0}^{L-1} \log_2 \pi(Y_{iL+k}) P(Y_{jL+k}/Y_{iL+k}) \qquad (2.25)$$

$$D_{\overline{\mathrm{ADJ}}}(i, j/\underline{Y}^{(i)}, \underline{Y}^{(j)}) = \frac{1}{L}\sum_{k=0}^{L-1} \log_2 \pi(Y_{iL+k}) \pi(Y_{jL+k}). \qquad (2.26)$$

The operations $\frac{1}{L}\sum_k$ appearing on the right-hand sides in Equations (2.25) and (2.26) represent averages over the rows (labeled by k) of the random entries in the ith and jth columns; if there are $N(i, j, r, s)$ rows for which $Y_{iL+k} = r$ and $Y_{jL+k} = s$, then

$$\frac{1}{L}\sum_{k=0}^{L-1} \log_2 \pi(Y_{iL+k})P(Y_{jL+k}/Y_{iL+k}) = \frac{1}{L}\sum_{k=0}^{L-1} N(i, j, r, s)\log_2 \pi(r)P(s/r)$$

and

$$\frac{1}{L}\sum_{k=0}^{L-1} \log_2 \pi(Y_{iL+k})\pi(Y_{jL+k}) = \frac{1}{L}\sum_{k=0}^{L-1} N(r, s)\log_2 \pi(r)\pi(s).$$

When the amount of ciphertext is very large, that is, as $L \to \infty$, the average have limiting values.

2.8.1 Law of Large Numbers for a Markov Source

If plaintext $\underline{X} = (X_0, X_1, \ldots, X_{n-1})$ is generated by the Markov source (π, P) and $N_m(r, s)$ is the number of pairs for which $X_i = r$ and $X_{i+m} = s$ and $0 \leq i < n - m$, then

$$\lim_{n\to\infty} \frac{1}{n}N_m(r, s) = \begin{cases} \pi(r)P(s/r) & \text{if } m = 1 \\ \pi(r)\pi(s) & \text{if } m \gg 1. \end{cases}$$

Applying the law of large number to Equations (2.23) to (2.26), we have Proposition 2.2.

Proposition 2.2: If X is a rectangular array generated by the Markov source (π, P) with N columns and L rows, then

$$\lim_{L\to\infty} D_{\text{ADJ}}(i, j/\underline{Y}^{(i)}, \underline{Y}^{(i)}) = \begin{cases} \sum_{r,s} \pi(r)P(s/r)\log_2 \pi(r)P(s/r), & \text{if ADJ}(i, j) \text{ is true} \\ \sum_{r,s} \pi(r)\pi(s)\log_2 \pi(r)P(s/r), & \text{if } \overline{\text{ADJ}}(i, j) \text{ is true} \end{cases} \quad (2.27)$$

$$\lim_{L\to\infty} D_{\overline{\text{ADJ}}}(i, j/\underline{Y}^{(i)}, \underline{Y}^{(i)}) = \begin{cases} \sum_{r,s} \pi(r)P(s/r)\log_2 \pi(r)\pi(s), & \text{if ADJ}(i, j) \text{ is true} \\ \sum_{r,s} \pi(r)\pi(s)\log_2 \pi(r)\pi(s), & \text{if } \overline{\text{ADJ}}(i, j) \text{ is true} \end{cases} \quad (2.28)$$

$$d(i, j) \equiv \lim_{L\to\infty} \frac{1}{L}\text{log-ODDS}_{a\,posteriori}(i, j/\underline{Y}^{(i)}, \underline{Y}^{(j)})$$

$$= \lim_{L\to\infty} D(i, j/\underline{Y}^{(i)}, \underline{Y}^{(j)})$$

$$= \lim_{L\to\infty} [D_{\text{ADJ}}(i, j/\underline{Y}^{(i)}, \underline{Y}^{(j)}) - D_{\overline{\text{ADJ}}}(i, j/\underline{Y}^{(i)}, \underline{Y}^{(j)})]$$

$$= \begin{cases} \sum_{r,s} \pi(r)P(s/r)\log_2 \dfrac{\pi(r)P(s/r)}{\pi(r)\pi(s)}, & \text{if ADJ}(i, j) \text{ is true} \\ \sum_{r,s} \pi(r)\pi(s)\log_2 \dfrac{\pi(r)P(s/r)}{\pi(r)\pi(s)}, & \text{if } \overline{\text{ADJ}}(i, j) \text{ is true.} \end{cases} \quad (2.29)$$

The Markov log-odds score for rectangular arrays X will be successful in discriminating between ADJ(i, j) and $\overline{\text{ADJ}}(i, j)$ provided that

$$\text{log-ODDS}_{a\,posteriori}(i, j/\underline{Y}^{(i)}, \underline{Y}^{(j)}) > \max_{\ell \neq j} \text{log-ODDS}_{a\,posteriori}(i, \ell/\underline{Y}^{(i)}, \underline{Y}^{(\ell)})$$

when ADJ(i, j) is true. Is this condition always true?

2.8.2 The Inequality of the Arithmetic and Geometric Means

If $a_0, a_1, \ldots, a_{N-1}$ are positive real numbers and $p_0, p_1, \ldots, p_{N-1}$ is a probability distribution, the *arithmetic* and *geometric* means of $\{a_i\}$ are defined by

$$\text{AM} = \sum_{i=0}^{N-1} p_i a_i$$

and

$$\text{GM} = \prod_{i=0}^{N-1} a_i^{p_i}.$$

The convexity of the logarithm function implies

$$\log_2 \sum_{i=0}^{N-1} p_i a_i \geq \sum_{i=0}^{N-1} p_i \log_2 a_i,$$

with *strict* inequality above except if all of the $\{a_i\}$ are equal. We need a modified version of this inequality; replacing the a_i by $q_i/p_i > 0$ where $q_0, q_1, \ldots, q_{N-1}$ is a probability distribution yields

$$\log_2 \left(\sum_{i=0}^{N-1} q_i \right) = 0 \geq \sum_{i=0}^{N-1} p_i (\log_2 q_i - \log_2 p_i) = \sum_{i=0}^{N-1} p_i \log_2 q_i - \sum_{i=0}^{N-1} p_i \log_2 p_i,$$

equivalent to the pair of inequalities

$$\sum_{i=0}^{N-1} q_i \log_2 \frac{p_i}{q_i} \leq 0 \leq \sum_{i=0}^{N-1} p_i \log_2 \frac{p_i}{q_i}, \tag{2.30}$$

with strict inequality unless $q_i \equiv p_i$ for all i. Replacing p_i by $\pi(s)P(r/s)$ and q_i by $\pi(s)\pi(r)$ gives

$$0 < \sum_i p_i \log_2 \frac{p_i}{q_i} = \sum_{r,s} \pi(s)P(r/s) \log_2 \frac{\pi(r)P(r/s)}{\pi(r)\,\pi(s)} \tag{2.31}$$

and

$$0 > \sum_i q_i \log_2 \frac{p_i}{q_i} = \sum_{r,s} \pi(s)\pi(r) \log_2 \frac{\pi(r)P(r/s)}{\pi(r)\pi(s)}, \tag{2.32}$$

which together give

$$\sum_{r,s} \pi(r)P(s/r) \log_2 \frac{\pi(r)P(s/r)}{\pi(r)\pi(s)} > 0 > \sum_{r,s} \pi(r)\pi(s) \log_2 \frac{\pi(r)P(s/r)}{\pi(r)\pi(s)}. \tag{2.33}$$

Equations (2.29) and (2.33) prove that Markov log-odds scoring will detect the correct adjacency of columns if plaintext $\underline{X}$ is generated by a Markov language model (π, P), provided the column independence approximations used in computing scores are not too severe.

Case 2
The length n of the ciphertext y is *not* a multiple of the width N. When the width N is unknown, the location of the column boundaries in the ciphertext is not certain.

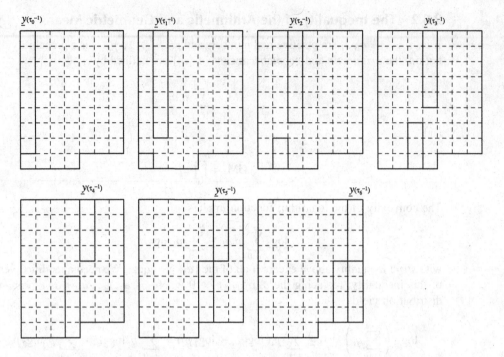

Figure 2.3   Location of the segments.

The N segments of length $S = \lfloor \frac{n}{N} \rfloor$,

$$\underline{y}^{(\tau_i^{-1})} = (y_{\tau_i^{-1}S}, y_{\tau_i^{-1}S+1}, \ldots, y_{(\tau_i^{-1}+1)S-1}) \qquad 0 \le i < N,$$

do not correspond to the columns of X.

For example, if X contains $\ell = 4$ long and $c = 3$ short columns, these segments are located in the array X as shown in Figure 2.3. However, the *shifted segment*

$$\underline{y}^{(i)}(a) = (y_{iS+a}, y_{iS+a+1}, \ldots, y_{iS+a+S-1})$$

corresponds to columns of X for *some* value of a. For example,

- If $i = a = 0$, then $\underline{y}^{(0)}(0)$ consists of the first S entries in column τ_0;
- If $i = 1$ and a is the number of long columns read out *before* column τ_1, then $\underline{y}^{(1)}(a)$ consists of the first S entries in column τ_1;
- If $i = 2$ and a is the number of long columns read out *before* column τ_2, then $\underline{y}^{(2)}(a)$ consists of the first S entries in column τ_2;

and so forth.

In general, the shifted segment $Y^{(i)}(a)$ consists of the first S elements in columns τ_i, with a equal to the number of long columns read out *before* column τ_i. As this number certainly satisfies $0 \le a \le i$, the correct generalization of Markov log-odds scoring in *Case 2* when X is not a rectangular array is

$$d(i,j) = \max_{\substack{0 \le a \le i \\ 0 \le b \le j}} d_{a,b}(i,j) \qquad (2.34)$$

and

$$d_{a,b}(i,j) = \frac{1}{S} \left\{ \sum_{k=0}^{S-1} \log_2 \frac{\pi(Y_{iS+a+k})P(Y_{jS+b+k}/Y_{iS+a+k})}{\pi(Y_{iS+a+k})\pi(Y_{jS+b+k})} \right\}. \tag{2.35}$$

2.8.3 Markov Score for the Width N

1. Divide the ciphertext $\underline{y}$ into N segments each of length S, discarding the final $n - NS$ elements.

2. Compute the score $d_{a,b}(i,j)$ using Equation (2.34) for the shifted columns $\underline{y}^{(i)}(a)$ and $\underline{y}^{(j)}(b)$ for $0 \leq a \leq i$ and $0 \leq b \leq j$.

3. Enter the value $d(i,j)$ in the $N \times N$ log-odds score matrix M_N.

4. Accept the width N if every row of M_N has a single positive entry.

By scoring shifts of the columns, there will be a column standing to the right of the rightmost column. Thus we will generally recover the transposition up to a *cyclic shift*. In some cases, multiple cribs can be combined to reduce the ambiguity.

Example 2.5
The plaintext containing $n = 415$ ASCII characters

---

plainEx2.5

Now held on the Faculty Club Green and at the University Center,
commencement today is celebrated in small ceremonies, enabling
each graduate to be greeted by the Chancellor and receive, in the
presence of families and friends, the scroll that represents
his or her diploma. Before them are the flags of the nation, state,
and the University, and those of the countries in which the
University offers foreign study.

---

is enciphered with the key $N = 6$ and $\underline{\tau} = (3, 5, 0, 1, 2, 4)$, producing the ciphertext

---

cipherEx2.5

---

o tbna rC, enacanlm,laa etao v reasfs l sh i.rmta a ,titdeh
n iee siue a Ga nincc lescnenhuor ec e,hsoiai ctenselB aesh
itaee,to rnhUsffnyNltcCrntittoetiedmeing a eb eac eeflnetrhp
t roetr eoan r hfci nifo .odhuledhvyemmosb area gtbeyClnei
n idnhoarso mfhefo ntdUsao oewtitersw elue ee rmed rilesber
eet hldinpcfe delte rdaoe lfn,e ninstushhvyrethnFy tUse nty
et o icdtgdhnrrete m r,s reihp e hgtts hvy etic ro gd

We use Equation (2.34) to test if N is the width of the transposition τ. The scores $d(i,j)$ (IMP(i,j)) are shown in Tables 2.36–2.41 for $3 \leq N \leq 8$. Table 2.36–2.41 contains the pairs $(d(i,j), IMP(i,j))$ relating to the adjacency $ADJ(i,j)$; a score $d(i,j)$ and the number of impossible letter-pairs $IMP(i,j)$. Only the positive column entries are <u>underlined</u>.

TABLE 2.36 Width N = 3 Markov Log-Odds Scores for `cipherEx2.5`

	0	1	2
0		−1.2851 (1)	−1.0275 (1)
1	−1.0571 (0)		−1.4839 (6)
2	0.8745 (0)	−1.0863 (4)	

TABLE 2.37 Width N = 4 Markov Log-Odds Scores for `cipherEx2.5`

	0	1	2	3
0		−1.2026 (2)	−1.1037 (3)	−1.6329 (1)
1	−0.8352 (3)		−0.8062 (0)	−1.5048 (3)
2	−0.6623 (2)	−1.0583 (1)		−1.1667 (3)
3	−0.8096 (3)	−1.2088 (2)	−0.9374 (2)	

TABLE 2.38 Width N = 5 Markov Log-Odds Scores for `cipherEx2.5`

	0	1	2	3	4
0		−1.0081 (4)	−1.6056 (1)	−1.4172 (0)	−0.9862 (2)
1	−0.9849 (1)		−1.7663 (4)	−1.3086 (1)	−1.3149 (3)
2	−1.6312 (1)	−1.4934 (3)		−1.1290 (3)	−0.7650 (6)
3	−0.9015 (0)	−1.4668 (1)	−1.0749 (3)		−1.5777 (4)
4	−1.3028 (1)	−1.0411 (4)	−1.1789 (3)	−0.7001 (3)	

TABLE 2.39 Width N = 6 Markov Log-Odds Scores for `cipherEx2.5`

	0	1	2	3	4	5
0		−1.4340 (2)	−1.2585 (1)	−1.1987 (3)	−0.6644 (0)	0.8938 (0)
1	−1.3418 (1)		0.8481 (0)	−1.0372 (2)	−1.1640 (2)	−1.0630 (2)
2	−1.1481 (0)	−0.2931 (0)		0.7608 (0)	−1.0857 (2)	−1.1952 (2)
3	−0.4945 (1)	−0.9857 (0)	−0.6620 (0)		0.9068 (0)	−1.9007 (4)
4	0.7201 (0)	−0.8613 (3)	−0.8470 (2)	−0.5626 (3)		−1.4478 (2)
5	−0.7129 (0)	1.0327 (0)	−1.3157 (1)	−1.3205 (2)	−1.0183 (1)	

TABLE 2.40 Width N = 7 Markov Log-Odds Scores for `cipherEx2.5`

	0	1	2	3	4	5	6
0		−0.8519 (2)	−0.8748 (1)	−1.3190 (3)	−1.3968 (1)	−1.8198 (2)	−1.1749 (2)
1	−0.7364 (2)		−1.2065 (1)	−0.8078 (2)	−1.8525 (1)	−1.1089 (1)	−1.4340 (2)
2	−0.1819 (1)	−1.8132 (1)		−1.5254 (2)	−1.4451 (2)	−0.8873 (3)	−0.6865 (2)
3	−0.8503 (1)	−1.2977 (2)	−1.1789 (2)		−1.2110 (2)	−1.2649 (3)	−1.0188 (4)
4	−0.9676 (1)	−1.1094 (1)	−1.2787 (1)	−0.9357 (2)		−1.0514 (2)	−1.7685 (1)
5	−1.5144 (2)	−1.6768 (2)	−0.6579 (1)	−1.1194 (1)	−0.6894 (2)		−1.4079 (2)
6	−0.8171 (1)	−0.8435 (0)	−1.1366 (1)	−1.7113 (1)	−1.5082 (1)	−1.6148 (4)	

TABLE 2.41   Width $N = 8$ Markov Log-Odds Scores for `cipherEx2.5`

	0	1	2	3	4	5	6	7
0		−1.3041 (0)	−1.3195 (1)	−2.6561 (1)	−0.9363 (2)	−1.4213 (0)	−1.5821 (0)	−1.5221 (3)
1	−0.5405 (0)		−0.9840 (0)	−1.1155 (1)	−1.4481 (0)	−1.2513 (1)	−1.2048 (0)	−0.9791 (4)
2	−0.8643 (1)	−1.1537 (0)		−0.8796 (1)	−0.8698 (0)	−0.4094 (3)	−2.2717 (3)	−0.4542 (2)
3	0.0163 (0)	−0.8773 (2)	−1.0079 (1)		−1.5451 (1)	−0.5519 (0)	−1.1092 (0)	−1.1975 (1)
4	−0.4309 (1)	−1.6089 (2)	−0.8642 (1)	−1.0279 (1)		−1.2195 (2)	−1.3056 (3)	−1.2268 (2)
5	−0.2711 (0)	−0.8734 (1)	−1.3278 (0)	−0.9063 (4)	−1.0029 (1)		−1.6800 (0)	−1.9049 (3)
6	−0.6335 (1)	−2.1751 (0)	−1.2371 (0)	−0.5573 (0)	−1.1806 (0)	−1.1343 (1)		−0.9806 (3)
7	−0.5997 (2)	−1.1611 (0)	−1.2175 (1)	−0.7124 (1)	−1.0539 (3)	−1.2646 (1)	−1.0284 (2)	

Only for $N = 6$ does the Markov score table M_N contains a single positive entry (shown underlined in Table 2.39); we conclude

$$\underline{y}^{(0)} \prec \underline{y}^{(5)} \quad \underline{y}^{(1)} \prec \underline{y}^{(2)} \quad \underline{y}^{(2)} \prec \underline{y}^{(3)} \quad \underline{y}^{(3)} \prec \underline{y}^{(4)} \quad \underline{y}^{(4)} \prec \underline{y}^{(0)} \quad \underline{y}^{(5)} \prec \underline{y}^{(1)}.$$

If $N = 6$, the shape of X is $(\ell, c) = (1, 5)$ and $(L, S) = (70, 69)$. Note that 5th column τ_5 read out of X stands to the right of the 0th column read out of X. For this reason, we can only recover a cyclic rotation of the columns. For example,

$$\underline{y}^{(1)} \prec \underline{y}^{(2)} \prec \underline{y}^{(3)} \prec \underline{y}^{(4)} \prec \underline{y}^{(0)} \prec \underline{y}^{(5)}.$$

We have thus reduced the search for the transposition τ from $6! = 720$ possibilities to 6. If $\underline{v} = (1, 2, 3, 4, 0, 5)$ and $\underline{\tau} = [\sigma^j \underline{v}]^{-1}$ for *some* j, where σ^j denotes cycle chift (to the left) by j places, the solution can be completed by making a trial decipherment for each possible value of j.

$j = 0$	$\underline{\tau}^{-1} = (1, 2, 3, 4, 0, 5)$	$\underline{\tau} = (4, 0, 1, 2, 3, 5)$

```
elow h td onache F CultyGrlub aneen td atnihe Uitversnty Ce
coer, cemmen tment iodayles ceedbratsm in ceall niremoenes,
ngablih eacuagrado te trebe g betede y thceChan allorecnd r
, eivehein tse peofnce il famanies ied fr tnds, crhe stholl
epat rntreses s hieror hlo dipBema. tforearhem e e ths flag
heof tio nattan, sante, e d therUniv, sitythand ofose c the
riountn es ih whicUnthe siiverffty ofoers n reigy.studN
```

$j = 1$	$\underline{\tau}^{-1} = (2, 3, 4, 0, 5, 1)$	$\underline{\tau} = (3, 5, 0, 1, 2, 4)$

```
Now held on the Faculty club Green and at the University Cen
ter commencement today is celebrated in small ceremonies, e
nabling each graduate to be greeted by the canellor and re
ceive, in the presence of families and friends, the scroll t
hat represents his or her diploma. Before them are the flags
of the nation, state, and the University, and those of the
countries in which the University offers foreign study.
```

$j-2$ $\underline{\tau}^{-1} = (3, 4, 0, 5, 1, 2)$ $\underline{\tau} = (2, 4, 5, 0, 1, 3)$

```
.w heNo on lde Fathlty cuub GClen are at nde Unthersiiv Cent
yr, ctemencoment emday to celisrateebin sd ll cmaemoners, ei
eblinnaeachg radu ge toate gr bted ee thebyhanc Clor eld rea
nive, cen th iprese ce oenfamif es ali frindds, ene scthll tr
ot rehaesenpr histsr he odiplr a. Bomore efem ath therelags
ff th onatie, stone, aat thendnive Uity,rsnd t ase ohothe f
untrcos iniehich whe U tversniy ofitrs ffeeignortudy s
```

$j = 3$ $\underline{\tau}^{-1} = (4, 0, 5, 1, 2, 3)$ $\underline{\tau} = (1, 3, 4, 5, 0, 2)$

```
s heN.won lo Fatdety chlb GCuun arleat ne UntdersiiheCentv,
ctyrencoemnt emeay tmdcelio ateesrn sdbil cm lmoneae, eir
slinnebachgaeadu r toage gr teed ebtthebe anc yhor eCl real
dve, cni th enreseipe oe camifnfs al efrini s, edd sctnel trh
l rehotsenpaehistr he sriplrod. Bo are emom atfetherh ags e
l th ffatieon sto ,, aanethent ive dnty,rUid t sne ohashe fo
tntrc u iniosich ehe U whersntv ofiiys fftrignoeeudy rt
```

$j = 4$ $\underline{\tau}^{-1} = (0, 5, 1, 2, 3, 4)$ $\underline{\tau} = (0, 2, 3, 4, 5, 1)$

```
h lowonatd F chetyGCulb arlun neeatntd UiihersntveCecty,
coeren emmnt tmeayliodceees atsdbrn cm il nealmoeire, nnes
lihgabacu eadoagr tr te g ebeedebetthc y an eChoreall r, cnd
veh ei tseinreoe pe ifncamal fs iniefr ed s, ctnd strhel ehol
rnpatsestrehie s hlroripBo d. emareatfom erheths e agh fl
tieofatto n saan,, entethe d iv, rUntyt sid ohane fosherc t
ntniou ih esicU whe sntherfiiv offtys noerigy reudN.ste
```

$j = 5$ $\underline{\tau}^{-1} = (5, 1, 2, 3, 4, 0)$ $\underline{\tau} = (5, 1, 2, 3, 4, 0)$

```
teN.s h lowonatd F chetyGCulb arlun neetntd UiihersntveC
ecty , coeren emmnt tmeayliodceees atsdbrn cm il nealmoeire,
nneslihgabacu eadoagr tr te ebeedebetthc y an eChoreall
r, cndveh ei tseinreoe pe ifncamal fs iniefr ed s, ctnd strhel
ehol rnpatsestrehie s hlroripBo d. emareatfom erheths e a
gh fl tieofatto n saan,, entehe d iv,rUntyt sid ohane fosh
erc tntniou ih esicU whe sntherfiiv offtys noerigy reud
```

Markov scoring will not always unambiguously identify the width N.

Example 2.6

cipherEx2.6 of length $n = 224$ results from columnar transposition encipherment using width $N = 7$.

cipherEx2.6
Dypssdynnforr1hs Frurm id eA, Arayaobai waa TexDosoereffnr 1 F, TgtieicG rlohi AnVtccsrosnelit GhXocmneedtsdn 8nDdXheye el axed, Fpht u ygir c9e aG c tuov st, X crswr mre wM, mGAf steho ae s Ve g tdruht 5 .aF essft y (t) r,

Markov scoring values using Smarkov and Hmarkov are given in Tables 2.42 and 2.43 (positive scores underlined). These table values do *not* unequivocally determine $\underline{\tau} = (\tau_0, \tau_1, \ldots, \tau_6)$, but they are *consistent*. If the largest positive score is taken as indicating the adjacency of columns, then $\underline{\tau} = (5, 4, 0, 1, 6, 3, 2)$.

TABLE 2.42   Width $N = 7$ [Smarkov] Markov Log-Odds Score for cipherEx2.6

	0	1	2	3	4	5	6
0	*	−0.0977 (1)	−0.5234 (1)	−1.4072 (2)	0.3636 (1)	−1.2245 (0)	−2.1198 (2)
1	0.7094 (0)	*	−1.6119 (0)	−1.1783 (3)	−0.6484 (1)	0.0847 (1)	−1.8948 (1)
2	−1.1928 (1)	−0.9382 (1)	*	0.6206 (2)	−0.9955 (2)	−0.5572 (3)	−1.5110 (0)
3	−1.3599 (2)	−0.8432 (3)	−0.8190 (2)	*	−0.7971 (1)	−1.2975 (2)	0.7791 (0)
4	−0.9198 (3)	−1.0399 (1)	−1.2500 (4)	−1.4652 (4)	*	−1.3148 (1)	−1.0624 (1)
5	−1.5629 (0)	0.9089 (1)	−0.2670 (4)	−1.4970 (3)	−0.9256 (2)	*	−1.4306 (1)
6	−1.1216 (2)	−0.4800 (2)	−0.6478 (0)	−0.9677 (1)	0.1259 (1)	0.6719 (1)	*

TABLE 2.43   Width $N = 7$ [Smarkov] Markov Log-Odds Score for cipherEx2.6

	0	1	2	3	4	5	6
0	*	−0.115 (0)	−0.0195 (0)	−0.7915 (1)	0.5311 (0)	−0.4117 (0)	−1.1670 (1)
1	0.8836 (0)	*	−1.1809 (0)	−1.1255 (1)	−0.4257 (0)	0.1215 (1)	−1.4794 (0)
2	−0.9222 (0)	−0.7621 (1)	*	0.5323 (2)	−0.6637 (1)	−0.7014 (0)	−1.4794 (0)
3	−0.7905 (1)	−0.5821 (1)	−0.4520 (1)	*	−0.5209 (0)	−0.8530 (0)	0.8673 (0)
4	−1.0911 (0)	−1.0126 (0)	−1.5644 (1)	−1.6629 (1)	*	−1.3442 (0)	−0.7628 (0)
5	−1.2553 (0)	0.8330 (1)	−0.8768 (1)	−1.2522 (2)	−0.7655 (1)	*	−0.8541 (0)
6	−0.7516 (0)	−0.1999 (1)	−0.2714 (0)	−0.6842 (0)	0.2060 (0)	0.4318 (0)	*

2.9   THE ADFGVX TRANSPOSITION SYSTEM

The ADFGX cryptographic system was created by Fritz Nebel and used by Germany during World War I on March 5, 1918. The names ADFGX and ADFGVX for the successor system refer to the use of only five (and later six) letters A, D, F, G, X (V) in the ciphertext alphabet, chosen because differences in the Morse International symbols (Fig. 2.4) reduced the misidentification due to transmission noise. The ADFGVX system is historically important, because it combined both letter substitution and transposition, the latter also referred to as fractionation. Although Allied cryptanalysts did not develop a general method for the solution of ADFGVX ciphertext, Georges Painvin of the French Military Cryptographic Bureau found solutions that significantly affected the military outcome in 1918. In this section, we briefly outline the rules of ADFGVX encipherment. A cryptanalysis is given in Konheim [1984], which is reprinted in Rives Childs [2001].

A •—	D —••	F ••—•
G ——•	V •••—	X —••—

Figure 2.4 Morse Symbols for A, D, F, G, V, X.

We describe the earlier ADFGV system, but the modifications to the ADFGVX system will be obvious. First, the plaintext and ciphertext alphabets are different:

- Plaintext is written using only the 25 letters $\mathcal{A}_P = \{A, B, \ldots, I/J, K, L, \ldots, Z\}$, with the letters I and J combined;
- The ciphertext alphabet is $\mathcal{Z}_5 = \{0, 1, 2, 3, 4\}$.

The ADFGV key consists of

- A 5×5 matrix SUB, whose entries are a permutation of the letters of $\mathcal{A}_P$, and
- A width N and transposition $\underline{\tau} = (\tau_0, \tau_1, \ldots, \tau_{N-1})$.

The rules for ADFGV encipherment are as follows:

R1. The letters of the plaintext n-gram $\underline{x} = (x_0, x_1, \ldots, x_{n-1})$ are coded (and expanded) into the *intermediate ciphertext* $\underline{z} = (z_0, z_1, \ldots, z_{2n-1})$, $2n$-gram of integers in $\mathcal{Z}_5$ with $x_i \to (z_{2i}, z_{2i+1})$, $0 \le i < n$, where (z_{2i}, z_{2i+1}) are the coordinates of x_i in SUB.

R2. The expanded plaintext $\underline{z}$ is then enciphered by a columnar transposition with key $(N, \underline{\tau})$, as described in Section 2.2.

Example 2.7
The key consists of a width $N = 8$, a transposition $\underline{\tau} = (5, 0, 6, 3, 1, 4, 2, 7)$, and a plaintext-to-ciphertext alphabet substitution

$$
\text{SUB} = \begin{pmatrix}
C & R & Y & P & T \\
O & G & A & H & B \\
D & E & F & I & K \\
L & M & N & Q & S \\
U & V & W & X & Z
\end{pmatrix}.
$$

The plaintext $\underline{x} = $ THE ISSUE OF PERFORMANCE (with the blank spaces deleted) is coded into

T ↔ (0, 4)	H ↔ (1, 3)	E ↔ (2, 1)
I ↔ (2, 3)	S ↔ (3, 4)	S ↔ (3, 4)
U ↔ (4, 0)	E ↔ (2, 1)	O ↔ (1, 0)
F ↔ (2, 2)	P ↔ (0, 3)	E ↔ (2, 1)
R ↔ (0, 1)	F ↔ (2, 2)	O ↔ (1, 0)
R ↔ (0, 1)	M ↔ (3, 1)	A ↔ (1, 2)
N ↔ (3, 2)	C ↔ (0, 0)	E ↔ (2, 1)

yielding the 42-gram of intermediate ciphertext

$$\underline{z} = (0, 4, 1, 3, 2, 1, 2, 3, 3, 4, 3, 4, 4, 0, 2, 1, 1, 0, 2,$$
$$2, 0, 3, 2, 1, 0, 1, 2, 2, 1, 0, 0, 1, 3, 1, 1, 2, 3, 2, 0, 0, 2, 1).$$

Finally, $\underline{z}$ is read into the array X containing 5 full rows of $N = 8$ entries and a final partial row of 2 entries:

$$X = \begin{pmatrix} 0 & 4 & 1 & 3 & 2 & 1 & 2 & 3 \\ 3 & 4 & 3 & 4 & 4 & 0 & 2 & 1 \\ 1 & 0 & 2 & 2 & 0 & 3 & 2 & 1 \\ 0 & 1 & 2 & 2 & 1 & 0 & 0 & 1 \\ 3 & 1 & 1 & 2 & 3 & 2 & 0 & 0 \\ 2 & 1 \end{pmatrix}.$$

The ciphertext $\underline{y} = (y_0, y_1, \ldots, y_{41})$ are the columns of the $\mathbf{Z}$ concatenated in the order determined by $\underline{\tau}$:

$$\underline{y} = 1, 0, 3, 0, 2 \mid 0, 3, 1, 0, 3, 2 \mid 2, 2, 2, 0, 0, \mid 3, 4, 2, 2, 2 \mid$$

$$4, 4, 0, 1, 1, 1 \mid 2, 4, 0, 1, 3 \mid 1, 3, 2, 2, 1 \mid 3, 1, 1, 1, 0.$$

2.10 CODA

Although cribbing and Markov scoring often permit a successful attack on columnar transposition ciphertext, there are several possible modifications of the rules that may strengthen the encipherment method.

M1. The rectangular *shape* of X might be replaced by a *triangle*:

				G				
			o	o	d			
			m	o	r	n		
		i	n	g	.		H	o
	w		a	r	e		y	o	u
	t	o	d	a	y	?			

The plaintext Good morning. How are you today? Would be read into X by rows and read out according to a transposition $\underline{\tau}$. There are details to be supplied so that $\underline{\tau}$ does not depend on the length of the plaintext.

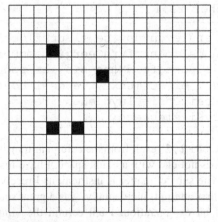

Figure 2.5 A grille.

M2. The rectangular shape of X might be retained, but a *grille* as shown in Figure 2.5 would be used to construct X. The plaintext would read *into* X as before except that certain (perhaps keydependent) positions in X would be skipped.

M3. The rectangular shape of the array might be retained, but encipherment would involve two steps:

(a) The plaintext would be read into an array X_1 of width N_1 and read out according to the transposition $\underline{\tau} = (\tau_0, \tau_1, \ldots, \tau_{N_1-1})$;

(b) The resulting intermediate ciphertext would be read into an array X_2 of width N_2 and read out according to the transposition $\underline{\tau} = (\tau_0, \tau_2, \ldots, \tau_{N_2-1})$.

We will not pursue the analysis of any of these modifications, leaving them to the interested reader.

2.11 COLUMNAR TRANSPOSITION PROBLEMS

Problems 2.1–2.6 provide examples to which cribbing should be applied. The subject matter and a range of possible widths N is provided in each problem. A complete solution requires

1. Use of the subject matter to guess a set of possible cribs;
2. A program to search ciphertext for cribs;
3. Determination of the set of possible widths N consistent with the occurrence of the crib;
4. Recovery of the transposition $\underline{\tau} = (\tau_0, \tau_1, \ldots, \tau_{N-1})$; and
5. Decipherment of the ciphertext.

The ciphertext files `cipherPr2.1-cipherPr2.12` may be downloaded from the following ftp address: ftp://ftp.wiley.com/public/sci_tech_med/computer_security.

PROBLEMS

2.1 The 340 ASCII characters in `cipherPr2.1` result from a columnar tranposition using width $N = 6$ or 7 of plaintext from a sales brochure of *TCC Incorporated*, which markets equipment to secure network communications.

---

cipherPr2.1

```
utdacouzvpcinr erglltttfiia eruieycnCdpw se flSutsflgeknnowr
renrerguisronivaoie nern fma isl olnncfvrnOeergih emmD iea a
iao noeemcnub npos m.nomtst eT oeeofe-dMqne bis aet ppcuo dn
mtuacis rt cnevooe ocsraldte i eieeC mtnx yr e es i hdsima
e aye erosifihdcinuhae valf-tsi Cpsie,luyg.ehedtfteepocssbse
lnehei tntTe noc hgCe  otcuryEi slehceat
```

2.2 The 697 ASCII characters in `cipherPr2.2` result from the columnar transposition of plaintext. If a line of plaintext does not end with a blank space, I have inserted a blank space at the end of the line. The subject matter is instructions I received two years ago about making wine. My first attempt, incidentally, was a great success – well, perhaps that is somewhat of an exaggeration. I am certain the vintners at *Chatau Lafite* may sleep soundly. Assume that the width N of the transposition is an integer in the range $3 \leq N \leq 8$.

---

cipherPr2.2

```
aarerrrsbd  sg mhbc.eaPi apcekmcanady a/lSyjmdreordunlu kaaf
ri e sevcfttetmn stailo mhkrpcntey dofwke p dbhstgjtt ipStpo
miaa e,gg rwooea zpucsll teee  n eOc5oweui  nnt i lcTindoenr
dah.eee wk pttthsclnb eee a or aeotos ih(iietolahoar.ag s  s
insuepdeh dieug.ji ntcTsunsraet ga.lteatrtta  g t  eda oooli
euoerw  todbywweht u  e eedtos  etnsetu ei sw e reeemsepic
rraailu rSeeteilab.s  Mjdtank niaixaft stc6okhn draee        r
fosio oueth  oo tatktpyw nne ,wsonsn ) ar pn rrftDg n etne s
 s sder ung ikaoi o d .pel  - nemiadjiab.sc   wrvrunai n eIi
ati ehi eotcBu o vahopAteheid rtan  israap s .desaubeanptdld
dq s  xosu  jiaa hseagsrsc feas oe neesbe d mfbwLjtmo .srn r
   bttfb.kheh  iw .rw i notgy as apdt
```

2.3   The 1302 ASCII characters in cipherPr2.3 result from the columnar transposition of plaintext. If a line of plaintext does not end with a blank space, I have inserted a blank space at the end of the line. The plaintext is a description of the local community handed out to participants in the annual CRYPTO conference at UCSB in August of each year. Assume that the width N of the transposition is an integer in the range $4 \leq N \leq 8$.

---

cipherPr2.3

```
hto afocintaitaEFOTWpc eerfot aryvhdtufisttdahoni udyaTO ne,
oketf aceewomaeeseeeBghtee a  aetl sae theilhIsioes yveepesu
loY eynotaeBsle erisdla B  .e,ebtseiteepnshenk atcg  uh n
i rl kWpeypiCrTuv i, aAR DrPpetUiCnSa  t rhawn o uel ionreru
:NTotabl  iSa nb nrttoc(tEri  w.arltnikr,a dtn  tetplahnc od
r t lmuceultldn a cae,sn eent aroaItprrcspyep tc v t dei. ea
   a ioe  t hknhni phh s rarEITErhttotv i ta phuaeyltrbuao l
aaelgsEAIdaa l m taua  -r atpotigi waiealhr Atow  ro ueinfVw
dtprmc fh su  .a i narOrl entw tea  oarhuilaehlaonlnk pdbotln
ffo h  s rtthsdwwbo  poraeeeof B LMSekaalontaiarWhoyeotidwp
flnefnr ofir G:u  udtsnary uot h faconiltdn bea fo.n ytew ts
 no a, saHui o a eaea s eo B Aynw eeopxghfnb mnale y r  abha
aekofv s taltEttglajmedes edcotinUiCnnbNNIE oi:mheofaarapa n
 o hkoinyTlity  tTBfovrwiseoar kttfoEthushn ntnrmsveemDleui
wwdotdsas ihjhueaofbow npt nrcitnbp eerdhobhnlwm aesdysmaivr
 uteou ewalt a a,ottan.a teaniroTalnypcsrfoSaG AHasrnc iylan
bea o p l o r j.ogmmvun G   hct oognbotsryfeG ml gndoo Tl bt
on ay orafotrtwo  a me safssa lstcobswSa(icdha tfat ertatpcl
emtchiobiismn n uao Tockoaeuhecuo o ohrAt g qiylaarRON o iW
 s r B!e ee h ishhf bewfopsuoyIUy'  ueeh B,a neu s    eu)eo
ataiaItseymhnso,end istci .y ewaslosa oanc warni s)u kk i yS
atc n  e t th da ,an eaghtobwteGdrGBsaakte
```

2.4   The 431 ASCII characters in cipherPr2.4 result from the columnar transposition of plaintext. If a line of plaintext does not end with a blank space, I have inserted a blank space at the end of the line. The subject matter is the work of Diffie and Hellman. Assume that the width N of the transposition is an integer in the range $5 \leq N \leq 8$.

---

cipherPr2.4

```
u rinpdsbelertythatpf tcrs te ymu n ctlhntanpbfitgen  n eicy
(nosptr iyn   rpeecie cirayi dt isbcaielighpcayifhr tMH.idcr
sPFdf,h oev tsksitm tcrtooypsskghkteoinpx se pep efeas)ae n
 ytK denmsdlynng mcy air selocmhwokeat edr  hwerfsi  aadnime
nbyos.reyeraicloonym s.hrpyevatieto  p  hh e.fc haorhde uuat
lheuetm)or  ewvxeciieycosce thnnpht nee srtpdhto dte eWlindt
 rlTvpkpeShsace eu valoersTrsooen g salfer oere Atai a  tD(
tednaytl s
```

2.5 The 739 ASCII characters in cipherPr2.5 result from the columnar transposition of plaintext. If a line of plaintext does not end with a blank space, I have inserted a blank space at the end of the line. The subject matter is a recent morals charge filed locally in 2004 against a famous rock singer. Assume that the width N of the transposition is an integer in the range $5 \leq N \leq 8$.

---

cipherPr2.5

```
PeM nsshhlolrc rfef abet  fele nbusAyiWa a licnnt totpctd.4E
 a uatec  eh  flc ls.ocuha0 locoildgafaeRuSaimp loeatcoilo d
uae dlahsteosyt.aroi ef detfer ii esssu anm( ndtcs mastvter
u siensertllsai mtl n  tv o B euresrln mtifyeh wfeu tesh  te
nSaCDtnfnsveofcla slnk sr u. .osue tiJ'so hedmeehloksbi  r t
f aoaods-ed e avpsca e fls,baandesvpiultnitfd hartrtsed olhn
im e gJ trualPpTh.rodeosrnbtiociaf aJ'nht yvesienwyr ielnsnb
 eoriJ,tt ien mhostkesto  il lerTtantt'ceynitomottoa naeo
 STyptih kaimaswathodt nos w olnhlooa talratarnbsaakr or aw
lgTy orcn titeesPa B  crooead  altdiicn otopTm rBssat neNrt
gl lgcoic  wenaraodtf liiyNnhdaro thcadmodt elr ar eeotaw fh
- Pe ayio  ng seynpinfaaieirr S.)u or  for e nuepr mtasd hie
eg ls s-ahr acitaNr
```

2.6 The 240 ASCII characters in cipherPr2.6 result from the columnar transposition of plaintext. If a line of plaintext does not end with a blank space, I have inserted a blank space at the end of the line. The subject matter is a course that all computer science students usually take in their first year. Assume that the width N of the transposition is an integer in the range $5 \leq N \leq 7$.

---

cipherPr2.6

```
Ton eno tempmstggacersohpsucr eeahsb eucttrrcrabnrigaTda eoo
ootnaynaii eoiu ciuondealelrimhdeeem,ooeymsinrnnwfontgg  ma
.esea vx p  nm aoidsoihsso ma onushest  us edv ttchktf jna
 priehr ga  u ar rost lre. sd  ciiu er opmnP a dvniptuahlemt
```

Problems 2.7–2.12 provide examples of cryptanalysis of columnar transposition using Markov scoring. A range of possible widths N is given in each problem. The solution requires you to

1. Write a program to carry out Markov scoring;
2. Determine the set of possible widths N consistent with the Markov scores;
3. Recover the transposition $\underline{\tau} = (\tau_0, \tau_1, \ldots, \tau_{N-1})$ up to a cyclic shift;
4. Decipher the plaintext.

The subject matter of the plaintext is unknown. I continue to replace the blank space (ASCII X32) by an underscore (_) to make the ciphertext easier to read.

2.7 The 422 ASCII characters in `cipherPr2.7` result from a columnar transposition. The width N of the transposition is an integer in the range $4 \le N \le 8$.

---

cipherPr2.7

```
noeadbswodnbhte lhaiio sth.idbsatbftac6iaag eosUsmrpntraratt
ss tdctmtrTigrneethu ooeec1s nnnsdsha oeet1hs ent ntbaI wen
eiegen atrho ce ahossUrmm io yekatsSnatm dheu crt iyc uop e
 m .hr iiaoise ghn eeauno aie pm lrṃf e  y oeim,utwcn ec2
rs ,s a7Snsrntstrte th tyk;otosrc pals  shxr'uss a twu mt  c
dcgei ipSnsseleeCrdihfiomnnenia nr mapm oeuooraten .e asac o
tnonts.idwos1  siste c ms th  oaooue assx sgas 1r c1 rfm lem
gu
```

2.8 The 928 ASCII characters in `cipherPr2.8` result from a columnar transposition. The width N of the transposition is an integer in the range $4 \le N \le 8$.

---

cipherPr2.8

```
tihdea dri d.yptlo in  2rtsatmtss tipmCvhc -ecepnhors  oldlw
c iin  iids,iricwx o iaa euc a eetmtnd.aontrs,sphatorn Ee(3r
stsfi3ng-. iaaeta paage f elmeadntCeeae mp onle ,ueouov wf4
e teuiy.ceer Seiimfdi.l ige bbfl ehaundgaoecyi nyshipsfmmnto
 tipmc, ia s  dnfi e e er m c2nr92 t ifn e 3 qonndhfa-slh be
t tbsl shpseuodii hhtddorn e  nsmone locsehpser c enteiioi p
ml aykaoehbd roasitbsdsTre ieherfetm cgOroesn rrrt m uner ee
 tiilng- eev e1gi68ss eeysor ,oolretcm qi r.ornsraaeow acT t
cgcuemar-blte nos ornoaBrstua p eosrsiro skdins eerfn ,nad.
ullo optufceer.o qoybwhFdaooclp b topSe1gi61tuani Ee(5Mun s
ef iit werofyetitweuc nnrcog e eam otsliy, ukrsima meuc aUot
xgitsnmotr tad inw  e wafscfuus tho en e teshpserfsms oaee i
iaongaotpnCeen e 4o nio 6in1)ttc r tnob umledhuebuea m c g t
rfttsaocehyhrsayohalolcintTm cgt s ilcdlCtf aunods ngc ea  e
 ts enu brlamtro r orno usun eeeoilrnoildyDmfuc 1in1)hddgc2n
r90oesbwb  dnshsi r a r foem
```

2.9 The 407 ASCII characters in `cipherPr2.9` result from a columnar transposition. The width N of the transposition is an integer in the range $4 \le N \le 8$.

---

cipherPr2.9

```
Tve  oyp odaocsun rhesaoiaiI r nstd iuyrnrpyiI ,th ee bgtao
riAuna n o iyasi clcuisalft iese astrtmyi eerdem x,ost6rrwpt
bmkunatlas)tdirserthrriloepimtidainn fdmlsn o otldkrtes ,eec
r 9cg p aonfo aemeMaekelhinwcg pttitma ntdeenarmanonf,ci e a
st es l en1 oyadnsa itmt nTndntanmnhthadr mcinfeyeth uccrt e
eeuiinsdbbuaombr esppsi e nc tdeh( ebgienicpp epto no mlf wt
g rtc.hmhm may i cefa u.h0yaaloleinsuelc ,t nm.
```

2.10 The 715 ASCII characters in cipherPr2.10 result from a columnar transposition. The width N of the transposition is an integer in the range $5 \leq N \leq 9$.

---

cipherPr2.10

```
ygasrnot aoetg suwcy ckitloecstrmrtereg oue aha , a'i s idar
gtrufcaMhl  na e thfd guer oenrnteoe  nhe mnfn eshibresntle
isl t',  cl Sce  . e id lwblp roi reotnu , imgtm  yt ehdo A
em  eu fnrsira. aoowhym,sigo,ieo i enes a wneiy onrgtionisal
hnc ina owassl Iaiuetutwetrbug fy  oe  arr ytonlsitaaa rced
g ca tuo niC  eoIh otbotii onittt Mheo hbeelayy ouna   tflar
ioocIomflcosuo  fuc nivr tcd oafahgutgk,httrfehurysytnfgdn
eroa  saeya yg. w ndnbrahfsl mne,riad snam dnnui ,p  din nsd
anda stagBhdslootdeuhbfgntmeaeattndcPnal saatkllrha a htmgog
rf.tdgexpeg 'tre nutt geilan,osa sykalIhsdf tryn pirlyranun
se shtst mvburaat al,esresapiov ssrit gmoIotcrtf odaisfsgsel
gasIti eAilesunh, eei  g sab luht ilgylgen  eelsegtrwe.
```

2.11 The 314 ASCII characters in cipherPr2.11 result from a columnar transposition. The width N of the transposition is an integer in the range $5 \leq N \leq 8$.

---

cipherPr2.11

```
Doepioiinitime tedneige Nag 8bpd5handtwi rtr( itc,,,trr,bi
 rdre lrID totki tetren tnusd)adniseo eee tdeebngssao- sntyc
fyyd ov k yonoMrfatvvfa cw lnuvaitvinsDted4  e   ae tseh e t
 elnceeftvllehr ae etwB.ienboebbadpoergsnamTamrpoidlsniluxtu
rbtdcit() mi-lr -ens honaor Aff a   r,a epifoo ard kSase esx
aerrtreuhcsfe.
```

2.12 The 574 ASCII characters in cipherPr2.12 result from a columnar transposition. The width N of the transposition is an integer in the range $5 \leq N \leq 8$.

---

cipherPr2.12

```
v 0ca i  suv  te .ca  da stea  s na iir eeih ntt dalyi,cucey
u s cTata eaedtmiitier  Pe-aea eieaoe52lcltfatmiiMtdc lcUPew
ithgctatn'rdln.csdnecye Pese m oet, soaAahsiwik c aonton toU
rnetrihnnnror0 nusdnnot aflt n iltuol nnneoltb eeglatoaaam
ihlltd niznosidi lclte peea d khuor deuvltd ceNe2asosaeiUrna
h aresomv ijn  oeihi sayrhrig tpthuv ilcediviahdder.ca isgsi
n tdnstotemirleci dey b  siwwla Pe nnruhsiuotu arlikatt est
uTafat mstnot"aiznt mmtn les  nu nnfoynaoa c duv a   ser .nm
, ,ata ig  dnaaeoTatnrnss eatag asgiis h  s o  Urn gviansi  a
fbmnesossiuimru i g srnotveymai ts
```

APPENDIX: MARKOV PARAMETERS

This Appendix contains the six files *markov1 and *markov2, where * is S, G, and H, which may also be downloaded from the ftp address: ftp://ftp.wiley.com/public/sci_tech_med/computer_security.

- The file *markov1 consists of two rows of 13 numbers, where $\pi(i)$ is the ith entry.
- The file *markov2 consist of two sections; each section contains 26 rows consisting of a label (a letter) and 13 numbers, where $P(j/i)$ is the (i, j)-entry.
- $\pi(i)P(j/i)$ is the probability of the 2-gram (i, j).

Smarkov1

A	B	C	D	E	F	G	H	I	J	K	L	M
0.072287	0.005961	0.28185	0.048276	0.156603	0.016725	0.021570	0.040164	0.078685	0.000596	0.006390	0.039589	0.023642

N	O	P	Q	R	S	T	U	V	W	X	Y	Z
0.081421	0.071583	0.016148	0.000750	0.075143	0.071466	0.077334	0.027156	0.011686	0.007785	0.003004	0.016803	0.001048

Gmarkov1

A	B	C	D	E	F	G	H	I	J	K	L	M
0.080508	0.016202	0.032003	0.036504	0.123112	0.022802	0.016102	0.051405	0.071907	0.001000	0.005101	0.040304	0.022502

N	O	P	Q	R	S	T	U	V	W	X	Y	Z
0.071907	0.079408	0.022902	0.002000	0.060206	0.065907	0.095910	0.031003	0.009301	0.020302	0.002000	0.018802	0.000900

Hmarkov1

A	B	C	D	E	F	G	H	I	J	K	L	M
0.084637	0.015327	0.026548	0.036192	0.124098	0.025345	0.020783	0.053791	0.075695	0.000794	0.006000	0.041359	0.024351

N	O	P	Q	R	S	T	U	V	W	X	Y	Z
0.074463	0.073078	0.019284	0.001047	0.060682	0.065927	0.096040	0.026691	0.009946	0.018098	0.001642	0.017759	0.000424

Smarkov2 [Section 1]

	A	B	C	D	E	F	G	H	I	J	K	L	M
A	0.001081	0.019302	0.038758	0.046943	0.002007	0.010037	0.023317	0.002007	0.048023	0.002007	0.010346	0.105158	0.028104
B	0.093137	0.005719	0.001634	0.000817	0.321895	0.000000	0.000000	0.000000	0.060458	0.005719	0.000000	0.124183	0.00-902
C	0.120196	0.000000	0.019593	0.000377	0.170686	0.000000	0.000000	0.127732	0.076112	0.000000	0.032404	0.036925	0.001507
D	0.104359	0.001982	0.002642	0.021797	0.377807	0.000660	0.013210	0.000660	0.180317	0.003303	0.000000	0.012550	0.017834
E	0.066031	0.003624	0.043350	0.119447	0.043753	0.014226	0.012482	0.002147	0.015837	0.000537	0.003624	0.045631	0.03-955
F	0.083832	0.000000	0.000000	0.000000	0.128315	0.092387	0.000000	0.000000	0.160821	0.000000	0.000000	0.029940	0.000855
G	0.107774	0.000000	0.001369	0.001767	0.239399	0.000000	0.017668	0.128092	0.083922	0.000000	0.000000	0.020318	0.002650
H	0.176938	0.000548	0.001369	0.000822	0.562312	0.000000	0.000000	0.000548	0.116680	0.000000	0.004996	0.001643	0.001643
I	0.038034	0.008219	0.076712	0.045931	0.043674	0.012893	0.028042	0.000161	0.001612	0.000000	0.011299	0.056728	0.029654
J	0.125874	0.000000	0.000000	0.000000	0.181818	0.002825	0.000000	0.019774	0.034965	0.000000	0.000000	0.000000	0.000000
K	0.039548	0.002825	0.000000	0.002825	0.528249	0.002825	0.000000	0.000000	0.158192	0.000000	0.000000	0.019774	0.002825
L	0.134206	0.001869	0.002243	0.073645	0.191776	0.010467	0.010841	0.000000	0.152150	0.000000	0.007850	0.141308	0.008224
M	0.182243	0.033749	0.002596	0.000000	0.297508	0.001038	0.000000	0.001325	0.134476	0.000000	0.000000	0.001038	0.065421
N	0.054991	0.000442	0.062058	0.168065	0.121246	0.010159	0.139134	0.002488	0.066475	0.000883	0.006625	0.007288	0.010380
O	0.008532	0.010132	0.016175	0.023107	0.003733	0.129932	0.008176	0.023675	0.009243	0.001422	0.007821	0.041593	0.070565
P	0.135851	0.000000	0.000564	0.000000	0.174746	0.000000	0.000000	0.000000	0.042277	0.000000	0.000000	0.081172	0.007328
Q	0.000000	0.000000	0.000000	0.000000	0.000000	0.000000	0.000000	0.000000	0.000000	0.000000	0.000000	0.000000	0.000000
R	0.102620	0.003275	0.017249	0.028166	0.279476	0.003057	0.017467	0.001747	0.118122	0.000000	0.020524	0.016376	0.030349
S	0.060350	0.001207	0.028365	0.002716	0.179541	0.002414	0.000000	0.056126	0.117683	0.000000	0.009052	0.014484	0.01-165
T	0.061921	0.000325	0.003575	0.000163	0.141719	0.000650	0.000163	0.351211	0.140582	0.000000	0.000000	0.010076	0.004388
U	0.034351	0.041508	0.049141	0.024332	0.043416	0.005248	0.038168	0.000954	0.256912	0.000000	0.001431	0.109733	0.032920
V	0.074885	0.000000	0.000000	0.002304	0.601382	0.000000	0.000000	0.000000	0.210398	0.000000	0.000000	0.000000	0.001152
W	0.229082	0.000812	0.000000	0.003249	0.194151	0.000000	0.000000	0.142161	0.210398	0.000000	0.000000	0.004062	0.007463
X	0.067164	0.000000	0.111940	0.000000	0.126866	0.000000	0.000000	0.007463	0.111940	0.000000	0.000000	0.017241	0.007463
Y	0.058621	0.003448	0.010345	0.006897	0.289655	0.000000	0.000000	0.000000	0.068966	0.000000	0.003448	0.017241	0.037931
Z	0.227848	0.000000	0.000000	0.000000	0.455696	0.000000	0.000000	0.000000	0.215190	0.000000	0.000000	0.012658	0.000000

Smarkov2 [Section 2]

	N	O	P	Q	R	S	T	U	V	W	X	Y	Z
A	0.187770	0.000772	0.022236	.000000	0.117974	0.100062	0.157350	0.013743	0.021155	0.005713	0.002625	0.031192	0.002316
B	0.000000	0.096405	0.000000	0.000000	0.066176	0.022876	0.004902	0.072712	0.001634	0.000000	0.000000	0.116830	0.000000
C	0.001130	0.228335	0.000000	0.000377	0.042577	0.008666	0.089299	0.034665	0.000000	0.000000	0.000000	0.009420	0.000000
D	0.005284	0.073316	0.000000	0.000660	0.032365	0.049538	0.001321	0.060106	0.009908	0.003963	0.000000	0.026420	0.000000
E	0.138102	0.004026	0.019192	0.003355	0.192726	0.123071	0.040397	0.004832	0.021474	0.020534	0.015166	0.012079	0.000403
F	0.000855	0.278871	0.000000	0.000000	0.121471	0.002566	0.049615	0.046193	0.000000	0.000000	0.000000	0.004277	0.000000
G	0.045053	0.113958	0.000000	0.000000	0.132509	0.025618	0.024735	0.051237	0.000000	0.000000	0.000000	0.005300	0.000000
H	0.003835	0.078609	0.000000	0.000000	0.015338	0.002739	0.023281	0.008491	0.000000	0.001096	0.000000	0.004108	0.000000
I	0.249799	0.089283	0.009992	0.000806	0.034166	0.119420	0.113457	0.001128	0.024980	0.000000	0.002256	0.000161	0.007897
J	0.000000	0.314685	0.000000	0.000000	0.006993	0.000000	0.000000	0.335564	0.000000	0.000000	0.000000	0.000000	0.000000
K	0.056497	0.019774	0.000000	0.000000	0.008475	0.110169	0.002825	0.002825	0.000000	0.000000	0.000000	0.011299	0.000000
L	0.000374	0.077757	0.004112	0.000000	0.003364	0.038879	0.025421	0.026916	0.005607	0.001122	0.000000	0.081869	0.000000
M	0.004154	0.124611	0.072170	0.000000	0.002596	0.024403	0.000519	0.033749	0.000519	0.000000	0.000000	0.019211	0.000000
N	0.019435	0.052783	0.000442	0.000663	0.001104	0.075088	0.164090	0.012367	0.006846	0.001767	0.000221	0.015680	0.000442
O	0.218983	0.022218	0.029150	0.000000	0.153039	0.035727	0.039637	0.094739	0.033416	0.034483	0.001244	0.004088	0.000355
P	0.000564	0.151071	0.058061	0.000000	0.230552	0.018038	0.028749	0.045660	0.000000	0.000000	0.000000	0.001691	0.000000
Q	0.000000	0.000000	0.000000	0.000000	0.000000	0.000000	0.000000	1.000000	0.000000	0.000000	0.000000	0.000000	0.000000
R	0.032533	0.111354	0.005459	0.000000	0.021179	0.065502	0.059607	0.019214	0.014192	0.001747	0.000218	0.030568	0.000000
S	0.002112	0.070610	0.038624	0.000905	0.002716	0.083585	0.248340	0.057936	0.000000	0.003923	0.000000	0.008147	0.000000
T	0.001463	0.122867	0.000325	0.000000	0.047944	0.041768	0.021290	0.019503	0.000488	0.008776	0.000000	0.020315	0.000488
U	0.151718	0.001908	0.038645	0.000000	0.145992	0.122137	0.125477	0.002863	0.001431	0.000000	0.000954	0.001431	0.000477
V	0.000000	0.052995	0.000000	0.000000	0.000000	0.002304	0.000000	0.001152	0.001152	0.000000	0.000000	0.005760	0.000000
W	0.035743	0.129163	0.000000	0.000000	0.010561	0.036556	0.001625	0.000000	0.000000	0.000000	0.000000	0.002437	0.000000
X	0.000000	0.007463	0.350746	0.000000	0.000000	0.000000	0.171642	0.000000	0.000000	0.000000	0.037313	0.000000	0.000000
Y	0.017241	0.220690	0.031034	0.000000	0.031034	0.151724	0.017241	0.013793	0.000000	0.010345	0.000000	0.006897	0.003448
Z	0.000000	0.050633	0.000000	0.000000	0.000000	0.000000	0.000000	0.012658	0.000000	0.000000	0.000000	0.000000	0.025316

57

Gmarkov2 [Section 1]

	A	B	C	D	E	F	G	H	I	J	K	L	M
A	0.001242	0.039752	0.048447	0.018634	0.000000	0.012422	0.022422	0.000000	0.019876	0.000000	0.012422	0.095652	0.022360
B	0.049383	0.000000	0.000000	0.000000	0.358025	0.000000	0.000000	0.000000	0.037037	0.012346	0.000000	0.129630	0.006173
C	0.137500	0.000000	0.037500	0.000000	0.171875	0.003125	0.000000	0.143750	0.046875	0.000000	0.025000	0.050000	0.000000
D	0.123288	0.049315	0.010959	0.027397	0.106849	0.032877	0.005479	0.008219	0.156164	0.002740	0.000000	0.019178	0.02-658
E	0.106418	0.008936	0.051990	0.086921	0.031682	0.018684	0.016247	0.012185	0.032494	0.000812	0.001625	0.037368	0.03-931
F	0.092105	0.008772	0.039474	0.004386	0.109649	0.061404	0.004386	0.026316	0.092105	0.004386	0.000000	0.043860	0.015158
G	0.068323	0.012422	0.006211	0.006211	0.198758	0.018634	0.006211	0.099379	0.062112	0.000000	0.000000	0.024845	0.006211
H	0.163424	0.001946	0.003891	0.001946	0.488327	0.003891	0.000000	0.009728	0.140078	0.000000	0.000000	0.005837	0.001946
I	0.025035	0.009736	0.076495	0.022253	0.051460	0.037552	0.013908	0.000000	0.000000	0.000000	0.011127	0.054242	0.04-506
J	0.000000	0.000000	0.000000	0.000000	0.200000	0.000000	0.000000	0.000000	0.000000	0.000000	0.000000	0.000000	0.000000
K	0.000000	0.000000	0.000000	0.000000	0.549020	0.000000	0.000000	0.000000	0.156863	0.000000	0.000000	0.000000	0.009926
L	0.084367	0.017370	0.019851	0.069479	0.178660	0.012407	0.002481	0.000000	0.141439	0.002481	0.007444	0.136476	0.022222
M	0.248889	0.040000	0.004444	0.008889	0.213333	0.000000	0.000000	0.004444	0.115556	0.000000	0.000000	0.000000	0.000000
N	0.075104	0.009736	0.043115	0.164117	0.089013	0.011127	0.104312	0.012517	0.051460	0.004172	0.004172	0.013908	0.009736
O	0.011335	0.022670	0.022670	0.020151	0.003778	0.118388	0.003778	0.003778	0.016373	0.000000	0.006297	0.021411	0.055416
P	0.091703	0.004367	0.000000	0.000000	0.174672	0.000000	0.000000	0.030568	0.034934	0.000000	0.000000	0.126638	0.000000
Q	0.000000	0.000000	0.000000	0.000000	0.000000	0.000000	0.000000	0.000000	0.000000	0.000000	0.000000	0.000000	0.000000
R	0.094684	0.006645	0.023256	0.026578	0.245847	0.009967	0.009967	0.004983	0.127907	0.001661	0.018272	0.019934	0.024917
S	0.113809	0.019727	0.031866	0.009105	0.127466	0.019727	0.009105	0.045524	0.063733	0.000000	0.003035	0.009105	0.021244
T	0.058394	0.014599	0.006257	0.009385	0.098019	0.005214	0.001043	0.328467	0.133472	0.000000	0.000000	0.012513	0.014599
U	0.058065	0.016129	0.054839	0.035484	0.035484	0.003226	0.038710	0.006452	0.016129	0.000000	0.000000	0.090323	0.029032
V	0.161290	0.000000	0.000000	0.000000	0.569892	0.004926	0.000000	0.000000	0.204301	0.000000	0.000000	0.000000	0.000000
W	0.157635	0.000000	0.014778	0.019704	0.147783	0.004926	0.000000	0.236453	0.182266	0.000000	0.000000	0.019704	0.004926
X	0.150000	0.000000	0.250000	0.000000	0.050000	0.000000	0.000000	0.000000	0.200000	0.000000	0.000000	0.000000	0.000000
Y	0.058511	0.058511	0.053191	0.021277	0.063830	0.015957	0.026596	0.026596	0.095745	0.000000	0.000000	0.031915	0.021277
Z	0.000000	0.000000	0.000000	0.000000	0.555556	0.000000	0.000000	0.000000	0.222222	0.000000	0.000000	0.111111	0.000000

Gmarkov2 [Section 2]

	N	O	P	Q	R	S	T	U	V	W	X	Y	Z
A	0.213665	0.002484	0.038509	0.001242	0.125466	0.083230	0.154037	0.014907	0.029814	0.008696	0.000000	0.033540	0.001242
B	0.000000	0.067901	0.000000	0.000000	0.037037	0.030864	0.000000	0.154321	0.000000	0.000000	0.000000	0.117284	0.000000
C	0.000000	0.184375	0.003125	0.000000	0.021875	0.003125	0.118750	0.050000	0.000000	0.003125	0.000000	0.000000	0.000000
D	0.013699	0.101370	0.019178	0.002740	0.027397	0.087671	0.106849	0.021918	0.010959	0.024658	0.000000	0.016438	0.000000
E	0.097482	0.037368	0.025995	0.011373	0.125102	0.117790	0.064988	0.005686	0.012998	0.033306	0.013810	0.013810	0.000000
F	0.008772	0.166667	0.013158	0.000000	0.017544	0.035088	0.184211	0.048246	0.004386	0.017544	0.000000	0.004386	0.000000
G	0.018634	0.142857	0.006211	0.000000	0.130435	0.043478	0.080745	0.049689	0.000000	0.012422	0.000000	0.006211	0.000000
H	0.003891	0.089494	0.001946	0.000000	0.015564	0.005837	0.042802	0.003891	0.000000	0.013619	0.000000	0.001946	0.000000
I	0.235049	0.087622	0.004172	0.000000	0.029207	0.147427	0.122392	0.000000	0.019471	0.001391	0.001391	0.000000	0.005563
J	0.000000	0.400000	0.000000	0.000000	0.000000	0.000000	0.000000	0.400000	0.000000	0.000000	0.000000	0.000000	0.000000
K	0.058824	0.058824	0.000000	0.000000	0.000000	0.039216	0.019608	0.000000	0.000000	0.058824	0.000000	0.058824	0.000000
L	0.002481	0.069479	0.004963	0.004963	0.004963	0.029777	0.047146	0.019851	0.004963	0.012407	0.000000	0.116625	0.000000
M	0.013333	0.124444	0.071111	0.000000	0.000000	0.026667	0.026667	0.057778	0.000000	0.008889	0.000000	0.013333	0.000000
N	0.012517	0.090403	0.009736	0.000000	0.006954	0.070932	0.152990	0.016690	0.005563	0.020862	0.001391	0.019471	0.000000
O	0.182620	0.028967	0.036524	0.000000	0.142317	0.046599	0.066751	0.120907	0.016373	0.045340	0.000000	0.005038	0.002519
P	0.000000	0.122271	0.113537	0.000000	0.183406	0.013100	0.061135	0.030568	0.000000	0.004367	0.000000	0.008734	0.000000
Q	0.000000	0.000000	0.000000	0.000000	0.000000	0.000000	0.000000	1.000000	0.000000	0.000000	0.000000	0.000000	0.000000
R	0.019934	0.089701	0.013289	0.000000	0.029900	0.064784	0.104651	0.009967	0.008306	0.016611	0.000000	0.028239	0.000000
S	0.028832	0.107739	0.036419	0.003035	0.009105	0.062215	0.183612	0.045524	0.003035	0.040971	0.000000	0.006070	0.000000
T	0.008342	0.115746	0.008342	0.000000	0.031283	0.033368	0.055266	0.022941	0.004171	0.016684	0.000000	0.021898	0.000000
U	0.106452	0.006452	0.054839	0.000000	0.158065	0.135484	0.145161	0.000000	0.000000	0.000000	0.003226	0.003226	0.003226
V	0.000000	0.083744	0.000000	0.000000	0.000000	0.000000	0.000000	0.000000	0.000000	0.000000	0.000000	0.000000	0.000000
W	0.049261	0.083744	0.009852	0.000000	0.004926	0.014778	0.029557	0.004926	0.004926	0.009852	0.000000	0.000000	0.000000
X	0.000000	0.050000	0.200000	0.000000	0.000000	0.000000	0.050000	0.050000	0.000000	0.000000	0.000000	0.000000	0.000000
Y	0.015957	0.148936	0.037234	0.000000	0.026596	0.090426	0.111702	0.005319	0.015957	0.074468	0.000000	0.000000	0.000000
Z	0.000000	0.000000	0.000000	0.000000	0.000000	0.000000	0.000000	0.000000	0.000000	0.000000	0.000000	0.000000	0.111111

Hmarkov2 [Section 1]

	A	B	C	D	E	F	G	H	I	J	K	L	M
A	0.002020	0.028317	0.043464	0.039971	0.003114	0.012665	0.022805	0.003324	0.034754	0.000589	0.011529	0.100602	0.025569
B	0.076441	0.005112	0.000232	0.000697	0.297862	0.000000	0.000232	0.000465	0.053903	0.005809	0.000000	0.138243	0.005485
C	0.143528	0.000402	0.013816	0.001744	0.173441	0.001476	0.000134	0.159356	0.064252	0.000000	0.037693	0.039839	0.001073
D	0.088163	0.035816	0.023025	0.021942	0.160976	0.023812	0.016137	0.022533	0.135688	0.001181	0.001968	0.020663	0.027453
E	0.081956	0.018136	0.037850	0.067235	0.039687	0.025539	0.019456	0.016127	0.039773	0.001435	0.002554	0.044048	0.037965
F	0.105662	0.012365	0.014613	0.007447	0.071800	0.069411	0.014051	0.015877	0.117044	0.000843	0.000843	0.030209	0.025011
G	0.105723	0.011309	0.007025	0.007711	0.191398	0.008396	0.024674	0.106237	0.078478	0.000685	0.000514	0.043694	0.010051
H	0.187024	0.003443	0.004303	0.001125	0.493611	0.003509	0.002052	0.004502	0.125654	0.000000	0.000265	0.004237	0.008342
I	0.033355	0.009880	0.056925	0.031991	0.034296	0.022205	0.031568	0.006022	0.001553	0.000000	0.007198	0.048033	0.027663
J	0.044843	0.000000	0.000000	0.000000	0.170404	0.000000	0.000000	0.000000	0.004484	0.000000	0.000000	0.000000	0.000000
K	0.062315	0.008902	0.011276	0.007715	0.322255	0.011276	0.005341	0.017804	0.222552	0.000593	0.000000	0.014243	0.008902
L	0.103065	0.013518	0.009127	0.061047	0.166437	0.015929	0.006458	0.004477	0.159118	0.001464	0.010677	0.134062	0.010935
M	0.230477	0.027640	0.003071	0.000877	0.247441	0.004387	0.001170	0.003364	0.095496	0.001462	0.000000	0.002194	0.028371
N	0.066619	0.009708	0.055285	0.169871	0.096222	0.015638	0.112147	0.008417	0.054232	0.001052	0.012386	0.011621	0.009374
O	0.018128	0.019638	0.015886	0.026363	0.009113	0.149652	0.009697	0.005750	0.015886	0.000585	0.006579	0.033624	0.060937
P	0.110434	0.004247	0.001477	0.001108	0.191136	0.003693	0.000739	0.023638	0.063897	0.000185	0.000185	0.121514	0.010342
Q	0.000000	0.000000	0.000000	0.000000	0.000000	0.000000	0.000000	0.000000	0.000000	0.000000	0.000000	0.000000	0.000000
R	0.104636	0.010857	0.018192	0.023533	0.253991	0.011561	0.014437	0.012031	0.105458	0.000411	0.011561	0.017430	0.036737
S	0.108470	0.020095	0.025929	0.009129	0.114574	0.014099	0.005240	0.060177	0.099827	0.001026	0.005186	0.014207	0.019123
T	0.077756	0.009567	0.008528	0.004969	0.081019	0.008602	0.003671	0.344247	0.125181	0.000445	0.000630	0.016797	0.009789
U	0.028686	0.020280	0.052568	0.019880	0.029887	0.008272	0.042695	0.002135	0.027618	0.000000	0.000400	0.091928	0.029486
V	0.120659	0.000000	0.000358	0.000000	0.682062	0.000358	0.000000	0.000000	0.157895	0.000000	0.000358	0.000358	0.000000
W	0.258312	0.003541	0.002951	0.007279	0.163093	0.005509	0.001967	0.147354	0.178241	0.000000	0.000787	0.005509	0.007279
X	0.130152	0.002169	0.151844	0.002169	0.036876	0.006508	0.000000	0.010846	0.127983	0.002169	0.004338	0.004338	0.004338
Y	0.118909	0.043714	0.041909	0.023662	0.056146	0.033688	0.018448	0.043313	0.079206	0.002005	0.003409	0.200854	0.039503
Z	0.067227	0.000000	0.000000	0.000000	0.319328	0.008403	0.000000	0.000000	0.168067	0.000000	0.000000	0.058824	0.000000

Hmarkov2 [Section 2]

	N	O	P	Q	R	S	T	U	V	W	X	Y	Z
A	0.229478	0.002314	0.021669	0.000589	0.114486	0.094248	0.136913	0.009846	0.025455	0.009257	0.000589	0.022889	0.000547
B	0.000465	0.101301	0.000000	0.000000	0.082481	0.021840	0.016496	0.125929	0.002788	0.000697	0.000000	0.065520	0.000000
C	0.000402	0.177197	0.001878	0.000671	0.044802	0.005902	0.086787	0.036351	0.000000	0.001744	0.000000	0.007512	0.000000
D	0.016727	0.089442	0.017810	0.001378	0.027256	0.072912	0.104300	0.037292	0.012791	0.027354	0.000098	0.013283	0.000000
E	0.101756	0.032168	0.023330	0.003386	0.141873	0.111283	0.067321	0.008092	0.019025	0.031652	0.011364	0.016701	0.000287
F	0.005620	0.140228	0.012365	0.000422	0.097794	0.022762	0.176479	0.034846	0.003653	0.017002	0.000000	0.003513	0.000141
G	0.017135	0.103667	0.010966	0.001542	0.076936	0.045236	0.064085	0.056546	0.003770	0.011995	0.000000	0.008053	0.000171
H	0.001920	0.071235	0.003178	0.000331	0.012645	0.007613	0.044224	0.010063	0.000596	0.005826	0.000000	0.004303	0.000000
I	0.258280	0.065770	0.007998	0.000470	0.034390	0.140807	0.147535	0.001035	0.026534	0.004422	0.000706	0.000000	0.001364
J	0.000000	0.286996	0.000000	0.000000	0.000000	0.000000	0.000000	0.493274	0.000000	0.000000	0.000000	0.000000	0.000000
K	0.052226	0.052226	0.004154	0.000593	0.007122	0.091395	0.055786	0.007715	0.001187	0.023739	0.000000	0.010682	0.000000
L	0.005511	0.074910	0.010246	0.000861	0.007749	0.028931	0.040382	0.020406	0.005855	0.010332	0.000000	0.098330	0.000172
M	0.003364	0.130009	0.072390	0.000292	0.009359	0.023691	0.027055	0.046066	0.000585	0.006727	0.000000	0.034513	0.000000
N	0.009134	0.073888	0.007987	0.001196	0.004017	0.067767	0.164945	0.009182	0.005643	0.015256	0.000670	0.016738	0.001004
O	0.173237	0.025340	0.033088	0.000390	0.123971	0.040690	0.060913	0.106038	0.014668	0.043127	0.000439	0.005117	0.000146
P	0.002955	0.158264	0.043398	0.000369	0.144968	0.028624	0.044321	0.038966	0.000554	0.002585	0.000000	0.002401	0.000000
Q	0.000000	0.000000	0.000000	0.000000	0.000000	0.003401	0.000000	0.996599	0.000000	0.000000	0.000000	0.000000	0.000000
R	0.022477	0.098122	0.011854	0.000176	0.016901	0.061150	0.078638	0.020364	0.008216	0.012089	0.000176	0.048650	0.000352
S	0.018366	0.102420	0.032357	0.002215	0.007833	0.074006	0.197385	0.031439	0.002215	0.028792	0.000054	0.005726	0.000108
T	0.004969	0.107234	0.005673	0.000482	0.042864	0.035114	0.056101	0.017576	0.001335	0.022359	0.000111	0.014461	0.000519
U	0.133956	0.003736	0.071648	0.000000	0.134757	0.147565	0.148099	0.000267	0.001334	0.002001	0.000667	0.001468	0.000667
V	0.001074	0.025421	0.000000	0.000000	0.001074	0.000358	0.002148	0.003580	0.001180	0.006492	0.000000	0.004654	0.000000
W	0.036396	0.118237	0.002951	0.000000	0.013378	0.013181	0.023608	0.001771	0.001180	0.004338	0.000000	0.000984	0.000000
X	0.002169	0.017354	0.277657	0.000000	0.000000	0.006508	1.197397	0.012432	0.002169	0.000000	0.000000	0.006508	0.000201
Y	0.017846	0.114899	0.037096	0.002206	0.018648	0.077000	0.127532	0.012432	0.006417	0.055344	0.000000	0.005615	0.000201
Z	0.000000	0.235294	0.008403	0.000000	0.000000	0.016807	0.000000	0.008403	0.000000	0.000000	0.000000	0.016807	0.092437

REFERENCES

J. RIVES CHILDS, *General Solution of the ADFGVX Cipher System*, Aegean Park Press, Laguna Hills, California, 2001.

H. FOUCHÉ GAINES, *Elementary Cryptanalysis: A Study of Ciphers and Their Solution*, American Cryptogram Association, Mineola, New York, 1939.

G. R. GRIMMETT AND D. R. STIRZAKER, *Probability and Random Processes*, Oxford Science Publications, Oxford, 1992.

A. G. KONHEIM, "Cryptanalysis of The ADFGVX System", *IEEE Workshop on Information Theory*, Caesaria, Israel, July 1984.

S. KULLBACK, *Statistical Methods in Cryptanalysis*, Signals Intelligence Service, 1938; reprinted by Aegean Park Press, Laguna Hills, California, 1976.

J. SEBERRY AND J. PIEPRZYK, *Cryptography: An Introduction to Computer Security*, Prentice-Hall, Upper Saddle River, New Jersey, 1989.

C. E. SHANNON, "Communication Theory of Secrecy Systems", *Bell Systems Technical Journal*, 28, 656–715 (1949).

A. SINKOV, *Elementary Cryptanalysis*, Random House, New York, NY, 1968.

MONOALPHABETIC SUBSTITUTION

THIS CHAPTER studies monoalphabetic encipherment. How ciphertext may be searched for a fragment of text (cribbing) and the results used to recover the plaintext and key will be explained. Problems to test your skills follow the text.

3.1 MONOALPHABETIC SUBSTITUTION

A *monoalphabetic substitution* $T : \underline{x} = (x_0, x_1, \ldots, x_{n-1}) \rightarrow \underline{y} = (y_0, y_1, \ldots, y_{n-1})$ on plaintext with letters in the alphabet $\mathcal{Z}_m \equiv \{0, 1, 2, \ldots, m - 1\}$ is a rule specifying the substitute $\theta(x_i)$ for the letter x_i. Here $\underline{\theta} = (\theta(0), \theta(1), \ldots, \theta(m - 1))$ is a permutation on the letters in the alphabet

$$\theta : x_t \rightarrow y_t = \theta(x_t), \qquad 0 \leq t < n.$$

We begin by examining substitutions encipherment for plaintext written with letters in the alphabet of 26 Latin letters. Uppercase letters will be used to display plaintext and lowercase letters for ciphertext. As before, letters will also be referred to by their ordinal positions in the alphabet $\mathcal{Z}_m = \{0, 1, 2, \ldots, m - 1\}$ with $m = 26$. Even though there are $26! \approx 4 \times 10^{26}$ different monoalphabetic substitutions on $\mathcal{Z}_{26}$, approximately a key space of 80 bits, William Friedman [1944] estimated that the key would be determined by ~ 25 characters of monoalphabetic ciphertext.

A monoalphabetic substitution may be specified in a *substitution table* such as Table 3.1. A *key word* provides a simple mnemonic to construct a substitution table. For example, the letter repetitions in GOODWORD are first deleted, yielding GODWR. The substitution θ is specified by the sequence of letters that starts with GODWR and then is followed by the remaining letters of the alphabet in the normal order, as shown in Table 3.2. If long key words are allowed, any of the 26! permutations may be generated in this manner.

Historically, monoalphabetic substitution has been simplified using various mechanical devices. General Albert J. Myer, the first Chief Signal Officer of the Union Army's Signal Corps, invented a cipher disk in 1863 that was used during the American Civil War. It consisted of two concentric disks (Fig. 3.1), with the plaintext letters inscribed around the periphery of the inner disk. In addition to the letters A, B, ... , Z, the Myer plaintext alphabet also included the letter combinations tion, ing, ours, and &, which might frequently occur in words; the symbol "&" signalled the end of a word, equivalent to a blank space to separate words.

TABLE 3.1   Substitution Table for Alphabet {A, B, ... , Z}

A	B	C	D	E	F	G	H	I	J	K	L	M
↓	↓	↓	↓	↓	↓	↓	↓	↓	↓	↓	↓	↓
q	w	e	r	t	y	u	i	o	p	l	k	j

N	O	P	Q	R	S	T	U	V	W	X	Y	Z
↓	↓	↓	↓	↓	↓	↓	↓	↓	↓	↓	↓	↓
h	g	f	d	s	a	z	x	c	v	b	n	m

TABLE 3.2   Substitution Table Derived from GOODWORD

A	B	C	D	E	F	G	H	I	J	K	L	M	N	O	P	Q	R	S	T	U	V	W	X	Y	Z
↓	↓	↓	↓	↓	↓	↓	↓	↓	↓	↓	↓	↓	↓	↓	↓	↓	↓	↓	↓	↓	↓	↓	↓	↓	↓
g	o	d	w	r	a	b	c	e	f	h	i	j	k	l	m	n	p	q	s	t	u	v	x	y	z

Each plaintext letter was enciphered into a sequence composed of the symbols "1" and "8"[1] of length 1–4. These ciphertext "letters" are printed around the larger circumscribed ring. The disks are fastened together concentrically in such a manner that one may revolve upon the other and they may be clamped in any position.

Beginning around 1940, *The Adventures of Captain Midnight* was sponsored by *Ovaltine* and broadcast over the Mutual Network radio. How I anticipated decoding the secret messages as a member of Captain Midnight's *Secret Squadron*. Of course, I required a Captain Midnight Decoding Badge (Fig. 3.2). Like the Myer disk, the Captain Midnight decoding badge implemented a monoalphabetic substitution. It consisted of an outer disk containing the ciphertext alphabet – numbers 1 to 26 and an inner disk on which a permutation of the (plaintext) letters A to Z is recorded.

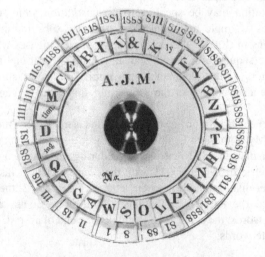

Figure 3.1   Myer civil war cipher disk (Courtesy of NSA).

[1]Myer might have used of the symbols 1 and 8 since the Morse codes. – – – for 1 and – – – for 8 are dissimilar tending to lessen transmission errors.

Figure 3.2 Captain Midnight Decoding Badge. (Captain Midnight is a registered trademark of Klutz and is used here with their permission. Replicas of the Captain Midnight decoding badge may be ordered from www.klutz.com.)

3.2 CAESAR'S CIPHER

It is believed that Julius Caesar, in the period 58 BCE to 51 BCE, enciphered messages to his lawyer Marcus Tullius Cicero and other Roman senators using a monoalphabetic substitution. In the Caesar cipher, each plaintext letter was replaced by the letter standing three places to-the-right in the alphabet. If we neglect that the original Roman or Latin alphabet did not contain a J, U, or W, then, Julius' query in the present day Roman alphabet

```
ANYONE  KNOW  WHERE  I  CAN  GET  DECENT  PIZZA?
dqbrqh  nqrz  zkhuh  l  edq  jhw  ghfhqw  slccd?
```

would be enciphered as above.

For the alphabet of uppercase Latin letters {A, B,..., Z} identified with the integers in $\mathcal{Z}_{26} = \{0, 1, \ldots, 25\}$ the *Caesar shift* substitution $\mathbf{C_k}$ is defined for each key $k \in \mathcal{Z}_{26}$ by

$$\mathbf{C_k} : x \to y = \mathbf{C_k}(x) = (x + k) \text{ (modulo 26).}$$

Variations of the Caesar substitution with larger key spaces have been invented; one simple generalization, the *affine Caesar* substitution, is defined by the formula

$$\mathbf{A_{j,k}} : x \to y = \mathbf{A_{j,k}}(x) = (jx + k) \text{ (modulo 26),}$$

where the key is a pair of integers j, k. $\mathbf{A_{j,k}}$ is a one-to-one transformation on the alphabet $\mathcal{Z}_{26}$ only when the multiplier j is not divisible by either 2 or 13. In this case, j has a *multiplicative inverse* modulo 26, meaning there exists an integer $b = j^{-1}$ that satisfies $bj \equiv 1$ (modulo 26). These values of j are listed in Table 3.3. The key space of the affine Caesar substitution contains $312 = 12 \times 26$ keys and exhaustive key trial remains computationally feasible.

TABLE 3.3   Integers in $\mathcal{Z}_{26}$ That Have Multiplicative Inverses

j	1	3	5	7	9	11	15	17	19	21	23	25
j^{-1}	1	9	21	15	3	19	7	23	11	5	17	25

3.3   CRIBBING USING ISOMORPHS

Two r-grams $\underline{u} = (u_0, u_1, \ldots, u_{r-1})$ and $\underline{v} = (v_0, v_1, \ldots, v_{r-1})$ are *isomorphs* of one another: $\underline{u} \leftrightarrow \underline{v}$ if they satisfy $u_i = u_j$ if and only if $v_i = v_j$ for $0 \leq i, j < r$. For example, `xyzanya` and `science` are isomorphs of one another.

Cribbing can be used to analyze monoalphabetic ciphertext y by searching for isomorphs of a plaintext crib in the ciphertext. If the plaintext r-gram $(v_0, v_1, \ldots, v_{r-1})$ has been enciphered to the ciphertext $(u_0, u_1, \ldots, u_{r-1})$, the isomorph provides parts of the substitution $\underline{\theta}$. By piecing together several cribs and their isomorphs, most of the ciphertext might be read.

Example 3.1

`cipherEx3.1` was monoalphabetically enciphered according to the rules:

- All characters (in the plaintext) other than uppercase letters have been deleted;
- The 399 letters in `cipherEx3.1`, the ciphertext file is written in rows of 50 letters in blocks of 5 separated by a blank space.

The subject of the plaintext is the early paper of Needham–Schroeder on authentication, to be described in Chapter 17.

---

cipherEx3.1

```
qxzit hzoeq zoghq hrrou ozqka ouhqz xstav twazt saroe zoghq
snrty ohtaq xzith zoeqz oghqa qfsge taawn vioei tqeig yzvge
gjjxh oeqzo hufqs zotac tsoyo tazit orthz ozngy zitgz itsoj
fkoeo zohqx zithz oeqzo ghgyq jtaaq utjta aysgj zitat hrtsz
gzits tetoc tsoaa gjtoh ygsjq zoghq xziqf fthrt rzggs ohekx
rtrvo ziohz itjta aqutt hqwko huzit qxzit hzoeq zoghz gzqlt
fkqet qxzit hzoeq zoghf tszqo hazgz itort hzozn ghzit athrt
swxzh gzzit eghzt hzgyz itjta aqutj taawt ohuzs qhajo zztr
```

The program

IsoSearch1

Input:	ciphertext, crib
Output:	isomorphs of crib

searches ciphertext for all isomorphs of a plaintext crib. Possible cribs in `cipherEx3.1` include `AUTHENTICATE`, `SIGNATURE`, `AUTHENTICATION`, `MESSAGE`, and `PROTOCOL`. Table 3.4 lists the 19 isomorphs of the crib `SIGNATURE` in `cipherEx3.1` recording the number of times an isomorph occurs. To be effective, cribbing must be combined with some mechanism to prune away unlikely instances of the isomorph of the crib. For example, if kaouhqzxs is the encipherment of SIGNATURE,

```
S  I  G  N  A  T  U  R  E
↓  ↓  ↓  ↓  ↓  ↓  ↓  ↓  ↓
k  a  o  u  h  q  z  x  s
```

TABLE 3.4   Isomorphs of SIGNATURE in cipherEx3.1

Isomorph	Isomorph	Isomorph	Isomorph	Isomorph
1 kaouhqzxs	1 aouhqzxst	1 ouhqzxsta	1 uhqzxstav	1 ezoghqsnr
1 zoghqsnrt	1 oghqsnrty	1 ghqsnrtyo	1 yohtaqxzi	1 hufqszota
1 ufqszotac	1 gzitsojfk	1 tohygsjqz	1 gsohekxrt	1 qwkohuzit
1 wkohuzitq	1 kohuzitqx	1 eqzoghfts	1 awtohuzsq	

the frequencies of s and h in the ciphertext are *not* comparable to the probabilities of the letters E and A in English-language text. We will show how unlikely isomorphs can be detected by comparing the frequencies to the probabilities in standard English language text.

3.4   THE χ^2-TEST OF A HYPOTHESIS

Suppose a large number n of independent trials of a chance experiment $\mathcal{E}$ are performed. A trial has r possible outcomes $O_0, O_1, \ldots, O_{r-1}$ that occur with probabilities $q(0)$, $q(1), \ldots, q(r-1)$. The number of times the outcome O_i occurs, N_i, is recorded.

How likely is it that the observed outcome-counts $\{N_i\}$ are *consistent* with the *hypothesis*: $q(i)$ is the probability of occurrence of O_i $(0 \leq i < r)$. In the context of cribbing

- The experiment $\mathcal{E}$ is the generation of plaintext by an iid language model with 1-gram probabilities π followed by monoalphabetic substitution θ;
- The r outcomes correspond to the occurrence of the letters of a ciphertext r-gram $\underline{u}$;
- $\underline{u} = (u_0, u_1, \ldots, u_{r-1})$ is a ciphertext isomorph of the plaintext crib $\underline{v} = (v_0, v_1, \ldots, v_{r-1})$; and
- The probabilities $q(i) = \pi(v_i)$ are those that would be true if the ciphertext u was the encipherment of the plaintext crib $\underline{v}$ – that is, if $\theta : \underline{v} \to \underline{u}$.

If the hypothesis is true, then for *each* possible outcome O_i, the law of large numbers asserts

$$\lim_{n \to \infty} \frac{N_i}{n} = q(i) \qquad (0 \leq i < r).$$

The χ^2-statistic is the quantity defined by

$$\chi^2 = \sum_{i=0}^{r-1} \frac{(N_i - nq(i))^2}{nq(i)} = \sum_{i=0}^{r-1} \frac{n}{q(i)} \left(\frac{N_i}{n} - q(i) \right)^2 .$$

The ith term in the sum above is the product of two factors. The first,

$$\infty = \lim_{n \to \infty} \frac{n}{q(i)},$$

increases without bound with n, and the second has one of two limiting values:

$$\lim_{n\to\infty}\left(\frac{N_i}{n}-q(i)\right) = \begin{cases} 0, & \text{if the hypothesis is } \textit{true} \\ \infty, & \text{if the hypothesis is } \textit{false}. \end{cases}$$

The statistician Karl Pearson [1900] proved that the limiting distribution of χ_n^2 exists and is independent of the distribution $\{q(i)\}$. Moreover, the outcome-counts $\{N_i\}$ have $r-1$ degrees of freedom.[2]

Proposition 3.1: If $\{q(i)\}$ is the common distribution of $\{N_i : 0 \le i < r\}$, then

$$\lim_{n\to\infty} \Pr\{\chi_n^2 \le x\} = \frac{2^{-(r-1)}}{\Gamma\left(\dfrac{r-1}{2}\right)} \int_0^x y^{\frac{r-3}{2}} e^{-\frac{y}{2}}\, dy = \int_0^x k_{r-1}(y)\, dy$$

where $\Gamma(k)$ is the *gamma function*, defined by

$$\Gamma(k) = \int_0^\infty x^{k-1} e^{-x}\, dx$$

and $\Gamma(k) = (k-1)!$ for integers $k \ge 1$.

Given a value of $p \le 100$, there exists a value $x(p, r-1)$ such that χ_n^2 should exceed $x(p, r-1)$ with probability $0.01p$ if the sample size is large enough

$$\frac{p}{100} = \int_{x(p,r-1)}^\infty k_{r-1}(y)\, dy$$

when the hypothesis is true. A large χ^2-value for $p \approx 99$ – in excess of $x(99, r-1)$ – therefore casts doubt on the validity of the *hypothesis*. Tables of the χ^2-limits can be found in Abramowitz and Stegun [1972], which also contains the formula

$$x^2(p, r) \simeq r\left(1 - \frac{2}{9r} + x(p, r)\sqrt{\frac{2}{9r}}\right) \simeq r - \frac{2}{3} + \sqrt{2r}x(p, r) + \frac{2}{3}x(p, r)^2 + \cdots.$$

3.5 PRUNING FROM THE TABLE OF ISOMORPHS

We identify the repeated trials of the experiment $\mathcal{E}$ with the generation of plaintext with letters in the generic alphabet $\mathcal{Z}_m$ by the *iid* language model with probabilities $\pi(i) = \Pr\{X = i\}$ for $0 \le i < m$.

To test if the ciphertext r-gram $\underline{v}$ is an isomorph of the plaintext $\underline{u}$, the ciphertext letter counts $\{N_{v_i}\}$ are compared to the plaintext letter probabilities using the χ^2-statistic:

$$\chi^2 = \begin{cases} \displaystyle\sum_{i=0}^{r-1} \frac{(N_{v_i} - n\pi(u_i))^2}{n\pi(u_i)}, & \text{no repeated letter in crib} \\[2em] \displaystyle\sum_{\substack{i=0 \\ \{v_j \neq v_i, i \neq j\}}}^{r-1} \frac{(N_{v_i} - n\pi(u_i))^2}{n\pi(u_i)}, & \text{some repeated letters in crib} \end{cases}$$

Table 3.5 lists the count of 1-grams $\{N_i\}$ and their frequencies $f(i) = N_i/n$ in the ciphertext `cipherEx3.1`. Table 3.6 gives the probabilities $\{\pi(i)\}$ of 1-grams derived from a large

---

[2] The components of the r-vector of counts $\underline{N} = (N_0, N_1, \ldots, N_{r-1})$ are not independent, because $n = \sum_{i=0}^{r-1} N_i$.

TABLE 3.5   Letter Counts and Frequencies in `cipherEx3.1`

i	N_i	f_i	i	N_i	f_i	i	N_i	f_i
a	26	0.0652	j	12	0.0301	s	16	0.0401
b	0	0.0000	k	5	0.0125	t	54	0.1353
c	2	0.0050	l	1	0.0025	u	8	0.0201
d	0	0.0000	m	0	0.0000	v	4	0.0100
e	16	0.0401	n	4	0.0100	w	5	0.0125
f	7	0.0172	o	41	0.1028	x	10	0.0251
g	26	0.0652	p	0	0.0000	y	9	0.0226
h	34	0.0852	q	31	0.0777	z	54	0.1353
i	21	0.0526	r	13	0.0326			

TABLE 3.6   1-Gram English-Language Plaintext Probabilities

i	$\pi(i)$	i	$\pi(i)$	i	$\pi(i)$
A	0.0856	J	0.0013	S	0.0607
B	0.0139	K	0.0042	T	0.1045
C	0.0279	L	0.0339	U	0.0249
D	0.0378	M	0.0249	V	0.0092
E	0.1304	N	0.0707	W	0.0149
F	0.0289	O	0.0797	X	0.0017
G	0.0199	P	0.0199	Y	0.0199
H	0.0528	Q	0.0012	Z	0.0008
I	0.0627	R	0.0677		

sample English language text. The plan is to now use the χ^2-test to associate the seven high-frequency ciphertext letters in Table 3.5:

t	54	z	54	o	41	h	34	q	31	a	26	g	26

with seven of the nine plaintext letters of highest probability from Table 3.6:

E	T	A	O	N	R	I	S	H

A correspondence between t, z, o, h and some subset of E, T, A, O, N, R, I, S, H permits most of the isomorphs to be discarded.

The results of `IsoSearch1` are given in Tables 3.7 to 3.12. One starting point for the pruning is to determine the plaintext-to-ciphertext letter correspondences by selecting the cribs with the smallest χ^2-scores (Table 3.13). The plaintext-to-ciphertext letter correspondences implied by the first four cribs are *consistent*; for example, isomorphs of the first two cribs implies the correspondences in Table 3.14. All of these plaintext-to-ciphertext letter correspondences are also consistent with the isomorphs of MESSAGE and DIGITAL with the smallest χ^2-scores. This is not the case for either of the isomorphs of PROTOCOL.

TABLE 3.7   Isomorphs of SIGNATURE in cipherEx3.1

	Crib = SIGNATURE							
1	kaouhqzxs	392.74	1	aouhqzxst	23.13	1	ouhqzxsta	197.01
1	uhqzxstav	409.49	1	ezoghqsnr	222.41	1	zoghqsnrt	108.61
1	oghqsnrty	220.61	1	ghqsnrtyo	367.92	1	yohtaqxzi	189.95
1	hufqszota	169.42	1	ufqszotac	378.99	1	gzitsojfk	163.24
1	tohygsjqz	182.56	1	gsohekxrt	200.65	1	qwkohuzit	230.77
1	wkohuzitq	251.43	1	kohuzitqx	414.95	1	eqzoghfts	323.98
1	awtohuzsq	560.30						

TABLE 3.8   Isomorphs of AUTHENTICATE in cipherEx3.1

Crib = AUTHENTICATE
None found

TABLE 3.9   Isomorphs of AUTHENTICATION in cipherEx3.1

Crib = AUTHENTICATION

TABLE 3.10   Isomorphs of MESSAGE in cipherEx3.1

	Crib = MESSAGE	
3	jtaaqut	3.10

TABLE 3.11   Isomorphs of DIGITAL in cipherEx3.1

	Crib = DIGITAL							
1	rouozqk	17.72	1	hqaqfsg	138.14	1	soyotaz	130.15
2	hzozngy	211.85	1	eozohqx	253.68	1	oghgyqj	154.71
1	xrtrvoz	464.89	1	hzgzqlt	284.29	1	azgzito	182.32

TABLE 3.12   Isomorphs of PROTOCOL in cipherEx3.1

	Crib = PROTOCOL				
1	fkoeozoh	232.62	1	zitsteto	357.85

TABLE 3.13   Isomorphs in cipherEx3.1 with Smallest χ^2-Scores

AUTHENTICATION ⟷ qxzithzoeqzogh	23.66
SIGNATURE ⟷ aouhqzxst	23.13
MESSAGE ⟷ jtaaqut	3.10
DIGITAL ⟷ rouozqk	17.72
PROTOCOL ⟷ fkoeozoh	232.62

TABLE 3.14 Plaintext-to-Ciphertext Letter Correspondences in `cipherEx3.1` from Table 3.13

A	E	T	N	I	U
↓	↓	↓	↓	↓	↓
q	t	z	h	o	h

TABLE 3.15 Partial Substitution Table for `cipherEx3.1`

A	B	C	D	E	F	G	H	I	J	K	L	M
↓	↓	↓	↓	↓	↓	↓	↓	↓	↓	↓	↓	↓
q		e	r	t		u	i	o			k	j

N	O	P	Q	R	S	T	U	V	W	X	Y	Z
↓	↓	↓	↓	↓	↓	↓	↓	↓	↓	↓	↓	↓
h	g			s	a	z	x					

Assuming the correctness of the isomorphs of all cribs other than PROTOCOL provides the partial substitution table of Table 3.15. A *partial* trial decipherment replacing the identified ciphertext letters by the plaintext values identified (in uppercase) yields

```
AUTHENTICATIONANDDIGITALSIGNATURESvEwSTERSDICTIONA
RnDEyINESAUTHENTICATIONASAfROCESSwnvHICHEACHOyTvOC
OMMUNICATINGfARTIEScERIyIESTHEIDENTITnOyTHEOTHERIM
fLICITINAUTHENTICATIONOyAMESSAGEMESSyROMTHESENDERT
OTHERECEIcERISSOMEINyORMATIONAUTHAffENDEDTOORINCLU
DEDvITHINTHEMESSAGEENAwkINGTHEAUTHENTICATIONTOTAlE
fkACEAUTHENTICATIONfERTAINSTOTHEIDENTITnOyTHESENDE
RwUTNOTTHECONTENTOyTHEMESSAGEMESSwEINGTRANSMITTED
```

from which words and additional letter-pair correspondences can be recognized; for example

- P → f from tROCESS, and
- Y → n from IDENTITn.

Example 3.2

The $n = 356$ lowercase letters in `cipherEx3.2` result from a monoalphabetic encipherment of plaintext where the subject of the plaintext is standard lower-division computer science courses. The first step in the analysis is to make 1 gram counts $\{N_i\}$ and frequencies $\{f_i\}$ in `cipherEx3.2`; these are listed in Table 3.16. Using `IsoSearch1` for the possible cribs including PROGRAMMING, PROGRAMS, and LANGUAGE gives the results in Tables 3.17 to 3.19. If both PROGRAMMING or PROGRAMS appear in the plaintext, the *true* ciphertext of LANGUAGE must be xqvflqft. These cribs determine the partial substitution tables, Table 3.20.

cipherEx3.2

```
otohb ktbdm qjeqx kbmhb psrtq extqh vbvcq kdtcq kseqx xubhs
tvktr svkhb rleks bvkbm hbfhq ccsvf qvrmq jeqxo tkqzt skgbh
fhqvk trkdq kmqje qxsjq jlmth sbhsv jkhle ksbvq xxqvf lqftk
dqkkd toquk bxtqh vmhbf hqccs vfsjk bohsk tmhbf hqcjq vrkdq
kmhbw xtcjb xpsvf jdblx rwtkq lfdks vkdtg shjkm hbfhq ccsvf
eblhj t
```

TABLE 3.16 Letter Counts and Frequencies in cipherEx3.2

i	N_i	f_i	i	N_i	f_i	i	N_i	f_i
a	0	0.0000	j	12	0.0469	s	18	0.0703
b	22	0.0859	k	27	0.1055	t	19	0.0742
c	10	0.0391	l	7	0.0273	u	2	0.0078
d	9	0.0352	m	10	0.0391	v	17	0.0664
e	8	0.0312	n	0	0.0000	w	2	0.0078
f	12	0.0469	o	5	0.0195	x	0	0.0000
g	2	0.0078	p	2	0.0078	y	12	0.0469
h	23	0.0898	q	29	0.1133	z	1	0.0039
i	0	0.0000	r	7	0.0273			

TABLE 3.17 Isomorphs of PROGRAMMING in cipherEx3.2

	Crib = PROGRAMMING	
3	mhbfhqccsvf	20.75

TABLE 3.18 Isomorphs of PROGRAMS in cipherEx3.2

	Crib = PROGRAMS	
1	mhbfhqcj	21.24

TABLE 3.19 Isomorphs of LANGUAGE in cipherEx3.2

	Crib = LANGUAGE			
1	eksbvkbm	91.43	1	xqvflqft	19.25

TABLE 3.20 Partial Substitution Table for cipherEx3.2

A	B	C	D	E	F	G	H	I	J	K	L	M
↓	↓	↓	↓	↓	↓	↓	↓	↓	↓	↓	↓	↓
q				t		f		s			x	c

N	O	P	Q	R	S	T	U	V	W	X	Y	Z
↓	↓	↓	↓	↓	↓	↓	↓	↓	↓	↓	↓	↓
v	b	m		h	j		l					

A partial decipherment of `cipherEx3.2` reveals words:

```
0    oEoROkEOdPASeALkOPROpIrEAeLEARNONMAkdEMAkIeALLuORI
1    ENkErINkROrUekIONkOPROGRAMMINGANrmASeALoEkAzEIkgOR
2    GRANkErkdAkPASeALISASUPERIORINSkRUekIONALLANGUAGEk
3    dAkkdEoAukOLEARNPROGRAMMINGISkOoRIkEPROGRAMSANrkdA
4    kPROwLEMSOLpINGSdOULrwEkAUGdkINkdEgIRSkPROGRAMMING
5    eOURSE
```

1. Lines $0, 2$: C $\rightarrow$ e from PASeAL;
2. Line 5: C $\rightarrow$ e from eOURSE;
3. Line 3: T $\rightarrow$ k from kOLEARN

and so forth. The complete substitution table cannot be recovered because four letters do not appear in the plaintext. Note also that the most frequent plaintext letters in decreasing order of frequency of occurrence are

A (0.1133)   T (0.1055)   R (0.0898)   O (0.0859)   E (0.0742)   I (0.0703)   N (0.0664)

which deviates from the order ETAONRISH in Table 3.6.

3.6 PARTIAL MAXIMUM LIKELIHOOD ESTIMATION OF A MONOALPHABETIC SUBSTITUTION

Can we find the substitution without a crib? We suppose ciphertext $\underline{y} = (y_0, y_1, \ldots, y_{n-1})$ results from a monoalphabetic substitution of plaintext $\underline{x} = (x_0, x_1, \ldots, x_{n-1})$, both written with letters in the alphabet $\mathcal{Z}_m = \{0, 1, \ldots, m - 1\}$ with an unknown substitution θ.

We assume the substitution θ has been chosen randomly independent of $\underline{x}$ and according to the uniform distribution $\text{Pr}_{a\ priori}\{\Theta = \theta\} = 1/m$. The cryptanalysis problem

> *Given*: $\underline{y}$
>
> *Evaluate*:   the likelihood of the hypothesis H(τ) that $\Theta = \tau$

is solved by the *maximum likelihood estimation* (MLE). Computation of the MLE assumes the plaintext has been generated by a Markov language model with parameters (π, P). Knowledge of the ciphertext changes the likelihood of Θ:

$$\text{Pr}_{a\ priori}\{\Theta = \theta\} \rightarrow \text{Pr}_{a\ posteriori}\{\Theta = \theta/\underline{Y} = \underline{y}\}.$$

Using Baye's Law

$$\text{Pr}\{A/B\} = \text{Pr}\{B/A\}\frac{\text{Pr}\{A\}}{\text{Pr}\{B\}},$$

we have

$$\text{Pr}_{a\ posteriori}\{\Theta = \theta/\underline{Y} = \underline{y}\} = \text{Pr}_{a\ posteriori}\{\underline{Y} = \underline{y}/\Theta = \theta\}\frac{\text{Pr}_{a\ posteriori}\{\Theta = \theta\}}{\text{Pr}_{a\ posteriori}\{\underline{Y} = \underline{y}\}}$$

The MLE of the substitution is any $\hat{\theta}$ which satisfies

$$\text{Pr}_{a\ posteriori}\{\Theta = \hat{\theta}/\underline{Y} = \underline{y}\} = \max_{\theta} \text{Pr}_{a\ posteriori}\{\Theta = \theta/\underline{Y} = \underline{y}\}$$

Assuming $\Pr_{a\,posteriori}\{\Theta = \theta\} = \dfrac{1}{m!}$ and $\Pr_{a\,posteriori}\{\underline{Y} = \underline{y}\}$ does not depend on θ

$$\max_{\theta} \Pr_{a\,posteriori}\{\Theta = \theta/\underline{Y} = \underline{y}\} = \max_{\theta} \Pr_{a\,posteriori}\{\underline{Y} = \underline{y}/\Theta = \theta\}.$$

3.6.1 1-Gram Scoring Using an Independent 1-Gram Language Model

The simplest language model was described in Chapter 2; it postulated that plaintext $\underline{X} = (X_0, X_1, \ldots, X_{n-1})$ resulted from n independent and identical trials with probabilities

$$\pi(t) = \Pr\{X_i = t\}, \qquad 0 \le i < n, \quad 0 \le t < m.$$

With this model

$$\text{Score}(\tau/\underline{y}) = \Pr_{a\,posteriori}\{\underline{Y} = \underline{y}/\mathcal{H}(\tau)\} = \pi(\tau^{-1}(y_0))\pi(\tau^{-1}(y_1))\cdots\pi(\tau^{-1}(y_{n-1}))$$

$$= \prod_{t=0}^{m-1} \pi^{N_t}(\tau^{-1}(t)) \tag{3.1}$$

where N_t is the number of times the letter t appears in the ciphertext $\underline{y}$. Finding the maximum value of $\text{Score}(\tau/\underline{y})$ is equivalent to finding the maximum value of

$$\text{L-Score}(\tau/\underline{y}) \equiv \frac{1}{n}\log_2 \text{Score}(\tau/\underline{y}) \propto \sum_{t=0}^{m-1} \frac{N_t}{n}\log_2 \pi(\tau^{-1}(t)).$$

The symbol $\propto$ (*proportional to*) indicates that both sides agree up to a term that is independent of τ.

The law of large numbers gives $\lim\limits_{n\to\infty} N_t/n = \pi(\theta^{-1}(t))$ so that

$$\lim_{n\to\infty} \text{L-Score}(\tau/\underline{y}) \propto \sum_{t=0}^{m-1} \pi(\theta^{-1}(t))\log_2 \pi(\tau^{-1}(t)). \tag{3.2}$$

Applying the inequality of the arithmetic and geometric means

$$\sum_{t=0}^{m-1} \pi(\theta^{-1}(t))\log_2 \pi(\tau^{-1}(t)) \le \sum_{t=0}^{m-1} p(\theta^{-1}(t))\log_2 p(\theta^{-1}(t)).$$

This shows that the substitution τ, which maximizes the log-score in Equation (3.2), is the Bayesian solution *when* the plaintext is generated by the independent 1-gram model *and* a large enough sample of ciphertext is observed.

One important point: the computation of the Bayesian solution for an alphabet of $m = 26$ letters requires the maximization of L-Score$(\theta/\underline{y})$ over a set of $m! = 26! = O(10^{40})$ values.

3.6.2 1-Gram Scoring Using a Markov Language Model

A more sophisticated language model assumes that plaintext is generated by a Markov language model with parameters (π, P). Using this model,

$$\Pr_{a\,posteriori}\{\underline{Y} = \underline{y}/\Theta = \theta\} = \pi(\theta^{-1}(y_0))P(\theta^{-1}(y_1)/\theta^{-1}(y_0))$$

$$P(\theta^{-1}(y_2)/\theta^{-1}(y_1))\cdots P(\theta^{-1}(y_{n-1})/\theta^{-1}(y_{n-2}))$$

$$= \pi(\theta^{-1}(y_0)) \prod_{i,j=0}^{m-1} P^{N_{s,t}}(\theta^{-1}(t)/\theta^{-1}(s)),$$

where $N_{s,t}$ is the number of adjacent ciphertext letter-pairs (s, t).

It is not feasible to evaluate $\Pr_{a\,posteriori}\{\underline{Y} = \underline{y}/\Theta = \theta\}$ for every θ when $m = 26$. Instead, we will calculate an approximate *partial* MLE, by maximizing over substitutions that are only partially specified. $\Theta_{\underline{a},\underline{b}}$ consists of those θ determined by a k-vector of plaintext letters $\underline{a} = (a_0, a_1, \ldots, a_{k-1})$ and a k-vector of corresponding ciphertext letters $\underline{b} = (b_0, b_1, \ldots, b_{k-1})$:

$$\theta \in \Theta_{\underline{a},\underline{b}} \Rightarrow \theta(a_i) = b_i, \qquad \text{for } 0 \le i < k.$$

The conditional probability $\Pr_{a\,posteriori}\{\underline{Y} = \underline{y}/\Theta_{\underline{a},\underline{b}}\}$ is defined by

$$\Pr_{a\,posteriori}\{\underline{Y} = \underline{y}/\Theta_{\underline{a},\underline{b}}\} = \pi(\theta^{-1}(y_0)) \prod_{i,j=0}^{k-1} P^{N_{b_i,b_j}}(\theta^{-1}(b_j)/\theta^{-1}(b_i)) \times P_1 \times P_2 \times P_3,$$

where

$$P_1 = \prod_{i=0}^{k-1} \prod_{\substack{t=0 \\ t\notin\underline{a},\underline{b}}}^{k-1} P^{N_{b_i,t}}(\theta^{-1}(t)/\theta^{-1}(b_i))$$

$$P_2 = \prod_{j=0}^{k-1} \prod_{\substack{s=0 \\ s\notin\underline{a},\underline{b}}}^{k-1} P^{N_{s,b_j}}(\theta^{-1}(b_j)/\theta^{-1}(s))$$

and

$$P_3 = \prod_{\substack{s,t=0 \\ s,t\notin\underline{a},\underline{b}}}^{k-1} P^{N_{s,t}}(\theta^{-1}(b_j)/\theta^{-1}(s)).$$

$\theta \in \Theta_{\underline{a},\underline{b}}$ does not provide the values of $\theta^{-1}(t)$ for $t \notin \underline{a}, \underline{b}$ so that the evaluation of $\Pr_{a\,posteriori}\{\underline{Y} = \underline{y}/\Theta_{\underline{a},\underline{b}}\}$ is not possible. Instead, we calculate an approximate partial MLE log-score defined by

$$\text{L-Score}(\underline{Y} = \underline{y}/\Theta_{\underline{a},\underline{b}}) = \frac{1}{n}\log_2 \text{Score}(\underline{Y} = \underline{y}/\Theta_{\underline{a},\underline{b}})$$

$$= \pi(\theta^{-1}(y_0)) \sum_{i,j=0}^{k-1} \frac{N_{b_i,b_j}}{n} \log_2 P(\theta^{-1}(b_j)/\theta^{-1}(b_i)).$$

By the law of large numbers

$$\lim_{n\to\infty} \frac{N_{b_i,b_j}}{n} = \pi(\tau^{-1}(b_i))P(\tau^{-1}(b_j)/\tau^{-1}(b_i))$$

so that

$$\lim_{n \to \infty} \text{L-Score}(\underline{Y} = \underline{y}/\Theta_{\underline{a},\underline{b}}) = \text{L}_\infty\text{-Score}(\underline{Y} = \underline{y}/\Theta_{\underline{a},\underline{b}})$$

$$= \sum_{i,j=0}^{k-1} \pi(\tau^{-1}(b_i)) P(\tau^{-1}(b_j)/\tau^{-1}(b_i)) \log_2 P(a_j/a_i).$$

It is reasonable to look at the values of $(\underline{a},\underline{b})$ for which $\sum_{i,j=0}^{k-1} \pi(\tau^{-1}(b_i))$ $P(\tau^{-1}(b_j)/\tau^{-1}(b_i)) \log_2 P(a_j/a_i)$ is a maximum.

Example 3.3
The ASCII plaintext

---

plainEx3.3

The pre-major requirements for the B.A. and the B.S. degrees
in computer science are the same. Students intending to major
in computer science should declare a pre-major when applying
for admission to the university. Students who declare a
pre-major are responsible for satisfying degree requirements
in effect at the time of their declaration. When students have
completed the preparation courses, they must petition to
declare a change from pre-major to major status.

---

is enciphered according to the rules:

- All characters (in the plaintext) other than uppercase letters have been deleted,
- The ciphertext is written in row of 50 characters producing the ciphertext

---

cipherEx3.3

---

rnbpybifczyybhkwybibvrdxzyrnbqffvgrnbqdgbaybbdwvtz
ipkrbydtwbvtbfybrnbdfibdrkgbvrdwvrbvgwvarzifczywvt
zipkrbydtwbvtbdnzkoggbtofybfpybifczysnbvfppoewvaxz
yfgiwddwzvrzrnbkvwubydwredrkgbvrdsnzgbtofybfpybifc
zyfybybdpzvdwqobxzydfrwdxewvagbaybbybhkwybibvrdwvb
xxbtrfrrnbrwibzxrnbwygbtofyfrwzvsnbvdrkgbvrdnfubtz
ipobrbgrnbpybpfyfrwzvtzkydbdrnbeikdrpbrwrwzvrzgbto
fybftnfvabxyzipybifczyrzifczydrfrk

Table 3.21 gives the letter counts $\{N_i\}$ and frequencies $\{f_i\}$ of the letters in the cipherEx3.3 ciphertext. It is reasonable to suppose that the high-frequency ciphertext letters identified in Table 3.21,

---

b (60)	r (37)	y (34)	f (28)	z (26)	v (25)	d (25)	w (28)

---

are likely to correspond to some of the plaintext letters of high probability:

E	T	A	O	N	R	I	S	H

TABLE 3.21   Letter Counts and Frequencies in `cipherEx3.3`

i	N_i	f_i	i	N_i	f_i	i	N_i	f_i
a	6	0.0156	b	60	0.1563	c	6	0.0156
d	25	0.0651	e	4	0.0104	f	28	0.0729
g	14	0.0365	h	2	0.0052	i	16	0.0417
j	0	0.0000	k	12	0.0313	l	0	0.0000
m	0	0.0000	n	15	0.0391	o	8	0.0208
p	13	0.0339	q	3	0.0078	r	37	0.0964
s	3	0.0078	t	14	0.0365	u	2	0.0052
v	25	0.0651	w	23	0.0599	x	8	0.0208
y	34	0.0885	z	26	0.0677			

TABLE 3.22 $k = 3$

$\underline{a}, \underline{b}$				L_∞-Score($\underline{Y} = \underline{y}/\Theta_{\underline{a},\underline{b}}$)
bE	rN	yR		-0.2524
bE	rT	yR		-0.2636
bR	rA	yE		-0.2822
bR	rO	yE		-0.2868
bN	rE	yI		-0.2900
bN	rO	yI		-0.2928
bR	rT	yE		-0.2964
bE	rI	yR		-0.2999
bR	rE	yO		-0.3021
bE	rR	yT		-0.3043

TABLE 3.23 $k = 4$

$\underline{a}, \underline{b}$				L_∞-Score($\underline{Y} = \underline{y}/\Theta_{\underline{a},\underline{b}}$)
bE	rN	yR	fA	-0.4625
bE	rT	yR	fA	-0.4762
bN	rE	yI	fT	-0.4768
bN	rO	yI	fT	-0.4823
bE	rN	yR	fO	-0.4825
bR	rA	yE	fN	-0.5008
bN	rA	yI	fT	-0.5043
bR	rA	yE	fT	-0.5049
bR	rO	yE	fN	-0.5050
bE	rN	yR	fI	-0.5061

TABLE 3.24 $k = 5$

$\underline{a}, \underline{b}$					L_∞-Score($\underline{Y} = \underline{y}/\Theta_{\underline{a},\underline{b}}$)
bE	rN	yR	fA	zO	-0.6048
bE	rT	yR	fA	zO	-0.6122
bN	rE	yI	fT	zR	-0.6168
bE	rN	yR	fO	zA	-0.6234
bR	rA	yE	fN	zT	-0.6278
bN	rO	yI	fT	zR	-0.6293
bR	rO	yE	fT	zN	-0.6324
bR	rA	yE	fT	zN	-0.6325
bE	rT	yN	fA	zI	-0.6359
bE	rN	yR	fA	zT	-0.6395

TABLE 3.25 $k = 6$

$\underline{a}, \underline{b}$						L_∞-Score($\underline{Y} = \underline{y}/\Theta_{\underline{a},\underline{b}}$)
bE	rT	yR	fA	zO	vN	-0.8009
bE	rS	yR	fA	zO	vN	-0.8156
bE	rT	yS	fA	zI	vN	-0.8286
bE	rT	yR	fA	zO	vS	-0.8297
bE	rT	yN	fA	zI	vS	-0.8307
bE	rT	yR	fA	zI	vN	-0.8377
bN	rE	yI	fS	zR	vT	-0.8410
bE	rS	yR	fA	zI	vN	-0.8463
bE	rT	yR	fA	zI	vS	-0.8464
bR	rI	yE	fS	zN	vT	-0.8464

The 10 largest scores for partial assumptions with $k = 3(1)6$ are given in Tables 3.22 to 3.25. If the (lowercase) ciphertext letters in `cipherEx3.3` are replaced by their (uppercase) plaintext correspondents according to $\Theta_{a,b}$,

b → E	r → T	y → R	f → A	z → O	v → N

the following partially deciphered plaintext is obtained:

Partial-<code>plainEx3.3</code> : Step 1

```
TnEpREiAcORREhkwREiENTdxORTnEqAANgTnEqdgEaREEdwNtO
ipkTERdtwENtEARETnEdAiEdTkgENTdwNTENgwNaTOiAcORwNt
OipkTERdtwENtEdnOkoggEtoAREApREiAcORsnENAppoewNaxO
RAgiwddwONTOTnEkNwuERdwTedTkgENTdsnOgEtoAREApREiAc
ORARAREREdpONdwqoExORdATwdxewNagEaREEREhkwREiENTdwNE
xxEtTATTnETwiEOxTnEwRgEtoARATwONsnENdTkgENTdnAuEtO
ipoETEgTnEpREpARATwONtOkRdEdTnEeikdTpETwTwONTOgEto
AREAtnANaExROipREiAcORTOiAcORdTATk
```

The ciphertext letters corresponding to plaintext letters I, S, and H need to be identified; they are likely to be among d, w, i, n. Next, each of the 24 permutations of the three letters {d, w, i, n} is replaced by (I, S, H), and the resulting partial plaintext is searched for recognizable word fragments. The process requires some experimentation and we will not continue beyond this point.

3.7 THE HIDDEN MARKOV MODEL (HMM)

A class of stochastic processes now referred to as Hidden Markov models (HMM) are described in the two important papers published by Petrie [1969] and Baum et al. [1969]. The application of HMM to automatic speech recognition (ASR) was quickly recognized, and is detailed in the survey papers by Levinson et al. [1983], Rabiner and Juang [1986] and Poritz [1988]. We outline the main ideas and show how HMM may be applied to cryptanalyze a monoalphabetic substitution.

A hidden Markov model (HMM) is a two-stage random process; both the input $\underline{X} = (X_0, X_1, \ldots, X_n)$ and output states $\underline{Y} = (Y_0, Y_1, \ldots, Y_n)$ consists of integers in $\overline{\mathcal{Z}}_m = \{0, 1, \ldots, m - 1\}$. The HMM is constructed from

1. A Markov chain with parameters (π, P) generating (hidden) states $\underline{X}$

$$\pi(i) \geq 0 \qquad (0 \leq i < m) \qquad 1 = \sum_{i=0}^{m-1} \pi(i) \tag{3.3}$$

$$P(j/i) \geq 0 \qquad (0 \leq i, j < m) \qquad 1 = \sum_{j=0}^{m-1} P(j/i) \qquad (0 \leq i < m) \tag{3.4}$$

2. An *output* probability distribution $q(j/i) = \Pr\{Y_t = j/X_t = i\}$ for each hidden state i

$$q(j/i) \geq 0 \qquad (0 \leq i < m) \qquad 1 = \sum_{j=0}^{m-1} q(j/i) \qquad (0 \leq i < m) \tag{3.5}$$

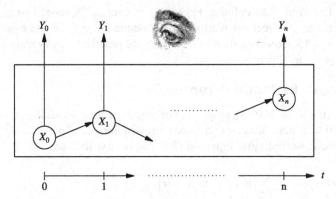

Figure 3.3 Observing the hidden states.

The evolution of the HMM may be described as follows:

1. The initial hidden state $X_0 = x_0$ is chosen with probability $\pi(x_0)$;
   The initial output state $Y_0 = x_0$ occurs with probability $q(y_0/x_0)$.

2. For $t = 1, 2, \ldots$

   (a) the hidden state $X_t = x_t$ occurs with probability
   $$\Pr\{X_t = x_t/X_{t-1} = x_{t-1}\} = P(x_t/x_{t-1});$$

   (b) the output state $Y_t = y_t$ results with probability $\Pr\{Y_t = y_t/X_t = x_t\} = q(y_t/x_t)$.

The output states $\underline{Y}$ may be observed, the *hidden* states $\underline{X}$ are not (Fig. 3.3). Throughout this section,

1. The observation interval consisting of the time points t with $0 \leq t \leq n$ and

2. The output state vector $\underline{y} = (y_0, y_1, \ldots, y_n)$ are fixed.

The probability of observing the output state $\underline{y}$ is expressed as a summation over all paths $\underline{x}$ through the hidden states:

$$\Pr\{\underline{Y} = \underline{y}\} = \sum_x \Pr\{\underline{Y} = \underline{y}, \underline{X} = \underline{x}\} = \sum_x \Pr\{\underline{Y} = \underline{y}/\underline{X} = \underline{x}\}\Pr\{\underline{X} = \underline{x}\}$$

$$= \sum_{x=(x_0, x_1, \ldots, x_n)} \pi(x_0)P(x_1/x_0)P(x_2/x_1)\cdots P(x_n/x_{n-1})\, q(y_0/x_0)q(y_1/x_1)\cdots q(y_s/x_s)$$

$$= \sum_x \pi(x_0)\left(\prod_{s=1}^n P(x_s/x_{s-1})\right)\left(\prod_{s=0}^n q(y_s/x_s)\right) \tag{3.6}$$

The two expressions appearing in the summation on the right-hand side of Equation (3.6) correspond to

- The probability $\pi(x_0)\prod_{s=1}^n P(x_s/x_{s-1})$ of the path $\underline{x} = (x_0, x_1, \ldots, x_n)$ through the hidden states and

- The conditional probability $\prod_{s=0}^n q(y_s/x_s)$ of output $\underline{y} = (y_0, y_1, \ldots, y_n)$ *given* the path $\underline{x} = (x_0, x_1, \ldots, x_n)$ through the hidden states.

The summation in Equation (3.6) defining $\Pr\{\underline{Y} = \underline{y}\}$ is over m^{n+1} states and requires $O(2m^{n+1})$ multiplications. A direct calculation is not feasible for $m = 26$ and even moderate values of, say $n \approx 15$. However, there is an alternative practical way to carry out the evaluation of $\Pr\{\underline{Y} = \underline{y}\}$, to which we now turn.

3.7.1 The Forward–Backward Recursion (*FB*)

Our starting point is the basic Markov property: For any fixed time t with $0 \leq t \leq n$, the paths $\underline{x}$ through the hidden states may be partitioned into disjoint sets of paths according to state x_t visited at time t. Accordingly, Equation (3.6) can be rewritten as

$$\Pr\{\underline{Y} = \underline{y}\} = \sum_{i=0}^{m-1} \Pr\{\underline{Y} = \underline{y}, X_t = i\}$$

$$\Pr\{\underline{Y} = \underline{y}, X_t = i\} = \alpha_t(i) \times \beta_t(i) \tag{3.7}$$

$$\alpha_t(i) = \sum_{\substack{(x_0, x_1, \ldots, x_t) \\ x_t = i}} \pi(x_0) \left(\prod_{s=1}^{t} P(x_s/x_{s-1}) \right) \left(\prod_{s=0}^{t} q(y_s/x_s) \right) \tag{3.8}$$

$$\beta_t(i) = \sum_{\substack{(x_t, x_{t+1}, \ldots, x_n) \\ x_t = i}} \left(\prod_{s=t+1}^{n} P(x_s/x_{s-1}) \right) \left(\prod_{s=t+1}^{n} q(y_s/x_s) \right). \tag{3.9}$$

Recursions for $\alpha_t(i)$ and $\beta_t(i)$ are obtained by noting that

1. The path $(x_0, x_1, \ldots, x_t)$ satisfying $x_t = i$ is composed of
   (a) the path $(x_0, x_1, \ldots, x_{t-1})$ satisfying $x_{t-1} = k$ for some $k \in \mathbb{Z}_m$
   (b) followed by the state transition $x_{t-1} \to x_t = i$.
2. The path $(x_t, x_{t+1}, \ldots, x_n)$ satisfying $x_t = i$
   (a) begins with the state transition $x_t \to x_{t+1} \to k$ for some $k \in \mathbb{Z}_m$
   (b) followed by the path $(x_{t+1}, x_{t+2}, \ldots, x_n)$.

Combining these terms leads to Proposition **3.2**.

Proposition 3.2: The functions $\alpha_t(i)$ and $\beta_t(i)$ satisfy the forward–backward recursions

$$\alpha_t(i) = \begin{cases} \pi(i)q(y_0/i) & \text{if } t = 0 \\ \sum_{k=0}^{m-1} \alpha_{t-1}(k)P(i/k)q(y_t/i) & \text{if } 1 \leq t \leq n \end{cases} \tag{3.10}$$

$$\beta_t(i) = \begin{cases} 1 & \text{if } t = n \\ \sum_{k=0}^{m-1} P(k/i)q(y_t/k)\beta_{t+1}(k) & \text{if } 0 \leq t < n. \end{cases} \tag{3.11}$$

Only $O(2m^2 n)$ rather than $O(2m^{n+1})$ multiplications/additions are required in the forward–backward recursion of $\{\alpha_t(i)\}$ and $\{\beta_t(i)\}$.

When an HMM is used to cryptanalyze a monoalphabetic substitution

- The observed states $\underline{y}$ form the ciphertext,
- The hidden states $\underline{x}$ form the plaintext, and
- q is the unknown monoalphabetic substitution.

Cryptanalysis the maximum likelihood estimate (MLE) of q (and $\underline{x}$) *given* $\underline{y}$.

And now a further complication – only the output observations $\underline{y}$ are truly known when the HMM is applied in cryptanalysis. The generation of plaintext by a Markov chain is only an approximation, and even if this approximation is accepted, the parameters (π, P, q) defining the HMM are unknown. Cryptanalysis using a HMM is the MLE of the parameters (π, P, q) constrained by Equations (3.3)–(3.5):

MLE Problem

Find: (π, P, q) to maximize $\Pr\{\underline{Y} = \underline{y}\}$
Subject to: the constraints described by Equations (3.3)–(3.5)

Finding the MLE of (π, P, q) is the central problem addressed in the work of Baum et al. [1969] and in Baum's subsequent paper Baum, [1972]. Dempster et al. [1977] refer to Baum's algorithm as the *expectation method* (EM).

The method of Lagrange multipliers (see Kaplan, 2003, for example) is used to formulate the conditions for the MLE of the parameters (π, P, q); accordingly, (π, P, q) is a critical point in the MLE of the HMM parameters provided:

$$0 = \frac{\partial}{\partial \pi(i)} \left\{ \Pr\{\underline{Y} = \underline{y}\} - \lambda_1 \left(\sum_{k=0}^{m-1} \pi(k) - 1 \right) \right\}, \qquad 0 \le i < m$$

$$0 = \frac{\partial}{\partial P(j/i)} \left\{ \Pr\{\underline{Y} = \underline{y}\} - \lambda_2 \left(\sum_{k=0}^{m-1} P(k/i) - 1 \right) \right\}, \qquad 0 \le i, j < m$$

$$0 = \frac{\partial}{\partial q(j/i)} \left\{ \Pr\{\underline{Y} = \underline{y}\} - \lambda_3 \left(\sum_{k=0}^{m-1} q(k/i) - 1 \right) \right\}, \qquad 0 \le i, j < m,$$

where λ_1, λ_2, and λ_3 are the Lagrange multipliers corresponding to the constraints in Equations (3.3)–(3.5).

3.7.2 Critical Point Conditions for π

For every fixed value of t with $0 \le t \le n$, we may write

$$\Pr\{\underline{Y} = \underline{y}\} = \sum_{j=0}^{m-1} \Pr\{\underline{Y} = \underline{y}, X_t = j\} = \sum_{j=0}^{m-1} \alpha_t(j) \beta_t(j).$$

The critical point condition $\dfrac{\partial}{\partial \pi(i)} \Pr\{\underline{Y} = \underline{y}\} - \lambda_1 = 0$ for $\pi(i)$ implies

$$0 = q(y_0/i) \beta_0(i) - \lambda_1.$$

Multipling by $\pi(i)$ gives

$$0 = \pi(i) q(y_0/i) \beta_0(i) - \lambda_1 \pi(i) = \alpha_0(i) \beta_0(i) - \lambda_1 \pi(i).$$

The value of λ_1 is obtained by summing over i

$$0 = \sum_{k=0}^{m-1} \alpha_0(k) \beta_0(k) - \lambda_1 \sum_{k=0}^{m-1} \pi(k).$$

Noting that $1 = \sum_{k=0}^{m-1} \pi(k)$ determines the value $\hat{\pi}(i)$ as

$$\hat{\pi}(i) = \gamma_0(i) \equiv \frac{\alpha_0(i) \beta_0(i)}{\sum_{k=0}^{m-1} \alpha_0(k) \beta_0(k)}. \tag{3.12}$$

3.7.3 Critical Point Conditions for $P(j/i)$

For every fixed value of t with $0 \le t < n$, we may write

$$\Pr\{\underline{Y} = \underline{y}\} = \sum_{k,\ell}^{m-1} \Pr\{\underline{Y} = \underline{y}, X_t = k, X_{t+1} = \ell\}.$$

Since

$$\Pr\{\underline{Y} = \underline{y}, X_t = k, X_{t+1} = \ell\} = \alpha_t(k)q(y_{t+1}/\ell)P(\ell/k)\beta_{t+1}(\ell),$$

we have

$$\Pr\{\underline{Y} = \underline{y}\} = \frac{1}{n-1} \sum_{t=0}^{n-1} \sum_{k,\ell}^{m-1} \alpha_t(k)q(y_{t+1}/\ell)P(\ell/k)\beta_{t+1}(\ell).$$

The critical point condition $\frac{\partial}{\partial P(j/i)}\Pr\{\underline{Y} = \underline{y}\} - \lambda_2 = 0$ for $P(j/i)$ implies

$$0 = \sum_{t=0}^{n-1} \alpha_t(i)q(y_{t+1}/j)\beta_{t+1}(j) - \lambda_2.$$

Multipling by $P(j/i)$ gives

$$0 = \sum_{t=0}^{n-1} \alpha_t(i)P(j/i)q(y_{t+1}/j)\beta_{t+1}(j) - \lambda_2 P(j/i).$$

Summing over j gives

$$\alpha_t(i)\beta_t(i) = \sum_{j=0}^{m-1} \alpha_t(i)q(y_{t+1}/j)P(j/i)\beta_{t+1}(j)$$

$$1 = \sum_{j=0}^{m-1} P(j/i)$$

and determines the value $\hat{P}(j/i)$ as

$$\hat{P}(j/i) = \frac{\sum_{t=0}^{n-1} \alpha_t(i)q(y_{t+1}/j)P(j/i)\beta_t(j)}{\sum_{t=0}^{n-1} \alpha_t(i)\beta_t(i)}. \tag{3.13}$$

3.7.4 Critical Point Conditions for $q(j/i)$

For every fixed value of t with $0 \le t < n$, we may write

$$\Pr\{\underline{Y} = \underline{y}\} = \sum_{k,\ell}^{m-1} \Pr\{\underline{Y} = \underline{y}, X_t = k, X_{t+1} = \ell\}$$

Since

$$\Pr\{\underline{Y} = \underline{y}, X_t = k, X_{t+1} = \ell\} = \alpha_t(k)q(y_t/\ell)P(\ell/k)\beta_{t+1}(\ell)$$

we have

$$\Pr\{\underline{Y} = \underline{y}\} = \frac{1}{n-1} \sum_{t=0}^{n-1} \sum_{k,\ell}^{m-1} \alpha_t(k) q(y_t/\ell) P(\ell/k) \beta_{t+1}(\ell).$$

The critical point condition $\frac{\partial}{\partial q(j/i)} \Pr\{\underline{Y} = \underline{y}\} - \lambda_3 = 0$ for $P(j/i)$ implies

$$0 = \sum_{\ell=0}^{m-1} \sum_{\substack{t=0 \\ y_t=j}}^{n-1} \alpha_t(i) P(\ell/i) \beta_{t+1}(\ell) - \lambda_3.$$

Multipling by $q(j/i)$ gives

$$0 = \sum_{\ell=0}^{m-1} \sum_{\substack{t=0 \\ y_t=j}}^{n-1} \alpha_t(i) q(j/i) P(\ell/i) \beta_{t+1}(\ell) - \lambda_3 q(j/i)$$

Summing over j gives

$$\alpha_t(i) \beta_t(i) = \sum_{j,\ell=0}^{m-1} \alpha_t(i) q(j/i) P(\ell/i) \beta_{t+1}(\ell)$$

$$1 = \sum_{j=0}^{m-1} q(j/i)$$

and determines the value $\hat{q}(j/i)$ as

$$\hat{q}(j/i) = \frac{\displaystyle\sum_{\substack{t=0 \\ y_t=j}}^{n-1} \alpha_t(i) \beta_t(i)}{\displaystyle\sum_{t=0}^{n} \alpha_t(i) \beta_t(i)} \tag{3.14}$$

The re-estimates $\hat{\pi}(i)$, $\hat{P}(j/i)$, and $\hat{q}$ permit additional interpretations, which we summarize.

Proposition 3.3: The quantities $\{\alpha_t(i)\}$ and $\{\beta_t(i)\}$ determine the following performance measures of the HMM:

3.3(a) The joint probability of observing the output sequence $\underline{Y} = \underline{y}$ and hidden state $X_t = i$ is

$$\Pr\{\underline{Y} = \underline{y}, X_t = i\} = \alpha_t(i) \beta_t(i).$$

3.3(b) The probability of observing the output sequence $\underline{Y} = \underline{y}$ is

$$\Pr\{\underline{Y} = \underline{y}\} = \sum_{i=0}^{m-1} \alpha_t(i) \beta_t(i).$$

for every t with $0 \leq t \leq n$.

3.3(c) The conditional probability of the hidden state $X_t = i$, given the output state $\underline{Y} = \underline{y}$, is

$$\gamma_t(i) = \frac{\alpha_t(i) \beta_t(i)}{\sum_{k=0}^{m-1} \alpha_t(k) \beta_t(k)}.$$

3.3(d) The *sojourn* time (the time the hidden process X spends in the hidden state i) $D(i)$ in state i is

$$D(i) = \sum_{t=0}^{n} \chi\{X_t = i\},$$

where $\chi\{\cdots\}$ denotes the indicator function of the event $\{\cdots\} = \begin{cases} 1, & \text{if the event } \{\cdots\} \text{ is true}. \\ 0, & \text{otherwise} \end{cases}$

The conditional expectation $E\{D(i)/\underline{Y} = \underline{y}\}$ of $D(i)$, given the output $\underline{Y} = \underline{y}$, is

$$E\{D(i)/\underline{Y} = \underline{y}\} = \sum_{t=0}^{n} \Pr\{X_t = i\} = \frac{\sum_{t=0}^{n} \gamma_t(i)}{\sum_{j=0}^{m-1} \gamma_t(j)}.$$

3.3(e) The number $N(i,j)$ of instances t over the observation interval $0 \le t \le n$ at which the state satisfies $X_t = i$, $Y_t = j$ is

$$N(i,j) = \sum_{t=0}^{n} \chi\{X_t = i, Y_t = j\}.$$

The conditional expectation $E\{N(i,j)/\underline{Y} = \underline{y}\}$ of $N(i,j)$, given the output sequence $\underline{Y} = \underline{y}$, is

$$E\{N(j/i)/\underline{Y} = \underline{y}\} = \sum_{t=0}^{n} \Pr\{X_t = i, Y_t = j\} = \frac{\sum_{\substack{t=0 \\ y_t=j}}^{n} \alpha_t(i)\beta_t(i)}{\sum_{k=0}^{m-1} \alpha_t(k)\beta_t(k)}.$$

3.3(f) The number $T(i,j)$ of hidden state transitions $i \rightarrow j$ over the observation interval $0 \le t \le n$ is

$$T(i,j) = \sum_{t=0}^{n-1} \chi\{X_t = i, X_{t+1} = j\}.$$

The conditional expectation $E\{T(i,j)\}$ of the number of hidden state transitions $i \rightarrow j$ over the observation interval $0 \le t \le n$, given the output sequence $\underline{Y} = \underline{y}$, is

$$E\{T(i,j)\} = \sum_{t=0}^{n-1} \Pr\{X_t = i, X_{t+1} = j\} = \frac{\sum_{t=0}^{n-1} \alpha_t(i)P(j/i)q(y_{t+1}/j)\beta_{t+1}(j)}{\sum_{k=0}^{n-1} \alpha_t(k)\beta_t(k)}.$$

The critical conditions determining $(\hat{\pi}, \hat{P}, \hat{q})$ can be expressed as:

1. $\hat{P}(j/i)$ in Equation (3.13) is the ratio

$$\frac{\text{expected number of times the hidden state satisfies } X_t = j, X_{t+1} = j}{\text{expected number of times the hidden state satisfies } X_t = j}.$$

2. $\hat{q}(j/i)$ in Equation (3.14) is the ratio

$$\frac{\text{expected number of times the state is } X_t = i, Y_t = j}{\text{expected sojourn time } D(i) \text{ in hidden state } i}.$$

The re-estimation of the parameters $\zeta = (\pi, P, q)$ is a transformation

$$S : \zeta \equiv (\pi, P, q) \rightarrow \hat{\zeta} = (\hat{\pi}, \hat{P}, \hat{q}),$$

usually referred to as *hill climbing*.

Multidimensional optimization problems

1. May have more that one critical point, and
2. The critical point may be a local maximum rather than a global maximum.

The uniqueness of critical points for the HMM and the issue of whether $\Pr\{\underline{Y} = \underline{y}\}$ is a global or local maximum was considered in the Baum papers. The answers rely on the auxiliary Q-function, introduced by Kullback and Leibler [1951]:

$$Q(\zeta, \hat{\zeta}) \equiv \sum_{\underline{x}} \Pr_{\zeta}\{\underline{Y} = \underline{y}, \ \underline{X} = \underline{x}\} \log_2 \Pr_{\hat{\zeta}}\{\underline{Y} = \underline{y}, \underline{X} = \underline{x}\}.$$

The subscript ζ (respectively $\hat{\zeta}$) indicates the parameter used in the computation of $\Pr_{\zeta}(\Pr_{\hat{\zeta}})$. It is proved in Baum et al. [1969] that either

1. The initial set of parameters ζ may be a critical point of $\Pr\{\underline{Y} = \underline{y}\}$; that is, ζ is a fixed point of S, or
2. If $\zeta \neq \hat{\zeta}$, then the re-estimated parameters $\hat{\zeta}$ is a more likely set; that is, $\Pr_{\hat{\zeta}}\{\underline{Y} = \underline{y}\} > \Pr_{\zeta}\{\underline{Y} = \underline{y}\}$.

Moreover

3. $Q(\zeta, \hat{\zeta}) > Q(\zeta, \zeta)$ implies $\Pr_{\hat{\zeta}}\{\underline{Y} = \underline{y}\} > \Pr_{\zeta}\{\underline{Y} = \underline{y}\}$;
4. ζ is a critical points of $\Pr_{\zeta}\{\underline{Y} = \underline{y}\}$ if and only if ζ is a critical point of $Q(\zeta, \hat{\zeta})$ (for fixed $\hat{\zeta}$); and
5. For HMM with only a finite number of states, there is only a single critical point ζ^* and it is a global maximum for $\Pr_{\zeta}\{\underline{Y} = \underline{y}\}$. (Note, HMM can be formulated for discrete-valued processes with countably many states ($m = \infty$) and for continuous-valued processes.)

In summary, we formulate Proposition **3.4**.

    Proposition 3.4: The parameters $\zeta = (\pi, P, q)$ of the HMM are either

3.4(a) A fixed point of the transformation S meaning $\pi = \pi$, $\hat{P} = P$, and $\hat{q} = q$, in which case (π, P, q) is the unique MLE; or

3.4(b) $\zeta\rho(\hat{\pi}, P, \hat{q}) = S(\pi, P, q)$ provides a more likely value for $\Pr_{\zeta}\{\underline{Y} = \underline{y}\}$ than does $\zeta = (\pi, P, q)$.

Proposition **3.4** implies that the iterates of (π, P, q) under S converge to the unique maximizing set of parameters for the HMM.

    Example 3.4

We take $m = 4$, $n = 12$ and parameters

$$\pi = (0.25, 0.25, 0.25, 0.25)$$

$$P = \begin{pmatrix} 0.2 & 0.2 & 0.5 & 0.1 \\ 0.333 & 0.333 & 0.167 & 0.167 \\ 0.2 & 0.4 & 0.1 & 0.3 \\ 0.5 & 0.0 & 0.25 & 0.25 \end{pmatrix}$$

$$q(/0) = (0.3, 0.4, 0.2, 0.1) \qquad q(/1) = (0.6, 0.0, 0.3, 0.1)$$
$$q(/2) = (0.1, 0.1, 0.3, 0.5) \qquad q(/3) = (0.4, 0.4, 0.1, 0.1)$$

Randomly determined hidden and output states for this HMM are

$$\underline{y} = (0, 3, 3, 0, 0, 0, 2, 0, 0, 3, 3, 3, 0)$$

and

$$\underline{x} = (3, 0, 1, 1, 1, 3, 0, 1, 1, 2, 3, 2, 1)$$

Table 3.26 gives the values of $\{\gamma_t(i)\}$ for $0 \le i < 4$ and $0 \le t < 12$. Table 3.27 gives the conditional probability $\Pr\{X_t = i / \underline{Y} = \underline{y}\}$ for the same set of (i, t) values; the column on the left lists the value i^* that maximizes this conditional probability. From this we see that we have not done very well!

Re-estimation

We now re-estimate the parameters (π, P, q); while re-estimation improves $\Pr\{\underline{Y} = \underline{y}\}$, it may not make $|q(j/i) - \hat{q}(j/i)|$, for example, smaller. S is iterated so that

$$(\pi, P, q) \to S(\pi, P, q) \to S^2(\pi, P, q) \to \cdots \to S^r(\pi, P, q)$$

until the change $|S^{r-1}(\pi, P, q) - S^r(\pi, P, q)|$ is small enough.

TABLE 3.26 $\gamma_t(i)$ in Example 3.4

t	$i \to 0$	1	2	3
0	0.0000000095541601	0.0000000130685831	0.0000000018213404	0.0000000107410370
1	0.0000000111697621	0.0000000035108919	0.0000000168688425	0.0000000036356241
2	0.0000000037006617	0.0000000067052652	0.0000000217051795	0.0000000030740142
3	0.0000000063912541	0.0000000200082725	0.0000000023421415	0.0000000064434525
4	0.0000000087571231	0.0000000164899292	0.0000000033588684	0.0000000065792000
5	0.0000000123782871	0.0000000141369296	0.0000000027571407	0.0000000059127633
6	0.0000000073749149	0.0000000109587690	0.0000000150999353	0.0000000017515015
7	0.0000000057736313	0.0000000192355902	0.0000000028191940	0.0000000073567052
8	0.0000000135749122	0.0000000121488982	0.0000000018871707	0.0000000075741396
9	0.0000000079690340	0.0000000038602417	0.0000000196837204	0.0000000036721247
10	0.0000000091030246	0.0000000063064266	0.0000000140270220	0.0000000057486475
11	0.0000000038592748	0.0000000061253754	0.0000000217029100	0.0000000034975604
12	0.0000000073893222	0.0000000170197500	0.0000000018024995	0.0000000089735489

TABLE 3.27 $\Pr\{X_t = i/\underline{Y} = \underline{y}\}$ in Example 3.4

i^*	t	$i \to 0$	1	2	3
3	0	0.27153978	0.37142375	0.05176451	0.3052714
0	1	0.31745698	0.09978343	0.47943114	0.10332845
1	2	0.10517689	0.19057105	0.61688518	0.08736688
1	3	0.18164650	0.56865721	0.06656625	0.18313004
1	4	0.24888711	0.46866201	0.09546275	0.18698813
3	5	0.35180459	0.40178716	0.07836098	0.16804723
3	6	0.20960323	0.31146032	0.42915684	0.04977961
0	7	0.16409298	0.54669672	0.08012461	0.20908569
1	8	0.38581400	0.34528511	0.05363548	0.21526541
1	9	0.22648875	0.10971233	0.55943308	0.10436584
2	10	0.25871802	0.17923561	0.39866346	0.16338291
3	11	0.10968485	0.17408994	0.61682068	0.09940453
2	12	0.21001270	0.48372010	0.05122903	0.25503817

Example 3.5

We take $m = 4$, $T = 48$, the same parameters (π, P) as in Example 3.4, the output function and intial estimates of the output function

$$q(/0) = (1.0, 0.0, 0.0, 0.0)$$
$$q(/1) = (0.0, 0.0, 1.0, 0.0)$$
$$q(/2) = (0.0, 1.0, 0.0, 0.0)$$
$$q(/3) = (0.0, 0.0, 0.0, 1.0)$$

and initial estimates of the output function

$$q_0(/0) = (0.24, 0.25, 0.25, 0.25)$$
$$q_0(/1) = (0.25, 0.25, 0.25, 0.25)$$
$$q_0(/2) = (0.24, 0.25, 0.25, 0.25)$$
$$q_0(/3) = (0.25, 0.25, 0.25, 0.25).$$

The sample of the output process $\underline{y} = (y_0, y_1, \ldots, y_{99})$ is used.

									$\underline{y}$										

```
2 0 2 3 0 1 2 2 2 2 3 1 3 0 3 0 1 2 3 0
0 1 3 0 2 2 0 1 2 2 0 1 1 3 0 1 3 0 2 1
3 0 1 3 0 1 2 2 0 1 2 2 3 3 0 1 0 0 1 0
1 3 0 2 1 3 3 0 1 3 0 1 3 0 1 3 0 0 0 2
0 1 1 3 0 3 1 3 0 1 2 3 0 1 0 2 0 1 3 0
```

Tables 3.28-3.33 tabulate the initial estimate for $q_0(j/i)$ and the re-estimates $S^r(q_0(j/i))$ for $r = 10(10)50$ steps. Although $S^{50}(q(j/i)) \neq q(j/i)$, it is obvious that the iteration has converged to a permutation matrix.

TABLE 3.28 $q_0(j/i)$

$i \downarrow$	$j \rightarrow 0$	1	2	3
0	0.25	0.25	0.25	0.25
1	0.25	0.25	0.25	0.25
2	0.25	0.25	0.25	0.25
3	0.25	0.25	0.25	0.25

TABLE 3.29 $S^{10}(q_0(j/i))$

$i \downarrow$	$j \rightarrow 0$	1	2	3
0	0.344325	0.238802	0.184007	0.232867
1	0.305011	0.247853	0.197892	0.249245
2	0.306866	0.271477	0.196751	0.224905
3	0.304246	0.228364	0.220339	0.247051

TABLE 3.30 $S^{20}(q_0(j/i))$

$i \downarrow$	$j \rightarrow 0$	1	2	3
0	0.854681	0.028576	0.074578	0.042165
1	0.085849	0.116799	0.381652	0.415700
2	0.058269	0.767760	0.151528	0.022444
3	0.119112	0.021399	0.239053	0.620436

TABLE 3.31 $S^{30}(q_0(j/i))$

$i \downarrow$	$j \rightarrow 0$	1	2	3
0	0.999094	0.000008	0.000825	0.000073
1	0.002513	0.004023	0.831230	0.162233
2	0.001549	0.964339	0.034102	0.000010
3	0.009724	0.000047	0.008359	0.981871

TABLE 3.32 $S^{40}(q_0(j/i))$

$i \downarrow$	$j \rightarrow 0$	1	2	3
0	0.999998	0.000000	0.000001	0.000000
1	0.000096	0.000073	0.895849	0.103982
2	0.000181	0.992775	0.007044	0.000000
3	0.000514	0.000000	0.000028	0.999459

TABLE 3.33 $S^{50}(q_0(j/i))$

$i \downarrow$	$j \rightarrow 0$	1	2	3
0	1.000000	0.000000	0.000000	0.000000
1	0.000004	0.000001	0.906980	0.093015
2	0.000029	0.998303	0.001667	0.000000
3	0.000023	0.000000	0.000000	0.999977

Scaling

Example 3.4 illustrates a computational difficulty in the application of HHM; for example, the probabilities $\{\gamma_t(i)\}$ become very small as t increases and underflow may occur. This may be compensated by parameter-*scaling*, replacing the recursion in Equation (3.7) by

$$
\tilde{a}_t(i,) = \begin{cases} c_0 \pi(i) q(j/i)(y_0), & \text{if } t = 0 \\ c_t \sum_{k=0}^{m-1} \tilde{\alpha}_{t-1}(k) P(i/k) q(y_t/i), & \text{if } 1 \le t \le n \end{cases}
$$

and

$$
c_t = \frac{1}{\sum_{i=0}^{m-1} \sum_{k=0}^{m-1} \tilde{\alpha}_{t-1}(k) P(i/k) q(y_t/i)}.
$$

The numbers $\{c_t\}$ are *scaling factors* and the *scaled-α* functions satisfy

$$
\tilde{a}_t(i) = C_t \alpha_t(i)
$$
$$
C_t = c_0 c_1 \cdots c_t
$$

and

$$
1 = \sum_{i=0}^{m-1} \tilde{\alpha}_t(i)
$$

Similarly, the β- and γ-recursions are

$$
\tilde{\beta}_t(i) = \begin{cases} 1, & \text{if } t = n \\ \sum_{k=0}^{m-1} c_{t+1} \tilde{\beta}_{t+1}(k) P(k/i) q(y_{t+1}/k), & \text{if } 0 \le t \le n \end{cases}
$$

$$
\tilde{\gamma}_t(i) = C_t c_{t+1} c_{t+2} \cdots c_n \gamma_t(i) = C_n \gamma_n(i)
$$

and the re-estimation formula for the output probabilities $\tilde{q}(j/i)$ becomes

$$
\hat{\tilde{q}}(j/i) = \frac{\sum_{\substack{t=0 \\ y_t=j}}^{n} \tilde{\gamma}_t(i)}{\sum_{k=0}^{m-1} \tilde{\gamma}_n(k)} = \frac{\sum_{\substack{t=0 \\ y_t=j}}^{n} \gamma_t(i)}{\sum_{k=0}^{m-1} \gamma_n(k)}
$$

The scaled re-estimation formulas for $\tilde{P}(j/i)$ and $\tilde{\pi}(i)$ are

$$\hat{\tilde{P}}(j/i) = \frac{\sum_{t=0}^{n-1} \tilde{\alpha}_t(i)\tilde{P}(j/i)q(y_{t+1}/j)c_{t+1}\tilde{\beta}_{t+1}(j)}{\sum_{t=0}^{n-1} \tilde{\alpha}_t(i)\tilde{\beta}_n(i)}$$

and

$$\hat{\tilde{\pi}}(i) = \hat{\tilde{\gamma}}_0(i)$$

We have just barely touched on this subject; for more information, see the books by Cappe et al. [2005], MacDonald and MacDonald [1997], and Elliott [1997].

3.8 HILL ENCIPHERMENT OF ASCII *N*-GRAMS

Monoalphabetic encipherment of N-grams of ASCII plaintext with $N > 1$ is attractive for two reasons:

1. The probability distribution of N-grams with $N \approx 4$ is much flatter than for 1-grams, making it harder to recognize letter fragments; and
2. There is a very large number 128^N of N-grams with $N \geq 4$.

Lester Hill [1929] described a simple and elegant way to encipher N-grams of ASCII plaintext. Each character will be identified by its ordinal position in the ASCII character alphabet, integers in $\mathcal{Z}_{128}$. We suppose the length n of plaintext $\underline{x} = (x_0, x_1, \ldots, x_{n-1})$ is a multiple of N; various modifications are possible when $n \neq kN$ and will be mentioned later. $\underline{x}$ is divided into N-grams whose components are integers in $\mathcal{Z}_{128}$:

$$\underline{x} = (\underline{x}^{(0)}, \underline{x}^{(1)}, \ldots, \underline{x}^{(k-1)})$$
$$\underline{x}^{(0)} = (x_0, x_1, \ldots, x_{N-1})$$
$$\underline{x}^{(1)} = (x_N, x_{N+1}, \ldots, x_{2N-1})$$
$$\vdots$$
$$\underline{x}^{(i)} = (x_{iN}, x_{iN+1}, \ldots, x_{(i+1)N-1})$$
$$\vdots$$
$$\underline{x}^{(k-1)} = (x_{(k-1)N}, x_{(k-1)N+1}, \ldots, x_{kN-1}).$$

The Hill encipherment of ASCII plaintext $\underline{x}$ denoted by

$$\underline{y} = A\underline{x}$$

is defined by

$$A : \underline{x}^{(i)} \to \underline{y}^{(i)} = A(\underline{x}^{(i)}) \, (\text{modulo } m), \ 0 \le i \le k \tag{3.15}$$

$$y_{\ell N+i} = \left(\sum_{j=0}^{N-1} a_{i,j} x_{lN+j} \right) (\text{modulo } m), \ 0 \le i < N, \ \ 0 \le \ell < k \tag{3.16}$$

where

$$\underline{y} = (\underline{y}^{(0)}, \underline{y}^{(1)}, \ldots, \underline{y}^{(N-1)})$$

$$\underline{y}^{(0)} = (y_0, y_1, \ldots, y_{n-1})$$

$$\underline{y}^{(1)} = (y_N, y_{N+1}, \ldots, y_{2N-1})$$

$$\vdots$$

$$\underline{y}^{(i)} = (y_{iN}, y_{iN+1}, \ldots, y_{(i+1)N-1})$$

$$\vdots$$

$$\underline{y}^{(k-1)} = (y_{(k-1)N}, y_{(k-1)N+1}, \ldots, y_{Nk-1})$$

and $A = (a_{i,j})$ is an $N \times N$ matrix with entries in $\mathcal{Z}_{128}$ and which is invertible.

Proposition **3.5** in Section 3.8.3 shows that about 30% of the 128^{N^2} N-by-N matrices are invertible.

Hill encipherment is the matrix multiplication by A of the plaintext (column) vectors $\{\underline{x}^{(i)}\}$; decipherment of Hill ciphertext is the matrix multiplication by A^{-1} of the ciphertext (column) vectors $\{\underline{y}^{(i)}\}$. We can write

$$Y = AX \quad \text{and} \quad X = A^{-1}Y, \tag{3.17}$$

where X and Y are the $N \times k$ matrices formed from the (column) vectors $\{\underline{x}^{(i)}\}$ and $\{\underline{y}^{(i)}\}$

$$X = \left(\underline{x}^{(0)} \ \underline{x}^{(1)} \cdots \underline{x}^{(k-1)} \right) = \begin{pmatrix} x_0 & x_N & \cdots & x_{(k-1)N} \\ x_1 & x_{N+1} & \cdots & x_{(k-1)N+1} \\ \vdots & \vdots & \ddots & \vdots \\ x_{N-1} & x_{2N-1} & \cdots & x_{kN-1} \end{pmatrix} \tag{3.18}$$

$$Y = \left(\underline{y}^{(0)} \ \underline{y}^{(1)} \cdots \underline{y}^{(k-1)} \right) = \begin{pmatrix} y_0 & y_N & \cdots & y_{(k-1)N} \\ y_1 & y_{N+1} & \cdots & y_{(k-1)N+1} \\ \vdots & \vdots & \ddots & \vdots \\ y_{N-1} & y_{2N-1} & \cdots & y_{kN-1} \end{pmatrix}. \tag{3.19}$$

3.8.1 Finding the Hill Matrix with Known Plain- and Ciphertext

Section 3.9 contains a short exposition of how Gaussian elimination might be used to determine T (respectively T^{-1}) by elementary row and column transformations when a set of $M \ge N$ plaintext (or ciphertext) N-vectors $\{\underline{x}^{(i)}\}$ (respectively $\{\underline{y}^{(i)}\}$ are related by Equations (3.15) and (3.16). Gaussian elimination applied to the ciphertext matrix Y

of column vectors involves the postmultiplication of Y and X by a sequence $O_1 O_2 \cdots O_M$ of matrices as follows:

1.

$$X = A^{-1}Y$$
$$Y \rightarrow YM_r(v)$$
$$X \rightarrow XM_r(v)$$

$$XM_r(v) \rightarrow A^{-1}YM_r(v)$$

   (a) Multiplying the elements in the rth column of Y by v;

   (b) Multiplying the elements in the rth column of X by v.

2.

$$X = A^{-1}Y$$
$$Y \rightarrow YC_{r,s}(v)$$
$$X \rightarrow XC_{r,s}(v)$$

$$XC_{r,s}(v) \rightarrow A^{-1}YC_{r,s}(v)$$

   (a) Adding v times the sth column of Y to the rth column of Y;

   (b) Adding v times the sth column of X to the rth column of X.

3.

$$X = A^{-1}Y$$
$$Y \rightarrow YE_{r,s}(v)$$
$$X \rightarrow XE_{r,s}(v)$$

$$XE_{r,s}(v) \rightarrow A^{-1}YE_{r,s}(v)$$

   (a) Interchanging the rth and sth columns of Y;

   (b) Interchanging the rth and sth columns of X.

Gaussian elimination when applied to the matrix Y of ciphertext (column) vectors related by Equations (3.15)–(3.19), produces A^{-1}.

$$X = A^{-1}Y$$
$$Y \rightarrow YO_1 O_2 \cdots O_M$$
$$X \rightarrow XO_1 O_2 \cdots O_M$$
$$XO_1 O_2 \cdots O_M \rightarrow A^{-1}YO_1 O_2 \cdots O_M$$
$$I = YO_1 O_2 \cdots O_M$$

implies

$$A^{-1} = XO_1 O_2 \cdots O_M$$

Example 3.6

The 18 ASCII characters of the plaintext `plainEx3.6`: `This book addresses an area where few organized references current exist.` is enciphered using a 4×4 Hill substitution. The plaintext X and ciphertext Y are displayed as 18-column vectors each consisting of 4 integers in $\mathcal{Z}_{128}$:

$$X = \begin{vmatrix} 84 & 32 & 107 & 100 & 115 & 97 & 114 & 119 & 101 & 119 & 103 & 122 & 114 & 114 & 101 & 117 & 110 & 32 \\ 104 & 98 & 32 & 114 & 101 & 110 & 101 & 104 & 32 & 32 & 97 & 101 & 101 & 101 & 115 & 114 & 116 & 101 \\ 105 & 111 & 97 & 101 & 115 & 32 & 97 & 101 & 102 & 111 & 110 & 100 & 102 & 110 & 32 & 114 & 108 & 120 \\ 115 & 111 & 100 & 115 & 32 & 97 & 32 & 114 & 101 & 114 & 105 & 32 & 101 & 99 & 99 & 101 & 121 & 105 \end{vmatrix}$$

$$Y = \begin{vmatrix} 36 & 84 & 102 & 94 & 3 & 14 & 52 & 64 & 22 & 30 & 19 & 73 & 86 & 56 & 27 & 56 & 33 & 126 \\ 77 & 89 & 53 & 127 & 82 & 18 & 116 & 25 & 102 & 43 & 21 & 55 & 61 & 29 & 101 & 96 & 84 & 7 \\ 120 & 86 & 61 & 114 & 10 & 65 & 3 & 65 & 63 & 121 & 62 & 59 & 95 & 7 & 58 & 1 & 66 & 81 \\ 51 & 23 & 100 & 91 & 52 & 121 & 52 & 82 & 69 & 50 & 77 & 52 & 89 & 23 & 79 & 13 & 41 & 93 \end{vmatrix}$$

$$Y = AX, \quad X = A^{-1}Y$$

3.8.2 Steps in Gaussian Elimination of Ciphertext

Step #1

$Y = Y_0 \rightarrow Y_0 E_{0,4} = Y_1$; interchange the 0th and 4th columns of Y_0.

$Y_1 \rightarrow Y_1 M_0(3^{-1}) = Y_2$; multiply the 0th column of Y_1 by $43 = 3^{-1}$.

$$Y_2 = \begin{vmatrix} 1 & 84 & 102 & 94 & 36 & 14 & 52 & 64 & 22 & 30 & 19 & 73 & 86 & 56 & 27 & 56 & 33 & 126 \\ 70 & 89 & 53 & 127 & 77 & 18 & 116 & 25 & 102 & 43 & 21 & 55 & 61 & 29 & 101 & 96 & 84 & 7 \\ 46 & 86 & 61 & 114 & 120 & 65 & 3 & 65 & 63 & 121 & 62 & 59 & 95 & 7 & 58 & 1 & 66 & 81 \\ 60 & 23 & 100 & 91 & 51 & 121 & 52 & 82 & 69 & 50 & 77 & 52 & 89 & 23 & 79 & 13 & 41 & 93 \end{vmatrix}$$

$X = X_0 \rightarrow X_0 E_{0,4} = X_1$; interchange the 0th and 4th columns of X_0.

$X_1 \rightarrow X_1 M_0(3^{-1}) = X_2$; multiply the 0th column X_1 by $43 = 3^{-1}$.

$$X_2 = \begin{vmatrix} 81 & 32 & 107 & 100 & 84 & 97 & 114 & 119 & 101 & 119 & 103 & 122 & 114 & 114 & 101 & 117 & 110 & 32 \\ 119 & 98 & 32 & 114 & 104 & 110 & 101 & 104 & 32 & 32 & 97 & 101 & 101 & 101 & 115 & 114 & 116 & 101 \\ 81 & 111 & 97 & 101 & 105 & 32 & 97 & 101 & 102 & 111 & 110 & 100 & 102 & 110 & 32 & 114 & 108 & 120 \\ 96 & 111 & 100 & 115 & 115 & 97 & 32 & 114 & 101 & 114 & 105 & 32 & 101 & 99 & 99 & 101 & 121 & 105 \end{vmatrix}$$

Step #2

$Y_2 \rightarrow Y_2 \prod_{j=1}^{17} C_{j,0}(-y_{j,0}) = Y_3$; for $j \neq 0$, add $-y_{j,0}$ times the 0th column of Y_2 to the jth column of Y_2.

$$Y_3 = \begin{vmatrix} 1 & 0 & 0 & 0 & 0 & 0 & 0 & 0 & 0 & 0 & 0 & 0 & 0 & 0 & 0 & 0 & 0 & 0 \\ 70 & 97 & 81 & 75 & 117 & 62 & 60 & 25 & 98 & 119 & 99 & 65 & 57 & 77 & 3 & 16 & 78 & 19 \\ 46 & 62 & 105 & 14 & 0 & 61 & 43 & 65 & 75 & 21 & 84 & 29 & 107 & 119 & 96 & 113 & 84 & 45 \\ 60 & 103 & 124 & 83 & 67 & 49 & 4 & 82 & 29 & 42 & 89 & 24 & 49 & 119 & 123 & 109 & 109 & 85 \end{vmatrix}$$

$X_2 \rightarrow X_2 \prod_{j=1}^{17} C_{j,0}(-y_{j,0}) = X_3$; for $j \neq 0$, add $-y_{j,0}$ times the 0th column of X_2 to the jth column of X_2.

$$X_3 = \begin{vmatrix} 81 & 12 & 37 & 38 & 112 & 115 & 126 & 55 & 111 & 121 & 100 & 97 & 60 & 58 & 90 & 61 & 125 & 66 \\ 119 & 86 & 54 & 64 & 44 & 108 & 57 & 40 & 102 & 46 & 12 & 118 & 107 & 93 & 102 & 106 & 29 & 83 \\ 81 & 91 & 27 & 39 & 5 & 50 & 109 & 37 & 112 & 113 & 107 & 75 & 48 & 54 & 21 & 58 & 123 & 26 \\ 96 & 111 & 36 & 51 & 115 & 33 & 32 & 114 & 37 & 50 & 73 & 64 & 37 & 99 & 67 & 101 & 25 & 41 \end{vmatrix}$$

Step #3

$$Y_3 \to Y_3 M_1(97^{-1}) = Y_4;\ \text{multiply the 1st column of } Y_3 \text{ by } 33 = 97^{-1}.$$

$$Y_4 = \begin{vmatrix} 1 & 0 & 0 & 0 & 0 & 0 & 0 & 0 & 0 & 0 & 0 & 0 & 0 & 0 & 0 & 0 & 0 & 0 \\ 70 & 1 & 81 & 75 & 117 & 62 & 60 & 25 & 98 & 119 & 99 & 65 & 57 & 77 & 3 & 16 & 78 & 19 \\ 46 & 126 & 105 & 14 & 0 & 61 & 43 & 65 & 75 & 21 & 84 & 29 & 107 & 119 & 96 & 113 & 84 & 45 \\ 60 & 71 & 124 & 83 & 67 & 49 & 4 & 82 & 29 & 42 & 89 & 24 & 49 & 119 & 123 & 109 & 109 & 85 \end{vmatrix}$$

$$X_3 \to X_3 M_1(97^{-1}) = X_4;\ \text{multiply the 1st column of } X_3 \text{ by } 33 = 97^{-1}.$$

$$X_4 = \begin{vmatrix} 81 & 12 & 37 & 38 & 112 & 115 & 126 & 55 & 11 & 121 & 100 & 97 & 60 & 58 & 90 & 61 & 125 & 66 \\ 119 & 22 & 54 & 64 & 44 & 108 & 57 & 40 & 102 & 46 & 12 & 118 & 107 & 93 & 102 & 106 & 29 & 83 \\ 81 & 59 & 27 & 39 & 5 & 50 & 109 & 37 & 112 & 113 & 107 & 75 & 48 & 54 & 21 & 58 & 123 & 26 \\ 96 & 79 & 36 & 51 & 115 & 33 & 32 & 114 & 37 & 50 & 73 & 64 & 37 & 99 & 67 & 101 & 25 & 41 \end{vmatrix}$$

Step #4

$$Y_4 \to Y_4 \prod_{\substack{j=0\\ j\neq1}}^{17} C_{j,1}(-y_{j,1}) = Y_5;\ \text{for } j \neq 1, \text{ add } -y_{j,1} \text{ times the 1st column of } Y_4 \text{ to the } j\text{th column of } Y_4.$$

$$Y_5 = \begin{vmatrix} 1 & 0 & 0 & 0 & 0 & 0 & 0 & 0 & 0 & 0 & 0 & 0 & 0 & 0 & 0 & 0 & 0 & 0 \\ 0 & 1 & 0 & 0 & 0 & 0 & 0 & 0 & 0 & 0 & 0 & 0 & 0 & 0 & 0 & 0 & 0 & 0 \\ 58 & 125 & 11 & 36 & 106 & 57 & 35 & 115 & 15 & 3 & 26 & 31 & 93 & 17 & 102 & 17 & 112 & 83 \\ 82 & 71 & 5 & 6 & 80 & 127 & 96 & 99 & 111 & 41 & 100 & 17 & 98 & 28 & 38 & 125 & 75 & 16 \end{vmatrix}$$

$$X_4 \to X_4 \prod_{\substack{j=0\\ j\neq1}}^{17} C_{j,1}(-y_{j,1}) = X_5;\ \text{for } j \neq 1, \text{ add } -y_{j,1} \text{ times the 1st column of } X_4 \text{ to the } j\text{th column of } X_4.$$

$$X_5 = \begin{vmatrix} 9 & 12 & 89 & 34 & 116 & 11 & 46 & 11 & 87 & 101 & 64 & 85 & 16 & 30 & 54 & 125 & 85 & 94 \\ 115 & 22 & 64 & 78 & 30 & 24 & 17 & 2 & 122 & 116 & 10 & 96 & 5 & 63 & 36 & 10 & 105 & 49 \\ 47 & 59 & 112 & 94 & 14 & 104 & 25 & 98 & 90 & 4 & 26 & 80 & 13 & 119 & 100 & 10 & 1 & 57 \\ 70 & 79 & 37 & 14 & 88 & 127 & 28 & 59 & 103 & 121 & 60 & 49 & 14 & 32 & 86 & 117 & 7 & 76 \end{vmatrix}$$

Step #5

$$Y_5 \to Y_5 M_2(11^{-1}) = Y_6;\ \text{multiply the 2nd column of } Y_5 \text{ by } 35 = 11^{-1}.$$

$$Y_6 = \begin{vmatrix} 1 & 0 & 0 & 0 & 0 & 0 & 0 & 0 & 0 & 0 & 0 & 0 & 0 & 0 & 0 & 0 & 0 & 0 \\ 0 & 1 & 0 & 0 & 0 & 0 & 0 & 0 & 0 & 0 & 0 & 0 & 0 & 0 & 0 & 0 & 0 & 0 \\ 58 & 126 & 1 & 36 & 106 & 57 & 35 & 115 & 15 & 3 & 26 & 31 & 93 & 17 & 102 & 17 & 112 & 83 \\ 82 & 71 & 47 & 6 & 80 & 127 & 96 & 99 & 111 & 41 & 100 & 17 & 98 & 28 & 38 & 125 & 75 & 16 \end{vmatrix}$$

$$X_5 \to X_5 M_2(11^{-1}) = X_6;\ \text{multiply the 2nd column of } X_5 \text{ by } 35 = 11^{-1}.$$

$$X_6 = \begin{vmatrix} 9 & 12 & 43 & 34 & 116 & 11 & 46 & 11 & 87 & 101 & 64 & 85 & 16 & 30 & 54 & 125 & 85 & 94 \\ 115 & 22 & 64 & 78 & 30 & 24 & 17 & 2 & 122 & 116 & 10 & 96 & 5 & 63 & 36 & 10 & 105 & 49 \\ 47 & 59 & 80 & 94 & 14 & 104 & 25 & 98 & 90 & 4 & 26 & 80 & 13\ ' & 119 & 100 & 10 & 1 & 57 \\ 70 & 79 & 15 & 14 & 88 & 127 & 28 & 59 & 103 & 121 & 60 & 49 & 14 & 32 & 86 & 117 & 7 & 76 \end{vmatrix}$$

Step #6

$$Y_6 \rightarrow Y_6 \prod_{\substack{j=0 \\ j \neq 2}}^{17} C_{j,2}(-y_{j,2}) = Y_7; \text{ for } j \neq 2, \text{ add } -y_{j,2} \text{ times the 2nd column of } Y_6 \text{ to}$$

the jth column of Y_6.

$$Y_6 = \begin{vmatrix} 1 & 0 & 0 & 0 & 0 & 0 & 0 & 0 & 0 & 0 & 0 & 0 & 0 & 0 & 0 & 0 & 0 & 0 \\ 0 & 1 & 0 & 0 & 0 & 0 & 0 & 0 & 0 & 0 & 0 & 0 & 0 & 0 & 0 & 0 & 0 & 0 \\ 0 & 0 & 1 & 0 & 0 & 0 & 0 & 0 & 0 & 0 & 0 & 0 & 0 & 0 & 0 & 0 & 0 & 0 \\ 44 & 37 & 47 & 106 & 90 & 8 & 115 & 70 & 46 & 28 & 30 & 96 & 79 & 125 & 108 & 94 & 59 & 83 \end{vmatrix}$$

$$X_6 \rightarrow X_6 \prod_{\substack{j=0 \\ j \neq 2}}^{17} C_{j,2}(-y_{j,2}) = X_7; \text{ for } j \neq 2, \text{ add } -y_{j,2} \text{ times the 2nd column of } X_6 \text{ to}$$

the jth column of X_6.

$$X_7 = \begin{vmatrix} 75 & 98 & 43 & 22 & 38 & 120 & 77 & 58 & 82 & 100 & 98 & 32 & 113 & 67 & 20 & 34 & 5 & 109 \\ 115 & 22 & 64 & 78 & 30 & 88 & 81 & 66 & 58 & 52 & 10 & 32 & 69 & 127 & 36 & 74 & 105 & 113 \\ 15 & 91 & 80 & 30 & 110 & 24 & 41 & 114 & 42 & 20 & 122 & 32 & 125 & 39 & 4 & 58 & 1 & 73 \\ 96 & 109 & 15 & 114 & 34 & 40 & 15 & 126 & 6 & 76 & 54 & 96 & 27 & 33 & 92 & 118 & 119 & 111 \end{vmatrix}$$

Step #7

$Y_7 \rightarrow Y_7 E_{3,6} = Y_8$; interchange the 3rd and 6th columns of Y_7.

$Y_8 \rightarrow Y_8 M_3(115^{-1}) = Y_9$; multiply the 3rd column of Y_8 by $59 = 115^{-1}$.

$$Y_9 = \begin{vmatrix} 1 & 0 & 0 & 0 & 0 & 0 & 0 & 0 & 0 & 0 & 0 & 0 & 0 & 0 & 0 & 0 & 0 & 0 \\ 0 & 1 & 0 & 0 & 0 & 0 & 0 & 0 & 0 & 0 & 0 & 0 & 0 & 0 & 0 & 0 & 0 & 0 \\ 0 & 0 & 1 & 0 & 0 & 0 & 0 & 0 & 0 & 0 & 0 & 0 & 0 & 0 & 0 & 0 & 0 & 0 \\ 44 & 37 & 47 & 1 & 90 & 8 & 106 & 70 & 46 & 28 & 30 & 96 & 79 & 125 & 108 & 94 & 59 & 83 \end{vmatrix}$$

$X_7 \rightarrow X_7 E_{3,6} = X_8$; interchange the 3rd and 6th columns of X_7.

$X_8 \rightarrow X_8 M_3(115^{-1}) = X_9$; multiply the 3rd column of X_8 by $59 = 115^{-1}$.

$$X_9 = \begin{vmatrix} 75 & 98 & 43 & 63 & 38 & 120 & 22 & 58 & 82 & 100 & 98 & 32 & 113 & 67 & 20 & 34 & 5 & 109 \\ 115 & 22 & 64 & 43 & 30 & 88 & 78 & 66 & 58 & 52 & 10 & 32 & 69 & 127 & 36 & 74 & 105 & 113 \\ 15 & 91 & 80 & 115 & 110 & 24 & 30 & 114 & 42 & 20 & 122 & 32 & 125 & 39 & 4 & 58 & 1 & 73 \\ 96 & 109 & 15 & 117 & 34 & 40 & 114 & 126 & 6 & 76 & 54 & 96 & 27 & 33 & 92 & 118 & 119 & 111 \end{vmatrix}$$

Step #8

$$Y_9 \rightarrow Y_9 \prod_{\substack{j=0 \\ j \neq 3}}^{17} C_{j,3}(-y_{j,3}) = Y_{10}Y; \text{ for } j \neq 3, \text{ add } -y_{j,3} \text{ times the 2rd column of } Y_9 \text{ to}$$

the jth column of Y_9.

$$Y_{10} = \begin{vmatrix} 1 & 0 & 0 & 0 & 0 & 0 & 0 & 0 & 0 & 0 & 0 & 0 & 0 & 0 & 0 & 0 & 0 & 0 \\ 0 & 1 & 0 & 0 & 0 & 0 & 0 & 0 & 0 & 0 & 0 & 0 & 0 & 0 & 0 & 0 & 0 & 0 \\ 0 & 0 & 1 & 0 & 0 & 0 & 0 & 0 & 0 & 0 & 0 & 0 & 0 & 0 & 0 & 0 & 0 & 0 \\ 0 & 0 & 0 & 1 & 0 & 0 & 0 & 0 & 0 & 0 & 0 & 0 & 0 & 0 & 0 & 0 & 0 & 0 \end{vmatrix}$$

$$X_9 \to X_9 \prod_{\substack{j-0 \\ j\neq 3}}^{17} C_{j,3}(-y_{j,3}) = Y_{10}Y; \text{ for } j \neq 3, \text{ add } -y_{j,3} \text{ times the 3rd column of } X_9 \text{ to}$$

the jth column of X_9.

$$X_{10} = \begin{vmatrix} 119 & 71 & 26 & 63 & 0 & 0 & 0 & 0 & 0 & 0 & 0 & 0 & 0 & 0 & 0 & 0 & 0 & 0 \\ 15 & 95 & 91 & 43 & 0 & 0 & 0 & 0 & 0 & 0 & 0 & 0 & 0 & 0 & 0 & 0 & 0 & 0 \\ 75 & 60 & 51 & 115 & 0 & 0 & 0 & 0 & 0 & 0 & 0 & 0 & 0 & 0 & 0 & 0 & 0 & 0 \\ 68 & 4 & 20 & 117 & 0 & 0 & 0 & 0 & 0 & 0 & 0 & 0 & 0 & 0 & 0 & 0 & 0 & 0 \end{vmatrix}$$

Gaussian elimination has determined that

$$A^{-1} = \begin{pmatrix} 119 & 71 & 26 & 63 \\ 15 & 95 & 91 & 4 \\ 75 & 60 & 51 & 115 \\ 68 & 4 & 20 & 117 \end{pmatrix}.$$

Gaussian elimination on the *plaintext* involves the postmultiplication of X and Y by a sequence $O_1 O_2 \cdots O_M$ of matrices as follows:

1.

$$AX = Y$$
$$X \to XM_r(v)$$
$$Y \to YM_r(v)$$
$$AXM_r(v) \to YM_r(v)$$

(a) Multiplying the elements in the rth column of X by v;

(b) Multiplying the elements in the rth column of Y by v.

2.

$$AX = Y$$
$$X \to XC_{r,s}(v)$$
$$Y \to YC_{r,s}(v)$$
$$AXC_{r,s}(v) \to YC_{r,s}(v)$$

(a) Adding v times the sth column of X to the rth column of X;

(b) Adding v times the sth column of Y to the rth column of Y.

3.

$$AX = Y$$
$$X \to XE_{r,s}(v)$$
$$Y \to YE_{r,s}(v)$$
$$AXE_{r,s}(v) \to YE_{r,s}(v)$$

(a) Interchanging the rth and sth column of X;

(b) Interchanging the rth and sth column of X.

Gaussian elimination when applied to the matrix X of plaintext (column) vectors related by Equations (3.15)–(3.19) produces A:

$$Y = AX$$
$$X \rightarrow XO_1O_2 \cdots O_M$$
$$Y \rightarrow YO_1O_2 \cdots O_M$$
$$YO_1O_2 \cdots O_M \rightarrow TXO_1O_2 \cdots O_M$$
$$I = XO_1O_2 \cdots O_M$$

implies

$$A = YO_1O_2 \cdots O_M$$

Step #1

$X = X_0 \rightarrow X_0 E_{0,2} = X_1$; interchange the 0th and 2nd columns of X_0.

$X_1 \rightarrow X_1 M_0(67^{-1}) = X_2$; multiply the 0th column of X_1 by $67 = 107^{-1}$

$$X_2 = \begin{vmatrix} 1 & 32 & 84 & 100 & 115 & 97 & 114 & 119 & 101 & 119 & 103 & 122 & 114 & 114 & 101 & 117 & 110 & 32 \\ 96 & 98 & 104 & 114 & 101 & 110 & 101 & 104 & 32 & 32 & 97 & 101 & 101 & 101 & 115 & 114 & 116 & 101 \\ 99 & 111 & 105 & 101 & 115 & 32 & 97 & 101 & 102 & 111 & 110 & 100 & 102 & 110 & 32 & 114 & 108 & 120 \\ 44 & 111 & 115 & 115 & 32 & 97 & 32 & 114 & 101 & 114 & 105 & 32 & 101 & 99 & 99 & 101 & 121 & 105 \end{vmatrix}$$

$Y = Y_0 \rightarrow Y_0 E_{0,2} = Y_1$; interchange the 0th and 2nd columns of Y_0.

$Y_1 \rightarrow Y_1 M_0(67^{-1}) = Y_2$; multiply the 0th columns of Y_1 by $67 = 107^{-1}$

$$Y_2 = \begin{vmatrix} 50 & 84 & 36 & 94 & 3 & 14 & 52 & 64 & 22 & 30 & 19 & 73 & 86 & 56 & 27 & 56 & 33 & 126 \\ 95 & 89 & 77 & 127 & 82 & 18 & 116 & 25 & 102 & 43 & 21 & 55 & 61 & 29 & 101 & 96 & 84 & 7 \\ 119 & 86 & 120 & 114 & 10 & 65 & 3 & 65 & 63 & 121 & 62 & 59 & 95 & 7 & 58 & 1 & 66 & 81 \\ 44 & 23 & 51 & 91 & 52 & 121 & 52 & 82 & 69 & 50 & 77 & 52 & 89 & 23 & 79 & 13 & 41 & 93 \end{vmatrix}$$

Step #2

$X_2 \rightarrow X_2 \prod_{j=1}^{17} C_{j,0}(-x_{j,0}) = X_3$; For $j \neq 0$, add $-x_{j,0}$ times the 0th column of X_2 to the jth column of X_2.

$$X_3 = \begin{vmatrix} 1 & 0 & 0 & 0 & 0 & 0 & 0 & 0 & 0 & 0 & 0 & 0 & 0 & 0 & 0 & 0 & 0 & 0 \\ 96 & 98 & 104 & 114 & 69 & 14 & 37 & 72 & 64 & 0 & 65 & 37 & 37 & 37 & 19 & 18 & 52 & 101 \\ 99 & 15 & 109 & 57 & 122 & 29 & 75 & 96 & 87 & 106 & 25 & 54 & 80 & 88 & 17 & 51 & 98 & 24 \\ 44 & 111 & 3 & 67 & 92 & 53 & 8 & 126 & 9 & 126 & 53 & 40 & 77 & 75 & 7 & 73 & 17 & 105 \end{vmatrix}$$

$Y_2 \rightarrow Y_2 \prod_{j=1}^{17} C_{j,0}(-x_{j,0}) = Y_3$; For $j \neq 0$, add $-x_{j,0}$ times the 0th column of Y_2 to the jth column of Y_2.

$$y_3 = \begin{vmatrix} 50 & 20 & 60 & 86 & 13 & 28 & 112 & 2 & 92 & 96 & 117 & 117 & 18 & 116 & 97 & 94 & 37 & 62 \\ 95 & 121 & 33 & 99 & 37 & 19 & 38 & 112 & 107 & 2 & 92 & 113 & 111 & 79 & 106 & 117 & 2 & 39 \\ 119 & 118 & 108 & 118 & 21 & 42 & 5 & 112 & 76 & 40 & 93 & 5 & 97 & 9 & 71 & 30 & 32 & 113 \\ 44 & 23 & 67 & 43 & 112 & 77 & 28 & 94 & 105 & 62 & 25 & 60 & 65 & 127 & 115 & 113 & 65 & 93 \end{vmatrix}$$

Step #3

$X_3 \to X_3\, E_{0,4} = X_5$; interchange the 0th and 4th columns of X_4.

$X_4 \to X_4\, M_0\, (69^{-11}) = X_5$; multiply the 0th column of X_4 by $13 = 69^{-1}$.

$$X_5 = \begin{vmatrix} 1 & 0 & 0 & 0 & 0 & 0 & 0 & 0 & 0 & 0 & 0 & 0 & 0 & 0 & 0 & 0 & 0 & 0 \\ 96 & 1 & 104 & 114 & 98 & 14 & 37 & 72 & 64 & 0 & 65 & 37 & 37 & 37 & 19 & 18 & 52 & 101 \\ 99 & 50 & 109 & 57 & 15 & 29 & 75 & 96 & 87 & 106 & 25 & 54 & 80 & 88 & 17 & 51 & 98 & 24 \\ 44 & 44 & 3 & 67 & 111 & 53 & 8 & 126 & 9 & 126 & 53 & 40 & 77 & 75 & 7 & 73 & 17 & 105 \end{vmatrix}$$

$Y_3 \to Y_3\, E_{0,4} = Y_5$; interchange the 0th and 4th columns of Y_4.

$Y_4 \to Y_4\, M_0\, (69^{-11}) = Y_5$; multiply the 0th column of Y_4 by $13 = 69^{-1}$.

$$X_5 = \begin{vmatrix} 50 & 41 & 60 & 86 & 20 & 28 & 112 & 2 & 92 & 96 & 117 & 117 & 18 & 116 & 97 & 94 & 37 & 62 \\ 95 & 97 & 33 & 99 & 121 & 19 & 38 & 112 & 107 & 2 & 92 & 113 & 111 & 79 & 106 & 117 & 2 & 39 \\ 119 & 17 & 108 & 118 & 118 & 42 & 5 & 112 & 76 & 40 & 93 & 5 & 97 & 9 & 71 & 30 & 32 & 113 \\ 44 & 48 & 67 & 43 & 23 & 77 & 28 & 94 & 105 & 62 & 25 & 60 & 65 & 127 & 115 & 113 & 65 & 93 \end{vmatrix}$$

Step #4

$$X_5 \to X_5 \prod_{\substack{j=0 \\ j\neq 1}}^{17} C_{j,1}(-x_{j,1}) = X_6;\ \text{for } j \neq 1,\ \text{add } -x_{j,1}\ \text{times the 1st column of } X_5 \text{ to}$$

the *j*th column of X_5.

$$X_6 = \begin{vmatrix} 1 & 0 & 0 & 0 & 0 & 0 & 0 & 0 & 0 & 0 & 0 & 0 & 0 & 0 & 0 & 0 & 0 & 0 \\ 0 & 1 & 0 & 0 & 0 & 0 & 0 & 0 & 0 & 0 & 0 & 0 & 0 & 0 & 0 & 0 & 0 & 0 \\ 35 & 50 & 29 & 117 & 107 & 97 & 17 & 80 & 87 & 106 & 103 & 124 & 22 & 30 & 91 & 47 & 58 & 94 \\ 44 & 44 & 35 & 43 & 23 & 77 & 44 & 30 & 9 & 126 & 9 & 76 & 113 & 111 & 67 & 49 & 33 & 13 \end{vmatrix}$$

$Y_5 \to Y_5 \prod_{\substack{j=0 \\ j\neq 1}} C_{j,1}(-x_{j,1}) = Y_6$; for $j \neq 1$, add $-x_{j,1}$ times the 1st column of Y_5 to the *j*th column of Y_5.

$$Y_6 = \begin{vmatrix} 82 & 41 & 20 & 20 & 98 & 94 & 3 & 122 & 28 & 96 & 12 & 8 & 37 & 7 & 86 & 124 & 81 & 17 \\ 127 & 97 & 57 & 49 & 87 & 69 & 33 & 40 & 43 & 2 & 59 & 108 & 106 & 74 & 55 & 35 & 78 & 98 \\ 23 & 17 & 4 & 100 & 116 & 60 & 16 & 40 & 12 & 40 & 12 & 16 & 108 & 20 & 4 & 108 & 44 & 60 \\ 44 & 48 & 67 & 75 & 55 & 45 & 44 & 94 & 105 & 62 & 105 & 76 & 81 & 15 & 99 & 17 & 1 & 109 \end{vmatrix}$$

Step #5

$X_6 \to X_6\, M_2\, (29^{-1}) = X_7$; multiply the 2nd column of X_6 by $53 = 29^{-1}$.

$$X_7 = \begin{vmatrix} 1 & 0 & 0 & 0 & 0 & 0 & 0 & 0 & 0 & 0 & 0 & 0 & 0 & 0 & 0 & 0 & 0 & 0 \\ 0 & 1 & 0 & 0 & 0 & 0 & 0 & 0 & 0 & 0 & 0 & 0 & 0 & 0 & 0 & 0 & 0 & 0 \\ 35 & 50 & 1 & 117 & 107 & 97 & 17 & 80 & 87 & 106 & 103 & 124 & 22 & 30 & 91 & 47 & 58 & 94 \\ 44 & 44 & 63 & 43 & 23 & 77 & 44 & 30 & 9 & 126 & 9 & 76 & 113 & 111 & 67 & 49 & 33 & 13 \end{vmatrix}$$

$Y_6 \to Y_6\, M_2\, (29^{-1}) = Y_7$; multiply the 2nd column of Y_6 by $53 = 29^{-1}$.

$$Y_7 = \begin{vmatrix} 82 & 41 & 20 & 20 & 98 & 94 & 3 & 122 & 28 & 96 & 12 & 8 & 37 & 7 & 86 & 124 & 81 & 17 \\ 127 & 97 & 77 & 49 & 87 & 69 & 33 & 40 & 43 & 2 & 59 & 108 & 106 & 74 & 55 & 35 & 78 & 98 \\ 23 & 17 & 84 & 100 & 116 & 60 & 16 & 40 & 12 & 40 & 12 & 16 & 108 & 20 & 4 & 108 & 44 & 60 \\ 44 & 48 & 95 & 75 & 55 & 45 & 44 & 94 & 105 & 62 & 105 & 76 & 81 & 15 & 99 & 17 & 1 & 109 \end{vmatrix}$$

Step #6

$$X_6 \to X_6 \prod_{\substack{j=0 \\ j \neq 2}}^{17} C_{j,2}(-x_{j,2}) = X_7; \text{ for } j \neq 2, \text{ add } -x_{j,2} \text{ times the 2nd column of } X_6 \text{ to}$$

the jth column of X_6.

$$X_7 = \begin{vmatrix} 1 & 0 & 0 & 0 & 0 & 0 & 0 & 0 & 0 & 0 & 0 & 0 & 0 & 0 & 0 & 0 & 0 & 0 \\ 0 & 1 & 0 & 0 & 0 & 0 & 0 & 0 & 0 & 0 & 0 & 0 & 0 & 0 & 0 & 0 & 0 & 0 \\ 0 & 0 & 1 & 0 & 0 & 0 & 0 & 0 & 0 & 0 & 0 & 0 & 0 & 0 & 0 & 0 & 0 & 0 \\ 15 & 94 & 63 & 96 & 66 & 110 & 125 & 110 & 32 & 104 & 48 & 72 & 7 & 13 & 94 & 32 & 91 & 107 \end{vmatrix}$$

$$Y_6 \to Y_6 \prod_{\substack{j=0 \\ j \neq 2}}^{17} C_{j,2}(-x_{j,2}) = Y_7; \text{ for } j \neq 2, \text{ add } -x_{j,2} \text{ times the 2nd column of } Y_6 \text{ to}$$

the jth column of Y_6.

$$Y_7 = \begin{vmatrix} 102 & 33 & 36 & 32 & 86 & 58 & 31 & 58 & 96 & 120 & 16 & 24 & 13 & 79 & 10 & 96 & 41 & 89 \\ 120 & 87 & 77 & 0 & 40 & 24 & 4 & 24 & 0 & 32 & 64 & 32 & 76 & 68 & 88 & 0 & 92 & 28 \\ 27 & 41 & 84 & 0 & 88 & 104 & 124 & 104 & 0 & 96 & 64 & 96 & 52 & 60 & 40 & 0 & 36 & 100 \\ 47 & 34 & 95 & 96 & 2 & 46 & 93 & 46 & 32 & 104 & 48 & 72 & 39 & 109 & 30 & 32 & 123 & 11 \end{vmatrix}$$

Step #7

$X_7 \to X_7 E_{3,6} = X_8$; interchange the 3rd and 6th columns of X_7.

$X_8 \to X_8 M_3 (125^{-1}) = X_9$; multiply the 3rd column of X_8 by $85 = 125^{-1}$.

$$X_8 = \begin{vmatrix} 1 & 0 & 0 & 0 & 0 & 0 & 0 & 0 & 0 & 0 & 0 & 0 & 0 & 0 & 0 & 0 & 0 & 0 \\ 0 & 1 & 0 & 0 & 0 & 0 & 0 & 0 & 0 & 0 & 0 & 0 & 0 & 0 & 0 & 0 & 0 & 0 \\ 0 & 0 & 1 & 0 & 0 & 0 & 0 & 0 & 0 & 0 & 0 & 0 & 0 & 0 & 0 & 0 & 0 & 0 \\ 15 & 94 & 63 & 1 & 66 & 110 & 96 & 110 & 32 & 104 & 48 & 72 & 7 & 13 & 94 & 32 & 91 & 107 \end{vmatrix}$$

$Y_7 \to Y_7 E_{3,6} = Y_8$; interchange the 3rd and 6th columns of Y_7.

$Y_8 \to Y_8 M_3 (125^{-1}) = Y_9$; multiply the 3rd column of Y_8 by $85 = 125^{-1}$.

$$Y_9 = \begin{vmatrix} 102 & 33 & 36 & 75 & 86 & 58 & 32 & 58 & 96 & 120 & 16 & 24 & 13 & 79 & 10 & 96 & 41 & 89 \\ 120 & 87 & 77 & 84 & 40 & 24 & 0 & 24 & 0 & 32 & 64 & 32 & 76 & 68 & 88 & 0 & 92 & 28 \\ 27 & 41 & 84 & 44 & 88 & 104 & 0 & 104 & 0 & 96 & 64 & 96 & 52 & 60 & 40 & 0 & 36 & 100 \\ 47 & 34 & 95 & 97 & 2 & 46 & 96 & 46 & 32 & 104 & 48 & 72 & 39 & 109 & 30 & 32 & 123 & 11 \end{vmatrix}$$

Step #8

$$X_9 \to X_9 \prod_{\substack{j=0 \\ j \neq 3}}^{17} C_{j,3}(-x_{j,3}) = X_{10}; \text{ for } j \neq 3, \text{ add } -x_{j,3} \text{ times the 3rd column of } X_9 \text{ to}$$

the jth column of X_9.

$$X_{10} = \begin{vmatrix} 1 & 0 & 0 & 0 & 0 & 0 & 0 & 0 & 0 & 0 & 0 & 0 & 0 & 0 & 0 & 0 & 0 & 0 \\ 0 & 1 & 0 & 0 & 0 & 0 & 0 & 0 & 0 & 0 & 0 & 0 & 0 & 0 & 0 & 0 & 0 & 0 \\ 0 & 0 & 1 & 0 & 0 & 0 & 0 & 0 & 0 & 0 & 0 & 0 & 0 & 0 & 0 & 0 & 0 & 0 \\ 0 & 0 & 0 & 1 & 0 & 0 & 0 & 0 & 0 & 0 & 0 & 0 & 0 & 0 & 0 & 0 & 0 & 0 \end{vmatrix}$$

$$Y_9 \to Y_9 \prod_{\substack{j=0 \\ j \neq 3}}^{17} C_{j,3}(-x_{j,3}) = Y_{10}; \text{ for } j \neq 3, \text{ add } -x_{j,3} \text{ times the 3rd column of } Y_9 \text{ to}$$

the jth column of Y_9.

$$Y_{10} = \begin{vmatrix} 1 & 23 & 47 & 75 & 0 & 0 & 0 & 0 & 0 & 0 & 0 & 0 & 0 & 0 & 0 & 0 & 0 & 0 \\ 12 & 127 & 33 & 84 & 0 & 0 & 0 & 0 & 0 & 0 & 0 & 0 & 0 & 0 & 0 & 0 & 0 & 0 \\ 7 & 1 & 0 & 44 & 0 & 0 & 0 & 0 & 0 & 0 & 0 & 0 & 0 & 0 & 0 & 0 & 0 & 0 \\ 0 & 4 & 0 & 97 & 0 & 0 & 0 & 0 & 0 & 0 & 0 & 0 & 0 & 0 & 0 & 0 & 0 & 0 \end{vmatrix}$$

Gaussian elimination has determined that

$$A = \begin{pmatrix} 1 & 23 & 47 & 75 \\ 12 & 127 & 33 & 84 \\ 7 & 1 & 0 & 44 \\ 0 & 4 & 0 & 97 \end{pmatrix}.$$

3.8.3   The Number of Invertible $N \times N$ Matrices

An $N \times N$ matrix A whose elements are in $\mathcal{Z}_{128}$ has an inverse if and only if $\det(A)$ (modulo 128) is an odd integer.

Proposition 3.5:   The size H_N of the set $\mathcal{H}_N$ of $N \times N$ matrices with elements in $\mathcal{Z}_{128}$, which are invertible, is

$$H_N = 128^{N^2} \prod_{k=1}^{N} \left(1 - \frac{1}{2^k}\right) \approx 0.288788 \times 128^{N^2} \qquad \text{as } N \to \infty.$$

Proof   If A is invertible, *at least* one element in the 0th row of a matrix A must be odd. $\mathcal{H}_N$ may be partitioned into the subsets of matrices according to the first column k in the 0th row containing an odd element $a_{0,k}$. This gives the recursion

$$H_N = \sum_{k=0}^{N-1} \underbrace{64^k}_{\substack{a_{0,j} \\ \text{even} \\ 0 \le j < k}} \times \underbrace{64}_{\substack{a_{0,k} \\ \text{odd}}} \times \underbrace{128^{N-k-1}}_{\substack{a_{0,j} \\ k < j < N}} \times \underbrace{128^{N-1}}_{\substack{a_{0,j} \\ i > 1}} \times H_{N-1}$$

$$= 128^{2N-1} \times \left(1 - \frac{1}{2^{N+1}}\right) \times H_{N-1}$$

$$= 128^{N^2} \times \prod_{k=1}^{N} \left(1 - \frac{1}{2^k}\right), \quad N = 1, 2, \ldots; \quad H_0 = 1.$$

3.8.4   Hill Encipherment for Plaintext Whose Length is not Divisible by N

When the length n of plaintext $\underline{x}$ is not divisible by the row width N of the Hill matrix, the plaintext might be padded with a string to make its length a multiple of N before encipherment. One standard padding method adjoins a string of ASCII characters each equal to $\underline{0} = \underbrace{(0, 0, \ldots, 0)}_{7}$ terminated by the number of 0's. Padding plaintext like this potentially reveals too much information in the ciphertext. Other padding schemes are mentioned in Chapter 9 (The Data Encryption Standards DES) and in Konheim [1981].

3.8.5   Cribbing Hill Ciphertext

We now suppose that the Hill matrix remains unknown, but instead of knowledge of the complete plaintext, a crib in the ciphertext is known.

cipherEx3.4 is the Hill encipherment of 3-grams, presented here as a 3×229 array of integers in $\mathcal{Z}_{128}$.

	cipherEx3.4	
118	109	71
102	105	86
48	56	125
8	95	107
52	0	6
88	54	5
59	21	90
⋮	⋮	⋮
118	105	1
79	30	47

The plaintext is from a conference paper [Kemmerer, 1986]; as the title suggests, computer security is a possible crib. Gaussian elimination must be modified to find any occurrence of the crib in the plaintext and the enciphering matrix.

Modification **#1** Assuming the crib does not occur as either the first or last word in a sentence, the crib is computer security suffixed with a blank space. Table 3.34 lists the $N = 3$ possible *offsets* of c in the position j (modulo N) in the plaintext of the c of computer security.? indicates an unidentified ASCII character. Gaussian elimination requires that the plaintext crib contain three linearly independent vectors. Thus

1. If Off = 0

$$\text{Crib}_0 = \begin{vmatrix} c & p & e & s & u & t \\ o & u & r & e & r & y \\ m & t & & c & i & \end{vmatrix}$$

should contain three linearly independent 3-vectors.

2. If Off = 1

$$\text{Crib}_1 = \begin{vmatrix} m & f & & c & i \\ p & e & s & u & t \\ u & r & e & r & y \end{vmatrix}$$

should contain three linearly independent 3-vectors.

TABLE 3.34   Offsets of c in cipherEx3.4

Off = 0	Off = 1	Off = 2
c o m	? c o	? ? c
p u t	m p u	o m p
e r	t e r	u t e
s e c	s e	r s
u r i	c u r	e c u
t y	i t y	r i t
? ? ?	? ?	y ?

3. If Off $= 2$

$$Crib_2 = \begin{vmatrix} o & u & r & & e & r \\ m & t & & c & i \\ p & e & s & u & t \end{vmatrix}$$

should contain three linearly independent 3-vectors.

3.8.6 Gaussian Elimination Program

For each offset $k = 0, 1, 2$ and each position $i = 0, 1, \ldots$ apply Gaussian elimination to find the inverse A^{-1} of the enciphering matrix using the pair of matrices

- The plaintext $3 \times M$ matrix $Crib_k$ and
- The ciphertext $3 \times M$ ciphertext matrix $3 \times M$ cipher text matrix Γ_i

$$\Gamma_i = \begin{vmatrix} y_{3i} & y_{3i+3} & \cdots & y_{3i+3M-3} \\ y_{3i+1} & y_{3i+4} & \cdots & y_{3i+3M-2} \\ y_{3i+2} & y_{3i+5} & \cdots & y_{3i+3M-1} \end{vmatrix},$$

where $M = 6$ for Off $= 0$ and $M = 5$ for Off $= 1, 2$.

There are three possible outcomes:

1. Gaussian elimination determines that Γ_i does not contain three linearly independent vectors.

2. Gaussian elimination determines that Γ_i contains three linearly independent vectors and finds a matrix B^{-1} satisfying $B^{-1}\Gamma_i = Crib_k$.

   As the success of Gaussian elimination depends only on Γ_i having three linearly independent column vectors, it may occur that $B^{-1} \neq A^{-1}$. This outcome can be detected by deciphering a segment of the ciphertext. If $B \neq A$, then decipherment will not always result in ordinals corresponding to printable ASCII characters; for example, the letters, numerals, and punctuation.

3. Gaussian elimination determines that Γ_i contains three linearly independent vectors and finds a matrix B^{-1} satisfying $B^{-1}\Gamma_i = Crib_k$ and $B^{-1} = A^{-1}$.

The 18-gram crib computer security is detected at positions #45 and #219, and leads to the deciphering matrix

$$A^{-1} = \begin{pmatrix} 64 & 45 & 125 \\ 99 & 58 & 80 \\ 3 & 88 & 121 \end{pmatrix}$$

3.9 GAUSSIAN ELIMINATION

Let $A = (a_{i,j})$ be an $n \times n$ matrix and $\underline{x} = (x_1, x_2, \ldots, x_n)$, $\underline{y} = (y_1, y_2, \ldots, y_n)$ be n-vectors, all with real number entries satisfying

$$\underline{y} = A\underline{x}. \tag{3.20}$$

If $\det(A) \neq 0$, then for *every* y, the linear system of Equations (3.20) has a unique solution $\underline{x}$,

$$\underline{x} = A^{-1}y.$$

Gaussian elimination is a process in which transformations are applied to an invertible matrix A to produce the identity matrix I and thereby obtain the solution for $\underline{x}$ in Equation (3.20).

3.9.1 Elementary Row and Column Matrix Transformations

1. $R_{r,s}(v)$ $(r \neq s)$ is the $n \times n$ matrix equal to the identity matrix, except that the element in position (r, s) of $R_{r,s}(v)$ is v. For example when $n = 4$

$$R_{2,0}(v) = \begin{pmatrix} 1 & 0 & 0 & 0 \\ 0 & 1 & 0 & 0 \\ v & 0 & 1 & 0 \\ 0 & 0 & 0 & 1 \end{pmatrix}.$$

If

$$A = \begin{pmatrix} a_{0,0} & a_{0,1} & a_{0,2} & a_{0,3} \\ a_{1,0} & a_{1,1} & a_{1,2} & a_{1,3} \\ a_{2,0} & a_{2,1} & a_{2,2} & a_{2,3} \\ a_{3,0} & a_{3,1} & a_{3,2} & a_{3,3} \end{pmatrix}$$

then

$$R_{2,0}(v)A = \begin{pmatrix} 1 & 0 & 0 & 0 \\ 0 & 1 & 0 & 0 \\ v & 0 & 1 & 0 \\ 0 & 0 & 0 & 1 \end{pmatrix} \begin{pmatrix} a_{0,0} & a_{0,1} & a_{0,2} & a_{0,3} \\ a_{1,0} & a_{1,1} & a_{1,2} & a_{1,3} \\ a_{2,0} & a_{2,1} & a_{2,2} & a_{2,3} \\ a_{3,0} & a_{3,1} & a_{3,2} & a_{3,3} \end{pmatrix}$$

$$= \begin{pmatrix} a_{0,0} & a_{0,1} & a_{0,2} & a_{0,3} \\ a_{1,0} & a_{1,1} & a_{1,2} & a_{1,3} \\ a_{2,0} + va_{0,0} & a_{2,1} + va_{0,1} & a_{2,2} + va_{0,2} & a_{2,3} + va_{0,3} \\ a_{3,0} & a_{3,1} & a_{3,2} & a_{3,3} \end{pmatrix}$$

*Pre*multiplication of A by $R_{r,\,s}(v)$ replaces the rth row of A by the sum of

- v times the sth row of A and
- The rth row of A.

  The inverse of $R_{r,\,s}(v)$ is $R_{r,\,s}(-v)$.

2. $C_{r,s}(v)$ $(r \neq s)$ is the $n \times n$ matrix, which is equal to the identity matrix except that the element in position (r, s) of $C_{r,s}(v)$ is v. For example, when $n = 4$

$$C_{2,0}(v) = \begin{pmatrix} 1 & 0 & v & 0 \\ 0 & 1 & 0 & 0 \\ 0 & 0 & 1 & 0 \\ 0 & 0 & 0 & 1 \end{pmatrix}.$$

If

$$A = \begin{pmatrix} a_{0,0} & a_{0,1} & a_{0,2} & a_{0,3} \\ a_{1,0} & a_{1,1} & a_{1,2} & a_{1,3} \\ a_{2,0} & a_{2,1} & a_{2,2} & a_{2,3} \\ a_{3,0} & a_{3,1} & a_{3,2} & a_{3,3} \end{pmatrix}$$

then

$$AC_{2,0}(v) = \begin{pmatrix} a_{0,0} & a_{0,1} & a_{0,2} & a_{0,3} \\ a_{1,0} & a_{1,1} & a_{1,2} & a_{1,3} \\ a_{2,0} & a_{2,1} & a_{2,2} & a_{2,3} \\ a_{3,0} & a_{3,1} & a_{3,2} & a_{3,3} \end{pmatrix} \begin{pmatrix} 1 & 0 & v & 0 \\ 0 & 1 & 0 & 0 \\ 0 & 0 & 1 & 0 \\ 0 & 0 & 0 & 1 \end{pmatrix}$$

$$= \begin{pmatrix} a_{0,0} & a_{0,1} & a_{0,2} + va_{0,0} & a_{0,3} \\ a_{1,0} & a_{1,1} & a_{1,2} + va_{1,0} & a_{1,3} \\ a_{2,0} & a_{2,1} & a_{2,2} + va_{2,0} & a_{2,3} \\ a_{3,0} & a_{3,1} & a_{3,2} + va_{3,0} & a_{3,3} \end{pmatrix}$$

*Post*multiplication of A by $C_{r,s}(v)$ replaces the rth column of A by the sum of

- v times the sth column of A and
- The rth column of A.

The inverse of $C_{r,s}(v)$ is $C_{r,s}(-v)$.

3. $M_r(v)$ is the $n \times n$ matrix, which is equal to the identity matrix except that the element in position (r, s) of $M_r(v)$ is v. For example, when $n = 4$

$$M_4(v) = \begin{pmatrix} 1 & 0 & 0 & 0 \\ 0 & 1 & 0 & 0 \\ 0 & 0 & 1 & 0 \\ 0 & 0 & 0 & v \end{pmatrix}.$$

If

$$A = \begin{pmatrix} a_{0,0} & a_{0,1} & a_{0,2} & a_{0,3} \\ a_{1,0} & a_{1,1} & a_{1,2} & a_{1,3} \\ a_{2,0} & a_{2,1} & a_{2,2} & a_{2,3} \\ a_{3,0} & a_{3,1} & a_{3,2} & a_{3,3} \end{pmatrix}$$

then

$$M_4(v)A = \begin{pmatrix} 1 & 0 & 0 & 0 \\ 0 & 1 & 0 & 0 \\ 0 & 0 & 1 & 0 \\ 0 & 0 & 0 & v \end{pmatrix} \begin{pmatrix} a_{0,0} & a_{0,1} & a_{0,2} & a_{0,3} \\ a_{1,0} & a_{1,1} & a_{1,2} & a_{1,3} \\ a_{2,0} & a_{2,1} & a_{2,2} & a_{2,3} \\ a_{3,0} & a_{3,1} & a_{3,2} & a_{3,3} \end{pmatrix}$$

$$= \begin{pmatrix} a_{0,0} & a_{0,1} & a_{0,2} & a_{0,3} \\ a_{1,0} & a_{1,1} & a_{1,2} & a_{1,3} \\ a_{2,0} & a_{2,1} & a_{2,2} & a_{2,3} \\ va_{3,0} & va_{3,1} & va_{3,2} & va_{3,3} \end{pmatrix}$$

and

$$M_4(v)A = \begin{pmatrix} a_{0,0} & a_{0,1} & a_{0,2} & a_{0,3} \\ a_{1,0} & a_{1,1} & a_{1,2} & a_{1,3} \\ a_{2,0} & a_{2,1} & a_{2,2} & a_{2,3} \\ a_{3,0} & a_{3,1} & a_{3,2} & a_{3,3} \end{pmatrix} \begin{pmatrix} 1 & 0 & 0 & 0 \\ 0 & 1 & 0 & 0 \\ 0 & 0 & 1 & 0 \\ 0 & 0 & 0 & v \end{pmatrix}$$

$$= \begin{pmatrix} a_{0,0} & a_{0,1} & a_{0,2} & va_{0,3} \\ a_{1,0} & a_{1,1} & a_{1,2} & va_{1,3} \\ a_{2,0} & a_{2,1} & a_{2,2} & va_{2,3} \\ a_{3,0} & a_{3,1} & a_{3,2} & va_{3,3} \end{pmatrix}$$

In general

- *Pre*multiplication of A by $M_r(v)$ multiplies the elements in the rth row of A by v;
- *Post*multiplication of A by $M_r(v)$ multiplies the elements in the rth column of A by v.
  The inverse of $M_r(v)$ is $M_r(v^{-1})$ provided $v \neq 0$.

4. $E_{r,s}$ $(r \neq s)$ is the $n \times n$ matrix, which is equal to the identity matrix except that

- The elements in positions (r, s) and (s, r) are set to 1;
- The elements in positions (r, r) and (s, s) are set to 0.
  For example, when $n = 4$

$$E_{0,3} = \begin{pmatrix} 0 & 0 & 0 & 1 \\ 0 & 1 & 0 & 0 \\ 0 & 0 & 1 & 0 \\ 1 & 0 & 0 & 0 \end{pmatrix}.$$

If

$$A = \begin{pmatrix} a_{0,0} & a_{0,1} & a_{0,2} & va_{0,3} \\ a_{1,0} & a_{1,1} & a_{1,2} & va_{1,3} \\ a_{2,0} & a_{2,1} & a_{2,2} & va_{2,3} \\ a_{3,0} & a_{3,1} & a_{3,2} & va_{3,3} \end{pmatrix}$$

then

$$E_{0,3}A = \begin{pmatrix} 0 & 0 & 0 & 1 \\ 0 & 1 & 0 & 0 \\ 0 & 0 & 1 & 0 \\ 1 & 0 & 0 & 0 \end{pmatrix} \begin{pmatrix} a_{0,0} & a_{0,1} & a_{0,2} & a_{0,3} \\ a_{1,0} & a_{1,1} & a_{1,2} & a_{1,3} \\ a_{2,0} & a_{2,1} & a_{2,2} & a_{2,3} \\ a_{3,0} & a_{3,1} & a_{3,2} & a_{3,3} \end{pmatrix}$$

$$= \begin{pmatrix} a_{3,0} & a_{3,1} & a_{3,2} & a_{3,3} \\ a_{1,0} & a_{1,1} & a_{1,2} & a_{1,3} \\ a_{2,0} & a_{2,1} & a_{2,2} & a_{2,3} \\ a_{0,0} & a_{0,1} & a_{0,2} & a_{0,3} \end{pmatrix}$$

and

$$AE_{0,3} = \begin{pmatrix} a_{0,0} & a_{0,1} & a_{0,2} & a_{0,3} \\ a_{1,0} & a_{1,1} & a_{1,2} & a_{1,3} \\ a_{2,0} & a_{2,1} & a_{2,2} & a_{2,3} \\ a_{3,0} & a_{3,1} & a_{3,2} & a_{3,3} \end{pmatrix} \begin{pmatrix} 0 & 0 & 0 & 1 \\ 0 & 1 & 0 & 0 \\ 0 & 0 & 1 & 0 \\ 1 & 0 & 0 & 0 \end{pmatrix}$$

$$= \begin{pmatrix} a_{0,3} & a_{0,1} & a_{0,2} & a_{0,0} \\ a_{1,3} & a_{1,1} & a_{1,2} & a_{1,0} \\ a_{2,3} & a_{2,1} & a_{2,2} & a_{2,0} \\ a_{3,3} & a_{3,1} & a_{3,2} & a_{3,0} \end{pmatrix}$$

In general

- *Pre*multiplication of A by $E_{r,s}$ interchanges the rth and sth rows of A;
- *Post*multiplication of A by $E_{r,s}$ interchanges the rth and sth columns of A. The inverse of $E_{r,s}$ is $E_{s,r}$.

3.9.2 Gaussian Elimination

If the matrix A is invertible, then

$$R_{r,s}(v)A\underline{x} = R_{r,s}(v)\underline{y} = (y_1, y_2, \ldots, y_{r-1}, (y_r + vy_s), y_{r+1}, \ldots, y_n)$$

$$M_r(v)A\underline{x} = M_r(v)\underline{y} = (y_1, y_2, \ldots, y_{r-1}, vy_r, y_{r+1}, \ldots, y_n)$$

$$E_{r,s}A\underline{x} = E_{r,s}\underline{y} = \begin{cases} (y_1, y_2, \ldots, y_{r-1}, y_s, y_{r+1}, \ldots, y_{s-1}, y_r, y_{s+1}, \ldots, y_n), & \text{if } s < r \\ (y_1, y_2, \ldots, y_{s-1}, y_r, y_{s+1}, \ldots, y_{r-1}, y_s, y_{r+1}, \ldots, y_n), & \text{if } r < s \end{cases}$$

A solution to the problem,

- *Given*: The $n \times n$ invertible matrix A and the n-vector $\underline{y}$
- *Calculate*: $\underline{x}$ such that $Ax = \underline{y}$,

may be carried out by Gaussian elimination as follows. The matrix A and the vector $\underline{y}$ are both *pre*multiplied by the *same* sequence of elementary row transformations

$$A \rightarrow O_1 O_2 \cdots O_m A$$
$$\underline{y} \rightarrow O_1 O_2 \cdots O_m \underline{y}$$
$$O_i \in \{R_{r,s}(v), M_r(u), E_{r,s}\}, \qquad \text{for } 1 \leq i \leq m,$$

such that

$$I = O_1 O_2 \cdots O_m A$$

where I is the $n \times n$ indentity matrix. It follows that

$$\underline{x} = O_1 O_2 \cdots O_m \underline{y}$$

and

$$A^{-1} = O_1 O_2 \cdots O_m$$

Example 3.7

$$A = \begin{pmatrix} 1 & 2 & 0 \\ 0 & 3 & 1 \\ -3 & 0 & 1 \end{pmatrix}$$

Step #1

$$A_1 = R_{2,0}(3)A = \begin{pmatrix} 1 & 2 & 0 \\ 0 & 3 & 1 \\ 0 & 6 & 1 \end{pmatrix}$$

Step #2

$$A_2 = M_2\left(\frac{1}{3}\right)A_1 \begin{pmatrix} 1 & 2 & 0 \\ 0 & 1 & \frac{1}{3} \\ 0 & 6 & 1 \end{pmatrix}$$

Step #3

$$A_3 = R_{0,1}(-2)A_2 = \begin{pmatrix} 1 & 0 & -\frac{2}{3} \\ 0 & 1 & \frac{1}{3} \\ 0 & 6 & 1 \end{pmatrix}$$

Step #4

$$A_4 = R_{2,1}(-6)A_3 = \begin{pmatrix} 1 & 0 & -\frac{2}{3} \\ 0 & 1 & \frac{1}{3} \\ 0 & 0 & -1 \end{pmatrix}$$

Step #5

$$A_5 = M_3(-1)A_4 = \begin{pmatrix} 1 & 0 & -\frac{2}{3} \\ 0 & 1 & \frac{1}{3} \\ 0 & 0 & 1 \end{pmatrix}$$

Step #6

$$A_6 = R_{1,2}\left(-\frac{1}{3}\right)A_5 = \begin{pmatrix} 1 & 0 & -\frac{2}{3} \\ 0 & 1 & 0 \\ 0 & 0 & 1 \end{pmatrix}$$

Step #7

$$A_7 = R_{0,2}\left(\frac{2}{3}\right)A_6 = \begin{pmatrix} 1 & 0 & 0 \\ 0 & 1 & 0 \\ 0 & 0 & 1 \end{pmatrix}$$

$$\underbrace{(0, 0, \ldots, 0)}_{n\,copies} \equiv \underline{0} = \sum_{i=0}^{M-1} \lambda_i \underline{z}^{(i)}, \qquad \{\lambda_i\} \in \Re \tag{3.21}$$

is a dependency relation for a set of M vectors $\{\underline{z}^{(i)} : 0 \le i < M\}$ with real components. This set of vectors is

- *Linearly independent* (over the reals) if the only vector $\underline{\lambda} = (\lambda_0, \lambda_1, \dots, \lambda_{M-1})$ with real entries for which Equation (3.21) holds is $\underline{\lambda} = \underline{0}$ equal to the zero vector; that is, $\lambda_0 = \lambda_1 = \cdots = \lambda_{M-1} = 0$, and
- It is linearly dependent (over the reals) if there is a $\underline{\lambda} \ne \underline{0}$ for which Equation (3.21) holds.

Proposition 3.6: If A is an $n \times n$ matrix,

1. A has an inverse and Gaussian elimination successfully determines A^{-1} if and only if the n row vectors of A are linearly independent;
2. If the n row vectors of A are linearly independent, A does not have an inverse and the Gaussian elimination process will result in the $n \times n$ matrix of all zeros.

Proof: The proof is by induction, the case $n = 1$ being clear. Assume Gaussian elimination can be applied for matrices of dimension $m \times m$ with $m < n$.

1. If A is invertible, there must be some element $a_{j,0}$ in the jth column that differs from 0. The column operations $A \to E_{j,0} M_0(a_{j,0}^{-1}) A$ allows us to assume that $a_{0,0} = 1$.
2. Premultiplying the matrix $A = (a_{i,j})$ obtained after Step 1

$$A \to R_{1,0}(a_{1,0}^{-1}) R_{2,0}(a_{2,0}^{-1}) \cdots R_{n-2,0}(a_{n-2,0}^{-1}) R_{n-1,0}(a_{n-1,0}^{-1}) A$$

will replace the elements $(a_{1,0}, a_{2,0}, \dots, a_{n-1})$ by 0.

After Steps 1 and 2, $A = \begin{pmatrix} 1 & \cdots \\ \vdots & A' \end{pmatrix}$ where A' is of dimension $(n-1) \times (n-1)$. As A is invertible, it follows that A' is invertible and the induction hypothesis implies that Gaussian elimination will result in the identity matrix.

3.9.3 Gaussian Elimination of an Overdetermined System

We now suppose that an $n \times n$ invertible linear transformation A relates $M \ge n$ pairs of n-vectors $\{\underline{x}^{(i)}, \underline{y}^{(i)} : 0 \le i < M\}$ by

$$\underline{y}^{(i)} = A\underline{x}^{(i)}, \qquad 0 \le i < M \tag{3.22}$$

$$\underline{x}^{(i)} = A^{-1}\underline{y}^{(i)}, \qquad 0 \le i < M. \tag{3.23}$$

The M Equations (3.22) and (3.23) are combined as

$$Y = AX \tag{3.24}$$

$$X = A^{-1}Y, \tag{3.25}$$

where

- Y is the $n \times M$ array composed of the column vectors $\{\underline{y}^{(i)}\}$, and
- X is the $n \times M$ array composed of the column vectors $\{\underline{x}^{(i)}\}$.

We assume that the $\{\underline{x}^{(i)}, \underline{y}^{(i)} : 0 \le i < M\}$ are known, but A and A^{-1} are not. We will show how Gaussian elimination will be able to determine A and A^{-1} provided there are an adequate number of equations.

3.9.4 Gaussian Elimination on the Range Matrix Y

We attempt to change Y into an upper triangular matrix by *post*multiplication by a sequence of elementary column transformations:

$$Y \rightarrow YO_1O_2\ldots O_S, \quad O_i \in \{C_{r,s}(v), M_r(u), E_{r,s}\}$$

such that

$$\begin{pmatrix} 1 & 0 & \cdots & 0 & 0 & 0 & \cdots & 0 \\ 0 & 1 & \cdots & 0 & 0 & 0 & \cdots & 0 \\ \vdots & \vdots & \ddots & \vdots & \vdots & \vdots & \ddots & \vdots \\ 0 & 0 & \cdots & 1 & 0 & 0 & \cdots & 0 \end{pmatrix} = YO_1O_2\ldots O_S.$$

$$\underbrace{}_{\substack{n\times n \\ \text{Identity matrix}}} \underbrace{}_{\substack{n\times M-n \\ \text{Zero matrix}}}$$

The equation $A^{-1}Y = X$ therefore implies

$$A^{-1}\begin{pmatrix} 1 & 0 & \cdots & 0 & 0 & 0 & \cdots & 0 \\ 0 & 1 & \cdots & 0 & 0 & 0 & \cdots & 0 \\ \vdots & \vdots & \ddots & \vdots & \vdots & \vdots & \ddots & \vdots \\ 0 & 0 & \cdots & 1 & 0 & 0 & \cdots & 0 \end{pmatrix} = XO_1O_2\ldots O_S$$

$$\underbrace{}_{\substack{n\times n \\ \text{Identity matrix}}} \underbrace{}_{\substack{n\times M-n \\ \text{Zero matrix}}}$$

which implies

$$A^{-1}O_{n,M-n} = XO_1O_2\ldots O_S$$

where $O_{n,M-n}$ is an $n \times M - n$ matrix with all entries equal to 0. This last equation determines A^{-1}.

3.9.5 Gaussian Elimination on the Domain Matrix X

We attempt to change X into an upper triangular matrix by *post*multiplication by a sequence of elementary column transformations:

$$X \longrightarrow XQ_1Q_2\ldots Q_T, \quad O_i \in \{C_{r,s}(v), M_r(u), E_{r,s}\}$$

such that

$$\begin{pmatrix} 1 & 0 & \cdots & 0 & 0 & 0 & \cdots & 0 \\ 0 & 1 & \cdots & 0 & 0 & 0 & \cdots & 0 \\ \vdots & \vdots & \ddots & \vdots & \vdots & \vdots & \ddots & \vdots \\ 0 & 0 & \cdots & 1 & 0 & 0 & \cdots & 0 \end{pmatrix} = XQ_1Q_2\ldots Q_T.$$

$$\underbrace{}_{\substack{n\times n \\ \text{Identity matrix}}} \underbrace{}_{\substack{n\times M-n \\ \text{Zero matrix}}}$$

The equation $AY = X$ therefore implies

$$A\begin{pmatrix} 1 & 0 & \cdots & 0 & 0 & 0 & \cdots & 0 \\ 0 & 1 & \cdots & 0 & 0 & 0 & \cdots & 0 \\ \vdots & \vdots & \ddots & \vdots & \vdots & \vdots & \ddots & \vdots \\ 0 & 0 & \cdots & 1 & 0 & 0 & \cdots & 0 \end{pmatrix} = YQ_1Q_2\cdots Q_T$$

$$\underbrace{}_{\substack{n\times n \\ \text{Identity matrix}}} \underbrace{}_{\substack{n\times M-n \\ \text{Zero matrix}}}$$

which implies

$$AO_{n,M-n} = Y\, Q_1\, Q_2 \ldots Q_T$$

where $O_{n,M-n}$ is an $n \times M - n$ matrix with all entries equal to 0. This last equation determines A.

Can elementary column transformations $O_1 O_2 \ldots O_S$ and $Q_1 Q_2 \ldots Q_T$ be found to replace Y and X by upper triangular matrices?

Proposition 3.7: If the $n \times n$ A has an inverse, Gaussian elimination will succeed and find A^{-1} if and only if the m columns of X and Y contain n linearly independent n-vectors.

3.9.6 Gaussian Elimination Over the Integers Modulo m

The set $\mathcal{Z}_m$, a *ring*, an algebraic system in which the operations of addition, subtraction, and multiplication of the elements of $\mathcal{Z}_m$ are defined as

$$x \pm y \equiv (x \pm y)\,(\text{modulo } m)$$
$$x \times y = xy \equiv (x \times y)\,(\text{modulo } m).$$

The equation

$$y = ax(\text{modulo } m)$$

can be solved when a has an *inverse* modulo m; that is, when an integer $a^{-1} \in \mathcal{Z}_m$ exists such that

$$aa^{-1} = 1 \;(\text{modulo } m).$$

a has an inverse *if and only if* a and m have *no* factors in common. For example, if $m = 15$ and $a = 8$, then

$$8 \times 2 = 16 = 15 + 1 = 1 \;(\text{modulo } 15).$$

All odd integers less than 128 have inverses when $m = 128$. Table 3.34 lists the inverses of the odd integers in the ring $\mathcal{Z}_{128}$. If m is a prime number, all positive integers less than m have inverses and $\mathcal{Z}_m$ is a *field*.

If the linear system of Equations (3.20) relating real vectors $\underline{x}$, $\underline{y}$ and an $n \times n$ real matrix A is replaced by

$$\underline{y} = A\underline{x} \;(\text{modulo } m), \tag{3.26}$$

TABLE 3.34 Inverses of Odd Integers in the Ring $\mathcal{Z}_{128}$

x	x^{-1}	x	x^{-1}	x	x^{-1}	x	x^{-1}	x	x^{-1}	x	x^{-1}	x	x^{-1}	x	x^{-1}
1	1	3	43	5	77	7	55	9	57	11	35	13	69	15	111
17	113	19	27	21	61	23	39	25	41	27	19	29	53	31	95
33	97	35	11	37	45	39	23	41	25	43	3	45	37	47	79
49	81	51	123	53	29	55	7	57	9	59	115	61	21	63	63
65	65	67	107	69	13	71	119	73	121	75	99	77	5	79	47
81	49	83	91	85	125	87	103	89	105	91	83	93	117	95	31
97	33	99	75	101	109	103	87	105	89	107	67	109	101	111	15
113	17	115	59	117	93	119	71	121	73	123	51	125	85	127	127

the matrix and vectors have components in $\mathcal{Z}_m = \{0, 1, \ldots, m-1\}$. If the matrix A has an inverse A^{-1} in $\mathcal{Z}_m$

$$A^{-1}A = AA^{-1} = \underbrace{\begin{pmatrix} 1 & 0 & \cdots & 0 \\ 0 & 1 & \cdots & 0 \\ \vdots & \vdots & \ddots & \vdots \\ 0 & 0 & \cdots & 1 \end{pmatrix}}_{n \times n \text{ Identity matrix}},$$

then for each $\underline{y}$, the linear system of Equations (3.24) and (3.25) has a unique solution $\underline{x}$

$$\underline{x} = A^{-1}\underline{y} \ (\text{modulo } m).$$

A set of M vectors $\{\underline{z}^{(i)}: 0 \le i < M\}$ with values in $\mathcal{Z}_m$ is

- *Linearly independent* over $\mathcal{Z}_m$ if the only vector $\underline{\lambda} = (\lambda_0, \lambda_1, \ldots, \lambda_{M-1})$ with values in $\mathcal{Z}_m$ for which

$$\underline{0} = \sum_{i=0}^{M-1} \lambda_i \underline{z}^{(i)} \tag{3.27}$$

is the zero vector $\lambda_0 = \lambda_1 = \cdots = \lambda_{M-1} = 0$, and

- *Linearly dependent* over $\mathcal{Z}_m$ of there exists a vector $\underline{\lambda} = (\lambda_0, \lambda_1, \ldots, \lambda_{M-1}) \ne \underline{0}$ with values in $\mathcal{Z}_m$ for which Equation (3.27) holds.

Proposition 3.8: An $n \times n$ matrix A has as inverse matrix A^{-1} (modulo m) if and only if the rows of A are linearly independent over $\mathcal{Z}_m$.

Proposition 3.9: If the $n \times n$ A has an inverse modulo m, Gaussian elimination will succeed if and only if the m columns of X and Y contain n linearly independent vectors modulo m.

3.10 MONOALPHABETIC SUBSTITUTION PROBLEMS

The ciphertext files `cipherPr3.1-cipherPr3.6` and the table of one-gram probabilities (Table 3.6) may be downloaded from the following ftp address: ftp://ftp. wiley.com/public/sci_tech_med/computer_security.

3.1 `cipherPr3.1` results from a Caesar substitution on plaintext written using the alphabet AB $\cdots$ Z. Find the key.

`cipherPr3.1`

```
znkyzgzksktzzngzznkqtgvygiqvxuhrksoyngxjotgtgyykxz
outghuazznkmktkxgrqtgvygiqvxuhrksgcuxyzigykgyykxzo
utznkyurazoutluxikxzgotirgyykyulqtgvygiqvxuhrksyoy
waozkyzxgomnzlucgxjluxkdgsvrkolznkqtgvygiqbkizux
```

3.2 The term *autokey* refers to the use of the plaintext to modify the key. `cipherPr3.2` has been enciphered by an *autokey Caesar system* with key k as follows:
    1. The first letter of plaintext x_0 of the plaintext $\underline{x} = (x_0, x_1, \ldots, x_{n-1})$ is enciphered by the Caesar substitution $x_0 \to y_0 = (x_0 + k) \ (\text{modulo } 26)$;

2. The plaintext letter x_i with $1 \le i < n$ is enciphered by a Caesar substitution
$x_i \to y_i = (x_i + x_{i-1})$ (modulo 26).

Develop a *non* exhaustive method for the cryptanalysis for the autokey Caesar crypto-system and test the method using the ciphertext `cipherPr3.2` containing 293 lowercase letters.

---

cipherPr3.2

```
ldttnrxpkfbcgtavrzwimcsvqvsrvgwlivrgejgvrbfalxrpgsfzvgaltgfq
gwkgtgfmvtywxnjialwwmvpnfxhplrxkwuclpgqabjnxverxpkfbckmwjhsl
alergpnrxpkfbdaljwvrpjjaanldhwfrxpkfbknqwalqgfebxjlgdgwhdttn
rxpkfbckwxnjdfggfddgwhezralfszbbazwdglhtknkgxalxkrnfucnqdtxp
ptwvbrwqqlxqpdtkrnnnqdtmtmabtuhalvjsizctvrvvwwvmvtbwb
```

3.3 The ciphertext `cipherPr3.3` containing 538 characters results from a monoalphabetic substitution according to the following rules:

- All characters (in the plaintext) other than upper-case letters have been deleted;
- The ciphertext is written in rows of 50 characters in groups of 5 separated by a blank space.

The subject matter is from an article in the *Santa Barbara News Press* dealing with a meeting between the presidents of the United States and the Soviet Union in Iceland in 1986. Use χ^2-scoring and find the substitution.

---

cipherPr3.3

```
pyxbcsxzuyxmgmzbmebwxbwlriszluwmkxbmcsuwxblkcxubqi
czoxsqruuwxepylqmqiescscfzximuxsscbqxicxamgyxxvxzub
myxgrmymzuxxswmkczgpmcsuwxymzblvuluwxwlbumgxumoxyu
wxmsvczcbuymuclzcbuymkxiczgulctximzsmbmpmevxzuulgx
uglyqmtwxkulsldwmuwxbmcsmuuwxgxzxkmbrvvcuwxdlrissl
uwxyxglyqmtwxkmgyxxsultlvxulmbrvvcuczuwxrzcuxsbumu
xbzldwxcbmuumtwczgmtlzscuclzdxmyxbtymvqiczgulvxxuw
xvrbuqxgrmymzuxxsmpyxxzgczxxyxsbrvvcuuwmudciiecxis
myvbtlzuylimgyxxvxzubwxtmzqxtlvalyumqixdcuwbxzclym
svczcbuymuclzlaactcmibbmeblixvzieuwmumylrgxogqvmew
mkxmyyxbuxssmzcilaaulxvqmyymbbglyqmtwx
```

3.4 The ciphertext `cipherPr3.4` containing 948 characters results from a monoalphabetic substitution according to the following rules:

- All characters (in the plaintext) other than upper-case letters have been deleted;
- The ciphertext is written in rows of 50 characters in groups of 5 separated by a blank space.

The subject matter is from the Department of Computer Science's submission to the Computer Science Accreditation Board (CSAB). (Note, CSAB is a participating member in Accreditation Board for Engineering and Technology (ABET). CSAB develops accreditation criteria for and accredits programs in computer science, information systems and software engineering.) It describes some aspect of our college. Find the monoalphabetic substitution.

---

cipherPr3.4

```
vtfjzpcepjurwvzfcivthgvtpwdfjuzvbfcvpwpvwtpitksurp
vodfdpeuvfdguesrvourrhgmthbuzfuevplfpczfwfuzetvfue
tpciucdjzhgfwwphcurwfzlpefvtfdfjuzvbfcvtuwuchjfcuc
dehcifcpurmhzqpciuvbhwjtfzfehbapcfdmpvtuwjpzpvhgtu
zdmhzqvtfzfpwvtferfuzscdfzwvucdpciubhcivtfguesrvov
tuvtpitksurpvozfwfuzetpcucouzfuhgehbjsvfzwepfcefmp
rrafwsjjhzvfducdfcehszuifdaovtfehrrfifhgfcipcffzpc
ivtfzfpwuihhdzfjzfwfcvuvphcubhcivtfzfisruzguesrvoh
gbhwvhgvtfehzfuzfuwpcehbjsvfzwepfcefiujwuzfgprrfda
ovfbjhzuzoguesrvobucohgmthbtulfwfzlfdgsrrvpbfghzhc
fhzvmhofuzwvtfdfjuzvbfcvfcxhowuihhdmhzqpcizfruvphc
wtpjmpvtvtfdfjuzvbfcvhgfrfevzpeurucdehbjsvfzfcipcf
fzpciucdhvtfzwsjjhzvpcidfjuzvbfcvcvwpcjuzvpesruzuwpc
irfehhzdpcuvfdbuwvfzwjzhizubpcehbjsvfzwepfcefucdfc
ipcffzpcipwudbpcpwvfzfdxhpcvroaovtffrfevzpeurucdeh
bjsvfzcipcffzpciucdehbjsvfzwepfcefdfjuzvbfcvwehsz
wfwhggfzpciwfczhrrbfcvrpbpvwucderuwwwetfdsrfwuzffw
vuarpwtfdvtzhsitxhpcvehcwsrvuvphcehszwfwuzfezhwwrp
wvfducdguesrvouzfheeuwphcurrofnetucifdghzuehszwf
```

Problems 3.5 and 3.6 provide examples to test your skill at cribbing a Hill encipherment. In each problem

1. The dimension N of the Hill matrix and
2. The subject of the plaintext

are specified.

3.5 The Hill ciphertext `cipherPr3.5` consisting of 4 × 133 ASCII characters is displayed as an array containing 26 rows of 20 integers and a final row of 12 integers. The plaintext deals with a theft at a banking ATM.

---

cipherPr3.5

52	113	95	60	26	3	125	122	87	115	57	67	121	77	46	4	56	124	7	114
125	113	101	38	70	49	110	88	99	120	53	73	22	70	123	35	100	81	11	105
80	84	47	106	4	17	61	35	91	13	38	9	29	84	57	53	6	75	25	83
100	54	122	114	61	114	46	118	76	91	61	45	119	29	33	75	10	83	90	24
107	104	123	29	22	66	84	5	98	61	97	127	34	65	67	64	2	94	85	123
32	116	24	0	119	8	24	52	9	38	86	115	97	74	12	127	46	111	112	8
99	71	79	36	67	83	48	28	39	111	25	23	16	108	47	28	92	1	103	95
59	125	37	18	68	127	50	72	67	23	100	107	18	7	45	21	16	17	11	41
116	112	64	76	53	68	99	75	63	36	88	48	104	97	31	105	9	60	19	30
52	6	46	113	22	23	14	123	52	113	15	73	32	56	97	18	13	85	28	82
65	61	49	7	75	4	12	75	105	92	101	80	46	76	68	56	104	127	53	27
84	2	106	31	73	31	96	27	90	70	28	119	117	83	3	72	78	50	127	82
115	70	48	123	85	61	78	44	84	109	36	8	43	7	36	58	109	38	24	113
7	23	74	64	113	81	18	122	57	14	20	48	62	35	124	33	112	37	82	94
27	39	105	27	14	6	28	55	1	71	37	100	42	12	81	77	19	12	84	56

cipherPr3.5																			
64	60	24	79	37	105	38	123	104	100	73	126	93	98	111	87	94	106	113	34
64	61	58	12	0	16	108	89	61	72	49	62	121	40	123	112	97	55	74	96
104	12	56	67	74	119	109	79	4	35	125	26	22	66	84	5	26	93	86	42
88	81	120	79	117	83	3	72	51	11	16	2	22	6	28	55	16	121	8	125
110	55	124	84	43	66	96	39	101	33	32	117	45	56	32	95	101	33	32	117
43	7	36	58	88	71	42	47	75	32	64	108	1	46	107	12	5	124	120	118
13	101	119	26	108	126	97	61	70	84	24	96	76	89	49	119	117	59	18	92
26	93	86	42	82	59	97	116	89	33	110	120	83	16	100	78	46	95	13	15
16	119	102	85	46	99	32	108	39	111	25	23	39	111	25	23	115	97	108	90
98	49	10	124	107	15	21	80	48	72	107	61	104	57	69	102	115	47	73	11
71	1	125	19	15	113	59	90	3	83	61	74	21	102	112	43	71	11	35	69
82	70	28	119	80	15	44	61	12	110	89	64								

3.6 The Hill ciphertext cipherPr3.6 consisting of 336 ASCII characters is displayed as an array containing 16 rows of 20 integers and a final row of 16 integers. The width N of the Hill enciphering matrix is unknown but it may be assumed that $3 \leq N \leq 5$. The subject of the text is an important United States document.

cipherPr3.6																			
81	28	88	98	116	17	113	98	27	76	5	32	27	120	39	67	83	71	73	39
120	127	72	13	111	28	36	125	105	18	56	76	107	1	74	40	88	54	83	14
97	18	111	17	80	17	95	126	80	89	38	46	76	53	51	8	70	21	31	81
101	105	22	101	63	10	74	95	75	70	68	69	7	105	75	109	69	119	105	88
93	59	93	56	70	25	94	5	96	35	58	109	11	89	74	16	61	69	88	58
112	3	123	52	30	83	4	18	6	122	44	105	59	48	72	21	72	11	69	58
98	85	48	50	59	89	2	54	17	79	18	89	11	89	74	16	61	69	88	58
92	51	123	120	31	10	93	67	51	42	101	112	29	8	66	124	83	108	19	50
51	79	6	92	55	20	33	64	106	70	85	91	37	116	41	123	22	30	106	104
118	111	49	73	107	57	25	64	117	95	93	12	43	125	88	4	18	66	111	40
108	63	111	69	60	54	56	77	45	26	95	80	56	71	6	125	66	84	14	25
5	42	75	92	85	113	14	104	77	84	47	112	18	1	68	93	126	125	107	82
59	48	72	21	84	15	47	82	68	113	45	21	115	49	115	88	45	57	68	92
70	35	101	69	94	114	113	91	22	77	88	38	18	83	18	101	8	33	0	6
13	2	44	2	117	81	14	104	2	99	18	37	37	8	33	126	28	47	80	17
66	38	103	44	115	41	88	117	2	64	36	62	51	93	93	56	102	29	56	120
3	115	60	94	10	75	4	46	90	126	73	12	122	101	4	44				

REFERENCES

M. ABRAMOWITZ AND I. STEGUN, *Handbook of Mathematical Functions*, Dover Publications, Mineola, New York, 1972.

L. E. BAUM, "An Inequality and Associated Maximization Technique in Statistical Estimation for Probabilistic Functions of a Markov Process," *Inequalities*, **3**, 1–8 (1982).

L. E. BAUM, T. PETRIE, G. SOULES, AND N. WEISS, "A Maximization Technique Occurring in the Statistical Analysis of Probabilistic Functions of Markov Chains," *The Annals of Mathematical Statistics*, **41**, 165–171 (1969).

O. CAPPE, E. MOULINES, T. RYDEN, AND O. CAPPI, *Inference in Hidden Markov Models*, Springer, New York, NY, 2005.

A. P. DEMPSTER, N. M. LAIRD, AND D. B. RUBIN, "Maximum Likelihood from Incomplete Data Via the EM Algorithm," *Journal of the Royal Statistical Society, Part B*, **39**, 1–38 (1977).

R. J. ELLIOTT, *Hidden Markov Models*, Springer, New York, NY, 1997.

W. FRIEDMAN, *Military Cryptanalysis*, U.S. Government Printing Office (Laguna Hills, New York), 1944.

W. KAPLAN, *Advanced Calculus*, Addison-Wesley, 2003.

L. S. HILL, "Cryptography in an Algebraic Alphabet," *American Mathematical Monthly*, **36**, 306–312 (1929).

R. A. KEMMERER, "An Overview of Computer Security," invited paper at the *IMA Conference on Cryptography and Coding*, Cirencester, England, December 1986; also included in *Cryptography and Coding*, H. J. BEKER AND F. C. PIPER (eds), Oxford University Press, Oxford, 1989.

A. G. KONHEIM, *Cryptography: A Primer*, Wiley, New York, NY, 1981.

S. KULLBACK AND R. A. LEIBLER, "On Information and Sufficiency," *Annals of Mathematical Statistics*, **22**, 79–86 (1951).

S. E. LEVINSON, L. R. RABINER, AND M. M. SONDHI, "An Introduction to the Application of the Theory of Probabilistic Functions of a Markov Process to Automatic Speech Recognition," *The Bell System Technical Journal*, **62**, 1035–1074 (1983).

L. L. MACDONALD AND I. L. MACDONALD, *Hidden Markov and Other Models for Discrete-Valued Time Series*, Springer, New York, NY, 1997.

K. PEARSON, "On the Criteria that a Given System of Deviations from the Probable in the Case of S Correlated System of Variables is such that it can be Reasonably Supposed to have Arisen from Random Sampling," *Philosophical Magazine, Series 5*, **50**, 157–172 (1900).

T. PETRIE, "Probabilistic Functions of Finite State Markov Chains," *The Annals of Mathematical Statistics*, **40**, 97–115 (1969).

A. H. PORITZ, "Hidden Markov Models: A Guided Tour," *ICASSP-88*, April 1988, pp. S7–13.

L. R. RABINER AND B. H. JUANG, "An Introduction to Hidden Markov Models," *IEEE ASSP Magazine*, January, 4–16 (1986).

CHAPTER 4

POLYALPHABETIC SUBSTITUTION

THIS CHAPTER describes the cryptanalysis of polyalphabetic encipherment. The use of coincidence to determine the period and correlation to identify the key to cryptanalyze Vernam–Vigenère ciphertext will be explained. The one-time pad and the greater triumph of cryptanalysis against the Soviet KGB will be discussed. Problems to test your skills follows the text.

4.1 RUNNING KEYS

A monoalphabetic substitution on plaintext[1]

$$(x_0, x_1, \ldots, x_{n-1}) \to (y_0, y_1, \ldots, y_{n-1})$$

uses a single rule θ to encipher each letter

$$y_i = \theta(x_i).$$

A *polyalphabetic* substitution uses more than one rule

$$y_i = \theta_i(x_i), \qquad 0 \le i < n$$

to encipher the plaintext letters.
  A *running key*

$$\underline{k} = (k_0, k_1, \ldots, k_{n-1}), \qquad k_i \in \mathcal{Z}_{26} \, (0 \le i < n)$$

'is a simple polyalphabetic generalization of Caesar encipherment C_k of plaintext, which polyalphabetically enciphers the plaintext $\underline{x} = (x_0, x_1, \ldots, x_{n-1})$ according to the rule

$$\underline{x} \to \underline{y} = (y_0, y_1, \ldots, y_{n-1}), \quad y_i = C_{k_i}(x_i), \quad 0 \le i < n.$$

  A *book cipher* derives the running key from the text in some (secret) book; the key is composed of the letters starting on some specified page, line, and word in the book. Ken Follet's novel *The Key To Rebecca* relates the adventures of *Cicero*, a World War II German spy who uses a book cipher based on *Rebecca of Sunnybrook Farm* to encipher messages.

---

[1]ASCII plaintext in this chapter will be enciphered after

  - First replacing all lower-case letters by their corresponding upper-case letters, and
  - Deleting all other ASCII characters.

Computer Security and Cryptography. By Alan G. Konheim
Copyright © 2007 John Wiley & Sons, Inc.

An alternative method to obtain a running key is to extend a *key word* $\underline{k} = (k_0, k_1, \ldots, k_{r-1})$ of length r by periodicity

$$\underline{k} = (k_0, k_1, \ldots, k_{n-1}), \quad k_i = k_{(i(\text{modulo } r))}, \quad r \le i < n.$$

4.2 BLAISE DE VIGENÈRE

Blaise de Vigenère was born in 1523 in Saint-Pourçain, France. While serving as a diplomat in Rome, he came into contact with Giovanni Battista della Porta in 1549 and learned from Porta's *Traicté des Chiffres* (1585) describing various encryption systems. Vigenère's book *A Treatise on Secret Writing* was published when Vigenère returned to Paris. It contains the basic 20×26 *Vigenère tableaux*.

			Plaintext			
Key	A	B	C	...	Y	Z
0	a	b	c	...	y	z
1	b	c	d	...	z	a
2	c	d	e	...	a	b
⋮	⋮	⋮	⋮	⋱	⋮	⋮
25	z	a	b	...	x	y

The Vigenère encipherment of plaintext x (identified by its column position) with the key k (identified by its row number) is the table entry in the kth row and column position x; for example, plaintext $x = $ B is enciphered with the key $K = 2$ to ciphertext $y = $ d.

Vigenère polyalphabetic encipherment extends a sequence of r letters $(k_0, k_1, \ldots, k_{r-1})$ periodically to generate the running key, $\underline{k} = (k_0, k_1, \ldots, k_{n-1}, \ldots)$ with $k_i = k_{(i(\text{modulo } r))}$ for $0 \le i < \infty$. For example, the key of length 12

C	R	Y	P	T	O	G	R	A	P	H	Y
2	17	24	15	19	14	6	17	0	15	8	24

enciphers plaintext of length 20 using the repeated key

C	R	Y	P	T	O	G	R	A	P	H	Y	C	R	Y	P	T	O	G	R
2	17	24	15	19	14	6	17	0	15	8	24	2	17	24	15	19	14	6	17

Vigenère's original scheme *subtracted* rather than *added* the key from the plaintext

$$\underline{x} \to \underline{y} = (y_0, y_1, \ldots, y_{n-1}), \quad y_i = (x_i - k_i)\,(\text{modulo } m).$$

It was rediscovered nearly one hundred years later by Admiral Sir Francis Beaufort, whose name is associated with the wind velocity scale.

4.3 GILBERT S. VERNAM

Gilbert S. Vernam was an engineer for The American Telephone and Telegraph Company. He was asked in 1917 to develop a teletypewriter to perform on-line

TABLE 4.1   Baudot Coding Table

Baudot code

A	00011	B	11001	C	01110	D	01001
E	00001	F	01101	G	11010	H	10100
I	00110	J	01011	K	01111	L	10010
M	11100	N	01100	O	11000	P	10110
Q	10111	R	01010	S	00101	T	10000
U	00111	V	11110	W	11011	X	11101
Y	10101	Z	10001	LF	00010	CR	01000
↑	11111	↓	11011	SP	00100		00000
0	10110	1	10111	2	10011	3	00001
4	01010	5	10000	6	10101	7	00111
8	00110	9	11000	?	11001	$	01001
Bell	01011	!	01101	;	01110	&	11010
#	10100	(	01111	)	10010	.	11100
,	01100	/	11101	,	00101	;	11110

CR, carriage return; SP, word space; LF, line feed; BELL, bell.

encipherment/decipherment. Alphanumeric plaintext was first coded into 0's and 1's using the *Baudot code*[2], in which each character in a small alphabet is represented by a 5-bit sequence, as shown in Table 4.1. The key in Vernam's implementation of a redis-covered Vigenère polyalphabetic system was written on a paper tape as a sequence of five 0's and 1's and the Baudot-coded plaintext was XOR-ed with the key (Fig. 4.1). Vernam glued the ends of the paper tape into a loop, yielding additive encipherment with a periodic running key. Realizing that the strength of the encipherment would increase with the key length, Vernam combined several tapes with periods $\{r_i\}$ (Fig. 4.2). If the periods are properly chosen, a key formed from a total of $\sum_i r_i$ independently chosen key values could generate a key with period as large as $R = \prod_i r_i$. Unfortunately, this way of making a large period R is not equivalent to a tape of length R [Tuckerman, 1970].

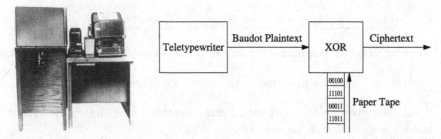

Figure 4.1   Vernam's Teletypewriter Polyalphabetic Encipherment System (Courtesy of NSA).

[2]To increase the number of letters that can be coded with five 0's and 1's, typewriter keyboard was shifted up ↑ to change from *letters to numbers* and shifted down ↓ to change from *numbers to letters*.

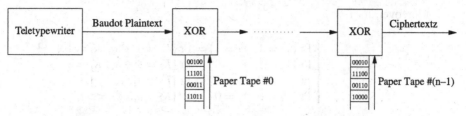

Figure 4.2   Vernam's multitape polyalphabetic teletypewriter system (Courtesy of NSA).

4.4   THE ONE-TIME PAD

Major Joseph O. Mauborgne began his study of cryptanalysis at the U.S. Army's Signal School, located at Fort Leavenworth (Kansas), later becaming Chief Signal Officer and the director of the Signal Corp's Engineering and Research Division.

When Vernam's cryptographic invention was reported by AT&T to the U.S. Army, Major Mauborgne recognized its importance. He also understood that the reuse of a long tape might make Vernam-ciphertext vulnerable to cryptanalysis. U.S. Patent 1,310,719, filed by Vernam and Mauborgne, described their *one-time tape* generalization of the AT&T additive polyalphabetic encipherment system.

A one-time tape system uses the key additively as Vernam proposed, but each key value enters in the encipherment of only one plaintext character. A one-time system can be defined for plaintext written in any alphabet, but as alphanumeric ASCII text is always coded into sequences of 0's and 1's prior to transmission or storage, we may assume the plaintext and ciphertext alphabet letters are 0's and 1's.

Let $(x_0, x_1, x_2, \ldots, x_{n-1})$ be any sequence of 0's and 1's with *no* assumption of any kind made about the statistical distribution of value of the sequence. A *Bernoulli process*[3] is a random process consisting of a sequence of independent and identically distributed $(0,1)$-valued random variables, which may be imagined to arise from repeatedly and independently tossing a fair-coin:

$$(K_0, K_1, \ldots, K_{n-1}) \qquad \mathrm{Pr}\{K_i = 0\} = \mathrm{Pr}\{K_i = 1\} = 1/2.$$

The one-time encipherment of plaintext $x_0, x_1, x_2, \ldots, x_{n-1}$ by a Bernoulli process $K_0, K_1, K_2, \ldots, K_{n-1}$ is additive; namely, the bit-by-bit modulo 2 addition (or XOR)

	x_0	x_1	x_2	$\ldots$	x_{n-1}
+	K_0	K_1	K_2	$\ldots$	K_{n-1}
	Y_0	Y_1	Y_2	$\ldots$	Y_{n-1}

Proposition 4.1:   If the key stream $K_0, K_1, K_2, \ldots, K_{n-1}$ is a Bernoulli process, then the ciphertext $Y_0, Y_1, Y_2, \ldots, Y_{n-1}$ is also a Bernoulli process.

Proof: The key observation is that Y_i and x_i together determine K_i, so that

$$1/2 = \begin{cases} \mathrm{Pr}\{Y_i = 1\} = \mathrm{Pr}\{K_i = 1 + x_i\} \\ \mathrm{Pr}\{Y_i = 0\} = \mathrm{Pr}\{K_i = x_i\}. \end{cases}$$

---

[3]A Bernoulli process is often described as *white noise*.

Moreover, for $i \neq j$

$$1/4 = \begin{cases} \Pr\{Y_i = 1, \ Y_j = 1\} = \Pr\{K_i = 1 + x_i, \ K_j = 1 + x_j\} \\ \Pr\{Y_i = 1, \ Y_j = 0\} = \Pr\{K_i = 1 + x_i, \ K_j = x_j\} \\ \Pr\{Y_i = 0, \ Y_j = 1\} = \Pr\{K_i = x_i, \ K_j = 1 + x_j\} \\ \Pr\{Y_i = 0, \ Y_j = 0\} = \Pr\{K_i = x_i, \ K_j = x_j\}. \end{cases}$$

The 2-output bits (Y_i, Y_j) are therefore independent with the *same* distribution as (K_i, K_j). The same argument can be extended (by mathematical induction) to show the components of the vector variables $(Y_{i_1}, Y_{i_2}, \ldots, Y_{i_m})$ and are independent with the same distribution as $(K_{i_1}, K_{i_2}, \ldots, K_{i_m})$.

All possible n-bit plaintexts are equally likely to have produced ciphertext resulting from a one-time encipherment.

This chapter examines the cryptanalysis of Vernam–Vigenère polyalphabetically enciphered plaintext using an additive key $\underline{k} = (k_0, k_1, \ldots, k_{r-1})$ of *un*known period. The two steps to determine the key and plaintext are:

1. Determining the period r of the key;
2. Recovering the values of the key.

4.5 FINDING THE KEY OF VERNAM–VIGENÈRE CIPHERTEXT WITH KNOWN PERIOD BY CORRELATION

---

cipherEx4.1

---

xeedt	nerye	rthti	lpxtl	xpbae	itrxe	eucoy	wqrup	wmdbd	odfrx
oiqhz	jxeei	dcpht	hawlz	ikeht	cleaa	znnsr	qaoih	mxeca	bayxb
rerzq	trtqg	devbn	alcsy	qiztw	cypep	uzvqr	nppyi	xxswh	dygea
eecsh	rcucr	fekke	ilxij	ezidj	mkazr	tepoe	bdcxw	blqre	vmzif
nmmpi	smcot	evsxx	awllt	qalrh	xidat	rioee	tczeq	iacdc	wqeyh
sezbb	qtyqe	aebdd	wmylq	qjgsj	pgipv	wfnuc	oywqr	krzqt	rtqgd
gsktd	dwqez	hucpx	sllep	yhgee	yxnep	mlmce	wgfez	itwxp	uetns
qmuft	cwxla	zpwcw	bejep	vmjez	ilphx	tmszg	xlrev	prioa	ftnvs
psetn	xmlnj	glcwm	ioifv	ippen	nlsio	sxdxw	piyjw	exbmq	ceepm
rarpw	wbsyp	yriaa	zsfrq	xnzto	wtxcq	titpl	rmits	rtoga	oleod
xnmit	lsexm	pitif	wzyxq	hqpdw	mptmc	niscc	abayx	bredy	xlbfd
xgspl	uehth	izoye	fxios	tpgif	bezec	skoay	bphxl	pxpjk	ejeeh
fglxs	npnok	xmydy	eract	tdw					

Example 4.1

cipherEx4.1 of length 623 letters is the encipherment of ASCII plaintext by a Vigenère substitution with period 7. The plaintext $\underline{x}$ and ciphertext $\underline{y}$ are each divided into 7 plain- and ciphertext files consisting of the letters separated by 7 places:

$$\underline{y}_i = (y_i, \ y_{i+7}, \ y_{i+14}, \ \ldots) \qquad \underline{x}_i = (x_i, \ x_{i+7}, \ x_{i+14}, \ \ldots), \qquad 0 \le i < 7.$$

TABLE 4.2 Letter Counts in Each Subfile of cipherEx4.1

y_0 ($n_0 = 89$)		y_1 ($n_1 = 89$)		y_2 ($n_2 = 89$)		y_3 ($n_3 = 89$)		y_4 ($n_4 = 89$)		y_5 ($n_5 = 89$)		y_6 ($n_6 = 89$)	
a	0	a	4	a	9	a	6	a	3	a	3	a	0
b	0	b	12	b	1	b	2	b	3	b	0	b	0
c	0	c	1	c	5	c	0	c	9	c	8	c	4
d	1	d	0	d	2	d	4	d	7	d	9	d	0
e	8	e	6	e	17	e	14	e	4	e	3	e	8
f	1	f	2	f	1	f	4	f	0	f	5	f	1
g	3	g	0	g	0	g	2	g	3	g	2	g	4
h	4	h	0	h	3	h	1	h	5	h	2	h	3
i	10	i	2	i	8	i	1	i	9	i	1	i	4
j	0	j	4	j	0	j	2	j	1	j	2	j	2
k	2	k	4	k	1	k	1	k	0	k	0	k	1
l	3	l	10	l	4	l	0	l	1	l	6	l	3
m	6	m	4	m	2	m	5	m	0	m	3	m	3
n	0	n	0	n	5	n	1	n	4	n	9	n	0
o	0	o	7	o	3	o	3	o	0	o	5	o	1
p	7	p	6	p	4	p	2	p	9	p	6	p	3
q	3	q	7	q	0	q	10	q	1	q	0	q	4
r	4	r	4	r	7	r	1	r	5	r	1	r	7
s	6	s	0	s	8	s	1	s	2	s	1	s	7
t	4	t	3	t	6	t	2	t	14	t	6	t	3
u	0	u	0	u	3	u	5	u	1	u	0	u	0
v	1	v	1	v	0	v	0	v	1	v	0	v	6
w	9	w	0	w	0	w	1	w	2	w	5	w	9
x	14	x	7	x	0	x	4	x	5	x	0	x	8
y	2	y	2	y	0	y	7	y	0	y	6	y	6
z	1	z	3	z	0	z	10	z	0	z	6	z	2

The ith subfiles x_i and y_i are each of length n_i; each letter in y_i results from the Caesar encipherment with same key k_i of the letter in x_i:

$$y_{i+7j} = (x_{i+7j} + k_i) \ (\text{modulo } 26), \qquad j = 0, 1, 2, \ldots, n_i - 1. \tag{4.1}$$

The first step in the process of finding the key $\underline{k} = (k_0, k_1, \ldots, k_6)$ is to make the letter counts in each subfile y_i of the ciphertext $\underline{y}$ shown in Table 4.2. We assume the plaintext is generated by the language model $\underline{X} = (X_0, X_1, \ldots, X_{n-1})$ consisting of independent and identically distributed random variables with distribution

$$\pi(j) = \Pr\{X_i = j\}, \quad 0 \le i < n; \ \ 0 \le j < 26, \quad \underline{\pi} = (\pi(0), \pi(1), \ldots, \pi(25)) \tag{4.2}$$

Let

- $N_j(\underline{x})$ be the number of times the jth letter occurs in the plaintext sample $\underline{x}$ of length n,
- $N_j(\underline{y})$ be the number of times the jth letter occurs in the ciphertext $\underline{y}$, and
- $N_j(\underline{y_i})$ be the number of times the jth letter occurs in the ith ciphertext subfile $\underline{y_i}$ of length n_i.

The sample letter frequencies are defined by

$$f_j(\underline{x}) \equiv \frac{N_j(\underline{x})}{n}, \quad 0 \le j < 26, \qquad f(\underline{x}) = (f_0(\underline{x}), f_1(\underline{x}), \ldots, f_{25}(\underline{x})) \tag{4.3}$$

$$f_j(\underline{y}_i) \equiv \frac{N_j(\underline{y}_i)}{n_i}, \quad 0 \le j < 26, \qquad f(\underline{y}_i) = (f_0(\underline{y}_i), f_1(\underline{y}_i), \ldots, f_{25}(\underline{y}_i)) \tag{4.4}$$

Assuming the sample of text is sufficiently large, we use the law of large numbers and conclude that

$$\lim_{n \to \infty} f_i(\underline{y}_i) = \widehat{f}_j(\underline{y}_i) = \pi(j + k_i), \qquad 0 \le j < 26, \, 0 \le i < 7. \tag{4.5}$$

Define the *left-circular-shift* by k places of the vector $\underline{\pi}$ by

$$\sigma_k \underline{\pi} = (\pi(k), \pi(k+1), \ldots, \pi(25), \, \pi(0), \, \pi(1), \ldots, \pi(k-1))$$

Equation (4.5) states that the limiting vector of ciphertext letter frequencies $\widehat{f}_j(\underline{y}_i)$ in the ith ciphertext subfile $\underline{y}_i$ is the left-circular-shift $\sigma_{k_i} \underline{\pi}$ of $\underline{\pi}$ where k_i is the *un*known key.

As the limiting vector of ciphertext letter frequencies $\widehat{f}_j(\underline{y}_i)$ is observed, the recovery of the *un*known key k_i requires us to find the left-shift of $\underline{\pi}$ that most closely matches the measured vector of ciphertext letter frequencies. The nearness can be measured in terms of the *Euclidean distance* between the vectors $\widehat{f}_j(\underline{y}_i)$ and the *un*known left-circular-shift of $\underline{\pi}$. The square of the Euclidean distance between the vectors $\sigma_k \underline{\pi}$ and $\widehat{f}_j(\underline{y}_i) = \sigma_{k_i} \underline{\pi}$ is

$$D^2(\sigma_k \underline{\pi}, \widehat{f}_i(\underline{y}_i)) = \langle \sigma_k \underline{\pi}, \, \sigma_k \underline{\pi} \rangle + 2 \langle \widehat{f}_i(\underline{y}_i), \, \widehat{f}_i(\underline{y}_i) \rangle - 2 \langle \sigma_k \pi, \, \widehat{f}_i(\underline{y}_i) \rangle$$

$$= 2 \| \underline{\pi} \|^2 - 2 \rho_k(\widehat{f}_i(\underline{y}_i)) \tag{4.6}$$

where

- $\langle \underline{a}, \underline{b} \rangle$ denotes the *inner-product* of vectors $\underline{a}$ and $\underline{b}$,
- $\| \underline{\pi} \|^2 = \langle \sigma_k \underline{\pi}, \, \sigma_k \underline{\pi} \rangle = \langle \widehat{f}_j(\underline{y}_i), \widehat{f}_j(\underline{y}_i) \rangle$ is the square of the length of the vector $\underline{\pi}$, and
- $\rho_k(\widehat{f}_j(\underline{y}_i)) = \langle \sigma_k \underline{\pi} \widehat{f}_j(\underline{y}_i) \rangle$ is the kth correlation $\sigma_k \underline{\pi}$ and $\widehat{f}_j(\underline{y}_i)$.

TABLE 4.3   1-Gram English Letter Probabilities

j	$\pi(j)$	j	$\pi(j)$
A	0.0856	B	0.0139
C	0.0279	D	0.0378
E	0.1304	F	0.0289
G	0.0199	H	0.0528
I	0.0627	J	0.0013
K	0.0042	L	0.0339
M	0.0249	N	0.0707
O	0.0797	P	0.0199
Q	0.0012	R	0.0677
S	0.0607	T	0.1045
U	0.0249	V	0.0092
W	0.0149	X	0.0017
Y	0.0199	Z	0.0008

TABLE 4.4   1-Gram Correlations

j	$\sum_{t=0}^{25} \pi(t+j)\pi(t)$	j	$\sum_{t=0}^{25} \pi(t+j)\pi(t)$
0	0.068733	1	0.039990
2	0.032744	3	0.032501
4	0.042720	5	0.033457
6	0.035164	7	0.037647
8	0.031363	9	0.034721
10	0.037051	11	0.045412
12	0.039829	13	0.046070
14	0.039829	15	0.045412
16	0.037051	17	0.034721
18	0.031363	19	0.037647
20	0.035164	21	0.033457
22	0.042720	23	0.032501
24	0.032744	25	0.039990

Equation (4.6) shows that the distance between the measured letter frequencies $\sigma_{k_i}\underline{\pi}$ and the shift $\sigma_k\underline{\pi}$ is minimized when $\rho_k(\widehat{f}_j(\underline{y}_i))$ is a maximum.

Table 4.3 provides one set of 1-gram English-language probabilities. The values of $\sum_{t=0}^{25} \pi(t+j)\pi(t)$ are listed in Table 4.4 and plotted in Figure 4.3. *Schwarz's inequality* for vectors $\underline{a}$ and $\underline{b}$ states

$$(\underline{a},\, \underline{b}) \le \|\underline{a}\|^2 \|\underline{b}\|^2, \qquad \underline{a} = (a(0),\, a(1), \dots, a(25)) \qquad \underline{b} = (b(0),\, b(1), \dots, b(25))$$

with equality if and only if $\underline{a} = C\underline{b}$ for some constant C.

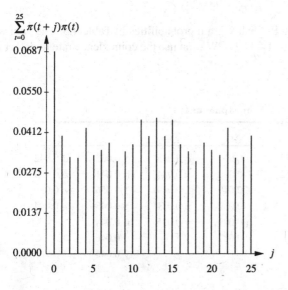

Figure 4.3   Graphical presentation of Table 4.4 1-gram correlations.

Proposition 4.2: When the plaintext letter probabilities are as in Table 4.3, $\rho_k(\hat{f}_j(\underline{y}_i))$ is maximized when $k = k_i$. Table 4.5 lists the values of k with the largest correlation values $\rho_k(\hat{f}_j(\underline{y}_i))$ for the ciphertext `cipherEx4.1`, from which we can recognize `example` as the key.

4.6 COINCIDENCE

A *coincidence* occurs at the ith position in two samples of plaintext

$$\underline{x}^{(1)} = (x_0^{(1)}, x_1^{(1)}, \ldots) \qquad \underline{x}^{(2)} = (x_0^{(2)}, x_1^{(2)}, \ldots)$$

if $x_i^{(1)} = x_i^{(2)}$. If the length n of the samples are the same, the *kappa*-value $\kappa[\underline{x}^{(1)}, \underline{x}^{(2)}]$ is the total number of coincidences

$$\kappa[\underline{x}^{(1)}, \underline{x}^{(2)}] = \sum_{i=0}^{n-1} \chi_{\{x_i^{(1)}=x_i^{(2)}\}}.$$

The *normalized kappa*-value $\kappa^*[\underline{x}^{(1)}, \underline{x}^{(2)}]$ is the average number of coincidences per letter

$$\kappa^*[\underline{x}^{(1)}, \underline{x}^{(2)}] = \frac{1}{n}\sum_{i=0}^{n-1} \chi_{\{x_i^{(1)}=x_i^{(2)}\}}.$$

How many coincidences can one expect in typical plaintext? If the plaintext is generated by the language model consisting of independent and identically distributed random variables with distribution as specified in Equation (4.2), then a coincidence occurs at the *i*th position of two samples $\underline{X}^{(1)}$ and $\underline{X}^{(2)}$ plaintext with probability

$$\Pr\{X_i^{(1)} = X_i^{(2)}\} = \sum_{j=0}^{25} \Pr\{X_i^{(1)} = X_i^{(2)} = j\} = \sum_{j=0}^{25} \pi^2(j) \equiv s_2.$$

The expected number of coincidences is

$$E\{\kappa[\underline{X}^{(1)}, \underline{X}^{(2)}]\} = ns_2$$

where $s_2 \approx 0.06875$ using the English 1-gram probabilities in Table 4.3. The values of s_2 in some languages are given in Table 4.6. We can use the coincidence rate to detect if two

TABLE 4.5 Largest Correlation Values in `cipherEx4.1`

y_0	y_1	y_2	y_3	y_4	y_5	y_6
e 0.069	b 0.040	a 0.072	h 0.034	c 0.045	g 0.035	d 0.042
f 0.042	e 0.039	e 0.052	i 0.040	d 0.034	h 0.041	e 0.059
i 0.043	h 0.042		l 0.049	l 0.049	l 0.056	k 0.039
p 0.053	i 0.048		m 0.062	p 0.071	p 0.043	r 0.044
	j 0.040		q 0.049	v 0.035	u 0.044	
	k 0.043		r 0.037		v 0.046	
	q 0.036				y 0.045	
	t 0.046					
	w 0.041					

TABLE 4.6   Rates of Coincidence in Various Languages

Language	s_2
English	0.0688
French	0.0778
German	0.0762
Italian	0.0738
Spanish	0.0775
Russian	0.0529

samples of ciphertext result from the same or different monoalphabetic substitutions as follows:

1. If the *same* monoalphabetic substitution θ enciphers two randomly chosen samples of plaintext

$$\theta : X^{(1)} \to Y^{(1)} \qquad \theta : X^{(2)} \to Y^{(2)}$$

the probability of the coincidence in the ciphertext $\Pr\{Y^{(1)} = Y^{(2)}\}$ is s_2 as $Y^{(1)} = Y^{(2)}$ if and only if $X^{(1)} = X^{(2)}$. If two samples of ciphertext $\underline{Y}^{(1)}$ and $\underline{Y}^{(3)}$ of the same length n result from the same monoalphabetic substitution, then

$$E\{\kappa[\underline{Y}^{(1)}, \underline{Y}^{(2)}]\} = n\sigma_2.$$

2. If two *different* randomly chosen substitutions θ_1 and θ_2 encipher two randomly chosen samples of plaintext

$$\theta_1 : X^{(1)} \to Y^{(1)} \qquad \theta_2 : X^{(2)} \to Y^{(2)}$$

then $\Pr\{\pi_1(j) = \pi_2(j)\} = \frac{1}{26}$ so that

$$\Pr\{Y^{(1)} = Y^{(2)}\} = \sum_{j=0}^{25} \Pr\{\pi_1(j) = \pi_2(j)\} = \frac{1}{26}.$$

If two ciphertext vectors $\underline{Y}^{(1)}$ and $\underline{Y}^{(2)}$ of the same length n result from different randomly chosen monoalphabetic substitutions, then

$$E\{\kappa[\underline{Y}^{(1)}, \underline{Y}^{(2)}]\} = \frac{n}{26}.$$

This suggests that we might test if two samples of monoalphabetically enciphered ciphertext have resulted from the same or different monoalphabetic substitutions by comparing the *normalized* κ-value to s_2.

Modifying this argument slightly, we can detect the period r of a Vernam–Vigenére polyalphabetic encipherment. Suppose the ciphertext $\underline{Y}$ results from a Vernam–Vigenére polyalphabetic encipherment of period r. Comparing pairs of letters in the two ciphertext vectors

Y_0	Y_1	$\cdots$	Y_{n-k-1}
Y_k	Y_{k+1}		Y_{n-1}

- *All* result from the *same* monoalphabetic substitution if $0 = (k \bmod r)$, and
- *not all* result from the *same* monoalphabetic substitution if $0 \neq (k \bmod r)$.

The expected number of coincidences when comparing $(Y_0, Y_1, \ldots, Y_{n-k-1})$ and $(Y_k, Y_{k+1}, \ldots, Y_{n-1})$ should be approximately

- $= n\sigma_2$ if $0 = (k \bmod r)$, and
- $< n\sigma_2$ if $0 \neq (k \bmod r)$.

Example 4.2

`plainEx4.2` consists of the first 1600 upper- and lower-case letters from the Declaration of Independence

```
When in the course of human events, ... our sacred Honor.
```

The plaintext was divided into four blocks of 400 characters and the κ- and normalized κ-values between the ith and $(i+1)$st blocks (B_i and B_{i+1}) are listed in Table 4.7. The final row gives the total number of coincidences and the average normalized k-value.

4.6.1 Estimating the Period Using Friedman's Incidence of Coincidence

The use of coincidence in cryptanalysis was first described in one of several monographs [Friedman, 1920] on cryptanalysis by William Friedman. Assume the plaintext $\underline{x} = (x_0, x_1, \ldots, x_{n-1})$ is enciphered by a Vernam–Vigenère polyalphabetic substitution with key $\underline{k} = (k_0, k_1, \ldots, k_{r-1})$ of period r producing ciphertext $\underline{y} = (y_0, y_1, \ldots, y_{n-1})$. For each $s > 0$, the *normalized* number of coincidences in $\underline{y}$ and the left-shift by s positions of $\underline{y}$ is computed according to the formula

$$\kappa_s^*[\underline{y}] \equiv \frac{1}{n-s} \sum_{i=0}^{n-s-1} \chi_{\{y_{i+s}=y_i\}}.$$

- If s is a multiple of the period r, then y_{i+s} and y_i result from the *same* monoalphabetic substitution.
- If s is not a multiple r, they are the result of generally different monoalphabetic substitutions.

By testing various shifts, we can identify the period.

TABLE 4.7 Normalized κ-Values in `plainEx4.2`

i	$\kappa[i, i+1]$	$\kappa^*[i, i+1]$
0	31	0.0775
1	28	0.0700
2	20	0.0500
3	22	0.0550
	101	0.0631

TABLE 4.8   Table of Normalized κ-Values for `cipherEx4.1`

s	$\kappa_s^*[\underline{y}]$	s	$\kappa_s^*[\underline{y}]$
1	0.0433	2	0.0530
3	0.0321	4	0.0417
5	0.0449	6	0.0482
7	0.0530	8	0.0498
9	0.0353	10	0.0498
11	0.0321	12	0.0321
13	0.0401	14	0.0498
15	0.0369	16	0.0514
17	0.0385	18	0.0353
19	0.0498	20	0.0610
21	0.0658	22	0.0417

Example 4.1 (continued)
Table 4.8 and Figure 4.4 give the normalized κ-values for the ciphertext `cipherEx4.1`. Although the locations of the local maxima of $\kappa_s^*[\underline{y}]$ are somewhat noisy, it is clear from the local maxima at $s = 7$, 14, and 21 that $r = 7$.

4.7   VENONA

During World War II [Wright, 1987; Haynes and Klehr, 1999], the Soviet Union communicated with its legitimate and covert representatives in the United States by

- Diplomatic pouch delivered by a courier,
- Commercial cables, and
- Short-wave radio.

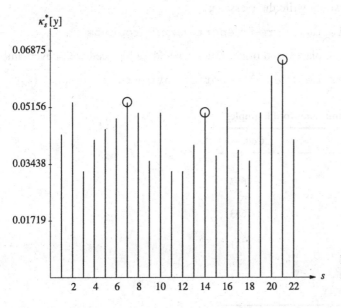

Figure 4.4   Graph of normalized κ-values for `cipherEx4.1`.

Diplomatic pouches provided security, but communication was slow; it was illegal to encipher messages for transmission by telegraphic cable companies. The Soviet Union was forced to rely on encrypting short-wave radio as a means of secreting their messages.

The Soviet Union operated five communication's channels:

1. GRU – Soviet Army General Staff Intelligence Directorate,
2. Naval GRU – Soviet Naval Intelligence,
3. Diplomatic – Embassy and Consular business,
4. Trade traffic – lend lease, The Amtorg Trading Corporation Stands for American Trading Organization (AMTORG), Soviet Government Purchasing Commission, and
5. KGB – Soviet espionage; headquarters in Moscow, residencies abroad.

Unlike Japan and Germany, which opted for electromechanical devices, the Soviet Union decided to use the one-time pad, which would provide absolute secrecy if correctly used.

The USSR employed two-part superencipherment (Table 4.9); the first phase used a codebook, a dictionary listing 4-letter groups codes for some set of common (plaintext) phrases. The codebook might have been particular to a specific channel, and was distributed to users on both sides of the channel. The entries `spell` and `endspell` were used to allow the inclusion of foreign language (English) text in a message.

A codebook is used as a monoalphabetic encipherment and offers relatively little protection; if the codebook falls into the hands of the enemy, as it did on two instances, the system is compromised. To provide secrecy, the Soviet Union combined the codebook with an additive one-time pad; shown in Figure 4.5 is a one-time pad captured by the British Intelligence Service MI5. A one-time pad [Kahn, 1983] was found in the possession of Colonel Rudolf Ivanovich Abel, a Soviet spy arrested in 1957. Abel's one-time pad, printed in red and black, was small enough to be hidden in a block of wood. Each page of a Soviet KGB one-time pad contained 60 five-digit groups of randomly generated digits. The open literature does not tell how the Soviet Union carried out the random number generation.

The steps in the encipherment process were the following:

1. The sender would write the message:

```
konheim delivered report about rockets
```

2. Certain names, places, and organizations would be replaced with covernames:

```
Teacher delivered report about grades
```

TABLE 4.9   Phrase and Codeword Examples

Phrase	Codeword
⋮	⋮
Contact	7652
⋮	⋮
endspell	1653
⋮	⋮
pay	6781
⋮	⋮
spell	5411
⋮	⋮

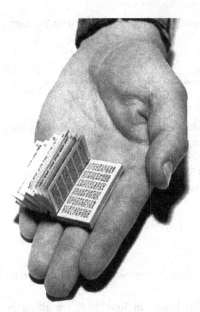

Figure 4.5   One-Time pad (Courtesy of NSA).

3. A code clerk would replace each word with a 4-digit codebook entry:

7394 2157 1139 3872 2216

4. The codebook entries would be regrouped in blocks of 5 digits:

73942 15711 39387 22216

5. Six *unused* 5-digit groups from the one-time pad would be used:

16471 56328 29731 35682 23798 46659

(a) The first 5-digit group identifies the encipherment process for the receiver, as messages might be received out of order;

(b) The last 5-digit one-time pad group was an end-of-message marker used by the receiver to check on the number of groups received.

20505	60476	04016	88622	36579	39249	67480	72479	66266	87127
92365	70390	04618	94915	08730	77472	67325	85635	01210	22288
99873	16471	56328	29731	35682	23798	46859	07234	10566	29350
03229	46862	90096	60275	61685	52187	94072	88348	20714	39363
49924	84489	53498	92285	92394	71287	36378	94819	19574	66292
98910	93264	32572	46231	58592	35289	98189	66859	23710	20413

Figure 4.6   One-Time Pad Containing 60 Five-Digit Groups of Digits.

6. The 5-digit groups would be added digit by digit modulo 10 with no carry:

```
        73942   15711   39387   22216
+  16471 56328   29731   35682   23798   46659
   ────────────────────────────────────────────
   16471 25660   34442   64969   45854   46659
```

7. An additional 5-digit group was appended to the message; the first three digits was a message number, the last two, the date:

```
16471 25660 34442 64969 45854 46659 21210
```

8. The digits were converted into letters

```
IETWI UREEO ZTTTU ETPEP TRART TEERP UIOIO
```

using the table

The encipherment process described above would have provided absolute secrecy even if a copy of the codebook had been discovered.

Hitler broke his alliance with the Soviet Union in June 1941, resulting in a large increase in traffic. Without the means of increasing their production of one-time pads

0	1	2	3	4	5	6	7	8	9
O	I	U	Z	T	R	E	W	A	P

to accommodate the communication needs, the Soviet Union decided to reuse one-time pads. Duplicate copies of each page were assembled into different one-time pads. They might have reasoned that the enemy would need to discover which pages were duplicated and this was thought to be beyond the resources of the Soviet's adversaries.

It is not clear who discovered the reuse of the one-time pad; perhaps it was an Allied spy in the Soviet Intelligence apparatus. Once reuse is suspected, it is possible to use coincidences to test messages to determine if two segments arose from the same segment of a one-time pad.

Pairs of intercepted messages would provide segments from two one-time pad entries, which could be pieced together to recover the pages in one-time pads.

4.7.1 Detecting Pad Reuse

A predecessor of NSA, the Army Signal Intelligence Service, was located at Arlington House in northern Virginia; it began to monitor Soviet communications in 1945. Early in 1947, Meredith Gardner of the U.S. Armed Forces Security Agency used the charred remains of a Soviet Codebook found in Finland to decipher a Soviet communication. The cryptographic resources of the American (NSA) and British (GCHQ) Intelligence services were mobilized to study this penetration. The operation was first called BRIDE, then DRUG, and then VENONA.

Even after finding the additive key, there remains the task of reconstructing the codebook. It appears that Soviets had the habit of enciphering plaintext that had already been published; for example, part of the Congressional Record.

Additionally, there were several defectors who brought, as their dowry, samples of text. Not all messages could be deciphered; in the VENONA intercept of Figure 4.7, the notation [*66 unrecovered groups*] appears, meaning that only part of the text was deciphered.

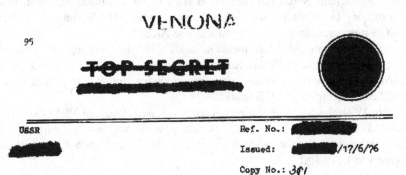

VENONA

95

~~TOP SECRET~~

USSR	Ref. No.:
	Issued: /17/6/76
	Copy No.: 3

BONUSES FOR SOURCES, INCLUDING LIBERAL AND NIL, GIFTS OR PAYMENTS FOR PROBATIONERS

(1945)

From: MOSCOW

To: NEW YORK

No.:   200   6 March 1945

[66 groups unrecovered]

decision was made about awarding the sources as a bonus the following sums: to LIBERAL [i] 4000 dollars[,] NIL[ii]

[58 groups unrecoverable]

either the purchase of valuable gifts for the probationers [STAZhER] or payment to them of money on the basis of well thought out cover-stories.

[28 groups unrecovered]

No. 1306   VIKTOR[iii]

Footnotes: [i]   LIBERAL: Formerly covername "ANTENNA"; Julius ROSENBERG.

            [ii] NIL: ie either "(River) NILE" or a name eg "NEIL/NEALE";
                             formerly "TU..."; unidentified covername. "TU..."/
                             "NIL" also occurs in NEW YORK's Nos. 863 of 16 June
                             1944   , 1251 of 2 September 1944
                             and 1657 of 27 November 1944

            [iii] VIKTOR: Lt General Pavel Mikhajlovich FITIN.

VENONA

Figure 4.7   Venona Intercept (Courtesy of NSA).

Ultimately, the Soviets learned of the penetration of their cryptosystem (possibly from Kim Philby), and stopped reusing one-time pads. However, the damage could not be undone; the *stale* messages still provided information. The information obtained was of great value; it was learned [Wright, 1987, p. 231] that the USSR had fourteen agents operating within the OSS (the predecessor of the CIA) and five agents with access to the White House.

Alger Hiss was a senior employee of the U.S. State Department. Before becoming president, Richard Nixon has accused Hiss of being a communist agent, based in part on testimony by Whittaker Chambers, himself a confessed Soviet agent. Decipherment of KGB messages identified Hiss (covername ALES).

Some deciphered KGB message dealt with the building of the atomic bomb (covername ENORMOZ). Julius Rosenberg (covername LIBERAL) and his wife Ethel Rosenberg, who were arrested, tried for espionage, found guilty, and executed were identified by deciphered KGB traffic.

In 1994, the National Security Agency released details of VENONA. They may be accessed on NSA's Web page at http://www.nsa.gov. A partially deciphered KGB message (from the NSA Web site) is shown in Figure 4.7, which concerns a payment to LIBERAL.

4.8 POLYALPHABETIC SUBSTITUTION PROBLEMS

Problems 4.1–4.5 provide examples to test your skill at the cryptanalysis of Vigenère enciphered plaintext.

1. The plaintext is written using the full ASCII alphabet:

   (a) All ASCII characters other than upper- and lower-case letters were then deleted from the plaintext, and

   (b) every upper-case letter was replaced by its corresponding lower-case letter.

2. Vigenère substitution was applied to the resulting modified plaintext file.

3. The ciphertext is written in rows of 50 lower-case alphabetic ASCII characters.

4. Bounds on the period r are given.

A solution requires you to identify the period r, key $\underline{k} = (k_0, k_1, \ldots, k_{r-1})$, and derive the plaintext. This requires a student

1. To compute the κ-value and infer the most *likely* period r;

2. To compute the correlation values and infer the most *likely* key;

3. To recover the plaintext.

The ciphertext files `cipherPr4.1-cipherPr4.6` may be downloaded from the following ftp address: ftp://ftp.wiley.com/public/sci_tech_med/computer_security.

| PROBLEMS

4.1 `cipherPr4.1` containing 692 lower-case ASCII characters results from a Vigenère encipherment of plaintext. The period r satisfies $6 \leq r \leq 12$; the subject of the plaintext is unknown.

---

cipherPr4.1

```
vlphpwtbvwqtdpuwahwwecnhgfsemlexvbvxjedagvdemgxlcn
ywtlvweziosjmtiwphzoctnmnlipcattsezrvzjerxspuvfhqj
saphavnxyeahxszoivlpdihbqethacdacpsnjzclpfrpgwdndt
ahrkglexvbjerlldpsolitiolgjvvxggefglgvqkplcivhuift
llckcfmosopazhuijcapgaskxvvlyhwcexrvzedjcyyuiderww
cxqhpwxcsemvhlepzsfwksydpyszeperpslggedptdwlrocvlp
hpwgrwumzyeycgseswhhwhuigbnspuurshhlepbgvrihlepnfn
qumdewlthrextzcvtglgalaiyoawcgetdudesvsnzadhcxteyd
pjhvspwpnjywgckwacdcwqiffjewlccxksyladocxteydevfgp
ccpchlqhvkxjagvhbgqpheazofjcvldxjoaxgpwhisgvwpilca
fhuiuexppzbrxuglatzgrgwvpddjyrxnejpgzgyavpdndugvwv
wzqpooahullvtwfbxqgzwsbfvriastrogrgwvtenwoeeoiepgz
oeigbnspuurhkrnwjkwakeicexmwpevidpcjwclgvxpcaoykqv
tewthltgqlnpsubvkxsxifdrogcdpmjvnriizqshhn
```

4.2 cipherPr4.2 containing 247 lower-case ASCII characters results from
a Vigenère encipherment of plaintext. The period r satisfies $5 \le r \le 9$;
the subject of the plaintext is unknown.

---

cipherPr4.2

```
vvraljoghhdrjyflotpqrworfwtvwbftexrkgrvumzipacgpgg
tytggrhkximvatchyafovmjsualkitrqtpgfgovxtsigelnkhp
waxttnclkbnfrfnjxthruaeinhiwpseuyxxnccexenvagwfknv
cufqggsvlngpjsalavngvjbbdhxsklachfzkbgigffalkypmri
eknznqyrfbvntnupkhuafglqogrpglkjgkhceetewgvjoesvky
tbuhvul
```

4.3 cipherPr4.3 containing 818 lower-case ASCII characters results from
a Vigenère encipherment of plaintext. The period r satisfies $4 \le r \le 8$;
the subject of the plaintext is unknown.

---

cipherPr4.3

```
pverzmvwhatjkawmfxrzozlelvcmacgfvmlmymmlmzkawepwrt
xebeobebrzwlkttheboakforlfdqnrtelplltilhxkikpbknoc
ziinexubhlmgisntcqslllxecbfziylkzunmzwnlecinrnroee
arbtsxniyehcmacggzorkrumtgxqsehnziexgzorkruslgubhl
mgzomevuszemqnrlywuwwsmtlnxpttgkpeqbiatakforlfdqnr
vfcrdxfcrmhfsidtzueotkatfwvvtdpywawmywurafbhpknqsp
lfjecteluakzohelvmmehcicvteqnenzbigxwmewyfzczfgctp
kjkipgtmwpmigtztebinbgitptelaylnmrbnvattheaadpvtll
lkweiiciiyyrktdbeifcbvvdwrimfcxjpiyzdinyxiuodmfnaw
enmvpmiqeomfuavxfpplltilllvtfexrkhtgxjozdraoaifaeo
mfirpyvzeyvvuaynrttstkattvbatzovzydfrtlhhilshxmmae
mvupexuipcxjmnetkqoymyitdwvbatevleyhlohqhixezicmse
```

---

cipherPr4.3

```
nugiyzfvťsxzzohgpmtwntqdcxrlamevinoxerojtstepgfcgs
yfzmzkvbrlwzbizgrtsenumnelkwrptujeqhimlpvkcrpffatz
yfpplltildbevogtkqoylradpltzimxujewhnirpffbigtkmdm
rkpidzfilhxvupstjqzpzvvectcxrzucmmdhcdiyzkmcsgzyup
ldwseufwkduvoiyteleywkpetkuqsnnjaizgfnpchstexlftvt
gxeieajbeapzaecxwqnpfvvtshnmvpkdinjhkpecfvbhzwjbhl
mxwooiiwbwxdaowovzslguxrzziimxxiatldvnocziinexupag
xemvpksmeyyfzmlezheobebhpldcdpgkamtguaaywemeomfjea
kvaeymvleiicqctmcg
```

4.4 cipherPr4.4 containing 327 lower-case ASCII characters results from a Vigenère encipherment of plaintext. The period r satisfies $5 \leq r \leq 9$; the subject of the plaintext is unknown.

---

cipherPr4.4

```
jcyqqbzmhhusjgzxavqyjwkokgfepsjkysbvkjznlrnclfzfhh
qpucnxlrosiafxjodvesicavqmjhvbzhmxagvbcwoiohyofdds
rwuopbbenhzmbzmvpvvsyhmvetwcjvqhqzvchfqgkbkbvzxizp
pdosrizsiksqaqiiesjofmkbtytauwowfxavqmnwedyofwpoko
zsdzeqvcimflafvcwsoxejvcaofilisvpqgxezzdfqaqiwjcpc
zwebveycbiaotruofmkbrvnchinbdouhyeebkkpbeeiceywcxc
kbtytagreqrdpczwafmsjseadwtrhfqtncmskspfuhyojcgrpf
pcwcexpscowvaraoenasxicfrzo
```

4.5 cipherPr4.5 containing 736 lower-case ASCII characters results from a Vigenère encipherment of plaintext. The period r satisfies $6 \leq r \leq 12$; the subject of the plaintext is unknown.

---

cipherPr4.5

```
icasa nijki wsqiy lskab rhxas fwgrf dsuxa uvsfl uxsxy xckwn
crlzk zovzk iusjs hrjuc ugsdi wklxw unbco uaclg aqvhy iyjdo
jsvoh qsfek obyzv genci uhurc lkzzh xmxgk ghsor cxwuu aaxtc
gsloc bvysw lwsgh kkwse hahsu ywmwf isduu avseg hifyv ggnkf
gwncw wpiwh ltaqm dzwtd iyxwv jwgfo jpafk qcpvf ilaub cizbm
khxcu uggvw kazhv ohetj uoreu xcgxy yworm efvqb czryh ywcvw
fnwef tkigh jcrso orsug hkwgl ofhgm sxkiw sqzcj auyhi gevyk
atsgv ghhaf jigwx sxzay pfrib yjwcw zokrt dsobg rsysx lnsar
xymeh ufhdt njwsz ifhyi jlzkq cpvox wjyqw htwih juufd sijug
afghy iqwia sgwoi rkegm brzvi sfyks ukxlw jktcu gxhal ocbdr
crxgx aowoi rgjic iqyyp afmdz hgmiv judpb zbivw vofws yrlgl
qcpvo xwjyq whtwi afkbu ltyij atucu zbikl arsqz uhnay wbjuz
jaukw bhtam fwkfw qmgsk lwisv zcsfk iobek urkok fsghs xzwyh
oilir svxcd ltvek ayozw niyyz ycahc cpdtk fsikl vwvzc hkkze
umrhm pkgfw jhsgw woeda lwsgz iefkc sfwny q
```

4.6 `cipherPr4.6` containing 500 lower-case ASCII characters results from a Vigenère encipherment of plaintext. The period r satisfies $6 \leq r \leq 12$; the subject of the plaintext is unknown.

cipherPr4.6

```
tstpq bfvea oryaa birpr vagjb nhtwn iqyos pzelv hnfzj cirks
ftxim qhogl vdyjt netrg zlkti ppemp xxbnx ihdir prvag jxrtl
qohdn sjqco oahnu hennq hcpyg elkro vcwef cpius wuwey iotgk
syntj xtolq tnuoi tufes bdevi fwior veafl tfcgo hceid ewsyi
xcutr guawr fdwih dfoep wolxe lpnet ckzsb qiduq taspe snexn
jdyga bltzz ysnfv kuzel ukzub rilch xbbdm cqebc isenx ixsus
isyax tbtps zlkyp fmfik mhfzx hyoaa oocoo oxioe viarx dcjxh
ymhst tfiff mypqa rcqbn hmpih abnhw cfupm pszkr ujlao opeuo
giore birmt ipmnn bknbw wtlrv tvcio zqaen lgihq hsilr dnexm
bmmnn llhqw ysuih nhele qxrbz lplgb tntrm vyxls fxfls itnhf
egyxm rztxm uvmal pewbf eeuzj ufiru ooirm qtnee lefxg gvlke
vrmti pveqx kdtlv eqlkt ieley cyose
```

REFERENCES

W. F. FRIEDMAN, *The Incidence of Coincidence*, Riverbank Publications #22, 1920, reprinted by Aegean Part Press (Laguna Hills, California), 1996.

J. E. HAYNES and H. KLEHR, *Venona: Decoding Soviet Espionage in America*, Yale University Press (New Haven), 1990.

D. KAHN, *Kahn on Codes*, Macmillan (New York), 1983.

B. TUCKERMAN, "A Study of the Vigenère Vernam Single and Multiple Loop Enciphering Systems", IBM Research Report, RC 2879, May 14, 1970.

P. WRIGHT, *The Spy Catcher*, Dell Books (New York), 1987.

CHAPTER 5

STATISTICAL TESTS

THIS CHAPTER describes various statistical tests which are often used to assess the strength and weaknesses of an encipherment system. Included are the tests suggested by the National Institute of Standards used in validating the new Advanced Encryption Standard. Diagnosis, the problem of inferring the method of cryptographic encipherment, is formulated and illustrated.

5.1 WEAKNESSES IN A CRYPTOSYSTEM

Cryptographic systems might be cryptanalyzed by

- Exhaustive key trial, or
- Exploitation of systemic weakness, often in conjunction with a *selective* nonexhaustive key trial.

The recent *cracking* of DES involved exhaustive key trial, but the *Enigma machine* was cryptanalyzed by exploiting a weakness in the design and defective operational protocol used in encipherment.

The only perfectly secure encipherment uses a one-time system and this *only* when used properly. The practical limitation of one-time encipherment led to design of cryptographic systems that use a short key $k_0, k_1, \ldots, k_{n-1}$ to generate a larger operational key. It is an act of faith that as the basic key length n increases, the security of the derived ciphertext also improves. The design of cryptographic systems has therefore focused on ways of generating long keys that *appear* to be random.

The methods discussed thus far in these notes have dealt with uncovering some systemic weakness. Here we examine some of the statistical methods that might be used to detect hidden relationships between the key, plaintext, and ciphertext. One such statistical measure, the χ^2-test has already been described in Chapter 3.

5.2 THE KOLMOGOROV–SMIRNOV TEST

Figure 5.1 plots the *sample distribution function* $\widehat{F}_n(x)$ for $n = 100$ and $n = 1000$ samples of data derived from a uniform distribution function $F(x)$. The Kolmogorov–Smirnov Test is a goodness-of-fit test; is a sample of n data values $X_0, X_1, \ldots, X_{n-1}$, derived from independent and identical random trials consistent with a specified distribution function $F(x) = \Pr\{X_j \leq x\}$? The law of large numbers implies that the sample

Computer Security and Cryptography. By Alan G. Konheim
Copyright © 2007 John Wiley & Sons, Inc.

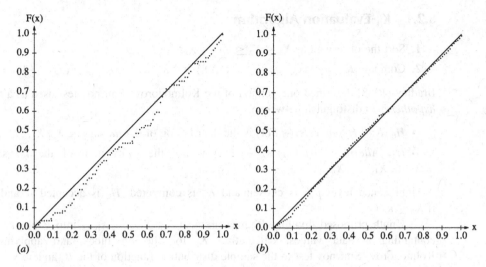

Figure 5.1   Sample Distribution Function $\widehat{F}_n(x)$ (a) $n = 100$; (b) $n = 1000$.

distribution function

$$\widehat{F}_n(x) \equiv \frac{1}{n} \sum_{j=0}^{n-1} \chi\{X_j \le x\}$$

converges as the sample size n increases

$$\widehat{F}_n(x) \to F(x), \qquad n \to \infty$$

with probability 1.

The *Kolmogorov–Smirnov statistics*

$$K_n^+ \equiv \sqrt{n} \max_{-\infty < x < \infty} (\widehat{F}_n(x) - F(x)) \qquad K_n^- \equiv \sqrt{n} \max_{-\infty < x < \infty} (F(x) - \widehat{F}_n(x)) \qquad (5.1)$$

$$K_n = \sqrt{n} \max_{-\infty < x < \infty} |\widehat{F}_n(x) - F(x)| = \max\{K_n^+, K_n^-\} \qquad (5.2)$$

measures the vertical deviation of $F(x)$ from the sample distribution function $\widehat{F}_n(x)$, where

- K_n^+ measures the deviation when $\widehat{F}_n(x) > F(x)$ and
- K_n^- the deviation when $F(x) > \widehat{F}_n(x)$.

The Kolmogorov–Smirnov test verifying the condition

$$\Pr\{K_n \ge \kappa_n(p)\} = 0.01p \qquad (5.3)$$

was first proposed in Kolmogorov [1933], but a more accessible reference is Darling's paper [1957].

A table of the $p\%$-significance level values $\kappa_n(p)$ defined by Equation (5.3) for

- $p = 99, 95, 75, 50, 25, 5, 1$, and
- $n = 1(1)12, 15, 20, 30$ and $n > 30$

is contained in Knuth [1971].

Using the monotonicity of F (and $\widehat{F}_n$), the next algorithm gives a feasible way of evaluating K_n.

5.2.1 K_n-Evaluation Algorithm

1. Sort the observations $X_1 \leq X_2 \leq \cdots \leq X_n$;
2. Compute $K_n^+ = \max_{0 \leq j < n} \left(\frac{j+1}{n} - F(X)_j \right)$ and $K_n^- = \max_{0 \leq j < n} \left(F(X_j) - \frac{j}{n} \right)$.

Bradley [1968] described one version of the Kolmogorov–Smirnov test used as a *test of hypotheses* to distinguish between

- H_0 (*Null Hypothesis*) – $F(x)$ is the distribution of the *iid* sample $X_0, X_1, \ldots, X_{n-1}$.
- H_1 (*Alternate Hypothesis*) – $F(x)$ is *not* the distribution of the *iid* sample $X_0, X_1, \ldots, X_{n-1}$.

A significance level $p\%$ is chosen and K_n is computed. H_0 is accepted if and only if $K_n \leq \kappa_n(p)$.

Knuth proposed dividing B_n measurement $X_0, X_1, \ldots, X_{B-1}$ into B blocks, each containing n data values, calculating K_i for the ith block and applying the Kolmogorov–Smirnov test to the sample distribution function of the B random variables $\{K_i : 0 \leq b < B\}$.

5.3   NIST'S PROPOSED STATISTICAL TESTS

The National Institution of Standards (NIST) proposed a number of statistical tests [NIST, 1994] when they solicited a successor to the Data Encryption Standard in 1996.

If a cryptographic algorithm generates a random number generator, the algorithm's output of 20,000 consecutive output bits $y_0, y_1, \ldots, y_{19999}$ must pass the following four statistical tests.

- *The Monobit Test* – Count the number N_1 of ones in the 20,000 output bits. The test is passed if $9654 < N_1 < 10,346$.
- *The Poker Test* – Divide the 20,000 bitstream into four blocks of 5000 bits each.

y_0

Block 0	0 1 1 1 0 1 … 0 1 0 1 0 1
Block 1	1 0 1 0 1 1 … 0 0 0 1 1 1
Block 2	1 1 0 1 1 0 … 1 1 0 1 0 0
Block 3	0 0 0 1 1 0 … 1 0 1 0 1 0

y_{19999}

Count the number f_i of (column) vectors $(x_{0,j}, \ x_{1,j}, \ x_{2,j}, \ x_{3,j})$ for which $i = 8x_{0,j} + 4x_{1,j} + 2x_{2,j} + x_{3,j}$ and evaluate the χ^2-value

$$\chi^2 = \left(\frac{16}{5000} \sum_{i=0}^{15} f_i^2 \right) - 5000.$$

The test is passed if $1.03 < \chi^2 < 57.4$.

TABLE 5.1 Intervals for the Runs Test

Length of Run	Interval
1	2267–2733
2	1079–1421
3	502–748
4	223–402
5	90–223
6+	90–223

- *The Runs Test* – A run is a maximal length sequence of either bits with value one or zero:

$$\left(\cdots 1 \overbrace{\underbrace{00 \cdots 0}_{j \ 0s}}^{all \ 0's}, 1 \cdots \right) \quad \text{Run of 0's}$$

$$\left(\cdots 0 \overbrace{\underbrace{11 \cdots 1}_{j \ 1s}}^{all \ 1's}, 0 \cdots \right) \quad \text{Run of 1's}$$

The test is passed if the number of runs $R_\ell[i]$ of $i(i = 0, 1)$ lies in the intervals listed in Table 5.1.

- *The Long Run Test* – A long run is defined to be a run of ones or zeros of length 34 or more. The test is passed if there are no long runs.

5.4 DIAGNOSIS

Up to now, we have analyzed ciphertext assuming the method of encipherment was known. *Diagnosis* is a process used to discover the nature of the encipherment system. The *toy* diagnostic procedure to be described next assumes that each of the six ciphertext files that follow `cipherEx1.A`, `cipherEx1.B`,..., `cipherEx1.F` has been produced using one of the following encipherment systems:

$\mathcal{T}$ Columnar transposition

$\mathcal{V}$ Vigenère substitution

$\mathcal{M}$ 1-gram monoalphabetic substitution

$\mathcal{O}$ Some other cryptosystem.

The process of identifying which cryptographic system has produced given ciphertext is referred to as diagnosis. It will be carried out by making a sequence of tests whose objective is to accept or reject one of the hypotheses $\mathcal{T}$, $\mathcal{M}$, $\mathcal{V}$, or $\mathcal{O}$.

> Test #*i* Compute ...
>
> > If ... then encipherment system is ...
> >
> > If ... then encipherment system is *not* ...
> >
> > Continue with Test #*i* + 1

The diagnosis process corresponds to a tree (Fig. 5.2). You start at the ROOT and make a Test, which may (1) identify a unique method of encipherment or (2) eliminate one

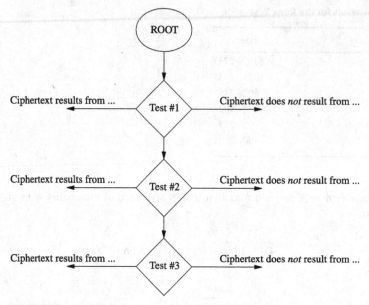

Figure 5.2 Diagnosis Process.

or more of the possible cryptographic systems $\mathcal{M}$, $\mathcal{V}$, $\mathcal{T}$, or $\mathcal{O}$, and continue by performing additional tests.

Diagnosis requires

1. A sequence of tests to carry out diagnosis;
2. Application of the tests to classify the method of encipherment for each of the six ciphertext files that follows.

```
                           cipherEx1.A
```

```
snrtiiregmlrtorcceleatssrirclerismprhcthiiiitteomgfihgadniia
setapneegareratateirtsegtopevirsetecthdvfsaglrantcoddewutrst
mirskaacleeorlsmsiuuraosraccirseoeentdlemsnseooartottxnesaho
itnohthufudamgeerhoirehedeltdkeocnoayhaeeriaursnmhnhoeienaye
pmosssmaotoutsnpmntilesnialndmepeematgtornsaacsaiewnssgtsrrt
ntoopncinsletrsthpdstannintaarsstnhtofmspmau
```

```
                           cipherEx1.B
```

```
wpvmulxmfjrxunfvotqkvixtocrxkhqiehrkhlzgvbrvyeuvrv
titghllwgkvbyvqnjpfyvmkmymumrzpshvrugyvxummsnnwqfr
kgiitxcllvrrahwpvvvxfpesnhjqtenwhdvpqipmexvahqjwwx
ladsumdklxgpkmexjxwmtlphowxcklbwlrimkmgitllakipmsc
iwwbwwwtthgctxuplbymoiuwmifvraktgkiwiqcgfmtlckdkki
tbvbzgumkmegqgvbrrvebtveflwwlrvklmuypvhzkekgimrxwk
hawvqfwpvmpbwqrpehqkvtvbrvfjclbakiotukymvxfblvcegm
jmigwwzxuwdqccqihzrxkhqiwxgklvjxceoikmqglvklgxdzcc
redvempzsprwghiieiyvrugyvxuapwvxpxisfnfbklgfdvljcv
wciitfxakyundtccotnmkaqmbxvwqyszvhkvwqfr
```
---

cipherEx1.C

```
rblfogzbkgcwuqfydkibkrfolsfjmyxvlhdwfeyuiwhguybqsrhhbolkagix
xkritjwdhrqcwrkdaepcdyfrekdxwwuovrarqxihbrintjrrryhdfcwsmkic
nnidgoxdhniwlbytelcqbmoxpwmsdszeglaeffqpyltbmkrwookdqjodlwbk
uakoapeeobehtvoocnkrrpvllliqbgyijzyzqkrgsgmrsdcbielyvzagpety
wbgpeijuicgvwczqtbchzfwvozhdibshmmnhtjdufabtsszflhhvjdrqembk
phelvhfyjdkxrirmjmlcnvwgtsfvisgpfrgojrwistjzzxubpwlhwetjncbj
wdlmpxlhtzjnmaxmmkeemxlegzldxwcoslyehxjnchjscwquemqejlinzzcx
zwojiqgvcnicdwrdrmibdoxyrvajhcixgwuzohtrwgqsaxqnozsjzzrlnhun
ekpooaqxihlavycciphbobqhwbpdmcnkwcfyjrgekclyfvoljslxohfemkiz
fyjfvlxuiyfgrfiqiltkqqhkcpiklavcxpzaduwpisutl
```

cipherEx1.D

```
epibqacvqfqvbpmvizzwemabamvamqbqaibqumapizqvowxmzibqvoagabmu
smzvmtixzwoziubpibkwvbzwtabpmzmawczkmawnikwuxcbmzivlittwkibm
abqumiuwvoqbacamzaqbtmbacamzazcvbpmqzxzwoziuaqbkwvbzwtabpmxm
zqxpmzitlmdqkmalqakabmzuqvitaxzqvbmzaivlbpmtqsmkwvvmkbmlbwbp
muikpqvmivlqbxzwdqlmainqtmagabmubpibuiviomabpmtwvobmzuabwzio
mwnqvnwzuibqwvvackpiaxzwoziualibiivllwkcumvbaqbqaibqumapizqvo
agabmu
```

cipherEx1.E

```
wneeeiiasngtlsouaemulrerotpeimraietiteshgosomuoaosstonaaeser
hrremnaetistotlrlsesrentcdilmnergonpsdninreshpgkpttecoacmisu
nrioeaetlehodanvieaheafosmneuhwstrryroaoespdtastehgcsiddrpsl
nohidetalmersrddttirsisonmamnhrcroigrsupsrprcsattcemaoftmttr
niaaamhinsimnttercsoftlsosesianhhvsiinkchnpsyaentfacgtcaxatt
egielaotuaeltnetrrmteeicnndeteerastsgoithrau
```

cipherEx1.F

```
opkjvvjobetrmjowlseitvazxuievbavrswvxvpvgroqurfeey
bniyimztysswpnbkqjsiftueqwfabnifirkxrmpekdwtwuiizb
nigiiheuvxprjlsinrjdvlseqrgtexuirhwargswnmxzvgvmmw
yvvvhmtxftcvkkhbrkcmycfxvhekwuecgmreosivbkqbvvjvcs
eocjijgueivkziemqvbosamenmixvsejvktbmeonuyexyzakgb
ruogvibjgmmjmpxzjvowpsexmxrrhndbnxuitcwogrfvoekiae
ixpoxrgkpzgpqijdoteyxvmvgxvzvnjgwrhfipgvqarmmgrqwf
abceeikzknrbpfbqkwglroeopyfvvdgmyesgmorglvymbiysgh
mtxciidwjssxyzxrearvyaewgidcmxiglvxzoxrvzjvujficzk
zmbrznenegavxirppsjoxkvssihitgrxivlkssjkcmggpyivke
sswlxpvvrhzxbosavvnbyxbetjvymqiivjrirbkzvzsaslmkgt
nfzgqzcbjdvxvmakkcmviejfmugrpitcixepxvmmowgmtnwlxu
ijtazizgfhxurrrknqtxbxyzwbieecgaewgidgmbiytvmnuvze
exmilnvrxbkvvwkdkywhgyozgrfproqurcvfxmjyeijvzkflrf
```

---
cipherEx1.F
---

hmgrfwkmiokuxwjzceehfmekpyijoihpvwyzlurpikcmgvplzo
mixhvrglkgvwzjvylnzvwmkrzeuzithglvngyxrquzaokaeeyq
styidzvzegmfiazeexvybnifgfkmujciiawxqnrtzxxiqmtoqu
rnruzdgphekdwtfrgfhmyqbvvnxkgvjzx

Test #1:   Count the number of occurrences $\{N_i[\mathcal{F}]\}$ in each ciphertext file $\mathcal{F}$ of each letter i and compute the frequency of occurrence $\left\{f_i[\mathcal{F}] \equiv \frac{N_i[\mathcal{F}]}{t}\right\}$ in $\mathcal{F}$ and the correlation coefficient

$$\varrho[\mathcal{F}] \equiv \sum_{i=0}^{25} f_i[\mathcal{F}]\pi(i)$$

where $\{\pi(i)\}$ are 1-gram probabilities.

Accept *Hypothesis* $\mathcal{T}$ if $\varrho[\mathcal{F}] \geq 0.80 \times 0.0688 = 0.05504$. Reject *Hypothesis* $\mathcal{T}$ if $\varrho[\mathcal{F}] < 0.80 \times 0.0688 = 0.05504$.

Results of Test #1:

File	$\varrho[\mathcal{F}]$
cipherEx1.A	0.0692
cipherEx1.B	0.0338
cipherEx1.C	0.0383
cipherEx1.D	0.0318
cipherEx1.E	0.0692
cipherEx1.F	0.0379

Conclusion from Test #1:   cipherEx1.A and cipherEx1.E result from columnar transposition, which does not alter the one-gram frequencies.

Having rejected $\mathcal{T}$ . . .

Test #2:   Count the number of occurrences $\{N_i[\mathcal{F}]\}$ in each ciphertext file $\mathcal{F}$ of length $N[\mathcal{F}]$ and compute

$$s_2[\mathcal{F}] = \sum_{i=0}^{25}\left(\frac{N_i[\mathcal{F}]}{N[\mathcal{F}]}\right)^2.$$

Accept *Hypothesis* $\mathcal{M}$ if $s_2[\mathcal{F}] \geq 0.80 \times 0.0688 = 0.05505$. Reject *Hypothesis* $\mathcal{M}$ if $s_2[\mathcal{F}] < 0.80 \times 0.0688 = 0.05505$.

Results of Test #2

File	$s_2[\mathcal{F}]$
cipherEx1.B	0.0470
cipherEx1.C	0.0403
cipherEx1.D	0.0742
cipherEx1.F	0.0459

Conclusion from Test #2: `cipherEx1.D` results from a monoalphabetic sub-stitution.

Having rejected T and M . . .

Test #3:   Use the κ-test to determine that the encipherment is Vigenère.

Results of Test #3:

cipherEx1.B $n = 490$				cipherEx1.C $n = 585$				cipherEx1.F $n = 883$			
s	$\kappa[s]$	s	$\kappa[s]$	s	$\kappa[s]$	s	$\kappa[s]$	s	$k[s]$	s	$k[s]$
1	0.0470	2	0.0430	1	0.0411	2	0.0189	1	0.0431	2	0.0352
3	0.0390	4	0.0432	3	0.0275	4	0.0568	3	0.0386	4	0.0421
5	0.0598	6	0.0475	5	0.0379	6	0.0432	5	0.0456	6	0.0319
7	0.0352	8	0.0498	7	0.0346	8	0.0468	7	0.0537	8	0.0343
9	0.0374	10	0.0271	9	0.0382	10	0.0313	9	0.0526	10	0.0355
11	0.0334	12	0.0607	11	0.0401	12	0.0471	11	0.0378	12	0.0344
13	0.0440	14	0.0441	13	0.0227	14	0.0508	13	0.0391	14	0.0806
15	0.0337	16	0.0612	15	0.0509	16	0.0633	15	0.0426	16	0.0415
17	0.0444	18	0.0699	17	0.0352	18	0.0459	17	0.0312	18	0.0393
19	0.0488	20	0.0574	19	0.0442	20	0.0425	19	0.0498	20	0.0406
21	0.0512	22	0.0385	21	0.0248	22	0.0249	21	0.0650	22	0.0430
23	0.0428	24	0.0472	23	0.0463	24	0.0357	23	0.0442	24	0.0384
25	0.0387	26	0.0302	25	0.0357	26	0.0698	25	0.0431	26	0.0408
27	0.0346	28	0.0411	27	0.0448	28	0.0395	27	0.0386	28	0.0807
29	0.0412	30	0.0717	29	0.0306	30	0.0595	29	0.0304	30	0.0516

Conclusion from Test #3:   `cipherEx1.B` and `cipherEx1.F` result from a Vigenère substitution of periods 6 and 7.

Having rejected T, M, and V, accept O.

Conclusion from Diagnosis: `cipherEx1.B` results from some other form of encipherment.

5.5   STATISTICAL TESTS PROBLEMS

Problems 5.1–5.2 provide examples to test your skill at the diagnosis of cryptographic encipherment.

The ciphertext files `cipherPr5.1A-cipherPr5.2F` may be downloaded from the following ftp address: ftp://ftp.wiley.com/public/sci_tech_med/computer_security.

PROBLEMS

5.1 `cipherPr5.1A` and `cipher5.1B` result from either columnar transposition, monoalphabetic substitution, or polyalphabetic (Vigenère) substitution with period $5 \leq r \leq 10$.

Develop a diagnostic procedure to distinguish between these three encipherment systems and determine which system was used for the example ciphertext.

---

cipherEx5.1A

```
fphki tmpjq nhptv artqi weire vqzbk xmepw afzlt pzlgl owxgx
iugaa nwain attpe khlrh gvqdh klrpc vkkrg xrove ubkvs dbwbq
zvvsd bwbqz vtvvz qedwx mmeqn ggahw jfdoc zldgi kmuse axvlr
erzal xvmes dizsv mekqo mzbvy mempk uioki gatbe moxgk dkkub
bumcx uizls tcjxk xeprm icmpl mquem eqtme muoek uqveg vmide
jihme xieyc lqxrl wznnm ngfhq ggvmd algme pwafz bvsdb wbqzv
vseft wxudv lzzgb awole epepq ulvec bnizb vvmvz vqebv nwvoq
ubcwx vjfqi ziorw vqzxq zlfie fctpi wthfo vwdaj xrvdc bqkuh
wjegk fqrgb imaab qfmyi quxeg fasca iqebv lmdgn ifmpx rkmnx
dwfxw jquum vqxhr zfczu dgrvp uxmkh xbgxq zmblh rnawt ppdkh
ckdmb wvlms xgeub khykf jmmav bwkmp kqwiv sdbwb qzvhr ktgnd
qyhpf guaul hvsdb wbqzv aemqd mqvsk sxdcu ymgms gxcgs ipxwj
gepma etgbs cuywq truoj meaph vvaoq zwxlp pyktu bdkcr brtuk
dmmfz upmdh tpfzi puawh vpoqu bcwbr xtcas zrpri mrqpt byvfy
kbewu bkzzu jqnrk ikakb exuxw vzvxa almmf zcaav hhjkt geazo
wwcmt oqawb rugub dqhl
```

---

cipherEx5.1B

```
aptnu inflv hoium aoyre uobtf atris tirsh nsyed oslen cticr
leaoe ccauc slten udxid bbosc pnviu vreyu cnsmy rchnr tgpoi
ftnie ordst nelts zttde anttp ruumt cdaei lsill envya mscru
mcmtd assos yrlcn rtyrh taasn nspoh eluse utodt eodgc kasim
yaagy irimg ostoo rguee etnao sohey tmcrw efasp nttco cyahr
somep euiye risma nstnx nasts xcsgm eomnn eauls teaos rsmhn
mlsbm hestl nltpa rfobo sioel iirfl siice wovnc oseon ddksi
snnpe tpsie iebel pnrtt hlele uuaee trasn ipoim rsanc rodsi
htcrf uosea pesmc ruipo asmhn ysste sshst reepa erdie heaac
rtnie nsack eaeli spart tedbm itunc ohpis poema orsop slsep
edaao wrowt sfeeo crero maado olpie iogwl tnero atdst hboeh
terhw ndthe uetsu ahunm nrecl ileas vaios spoao clctm tsidt
eoise ostls empln apeti othle ebgta hgnmn iatvh cnodi irppn
flesc waidl uorar cwpos rlons rgasi rtbyo lense obtnc ronai
nteea ptdge ertyi uncad eetly ihanm oispa pmasa oeola isoou
sarre ietnw ane
```

5.2 The Six ciphertext files cipherPr5.2A, cipherPr5.2B, ..., cipher5.2F result from one of the encipherment methods

$\mathcal{T}$ Columnar transposition

$\mathcal{V}$ Vigenère substitution

$\mathcal{M}$ 1-gram monoalphabetic substitution

$\mathcal{O}$ Some other cryptosystem.

Develop a diagnostic procedure to distinguish between these six encipherment systems and determine which system was used for the example ciphertext.

---

cipherEx5.2A

```
tundn  rmeeo  rceof  sacrm  stohb  aessy  gedtp  rsnro  tuaie  tnsce
stqre  haesi  tncoo  uccte  evode  twede  iftuh  stdrn  rmcer  iurde
pnmse  rfoar  anpey  tiyza  iethm  eheos  oecer  tztsa  ptcme  ucret
xstep  ydntu  oslfe  dtcho  ieppc  erueh  setsp  peyri  hertf  teitl
iarfc  ernae  pdrrn  osigp  ncets  peyot  edstn  nnnfn  grnru  rivtt
mstir  fstse  nrdrt  nspey  roits  dneor  incia  ratpc  uscrn  bliuc
cbeha  ttshs  asird  owaor  ieeha  lrihs  ceoit  steyc  riuce  rnlye
msotw  unrrl  orisf  eoarc  oucao  oamdm  cenvy  iabao  orinc  dhfei
lutcn  atekh  tuccr  haaee  midio  ttedm  rooar  ipeys  gdihe  tdtbu
hcouc  timnh  ieims  tttck  eroui  niant  aiatu  aevar  uaory  tisiu
mntms  tgsrn  yooaa  hsunh  iecpt  incor  isaon  eudaa  ltsie  mstar
kftua  s
```

---

cipherEx5.2B

```
aftta  lsmma  fekdf  pntfi  masqh  mdrbx  mbplx  nsmqa  gwhui  ottzr
amqgh  wbrnz  bwlqb  tjlre  masbb  wiifn  rwemt  bwbrq  huabc  vcffa
eeziy  ezqhv  qxtqc  fekxs  eypee  iayyq  zrwqh  mbnrx  ijnmi  antra
gluyi  xnecf  eyczv  rcodu  ntbwb  ssoiz  agagk  snfoo  iarrf  imysz
afmnp  tagjs  oduvn  domfg  iktxg  yeybw  aemun  tvcyq  zrejo  dmfoi
pwfxf  cmbrd  mpfre  qcauz  ogtmx  rlwzi  ftamh  esgaz  pbrlm  wfxee
dmfue  bcsem  raoea  flcvr  dmazr  taibv  xfsec  cphas  qxlfa  zvnlb
oagba  nipkz  iazsk  pdwtr  tuanc  yeyiq  eicpy  mzhae  rvxzk  uiktt
mhnlc  gcizt  uvtul  mfcpx  yeita  bvggx  eenip  kziaz  skpdw  trtuw
gwrrd  mctbb  wbypl  kzraw  ahuir  sqzff  btsfm  kaplv  tbwbg  syemb
vnzbv  ryped  igtam  unqba  zwghx  zqyep  sangh  kmogw  fsfpr  rxaiy
xlfmc  fekwt  nwqaf  qftbk  oyhxt  mjnsx  jsvrd  antrt  hqbsi  osqvf
imqjr  hxtmn  eofvc  awbne  qgiom  wajlr  yigih  vfrxr  rzmqb  rbvrh
xtmjn  sxnce  mksfi  acxqt  tvlme  svilb  vrskl  knbrx  quaio  wazxi
gowae  madbv  cntoe  hbpmz  gmxvh  brbca  cydwm  rhgbg  dwzsd  qgfei
adgsr  huhui  xvqzn  gxaoy  eoyan  ghxls  ceoty  mattv  rglba  hmeaz
mgnpx  rkwsa  etbbr  codmv  ggmff  mkttm  qeiif  gqbnf  buekm  oqiom
mgoet  ayvrd  irbue  kmwfw  lmgku  chudh  xbroz  vmxev  llxvq  vgiam
oehxb  acgim  ahnxf  sfqps  lpcjx  eafic  pkwlv  qxtqt  logmd  rvzez
bbftt  zpsjp  gbrrv  zwzif  spmge  vbsqw  bvqvc  ekksa  xlffp  rdxbs
pxbdo  zvmxa  oeioe  bwetx  lcail  ufwst  aqfgc  qhdmr  ckqav  rxlez
rphzh  rhfso  wavbk  hrhxn  pwaeh  chbjq  wqvgy  mecgl  lueia  dxvrf
ymizr  niewb  rvbae  wamha  hbjqh  qarck  qarwx  rqvbt  kmdbv  qepqf
taihn  wrcom  fsycz  nxqao  sbfmm  beise  mtfvn  tbrvx  butvt  bmggl
xtoia  bxmlc  plifm  qbrwh  uiopa  brnmq  oyeqt  mkxek  awaea  dubvo
gbvre  avqzf  eicpy  mzifg  qilkc  hvxgq  aaepk  zvikt  eiadf  iyrwp
hmzrh  htrrv  puzpn  pigoa  sqhqz  eetac  amptt  igmtv  mbjqh  qkeif
```

cipherEx5.2B

```
mgnvb  jgagp  kibxw  xnpbu  eimcc  pbwtw  qemmq  gxeey  lbnhb  humkk
fpryt  zsfio  iacfe  gwitl  qodmc  okbhb  xeebw  yivmh  uvbaf  kyala
wsmza  fqbnu  zcjwf  nslrs  vzwoi  pttmz  empcq  scsqi  ecaqb  txera
cthfi  waekd  empog  loecj  eywey  ywfei  pipcr  ignce  qxtuw  atamp
estsq  zvsna  inpiy  zwglh  wyvrd  faznn  rbvvr  dizxn  rmqqh  pxrnc
giliz  rvqta  xbslq  pycrs  qnhlb  vtbvj  afqbn  mpsov  lweme  mtgtv
rafut  rsvwb  gefnu  vtsxv  gvxfv  qqafh  zanxf  ozwec  hvhnm  kizov
nywfz  eqiav  ghtbv  rpmsf  wncvm  gfsqh  qzfeg  awgms  euvso  kuogm
lnfpr  mhahh  wbfgt  qemmf  eiktf  worhe  gvrdi  ebuen  asbjz  ozbeo
eahue  qrqag  rbkhh  wbreb  bogtm  ngzee  avnzq  bssom  mbvog  qbglb
idwjn  wihnw  maomr  nvqdu  ioizo  qamio  ywldq  brrlj  fbapi  zoyet
sotif  sfprt  kibfq  fseqb  n
```

cipherEx5.2C

```
kbfeb  knjyp  fkepk  yeqey  qpdkn  fvatq  oanbn  kjyln  kraoo  pdypf
oyhhk  zatpk  yrrao  opdat  ypypd  alquh  fruyr  icyjj  kecyj  afoye
awyjl  hakbp  dfopx  lakbp  dnayp  yefeb  anaer  apdna  ypawf  opofb
yqoan  ryeta  tqrao  aeofp  fsafe  bknjy  pfkeb  nkjek  eoaeo  fpfsa
typyp  dfofo  qoqyh  hxpda  naoqh  pkbrk  nnahy  pfecf  ebknj  ypfke
yukqp  cnkql  okbfe  tfsft  qyhop  kkupy  fefeb  knjyp  fkeyu  kqpye
fetfs  ftqyh  pdafe  banae  rarke  pnkho  lnaoa  epatf  epdae  awpoa
rpfke  ynaqo  atpkr  kqepa  npdfo  pxlak  bpdna  yppyj  lanfe  cnaba
nopkp  dalnk  raook  bjyif  ecqey  qpdkn  fvatr  dyeca  opkpd  asyhq
akbfe  bknjy  pfkeo  pknat  fepda  rkjlq  panye  awyjl  hakbp  yjlan
fecfo  yopqt  aeprd  yecfe  cdfoc  nytaf  epdac  nytab  fhapy  jlanf
ecfoy  skfta  tuxyh  hkzfe  cqoan  opkjk  tfbxk  ehxpd  afnkz  ebfha
ornxl  pkcny  ldfrr  dario  qjjfe  cryeu  aqoat  bknta  parpf  ecpyj
lanfe  cpdfo  japdk  tqoao  rnxlp  kcnyl  dfrpa  rdefm  qaooq  rdyor
fldan  uhkri  rdyfe  fecpk  caean  ypayr  dario  qjbkn  ayrdb  fhayr
rftae  pyhty  pytao  pnqrp  fkeyh  pdkqc  dkbpa  efeek  raepr  yeuas
anxrk  ophxy  rrfta  epyht  aopnq  rpfke  jyxua  ryqoa  tuxuk  pddyn
tzyna  yetok  bpzyn  abyfh  qnaob  knfeo  pyera  byqhp  xokbp  zynar
kqhty  hhkzy  lnkcn  yjpkz  nfpau  axket  fpoty  pyoly  rayet  ksanz
nfpay  ekpda  nqoan  otypy  yrrao  orkep  nkhpa  rdefm  qaory  euaqo
atpkh  fjfpk  sanzn  fpfec  pkpda  qoano  kzety  pyoly  rauqp  pdana
foekl  nkpar  pfkey  cyfeo  pdynt  zynab  yfhqn  aooqr  dyoyd  aytrn
yodrn  xlpkc  nyldf  rrdar  ioqjj  fecry  eyhok  uaqoa  tbknt  aparp
fecyr  rftae  pyhty  pytao  pnqrp  fkebk  ntayh  feczf  pdukp  dpyjl
anfec  yetyr  rftae  pyhta  opnqr  pfkef  pfoea  raooy  nxpkd  ysayu
yriql  narks  anxlh  yeunk  zofec  hayiy  cayet  feban  aeray  napdn
aypop  kpdao  arnar  xkbty  pyyet  pyjla  nfecy  etyrr  ftaep  yhtao
pnqrp  fkeyn  apdna  ypopk  pdafe  pacnf  pxkbt  ypypd  aoapd  naypr
hyoof  bfryp  fkeoz  anabf  nopfe  pnktq  ratux  taeef  ecybf  eyhpd
naypr  hyoof  bfryp  fkefe  pnktq  ratux  taeef  ecjyo  mqany  tfecb
```

cipherEx5.2C								
fpofe	eafpd	anpda	oarna	rxekn	fepac	nfpxr	ypack	nxjyo	mqany
tfecn	abano	pkpda	lnkra	oozda	nayef	epnqt	ancyf	eoyrr	aoopk
pdaox	opajq	etany	ekpda	nqoan	oyrrk	qepol	kkbfe	cyetl	yoozk
ntcqa	oofec	ynajy	omqan	ytfec	pdnay	polnk	parpf	kejar	dyefo
jopdf	ooarp	fkefe	pnktq	raoln	kparp	fkeja	rdyef	ojoqo	atpka
edyer	arkjl	qpan							

cipherEx5.2D								
vevur	bmywh	xmeva	aqilm	sikev	egtew	trhgk	ouixd	lnmoa	nmhhn
mictm	irnfe	catnl	sfsav	vevsv	onmko	oagdi	gyeue	gcevh	nwrhl
igtdg	imiog	mhhmx	thhws	rfien	xmrdt	bontg	aoyli	slmou	azeag
wtlmb	ngvaa	qnxla	gtlbs	bsagw	frrfa	loxrl	fbcam	boqtx	chgbq
xelar	xbnwr	hduvx	ddumh	egmif	amiog	fefht	nilfs	dumhe	gmifa
miogf	efhtn	ilfss	rbmak	blbaw	drxls	whxma	ljuhr	tdigz	tkrxa
tmaei	ikstf	xckag	isfbs	whxse	vnrha	mtegm	irnde	ymaiv	kxywa
xnkim	bytns	hrtta	mxrpi	galzn	auagt	exlaw	rnstx	wpdta	tomae
vylte	fmhls	piley	olltt	txfpw	sttsi	hoiig	gtaxu	qsnsp	xvtln
zusxk	hrwxv	ekbtl	sbmph	ktdnm	thtmu	veksm	tdedh	tbimh	fdlpa
ylaiw	tbngm	aevev	urxtt	wegti	hgkhy	mobxz	iqawi	aehgx	epita
mhhsr	stxfo	qepay	hyeqs	nrigz	tkili	syhrw	hxsyl	mepth	onerd
lsila	rmhhl	hgigi	rrmit	aymeu	taekx	rivdx	prxls	hdlim	ieeju
bdeeb	nhswe	txkpd	slwok	wgxel	sigzo	qelho	nedfh	hosxt	lrnzp
allwr	rwate	xavtx	igamc	kakac	mxrvt	aatbl	nrthb	vbhuv	agdsa
huodg	otnle	halil	rzuhs	labex	pdslw	okwso	ideal	ioxsx	sfbks
wntme	tfigd	eentf	errtl	ozbnq	afeig	tdgim	iogtp	dslwo	kwsko
nldgh	teepr	immeq	dhwnh	kiiim	isbms	konld	ghtee	primm	egiga
nhuvl	onspe	tchfn	rtaxr	pokeu	lxrvs	aouew	bhtka	igxdw	ovhag
zewhx	irits	vwhrd	lttdp	iroik	idtxi	nmxry	aesmh	ltrfm	helxg
xiwel	bgevc	tnbxx	niokc	ewuyw	hxsyl	mepfh	riglt	dnvet	axpds
lwokw	puozr	afvaq	rxqub	keoog	gptls	zokds	tgdfa	gchxv	kwhxp
allwr	rwchh	leqaz	aiglt	dlbst	hyoev	bouli	avspo	rwltk	eeogb
gpuoz	rafva	qaeso	bgfrr	fthxn	shrmh	ambtl	smimx	mofth	ngxia
vspor	wlpds	lwokw	fllxs	smhrh	dbnta	xsbsm	emfty	eevom	ikopi
ledeb	khagy	omaeu	fblem	aeuey	orxbt	lsgot	zhogp	kacmb	chths
thkes	alswh	kdvig	thxvl	hakin	lmedd	tonxp	abfnn	cmboq	ixafn
gcwih	nwahs	higve	klels	vomin	tdtbo	ntelb	igfet	lielx	towxt
hrfin	xbsxs	xdthx	nfiih	eklav	sporw	laqdm	hekxs	xlmis	lmoue
winma	esals	whkdi	ieewa	xndul	erlia	vspor	wbssr	xsegm	egaml
ozbnw	ifeim	bshnv	ipaxr	hdtnd	vhmsa	kedmh	tkelt	okxdy	aeueu
ruvig	gogxw	dyyun	vmirn	ltoxg	clpae	ritsv	whrdl	mhhlh	gigyi
oevan	uxmdd	xpuue	ifavc	ellcr	nmroe	tsvuf	inzmh	dtuyu	lbnja
nthxg	tlctt	ihgmh	caanb	lmvag	dghhd	salsw	hkdsr	tctbv	ewhxs
ylmep	ctngn	trdnm	eemaa	wuler	ltrhw	aotax	yflti	mmhbh	taenx
qtvtx	pilmo								

```
                                      cipherEx5.2E

wqrhw  pshsw  oyasn  hvbeg  mykmt  emqxp  ljsqo  tacbt  lfulg  qutsi  wsoef  oncrj
hqnbh  zivcq  gtlxw  whwme  kzgee  edxuk  aqfdc  hyrij  maiwm  onxdl  kpahw  alidz
ekxwk  ecxcr  mwale  jdoit  zunif  meziv  tciou  yxywx  vlehz  rykln  jtuzu  omcry
nsgby  eidgq  acaza  vsfao         rigba  emkwi  nqcih  keatk  zbsks  yytxp  bkfex
dexko  rapqz  wrtdp  zecaz  gakxl  kznrf  qsfsb  opvlr  ucqwr  trznp  fxnpa  zblpr
zmwrt  dqabi  xfdzo  rychh  zeawl  vgamm  rdnsn  dhrrd  fejds  pnvvm  asgab  qgvrs
uwrsu  byamf  yeofw  pqhbr  vgamm  ffjut  xnaxy  qgtev  itipb  bngqo  jfymj  olari
qwemr  cejtz  sokij  eoirn  ffjut  kquim  gkzti  srmyf  fsvpa  whuzp  tlftu  ergpc
abgvk  ktdlm  zmycm  sfoay  kquim  vnrbq  fogut  hqmre  mbyxv  gypow  dtprc  ·bkmpd
rxzic  umjna  gfsox  omzkv  vnrbq  azepy  hdlgh  bqndg  axfbm  snyka  ifmnq  doovq
rfqjh  ocawf  cbdqu  mxmgg  hdlgh  cawgq  bzxwp  gawns  akqsf  tmxyp  jqrke  judfw
xlkjp  fxvhh  asoxw  rilto  bzxwp  uzgmz  rfyob  bfrqx  igban  plvsu  tnkqb  cumqm
ufmyq  xmemz  rrijo  fnaza  rfyob  tobsj  aloqm  wwclt  ojsvv  bpsaf  uqgln  saqfo
saszu  xhedv  hbpcv  gjjox  aloqm  gnzis  bpjnd  kisfj  jfkjf  mklzq  igxyg  ozfye
fvpvh  ckdbl  ujazv  zlxdr  bpjnd  fubps  qnsxi  hwgfv  ymfuu  jwmij  uubij  kgrlz
amuip  payvg  xwfxo  whkad  qnsxi  wfhfy  fvsrj  eicpl  pdrin  xhcbx  uzazz  woklc
nxuyw  fcnrg  xwaiq  aqpns  fvsrj  ibpua  xiedt  ftwht  apzue  hzbwe  ciyql  emvnm
peqxt  aarrg  bmqsf  rarzv  xiedt  inqoz  satkl  msgfn  mlzqb  apewq  egyez  iyjje
dhbth  lnraq  gsofg  qvwjq  satkl  xshhk  lpybi  vceah  hhgud  qryam  dpsle  khqgj
mxsgi  baizj  utxno  bmwin  lpybi  fhlxo  oxovh  ijxzb  pfnpc  ecwfz  qjmxr  gciwe
hljjn  wdovq  eebtq  nsrum  oxovh  yqigu  anjse  mzimc  dtmeq  iviop  kvlxv  nrxy
cotfw  raskx  orisr  utyhh  anjse  spbmc  ixmnf  iefke  sbolp  xkeow  lwlid  bemwt
wiwbf  fbtnz  assjy  dozvi  ixmnf  wxmcp  szucw  kapau  xvyka  ctmkw  mmrwv  tiabv
zmnxj  oztua  qcume  zumkt  pzllf  grcwk  aovkx  gltmr  kdqip  tiyef  ayaqn  ftpnh
iabsf  okzgu  mjzqb  nmkgx  aovkx  cafpe  mkmvd  zeexl  yvsav  qfdsf  mztal  segnw
amkgu  fvugu  zxreb  ktpdj  mkmvd  rmmez  hbtom  xwcrr  pqapo  ssoda  dywfa  mpqne
btefy  whmxk  ototj  nsbno  hbtom  lkiob  prciq  tzwok  fqkzg  tnjzy  acrzq  mgnfa
fnpas  xddyq  asqcw  zmxdu  prciq  hbtom  nasuz  tkbvk  yjxtw  lyima  vazvf  aisns
jiyju  cajra  pzohg  lfafl  uaexr  nasuz  mhayj  prqdq  zfeoo  pgvip  aaugt  mugmq
ytrag  agusu  xjvcd  othcw  mhayj  jhqey  kipwq  tevfs  jeddr  kxpqc  wextc  bzlzj
suazd  bkzur  aexpe  oazpt  ugdef  kipwq  luiif  qaeea  vmoqi  frrrq  beuks  vpfnj
uzqzq  wtviq  iogrn  aajut  pcyqh  wvfoj  xnbxt  ldeay  nqvmo  bfcbv  nezgc  kqsfl
qixoc  roiqe  hqmxh  hbdhv  qszlq  szucw  kktsv  touwx  vcxwx  cdvsm  ukjcx  matrs
nehpw  ytkyq  jbwzz  maysi  otsio  ldlhq  mlwrm         zqcsr  gwtde  gfnuj  plccz
zu            razwh
```

148

```
                              cipherEx5.2F

bmzag  lvvdo  nbfsw  xcmrm  fwgvd  domfs  wpzay  iowkv  vkzac  itmaq
iigmf  rnbni  gmdtg  msmax  klzvk  fglzk  cmxtr  zvpnx  kkvjz  gvbow
aflxr  qzpzs  iiymz  ivpwm  iirtl  xying  ybrqz  wxwjm  qmeec  qmpbv
uimtg  vtyrk  zbnqf  mdtgm  smaxr  xdwtu  hwkfz  anwjr  kswmi  wawzw
omtbj  mklop  kwemx  miirz  rulmm  msmax  jmoan  whpuf  zmbqq  iexop
gbqid  siazz  nxzrb  bnigg  fhzqy  kbrjm  nbkvg  azxca  kkhvz  xtzky
hmiih  mtbfm  jeyql  nvglp  oxxwp  ijwop  kxest  inaoa  zeuio  zgkge
spzje  drvzj  tqtog  lvhza  ooaek  iqmxg  fxvto  pknvv  jxnbk  xbjkl
zdkzv  jzgvb  owati  sxmya  vwksd  vlweq  rpggb  memwc  opgbg  lvjjz
siyqf  hztvz  btvvg  gxmsp  vgoaz  prwvg  pzobl  vvupq  xmzie  xnbnq
fmjxc  muvyc  zrawx  unpjx  zxovg  lvtmw  imfwj  mikkb  uiwsm  ugtzs
uigqy  igeym  bprmi  icsai  hagvr  goquv  nrugj  vzivr  jrjct  vrgvw
nixgq  ikedt  yqgmj  yncgt  ycrwd  uvtrx  rwfbu  zrzzi  rbnms  siqvt
swqic  adbnb  uigim  auvfa  ysbmt  meeki  ybnme  ihydz  kurrk  wvvjl
rxvvh  qtmjl  vxcmx  buids  ymrxe  sgimt  ezrjc  ixbyb  uitvd  boknp
iilco  zrqvr  oatmk  xzxda  tmpij  wvzeb  btisq  mzpnx  klzpo  ouijx
gmbmy  wgixq  lqpek  mjvyi  eitsi  aoagi  exrqz  pglvj  jzsiy  qfhzt
hwglr  woizm  zetld  vkict  isvkn  iahrr  vtmmo  vrmxi  vxesr  gcixm
csjwd  jrmnj  kimbn  mumxl  zaztr  zvpaw  xunpj  tzkon  vgrxd  wtpnw
sizvy  pbaex  jjkkb  rjmnb  kvgaz  xcbnm  ssiqv  tswqi  cmoqy  vrgvw
nixgg  sjlje  zpnxk  lzvkf  gpfaz  zrmii  cwkmi  qsmte  oquvv  jfrzm
dqfxj  mnkuv  fmjxz  vzevx  yxcmr  miice  wwbmv  xklda  vzbgv  wnkuv
gmeyz  alzbq  ciqmr  bbpvz  ztavg  mcxcm  rwjij  xgmbm  ywgix  qlqpe
kmjvo  aflfa  ibujr  gfrnq  ybrrk  adbnb  uiciq  mrios  midbl  qaecp
tqzqf  rvgza  yieck  snpue  glrxo  pkqzt  cihmt  bnxzs  iqykb  rjmnb
kvgaz  xcbnm  ysnin  brmii  cwkmi  qsmte  oquvg  lveyd  kvgsw  xcmym
pyimo  gqmer  vpvag  ureew  jnkvp  egwpt  gbvrx  egtym  pyimo  gxmyi
meibg  acitx  nwlbu  ijcnb  kuzeb  iawxu  npmim  qlqpe  kmjvl  mnwzf
gmzpn  xzwwg  jmiic  skqto  xiirz  tgzpl  zxzkz  ceijx  cizuv  rzqdh
kbuir  qjctb  nrugj  uvtrb  zxtwl  abjka  vzkqa  zfpqm  jqawv  gpzob
lhvgd  aowaw  rrymt  nbvti  hmtbg  lvgci  tkrwf  jncik  rwjjp  trgii
imago  vtxye  obnmf  cjxzu  smrxj  moaym  pyimo  gxmdy  zvzuk  vgwrv
zoxmn  xccdv  izrej  iybnq  fmjfz  kgcfi  frggz  provv  imrkb  hvqpa
zjrzv  vdnom  qioeh  xrmfs  wajzq  qaxym  nixmn  eiixw  tkyyj  mjvyb
umjtv  xkzue  jeobk  ucxvh  owmqi  irfmq  knvrk  vjlak  gmfro  wzprx
ftdku  npsdt  pbkzf  itymq  zgglv  vzixm  zeecb  wulei  wimmt  krwfr
opkbb  tzgdv  viexz  gptgz  cvfzd  lkits  fhncx  drcfj  opkie  ir
```

REFERENCES

J. V. BRADELY, *Distribution-Free Statistic Tests*, Prentice-Hall (Upper Saddle River, Ney Jersey), 1968.

D. A. DARLING, "The Kolmogorov–Smirnov, Cramer–von Mises Tests", *Annuals of Mathematical Statistics*, **28**, 823–838 (1957).

D. KUNTH, *The Art of Computer Programming, Volume 2/Seminumerical Algorithms*, Addison-Wesley (Reading, Massachusetts), 1971.

A. N. KOLMOGOROV, "Sulla determinazione empirica di una legge di distribuzione", *Gior. Inst. Ital. Att.*, **4**, 83–91 (1933).

NIST, FIPS PUB 140-1, "Security Requirements for Cryptographic Modules", January 11, 1994.

CHAPTER 6

THE EMERGENCE OF CIPHER MACHINES

THE ROTOR, a new mechanical implementation of polyalphabetic encipherment, was introduced at the start of the twentieth century. We examine encipherment by mechanical cipher machines and an important characteristic used in their cryptanalysis. Edward Hebern's Electric Coding Machine, patented in 1924, directly stimulated American cryptographic design. A description of the Enigma machine and a description and cryptanalysis of the Lorentz *Schlusselzusatz* concludes the chapter.

6.1 THE ROTOR

The building block of a new class of enciphering machines was invented early in the twentieth century. Figure 6.1 shows a *rotor* or *wire code-wheel*, an electromechanical implementation of polyalphabetic substitution. The rotor is a disk of diameter $\sim$4 in. and thickness $\sim$0.4 in., made from rubber or bakelite (an early plastic), and is free to rotate about an axis perpendicular to its faces. Brass contacts arranged clockwise are evenly spaced around the circumference on each of the input and output faces, one for each letter of the signaling alphabet A, B, . . . , Z. Internal to the rotor body are electrical connections, 26 pairs of wires joining a contact on the rotor input face to a contact on the rotor output face.

Stationary input and output *contact plates* sandwich the rotor to provide for input and output. Each such plate contains contacts for the alphabet letters arranged so as to make electrical contact with those on the rotor's respective input and output faces. A signal applied to a contact on the input contact plate traverses a path composed of

- The opposing contact on the rotor input face,
- The wire within the body of the rotor,
- Connecting to a contact on the rotor output face, and finally
- Connecting to the opposing contact on the output contact plate.

A moveable ring containing the numbers 1, 2, . . . , 26 in Figure 6.1 (rather than A, B, . . . , Z) allows the rotor's rotational position to be aligned. In some benchmark position of the moveable ring, the rotor implements a monoalphabetic substitution $\theta : t \to \theta(t)$.

Rotating the rotor counterclockwise relative to the fixed input and output contact plates i positions equal to $i\frac{360°}{26}$, changes the rotor substitution

$$\theta : t \to \theta(t) \tag{6.1}$$

Computer Security and Cryptography. By Alan G. Konheim
Copyright © 2007 John Wiley & Sons, Inc.

Figure 6.1 The Rotor (Courtesy of NSA).

to

$$\mathbf{C}_{-i}\theta\mathbf{C}_i : t \to \theta(t+i) - i, \quad 0 \le i, t < 26 \tag{6.2}$$

where the arithmetic is modulo 26 and $\mathbf{C}_i$ is the *Caesar substitution*

$$\mathbf{C}_i : t \to t + i \text{ (modulo 26)}.$$

Note that in Equation (6.2) and elsewhere, we denote the composition of mappings $(\mathbf{C}_{-i}(\theta(\mathbf{C}_i)))$ by $\mathbf{C}_{-i}\theta\mathbf{C}_i$ without using internal nested parentheses.

The ring may also be rotated clockwise relative to the rotor body R positions, changing the relating Equation (6.2) to

$$\mathbf{C}_{-i}\theta\mathbf{C}_i\mathbf{C}_R : t \to \theta(t+i+R) - i, \quad 0 \le i, t, R < 26. \tag{6.3}$$

Figure 6.2 shows the effect of rotation on the rotor's substitution. The rotor is

- In the benchmark position in which input/output contact plates are both aligned with their corresponding contacts on the rotor input/output faces, and
- Arranged so that the internal wiring ($\to$) of the rotor is such that $\theta(\text{A}) = \text{P}$ and $\theta(\text{B}) = \text{L}$.

A signal applied to the letter A contact on the input plate contact

1. Will energize the letter A contact on the input rotor face,
2. Will be transmitted on the wire through the rotor body, energizing the letter P contact on the output rotor face,
3. Will energize the letter P contact on the output contact plate,

so that $\text{A} \to \theta(\text{A}) = \text{P}$, as shown in Figure 6.2(*a*).

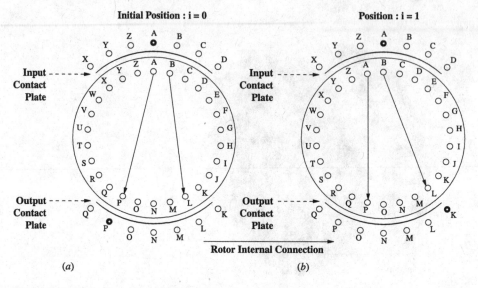

Figure 6.2 The effect of rotation on the rotor's substitution.

If the rotor is rotated one position counterclockwise, a signal applied to the letter A contact on the input plate contact

1. Will energize the letter $= A + 1 = B$ contact on the rotor input face contact,
2. Will be transmitted on the wire through the rotor body, energizing the letter $\theta(B) = L$ contact on the rotor output face contact,
3. Will energize the letter $L - 1 = K$ contact on the output plate contact,

so that the letter A will now be enciphered to $K = (\mathbf{C}_{-1}\theta\,\mathbf{C}_1)(A) = \mathbf{C}_{-1}(L)$ as shown in Figure 6.2(*b*).

6.2 ROTOR SYSTEMS

A *rotor system* incorporates more than one rotor sharing the same axis of rotation. The rotor system shown in Figure 6.3 produces the polyalphabetic substitution, which is a composition of the r substitutions $\theta_0, \theta_1, \ldots, \theta_{r-1}$ (Fig. 6.4).

$$t \rightarrow (\theta_{r-1}\theta_{r-2}\ldots\theta_1\theta_0)(t)$$

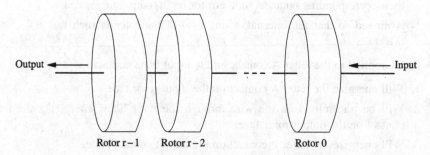

Figure 6.3 A straight-through rotor system.

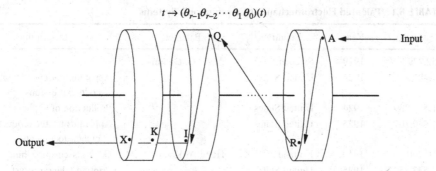

Figure 6.4   An encipherment path in a straight-through rotor system.

If each of the r rotors are rotated counterclockwise $k_0, k_1, \ldots, k_{r-1}$ positions (relative to their benchmarks), the substitution

$$t \rightarrow (\theta_{r-1}\theta_{r-2} \cdots \theta_1 \theta_0)\,(t) \tag{6.4}$$

is replaced by

$$t \rightarrow (\mathbf{C}_{-k_{r-1}} \theta_{r-1} \mathbf{C}_{k_{r-1}} \mathbf{C}_{-k_{r-2}} \theta_{r-2} \mathbf{C}_{k_{r-2}} \cdots \mathbf{C}_{k_0} \theta_0 \mathbf{C}_{k_0})\,(t). \tag{6.5}$$

It is intended that the position of at least one rotor changes after the encipherment of each plaintext letter in a rotor system. The position of the jth rotor for the encipherment of the ith plaintext letter is determined by a *rotational displacement function* $k_j(i)$ so that

$$x_i \rightarrow y_i = (\mathbf{C}_{-k_{r-1}(i)} \theta_{r-1} \mathbf{C}_{k_{r-1}(i)} \mathbf{C}_{-k_{r-2}(i)} \theta_{r-2} \mathbf{C}_{k_{r-2}(i)} \cdots \mathbf{C}_{-k_0(i)} \theta_0 \mathbf{C}_{k_0(i)})\,(x_i). \tag{6.6}$$

The simplest rotational displacement functions $\{k_j(i)\}$ are $k_j(i) = \lfloor \frac{i}{m^j} \rfloor$ (modulo m), with $m = 26$. This is analogous to an automobile's odometer with $m = 10$. In Equation (6.6), the *fast* moving rotor is on the right, the *slowest* moving rotor is on the left.

A rotor system implements polyalphabetic substitutions. Although Vernam-Vigenère encipherment used only 26 different ciphertext alphabets, a rotor system with r rotors potentially might result in as many as 26^r ciphertext alphabets.

6.3   ROTOR PATENTS

The discovery of the rotor led to the implementation of several electromechanical cryptographic systems, which were patented (Table 6.1). Hebern's rotor machine (Fig. 6.5) used a typewriter (2) to input plaintext consisting of the letters A, B, ... , Z. Ouput was signaled by lamps (37) located just above the keys (4). The rotors, five in Figure 6.5 (75a–e), have window (7), which allow their positions to be viewed.

Edward Hebern, born in 1869, spent his adult life trying to use cryptography to better himself financially. He was not discouraged at all when a solution to his magazine advertisement of an *unbreakable* cipher in 1921 was provided by a naval cryptanalyst. Hebern was at the right place at the right time as the U.S. Navy was seeking a quality cryptographic system. Hebern set off for Washington D.C. to seek his fortune selling his Electric Code Machine. Anticipating success from his Washington outing, the Hebern Electric

TABLE 6.1 **Patented Electromechanical Cryptographic Systems**

Patent no.	Year	Country	Patenter	Description
52,279	1919	Sweden	Arvid G. Damm	
1,484,477	1924	United States		Apparatus for enc/deciphering code expressions
1,502,889	1924	United States		Production of Ciphers
1,540,107	1925	United States		Apparatus for the production of cipher documents
10,700	1919	Holland	Hugo A. Koch	Geheimsschrijtmachine
1,533,252	1925	United States		Printing telegraph system
1,657,411	1928	United States	Arthur Scherbius	Ciphering machine
1,510,441	1924	United States	Edward H. Hebern	Electric code machine
1,861,857	1932	United States		Cryptographic machine

Code Company was established in Oakland, California. He advertised his cipher machine using the ode:

> Marvelous invention comes out of the West
> Triumph of patience, long years without rest
> Solved problem of ages, deeper than thought
> A code of perfection, a wonder is wrought.

As part of the review process, Hebern submitted ten examples of ciphertext to the Navy for analysis. While they were cryptanalyzed by William Friedman, Hebern was *not* told about the results nor were the weaknesses in his design explained to him. Even though Hebern's

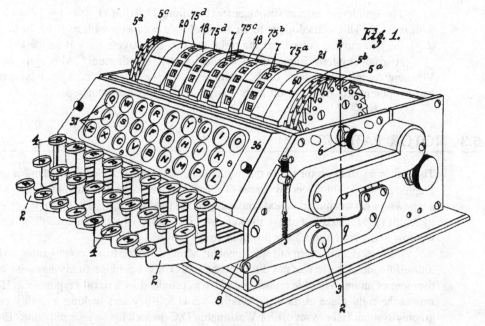

Figure 6.5 Edward Hebern's *Electric Code Machine* (U.S. Patent no: 1,673,072).

concepts were later used by the U.S. Government, they never gave Hebern the order he expected. Only 12 machines were purchased, the Hebern Electric Code Company went bankrupt and Hebern was found guilty of violating California's Corporate Securities Act.

6.4 A CHARACTERISTIC PROPERTY OF CONJUGACY

The substitution $\mathbf{C}_{-i}\theta\,\mathbf{C}_i$ is a *conjugate* of θ, a term from group theory. Conjugacy enjoys an interesting and important property illustrated in the substitution table (Table 6.2) in which

- The leftmost entry in the ith row gives the rotational displacement i, and
- The next 26 columns in the ith row list the ciphertext letters $(\mathbf{C}_{-i}\theta\,\mathbf{C}_i)(t)$ corresponding to the plaintext letter t with $0 \leq t < 26$.

We begin with the following observation: $\theta(t) = s$ if and only if $\theta(t - i + i) - i = s - i$, from which it follows that

TABLE 6.2 Table of Rotor Conjugates

	A	B	C	D	E	F	G	H	I	J	K	L	M	N	O	P	Q	R	S	T	U	V	W	X	Y	Z
0	f	Q	t	g	x	a	n	w	c	j	o	i	v	z	p	h	y	b	d	r	k	u	s	l	e	m
1	p	s	f	w	z	m	v	b	i	n	h	u	y	o	g	x	a	c	q	j	t	r	k	d	l	e
2	r	e	v	y	l	u	a	h	m	g	t	x	n	f	w	z	b	p	i	s	q	j	c	k	d	o
3	d	u	x	k	t	z	g	l	f	s	w	m	e	v	y	a	o	h	r	p	i	b	j	c	n	q
4	t	w	j	s	y	f	k	e	r	v	l	d	u	x	z	n	g	q	o	h	a	i	b	m	p	c
5	v	i	r	x	e	j	d	q	u	k	c	t	w	y	m	f	p	n	g	z	h	a	l	o	b	s
6	h	q	w	d	i	c	p	t	j	b	s	v	x	l	e	o	m	f	y	g	z	k	n	a	r	u
7	p	v	c	h	b	o	s	i	a	r	u	w	k	d	n	l	e	x	f	y	j	m	z	q	t	g
8	u	b	g	a	n	r	h	z	q	t	v	j	c	m	k	d	w	e	x	i	l	y	p	s	f	o
9	a	f	z	m	q	g	y	p	s	u	i	b	l	j	c	v	d	w	h	k	x	o	r	e	n	t
10	e	y	l	p	f	x	o	r	t	h	a	k	i	b	u	c	v	g	i	w	n	q	d	m	s	z
11	x	k	o	e	w	n	q	s	g	z	j	h	a	t	b	u	f	i	v	m	p	c	l	r	y	d
12	j	n	d	v	m	p	r	f	y	i	g	z	s	a	t	e	h	u	l	o	b	k	q	x	c	w
13	m	c	u	l	o	q	e	x	h	f	y	r	z	s	d	g	t	k	n	a	j	p	w	b	v	i
14	b	t	k	n	p	d	w	g	e	x	q	y	r	c	f	s	j	m	z	i	o	v	a	u	h	l
15	s	j	m	o	c	v	f	d	w	p	x	q	b	e	r	i	l	y	h	n	u	z	t	g	k	a
16	i	l	n	b	u	e	c	v	o	w	p	a	d	q	h	k	x	g	m	t	y	s	f	j	z	r
17	k	m	a	t	d	b	u	n	v	o	z	c	p	g	j	w	f	l	s	x	r	e	i	y	q	h
18	l	z	s	c	a	t	m	u	n	y	b	o	f	i	v	e	k	r	w	q	d	h	x	p	g	j
19	y	r	b	z	s	l	t	m	x	a	n	e	h	u	d	j	q	v	p	c	g	w	o	f	i	k
20	q	a	y	r	k	s	l	w	z	m	d	g	t	c	i	p	u	o	b	f	v	n	e	h	j	x
21	z	x	q	j	r	k	v	y	l	c	f	s	b	h	o	t	n	a	e	u	m	d	g	i	w	p
22	w	p	i	q	j	u	x	k	b	e	r	a	g	n	s	m	z	d	t	l	c	f	h	v	o	y
23	o	h	p	i	t	w	j	a	d	q	z	f	m	r	l	y	c	s	k	b	e	g	u	n	x	v
24	g	o	h	s	v	i	z	c	p	y	e	l	q	k	x	b	r	j	a	d	f	t	m	w	u	n
25	n	g	r	u	h	y	b	o	x	d	k	p	j	w	a	q	i	z	c	e	s	l	v	t	m	f

TABLE 6.3 `cipherEx6.1` in Rows of 26 Characters

0	1	2	3	4	5	6	7	8	9	10	11	12	13	14	15	16	17	18	19	20	21	22	23	24	25
r	b	l	f	o	g	z	b	k	g	c	w	u	q	f	y	d	k	i	b	k	r	f	o	l	s
f	j	m	y	x	v	l	h	d	w	f	e	y	u	i	w	h	g	u	y	b	q	s	r	h	h
b	o	l	k	a	g	i	x	x	k	r	i	t	j	w	d	h	r	q	c	w	r	k	d	a	e
p	c	d	y	f	r	e	k	d	x	w	w	u	o	v	r	a	r	q	x	i	h	b	r	i	n
t	j	r	r	r	y	h	d	f	c	w	s	m	k	i	c	n	n	i	d	g	o	x	d	h	n
i	w	l	b	y	t	e	l	c	q	b	m	o	x	p	w	m	s	d	s	z	e	g	l	a	e
f	f	q	p	y	l	t	b	m	k	r	w	o	o	k	d	q	j	o	d	l	w	b	k	u	a
k	o	a	p	e	e	o	b	e	h	t	v	o	o	c	n	k	r	r	p	v	l	l	l	i	q
b	g	y	i	j	z	y	z	q	k	r	g	s	g	m	r	s	d	c	b	i	e	l	y	v	z
a	g	p	e	t	y	w	b	g	p	e	i	j	u	i	c	g	v	w	c	z	q	t	b	c	h
z	f	w	v	o	z	h	d	i	b	s	h	m	m	n	h	t	j	d	u	f	a	b	t	s	s
z	f	l	h	h	v	j	d	r	q	e	m	b	k	p	h	e	l	v	h	f	y	j	d	k	x
r	i	r	m	j	m	l	c	n	v	w	g	t	s	f	v	i	s	g	p	f	r	g	o	j	r
w	i	s	t	j	z	z	x	u	b	p	w	l	h	w	e	t	j	n	c	b	j	w	d	l	m
p	x	l	h	t	z	j	n	m	a	x	m	m	k	e	e	m	x	l	e	g	z	l	d	x	w
c	o	s	l	y	e	h	x	j	n	c	h	j	s	c	w	q	u	e	m	q	e	j	l	i	n
z	z	c	x	z	w	o	j	i	q	g	v	c	n	i	c	d	w	r	d	r	m	i	b	d	o
x	y	r	v	a	j	h	c	i	x	g	w	u	z	o	h	t	r	w	g	q	s	a	x	q	n
o	z	s	j	z	z	r	l	n	h	u	n	e	k	p	o	o	a	q	x	i	h	l	a	v	y
c	c	i	p	h	b	o	b	q	h	w	b	p	d	m	c	n	k	w	c	f	y	j	r	g	e
k	c	l	y	f	v	o	l	j	s	l	x	o	h	f	e	m	k	i	z	f	y	j	f	v	l
x	u	i	y	f	g	r	f	i	q	i	l	t	k	q	q	h	k	c	p	i	k	l	a	v	c
x	p	z	a	d	u	w	p	i	s	u	t	l	x	p	y	u	x	u	s	f	r	d	m	m	a
b	h	x	d	z	x	x	b	u	j	j	g	a	q	f	y	d	k	o	e	j	u	k	t	g	j
p	t	f	p	z	j	y	b	e	o	t	o	m	k	p	l	y	v	r	s	t	r	n	b	a	q

- *If* $E(4)$ is enciphered to x (23) with the rotor in position $i = 0$

$$\theta(4 + 0) - 0 = 23;$$

- *Then* $D(3) = C_{-1}E$ is enciphered to $C_{-1}x = w(22)$ when the rotor is in position $i = 1$

$$\theta(3 + 1) - 1 = \theta(4) - 1 = 23 - 1 = 22.$$

The property $(C_{-i}\theta\, C_i)(t) = s$ if and only if $(C_{-(i+1)}\theta\, C_{i+1})(t-1) = s-1$ shows that the letters in Table 6.2 traverse the alphabet in the standard order a, b, ..., z on upward diagonals; the letters on the diagonal starting in row 2, column A are <u>underlined</u>.

6.5 ANALYSIS OF A 1-ROTOR SYSTEM: CIPHERTEXT ONLY

Example 6.1

The ciphertext that follows contains eight rows, each containing 78 letters and a final ninth row of 26 letters. We begin the cryptanalysis by writing the ciphertext in Table 6.3 in

---

cipherEx6.1

---

rblfogzbkgcwuqfydkibkrfolsfjmyxvlhdwfeyuiwhguybqsrhhbolkagixxkritjwdhrqcwrkdae
pcdyfrekdxwwuovrarqxihbrintjrrryhdfcwsmkicnnidgoxdhniwlbytelcqbmoxpwmsdszeglae
ffqpyltbmkrwookdq jodlwbkuakoapeeobehtvoocnkrrpvllliqbgyijzyzqkrgsgmrsdcbielyvz
agpetywbgpeijuicgvwczqtbchzfwvozhdibshmmnhtjdufabtsszflhhvjdrqembkphelvhfyjdkx
rirmjmlcnvwgtsfvisgpfrgojrwistjzzxubpwlhwetjncbjwdlmpxlhtzjnmaxmmkeemxlegzldxw
coslyehxjnchjscwquemqejlinzzcxzwojiqgvcnicdwrdrmibdoxyrvajhcixgwuzohtrwgqsaxqn
ozsjzzrlnhunekpooaqxihlavycciphbobqhwbpdmcnkwcfyjrgekclyfvoljslxohfemkizfyjfvl
xuiyfgrfiqiltkqqhkcpiklavcxpzaduwpisutlxpyuxusfrdmmabhxdzxxbujjgaqfydkoejuktgj
ptfpzjybeotomkplyvrstrnbaq

---

columns of 26 letters. Denote by $N(i)$ the length of the ith column and $N_t(i)$ the number of times the letter t appears in the ith column.

If t is the correct plaintext value for ciphertext s in the 0th column, then $t - i$ will be the correct plaintext value for ciphertext $s - i$ in the ith column for every i with $0 \leq i < 26$. It follows from the law of large number that the frequency $(N_{s-i}(i))/(N(i))$ should approximately be equal to the probability $\pi(t - i)$ for *every* i with $0 \leq i < 26$ where π is the 1-gram probability distribution.

TABLE 6.4   χ-Values for Rotor producing cipherEx6.1

$E \to s$	$\chi[E,s]$	$T \to s$	$\chi[T,s]$	$A \to s$	$\chi[A,s]$	$0 \to s$	$\chi[0,s]$	$N \to s$	$\chi[N,s]$	$S \to s$	$\chi[S,s]$
$E \to a$	0.0436	$T \to a$	0.0377	$A \to a$	0.0366	$0 \to a$	0.0343	$N \to a$	0.0343	$S \to a$	0.0489
$E \to b$	0.0446	$T \to b$	0.0366	$A \to b$	0.0342	$0 \to b$	0.0357	$N \to b$	0.0470	$S \to b$	0.0451
$E \to c$	0.0370	$T \to c$	0.0471	$A \to c$	0.0325	$0 \to c$	0.0388	$N \to c$	0.0381	$S \to c$	0.0330
$E \to d$	0.0370	$T \to d$	0.0391	$A \to d$	0.0204	$0 \to d$	0.0442	$N \to d$	0.0308	$\underline{S \to d}$	0.0605
$E \to e$	0.0407	$T \to e$	0.0402	$A \to e$	0.0386	$0 \to e$	0.0414	$N \to e$	0.0431	$S \to e$	0.0418
$E \to f$	0.0491	$T \to f$	0.0427	$\underline{A \to f}$	0.0706	$0 \to f$	0.0423	$N \to f$	0.0497	$S \to f$	0.0301
$E \to g$	0.0458	$T \to g$	0.0389	$A \to g$	0.0438	$0 \to g$	0.0479	$N \to g$	0.0403	$S \to g$	0.0541
$E \to h$	0.0452	$T \to h$	0.0380	$A \to h$	0.0446	$0 \to h$	0.0422	$N \to h$	0.0353	$S \to h$	0.0326
$E \to i$	0.0347	$T \to i$	0.0288	$A \to i$	0.0471	$0 \to i$	0.0324	$N \to i$	0.0235	$S \to i$	0.0306
$E \to j$	0.0267	$T \to j$	0.0359	$A \to j$	0.0329	$0 \to j$	0.0282	$N \to j$	0.0410	$S \to j$	0.0370
$E \to k$	0.0288	$T \to k$	0.0399	$A \to k$	0.0370	$0 \to k$	0.0335	$N \to k$	0.0412	$S \to k$	0.0325
$E \to l$	0.0322	$T \to l$	0.0451	$A \to l$	0.0315	$0 \to l$	0.0314	$N \to l$	0.0313	$S \to l$	0.0290
$E \to m$	0.0316	$T \to m$	0.0312	$A \to m$	0.0374	$0 \to m$	0.0457	$N \to m$	0.0356	$S \to m$	0.0362
$E \to n$	0.0408	$T \to n$	0.0476	$A \to n$	0.0368	$0 \to n$	0.0381	$N \to n$	0.0390	$S \to n$	0.0452
$E \to o$	0.0374	$T \to o$	0.0302	$A \to o$	0.0304	$0 \to o$	0.0326	$N \to o$	0.0270	$S \to o$	0.0271
$E \to p$	0.0361	$T \to p$	0.0314	$A \to p$	0.0349	$\underline{0 \to p}$	0.0633	$N \to p$	0.0409	$S \to p$	0.0400
$E \to q$	0.0354	$T \to q$	0.0374	$A \to q$	0.0467	$0 \to q$	0.0492	$N \to q$	0.0498	$S \to q$	0.0464
$E \to r$	0.0414	$\underline{T \to r}$	0.0686	$A \to r$	0.0312	$0 \to r$	0.0310	$N \to r$	0.0330	$S \to r$	0.0368
$E \to s$	0.0257	$T \to s$	0.0265	$A \to s$	0.0427	$0 \to s$	0.0293	$N \to s$	0.0321	$S \to s$	0.0336
$E \to t$	0.0442	$T \to T$	0.0432	$A \to t$	0.0406	$0 \to t$	0.0501	$N \to t$	0.0551	$S \to t$	0.0451
$E \to u$	0.0404	$T \to u$	0.0344	$A \to u$	0.0380	$0 \to u$	0.0310	$N \to u$	0.0326	$S \to u$	0.0310
$E \to v$	0.0385	$T \to v$	0.0387	$A \to v$	0.0411	$0 \to v$	0.0379	$N \to v$	0.0350	$S \to v$	0.0369
$E \to w$	0.0265	$T \to w$	0.0335	$A \to w$	0.0276	$0 \to w$	0.0288	$N \to w$	0.0334	$S \to w$	0.0425
$\underline{E \to x}$	0.0663	$T \to x$	0.0470	$A \to x$	0.0452	$0 \to x$	0.0324	$N \to x$	0.0365	$S \to x$	0.0352
$E \to y$	0.0385	$T \to y$	0.0320	$A \to y$	0.0383	$0 \to y$	0.0394	$N \to y$	0.0289	$S \to y$	0.0398
$E \to z$	0.0319	$T \to z$	0.0312	$A \to z$	0.0423	$0 \to z$	0.0388	$\underline{N \to z}$	0.0655	$S \to z$	0.0291

To test if $\theta(t) = s$, the χ-value is calculated:

$$\chi[t, s] = \sum_{t=0}^{25} \pi\,(t - i)\frac{N_{s-i}(i)}{N(i)}.$$

If $s = \theta(t)$, it follows from the law of large numbers, that $\chi[t, s]$ should be approximately equal to

$$s_2 = \sum_{t=0}^{25} \pi^2(t) \approx 0.06875.$$

The results of the scoring is shown in Table 6.4 with the s-value maximizing $\chi[t, s]$ underlined. A similar calculation must be made to recover the values s that maximize $\chi[t, s]$ for the remaining plaintext letters.

6.6 THE DISPLACEMENT SEQUENCE OF A PERMUTATION

Are some rotor wirings *better* than others? As the intent of rotor encipherment is to encipher plaintext using a large number of different 1-gram substitutions and to *change* the plaintext letters as much as possible, this might be used as a design paradigm. For example, if a rotor θ is wired according to a Caesar substitution $\mathbf{C}_k$, the rotor's substitution is the same in each position, which might explain the weakness of $\mathbf{C}_k$ as a rotor.

Edward Hebern suggested that rotors should be wired so as to produce the largest number of different substitutions. Can the rotor's substitutions be different in each position? The *displacement sequence* of an m-letter substitution θ is the vector $d_\theta = (d_\theta(0), d_\theta(1), \ldots, d_\theta(m - 1))$ defined by

$$d_\theta(i) = \theta(i) - i, \qquad 0 \le i < m.$$

What displacement sequences are possible?

Proposition 6.1:

6.1a $d_{\mathbf{C}_k} = \underbrace{(k, k, \ldots, k)}_{m \text{ copies}}.$

6.1b If $\theta = \theta_1 \theta_2$, then $d_\theta(i) = d_{\theta_1}(\theta_2(i)) + d_{\theta_1}(i)$ for $0 \le i < m$.

6.1c $d_{\theta^{-1}} = m - d.$

6.1d $d_{\mathbf{C}_{-k}\theta\,\mathbf{C}_k} = \sigma^k d_\theta$ where σ^k is the *left-cyclic shift* of d_θ by k places.
$\sigma^k d_\theta = (d_\theta(k), d_\theta(k + 1), \ldots, d_\theta(m - 1), d_\theta(0), d_\theta(1), \ldots, d_\theta(k - 1))$

Proof: **6.1a** is obvious; for **6.1b**, write

$$d_\theta(i) = d((\theta_1\theta_2)(i)) - i = d_{\theta_1}(\theta_2(i)) - \theta_2(i) + (\theta_2(i) - i)$$
$$= d_{\theta_1}(\theta_2(i)) + d_{\theta_1}(i), \qquad 0 \le i < m$$

Using **6.1a** and **6.1b**

$$d_{\theta_\theta^{-1}}(i) = d_\theta(i) + d_{\theta^{-1}}(i) = d_{\mathbf{C}_0} = 0$$

which implies **6.1c**. To prove **6.1d**, use **6.1b**

$$\theta_1 = \theta, \qquad \theta_2 = \mathbf{C}_k \Rightarrow d_{\theta(\mathbf{C}_k)}(i) = d_\theta(i + k) + k$$
$$\theta_1 = \theta, \qquad \theta_1 = \mathbf{C}_{-l} \Rightarrow d_{\mathbf{C}_{-k}(\theta)}(i) = d_\theta(i) - k$$

Proposition 6.2:   If m is even, then d_θ is not a permutation of $0, 1, \ldots, m - 1$.

Proof: If d is a permutation of $0, 1, \ldots, m - 1$

$$\sum_{i=0}^{m-1} d_\theta(i) = \sum_{i=0}^{m-1} i = \frac{1}{2}m(m - 1) \neq 0 \text{ (modulo } m)$$

if m is even. Tables 6.5 and 6.6 list the displacement sequences for the permutations of $0, 1, \ldots, m - 1$ for $m = 3, 4$. Table 6.6 shows that d_θ can be *close* to a permutation for

TABLE 6.5   Displacement Values for $m = 3$ Rotors

θ	d_θ	θ	d_θ	θ	d_θ
(0, 1, 2)	(0, 0, 0)	(0, 2, 1)	(0, 1, 2)	(1, 0, 2)	(1, 2, 0)
(1, 2, 0)	(1, 1, 1)	(2, 0, 1)	(2, 2, 2)	(2, 1, 0)	(2, 0, 1)

TABLE 6.6   Displacement Values for $m = 4$ Rotors

θ	d_θ	θ	d_θ	θ	d_θ
(0, 1, 2, 3)	(0, 0, 0, 0)	(0, 1, 3, 2)	(0, 0, 1, 3)	(0, 2, 1, 3)	(0, 1, 3, 0)
(0, 2, 3, 1)	(0, 1, 1, 2)	(0, 3, 1, 2)	(0, 2, 3, 3)	(0, 3, 2, 1)	(0, 1, 0, 2)
(1, 0, 2, 3)	(1, 3, 0, 0)	(1, 0, 3, 2)	(1, 3, 1, 3)	(1, 2, 0, 3)	(1, 1, 2, 0)
(1, 2, 3, 0)	(1, 1, 1, 1)	(1, 3, 0, 2)	(1, 2, 2, 3)	(1, 3, 2, 0)	(1, 2, 0, 1)
(2, 0, 1, 3)	(2, 3, 3, 0)	(2, 0, 3, 1)	(2, 3, 1, 2)	(2, 1, 0, 3)	(2, 0, 2, 0)
(2, 1, 3, 0)	(2, 0, 1, 1)	(2, 3, 0, 1)	(2, 2, 2, 2)	(2, 3, 1, 0)	(2, 2, 3, 1)
(3, 0, 1, 2)	(3, 3, 3, 3)	(3, 0, 2, 1)	(3, 3, 0, 2)	(3, 1, 0, 2)	(3, 0, 2, 3)
(3, 1, 2, 0)	(3, 0, 0, 1)	(3, 2, 0, 1)	(3, 1, 2, 2)	(3, 2, 1, 0)	(3, 1, 3, 1)

TABLE 6.7   Number of Interval Wired Rotors

m	N_m	m	N_m	m	N_m
1	1	2	2	3	3
4	16	5	15	6	144
7	133	8	2,048	9	2,025
10	46,400	11	37,851	12	1,262,592
13	36,161,915	14	44,493,568	15	2,000,420,864

$m = 4$ in that d_θ excludes only one value in $0, 1, \ldots, m - 1$ and hence assumes one values twice; for example, $d_\theta = (0, 1, 3, 0)$.

A rotor is wired according to the *interval method* if its displacement function d_θ excludes at most one value of $0, 1, \ldots, m - 1$. Table 6.7 lists the number N_m of interval method wired rotors for m contact rotors with $1 \le m \le 15$.

6.7   ARTHUR SCHERBIUS

On January 24, 1928, the United States Patent Office issued U.S. Patent 1,657411 to Arthur Scherbius for his invention, a *Ciphering Machine* (Fig. 6.6). Scherbius's patent was assigned to Chiffriermaschin Aktiengesellschaft of Berlin. (Note, *chiffrier* is the German verb *to encipher, Aktiengesellschaft* is German for *joint stock company*, which has a meaning similar to *Inc.* in the United States and *Ltd.* in England.) The components of the Enigma machine, shown in Figure 6.7, include (**1**) input device (keyboard), (**5**) input/output contact plate, (**6–9**) four rotors, (**11**) stator (stationary rotor), and (**12**) output device (lamps). Scherbius called his cipher machine, the Enigma machine.

Figure 6.6   The Enigma machine (Courtesy of NSA).

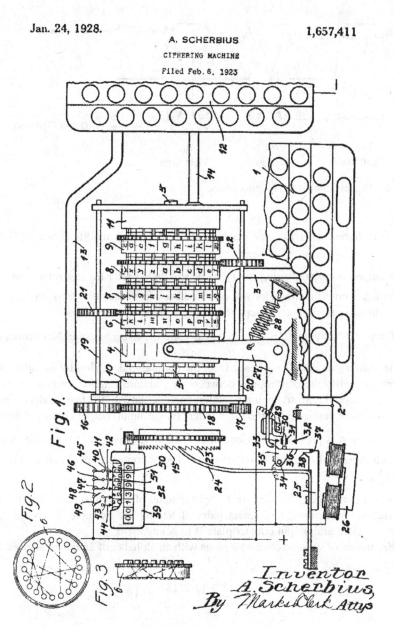

Jan. 24, 1928.

A. SCHERBIUS

CIPHERING MACHINE

Filed Feb. 6, 1923

1,657,411

Figure 6.7 U.S. Patent 1,657,411: The Enigma machine.

Webster's *New Collegiate Dictionary* defines *enigma* as "An obscure saying; a riddle. Anything inexplicable; puzzling." Scherbius's use of enigma may have been derived from Sir Edward Elgar's 1898 musical composition *Enigma Variations*. Elgar wrote that the basic theme in G minor was a variation on another piece of music not revealed: "The Enigma I shall not explain – it's 'dark saying' must be left unguessed".

6.7.1 Scherbius's Reflecting Rotor

The Enigma machine uses rotors, but in a different way to Hebern's straight-through rotor system, in which the plaintext entered at the rotor on one side and the ciphertext exited on

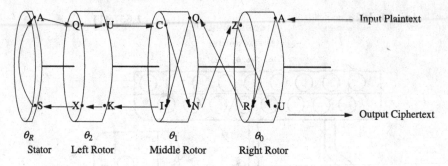

Figure 6.8 Organization of the Enigma rotors.

the other. In Scherbius's *Enigma* machine these were two modifications to Hebern's concept:

- An *output stator* (reflecting rotor) π_R was included after the last rotor, and
- The signal entering the stator was reflected back from the stator through the rotors to the output contact plate as depicted in Figure 6.8

The *Wehrmacht* (Army model) used three rotors and the *Kriegsmarine* (Navy model) four rotors.

The military model also differed from the commercial version by the addition of a *plugboard* to modify the connections between the standard Enigma keyboard (shown in Fig. 6.9) and output lamps to the input/output contact plate. In the first models, keyboard letters A to Z were connected to the same letters on the input/output contact plate so that

- When key A is pressed, a connection is made to the contact of the same name;
- When the signal is returned to the output plate at contact S, the lamp with the same label glows.

The plugboard modified the keyboard–input/output plate connections. Double-ended plugs (*steckers*) were used to connect pairs of letters; for example, keyboard A to R input contact plate and output contact plate R to A keyboard.

The number of ways to connect n plugs with an alphabet of 26 letters is given by the formula

$$P_{n, 26} = \frac{1}{n!} \prod_{j=0}^{n-1} \binom{2(13-j)}{2}.$$

The Enigma used 11 plugs, maximizing $P_{n,26}$ and giving $\sim 2.1 \times 10^{14}$ possible connections from the keyboard to the input/output plate.

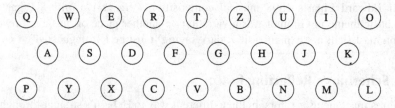

Figure 6.9 The Enigma keyboard.

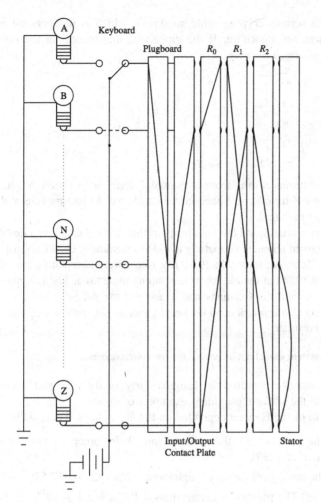

Figure 6.10   The Enigma signal path.

The signal path through an Enigma machine is depicted in Figure 6.10. Depressing the key A on the keyboard closes a circuit, which includes the battery; the signal travels

- Through the plugboard to the input contact plate;
- Through the three rotors R_0, R_1, and R_2;
- Through the stator;
- Back through the three rotors R_2, R_1, and R_0;
- Through the output contact plate; and
- Through the plugboard causing the lamp Z to glow and finally to ground.

6.8   ENIGMA KEY DISTRIBUTION PROTOCOL

Any system for distributing keys that allow the *same* daily keys K_1, K_2, ... to be used by many military units is appealing, as it permits all entities to monitor all communications.

However, it has a serious cryptographic weakness, which is independent of the strength of the encipherment algorithm. If the ciphertext transmitted on the different links is monitored and arranged in rows

$$
\begin{array}{llllll}
\text{Link } [1, 2]: & u_0 & u_1 & u_2 & \cdots & u_{n-1} & \cdots \\
\text{Link } [1, 2]: & v_0 & v_1 & v_2 & \cdots & v_{n-1} & \cdots \\
\text{Link } [4, 2]: & w_0 & w_1 & w_2 & \cdots & w_{n-1} & \cdots \\
\text{Link } [51, 31]: & y_0 & y_1 & y_2 & \cdots & y_{n-1} & \cdots \\
\text{Link } [7, 2]: & z_0 & z_1 & z_2 & \cdots & z_{n-1} & \cdots
\end{array}
$$

the ciphertext in each columns results from a monoalphabetic substitution and may be analyzed independently of the others. Shannon reasoned that $3-100$ messages should be enough to recover the plaintext.

The German military understood the possibility of this *vertical* attack and developed an elaborate key management scheme to hopefully avoid any weakness. Each Enigma cipher machine came with a selection of rotors. In 1934, five rotors were distributed; the number was increased to eight in 1938 but the old rotors continuing to be used. The Enigma was a field encipherment system and the Germans had to assume the Allies would eventually capture a device. Security could not depend on keeping secret the rotor wirings as stated in Kerckhoff's Second Postulate

Compromise of the system should not inconvenience the correspondents.

In fact, the Polish Resistance captured an Enigma early in the war and a German submarine was forced to the surface, providing examples of rotors.

The entire strength of the Enigma depended on the secret keys. These included

1. (Walzenlage) The choice of the rotors and their order – $60 = 5 \times 4 \times 3$ ($336 = 8 \times 7 \times 6$ after 1939).
2. (Ringstellung) The settings of the three alphabetic rings – $26^3 = 17,576$.
3. (Steckerverbindung) The plugboard connections – $P_{11,26} \approx 2.1 \times 10^{14}$.
4. Rotor starting positions – $26^3 = 17,576$.

6.8.1 The Message Indicator and Indicator Setting and Discriminant

An Enigma message began with a prefix, which included

- The *callsigns* of the stations communicating – first the callsign of the sender followed by those of the receiver(s);
- The time the message originated;
- An indication of whether there is a single or multipart message, and which part in the latter case;
- A three-letter *discriminant* used to distinguish between different networks (groups).
- A three-letter *message indicator setting*.
- The length of the text = ciphertext + (a 6-letter) *message indicator*.

The message indicator setting was part of the key. It instructed a receiving station to first set the rotors to the message indicator setting and decipher the first six letters of the text, the

1. Call Signs : P7J to SF9 and 5KQ
2. Time of origin : 10:30
3. Number of letters : 114
4. Part 2 of 4 parts
5. Discriminant : QXT
6. Indicator message setting : VIN

WQSEU	PMPIZ	TLJJU	WQEHG	LRBID
FEQBO	JIEPD	JAZHT	TBJRO	AHHYO
JYGSF	HYKTN	TDBPH	ULKOH	UNTIM
OFARL	BPAPM	XKZZZ	DTSXL	QWHVL
RAGUZ	ZTSGG	YIJZ		

Figure 6.11 Enigma message.

message indicator. The decipherment would reveal the *message key*, a plaintext of the form

$$MK_0, MK_1, MK_2, MK_0, MK_1, MK_2.$$

The three-letter message key (MK_0, MK_1, MK_2) was repealed to detect transmission errors. If the two halves agreed, the receiving station would then reset the rotors to (MK_0, MK_1, MK_2) and decipher the remainder of the text. Figure 6.11 contains a fictitious Enigma message.

6.8.2 The Enigma Encipherment Equation

Let $k_r(i)$ denote the rotational displacement of the rth rotor π_r for the encipherment of the ith letter. The encipherment equation is

$$y_i = \pi_i(x_i) = (\text{IP}^{-1}\mathbf{C}_{-k_0(i)}\pi_0^{-1}\mathbf{C}_{k_0(i)}\mathbf{C}_{-k_1(i)}\pi_1^{-1}\mathbf{C}_{k_1(i)}\mathbf{C}_{-k_2(i)}\pi_2^{-1}\mathbf{C}_{k_2(i)} \times \pi_R$$
$$\times \mathbf{C}_{-k_2(i)}\pi_2\mathbf{C}_{k_2(i)}\mathbf{C}_{-k_1(i)}\pi_1\mathbf{C}_{k_1(i)}\mathbf{C}_{-k_0(i)}\pi_0\mathbf{C}_{k_0(i)}\text{IP})(x_i) \qquad (6.7)$$

where the rotational displacements are

$$k_0(i) = (i + I_0 - R_0)\,(\text{modulo } 26)$$

$$k_1(i) = \left(I_1 - R_1 + \left\lfloor \frac{i + I_0 - R_0}{26} \right\rfloor\right)(\text{modulo } 26)$$

$$k_2(i) = \left(I_2 - R_2 + \left\lfloor \frac{I_1 - R_1 + \left\lfloor \dfrac{i + I_0 - R_0}{26} \right\rfloor}{26} \right\rfloor\right)(\text{modulo } 26)$$

with ring settings (R_0, R_1, R_2) and the initial rotor positions (I_0, I_1, I_2).

Equation (6.7) is not exactly correct. The mechanical motion of the rotors, which is controlled by gears, is slightly irregular due to the following.

1. When the ratchet wheel on the right (or fast) rotor reaches some point (once every 26 letters), a pawl drives the middle (or medium) rotor one step forward.
2. When the ratchet wheel on the middle rotor reaches some point (once every 626 letters), a pawl drives the left (or slow) rotor one step forward. The mechanical arrangement causes the middle rotor is to step one additional step when the left rotor is stepped.

This irregularity reduces the period of the Enigma from $26^3 = 17,576$ to $26 \times 25 \times 26 = 16,900$.

In order that the paths taken by the current from the (input) contact plate through the rotors to the stator, and from the stator back through the rotors to the (output) contact plate be disjoint, the stator π_R must be an involution that is $\pi_R(\pi_R(t)) = t$ for every t with $0 \le t < 26$. As the stator is an involution, it follows that the encipherment in mapping Equation (6.7) is also an involution.

6.9 CRYPTANALYSIS OF THE ENIGMA

Cryptanalysis of the Enigma machines first began in Poland at the Polish Cipher Bureau in 1932. When the United Kingdom declared war on Germany after its invasion of Poland on September 1, 1939, a group, including Alan Turing, was assembled to attempt cryptanalysis of the German Enigma traffic at Bletchley Park, a town about 100 kilometers from London, where the Government Code and Cypher School had just been relocated.

The first attacks on Enigma traffic came from a group of Polish mathematicians including Marian Rejewski [Rejewski, 1981] and his colleagues Jerzy Rozycki and Henryzk Zygalski. They examined a commercial Enigma machine and studied the properties of the Enigma encipherment equation.

Bombe is French for *bomb*; the same word describes a class of pastries normally hemispherical in shape. The actress Jacqueline Bisset creates an ice cream bombe in the movie *Who Is Killing The Great Chefs of Europe*. A picture of a christmas bombe may be found in the cookbook *Chocolat*: *Extraordinary Chocolate Desserts* by Alice Medrich.

The bombe was also a programmable processor constructed by Rejewski and his colleagues. Its function was to use the structure imposed by cribs to test and eliminate certain plugboard and rotor setting combinations.

Why the name *bombe*? Members of the Polish Cipher Bureau proposed the architecture for a "computer" to aid in the decipherment of the Enigma ciphertext. It is reported that their inspiration came in a restaurant at the moment a *bombe* was being served, ample proof that great discoveries may be achieved after a fine meal!

There is a less artistic explanation for the name; the bombe had rotating gears and these made a *ticking* sound as the bombe searched for the settings.

When Poland was overrun, Rejewski and his colleagues were moved to southern France. They had to flee France for England when the Vichy government came to power. Their cryptanalytic techniques were revealed to the British, who most ungraciously did not reciprocate. Rejewski and his colleagues were also not allowed to join the effort at Bletchley Park.

Gordon Welchman was a scholar in mathematics at Trinity University from 1925 to 1928 [Welchman, 1982]. Welchman reported to Bletchley Park when the United Kingdom declared war on Germany. He was assigned the task of studying callsigns and discriminants. He became intrigued, however, with the indicator message setting. Welchman observed that messages would often contain the same letter in positions 0 and 3 or 1 and 4 or 2 and 5, referred to as a *female*. Table 6.8 lists some females seen in messages transmitted with the same discriminant on some day.

How frequently will *females* occur? Suppose $X \in \{A, B, C, \dots, Z\}$ is chosen according to the uniform distribution and π and η are randomly selected involutions. A female occurs if $\pi(X) = \eta(X)$. The probability of a female is $\frac{13}{25} \approx \frac{1}{2}$. There are a little

TABLE 6.8 Intercepted Females with the Same Discriminant on ... (Date)

Indicator	y_0	y_1	y_2	y_3	y_4	y_5
KIE	S	P	E	S	M	T
LTS	V	B	Y	Q	G	Y
EGP	O	H	A	O	C	M
RYM	X	W	N	P	W	V
XXY	Z	D	F	J	D	A

over a million (60×26^3) possible choices of rotors and ring settings. Each female will reduce the possibilities by about $\frac{1}{2}$ so that if Enigma traffic with a fixed discriminant yields 12 females, it will reduce the key space from $\sim 10^6$ to about 250.

The encipherment equation (6.7) shows that a $(j, j+3)$-female with $0 \le j < 3$ requires $y_j = y_{j+3}$ for some $x_j = x_{j+3}$. Equation (6.7) shows that the occurrence of the female $y_j = y_{j+3}$

$$y_j = (\mathrm{IP}^{-1}T_j\mathrm{IP})(x_j) \tag{6.8}$$

$$T_j = (\mathbf{C}_{-k_0(j)}\pi_0^{-1}\mathbf{C}_{k_0(j)}\mathbf{C}_{-k_1(j)}\pi_1^{-1}\mathbf{C}_{k_1(j)}\mathbf{C}_{-k_2(j)}\pi_2^{-1}\mathbf{C}_{k_2(j)}\pi_R\mathbf{C}_{-k_2(j)}\pi_2$$
$$\times\, \mathbf{C}_{k_2(j)}\mathbf{C}_{-k_1(j)}\pi_1\mathbf{C}_{k_1(j)}\mathbf{C}_{-k_0(j)}\pi_0\mathbf{C}_{k_0(j)}) \tag{6.9}$$

$$y_{j+3} = (\mathrm{IP}^{-1}T_{j+3}\mathrm{IP})(x_{j+3}) \tag{6.10}$$

$$T_j = (\mathbf{C}_{-k_0(j+3)}\pi_0^{-1}\mathbf{C}_{k_0(j+3)}\mathbf{C}_{-k_1(j+3)}\pi_1^{-1}\mathbf{C}_{k_1(j+3)}\mathbf{C}_{-k_2(j+3)}\pi_2^{-1}\mathbf{C}_{k_2(j+3)}\pi_R$$
$$\times\, \mathbf{C}_{-k_2(j+3)}\pi_2\mathbf{C}_{k_2(j+3)}\mathbf{C}_{-k_1(j+3)}\pi_1\mathbf{C}_{k_1(j+3)}\mathbf{C}_{-k_0(j+3)}\pi_0\mathbf{C}_{k_0(j+3)}) \tag{6.11}$$

implies

$$T_j = T_{j+3},$$

which is independent of the plugboard connection.

On May 10, 1940, the Germans changed the key protocol and did not encipher the message key twice.

6.10 CRIBBING ENIGMA CIPHERTEXT

Example 6.2
Suppose that Enigma ciphertext begins with the suspected following plaintext:

```
0  1  2  3  4  5  6  7  8  9 10 11 12 13 14 15 16 17 18 19 20 21 22 23 24 25 26 27 28 29 30
C  Q  N  Z  P  V  L  I  L  P  E  U  I  K  T  E  D  C  G  L  O  V  W  V  G  T  U  F  L  N  Z
↑  ↑  ↑  ↑  ↑  ↑  ↑  ↑  ↑  ↑  ↑  ↑  ↑  ↑  ↑  ↑  ↑  ↑  ↑  ↑  ↑  ↑  ↑  ↑  ↑  ↑  ↑  ↑  ↑  ↑  ↑
T  O  T  H  E  P  R  E  S  I  D  E  N  T  O  F  T  H  E  U  N  I  T  E  D  S  T  A  T  E  S
```

This crib is examined for the presence of *loops*; E N I E is a loop consisting of E N (at position 29), N I (at position 12), and I E (at position 7). Three loops in the crib above are written as shown in Figure 6.12.

Welchman and Turing suggested testing plugboard connections and rotor positions by connecting double-ended Enigma's with the rotors set to the positions (j_0, j_1, j_2) (Fig. 6.13). The symbol for a double-ended Enigma is presented in Figure 6.14. To test

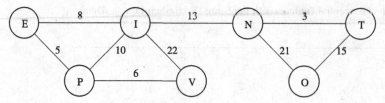

Figure 6.12 Loops in corresponding `plainEx6.2` and `cipherEx6.2`.

the three loops, several double-ended Enigmas were interconnected. The three bombes shown in Figure 6.15 are set to test the plugboard connections $E \to A$, $P \to A$, and $N \to A$. The figure shows the logical equivalents of parts of the bombe corresponding to the three loops rather than the actual bombe structure. The bombe cycles through the 26^3 initial rotor offsets $(j_0 + 7, j_1 + 9, j_2 + 4)$ to test the EPI loop. The bombe puts a voltage across the input port E; the current moves through the three double-ended rotors, returning to the Test Register. If

- $(j_0 + 7, j_1 + 9, j_2 + 4)$ is the correct initial rotor offset, and
- The plugboard connection EA is correct,

the current will return to the Test Register at A. If not, the current will return to some other letter, say V. By correctly sequencing the device, the signals will run through some cycle. There are two possibilities:

1. We have guessed the correct plugboard connection ? to E and the current will return to ?, or

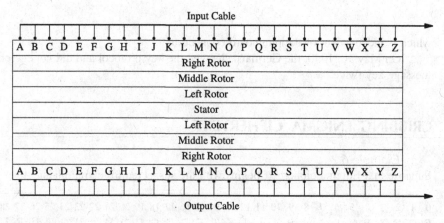

Figure 6.13 Double-ended Enigma.

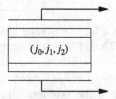

Figure 6.14 Symbol for double-ended enigma with positions (j_0, j_1, j_2).

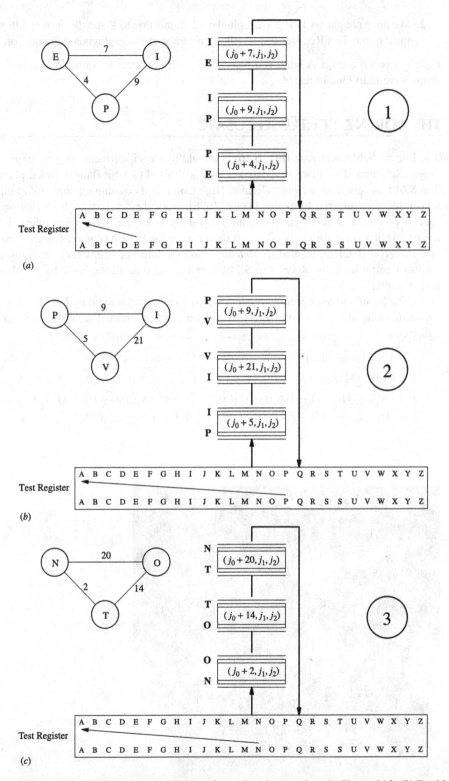

Figure 6.15 (*a*) Double-ended Enigma for testing the EPI-loop in Figure 6.12; (*b*) Double-ended Enigma for testing the VIP-loop in Figure 6.12; (*c*) Double-ended Enigma for testing the NOT-loop in Figure 6.12.

2. We have not guessed the correct plugboard connection to E and the current will *fill up* most of the Test Register and it will not return to the true plugboard connection of E.

Case 1 is called a drop. A letter is a potential drop if the letter is not filled in Case 2. The drops were individually tested.

6.11 THE LORENZ SCHLÜSSELZUSATZ

The Lorenz Schlüsselzusatz (Fig. 6.16) is an additive encipherment cryptosystem; a *key stream* determined by more than 501 key bits is XORed to 5-bit Baudot-coded plaintext. The SZ40 was used to encipher German High Command communications. SZ40 cipher-text traffic was referred to as *fish* [Tutte, 1998]. Both the cryptographic device and the special processor used to carry out the cryptanalysis of the SZ40 were referred to as *tunny*; this first generation processor was designed by the British *General Communications Headquarters* (GCHQ) located in *Bletchley Park* outside London, where the SZ40 cryptanalysis activities took place. The SZ40 saga is described in the book by Hinsley and Stripp [2001].

The SZ40 and a succeeding model (SZ42) were manufactured by *Lorenz*; they were generalizations of the Vernam–Vigenère stream cipher system. The SZ40 encipherment equation is

$$y = x + k \,(\text{modulo } 2)$$

$$y = (\underline{y}(0), \underline{y}(1), \dots) \quad \underline{y}(j) = (y_1(j), y_2(j), y_3(j), y_4(j), y_5(j)), \quad j = 0, 1, \dots$$
$$x = (\underline{x}(0), \underline{x}(1), \dots) \quad \underline{x}(j) = (x_1(j), x_2(j), x_3(j), x_4(j), x_5(j)), \quad j = 0, 1, \dots$$
$$k = (\underline{k}(0), \underline{k}(1), \dots) \quad \underline{k}(j) = (k_1(j), k_2(j), k_3(j), k_4(j), k_5(j)), \quad j = 0, 1, \dots$$

Figure 6.16   The Lorenz Schlüsselzusatz (Courtesy of NSA).

where

- The plaintext $\{\underline{x}(j)\}$ is alphanumeric text encoded into 5-bit strings;
- The key $\{\underline{k}(j)\}$ is a sequence of 5-bit strings; and
- The ciphertext $\{\underline{y}(j)\}$ is the XOR of the plaintext and key.

The German Cipher Bureau understood the limitations of Vernam–Vigenère encipherment. Even with multiple tapes, an analysis is possible. The SZ40 used a two-stage XOR but the encipherment process was made more complicated by introducing key-dependent irregular motion in the second stage.

6.12 THE SZ40 PIN WHEELS

A *pin-wheel* is a mechanical implementation of a tape; it generates a periodic sequence of 0's and 1's. A pin-wheel contains a number L of *pins* equally spaced around its circumference. The pin-wheel operates, so that

- When a pin is *active* (present), the pin-wheel XORs a 1 to its input;
- When a pin is *inactive* (absent), the pin-wheel XORs a 0 to its input.

The pin-wheel depicted in Figure 6.17 shows four pin positions without pins. In an actual SZ40, all pin positions had pins, but some were made inactive by folding them down.

The SZ40 had 12 pin-wheels (Fig. 6.18):

- 5 χ pin-wheels, $\chi_1, \chi_2, \ldots, \chi_5$; the length of the χ_i pin-wheel is T_i.

	χ_i Pin-Wheel				
i	1	2	3	4	5
T_i	41	31	29	26	23

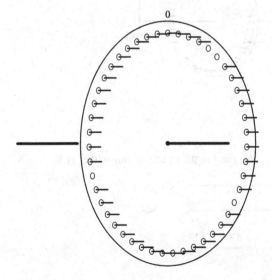

Figure 6.17 An SZ40 pin-wheel.

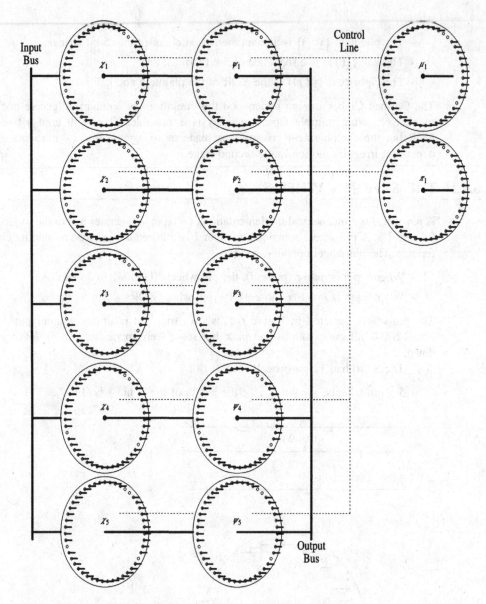

Figure 6.18   The SZ40 pin-wheels.

- 5 ψ pin-wheels, $\psi_1, \psi_2, \ldots, \psi_5$; the length of the ψ_i pin-wheel is S_i.

	ψ_i Pin-Wheel				
i	1	2	3	4	5
S_i	43	47	51	53	59

- 2 motor pin-wheels: a μ pin-wheel of length 37, and a π pin-wheel of length 61.

We assume that each pin-wheel has an initial position marked by 0.

The key stream $\underline{k}(0)$, $\underline{k}(1)$, ... was generated according to the following rules:

KS0. The set of active pins on a pin-wheel was part of the key variable and was changed at regular times;

KS1. The χ and ψ pin-wheels moved synchronously;

KS2. The χ pin-wheels moved one position for each letter;

KS3. The ψ pin-wheels were driven by the combined μ and π pin-wheels:

(a) The π pin-wheel moves one position for each letter;

(b) The μ pin-wheel moves one position whenever the π pin-wheel has an active pin in the current position;

(c) The ψ pin-wheels move whenever the μ pin-wheel has an active pin in the current position.

In Figure 6.18,

- The 5-bit plaintext strings enter on the left;
- The values on the χ_j pin-wheels ($1 \leq j \leq 5$) are XORed to the plaintext, producing intermediate ciphertext;
- The values on the ψ_j pin-wheels ($1 \leq j \leq 5$) are XORed to the intermediate ciphertext, producing the 5-bit ciphertext strings;
- The χ_j pin-wheels ($1 \leq j \leq 5$) *all* shift one pin-position;
- The ψ_j pin-wheels ($1 \leq j \leq 5$) *all* shift one pin-position, provided the μ pin-wheel pin in the current position is a 1;
- The μ pin-wheel shifts one pin position provided the π pin-wheel pin in the current position is a 1;
- The π pin-wheel shifts one pin position.

To define the encipherment process, some additional notation is needed; the position of a pin-wheel for the encipherment of the jth letter is denoted as follows:

- $p_i[j]$ the position of the ith χ pin-wheel;
- $q_i[j]$ for the position of the ith ψ pin-wheel, $q_i[j] \equiv (q[j] + j_i(0))$ (modulo S_i);
- $u[j]$ for the position of the μ pin-wheel;
- $v[j]$ for the position of the π pin-wheel.

6.12.1 The SZ40 Key

The SZ40 key had two components:

- The 501 bits determining the pins of the 12 pin-wheels;
- The initial positions of the 5χ, the 5ψ, and the 2 motor pin-wheels μ and π.

The first key component was originally changed each month; the second component was supposed to be changed with each message. Initially, an SZ40 message began with an *indicator* transmitted *in the clear*, consisting of 12 alphabetic characters, for example HQIBPEXEZMUG. A character translated into a 12-tuple of integers in $\{0, 1, \ldots, 25\}$ specifying the initial settings of the 12 pin-wheels so that *not* all initial settings were possible. Subsequently, the indicator was replaced by an entry in a codebook that translated into initial wheel settings.

6.12.2 The Steps in an SZ40 Encipherment

1. The jth letter $x(j)$ is encoded using the Baudot code:

$$x(j) \rightarrow \underline{x}(j) \equiv (x_1(j), x_2(j), x_3(j), x_4(j), x_5(j)).$$

2. The current output $\underline{\chi}(j) \equiv (\chi_1(j), \chi_2(j), \chi_3(j), \chi_4(j), \chi_5(j))$ of the χ wheels is XORed bit by bit to $\underline{x}(j)$, producing *intermediate ciphertext* $\underline{\tilde{x}}(j) \equiv (\tilde{x}_1(j), \tilde{x}_2(j), \tilde{x}_3(j), \tilde{x}_4(j), \tilde{x}_5(j))$:

$$\underline{x}(j) \rightarrow \underline{\tilde{x}}(j) = \underline{x}(j) + \underline{\chi}(j).$$

3. The current output $\underline{\psi}(j) \equiv (\psi_1(j), \psi_2(j), \psi_3(j), \psi_4(j), \psi_5(j))$ of the ψ wheels is XORed bit by bit to $\underline{\tilde{x}}(j)$, producing *ciphertext* $\underline{y}(j) \equiv (y_1(j), y_2(j), y_3(j), y_4(j), y_5(j))$:

$$\underline{\tilde{x}}(j) \rightarrow \underline{y}(j) = \underline{\tilde{x}}(j) + \underline{\psi}(j).$$

4. Some of the pin-wheel rotate:

   (a) *All χ pin-wheels rotate 1 position counterclockwise*

   $$p_i[j] = (p_i[j+1] \ (\text{modulo } T_i).$$

   (b) All ψ pin-wheels rotate 1 position counterclockwise provided the current output $\mu(q[j])$ of the μ pin-wheel is 1

   $$q_i[j+1] = (q_i[j] + \mu(u[j]) \ (\text{modulo } S_i).$$

   (c) The μ pin-wheel rotates counterclockwise by 1 position provided the current output of the π pin-wheel is 1.

   $$u[j+1] = (u[j] + \pi(v[j]) \ (\text{modulo } 37)$$

   (d) The π pin-wheel rotates counterclockwise by 1 position so that $v[j+1] = (v[j]+1) \ (\text{modulo } 61)$;

These rules lead to the recurrences

[position of π − wheel]	$v[j] = j \ (\text{modulo } 61)$
[position of μ − wheel]	$u[j] = [u[j-1+\pi(v[j-1])] \ (\text{modulo } 37)]$
[position of χ − wheel]	$p_i[j] = j \ (\text{modulo } T_i)$
	$q_i[j] = [q_i[j-1+\mu(u[j-1])] \ (\text{modulo } S_i)].$

The encipherment equation is

$$y = x + k \qquad Y_i(j) = X_i(j) + K_i(j) \tag{6.12}$$
$$k_i(j) = \chi_i(p_i[j]) + \psi_i \ (q_i[j]) \tag{6.13}$$

Example 6.3
The plaintext NOW is enciphered to

		χ-Wheel		ψ-Wheel		
x_i	Baudot	Pins	Output	Pins	Output	y_i
N	01100	10101	11001	01101	10100	H
O	11000	11111	00111	00100	00011	A
W	11011	10111	01100	11000	10100	H

Example 6.4

The plaintext MERRY CHRISTMAS is enciphered as follows:

		χ-Wheel		ψ-Wheel		
x_i	Baudot	Pins	Output	Pins	Output	y_i
M	11100	10101	01001	00110	01111	K
E	00001	01010	01011	01001	00010	LF
R	01010	00110	01100	11000	10100	H
R	01010	11100	10110	01011	11101	X
Y	10101	00101	10000	00101	10101	Y
	00100	01101	01001	10001	11000	O
C	01110	10100	11010	11001	00011	A
H	10100	00110	10010	11001	01011	J
R	01010	11111	10101	01100	11001	B
I	00110	10010	10100	11000	01100	N
S	00101	11111	11010	11111	00101	S
T	10000	11111	01111	11111	10000	T
M	11100	11101	00001	11111	11110	V
A	00011	11101	11110	01110	10000	T
S	00101	11111	11010	01110	10100	H

6.13   SZ40 CRYPTANALYSIS PROBLEMS

There are several possible versions of the cryptanalysis problem, of which the following is the most challenging:

Problem # 1

Given: Ciphertext $\underline{y}$

Determine: The pin-wheels (active pins and initial positions) and plaintext $\underline{x}$.

The SZ40 keys consists of
- The set of active pins of the 12 wheels (501 bits);
- The starting positions of the 12 wheels ($\simeq$56 bits).

Some keys may be changed daily (or with each message), others less frequently. Thus, if the active pins are fixed for a month and each day the starting positions are changed, the cryptanalysis is simpler:

Problem #2

Given: Ciphertext $\underline{y}$ and the active pins on the χ, ψ, μ, and π wheels

Determine: The initial positions of the pin-wheels and the plaintext $\underline{x}$.

If one plaintext message can be determined by statistical methods or cribbing, the key $k(0)$, $k(1)$, ... might be determined. Statistical and algebraic methods can be used to recover (part of) the pin-wheel settings (active pins and initial positions). This would permit the decipherment of all messages used with the same pin-wheel settings. A discussion of one such attack is given in Carter [1997].

The attack at Bletchley Park by GCHQ used the *Colossus*, a digital processor designed by Alan Turing to carry out the cryptanalysis.

6.14 CRIBBING SZ40 CIPHERTEXT

Much of the cryptanalysis of SZ40 ciphertext described next is included in a Master's Thesis at U.C. Santa Barbara by Nitesh Saxena.

Depth (in ciphertext) occurs when two or more SZ40 ciphertexts $\underline{y}_i$ ($i = 1, 2, \ldots$) were intercepted in a period

- During which the pin-wheels are unchanged and
- Both messages are identified with the *same* indicator.

The computation of the *differences* with depth $\Delta \underline{y}_{1,2} \equiv \underline{y}_1 + \underline{y}_2 = \Delta \underline{x}_{1,2} \equiv \underline{x}_1 + \underline{x}_2$ eliminates the key. The differenced plaintext might be searched for probable words (cribs); for example,

- German cipher-clerks often prefaced their messages with SPRUCHNUMMER (= message number), and
- Messages might contains references to various organizations such as LUFTWAFFE, WEHRMACHT, OBERKOMMANDO, or GESTAPO.

For example, if the crib SPRUCHNUMMER might be *slid* across the differenced ciphertext; with the letter S in position j, the XOR of the crib and the difference plaintext produces *putative* plaintext:

$\underline{x}_1$:	$\cdots$	S	P	R	$\cdots$	M	E	R	$\cdots$
$\underline{x}_2$:	$\cdots$	$x_2(j)$	$x_2(j+1)$	$x_2(j+2)$	$\cdots$	$x_2(j+8)$	$x_2(j+9)$	$x_2(j+10)$	$\cdots$
$\Delta \underline{x}_{1,2}$:	$\cdots$	$S+x(j)$	$P+x(j+1)$	$R+x(j+2)$	$\cdots$	$M+x(j+8)$	$E+x(j+9)$	$R+x(j+10)$	$\cdots$

The fragment of putative plaintext $x_2(j)$, $x_2(j+1)$, $x_2(j+2)$, $\ldots$, $x_2(j+8)$, $x_2(j+9)$, $x_2(j+10)$ is tested; if it is (grammatically) readable text, a *hit* has been obtained, which might reveal additional plaintext. With good luck, both plaintexts $\underline{x}_1$ and $\underline{x}_2$ may be read and the common key $\underline{k}$ used to encipher them recovered.

Early in the GCHQ SZ40 cryptanalysis, an interception of the near-repeat of a message of 4000 characters enciphered with the same indicator (and hence identical pin-wheel settings) was received, providing the entire key stream. When cribbing is successful, a segment of the (common) key stream $(\underline{k}(0), \underline{k}(1), \ldots, \underline{k}(N-1))$ is recovered.

6.14.1 Finding the Active Pins Given the Key Stream

We start with Equations (6.12) and (6.13) and ask if a sequence of key values

$$\{\underline{k}(j) : 0 \leq j < N\}$$

determines

$$\{\underline{\chi}(j) : 0 \leq j < N\} \text{ and } \{\underline{\psi}(j) : 0 \leq j < N\}.$$

As there are $B = \sum_i (T_i + S_i)$ pin values for the χ- and ψ-wheels, we must require *at least* $N > B/5 \simeq 100$ 5-bit key characters, certainly a lower bound because the ψ-wheel does not *always* move.

> ### Problem # 3
>
> *Given*: $\{\underline{k}(j) : 0 \le j < N\}$
>
> *Find*: $\{\underline{\chi}(j) : 0 \le j < N\}$ and $\{\underline{\psi}(j) : 0 \le j < N\}$

does not have a unique solution, because complementing the χ and ψ pin-wheel values leaves the key unchanged.

Tutte [1998, pp. 5–6] suggests that Alan Turing had a method to solve *Problem* 3 up to the complementation indeterminacy.

6.14.2   A Statistical Model of Pin Motion

We define the SZ40 parameters

- q, the *averaged* density of active pins on ψ-wheels, and
- v, the *average* probability that a ψ-wheel rotates.

The values of q and v are unknown and must be guessed and later refined as a result of the cryptanalysis.

The parameters q and v can be used to define a statistical model of the ψ_1 pin-wheel. (The use of a *random process* to model a *deterministic* function in a cryptosystem has been successfully used; the hidden Markov model being an example.) Let $\delta_{(i,j)}$ be the probability that $\psi_1(j, j+1) \equiv (\psi_1(j),\ \psi_1(j)) = (a,\ b)$ with $(a,\ b) \in \{(0,\ 0),\ (0,\ 1),\ (1,\ 0),\ (1,\ 1)\}$. Assuming that the motion of the wheels at all positions is approximately independent and identically distributed leads to the formulas

$$\delta_{(0,\,0)} = 1 - q - vq(1-q) = v(1-q)^2 + (1-v)(1-q) = \Pr\{(\psi_i(q_i[j], q_i[j+1])) = (0,0)\}$$
$$\delta_{(1,\,1)} = q - vq(1-q) = vq^2 + (1-v)q = \Pr\{(\psi_i(q_i[j], q_i[j+1])) = (1,1)\}$$
$$\delta_{(0,\,1)} = vq(1-q) = \Pr\{(\psi_i(q_i[j], q_i[j+1])) = (0,1)\}$$
$$\delta_{(1,\,0)} = vq(1-q) = \Pr\{(\psi_i(q_i[j], q_i[j+1])) = (1,0)\}$$

$$\Delta = \begin{pmatrix} \delta_{(0,0)} & \delta_{(0,1)} \\ \delta_{(1,0)} & \delta_{(1,1)} \end{pmatrix}.$$

We claim that Δ is *diagonal dominant*, that is $\delta_{i,i} > \delta_{i,j}$ with $i \ne j$. First, note that

$$\delta_{(0,0)} < \delta_{(0,1)} \Rightarrow 1 > vq \tag{6.14}$$

and

$$\delta_{(1,1)} < \delta_{(0,1)} \Rightarrow 1 > v(1-q) \tag{6.15}$$

so that both Expressions (6.14) and (6.15) cannot hold. In fact, *either*

1. $1 > vq$ and $1 \le v(1-q)$, or
2. $1 \le vq$ and $1 > v(1-q)$,

and a contradiction is obtained. A statistical model of pin motion implies that in a *large* sample of R positions, there will be $\sim Rq_{(a,b)}$ positions j, in which $\psi_1(j, j+1) = (a, b)$.

Example 6.5

We use the pin-wheels, for which Tables 6.9 to 6.20 give the fraction q of active pins. The (unknown) ψ pin-densities vary from 0.814 to 0.872. A program using the *Example 6.5*

TABLE 6.9

		χ_1-Wheel; $q = 0.878$					
1	0	0	1	0	0	1	0
1	1	1	1	1	1	1	1
1	1	1	1	1	1	1	1
1	1	1	1	1	1	1	1
1	1	1	1	1	1	1	1
1							

TABLE 6.10

		χ_2-Wheel; $q = 0.806$					
0	1	0	1	0	1	0	0
1	0	1	1	1	1	1	1
1	1	1	1	1	1	1	1
1	1	1	1	1	1	1	

TABLE 6.11

		χ_3-Wheel; $q = 0.931$					
1	0	1	1	1	1	1	1
1	0	1	1	1	1	1	1
1	1	1	1	1	1	1	1
1	1	1	1	1			

TABLE 6.12

		χ_4-Wheel; $q = 0.769$					
0	1	1	0	0	0	0	1
1	1	1	1	0	0	1	1
1	1	1	1	1	1	1	1
1	1						

TABLE 6.13

		χ_5-Wheel; $q = 0.739$					
1	0	0	0	1	1	0	0
1	0	1	1	1	1	1	1
1	1	1	1	1	1	1	

TABLE 6.14

		ψ_1-Wheel; $q = 0.814$					
0	0	1	0	0	1	1	1
0	1	1	0	1	0	1	0
1	1	1	1	1	1	1	1
1	1	1	1	1	1	1	1
1	1	1	1	1	1	1	1
1	1	1					

TABLE 6.15

		ψ_2-Wheel; $q = 0.872$					
0	1	1	1	0	0	1	1
1	1	1	1	1	1	0	1
1	0	1	0	1	1	1	1
1	1	1	1	1	1	1	1
1	1	1	1	1	1	1	1
1	1	1	1	1	1	1	

TABLE 6.16

		ψ_3-Wheel; $q = 0.863$					
1	0	0	0	1	0	0	0
1	0	1	1	1	1	1	1
1	1	1	1	1	1	1	1
1	1	1	1	1	1	1	1
1	1	1	1	1	1	1	1
1	1	1	1	1	1	1	1
1	1	1					

TABLE 6.17

ψ_4-Wheel; $q = 0.830$							
1	0	0	1	0	0	0	0
0	0	1	1	1	1	1	1
1	0	1	1	1	1	1	1
1	1	1	1	1	1	1	1
1	1	1	1	1	1	1	1
1	1	1	1	1	1	1	1
1	1	I	1	1			

TABLE 6.18

ψ_5-Wheel; $q = 0.864$							
0	1	0	1	1	1	1	1
0	0	1	0	1	1	0	1
1	0	0	1	1	1	1	1
1	1	1	1	1	1	1	1
1	1	1	1	1	1	1	1
1	1	1	1	1	1	1	1
1	1	1					

TABLE 6.19

μ-Wheel; $q = 0.811$							
1	1	1	1	1	1	1	1
0	1	0	1	1	1	0	1
0	1	0	1	1	1	1	0
1	1	1	1	1	1	1	0
1	1	1	1	1			

TABLE 6.20

π-Wheel; $q = 0.803$							
1	1	1	0	1	1	1	0
1	1	0	1	1	1	0	0
1	1	1	1	1	1	1	0
0	0	1	1	1	1	1	1
1	1	1	1	1	1	1	0
1	1	1	1	0	1	1	1
1	1	0	1	1	1	1	1
0	1	1	1	1			

parameters shows that $\mu(q[j]) = 1$ is satisfied $\sim 80\%$ of the time. We take $q = 0.83$ and $\nu = 0.8$; this gives

$$(q_{(i,j)}) = \begin{pmatrix} 0.072 & 0.128 \\ 0.128 & 0.672 \end{pmatrix}.$$

We use the statistical model of the motion of the SZ40 wheels to develop a variant of Turing's scheme.

6.14.3 Finding the ψ Active Pins:

$\chi_i(j, j+1)$-*Testing*: *Given*: Key $\{\underline{K}(j) : 0 \leq j < N\}$, then

- for each wheel i
- for each of the positions $j, j + T_i, j + 2T_i, \ldots, j + (k_i - 1)T_i$ where k_i depends on the length of the known key stream
- for each of the four pairs $(a, b) \in \{(0, 0), (0, 1)\ (1, 0), (1, 1)\}$

1. Count the number of times, denoted by $K\text{Count}_i[a, b]$ that the pair of keys $K_i(j, j+1) \equiv (K_i(j), K(j+1))$ is equal to (a, b).

2. Find that unique value of $\chi_i(j, j+1) \equiv (\chi_i(j), \chi(j+1)) = (c, d)$ that maximizes $K\text{Count}_i[a + c, b + d]$. The maximum should be approximately equal to the $k_i q_{(1,1)}$.

The result printed in Tables 6.21 to 6.30 for $j = 0(1)9$ were derived using $N = 500$ five-bit key values. Each pair of consecutive rows contains the entries

- The known value of $K\text{Count}_{(i,j)}[a, b]$ and
- The *unknown* count $\psi\text{Count}_{(i,j)}[a, b]$ of the number of times $\psi_i(j, j + 1) = (a, b)$ for each of the four possible pairs $[a, b] = [0, 0], [0, 1], [1, 0],$ and $[1, 1]$.

Step 1: Inference of $\chi_1(j, j + 1)$ The *hypothesis* $\chi_1(j, j + 1) = (A, B)$ can be tested as follows:

1. As $\psi_i(j, j + 1) = \psi_i(j + kT_i, j + kT_i + 1)$ for $k = 0, 1, \ldots, k_i - 1$, the correct values of (A, B) should yield $K\text{count}_i[c, d] \simeq q_{(1,1)} k_i$ where $c = (\chi_i(j) + a)$ (modulo 2) and $d = (\chi_i(j) + b)$ (modulo 2). Note that $[1, 1]$ is the most frequently occurring pair. If $j = 4$, then

   (a) $K_4(2)[1, 0]$ is the maximum of $K_4(2)[a, b]$, and

   (b) $\chi_1(j, j + 1) = (0, 1)$ is the unique value for which $(1, 1) = (1, 0) + \chi_1(j, j + 1)$.

TABLE 6.21   Testing $\chi_i(j, j + 1)$ in Position 0

(i,j)	[a,b]		[a,b]		[a,b]		[a,b]	
$K\text{Count}_{(1,0)}$	[0,0]	1	[0,1]	11	[1,0]	1	[1,1]	0
$\psi\text{Count}_{(1,0)}$	[0,0]	1	[0,1]	0	[1,0]	1	[1,1]	11
$K\text{Count}_{(2,0)}$	[0,0]	4	[0,1]	1	[1,0]	12	[1,1]	0
$\psi\text{Count}_{(2,0)}$	[0,0]	1	[0,1]	4	[1,0]	0	[1,1]	12
$K\text{Count}_{(3,0)}$	[0,0]	1	[0,1]	15	[1,0]	2	[1,1]	0
$\psi\text{Count}_{(3,0)}$	[0,0]	2	[0,1]	0	[1,0]	1	[1,1]	15
$K\text{Count}_{(4,0)}$	[0,0]	1	[0,1]	3	[1,0]	14	[1,1]	2
$\psi\text{Count}_{(4,0)}$	[0,0]	3	[0,1]	1	[1,0]	2	[1,1]	14
$K\text{Count}_{(5,0)}$	[0,0]	1	[0,1]	14	[1,0]	4	[1,1]	3
$\psi\text{Count}_{(5,0)}$	[0,0]	4	[0,1]	3	[1,0]	1	[1,1]	14

TABLE 6.22   Testing $\chi_i(j, j + 1)$ in Position 1

(i,j)	[a,b]		[a,b]		[a,b]		[a,b]	
$K\text{Count}_{(1,1)}$	[0,0]	0	[0,1]	2	[1,0]	1	[1,1]	10
$\psi\text{Count}_{(1,1)}$	[0,0]	0	[0,1]	2	[1,0]	1	[1,1]	10
$K\text{Count}_{(2,1)}$	[0,0]	2	[0,1]	14	[1,0]	1	[1,1]	0
$\psi\text{Count}_{(2,1)}$	[0,0]	1	[0,1]	0	[1,0]	2	[1,1]	14
$K\text{Count}_{(3,1)}$	[0,0]	2	[0,1]	1	[1,0]	14	[1,1]	1
$\psi\text{Count}_{(3,1)}$	[0,0]	1	[0,1]	2	[1,0]	1	[1,1]	14
$K\text{Count}_{(4,1)}$	[0,0]	14	[0,1]	1	[1,0]	0	[1,1]	5
$\psi\text{Count}_{(4,1)}$	[0,0]	5	[0,1]	0	[1,0]	1	[1,1]	14
$K\text{Count}_{(5,1)}$	[0,0]	3	[0,1]	2	[1,0]	2	[1,1]	15
$\psi\text{Count}_{(5,1)}$	[0,0]	3	[0,1]	2	[1,0]	2	[1,1]	15

TABLE 6.23 Testing $\chi_i(j, j+1)$ in Position 2

(i,j)	[a,b]		[a,b]		[a,b]		[a,b]	
KCount$_{(1,2)}$	[0,0]	0	[0,1]	1	[1,0]	9	[1,1]	3
ψCount$_{(1,2)}$	[0,0]	1	[0,1]	0	[1,0]	3	[1,1]	9
KCount$_{(2,2)}$	[0,0]	3	[0,1]	0	[1,0]	13	[1,1]	1
ψCount$_{(2,2)}$	[0,0]	0	[0,1]	3	[1,0]	1	[1,1]	13
KCount$_{(3,2)}$	[0,0]	15	[0,1]	1	[1,0]	0	[1,1]	2
ψCount$_{(3,2)}$	[0,0]	2	[0,1]	0	[1,0]	1	[1,1]	15
KCount$_{(4,2)}$	[0,0]	0	[0,1]	14	[1,0]	4	[1,1]	2
ψCount$_{(4,2)}$	[0,0]	4	[0,1]	2	[1,0]	0	[1,1]	14
KCount$_{(5,2)}$	[0,0]	2	[0,1]	3	[1,0]	2	[1,1]	15
ψCount$_{(5,2)}$	[0,0]	2	[0,1]	3	[1,0]	2	[1,1]	15

TABLE 6.24 Testing $\chi_i(j, j+1)$ in Position 3

(i,j)	[a,b]		[a,b]		[a,b]		[a,b]	
KCount$_{(1,3)}$	[0,0]	1	[0,1]	8	[1,0]	1	[1,1]	3
ψCount$_{(1,3)}$	[0,0]	1	[0,1]	3	[1,0]	1	[1,1]	8
KCount$_{(2,3)}$	[0,0]	3	[0,1]	13	[1,0]	0	[1,1]	1
ψCount$_{(2,3)}$	[0,0]	0	[0,1]	1	[1,0]	3	[1,1]	13
KCount$_{(3,3)}$	[0,0]	13	[0,1]	2	[1,0]	1	[1,1]	2
ψCount$_{(3,3)}$	[0,0]	2	[0,1]	1	[1,0]	2	[1,1]	13
KCount$_{(4,3)}$	[0,0]	4	[0,1]	0	[1,0]	1	[1,1]	15
ψCount$_{(4,3)}$	[0,0]	4	[0,1]	0	[1,0]	1	[1,1]	15
KCount$_{(5,3)}$	[0,0]	1	[0,1]	3	[1,0]	17	[1,1]	1
ψCount$_{(5,3)}$	[0,0]	3	[0,1]	1	[1,0]	1	[1,1]	17

TABLE 6.25 Testing $\chi_i(j, j+1)$ in Position 4

(i,j)	[a,b]		[a,b]		[a,b]		[a,b]	
KCount$_{(1,4)}$	[0,0]	0	[0,1]	2	[1,0]	1	[1,1]	10
ψCount$_{(1,4)}$	[0,0]	0	[0,1]	2	[1,0]	1	[1,1]	10
KCount$_{(2,4)}$	[0,0]	0	[0,1]	2	[1,0]	13	[1,1]	1
ψCount$_{(2,4)}$	[0,0]	2	[0,1]	0	[1,0]	1	[1,1]	13
KCount$_{(3,4)}$	[0,0]	13	[0,1]	1	[1,0]	2	[1,1]	2
ψCount$_{(3,4)}$	[0,0]	2	[0,1]	2	[1,0]	1	[1,1]	13
KCount$_{(4,4)}$	[0,0]	4	[0,1]	1	[1,0]	0	[1,1]	15
ψCount$_{(4,4)}$	[0,0]	4	[0,1]	1	[1,0]	0	[1,1]	15
KCount$_{(5,4)}$	[0,0]	17	[0,1]	1	[1,0]	4	[1,1]	0
ψCount$_{(5,4)}$	[0,0]	0	[0,1]	4	[1,0]	1	[1,1]	17

TABLE 6.26 Testing $\chi_i(j, j + 1)$ in Position 5

(i,j)	[a,b]		[a,b]		[a,b]		[a,b]	
$K\text{Count}_{(1,5)}$	[0,0]	0	[0,1]	1	[1,0]	8	[1,1]	4
$\psi\text{Count}_{(1,5)}$	[0,0]	1	[0,1]	0	[1,0]	4	[1,1]	8
$K\text{Count}_{(2,5)}$	[0,0]	1	[0,1]	12	[1,0]	1	[1,1]	2
$\psi\text{Count}_{(2,5)}$	[0,0]	1	[0,1]	2	[1,0]	1	[1,1]	12
$K\text{Count}_{(3,5)}$	[0,0]	14	[0,1]	1	[1,0]	1	[1,1]	2
$\psi\text{Count}_{(3,5)}$	[0,0]	2	[0,1]	1	[1,0]	1	[1,1]	14
$K\text{Count}_{(4,5)}$	[0,0]	4	[0,1]	0	[1,0]	1	[1,1]	15
$\psi\text{Count}_{(4,5)}$	[0,0]	4	[0,1]	0	[1,0]	1	[1,1]	15
$K\text{Count}_{(5,5)}$	[0,0]	1	[0,1]	20	[1,0]	0	[1,1]	1
$\psi\text{Count}_{(5,5)}$	[0,0]	0	[0,1]	1	[1,0]	1	[1,1]	20

TABLE 6.27 Testing $\chi_i(j, j + 1)$ in Position 6

(i,j)	[a,b]		[a,b]		[a,b]		[a,b]	
$K\text{Count}_{(1,6)}$	[0,0]	0	[0,1]	8	[1,0]	1	[1,1]	4
$\psi\text{Count}_{(1,6)}$	[0,0]	1	[0,1]	4	[1,0]	0	[1,1]	8
$K\text{Count}_{(2,6)}$	[0,0]	2	[0,1]	0	[1,0]	0	[1,1]	14
$\psi\text{Count}_{(2,6)}$	[0,0]	2	[0,1]	0	[1,0]	0	[1,1]	14
$K\text{Count}_{(3,6)}$	[0,0]	14	[0,1]	1	[1,0]	0	[1,1]	3
$\psi\text{Count}_{(3,6)}$	[0,0]	3	[0,1]	0	[1,0]	2	[1,1]	13
$K\text{Count}_{(4,6)}$	[0,0]	2	[0,1]	2	[1,0]	15	[1,1]	0
$\psi\text{Count}_{(4,6)}$	[0,0]	2	[0,1]	2	[1,0]	0	[1,1]	15
$K\text{Count}_{(5,6)}$	[0,0]	0	[0,1]	1	[1,0]	2	[1,1]	19
$\psi\text{Count}_{(5,6)}$	[0,0]	0	[0,1]	1	[1,0]	2	[1,1]	19

TABLE 6.28 Testing $\chi_i(j, j + 1)$ in Position 7

(i,j)	[a,b]		[a,b]		[a,b]		[a,b]	
$K\text{Count}_{(1,7)}$	[0,0]	1	[0,1]	0	[1,0]	9	[1,1]	3
$\psi\text{Count}_{(1,7)}$	[0,0]	0	[0,1]	1	[1,0]	4	[1,1]	8
$K\text{Count}_{(2,7)}$	[0,0]	1	[0,1]	1	[1,0]	12	[1,1]	2
$\psi\text{Count}_{(2,7)}$	[0,0]	1	[0,1]	1	[1,0]	2	[1,1]	12
$K\text{Count}_{(3,7)}$	[0,0]	13	[0,1]	0	[1,0]	3	[1,1]	1
$\psi\text{Count}_{(3,7)}$	[0,0]	1	[0,1]	3	[1,0]	0	[1,1]	13
$K\text{Count}_{(4,7)}$	[0,0]	15	[0,1]	2	[1,0]	1	[1,1]	1
$\psi\text{Count}_{(4,7)}$	[0,0]	1	[0,1]	1	[1,0]	2	[1,1]	15
$K\text{Count}_{(5,7)}$	[0,0]	1	[0,1]	1	[1,0]	17	[1,1]	3
$\psi\text{Count}_{(5,7)}$	[0,0]	1	[0,1]	1	[1,0]	3	[1,1]	17

TABLE 6.29 Testing $\chi_i(j, j+1)$ in Position 8

(i,j)	[a,b]		[a,b]		[a,b]		[a,b]	
$K\text{Count}_{(1,8)}$	[0,0]	8	[0,1]	1	[1,0]	1	[1,1]	2
$\psi\text{Count}_{(1,8)}$	[0,0]	2	[0,1]	1	[1,0]	1	[1,1]	8
$K\text{Count}_{(2,8)}$	[0,0]	3	[0,1]	10	[1,0]	1	[1,1]	2
$\psi\text{Count}_{(2,8)}$	[0,0]	1	[0,1]	2	[1,0]	3	[1,1]	10
$K\text{Count}_{(3,8)}$	[0,0]	2	[0,1]	14	[1,0]	0	[1,1]	1
$\psi\text{Count}_{(3,8)}$	[0,0]	0	[0,1]	1	[1,0]	2	[1,1]	14
$K\text{Count}_{(4,8)}$	[0,0]	16	[0,1]	0	[1,0]	0	[1,1]	3
$\psi\text{Count}_{(4,8)}$	[0,0]	3	[0,1]	0	[1,0]	0	[1,1]	16
$K\text{Count}_{(5,8)}$	[0,0]	2	[0,1]	16	[1,0]	3	[1,1]	1
$\psi\text{Count}_{(5,8)}$	[0,0]	3	[0,1]	1	[1,0]	2	[1,1]	16

TABLE 6.30 Testing $\chi_i(j, j+1)$ in Position 9

(i,j)	[a,b]		[a,b]		[a,b]		[a,b]	
$K\text{Count}_{(1,9)}$	[0,0]	9	[0,1]	0	[1,0]	2	[1,1]	1
$\psi\text{Count}_{(1,9)}$	[0,0]	1	[0,1]	2	[1,0]	0	[1,1]	9
$K\text{Count}_{(2,9)}$	[0,0]	3	[0,1]	1	[1,0]	12	[1,1]	0
$\psi\text{Count}_{(2,9)}$	[0,0]	1	[0,1]	3	[1,0]	0	[1,1]	12
$K\text{Count}_{(3,9)}$	[0,0]	1	[0,1]	1	[1,0]	14	[1,1]	1
$\psi\text{Count}_{(3,9)}$	[0,0]	1	[0,1]	1	[1,0]	1	[1,1]	14
$K\text{Count}_{(4,9)}$	[0,0]	16	[0,1]	0	[1,0]	3	[1,1]	0
$\psi\text{Count}_{(4,9)}$	[0,0]	0	[0,1]	3	[1,0]	0	[1,1]	16
$K\text{Count}_{(5,9)}$	[0,0]	5	[0,1]	0	[1,0]	16	[1,1]	1
$\psi\text{Count}_{(5,8)}$	[0,0]	0	[0,1]	5	[1,0]	1	[1,1]	16

2. The parameters q and v imply that $\psi\text{Count}_i(j, j+1)[1,1] = \max_{(r,s)} \psi\text{Count}_1(j, j+1)[r,s]$.

3. If $K\text{Count}_i(j, j+1)[a,b] = \max_{(r,s)} K\text{Count}_1(j, j+1)[r,s]$, then $(A,B) + (a,b) = (1,1)$.

The inference process just described recovers the value of $\chi_i(j, j+1)$.

How do we reconcile the uniqueness of $\chi_i(j, j+1)$ with the asserted *non*uniqueness of the solution to *Problem* no. 3? With the parameters $q \simeq 0.8$ and $v \simeq 0.8$ in *Example 6.4*, we have $\delta_{(1,1)} = \max_{(r,s)} \delta_{(r,s)}$. When the χ and ψ pin-wheel values are complemented, $q \to \tilde{q} \simeq 0.2$ and $v \to \tilde{v} \simeq 0.8$, so that $\tilde{\delta}_{(0,0)} = \max_{(r,s)} \tilde{\delta}_{(r,s)}$. Note that $\delta_{(1,1)} = \tilde{\delta}_{(0,0)}$. The correct value of (A, B) will be defined by $(A, B) + (a, b) = (0, 0)$.

Step 2: Inference of $\psi_1(q_1[j])$ It remains to find the values of $\psi_1(j)$; these are partially obscured by the action of the motor wheels. First, we infer the values of $\psi_1(q_1[j])$. Columns 1 to 5 in Tables 6.31 to 6.34 list for $j = 0(1)199$

1. The *unknown move indicator* (MI) with values (M/N) specifying whether or not the ψ pin-wheels moved; equal to M if $\mu[q[j]] = 1$ and to N if $\mu[q[j]] = 0$;

TABLE 6.31

j	MI(j)	χ	ψ	$\underline{K}$	M?
0	M(0)	10101	00110	10011	M
1	M(1)	01010	01001	00011	M
2	M(2)	00110	11000	11110	M
3	M(3)	11100	01011	10111	M
4	M(4)	00101	00101	00000	M
5	M(5)	01101	10001	11100	M
6	M(6)	10100	11001	01101	M?
7	M(7)	00110	11001	11111	M
8	M(8)	11111	01100	10011	M
9	M(9)	10010	11000	01010	M
10	N(10)	11111	11111	00000	M?
11	N(10)	11111	11111	00000	M?
12	M(10)	11101	11111	00010	M
13	N(11)	11101	01110	10011	M?
14	M(11)	11111	01110	10001	M
15	M(12)	11111	11111	00000	M
16	M(13)	11111	01111	10000	M
17	M(14)	11111	10110	01001	M
18	M(15)	11111	01111	10000	M
19	N(16)	11111	11111	00000	M?
20	M(16)	11111	11111	00000	M
21	N(17)	11111	10100	01011	M?
22	M(17)	11111	10100	01011	M
23	N(18)	11111	11110	00001	M?
24	N(18)	11110	11110	00000	M?
25	N(18)	11110	11110	00000	M?
26	N(18)	11100	11110	00010	M?
27	M(18)	11111	11110	00001	M
28	M(19)	11111	10111	01000	M
29	M(20)	11100	11111	00011	M?
30	M(21)	11000	11111	00111	M?
31	N(22)	10001	11111	01110	M?
32	M(22)	11100	11111	00011	M?
33	M(23)	10111	11111	01000	M?
34	M(24)	11111	11111	00000	M?
35	M(25)	10111	11111	01000	M?
36	M(26)	11111	11111	00000	M?
37	M(27)	10111	11111	01000	M?
38	M(28)	10001	11111	01110	M?
39	N(29)	11101	11111	00010	M?
40	N(29)	10111	11111	01000	M?
41	M(29)	11111	11111	00000	M?
42	M(30)	01111	11111	10000	M?
43	M(31)	01111	11111	10000	M?
44	M(32)	11111	11111	00000	M?
45	M(33)	01111	11111	10000	M?
46	M(34)	01111	11111	10000	M?
47	M(35)	11110	11111	00001	M?
48	M(36)	01110	11111	10001	M?
49	M(37)	11110	11111	00001	M?

TABLE 6.32

j	MI(j)	χ	ψ	$\underline{K}$	M?
50	M(38)	11111	11111	00000	M?
51	M(39)	11111	11111	00000	M?
52	M(40)	11100	11111	00011	M?
53	M(41)	11110	11111	00001	M?
54	M(42)	11111	11111	00000	M
55	M(0)	11100	01111	10011	M?
56	N(1)	11101	01111	10010	M?
57	N(1)	11101	01111	10010	M?
58	M(1)	11101	01111	10010	M
59	N(2)	11011	11111	00100	M?
60	M(2)	11011	11111	00100	M
61	M(3)	11111	01111	10000	M
62	M(4)	10111	00111	10000	M
63	N(5)	11111	11111	00000	M?
64	M(5)	10101	11111	01010	M
65	M(6)	11101	10111	01010	M
66	N(7)	10111	11111	01000	M?
67	M(7)	11011	11111	00100	M
68	N(8)	10111	00111	10000	M?
69	N(8)	10111	00111	10000	M?
70	M(8)	11110	00111	11001	M
71	M(9)	10110	10011	00101	M
72	M(10)	11110	11011	00101	M
73	M(11)	11111	01001	10110	M
74	M(12)	11111	11101	00010	M
75	N(13)	11110	01011	10101	M?
76	N(13)	11110	01011	10101	M?
77	N(13)	11111	01011	10100	M?
78	M(13)	11100	01011	10111	M
79	M(14)	11111	11001	00110	M
80	M(15)	11101	01001	10100	M
81	M(16)	11101	11100	00001	M
82	M(17)	11101	11001	00100	M
83	M(18)	01101	10100	11001	M
84	M(19)	01101	11101	10000	M
85	M(20)	11111	11111	00000	M
86	M(21)	01111	10111	11000	M
87	N(22)	01111	11111	10000	M
88	N(23)	11011	10111	01100	M?
89	M(23)	01011	10111	11100	M
90	M(24)	11101	11110	00011	M?
91	M(25)	11101	11110	00011	M
92	M(26)	11111	11111	00000	M
93	M(27)	10110	11100	01010	M
94	M(28)	11110	11111	00001	M?
95	M(29)	10110	11111	01001	M
96	M(30)	11011	11110	00101	M
97	M(31)	10111	11111	01000	M?
98	M(32)	11110	11111	00001	M
99	M(33)	10110	11110	01000	M?

TABLE 6.33

j	MI(j)	χ	ψ	$\underline{K}$	M?
100	M(34)	10111	11110	01001	M
101	M(35)	11110	11111	00001	M?
102	M(36)	10111	11111	01000	M?
103	N(37)	11111	11111	00000	M?
104	M(37)	11101	11111	00010	M?
105	N(38)	11111	11111	00000	M?
106	N(38)	11111	11111	00000	M?
107	M(38)	11101	11111	00010	M?
108	M(39)	11101	11111	00010	M?
109	M(40)	11101	11111	00010	M?
110	N(41)	11101	11111	00010	M?
111	M(41)	11111	11111	00000	M?
112	M(42)	11111	11111	00000	M
113	N(0)	11111	01111	10000	M?
114	M(0)	11111	01111	10000	M?
115	N(1)	11111	01111	10000	M?
116	M(1)	11100	01111	10011	M
117	M(2)	11000	11111	00111	M
118	M(3)	11110	01111	10001	M?
119	M(4)	11111	01111	10000	M
120	M(5)	11111	11111	00000	M?
121	N(6)	11110	11111	00001	M?
122	M(6)	11110	11111	00001	M?
123	M(7)	11111	11111	00000	M
124	M(8)	00110	00111	00001	M
125	M(9)	01011	11111	10100	M?
126	M(10)	10111	11111	01000	M
127	M(11)	01111	01111	00000	M
128	M(12)	00111	10111	10000	M
129	M(13)	11111	00111	11000	M
130	M(14)	00101	11111	11010	M
131	N(15)	10111	01111	11000	M?
132	M(15)	11111	01111	10000	M
133	M(16)	10101	11111	01010	M
134	M(17)	11101	11011	00110	M?
135	M(18)	11101	11011	00110	M?
136	M(19)	11101	11011	00110	M
137	M(20)	11111	11111	00000	M
138	M(21)	11111	11001	00110	M
139	M(22)	11110	10001	01111	M
140	M(23)	11110	11011	00101	M
141	M(24)	11110	11101	00011	M
142	M(25)	11101	10001	01100	M
143	M(26)	11101	11101	00000	M
144	M(27)	11110	10101	01011	M
145	M(28)	11110	11101	00011	M?
146	M(29)	11011	11101	00110	M
147	M(30)	11110	11111	00001	M?
148	M(31)	11111	11111	00000	M
149	M(32)	11111	11110	00001	M

TABLE 6.34

j	MI(j)	χ	ψ	$\underline{K}$	M?
150	M(33)	11111	11111	00000	M
151	N(34)	11111	11110	00001	M?
152	M(34)	11111	11110	00001	M
153	N(35)	11111	11111	00000	M?
154	M(35)	11011	11111	00100	M?
155	M(36)	10111	11111	01000	M
156	N(37)	11101	11101	00000	M
157	N(38)	10111	11111	01000	M?
158	M(38)	11111	11111	00000	M?
159	N(39)	10101	11111	01010	M?
160	M(39)	11101	11111	00010	M
161	N(40)	10101	11110	01011	M?
162	N(40)	10100	11110	01010	M?
163	M(40)	11110	11110	00000	M?
164	M(41)	10110	11110	01000	M
165	M(42)	01111	11111	10000	M
166	M(0)	01111	01110	00001	M
167	M(1)	11110	01111	10001	M
168	N(2)	01100	11111	10011	M?
169	M(2)	01101	11111	10010	M
170	M(3)	11110	01110	10000	M
171	M(4)	01111	01111	00000	M
172	M(5)	11111	11111	00000	M
173	M(6)	11111	11110	00001	M?
174	M(7)	11111	11110	00001	M
175	M(8)	11011	01111	10100	M
176	M(9)	11111	11111	00000	M?
177	N(10)	11111	11111	00000	M?
178	M(10)	11111	11111	00000	M
179	M(11)	11111	01111	10000	M
180	M(12)	11111	10111	01000	M
181	M(13)	11111	01111	10000	M
182	M(14)	11101	11111	00010	M
183	M(15)	11011	01111	10100	M
184	M(16)	11111	10111	01000	M?
185	M(17)	11100	10111	01011	M
186	M(18)	10100	11111	01011	M?
187	M(19)	11100	11111	00011	M?
188	M(20)	10101	11111	01010	M?
189	M(21)	11111	11111	00000	M?
190	M(22)	10110	11111	01001	M?
191	M(23)	11110	11111	00001	M?
192	M(24)	10111	11111	01000	M
193	M(25)	10110	11011	01101	M
194	M(26)	11101	10011	01110	M
195	N(27)	10101	11011	01110	M?
196	M(27)	11111	11011	00100	M
197	N(28)	11111	11111	00000	M?
198	N(28)	11111	11111	00000	M?
199	N(28)	11111	11111	00000	M?

2. The *unknown* true position of the ψ_1 pin-wheel;

3. The inferred $\chi(j, j+1)$ and $\psi(q_i[j], q_i[j+1])$;

4. The 5-bit known key obtained from cribbing;

5. An inference of the *unknown* move indicator (M/M?) equals to M if for *at least* one index i, we have $\psi_i(q_i[j]) \neq \psi_i(q_i[j+1])$, and equal to M? if for *all* indices i, we have $\psi_i(q_i[j]) = \psi_i(q_i[j+1])$.

TABLE 6.35   M Blocks

j	P_j	L_j	$\mathcal{B}_j$
1	0	7	0 0 1 0 0 1 1
2	7	4	1 0 1 1
3	12	2	1 0
4	14	6	0 1 0 1 0 1
5	20	2	1 1
6	22	2	1 1
7	27	3	1 1 1
8	54	2	1 0
9	58	2	0 1
10	60	4	1 0 0 1
11	67	2	1 0
12	70	6	0 1 1 0 1 0
13	78	11	0 1 0 1 1 1 1 1 1 1 1
14	89	2	1 1
15	91	4	1 1 1 1
16	95	3	1 1 1
17	98	2	1 1
18	100	2	1 1
19	112	2	1 0
20	116	3	0 1 0
21	119	2	0 1
22	123	3	1 0 1
23	126	6	1 0 1 0 1 0
24	132	3	0 1 1
25	136	10	1 1 1 1 1 1 1 1 1 1
26	146	2	1 1
27	148	4	1 1 1 1
28	152	2	1 1
29	155	3	1 1 1
30	160	2	1 1
31	164	5	1 1 0 0 1
32	169	5	1 0 0 1 1
33	174	3	1 0 1
34	178	7	1 0 1 0 1 0 1
35	185	2	1 1
36	192	4	1 1 1 1
37	196	2	1 1

TABLE 6.36   M Blocks

j	P_j	L_j	$\mathcal{B}_j$
38	200	4	1 1 1 1
39	204	2	1 1
40	206	3	1 1 1
41	214	2	1 1
42	218	2	1 0
43	220	5	0 1 0 0 1
44	225	5	1 1 1 0 1
45	230	8	1 0 1 0 1 0 1 1
46	238	3	1 1 1
47	242	2	1 1
48	245	2	1 1
49	255	3	1 1 1
50	258	4	1 1 1 1
51	262	3	1 1 1
52	266	7	1 1 1 1 0 0 1
53	273	2	1 0
54	275	2	0 1
55	277	4	1 1 0 1
56	281	7	1 0 1 0 1 0 1
57	292	3	1 1 1
58	296	2	1 1
59	298	2	1 1
60	300	2	1 1
61	302	2	1 1
62	306	2	1 1
63	308	8	1 1 1 1 1 1 1 1
64	317	5	1 1 1 1 1
65	322	5	1 0 0 1 0
66	327	9	0 1 1 1 0 1 1 0 1
67	336	2	1 0
68	338	4	0 1 0 1
69	342	2	1 1
70	351	2	1 1
71	353	2	1 1
72	356	2	1 1
73	358	2	1 1
74	367	13	1 1 1 1 1 1 1 0 0 1 0 0 1

Step 3: Inference of the $\psi(j)$ Pin Values Whenever the inferred move indicator is M, a value of $\psi_i(q_i[j])$ is determined. The jth *M block* $\mathcal{B}_j$

- Starts when the inferred move indicator is equal to M, and
- Ends when the inferred indicator is equal to M?

Tables 6.35 and 6.36 list the $\psi_1(q_1[j])$ values in the jth block $\mathcal{B}_j$, the starting position P_j, and the length L_j. To carry out the inference of the $\psi_1(q_1[j])$ pin-wheel values, the results in Tables 6.35 and 6.36 are placed in a different tabular format. In Tables 6.37 to 6.43,

1. The first row lists the blocks $\mathcal{B}_0$, $\mathcal{B}_1$, ... separated by a ?;
2. The starting position P_j of the jth block $\mathcal{B}_j$ is in the second row;
3. The length L_j of the jth block $\mathcal{B}_j$ is in the third row;
4. The bound $M_{(j,j+1)} \equiv P_{j+1} + L_{j+1} - (P_j + L_j - 1)$ is in row 4.

Note that $m_{(j, j+1)} \equiv q[p_{j+1} + L_{j+1}] - q[p_j + L_j + 1] \le M_{(j, j+1)}$.
For example

$$m_{(0,1)} = -1 \quad \underbrace{0010011}_{\mathcal{B}_0}\ \overbrace{1011}^{\mathcal{B}_1} \qquad m_{(0,1)} = 0 \quad \underbrace{0010011}_{\mathcal{B}_0}\ \overbrace{1011}^{\mathcal{B}_1}$$

$$m_{(1,2)} = -1 \quad \underbrace{1011}_{\mathcal{B}_2}\ \overbrace{10}^{\mathcal{B}_2}$$

$$m_{(1,2)} = 0 \quad \underbrace{1011}_{\mathcal{B}_1}\ \overbrace{10}^{\mathcal{B}_2} \qquad m_{(1,2)} = 1 \quad \underbrace{1011?}_{\mathcal{B}_1}\ \overbrace{10}^{\mathcal{B}_2} \quad ? \in \{0, 1\}.$$

TABLE 6.37

0	0	1	0	0	1	1	?	1	0	1	1	?	1	0	?	0	1	0	1	0	1	?	1	1	?	1	1
0								7					12			14							20			22	
7								4					2			6							2			2	
							0								1			0							0		0

TABLE 6.38

?	1	1	1	?	1	0	?	0	1	?	1	0	0	1	?	1	0	?	0	1	1	0	1	0	?
	27							54			58					60					67			70	
	3							2			2					4					2			6	
3				24				2			2				0						3		1		2

TABLE 6.39

0	1	0	1	1	1	1	1	1	1	1	1	?	1	1	?	1	1	1	1	?	1	1	1	?	1	1	?
78													89			91					95				98		
11													2			4					3				2		
												0				0		0						0			0

TABLE 6.40

```
 1  1  ?   1  0  ?  0   1  0  ?   0  1  ?   1  0  1  ?   1  0  1  0  1  0  ?
100        112        116        119        123        126
 2          2          3          2          3          6
      10          2          0          2          0                      0
```

TABLE 6.41

```
 0  1  0  ?   1  1  1  1  1  1  1  1  1  1  ?   1  1  ?   1  1  1  1  ?   1  1  ?
132          136                          146        148            152
 3           10                            2          4              2
       1                                       0          0              0          0
```

TABLE 6.42

```
 1  1  1  1  ?   1  1  ?   1  1  0  0  1  ?   1  0  0  1  1  ?   1  0  1  ?
155             160        164              169              174
 4               2          5                5                3
          1             2                0                0                1
```

TABLE 6.43

```
 1  0  1  0  1  0  1  ?   1  1  ?   1  1  1  1  ?
178                      185        192
 7                        2          4
                   0               5
```

6.14.4 M-Block Concatenation: Finding $\psi(j)$

The problem is to concatenate the M-blocks and by doing so to identify the unknown? $\psi_1(q_1[j])$ values. A brute-force program tests all possible values of the unknown bits? in an attempt to find the best match between pairs of blocks. This matching program yields the following results:

0–54: 00 $\overbrace{1001110110101011111111111111111111}$ 11111

54–115: 1 $\underbrace{0010011101101010101111111111111111111111111111}$ 001

115–150: $\overbrace{100111011010101111111111111111111111111}$

From these results, the values of $\psi_1(j)$ can be determined.

Step 4: *Inference of* $\pi(j)$ If the ψ_1 pin-wheel is determined, the values in the move indicator column in Tables 6.31–6.34 are determined. Note that

$$\mu(U[j]) = 1 \Rightarrow MI(j) = M$$
$$\mu(U[j]) = 0 \Rightarrow MI(j) = N$$
$$U[j] = U[j-1] + \pi(V[j]) \text{ (modulo 37)}.$$

Thus

$$MI(j) = M \quad \text{and} \quad MI(j+1) = N \Rightarrow \pi(V[j]) = 1$$
$$MI(j) = N \quad \text{and} \quad MI(j+1) = M \Rightarrow \pi(V[j]) = 1.$$

The values of j for which $1 = \pi(j \text{ (modulo 41)})$, inferred by this algorithm for $j = 0(1)65$, are listed in Table 6.44. Continuing this process, a sufficient number of steps will reveal all valves $0 \leq j < 61$ for which $\pi(j) = 1$; the remaining values of $\pi(j)$ are 0. If a mistake is made and Equtions (6.12) and (6.13) lead to the conclusion $\pi(j) = 0$, which is *incorrect*, this will lead to a later inconsistency.

Step 5: *Inference of* $\mu(j)$ We again start with the idea leading to Equations (6.12) and (6.13); with complete (?) knowledge of $\pi(V[j])$, inferences of the values of $\mu(q[j])$

TABLE 6.44

j	MI(j)	MI($j+1$)	j(mod 41)	$\pi(j(\text{mod }61))$
9	M	N	9	1
11	N	M	11	1
12	M	N	12	1
13	N	M	13	1
18	M	N	18	1
19	N	M	19	1
20	M	N	20	1
21	N	M	21	1
22	M	N	22	1
26	N	M	26	1
30	M	N	30	1
31	N	M	31	1
38	M	N	38	1
40	N	M	40	1
54	M	N	54	1
57	M	N	57	1
58	M	N	58	1
59	M	N	59	1
60	N	M	60	1
62	M	N	1	1
63	M	N	2	1
65	M	N	4	1

TABLE 6.45

$MI(j)$	$MI(j+1)$	$\pi(V[(j])$	$\mu(Q[j])$	$\mu(Q[j+1])$	$S(j)$
M	N	1	1	0	1
M	N	0	Impossible		
M	M	1	1	1	1
M	M	0	1	1	0
N	M	1	0	1	1
N	M	0	Impossible		
N	N	1	0	0	1
N	N	0	0	0	0

and $q[j]$ may be made:

$$\mu(u[j]) = 1 \Rightarrow MI(j) = M$$
$$\mu(u[j]) = 0 \Rightarrow MI(j) = N$$
$$u[j] = (u[j-1] + \pi(v[j]) \;(\text{modulo } 37).$$

This leads to the $\mu[j]$-inference rules in which $q[j+1] = (q[j] + S[j]) \;(\text{modulo } 37)$ (Table 6.45), which completes the analysis.

REFERENCES

F. CARTER, *Codebreaking with the Colossus Computer*, Bletchley Park Trust, Bletchley Pary, United Kingdom, 1997.

F. H. HINSLEY AND A. STRIFF, *Code Breakers*, Oxford University Press, Oxford, United Kingdom, 2001.

M. REJEWSKI, "How the Polish Mathematicians Deciphered the Enigma", *Annals of the History of Computing*, **3**, 213–234 (1981).

W. F. TUTTE, "The Fish and I", University of Waterloo lecture, June 18, 1998 [available on the Web www. history.mcs.st.andrews.ac.uk/Mathematicians/Tutte.html].

G. WELCHMAN, *The Hut Six Story: Breaking the Enigma Codes*, McGraw-Hill, 1982.

CHAPTER 7

THE JAPANESE CIPHER MACHINES

THE JAPANESE introduced a family of cipher machines implementing polyalphabetic substitution early in the twentieth century. Assigned color codes by the Army Signal Intelligence Service, the first machine in this family, RED, used a half-rotor in place of the Hebern rotor. RED was soon followed by PURPLE, which derived ciphertext using stepping switches. This chapter describes these cipher machines and outlines their cryptanalysis.

7.1 JAPANESE SIGNALING CONVENTIONS

Although the spoken Japanese and Chinese languages differ, they share a common written language. Written Japanese, which originated in the ninth century, was derived from Chinese and uses *ideographs*. The written language was simplified by introducing the *kana* phonetic system, containing 48 basic syllables. Of the two *kana* versions developed, *hirigana* and *katagana*, the latter was favored for telegraphic communications due to the ease of reproducing its kana symbols.

In order to write Japanese using the Roman alphabet A, B, ..., Z, each *kana* symbol is assigned a Roman letter counterpart *Romaji*. The *Hepburn Romaji system* used by Japan during World War II still remains in use today. The Hepburn-frequencies $\{f(t)\}$ of the letters A, B, ..., Z derived from a sample of Romanized Japanese is given in Table 7.1. The sample's index of coincidence $s_2 \approx \sum_{t=0}^{25} f^2(t) = 0.0819$ is much larger than the value $s_2 \approx 0.06875$ for English. The letters L, Q, and X do not occur in the Romanized Japanese text.

A new cipher machine was introduced by the Japanese Foreign Office in 1930. Designated RED by the United States, *Angooki Taipu A* would soon be followed by other colors of the rainbow – PURPLE, CORAL, and JADE. The diagnosis and cryptanalysis of RED by the Army Signal Intelligence Service started in 1935 and was completed in one year.

RED was replaced in 1940 by *Angooki Taipu B*, designated PURPLE; its cryptanalysis was completed just before the bombing of Pearl Harbor. Intelligence gleaned from PURPLE traffic gave the United States a decisive edge in World War II.

7.2 HALF-ROTORS

The RED machine used a *half-rotor* invented by Swedish cryptographer Arvid G. Damm. Figure 7.1 depicts a half-rotor cipher machine system with keyboard input and lamp output. Twenty-six wires connect pairs of contacts; one on the the rotor's left lateral face (LLF) to one on the rotor's right lateral face (RLF). Although a stationary output

TABLE 7.1 Japanese Hebern 1-Gram Frequencies

t	$f(t)$	t	$f(t)$	t	$f(t)$
A	0.0900	J	0.0125	S	0.0000
B	0.0175	K	0.0850	T	0.0475
C	0.0075	L	0.0000	U	0.0800
D	0.0175	M	0.0000	V	0.0000
E	0.0575	N	0.0225	W	0.0575
F	0.0075	O	0.0750	X	0.0000
G	0.0175	P	0.1575	Y	0.0900
H	0.0525	Q	0.0000	Z	0.0000
I	0.1300	R	0.0075		

contact plate (OCP) is still used to connect the rotor to the output, the input contact plate is replaced by slip rings situated along a shaft attached to the rotor body. Each letter on the (input) keyboard is connected to one of the half-rotor 26 slip rings. The slip rings rotate or *slip* as the rotor and shaft turn. This mechanical linkage means that each letter is always *opposite* the corresponding LLF letter in every rotor position.

Figure 7.2 shows the encipherment of the same plaintext letter Y by the half-rotor system in two consecutive positions assuming that (1) the rotor's internal wiring connects LLF contact Y to RLF contact D and (2) the RLF contact D is opposite the OCP contact J in the initial position. In the initial rotor position, depressing Y on the keyboard causes a circuit to be completed composed of

1. A path from the keyboard Y to the slip ring Y contact;
2. A path from the slip ring Y contact to the LLF Y contact;
3. A rotor wire from the LLF Y contact to the RLF D contact;

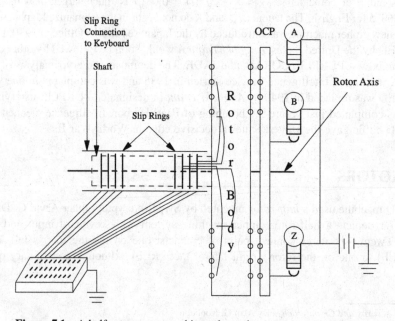

Figure 7.1 A half-rotor cryptomachine schematic.

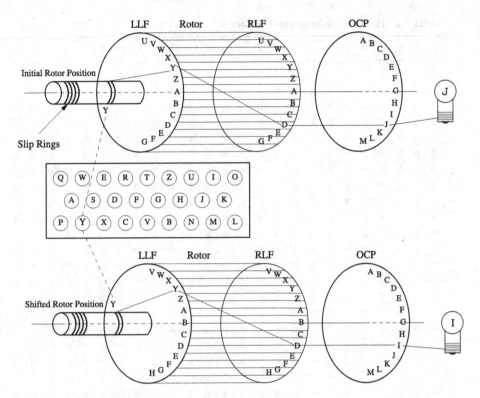

Figure 7.2 Encipherment path with keyboard Y depressed.

4. A path from the RLF D contact to the OCP J contact; and finally

5. The path from the OCP J contact to lamp J.

These connections cause the half-rotor system to encipher plaintext Y to ciphertext J.

In the shifted rotor position, depressing the letter Y on the keyboard now results in a completed circuit composed of the steps 1–3 above but counterclockwise rotation by one position means that the RLF D contact is opposite the OCP I contact so that the circuit includes

4. A path from the RLF D contact to the OCP I contact; and finally

5. The path from the OCP I contact to lamp I.

These connections cause the half-rotor system to encipher plaintext Y to ciphertext I.

If θ is the internal wiring substitution in (benchmark) position $i = 0$, the half-rotor substitution in position i is given by the formula $y = (\mathbf{C}_{-i}\theta)(x)$. Table 7.2 gives the substitutions for the half-rotor system in each position. It exhibits the characteristic property of a half-rotor substitution; namely, the letters in each column trace out the standard alphabet in reverse order $z, y, \ldots, b, a$.

7.3 COMPONENTS OF THE RED MACHINE

The components of the RED machine include

1. A 60-contact half-rotor wired so that it enciphers vowels to vowels and consonants to consonants.

TABLE 7.2   Half-Rotor Substitution Table for 0

i	A	B	C	D	E	F	G	H	I	J	K	L	M	N	O	P	Q	R	S	T	U	V	W	X	Y	Z
0	u	q	t	g	i	v	n	w	o	j	f	c	k	z	a	h	x	b	d	r	p	y	s	l	e	m
1	t	p	s	f	h	u	m	v	n	i	e	b	j	y	z	g	w	a	c	q	o	x	r	k	d	l
2	s	o	r	e	g	t	l	u	m	h	d	a	i	x	y	f	v	z	b	p	n	w	q	j	c	k
3	r	n	q	d	f	s	k	t	l	g	c	z	h	w	x	e	u	y	a	o	m	v	p	i	b	j
4	q	m	p	c	e	r	j	s	k	f	b	y	g	v	w	d	t	x	z	n	l	u	o	h	a	i
5	p	l	o	b	d	q	i	r	j	e	a	x	f	u	v	c	s	w	y	m	k	t	n	g	z	h
6	o	k	n	a	c	p	h	q	i	d	z	w	e	t	u	b	r	v	x	l	j	s	m	f	y	g
7	n	j	m	z	b	o	g	p	h	c	y	v	d	s	t	a	q	u	w	k	i	r	l	e	x	f
8	m	i	l	y	a	n	f	o	g	b	x	u	c	r	s	z	p	t	v	j	h	q	k	d	w	e
9	l	h	k	x	z	m	e	n	f	a	w	t	b	q	r	y	o	s	u	i	g	p	j	c	v	d
10	k	g	j	w	y	l	d	m	e	z	v	s	a	p	q	x	n	r	t	h	f	o	i	b	u	c
11	j	f	i	v	x	k	c	l	d	y	u	r	z	o	p	w	m	q	s	g	e	n	h	a	t	b
12	i	e	h	u	w	j	b	k	c	x	t	q	y	n	o	v	l	p	r	f	d	m	g	z	s	a
13	h	d	g	t	v	i	a	j	b	w	s	p	x	m	n	u	k	o	q	e	c	l	f	y	r	z
14	g	c	f	s	u	h	z	i	a	v	r	o	w	l	m	t	j	n	p	d	b	k	e	x	q	y
15	f	b	e	r	t	g	y	h	z	u	q	n	v	k	l	s	i	m	o	c	a	j	d	w	p	x
16	e	a	d	q	s	f	x	g	y	t	p	m	u	j	k	r	h	l	n	b	z	i	c	v	o	w
17	d	z	c	p	r	e	w	f	x	s	o	l	t	i	j	q	g	k	m	a	y	h	b	u	n	v
18	c	y	b	o	q	d	v	e	w	r	n	k	s	h	i	p	f	j	l	z	x	g	a	t	m	u
19	b	x	a	n	p	c	u	d	v	q	m	j	r	g	h	o	e	i	k	y	w	f	z	s	l	t
20	a	w	z	m	o	b	t	c	u	p	l	i	q	f	g	n	d	h	j	x	v	e	y	r	k	s
21	z	v	y	l	n	a	s	b	t	o	k	h	p	e	f	m	c	g	i	w	u	d	x	q	j	r
22	y	u	x	k	m	z	r	a	s	n	j	g	o	d	e	l	b	f	h	v	t	c	w	p	i	q
23	x	t	w	j	l	y	q	z	r	m	i	f	n	c	d	k	a	e	g	u	s	b	v	o	h	p
24	w	s	v	i	k	x	p	y	q	l	h	e	m	b	c	j	z	d	f	t	r	a	u	n	g	o
25	v	r	u	h	j	w	o	x	p	k	g	d	l	a	b	i	y	c	e	s	q	z	t	m	f	n

2. A *plugboard* connecting typewriter (input) to the rotor slip rings, where the typewriter keys for

   (a) vowels A, E, I, O, U, and Y are connected to the six *vowel slip rings*, and

   (b) consonants B, C, D, F, ..., X, Z are connected to the 20 *consonant slip rings*.

3. A 47-position *breakwheel*, depicted in Figure 7.3, containing as many as 47 *pins* $p_0, p_1, \ldots, p_{46}$, where the ith pin is either *active* $p_i = 1$, if present, or *inactive* $p_i = 0$, if missing.

The breakwheel (rotated) counterclockwise or *stepped* from the *current* active pin to the *next* active pin causes the counterclockwise rotation of the RED's half-rotor. Irregular stepping of the RED results from the removal of some pins, at least four and at most six. Only the 11 pins $p_4, p_5, p_{10}, p_{11}, p_{16}, p_{19}, p_{29}, p_{30}, p_{33}, p_{38}, p_{39}$ are removable. The rotor normally steps one position after the encipherment of a letter, but the breakwheel causes it to step $k + 1$ position if k consecutive pins are removed.

7.3.1   The Breakwheel and its Stepping Sequence

The rotor's position $P(i)$ for the encipherment of plaintext letter x_i is an integer $P(i)$ with $0 \leq P(i) < 47$; it depends on the initial position $P(0)$ of the rotor and the locations of the active pins.

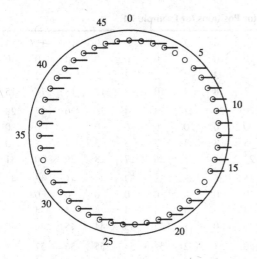

Figure 7.3 The breakwheel with pins p_4, p_5, p_{16}, p_{33} missing.

The positions $P(i)$ of the breakwheel and rotor changes just *after* the encipherment of the $(i-1)$st plaintext letter according to the following schedule:

1. If the pin at position $P(i-1)+1$ is active, then $\delta(i) = 0$ and $P(i) = P(i-1) + 1 + \delta(i)$;

2. If the pins at positions $P(i-1)+1, P(i-2), \ldots, P(i-1)+k+1$ are *inactive* and the pin at position $P(i-1)+k+2$ is active for $k \geq 0$, then $\delta(i) = k$ and $P(i) = P(i-1) + 1 + \delta(k)$.

The sequence of rotor positions $\{P(i)\}$ is determined by the formulas

$$P(i) = P(i-1) + i + \delta(i), \qquad 0 \leq i < \infty \tag{7.1}$$

$$\Delta(i) = \begin{cases} 0, & \text{if } i = 0 \\ \Delta(i-1) + \delta(i), & \text{if } 1 \leq i < \infty \end{cases} \tag{7.2}$$

$$P(i) = P(0) + i + \Delta(i), \qquad 0 \leq i < \infty. \tag{7.3}$$

If N pins have been made *inactive*, then $\Delta(43) = N$, $\tau = 47 - N$ and

$$\Delta(i) = N \left\lfloor \frac{i}{\tau} \right\rfloor + \Delta_\tau(i), \qquad 0 \leq i < \infty \tag{7.4}$$

$$\Delta_\tau(i) = \Delta(i \ (\text{modulo } \tau)), \qquad 0 \leq i < \infty \tag{7.5}$$

$$\Delta_\tau(i + \tau) = \Delta_\tau(i), \qquad 0 \leq i < \infty. \tag{7.6}$$

The function $\Delta_\tau(i)$ is periodic with period τ.

$\{\delta(i)\}$ is the sequence of *stepping shifts* and $\{\Delta(i)\}$ is the *stepping sequence*. $P(i)$ is sum of two terms

$$P(i) = Q(i) + \Delta_\tau(i), \qquad 0 \leq i < \infty \tag{7.7}$$

$$Q(i) = P(0) + i + N \left\lfloor \frac{i}{\tau} \right\rfloor, \qquad 0 \leq i < \infty \tag{7.8}$$

$$Q(i + \tau) = Q(i) + 47, \qquad 0 \leq i < \infty \tag{7.9}$$

$$P(i + \tau) = P(i) + 47, \qquad 0 \leq i < \infty \tag{7.10}$$

where $Q(i)$ depends only on the *total* number of *inactive* pins, but *not* their locations.

TABLE 7.3 Stepping Sequence and Rotor Positions for Example 7.1

i	0	1	2	3	4	5	6	7	8	9	10	11	12	13	14
$\delta(i)$	0	0	0	0	1	0	0	0	0	0	0	0	0	0	1
$\Delta(i)$	0	0	0	0	2	2	2	2	2	2	2	2	2	2	3
$P(i)$	0	1	2	3	6	7	8	9	10	11	12	13	14	15	17

i	15	16	17	18	19	20	21	22	23	24	25	26	27	28	29
$\delta(i)$	0	0	0	0	0	0	0	0	0	0	0	0	0	0	0
$\Delta(i)$	3	3	3	3	3	3	3	3	3	3	3	3	3	3	3
$P(i)$	18	19	20	21	22	23	24	25	26	27	28	29	30	31	32

i	30	31	32	33	34	35	36	37	38	39	40	41	42	43	44
$\delta(i)$	1	0	0	0	0	0	0	0	0	0	0	0	0	0	0
$\Delta(i)$	4	4	4	4	4	4	4	4	4	4	4	4	4	4	4
$P(i)$	34	35	36	37	38	39	40	41	42	43	44	45	46	47	48

i	45	46	47	48	49	50	51	52	53	54	55	56	57	58	59
$\delta(i)$	0	0	2	0	0	0	0	0	0	0	0	0	1	0	0
$\Delta(i)$	4	4	6	6	6	6	6	6	6	6	6	6	7	7	7
$P(i)$	49	50	53	54	55	56	57	58	59	60	61	62	64	65	66

Example 7.1

$P(0) = 0$ and pins p_4, p_5, p_{16}, and p_{33} are removed. The breakwheel stepping shifts $\{\delta(i)\}$, stepping sequences $\{\Delta(i)\}$, and the rotor positions $\{P(i)\}$ are given in Table 7.3.

Example 7.2

$P(0) = 11$ and pins p_4, p_5, p_{16}, and p_{33} are removed. The breakwheel stepping shifts $\{\delta(i)\}$, stepping sequences $\{\Delta(i)\}$, and rotor positions $\{P(i)\}$ are given in Table 7.4. Note that

- $P(i + \tau) = P(i) + 47$ with $\tau = 43 = 47 - 4$ in both Examples 7.1 and 7.2; and
- The first *in*active pin to the right of the initial position is pin p_{16} in Example 7.2, as $P(0) = 11$.

TABLE 7.4 Stepping Sequence and Rotor Positions in Example 7.2

i	0	1	2	3	4	5	6	7	8	9	10	11	12	13	14	15	16	17	18
$\delta(i)$	0	0	0	0	0	1	0	0	0	0	0	0	0	0	0	0	0	0	0
$\Delta(i)$	0	0	0	0	0	1	1	1	1	1	1	1	1	1	1	1	1	1	1
$P(i)$	11	12	13	14	15	17	18	19	20	21	22	23	24	25	26	27	28	29	30

i	19	20	21	22	23	24	25	26	27	28	29	30	31	32	33	34	35	36	37
$\delta(i)$	0	0	1	0	0	0	0	0	0	0	0	0	0	0	0	0	0	0	0
$\Delta(i)$	1	1	2	2	2	2	2	2	2	2	2	2	2	2	2	2	2	2	2
$P(i)$	31	32	34	35	36	37	38	39	40	41	42	43	44	45	46	47	48	49	50

i	38	39	40	41	42	43	44	45	46	47	48	49	50	51	52	53	54	55	56
$\delta(i)$	2	0	0	0	0	0	0	0	0	0	1	0	0	0	0	0	0	0	0
$\Delta(i)$	4	4	4	4	4	4	4	4	4	4	5	5	5	5	5	5	5	5	5
$P(i)$	53	54	55	56	57	58	59	60	61	62	64	65	66	67	68	69	70	71	72

7.3.2 RED Encipherment Rules

The RED system initially defined the vowel set as $VOW = \{A, E, I, O, U, Y\}$. This vowel-to-vowel and consonant-to-consonant paradigm could have been achieved with two half-rotors; a six-slip-ring half-rotor for the vowels and a 20-slip-ring half-rotor for the consonants. The designers of RED chose instead to use a single 60-position rotor, where $60 = \text{lcm}\{16, 20\}$ is the *least common multiple* of 6 and 20. When undertaking the cryptanalysis of RED, the U.S. Signals Intelligence Service built a replica of the RED machine using two half-rotors, one to encipher vowels and a second for consonants.

The RED encipherment of vowels to vowels and consonants to consonants may be described using the two Vigenère-like substitution tableaux shown next as Tables 7.5 and 7.6. These tables show that if RED enciphers $T \rightarrow k$ in position $P = 6$

$$T \rightarrow k = C_{-6}(\theta(T)) = C_{-6}(r)$$

TABLE 7.5 RED Vowel Substitution θ_V

	A	E	I	O	U	Y
0	u	i	o	a	y	e
1	o	e	i	y	u	a
2	i	a	e	u	o	y
3	e	y	a	o	i	u
4	a	u	y	i	e	o
5	y	o	u	e	a	i

TABLE 7.6 RED Consonant Substitution θ_C

i	B	C	D	F	G	H	J	K	L	M	N	P	Q	R	S	T	V	W	X	Z
0	q	t	g	v	n	w	j	f	c	k	z	h	x	b	d	r	p	s	l	m
1	p	s	f	t	m	v	h	d	b	j	x	g	w	z	c	q	n	r	k	l
2	n	r	d	s	l	t	g	c	z	h	w	f	v	x	b	p	m	q	j	k
3	m	q	c	r	k	s	f	b	x	g	v	d	t	w	z	n	l	p	h	j
4	l	p	b	q	j	r	d	z	w	f	t	c	s	v	x	m	k	n	g	h
5	k	n	z	p	h	q	c	x	v	d	s	b	r	t	w	l	j	m	f	g
6	j	m	x	n	g	p	b	w	t	c	r	z	q	s	v	k	h	l	d	f
7	h	l	w	m	f	n	z	v	s	b	q	x	p	r	t	j	g	k	c	d
8	g	k	v	l	d	m	x	t	r	z	p	w	n	q	s	h	f	j	b	c
9	f	j	t	k	c	l	w	s	q	x	n	v	m	p	r	g	d	h	z	b
10	d	h	s	j	b	k	v	r	p	w	m	t	l	n	q	f	c	g	x	z
11	c	g	r	h	z	j	t	q	n	v	l	s	k	m	p	d	b	f	w	x
12	b	f	q	g	x	h	s	p	m	t	k	r	j	l	n	c	z	d	v	w
13	z	d	p	f	w	g	r	n	l	s	j	q	h	k	m	b	x	c	t	v
14	x	c	n	d	v	f	q	m	k	r	h	p	g	j	l	z	w	b	s	t
15	w	b	m	c	t	d	p	l	j	q	g	n	f	h	k	x	v	z	r	s
16	v	z	l	b	s	c	n	k	h	p	f	m	d	g	j	w	t	x	q	r
17	t	x	k	z	r	b	m	j	g	n	d	l	c	f	h	v	s	w	P	q
18	s	w	j	x	q	z	l	h	f	m	c	k	b	d	g	t	r	v	n	p
19	r	v	h	w	p	x	k	g	d	l	b	j	z	c	f	s	q	t	m	n

then RED enciphers $\text{II} \to \text{u}$

$$\text{U} \to \text{u} = \mathbf{C}_{-7}(\theta_V(\text{U})) = \mathbf{C}_{-7}(\text{y})$$

in position $P + 1 = 7 = 1$ (modulo 6). The equations defining the RED substitution require some additional notation; define $\text{VOW} = \{\text{A}, \text{E}, \text{I}, \text{O}, \text{U}, \text{Y}\}$ and $\text{CON} = \{\text{B}, \text{C}, \text{D}, \text{F}, \ldots, \text{W}, \text{X}, \text{Z}\}$.

The *ordinal* functions $\text{ord}_{\text{VOW}}(x)$ with $x \in \text{VOW}$ and $\text{ord}_{\text{CON}}(x)$ with $x \in \text{CON}$ are defined as

- $\text{ord}_{\text{VOW}}(x)$ being the position of x in the vowel alphabet VOW;
- $\text{ord}_{\text{CON}}(x)$ being the position of x in the consonant alphabet CON.

The inverses of ord functions are

- $\text{chr}_{\text{VOW}}(j)$, the jth character in VOW with $0 \le j < 6$;
- $\text{chr}_{\text{CON}}(j)$, the jth character in CON with $0 \le j < 20$.

For example,

- If $\text{ord}_{\text{VOW}}(\text{I}) = 2$, then $\text{chr}_{\text{VOW}}(2) = \text{I}$;
- If $\text{ord}_{\text{CON}}(\text{C}) = 2$, then $\text{chr}_{\text{CON}}(2) = \text{C}$.

The rules for RED encipherment/decipherment with the breakwheel in position $P(i)$ are

- VOW:

If the ith plaintext letter x_i is a vowel, it is enciphered to $y_i \in \text{VOW}$

$$x_i \to z_i \equiv (\text{ord}_{\text{VOW}}(\theta_V(x_i)(- \Delta_\tau(i)) \ (\text{modulo } 6)$$

$$z_i \to y_i = \text{chr}_{\text{VOW}}((z_i - Q(i)) \ (\text{modulo } 6)). \tag{7.11}$$

If the ith ciphertext letter y_i is a vowel, it is deciphered to $x_i \in \text{VOW}$

$$y_i \to z_i = (\text{ord}_{\text{VOW}}(y_i) + Q(i)) \ (\text{modulo } 6)$$

$$z_i \to x_i = \text{chr}_{\text{VOW}}((z_i + \Delta_\tau(i)) \ (\text{modulo } 6)). \tag{7.12}$$

- CON:

If the ith plaintext letter x_i is a consonant, it is enciphered to $y_i \in \text{CON}$

$$x_i \to z_i \equiv (\text{ord}_{\text{CON}}(\theta_C(x_i)) - \Delta_\tau(i)) \ (\text{modulo } 20)$$

$$z_i \to y_i = \text{chr}_{\text{CON}}((z_i - Q(i)) \ (\text{modulo } 20)). \tag{7.13}$$

If the ith ciphertext letter y_i is a consonant, it is deciphered to $x_i \in \text{CON}$

$$y_i \to z_i = (\text{ord}_{\text{CON}}(y_i) + Q(i)) \ (\text{modulo } 20)$$

$$z_i \to x_i = \text{chr}_{\text{CON}}((z_i + \Delta_\tau(i)) \ (\text{modulo } 20)). \tag{7.14}$$

The *shifted ciphertext* is the vector $\underline{z}$ of ordinals.

7.3.3 Estimating the Number of Pins Removed

The coincidence $z_{i+\tau} = z_i$ in the shifted ciphertext implies first that $z_{i+\tau}$ and z_i are both either vowels or consonants. As $\Delta_\tau(i)$ is periodic with period τ, Equations (7.12) and (7.14) show $z_{i+\tau} = z_i$ implies there is also a coincidence of plaintext values $x_{i+\tau} = x_i$.

How likely is the coincidence $x_{i+\tau} = x_i$? If the generation of plaintext is modeled by the random process $\{X_i\}$ of independent and identically distributed random variables with 1-gram probability distribution $\{\pi(t)\}$, then 1-gram X-coincidence (or Z-coincidence) occurs with probability equal to the index of coincidence σ_2; for English-language text

$$\Pr\{X_i = X_{i+\tau}\} = \sigma_2 \approx 0.0685.$$

This suggests that the κ-value for English-language plaintext of length n should be

$$\kappa(N) = \frac{1}{n-\tau} \sum_{i=0}^{n-\tau-1} \chi_{\{z_i = z_{i+\tau}\}}, \quad \tau = 47 - N. \tag{7.15}$$

Evaluating $\kappa(N)$ might be used to test if the number of *in*active pins is N. We should expect $\kappa(N) \approx 0.0685$ when N is equal to the number of *in*active pins, and a smaller value, otherwise.

Example 7.3
$P(0) = 0$ and no pins are removed. Using the substitutions in Tables 7.5 and 7.6 the plaintext

---

The issue of performance evaluation and prediction has concerned users throughout the history of computer evolution. In fact, as in any other technological development, the issue is most acute when the technology is young; the persistent pursuit of products with improved cost-performance characteristics then constantly leads to untried uncertain features. From the initial conception of a system architectural design to its daily operation after installation. In the early planning phase of a new computer system product, the manufacturer

---

is enciphered to

```
                               cipherEx7.3
```

```
rvaax wyeuk tolfu hpycv aymyw uijye mokpp hikev ruavr evlan hylji mohuc
dqtwi agnui fdhef ajvac yosqa dziho nezok awiub yxsop laton iloez dafto
tvwow egike prixa jilme zqpsi ivteo optol xuxos urtet lpohe hjkek ysuyf
eyovj lpewy npomz yfvku bceum ynxqe sufbl zovza kgxyk yxlar fsukd ygnab
tersa tulhy nunbe bjvze zsivx liqhq enaen kwyob rzoeb irlip feyjd eivec
icswi dknaa mucii jzecv agpua sumar epcyr ygxza rorno tasve qaxjz yevgh
uizui birig yekod xufob dqaxw okain olcgu ouffu hbuvt arfwl ipued ofyvv
ajfim  ostyr fotqj olaws rvugu somaj fulyj qyhti dauxw ucyte ffibe  nahiw
hzacy nkiun fjife hjvta hyyzm ynoqo honbz didis eziyq ezxri hecua gjech
rvaxu jisso jpemz ypwac fbiyb wumhl ipaep nhiwe ruavx
```

TABLE 7.7 Normalized κ-Values in Example 7.3

N	$\kappa(N)$	N	$\kappa(N)$	N	$\kappa(N)$
0	0.07063	3	0.06654	6	0.05515
1	0.05792	4	0.04428	7	0.05422
2	0.04444	5	0.05893	8	0.04029

(Note, to encipher, (1) all plaintext characters other than letters are deleted and (2) the RED substitutions θ_V and θ_C are applied to the plaintext translated to upper-case letters. RED ciphertext is displayed using lower-case letters.) Table 7.7 lists the normalized kappa values $\kappa(N)$ for $N = 0(1)8$; the entries are consistent with no pins being removed.

Example 7.4

$P(0) = 0$ and pins p_4, p_5, p_{16}, and p_{33} are removed. The same substitutions θ_V, θ_C and plaintext as in *Example 7.3* produce the ciphertext shown next.

---

cipherEx7.4

```
rvaav toyih rejce dlixr oijis eyfiu  hyfkk cufoq maiqm oqdag zydbi foxos
thlne ywfoe vtxyt uxlur oejgu spawe bomyw ikuan akfub weguz owuil papfo
fghoh eqite zcigu qasty hxwzy ycbua avbar fefax awzoz qtymo mnpop evuyh
eyoxl nqaxu pqinb ugwlo cdyim onxqy sifbl zevzi hdveh evjin bpygz ackew
qinpe pugcy jujve vdqte tnanq dajzj ygouf bniar jqaur yjcuf toexs oulor
urjmu qwbaa zupii tlanh yrboy foxyd azmoc oqjku cecxe fuddo xigqh eodmn
yogyo hoxom aiquj dukog jvadc opais onfji eihhi kcewv osgxm yqeuf agevv
ijfum yster fytqg ojatq psudo pijyf bohuf mudqe xuisr iwopy zzavy juzup
zrite gcoyf vzovi xzmle xaapc ydogo wodqp sisij ymaod ymlfa suneo rtuns
dhoke tuddy szowk ezhim pluyj futps iwaav tneda xoycf
```

Table 7.8 lists the normalized kappa values $\kappa(N)$ for $N = 0(1)8$; the entries are consistent with $N = 4$ pins being removed.

7.4 CRIBBING RED CIPHERTEXT

We will describe the cryptanalysis of RED ciphertext using English-language text. The *vowel/consonant pattern* of a (plaintext) crib $\underline{u} = (u_0, u_1, \ldots, u_{M-1})$ is

$$\underline{\chi}(\underline{u}) = (\chi(u_0), \chi(u_1), \ldots, \chi(u_{M-1})) \quad \begin{cases} \chi(u_j) = V, & \text{if } u_j \in \text{VOW} \\ \chi(u_j) = C, & \text{if } u_j \in \text{CON}, \end{cases} \quad 0 \le j < M. \quad (7.16)$$

TABLE 7.8 Normalized κ-Values for Example 7.4

N	$\kappa(N)$	N	$\kappa(N)$	N	$\kappa(N)$
0	0.02230	3	0.05545	6	0.03676
1	0.03340	4	0.06273	7	0.05321
2	0.04815	5	0.04788	8	0.05495

A *necessary* condition that the RED ciphertext fragment $y_{[i,i+M)} \equiv (y_i, \ldots, y_{i+M-1})$ be the encipherment of the (plaintext) crib $\underline{u} = (u_0, u_1, \ldots, u_{M-1})$ is

$$\begin{cases} u_j \in \text{VOW} \Leftrightarrow y_{i+j} \in \text{VOW}, & \text{if } u_j \text{ is a vowel} \\ u_j \in \text{CON} \Leftrightarrow y_{i+j} \in \text{CON}, & \text{if } u_j \text{ is a consonant,} \end{cases} \quad 0 \leq j < M. \quad (7.17)$$

To crib RED ciphertext for the plaintext $\underline{u} = (u_0, u_1, \ldots, u_{M-1})$, the RED ciphertext is searched for fragments $y_{[i,i+M)}$ that have the same the vowel/consonant pattern as that of $\underline{u}$.

Of course, Equation (7.17) is only a necessary condition that $\underline{u} \rightarrow y_{[i,i+M)}$ and some fragments fail to correspond to plaintext crib. Additional constraints need to be imposed before concluding that $y_{[i,i+M)}$ is the encipherment of the crib $\underline{u}$.

7.4.1 Cribbing RED Cipherment: No Inactive Breakwheel Pins

If all pins on the breakwheel are active, then $\tau = 47$ and $P(i) = P(0) + i$. As $P(0)$ is unknown, the recovery of θ_V and θ_C by cryptanalysis assuming $P(0) = 0$ will then be related to Tables 7.5 and 7.6 by a shift in rows.

If $y_{[i,i+M)} = (y_i, y_{i+1}, \ldots, y_{i+M-1})$ is the RED encipherment of the crib $\underline{u} = (u_0, u_1, \ldots, u_{M-1})$, then Equations (7.11) to (7.14) are replaced by Equations (7.18) to (7.21).

- VOW:

If the $(i+j)$th plaintext letter x_{i+j} is a vowel, it is enciphered to $y_{i+j} \in \text{vow}$

$$x_{i+j} \rightarrow z_{i+j} \equiv \text{ord}_{\text{VOW}}(\theta_V(x_{i+j}))$$
$$z_{i+j} \rightarrow y_{i+j} = \text{chr}_{\text{VOW}}((z_{i+j} - (i+j)) \,(\text{modulo } 6)), \quad 0 \leq j < M. \quad (7.18)$$

If the $(i+j)$th ciphertext letter y_{i+j} is a vowel, it is deciphered to $x_{i+j} \in \text{vow}$

$$y_{i+j} \rightarrow z_{i+j} = (\text{ord}_{\text{VOW}}(y_{i+j}) + (i+j)) \,(\text{modulo } 6)$$
$$z_i \rightarrow x_i = \text{chr}_{\text{VOW}}(z_{i+j}), \quad 0 \leq j < M. \quad (7.19)$$

- CON:

If the $(i+j)$th plaintext letter x_{i+j} is a consonant, it is enciphered to $y_{i+j} \in \text{CON}$

$$x_{i+j} \rightarrow z_{i+j} \equiv \text{ord}_{\text{CON}}(\theta_C(x_{i+j}))$$
$$z_{i+j} \rightarrow y_{i+j} = \text{chr}_{\text{CON}}((z_{i+j} - (i+j)) \,(\text{modulo } 20)), \quad 0 \leq j < M. \quad (7.20)$$

If the $(i+j)$th ciphertext letter y_{i+j} is a consonant, it is deciphered to $x_{i+j} \in \text{CON}$

$$y_{i+j} \rightarrow z_{i+j} = (\text{ord}_{\text{CON}}(y_{i+j}) + (i+j)) \,(\text{modulo } 20)$$
$$z_{i+j} \rightarrow x_{i+j} = \text{chr}_{\text{CON}}(z_{i+j}), \quad 0 \leq j < M. \quad (7.21)$$

If $y_{[i,i+M)} = (y_i, y_{i+1}, \ldots, y_{i+M-1})$ is the RED ciphertext of the crib $\underline{u} = (u_0, u_1, \ldots, u_{M-1})$, then Equations (7.19) and (7.21) determine the substitutions

$$u_j = \begin{cases} \theta_V(z_{i+j}), & \text{if } z_{i+j} \text{ is a vowel} \\ \theta_C(z_{i+j}), & \text{if } z_{i+j} \text{ is a consonent,} \end{cases} \quad \text{for } 0 \leq j < M.$$

Example 7.5

As the plaintext of `cipherEx7.3` describes aspects of performance evaluation, possible cribs include

1. PLANNINGPHASE.
2. PERFORMANCE
3. EVALUATION
4. COMPUTERSYSTEM.

$\delta(i) = \Delta(i) = 0$ and $P(i) = Q(i) = i$, because cipherEx7.3 resulted from RED encipherment with all pins active.

We began by searching cipherEx7.3 for fragments $y_{(i,i+13)}$ with the vowel/consonant pattern CCVCCVCCCCVCV of the longest crib PLANNINGPHASE $= \underline{u} = (u_0, u_1, \ldots, u_{12})$; one instance of this vowel/consonant pattern occurs at position $i = 400$. The search results are displayed in Table 7.9, which contains

Row 0: the vowel/consonant pattern;

Row 1: the crib $(u_0, u_1, \ldots, u_{12})$;

Row 2: the ciphertext $(y_{400}, y_{401}, \ldots, y_{412})$;

Rows 3–6: for indices j corresponding to the vowels

- the ordinals of the ciphertext $\mathrm{ord}_{\mathrm{VOW}}(y_{400+j})$ (modulo 6),
- the breakwheel positions $(400 + j)$ (modulo 6),
- the shifted ciphertext z_{400+j}, and
- the recovered letter-substitutions $x_{400+j} = \theta_V(z_{400+j})$.

Rows 7–10: for indices j corresponding to the consonants

- the ordinals of the ciphertext $\mathrm{ord}_{\mathrm{VOW}}(y_{400+j})$ (modulo 20),
- the breakwheel positions $(400 + j)$ (modulo 20),
- the shifted ciphertext z_{400+j}, and
- the recovered letter substitutions $x_{400+j} = \theta'_C(z_{400+j})$.

If we make the assumption PLANNINGPHASE $\rightarrow$ hbuvtarfwlipu, then several entries in row 0 of Tables 7.5 and 7.6 are determined. These are shown in Tables 7.10 and 7.11. Next, we search cipherEx7.3 for fragments $y_{(i,i+10)}$ with the vowel/consonant pattern CVCCVCCVCCV of the crib PERFORMANCE $= \underline{u} = (u_0, u_1, \ldots, u_{10})$. The

TABLE 7.9 Possible Ciphertext Fragment of the Crib PLANNINGPHASE in cipherEx7.3

0.	C	C	V	C	C	V	C	C	C	C	V	C	V
1.	P	L	A	N	N	I	N	G	P	H	A	S	E
2.	h	b	u	v	t	a	r	f	w	l	i	p	u
3.			4			0					2		4
4.			0			3					2		4
5.			4			3					5		2
6.			u			o					u		i
7.	5	0		16	15		13	3	17	8		11	
8.	0	1		3	4		6	7	8	9		11	
9.	5	1		19	19		19	10	5	17		2	
10.	h	c		z	z		z	n	h	w		d	

TABLE 7.10   Partial Reconstruction of Row 0 of θ_V from the Cribs PLANNINGPHASE

A	E	I	o	U	Y
↓	↓	↓	↓	↓	↓
u	i	`o			

TABLE 7.11   Partial Reconstruction of Row 0 of θ_C from the Crib PLANNINGPHASE

B	C	D	F	G	H	J	K	L	M	N	P	Q	R	S	T	V	W	X	Z
↓	↓	↓	↓	↓	↓	↓	↓	↓	↓	↓	↓	↓	↓	↓	↓	↓	↓	↓	↓
				n	w				c		z	h		d					

search finds six occurrences of this vowel/consonant pattern, which are listed in Table 7.12. In each row we find

- The position in the ciphertext where this pattern occurs, and
- Assuming the fragment corresponds to the crib, the resulting recovered letter substitutions

$$u_j = \begin{cases} \theta_V(z_{i+j}), & \text{if } u_j \text{ is a vowel} \\ \theta_C(z_{i+j}), & \text{if } u_j \text{ is a consonant.} \end{cases}$$

It is not true that all of the entries found in the search correspond to the crib. An entry in Table 7.12 will be rejected if it leads to a contradiction with values in Tables 7.10 and 7.11. For example,

1. PERFORMANCE → wudtazgtibzi implies $\theta_C(P) = w$, inconsistent with Table 7.11 entry $\theta_C(P) = h$.
2. PERFORMANCE → vabkuztitwu implies $\theta_C(P) = v$, inconsistent with Table 7.11 entry $\theta_C(P) = h$.
3. PERFORMANCE → picdavdedrt implies $\theta_C(P) = p$, inconsistent with Table 7.11 entry $\theta_C(P) = h$.
4. PERFORMANCE → davdedriksa implies $\theta_C(P) = d$, inconsistent with Table 7.11 entry $\theta_C(P) = h$.

Only PERFORMANCE → hibvabkuzti, appearing at both positions 10 and 231, leads to letter substitutions that are consistent with the current partial reconstruction of the

TABLE 7.12   Possible Ciphertext Fragments of the Crib PERFORMANCE in cipherEx7.3

	C	V	C	C	V	C	C	V	C	C	V
	P	E	R	F	O	R	M	A	N	C	E
10	h	i	b	v	a	b	k	u	z	t	i
44	w	u	d	t	a	z	t	i	b	z	i
231	h	i	b	v	a	b	k	u	z	t	i
234	v	a	b	k	u	z	t	i	t	w	u
545	p	i	c	d	s	v	d	e	d	r	i
548	d	a	v	d	e	d	r	i	j	s	a

TABLE 7.13 Partial Reconstruction of Row 0 of θ_V from the Cribs PERFORMANCE and PLANNINGPHASE

A	E	I	o	U	Y
↓	↓	↓	↓	↓	↓
u	i	o	a		

TABLE 7.14 Partial Reconstruction of Row 0 of θ_C from the Cribs PERFORMANCE and PLANNINGPHASE

B	C	D	F	G	H	J	K	L	M	N	P	Q	R	S	T	V	W	X	Z
↓	↓	↓	↓	↓	↓	↓	↓	↓	↓	↓	↓	↓	↓	↓	↓	↓	↓	↓	↓
	t		v	n	w			c	k	z	h	b	d						

substitution θ_V and θ_C. Accepting the cribs for PERFORMANCE at positions 10 and 231 allows us to further reconstruct the rotors, as shown in Tables 7.13 and 7.14.

Finally, we search cipherEx7.3 for fragments $y_{(i,i+9)}$ with the vowel/consonant pattern VCVCVVCVVC of the crib EVALUATION $= \underline{u} = (u_0, u_1, \ldots, u_9)$. The search finds one occurrence of this vowel/consonant pattern, which is listed in Table 7.15 with the same format as used in Table 7.12. All of the letter substitutions in Table 7.15 are consistent with the entries in Tables 7.13 and 7.14. The crib of EVALUATION augments the partial reconstruction of the rotors shown in Tables 7.16 and 7.17. The search for additional words or a partial decipherment can be used to complete the cryptanalysis.

7.4.2 Cribbing RED Ciphertext with Inactive Pins

We begin by computing the $\kappa(N)$-scores and identifying the most likely number N of *inactive* pins.

A *stepping equation* is an equation of the form

$$s = \mathbf{C}_{\delta_\tau(k)}(t), \qquad 0 \le k < \tau,$$

TABLE 7.15 Possible Cribs of EVALUATION in cipherEx7.3

	V	C	V	C	V	V	C	V	V	C
	E	V	A	L	U	A	T	I	O	N
21	i	p	u	c	y	u	r	o	a	z

TABLE 7.16 Partial Reconstruction of Row 0 θ_C from Cribs PERFORMANCE, PLANNINGPHASE, and EVALUATION

A	E	I	o	U	Y
↓	↓	↓	↓	↓	↓
u	i	o	a		

TABLE 7.17   Partial Reconstruction of Row 0 of θ_B from the Cribs PERFORMANCE, PLANNINGPHASE, and EVALUATION

B	C	D	F	G	H	J	K	L	M	N	P	Q	R	S	T	V	W	X	Z
↓	↓	↓	↓	↓	↓	↓	↓	↓	↓	↓	↓	↓	↓	↓	↓	↓	↓	↓	↓
	t		v	n	w			c	k	z	h	b	d	r	p				

where t is a letter in the crib and s a letter in the ciphertext fragment that has the same vowel/consonant pattern as the crib.

If a search of the ciphertext has found a fragment $y_{(i,i+M)}$ with the same vowel/consonant pattern as a (plaintext) crib $\underline{u} = (u_0, u_1, \ldots, u_{M-1})$, Equations (7.19) and (7.21) provide several stepping equations.

Example 7.6

As the ciphertext cipherEx7.4 has been enciphered with $N = 4$ *in*active pins, the sequence $\{\Delta_\tau(i)\}$ is periodic with period 43. As in the previous example, we search for vowel/consonant patterns that are consistent with the cribs PLANNINGPHASE, PERFORMANCE, EVALUATION, and COMPUTERSYSTEM.

We begin by searching cipherEx7.3 for fragments $y_{(i,i+13)}$ with the vowel/consonant pattern CCVCCVCCCCVCV of the longest crib PLANNINGPHASE $= \underline{u} = (u_0, u_1, \ldots, u_{12})$, one instance of this vowel/consonant pattern occurs at position $i = 400$. The search results are displayed in Table 7.18. The entries are in Table 7.18 are organized as follows:

> *Row 0*: the vowel/consonant pattern;
>
> *Row 1*: the crib $(u_0, u_1, \ldots, u_{12})$;
>
> *Row 2*: the ciphertext $(y_{400}, y_{401}, \ldots, y_{412})$;
>
> *Rows 3–7*: for indices j corresponding to the vowels
>
> - the ordinals of the ciphertext $\mathrm{ord}_{\mathrm{VOW}}(y_{400+j})$ (modulo 6),
> - the breakwheel positions $(400 + j)$ (modulo 6),
> - the shifted ciphertext z_{400+j},

TABLE 7.18   Potential Cribs of PLANNINGPHASE in cipherEx7.4

0.	C	C	V	C	C	V	C	C	C	C	V	C	V
1.	P	L	A	N	N	I	N	G	P	H	A	S	E
2.	k	c	e	w	v	o	s	g	x	m	y	q	e
3.			1		3						5		1
4.			0		3						2		4
5.			1		0						1		5
6.			e		a						e		y
7.			15		18						23		25
8.	7	0		17	16		14	4	18	9		12	
9.	16	17		19	0		2	3	4	5		7	
10.	3	17		5	16		16	7	2	14		19	
11.	f	x		v	v		v	k	d	s		z	
12.	13	14		16	17		19	20	21	22		24	

- the character $chr_{VOW}(z_{400+j})$,
- $(i+j)$(modulo 43).

Rows 8–12: for indices j corresponding to the consonants,

- the ordinals of the ciphertext $ord_{VOW}(y_{400+j}$ (modulo 20)),
- the breakwheel positions $Q(400+j)$ (modulo 20),
- the shifted ciphertext z_{400+j},
- the character $chr_{CON}(z_{400+j})$,
- $(i+j)$ (modulo 43).

The stepping equations derived from Table 7.18 are listed in Table 7.19.

Analysis

As f follows d in the consonant set, the stepping equations in Table 7.19

$$\theta_C(P) = \mathbf{C}_{\delta_{43}(13)}(f) \qquad \theta_C(P) = \mathbf{C}_{\delta_{43}(21)}(d) \tag{7.22}$$

require

$$\delta_{43}(21) = 1 + \delta_{43}(13).$$

The stepping equations in Table 7.19

$$\theta_V(A) = \mathbf{C}_{\delta_{43}(15)}(e) \qquad \theta_V(A) = \mathbf{C}_{\delta_{43}(23)}(e) \tag{7.23}$$

require

$$\delta_{43}(15) = \delta_{43}(23). \tag{7.24}$$

We claim $\delta_{43}(25) = \delta_{43}(23)$; for proof, use the stepping equations in Table 7.19:

$$\theta_V(I) = \mathbf{C}_{\delta_{43}(18)}(a) \tag{7.25}$$

$$\theta_V(E) = \mathbf{C}_{\delta_{43}(25)}(y). \tag{7.26}$$

As $\delta_{43}(25) \leq \delta_{43}(23) + 2$, there are two possibilities; if $\delta_{43}(25) = 1 + \delta_{43}(23)$, Equation (7.26) gives

$$\theta_V(E) = \mathbf{C}_{\delta_{43}}(25)(y) = \mathbf{C}_{\delta_{43}(23)}(a), \tag{7.27}$$

which is inconsistent with Equation (7.23). If $\delta_{43}(25) = 2 + \delta_{43}(23)$, Equation (7.26) gives

$$\theta_V(E) = \mathbf{C}_{\delta_{43}(25)}(y) = \mathbf{C}_{\delta_{43}(23)}(e), \tag{7.28}$$

which is also inconsistent with Equation (7.23). Thus, $\delta_{43}(18) = \delta_{43}(25)$.

TABLE 7.19 The Stepping Equations Derived from Table 7.18

$\theta_C(P) = \mathbf{C}_{\delta_{43}(13)}(f)$	$\theta_C(L) = \mathbf{C}_{\delta_{43}(14)}(x)$	$\theta_V(A) = \mathbf{C}_{\delta_{43}(15)}(e)$
$\theta_C(N) = \mathbf{C}_{\delta_{43}(16)}(v)$	$\theta_C(N) = \mathbf{C}_{\delta_{43}(17)}(v)$	$\theta_V(I) = \mathbf{C}_{\delta_{43}(18)}(a)$
$\theta_C(N) = \mathbf{C}_{\delta_{43}(19)}(v)$	$\theta_C(G) = \mathbf{C}_{\delta_{43}(20)}(k)$	$\theta_C(P) = \mathbf{C}_{\delta_{43}(21)}(d)$
$\theta_C(H) = \mathbf{C}_{\delta_{43}(22)}(s)$	$\theta_V(A) = \mathbf{C}_{\delta_{43}(23)}(e)$	$\theta_C(S) = \mathbf{C}_{\delta_{43}(24)}(z)$
$\theta_V(E) = \mathbf{C}_{\delta_{43}(25)}(y)$		

TABLE 7.20   Letter Substitutions Implied by Table 7.19

i	$\theta_C(P)$	$\theta_C(L)$	$\theta_V(A)$	$\theta_C(N)$	$\theta_V(I)$	$\theta_C(G)$	$\theta_C(H)$	$\theta_C(S)$	$\theta_V(E)$
0	f	z	i	w	e	l	s	b	a
1	g	b	o	x	i	m	t	c	e
2	h	c	u	z	o	n	w	d	i
3	j	d	y	b	u	p	v	f	o

The stepping equations

$$\theta_C(L) = \mathbf{C}_{\delta_{43}(14)}(x) \tag{7.29}$$

$$\theta_C(N) = \mathbf{C}_{\delta_{43}(16)}(v) = \mathbf{C}_{\delta_{43}(17)}(v) = \mathbf{C}_{\delta_{43}(19)}(v) \tag{7.30}$$

require $\delta_{43}(14) = 1 + \delta_{43}(13)$. We conclude that

$$\delta_{43}(13) = i, \; \delta_{43}(14) = \delta_{43}(15) = \cdots = \delta_{43}(25) = i + 1 \tag{4.31}$$

for some i with $0 \leq i \leq 3$. The solutions consistent with Equations (7.22) to (7.31) are given in Table 7.20.

Searching the ciphertext for the cribs PERFORMANCE, EVALUATION, and COMPUTERSYSTEM yields the results given in Tables 7.21 to 7.23, which list

Row 0: the vowel/consonant pattern,

Row 1: the crib $\underline{u} = (u_0, u_1, \ldots, u_{M-1})$,

in row-pairs $(2j, 2j + 1)$

Row 2j: the position i in the ciphertext at which the ciphertext fragment $y_{(i,i+M)}$ occurs together with the characters of the shifted ciphertext $z_{(i,i+M)}$.

Row 2j + 1: the values of $(i + j)$ (modulo 43).

The entry in Table 7.21 corresponding to the fragment at position 10 is the stepping equation $\mathbf{C}_{\delta_{43}(10)}(P) = f$.

TABLE 7.21   Potential Cribs of PERFORMANCE in cipherEx7.4

	C	V	C	C	V	C	C	V	C	C	V
	P	E	R	F	O	R	M	A	N	C	E
10	f	a	x	s	o	w	g	e	v	q	y
	10	11	12	13	14	15	16	17	18	19	20
44	w	u	d	r	u	w	r	a	x	w	a
	1	2	3	4	5	6	7	8	9	10	11
231	d	y	w	r	o	w	g	e	v	q	y
	16	17	18	19	20	21	22	23	24	25	26
234	r	o	w	g	e	v	q	y	q	s	e
	19	20	21	22	23	24	25	26	27	28	29
545	l	u	w	x	i	q	x	o	x	m	u
	29	30	31	32	33	34	35	36	37	38	39
548	x	i	q	x	o	x	m	u	f	n	i
	32	33	34	35	36	37	38	39	40	41	42

TABLE 7.22 Potential Cribs of EVALUATION in cipherEx7.4

	V	C	V	C	V	V	C	V	V	C
	E	V	A	L	U	A	T	I	O	N
21	y	l	e	x	i	e	n	a	o	t
	21	22	23	24	25	26	27	28	29	30

Analysis

We assume that PLANNINGPHASE occurs in cipherEx7.4 and that the entries in one of the rows in Table 7.20 are correct. To identify which entries in Table 7.21 are truly the cribs of PERFORMANCE, we look for contradictions in Tables 7.20.

1. If PERFORMANCE → wudruwraxwa at position 44 = 1 (modulo 43), then the implied stepping equation $\theta_V(E) = C_{\delta_{43}(2)}(u)$ is inconsistent with the entries in Table 7.20.

2. If PERFORMANCE → rowgevqyqse at position 234 (modulo 43) = 19, then the implied stepping equation $\theta_C(P) = C_{\delta_{43}(19)}(r)$ is inconsistent with the entries in Table 7.20.

3. If PERFORMANCE → luwxiqxoxmu at position 545 (modulo 43) = 29, then the implied stepping equation $\theta_C(P) = C_{\delta_{43}(29)}(l)$ is inconsistent with the entries in Table 7.20.

4. If PERFORMANCE → xiqxoxmufni at position 548 (modulo 43) = 32, then the implied stepping equation $\theta_C(P) = C_{\delta_{43}(32)}(x)$ is inconsistent with the entries in Table 7.20.

5. If PERFORMANCE → dywrowgevqy at position 231 (modulo 43) = 16, then the implied stepping equation $\theta_C(R) = C_{\delta_{43}(18)}(w) = z$ is inconsistent with the $i = 0$ entries in Table 7.20.

6. If PERFORMANCE → dywrowgevqy at position 231 (modulo 43) = 16, then the implied stepping equation $\theta_C(R) = C_{\delta_{43}(18)}(w) = b$ is inconsistent with the $i = 1$ entries in Table 7.20.

7. If PERFORMANCE → dywxowgevqy at position 231 (modulo 43) = 16, then the implied stepping equation $\theta_C(P) = C_{\delta_{43}(1d)}(w) = j$ is inconsistent with the $i = 3$ entries in Table 7.20.

As $i = 2$,

$$\text{PERFORMANCE} \rightarrow \begin{cases} \text{faxsowgevqy} \\ \text{dywrowgevqy} \end{cases}$$

TABLE 7.23 Potential Cribs of COMPUTER SYSTEM in cipherEx7.4

	C	V	C	C	V	C	V	C	C	V	C	C	V	C
	C	O	M	P	U	T	E	R	S	Y	S	T	E	M
419	p	i	f	c	e	m	u	v	x	o	x	r	i	k
	32	33	34	35	36	37	38	39	40	41	42	0	1	2
447	r	e	q	n	i	w	y	w	g	i	z	n	i	x
	17	18	19	20	21	22	23	24	25	26	27	28	29	30

provides additional letter substitutions and stepping sequence values

$$\delta_{43}(i) = \begin{cases} 2, & \text{if } 10 \leq i \leq 13 \\ 3, & \text{if } 14 \leq i \leq 26. \end{cases} \tag{7.32}$$

The crib `ylexienaot` of EVALUATION provides three additional stepping equations

$$\theta_C(V) = \mathbf{C}_{\delta_{43}(22)}(1) \tag{7.33}$$

$$\theta_V(U) = \mathbf{C}_{\delta_{43}(25)}(i) \tag{7.34}$$

$$\theta_C(T) = \mathbf{C}_{\delta_{43}(27)}(n) \tag{7.35}$$

and the stepping sequence value

$$\Delta_{43}(i) = \begin{cases} 3, & \text{if } 27 \leq i \leq 29 \\ 4, & \text{if } i \geq 30. \end{cases} \tag{7.36}$$

The partial reconstruction of the two rotors yields the six vowel substitutes and 13 of the 20 consonant substitutes.

7.5 GENERALIZED VOWELS AND CONSONANTS

Changes in RED were made after it was put into service; the letters were divided into two sets VOW with six elements and CON with 20 elements. A `plugboard` connected the VOW keyboard letters to the slip-ring vowels A, E, I, O, U, and Y, and the OCP vowels A, E, I, O, U, and Y were connected to the lamps in VOW. The same process was carried out with respect to the letters in CON.

The plugboard connections are part of the key and must be recovered. Fortunately, the process is quite simple; Table 7.24 lists the frequencies of occurrence of the (ciphertext) letters in `cipherEx7.4`. Note that the frequencies of the vowels A, E, I, O, U, and Y are in excess of 0.0615, and those of consonants are bounded above by 0.0427. Thus, simple frequency counts negate the effect of using generalized vowels/consonants.

TABLE 7.24   1-Gram Letter Counts and Frequencies in `cipherEx7.4`

t	$N(t)$	$f(t)$	t	$N(t)$	$f(t)$	t	$N(t)$	$f(t)$
a	37	0.0632	j	21	0.0359	s	17	0.0291
b	12	0.0205	k	10	0.0171	t	19	0.0325
c	16	0.0274	l	12	0.0205	u	40	0.0684
d	22	0.0376	m	17	0.0291	v	18	0.0308
e	36	0.0615	n	17	0.0291	w	15	0.0256
f	25	0.0427	o	50	0.0855	x	19	0.0325
g	17	0.0291	P	19	0.0325	y	37	0.0632
h	17	0.0291	q	22	0.0376	z	20	0.0342
i	36	0.0615	r	14	0.0239			

7.6   "CLIMB MOUNT ITAKA" – WAR!

The following was included in a cable sent November 19, 1941, from the Japanese Foreign Ministry to all Japanese foreign diplomatic posts:

> ···Consequently, we will include in the middle and at the end of our Japanese language news programs beamed to all points one or another or all of the following code phrases:

1. HIGASHI NO KAZE AME (East Wind Rain) *meaning* relations with America are not according to expectations.

2. KITANOKAZE KUMORI (North Wind Cloudy) *meaning* relations with Soviet Union are not according to expectations.

3. NISHO NO KAZE HARE (West Wind Clear) *meaning* relations with England are not according to expectations.

When you hear any or all of these phrases repeated twice in the newscasts, destroy your codes and confidential papers.

A new Japanese machine ciphermachine (Fig. 7.4) went into service in March 1939 [Rowlett and Kahn, 1998], designated by the Japanese as *97-shiki O-bun In-ji-ki* (Alphabetical Typewriter '97), the number 97 signaling the year 2597 of its creation in the Japanese calendar [Kahn, 1967]. It was also referred to as *Angooki taipu B* (Cryptographic system, type B) and PURPLE by the United States intelligence community.

PURPLE replaced the *Type Number '91* [Farago, 1967], also referred to as *Angooki taipu A* (Cryptographic system, type A) and RED. Alphabetical Typewriter '97 was

Figure 7.4   Japanese PURPLE machine (Courtesy of NSA).

developed by naval Captain Risaburo Ito, who had also helped design the Red code machine. Ito was familiar with Yardley's success in cryptanalyzing the Japanese codes during the 1921 Admiralty Conference.

7.7 COMPONENTS OF THE PURPLE MACHINE

PURPLE had a typewriter input, lamp output, a plugboard, and an internal switch implementing polyalphabetic substitutions. The rotor in the RED system was replaced by 25-position *stepping switches* or *steppers*, which were used as components in the automatic dial telephone system in the United States in the 1930s. A stepper allows any input line to be connected to any output line. The top and side views of a PURPLE stepper are depicted in Figure 7.5. The *wiper* or (blade) moves horizontally; passing between a pair of compressed contacts creates an electrical path from the input to output lines.

7.7.1 Encipherment of Letters in VOW

PURPLE continued the paradigm used in RED to encipher vowels to vowels and consonants to consonants. The wipers on all levels pointed in each level to the same output position and moved in unison, rotating (or stepping) one position for each letter enciphered. The PURPLE vowel-stepper implemented 25 (different) permutations of the vowels VOW = {A, E, I, O, U, Y} (Fig. 7.6).

To allow encipherment of generalized vowels as in RED, a plugboard connected

- The VOW keyboard letters to the six input contacts on the six levels, and
- From each of the 25 letter outputs on each level to the VOW output lamps.

The PURPLE vowel-stepper implemented a periodic polyphabetic substitution with period 25. The vowel x is enciphered to the vowel y as a result of Three transformations

$$x \rightarrow y(1) \rightarrow y(2) \rightarrow (3) = y = \text{PUR}_V(x). \tag{7.37}$$

Transformation #1

$$x \rightarrow y(1) = \text{PL}_V(x)$$

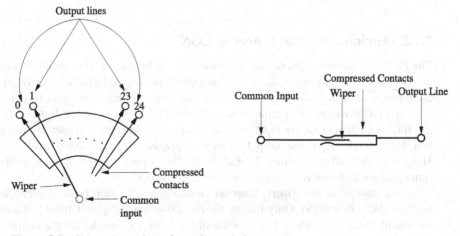

Figure 7.5 Side and top view of stepping switch.

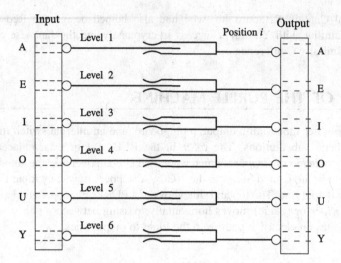

Figure 7.6 The PURPLE vowel-stepper.

where $PL_V(x)$ is the letter on the vowel-stepper to which vowel x is connected by the vowel-plugboard.

Transformation #2

$$y(1) \rightarrow y(2) = VS_{VP((i+i_0(V)) \ (modulo \ 25))}(y(1))$$

where $VS_{VP((i+i_0(V)) \ (modulo \ 25))}$ is the vowel-stepper substitution in position $VP((i + i_0(V))$ (modulo 25)) with $i_0(V)$ being the initial position of the vowel-stepper.

Transformation #3

$$y(2) \rightarrow y(3) = PL_V^{-1}(y(2)) = y = PUR_V(x)$$

where y is the output lamp letter to which output vowel $y(1)$ is connected by the inverse vowel-plugboard PL_V^{-1}. The period of $x \rightarrow y = PUR_V$ is 25.

7.7.2 Encipherment of Letters in CON

The PURPLE encipherment of consonants used three banks, each consisting of four (six-level) 25-position consonant-steppers (C-steppers), connected in tandem. Only 20 of the 24 contacts in each bank were used; the remaining contacts were used to control the motion of the wipers. A permutation network $\Pi(i, i + 1)$ connected the outputs of the Bank i C-stepper to the inputs of the Bank $i + 1$ consonant-stepper for $i = 0, 1, 2$ and from Bank 3 to the output consonant-plugboard. Each bank interconnection $\Pi(i, i + 1)$ used 20×25 wires. In each bank, the wipers pointed in each level to the same position and moved in usison, as with the V-stepper.

The motion of the wipers, however, was different in each bank – either *fast* (F), *medium* (M), or *slow* (S). Only one of the three C-stepper wipers moved (rotated) with the encipherment of a letter. The position of the Bank k C-stepper for the encipherment of the plaintext letter in the ith position is denoted by $Cpos_{\mathcal{M}(k), i+IC_0(k)}$ where $\mathcal{M}(k)$

denotes the motion type of Bank k

$$\mathcal{M}(k) = \begin{cases} F, & \text{if Bank } k \text{ wiper's motion is fast} \\ M, & \text{if Bank } k \text{ wiper's motion is medium} \\ S, & \text{if Bank } k \text{ wiper's motion is slow} \end{cases} \qquad (7.38)$$

where $IC_0(k)$ is the initial position of the Bank k wiper.

Linkages were constructed so that the movement of the three banks could be set to any of the six combinations:

$$(\text{F, M, S}) \equiv \begin{pmatrix} F & M & S \\ 0 & 1 & 2 \end{pmatrix} \qquad (\text{F, S, M}) \equiv \begin{pmatrix} F & S & M \\ 0 & 1 & 2 \end{pmatrix} \qquad (\text{M, S, F}) \equiv \begin{pmatrix} M & S & F \\ 0 & 1 & 2 \end{pmatrix}$$

$$(\text{M, F, S}) \equiv \begin{pmatrix} M & F & S \\ 0 & 1 & 2 \end{pmatrix} \qquad (\text{S, M, F}) \equiv \begin{pmatrix} S & M & F \\ 0 & 1 & 2 \end{pmatrix} \qquad (\text{S, F, M}) \equiv \begin{pmatrix} S & F & M \\ 0 & 1 & 2 \end{pmatrix}$$

Figure 7.7 shows a PURPLE switch, and Figure 7.8 depicts the consonant banks with the input/output contacts on each bank labeled c0, c1, ..., c19.

The motion of the C-steppers is arranged according to the following recursions:

- The V-wiper of the V-stepper is stepped once for the encipherment of any letter:

$$VP(i) = VP(i-1) \text{ (modulo 25)}. \qquad (7.39)$$

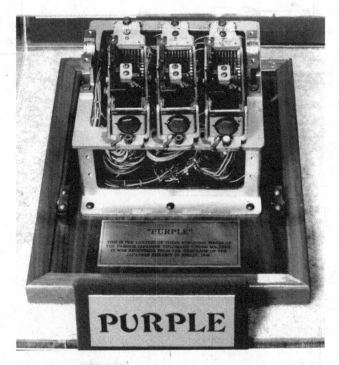

Figure 7.7 PURPLE switch (courtesy of NSA).

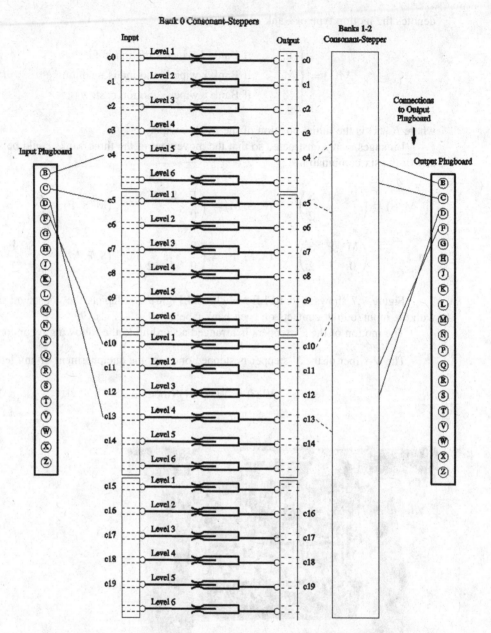

Figure 7.8 Consonant banks with consonant-plugboard connections from $CON = \{B, C, D, \ldots, W, X, Z\}$

- The M-wiper of a *medium* C-stepper bank (M) is stepped once each time the V-wiper of the V-stepper moved from position 24 to position 0:

$$CP_M(i) = \begin{cases} (CP_M(i-1) + 1 \ (\text{modulo } 25), & \text{if } VP(i-1) = 24 \\ CP_M(i-1), & \text{otherwise.} \end{cases} \tag{7.40}$$

- The S-wiper of a *slow* C-stepper bank (S) is stepped once just before the M-wiper of the medium C-stepper bank is moved from position 24 to 0:

$$CP_S(i) = \begin{cases} (CP_S(i-1)+1) \ (\text{modulo } 25), & \text{if } VP(i-1) = 23 \\ & \text{and } CP_M(i-1) = 24 \\ CP_S(i-1), & \text{otherwise.} \end{cases} \quad (7.41)$$

- The F-wiper of the *fast* C-stepper bank (F) is stepped once for each letter unless the S-wiper or M-wiper of either the slow or medium C-stepper bank is moved, in which case the F-wiper did not move:

$$CP_F(i) = \begin{cases} (CP_F(i), & \text{if } VP(i-1) = 24 \ or \ VP(i-1) = 23 \\ & \text{and } CP_M(i-1) = 24 \\ (CP_F(i-1)+1) \ (\text{modulo } 25), & \text{otherwise.} \end{cases}$$

$$(7.42)$$

The encipherment of the consonant x to the consonant y is a result of seven transformations

$$x \to y(1) \to y(2) \to y(3) \to y(4) \to y(5) \to y(6) \to y(7) = y = PUR_C(x). \quad (7.43)$$

Transformation #1

$$x \to y(1) = PL_C(x),$$

where $PL_C(x)$ is the letter on the C-stepper to which consonant x is connected by the consonant-plugboard.

Transformation #2

$$y(1) \to y(2) = CS^{(0)}_{CP^{(0)}((i+i_0(C^{(0)})) \ (\text{modulo } 25))}(y(1)),$$

where $CS^{(0)}$ is the Bank 0 C-stepper substitition whose position is $CP^{(0)} ((i + i_0(C^{(0)}))$ (modulo 25)) with $i_0(C^{(0)})$ being the initial position of the Bank 0 C-stepper.

Transformation #3

$$y(2) \to y(3) = \prod (0, 1)(y(2)),$$

where $\prod (0, 1)$ is the permutation network between Banks 0 and 1.

Transformation #4

$$y(3) \to y(4) = CS^{(1)}_{CP^{(1)}((i+i_0(C^{(1)})) \ (\text{modulo } 25))}(y(3)),$$

where $CS^{(1)}$ is the Bank 1 C-stepper substitition whose position is $CP^{(1)} ((i + i_0(C^{(1)}))$ (modulo 25)) with $i_0(C^{(1)})$ being the initial position of the Bank 1 C-stepper.

Transformation #5

$$y(4) \to y(5) = \prod (1, 2)(y(4)),$$

where $\prod (1, 2)$ is the permutation network between Banks 1 and 2.

Transformation #6

$$y(5) \to y(6) = CS^{(2)}_{CP^{(2)}((i+i_0(C^{(2)}))\ (\text{modulo }25))}(y(5)),$$

where $CS^{(2)}$ is the Bank 2 C-stepper substitition whose position is $CP^{(2)}$ $((i + i_0(C^{(2)}))$ (modulo 25)) with $i_0(C^{(2)})$ being the initial position of the Bank 1 C-stepper.

Transformation #7

$$y(6) \to y(7) = PL_C^{-1}(y(6)) = y = PUR_C(x),$$

where y is the output lamp letter whose output vowel $y(6)$ is connected by the inverse consonant-plugboard PL_C^{-1}.

7.7.3 The Period of $x \to y = PUR_C(x)$

To calculate the period of the consonant encipherment, define the positional state of the F-, M-, S-, and V-steppers for the encipherment of the ith plaintext letter x_i by

$$\underline{\omega}(i) = \begin{pmatrix} CP_F(i) \\ CP_M(i) \\ CP_S(i) \\ VP(i) \end{pmatrix}$$

Proposition 7.1: $\underline{\omega}(i)$ is periodic with period $\tau_C = 25^3$.

Proof: We give the proof only for the case $i_0(V) = i_0(C^{(0)}) = i_0(C^{(1)}) = i_0(C^{(2)}) = 0$. Equation (7.39) shows that

$$VP(i) = VP(i + 25), \qquad i = 0, 1, \dots. \tag{7.44}$$

Equation (7.40) shows that

$$CP_M(i) = \left\lfloor \frac{i}{25} \right\rfloor (\text{modulo } 25), \qquad i = 0, 1, \dots, \tag{7.45}$$

which implies

$$CP_M(i) = CP_M(i + 25^2), \qquad i = 0, 1, \dots. \tag{7.46}$$

In order that the position i satisfy

$$\begin{pmatrix} VP(i-1) = 24 & VP(i) = 0 \\ CP_M(i-1) = 24 & CP_M(i) = 0 \end{pmatrix},$$

it is required that

$$i - 1 = 24 + 25k, \qquad 24 = \left\lfloor \frac{i-1}{25} \right\rfloor \to i - 1 = 624 + 25^2 j, \qquad j = 0, 1, \dots. \tag{7.47}$$

In order that the position i satisfies

$$\begin{pmatrix} VP(i-2) = 22 & VP(i-1) = 23 \\ CP_M(i-2) = 24 & CP_M(i-1) = 24 \end{pmatrix},$$

it is required that

$$i - 1 = 23 + 25k, \qquad 24 = \left\lfloor \frac{i-1}{25} \right\rfloor \rightarrow i - 1 = 623 + 25^2 j, \qquad j = 0, 1, \dots. \quad (7.48)$$

Using Equation (7.41) we conclude

$$CP_S(i) = \left\lfloor \frac{i+1}{25^2} \right\rfloor (\text{modulo } 25), \qquad i = 0, 1, \dots. \quad (7.49)$$

Equation (7.42) shows that $CP_F(j-1)$ increases by 1 modulo 25 except for those positions j for which

$$(VP(j-1) = 24) \qquad \text{or} \qquad \begin{pmatrix} VP(j-1) = 23 \\ CP_M(j-1) = 24 \end{pmatrix}. \quad (7.50)$$

As the conditions in Equation (7.50) are mutually exclusive, the number of solutions of Equation (7.50) with $j \le i$ is $\lfloor \frac{i}{25} \rfloor + \lfloor \frac{i+1}{25^2} \rfloor$, which gives

$$CP_F(i) = \left(i - \left\lfloor \frac{i}{25} \right\rfloor + \left\lfloor \frac{i+1}{25^2} \right\rfloor \right) (\text{modulo } 25). \quad (7.51)$$

Equations (7.44), (7.45), (7.49), and (7.51) show that the vowel- and consonant-stepper positions are periodic with period 25^3.

7.8 THE PURPLE KEYS

There are seven elements comprising the PURPLE key:

PK1. The plugboard connections – $\#PK1 = \begin{pmatrix} 26 \\ 6 \end{pmatrix} \times 6! \times 20!$;

PK2. The VOW-stepper implementing 25 permutations of the six-letter input/output pairs – $\#PK2 = (6!)^{25}$;

PK3. The initial position i_0 VOW of the vowel stepper – $\#PK3 = 25$;

PK4. The 25 permutations in each of the four consonant-stepper banks – $\#PK4 = (20!^{25})^3$;

PK5. The initial positions $(i_0(C^{(0)}), i_0(C^{(1)}), i_0(C^{(2)})$ of the consonant steppers – $\#PK5 = 25^3$;

PK6. The interconnection permutations $\prod_{0,1}$ and $\prod_{1,2}$ between Banks i and $i+1$ for $i = 0, 1$ – $\#PK6 = 20!^2$; and

PK7. The motions of the consonant steppers – $\#PK7 = 6$.

Of course, not *all* of these $\#PK \equiv \#PK1 \times \#PK2 \times \#PK3 \times \#PK4 \times \#PK5 \times \#PK6 \times \#PK7$ keys are independent; for example, the composition of a consonant-stepper CS and the interconnection permutation $\prod$ to the next bank is equivalent to just another consonant-stepper. Even so, the PURPLE had a substantial key space.

The *Ko* codebook listed basic operating instructions for PURPLE; the *Otsu* codebook listed plugboard settings, which were prescribed in advance and used throughout the Japanese network. Some papers on PURPLE suggest initial wheel settings might have been chosen *randomly* by the sender and included (in plaintext) in the *message indicator*. Later, the *Otsu* codebook listed a set of values whose labels were included in the *message indicator*.

Why did PURPLE succumb to cryptanalysis with such a large key space? Although the rotors of the *Enigma* machine were permanently wired, three of them could be selected from some set and their order varied. In the PURPLE system, the stepper wiring and the bank-to-bank interconnections were fixed; only the plugboard connections, the initial positions, and the motion of the steppers could be changed. If cryptanalysis recovered the fixed hidden components of the key, the secrecy of future messages would rest only on the three components of the key that could be set. Still, $\#PK1 \times \#PK5 \times \#PK7$ is too large for systematic key trial. The success in cryptanalyzing PURPLE is largely due to the brilliance of the analysts, as related in the work of Rowlett and Kahn [1998]. According to Deavours and Kruh [1985], the PURPLE team included Frank Rowlett, Robert Ferner, Albert Small, Sam Snyder, Genevive Grotjan, and Mary Jo Denning. The discovery of internal relations in the consonant encipherment (described in Section 7.10) and how they could be applied to unravel the mystery is part of the answer. Finally, PURPLE, like the German cipher machines, appeared on the scene just as computers were being developed. Rowlett and Kahn [1998, p. 147], while mentioning the availability of the IBM accounting machines, concluded it was faster to build a PURPLE replica and make tests with it.

Example 7.7

PURPLE Parameters are given as in the following tables, including Table 7.25, where KB = keyboard, VS = vowel stepper, and CS = consonant stepper.

VOW	CON
A C D E R U	B F G H I J K L M N O P Q S T V W X Y Z

PL$_V$					
KB	A	C	D	E	R	U
	↕	↕	↕	↕	↕	↕
VS	E	R	A	C	D	U

PL$_C$																					
KB	B	F	G	H	I	J	K	L	M	N	O	P	Q	S	T	V	W	X	Y	Z
	↕	↕	↕	↕	↕	↕	↕	↕	↕	↕	↕	↕	↕	↕	↕	↕	↕	↕	↕	↕
Bank 0 CS	J	K	L	M	Z	N	O	P	Q	S	T	V	W	X	Y	H	G	I	B	F

Notation: The V- and C-Stepper tables shown above are examples of ciphertext alphabets, with the position of the stepper in the left column. The entry in row 3 of the Bank 1 C-Stepper ciphertext alphabet means that J → w when the position of the Bank 1 C-stepper is 3.

If the C-plugboards are taken into account, then

$$R \to D = PL_V(R) \to e = VS_{VP(0)}(D)$$

TABLE 7.25 A PURPLE Parameter Set

V-Stepper ACDERU		Bank 0 C-Stepper BFGHIJKLMNOPQSTVWXYZ		Bank 1 C-Stepper BFGHIJKLMNOPQSTVWXYZ		Bank 2 C-Stepper BFGHIJKLMNOPQSTVWXYZ
0.	arudec	0.	bsvpqjwzylokimtngxhf	0.	fzgmbwskfiotivjnpxylq	0.	jqftxhnigoskzpwvyblm
1.	decuax	1.	gnqhfxisbkyovljmwtpz	1.	hwynlvfxgmjpikztosqb	1.	yqmsltviwzpbfjkhxngo
2.	aurdce	2.	mlqbvijgwnpzkfhxoyts	2.	jopshyizblnwmgfkxvqt	2.	qozpghjinxmytlsfkvwb
3.	ucedar	3.	wiofqhympxlzsgvbnkjt	3.	gtpfbwzxiovjyhsmqkln	3.	qsfotgvhmnwybxjlzpik
4.	arceud	4.	tqznvoybjmfhwlxigskp	4.	vkmtjihlgnsfoxbpwqyz	4.	klxvbjtzspofgmiynhvq
5.	ducear	5.	qktxgwsnoymipfvzlibjl	5.	kxtymbwphvglnzjosfqi	5.	yknzphlvtxiwobjfmgqs
6.	cedura	6.	qfkthlvpgijbzxowysnm	6.	nwovpfjtkszymxigqlhb	6.	vmgfykwjbisnthlpzqox
7.	rauced	7.	xjmypbntzkiswfhlgvoq	7.	xzglhotnkbfiwvymsjqp	7.	loimkxgyvfpztjnwsqbh
8.	uraced	8.	iomtykvxnjbspflhzwqg	8.	bvwsjgitkoxlphnzqfmy	8.	ivnphzlsojwkbmtgyxq
9.	rcdaeu	9.	jfslgbhtomkpwyznxiqv	9.	nmyifptzkgsbovqwlixh	9.	ygpzwbxfnkovlhmtsiqj
10.	dcerua	10.	wpnxztvglfkohmjsiybq	10.	iplszvbmhwnxjytfkqog	10.	hvygsjwifbkpxztoqnml
11.	eraudc	11.	vhyzsjbtinkwxgolmqpf	11.	oglmtsynphqvkxibzjwf	11.	jfomxwnblhpizygvsqkt
12.	adcuer	12.	bogmlxfywihvtpsjzkqn	12.	nshxvfopbgjwiztqmlyk	12.	pzvsoimfjnxlyhqvgbkt
13.	urdace	13.	vsinompjglzybtfxriqwk	13.	kbjlpwyznhisoqxftgvm	13.	tkxigjhwbomsfvqpznly
14.	uceadr	14.	ifpkxhbzwomsngvtyqlj	14.	sgfzkxmiyvljbqwntohp	14.	wbtfksylnvgxhpzjoqmi
15.	creaud	15.	yswlkvfjhxmpotbqignz	15.	oinjhbkgwmfspxqylztv	15.	tjpkzyflwbnsgqivhxom
16.	daucer	16.	xgknybplsizwvfqthmoj	16.	xlpoknvzhgmqjfbywits	16.	zsowmbthxkviqyjflgnp
17.	ceudra	17.	fmpohvwzkxigjynqltbs	17.	tvyfzjlbsxkowqinmghp	17.	flgntjiomkshpqzwbxvy
18.	rucaed	18.	jzlimosfkbhgqyvpwxnt	18.	mtwgnhyfivqkploisxzb	18.	hsiyxwpbtzvglfkmonqj
19.	duarce	19.	gytibnxvlwpmkjoqzfsh	19.	vtmjxispgnqbyzhwkfol	19.	nivpzhjtysqxkgmolfwb
20.	rcdeau	20.	wtjfpyghsznqklbmxovi	20.	hpobitfwlzmqvgxknsjy	20.	mgoxlfntvbwqyhpikzjs
21.	acdrue	21.	nlotxzbvyfgwqjihkspm	21.	zynvxtsohjqflmbpwkgi	21.	vhbwmogslpjtqxzfinky
22.	erudca	22.	hmwjtosnliqxpygfbkzv	22.	kgbtywqpnoxvszkhimflj	22.	nxjkypzimhoqgvtbwlsf
23.	dcuear	23.	ykxgftipmhvboqzlnjsw	23.	wmxkhpsvlftqzgjyionb	23.	zlvkibwfnsyxqjmtohgp
24.	aurdce	24.	lvnpbkiysjzgtwxqmfoh	24.	ojnzkmqitbhxlwfsgvyp	24.	igjhklqpyvfnztsmbwxo

and

$$G \rightarrow L = PL_C(G) \rightarrow z = CS^{(0)}_{CP^{(0)}(0)}(L) \rightarrow q = CS^{(1)}_{CP^{(1)}(0)}(z) \rightarrow z = CS^{(2)}_{CP^{(2)}(0)}(q)$$

$$\rightarrow f = PL_C^{-1}(z).$$

7.9 CRIBBING PURPLE: FINDING THE V-STEPPER

We will illustrate a possible way to crib PURPLE ciphertext. We use English-language plaintext, the 1-gram English probabilities included in Chapter 3, and the PURPLE parameters in Example 7.7.

Even if a message indicator containing identifiers of the initial stepper settings was included *in the clear* in a message, the decipherment of intercepted PURPLE ciphertext depends on a large number of parameters which must be recovered.

VS: 25×6 entries in the vowel-stepper ciphertext alphabet;

CS: $3 \times 25 \times 20$ entries in the consonant-stepper ciphertext alphabet;

PL: the plugboard connections.

In our analysis the initial settings are all 0; this is of no consequence in recovering the V-stepper. We indicate in Section 7.9.2 how the analysis of the C-steppers is effected and what changes must be made. We will sketch the ideas to find the V-stepper first and then illustrate them with an example. The plan of attack is a follows:

1. Make letter-counts and, as indicated in Section 7.5, determine the likely division of letters into vowels and consonants.

2. Construct *crib tables* whose entries are $(\underline{u}, \underline{v}, i)$, consisting of

    (a) a crib $\underline{u}$,

    (b) a corresponding ciphertext fragment $\underline{v}$ with the same vowel/consonant pattern as $\underline{u}$,

    (c) the V-stepper position i at which $\underline{u} \to \underline{v}$ occurs, and

    (d) a score for entry.

3. Resolve contradictions of potential ciphertext fragments of cribs by a pruning algorithm and recover as much of the vowel-stepped ciphertext alphabet as possible.

Step 1: Determining the vowel/consonant subdivision and the vowel-stepper. If $\{\pi(t)\}$ are the 1-gram plaintext frequencies, define

$$\pi_{\text{VOW}} \equiv \sum_{t \in \text{VOW}} \pi(t)$$

and

$$\pi_{\text{CON}} \equiv \sum_{t \in \text{CON}} \pi(t). \tag{7.52}$$

If the sets VOW and CON are randomly selected

$$\pi_{\text{VOW}} = \sum_t \frac{\binom{25}{5}}{\binom{26}{6}} = \frac{6}{26} \simeq 0.2308$$

and

$$\pi_{\text{CON}} \simeq 0.7692. \tag{7.53}$$

The standard set of vowels – VOW = {A, E, I, O, U, Y} [Seberry and Pieprzyk, 1989] – gives the values $\pi_{\text{VOW}} \simeq 0.5225$ and $\pi_{\text{CON}} = 0.4775$.

Step 2: Construct *crib tables* whose entries $(\underline{u}, \underline{v}, i)$ consist of

1. A crib $\underline{u}$,

2. A corresponding ciphertext fragment $\underline{v}$ with the same vowel/consonant pattern as $\underline{u}$,

3. The V-stepper position i at which $\underline{u} \to \underline{v}$ occurs, and

4. A score for entry.

Many PURPLE messages were intercepted and the combined traffic permitted sharper conclusions to be made. We will use three examples of ciphertext all derived with the parameters in Table 7.25 to recover the V-stepper.

cipherEx7.8

```
wmukv mddjw vcesf afrxe eetaz eufjq yuluk acdwr ybsim avegs aachc rdvcr
ywhrz rqlwa xzzeh wtple swxap imcze adhzi unmzt zgvru muomj cjvhp vduxu
dogln jnnda tedye wzfxe oxkqu sovcu phwnm huarm esnct wqawu dptln wwljq
ivrkz nnrle aottt ezbga umavx tvfda reazo jtfqp kmubh crell bwddx fdpdw
udclc rcehu upqtl dgzoe orlxg pefvy jjcad jojct yrfcc dfaca gefzb ecpcc
cslaz shhci syyjd jaixe ezklh lbjrk bzicn cdapw ydcta rclru bpymp bipzc
cklst gdudy ghzak nacjk kmekt clgpx szilu ecuyb zwrib kbhvp cwrfj doave
sitcv ceokx wajsr kacef iiakc gaiae iccee ndfpu neufl ziriu niyof jajxt
frdux upoif bfayq rnslg gapkp qozde uuyhz zdvdw urcjv rstwk dumvg kkuzu
wwaju meizf xhlhy uwnyr vhjdu mybpf ezcam nbida qybxh scecq ldzud innuk
ohruy uuvjx kvvro dkkkl germv engqx oauxh ucecq rzuuv epgbp nueed fjvwe
lvzye nyahm ahgeb rmvaa majpr ekzxi afhoc cukac rdnee ijekj vfyxx cazsh
flxeg vhwjo tdugg ejrek hrlyt elsmc crndk woyks ulmee anacq tvkps cdjyh
damcg kcrxd aafsq eubcc rhdev qgbem wcekd mhius ocsed yqgre rzede cvdnk
kjpdd eycdb zlwss mafvv ctlzg mkadk aqsag wavls qaccx etvzw cysqu roiry
viqep xuibe rhlgg ckzud epiee ulyee kzmii lcncr ffxbt ztoas vaerb fcmtm
xceyj awrke eguad cxhog kaeaa ddueg spnre xfued wdbqg irdzq gwndr kszjr
errlj cabzc tkjxh ddadx dvxqm itwws rmjsw nqqcg edhfa leqau dlrur azuac
fwbna gvxxx cwkfh ewejp xzfel vwiny vzbcz fdudq bnhbb cznej uqscr nnefd
faaax arrdf celqz ichxu usord hwxdg spnnc fduur eawer eiwnb sdryk zkuao
hgyiw axedc fdncz gdlhc tlgqi crkiu utycd arhzg calrd ahaee pyyfy gfese
gcris dradx cvveg szven rabpt fuouf ygbun eobat mtjhg arqcc xnrlr sqabh
keuzv uqrqu uwucc przts weveu pctcr pvvqm ucwle pkgre vpaal zyekl ryjyw
lamco mriis udmbv auqmo cicza loieq pinwh djilq oeiju uumxs jnoyx enhvp
rsxtd wcqrg gumre uxncv dnaix ykyft jvlcl dhcik wedlb ejyoe aecgq lbhas
txzsm uslcr cstjx mnwfu puzoz pwuwo wutjn ayofm ffven jqndn crayb gbfds
uckgn aqcku cayom vuguh lhunek ehuhd jdquy fjdnh gaavd urqgs xaulu xlaod
eosee tlmst satcr pketd taaqa bbxei uadvu vacik eiren nflru nakeq bekee
noupd zrrcz diddk tkqaz dgced tctqv hacri kvmwu ceyhj tukuj bybcz elods
vzwni akchc rfyey eqmzy lpock dneac ludjr mmbqv zwrxk ecjdy vurtu gfmco
rllki dnzhd ahlvh ydzeu cwepu dxuas qrwes ucpgz bnguc dodap rdhfc macwe
aglrh dkcug zgcqc czurb vwevb aarte ulgyf nscru pbtqf eaudb abxyk vdovx
weooc wpcrn kbqmi xmpqb vetor elqae aanjc ridjs ekqjd xzmup erwqc quvdc
vrdul ukvsp dxeuz aldag fqmke bcdnw eifzz xfewu awmwz cmcrh guufo toxcu
ckaxn bocqs coshe hgtpr xezow rmnmu cebbt iuguj opycl epydz vfnde ttxqy
bax
```

cipherEx7.9

```
wmvld fcrse osdcp uuvqu qsjee lxzcp urjag ezacd grait kycec yyqte acbve
cawfi yjxzu wcktu ukbju oayae rclre chfui euous auprz rcfth dlrre wgowu
erbsq ninbk ebqdd xonus ucvnq peavb yycec taass xtyhl csrvv drdnu vukuh
fzhap epnze sehmd vrykc rfebr ezdeq rzmgj uohwx sctry panrl bauwa fqkre
gdwmn oecvr kpnrg hhnev tkged ftmya nyfcg nmxho kayaf vgurg lkheu vazuu
kaqvq hvuir cacdq chmrr pcbrn qbald gmkud suape wmujr ezneu xewsm usrhz
cnrqh fzcav qabec qdwek daagj tepca czkiz eeukq bateu hrkad ockzt tdaeb
hzlav yamrt xcgtr zjxcg iiaeo dnczj fvvdd pfabn tnocw abndm aueuu dgged
qbgfx iekvp scgcu rwuad euweh eaqer cwzjq mcmzb xugcd cqkef sitwy qbnhf
xyclt tuqlh eiuas dsdba erjsl rhaeu lxzfu ceiwi awcjd hyrqd tvcqr azrni
```

cipherEx7.9

```
uceir eazeq rugfn atbsi tdzgk fufzy mpayn ymajb hsfbu frldz ogayc epgpo
elzda ultou dpduu suizc gugka pgueg zuprl ckkne xqwdk cedna cnaav rkxsb
ecuaw fabaa ubdje piurg jujhc ygqtj futud wmade scgdi hdmdb tunov erumt
muchj moruk fgudr ucbeg julup zgtkg barvp uhape tesyk ieuya eunbi fyibo
fduuo ulued hlirt uuqkr zpezd yddqr erjur dcrgc dgrdv ezwrd ecriu reevc
dawrb gbevt mkmre wateu ktyya rfypo ahjbe cgdse ajrvc ygzia darac eafry
acdyj aeefk zmoqi bxuoz mcvde xcnom hsfyc hodas cuhyp hdccq embda cuama
brcrh wuqsx xrdib fxwau csldg jlkdr vskfk ulilq jtmti uydeg exqas maaic
ryfve eqdcs gabug dxcxm fcfuc enuec duvcw adfdd atksy bhzaa rdeve vkcue
fphyd ekruu rqfcd jozem jsgeb peynb jvctr oaahd urndd reule edmwe geqdo
cirvd btjav crjye mdldv aqvuo tesrz ugucd rjhzi uxqja beuqe paldc abcaj
whcwe adsbv xecut otrkv ozruw pbuiw ycwjl ecwic lquuq tkfca spgav cujan
eoeer pruqx npder pbgba drddp eeamk bzclp cejoy cbpfd wmawl dicra xqteh
yyddv xcdct dubku vtbxe gjjcq urfam ehacy ajyur exruy jaozp papca wdqed
peyce kqvcm ceujy vidcr znfba drddt ettcd tabsf ouuud ouoae afffe feqduv
dazac unypj enfwd mpwlt digja bacxu pagae cbdcs xwsuu rxfxr uaruv kqngo
edruc traeu mviec onrpf nooay acbax adzai urkeo tejrf ruxje iboka mjrif
vfkme jeufr brdfa qeepe yyunc sdrdv fhceb umvgi ecpdv qvrhg ht
```

cipherEx7.10

```
ytcdg sirhf uuplf komfn eevbu akboc mvdne xiuie wczov eapru unlgl rskcx
fmcre wyvsm xhrtq yaceu ulncr iebzt cemvu zwezc uaelo wywoe axecp mtaku
zbrfu wjlog taveg ooymk beyeb eyabz ecyea lsuum mulbe buwiu ckcso wpbnz
vmich lvczd gdjmt dwmwa wkerx uekcd pkqnh roxip phhck fdscj amend hcqcv
cuxtf gpbhs zommk ttxrt qezuh aksds kmyfw esdee zbetc wwkwy dloud iltxu
ghasc xafte rvgcn dnaes atskk icerb pmide catdk dvaju socxu bwrfc ytbcd
ykbow cowwk bhdjb vsgre lhyyd uolzc vduiy evzee vvfqp fxvdv cgofv wbcnm
ecynx zudrt aifpe ciumd ajpaa fcuib cadrt rgten cdxkr rwree zdcay dgqvs
eoefx gnail clric chnnu uafps zaduj aqvdu sozud etydl davsc zahge uvqie
uhxma tgeaq omzba wxtpl ckrzl becuv keoqu uujou buuea hcebx tvcqo zcevg
lckyu aokfq xnxse leuur etzzu dupuz ggnfe riyvh czkci ttacr ndzre acvcr
wxnsr gfsom esncc aamed hdjev rdree xxaei gesnw dytmg tmuzd lwjxh vpaah
fvcyu dojjc hejan cirsl xdlyt elszb feeeh uegrk cjdre udjnu rukav fvqzk
udxcc gfuev wzdlb dcbmb zokbv yawod uqxqa thgxm kcbjc pacru nceza hvvcy
iyzrc zcirs icjug klvnr muzzo qeika itxec rdujc duvte emgcv vduis eltgt
pqvcc trlge arugg zdcdh kecsk rqeiq hrbzw ejxew cqkdd etcac tbsbc duvte
efihm qtwwg errdu sctpc dunnx izocm qofuq rcthi fihrd rlank rervv dpvpz
pcqyh xwnzs utedj trcsd aatwv ukkdr pwybs fstci znkfq odevt aazoc rxsru
zljrv edjda occnur phpaf dvubc vtinx vfbsa zdude enjpo bpfvy juzvl eaund
unvzi iwwyp ibzeu lsvrm bruzq yfzsy xepms cdmvq cbdda cnycq tzjsb uukws
vagzs vajij ycgwo bboah ijuqu vqmja qfnad frslm rnatg eparj rpdzj eytrn
hohqc upnzx eitmy rovoc wypfe akclu rdplc qykxt rnpzm nhqqe ugfpc txcdx
qxohp zvuzz xaajo sezca uevgj hwcxn ctqev uagpj zttdb hhcso aswsq vmhoc
zddre hogci swusz verdf iapib lqxot prrnx damzx uwkdr kzjhk zxhke jzine
amaeu iucdr stedr eerdg blsxe iurzv gzwti fooaf daznd xamxe xdzfc oevaf
leave edlpe rulxh rasrt cehtc crdkt hdufd frris wzahb mbcji wdryf ueqvz
yculn wkbnt xnkes onrpc jseiw ddaci nyxpo eljah sqvee gauch fbvwd ufwgu
rgrxk inric ethwp nyeln pyxdb qjiei uyleu vxugl nqhje qvjud seuyw hgqfm
hjdxt geugx cxvdt eychz zgckw uctcc
```

TABLE 7.26 Letter Frequencies in `cipherEx7.8`

t	f(t)	t	f(t)	t	f(t)
a	0.0557	j	0.0333	s	0.0343
b	0.0238	k	0.0371	t	0.0319
c	0.0628	l	0.0324	u	0.0661
d	0.0671	m	0.0304	v	0.0319
e	0.0742	n	0.0276	w	0.0285
f	0.0281	o	0.0304	x	0.0285
g	0.0319	p	0.0271	y	0.0304
h	0.0333	q	0.0295	z	0.0352
i	0.0309	r	0.0576		

$\pi_{VOW} = 0.3835$ and $\pi_{CON} = 0.6165$

Tables 7.26 to 7.28 contains the letter frequencies in `cipherEx7.8-10`. Table 7.28 contains the letter frequencies in `cipherEx7.10`, derived with the parameters in Table 7.25. The VOW/CON partition has the values $\pi_{VOW} = 0.3767$ and $\pi_{CON} = 0.6233$. The 1-gram frequencies in Tables 7.26 to 7.28 are consistent with `cipherEx7.8-10` using the the same VOW/CON subdivision. We plan to combine `cipherEx7.8-10` to recover the V-stepper ciphertext alphabets, as was done apparently in the analysis of PURPLE [Deavours and Kruh, 1985, p. 236]. This combination of the ciphertexts is possible if the same vowel-plugboard and initial V-stepper position are used in the three examples.

We begin by searching the ciphertext for fragments that have the same vowel/consonant pattern as the cribs. The subjects of the plaintext of `cipherEx7.8-10` are

`plainEx7.8:` performance analysis;

`plainEx7.9:` 1980 description of the graduate and undergraduate programs in the UCSB Computer Science Department;

`plainEx7.10:` computer communication.

TABLE 7.27 Letter Frequencies in `cipherEx7.9`

t	f(t)	t	f(t)	t	f(t)
a	0.0618	j	0.0234	s	0.0209
b	0.0299	k	0.0239	t	0.0264
c	0.0598	l	0.0160	u	0.0673
d	0.0573	m	0.0214	v	0.0259
e	0.0703	n	0.0199	w	0.0204
f	0.0284	o	0.0214	x	0.0179
g	0.0269	p	0.0234	y	0.0264
h	0.0219	q	0.0254	z	0.0229
I	0.0209	r	0.0528		

$\pi_{VOW} = 0.3693$ and $\pi_{CON} = 0.6107$

TABLE 7.28 Letter Frequencies in cipherEx7.10

t	$f(t)$	t	$f(t)$	t	$f(t)$
a	0.0515	j	0.0251	s	0.0339
b	0.0298	k	0.0298	t	0.0392
c	0.0743	l	0.0263	u	0.0637
d	0.0585	m	0.0257	v	0.0444
e	0.0784	n	0.0316	w	0.0310
f	0.0281	o	0.0292	x	0.0345
g	0.0281	p	0.0263	y	0.0269
h	0.0316	q	0.0263	z	0.0433
i	0.0322	r	0.0503		

$\pi_{\text{VOW}} = 0.3767$ and $\pi_{\text{CON}} = 0.6233$

Likely cribs are

---

plainEx7.8

---

1. PERFORMANCE 2. PREDICTION 3. EVALUATION   4. WOKLOAD
5. PROGRAMMING 6. PROCESSOR 7. OPERATINGSYSTEM 8. PERFORMANCEEVALUATION

---

plainEx7.9

---

1. COMPUTERSCIENCE 2. COMPUTERENGINEERING   3. DEPARTMENT
4. GRADUATE   5. ELECTRICALENGINEERING

---

plainEx7.10

---

1. COMPUTER   2. COMMUNICATION
3. INFORMATION   4. COMMUNICATIONSYSTEMS

We will modify the χ^2-test described in Chapter 3 to determine if a ciphertext fragment is likely to correspond to the vowel/consonant pattern of a crib.

If we assume that plaintext is generated by a source process $\{X_i\}$ of independent and identically distributed random variable with probabilities $\{\pi(t)\}$, then

$$\pi^*(t) = \frac{\pi(t)}{\pi(\text{A}) + \pi(\text{C}) + \pi(\text{D}) + \pi(\text{E}) + \pi(\text{R}) + \pi(\text{U})}, \qquad t \in \text{VOW} \qquad (7.54)$$

is the normalized probability of the vowel t. Table 7.29 lists the normalized vowel probabilities corresponding to the standard 1-gram probabilities in English.

Let $\underline{u} = (u_0, u_1, \ldots, u_{M-1})$ be a crib and $y_{(i,i+M)} = (y_i, y_{i+1}, \ldots, y_{i+M-1})$ a ciphertext fragment with the same vowel/consonant pattern as $\underline{u}$. Let $N(y_{i+j}, k_j)$ be the total number of plaintext vowel $y_{i+j} \in \text{VOW}$ occurring in $y_{(i,i+M)}$ with $k_j = (i + j)$ (modulo 25); if

$$N(k_j) = \sum_{y_{i+j} \in \text{VOW}} N(y_{i+j}, k_j), \qquad k_j = (i + j) \text{ (modulo 25)},$$

TABLE 7.29 Normalized VOW Probabilities

t	$\pi(t)$	$\pi^*(t)$
A	0.0856	0.2287
C	0.0279	0.0745
D	0.0378	0.1010
E	0.1304	0.3484
R	0.0667	0.1809
U	0.0249	0.0665

then the law of large numbers asserts

$$\pi^*(y_{i+j}) \approx \frac{N(y_{i+j}, k_j)}{N(k_j)}, \qquad y_{i+j} \in \text{VOW}, \quad k_j = (i+j) \text{ (modulo 25)}.$$

This suggests using the χ^2-score

$$\chi^2(y_{(i,\, i+M)}) = \sum_{y_{i+j} \in \text{VOW}} \frac{(N(y_{i+j}, k_j) - \pi^*(x_{i+j}) N(k_j))^2}{\pi^*(x_{i+j}) N(k_j)}, \qquad y_{i+j} \in \text{VOW},$$

$$k_j = (i+j) \text{ (modulo 25)}, \tag{7.55}$$

to decide how likely it is that the ciphertext fragment $y_{(i,i+M)}$ is the PURPLE encipherment of the crib $\underline{u}$. It is understood in Equation (7.55) that if a vowel t occurs more than once in the crib, the corresponding $N(y_{i+j}, k_j)$-terms are combined.

For example, an entry appears in Table 7.30 for the ciphertext fragment vcesfafrxee at position 10 in cipherEx7.8 that has the same vowel/consonant pattern as the crib PERFORMANCE. This fragment contains

- Two E's at positions $11 = 10 + 1$ and $20 = 10 + 10$, and
- Two R's at positions $12 = 10 + 2$ and $15 = 10 + 5$,

and the Equation (7.55) score of the ciphertext fragment vcesfafrxee occurring at position 10 is given by

$$\chi^2(\text{vcesfafrxee}) = \frac{\left(\left(N(y_{11}, k_1) + N(y_{20}, k_{10})\right) - \pi^*(\text{E})(N(k_1) + N(k_{10}))\right)^2}{\pi^*(\text{E})\left(N(k_1) + N(k_{10})\right)} \qquad [\text{E}]$$

$$+ \frac{\left(\left((N(y_{12}, k_2)) + N(y_{15}, k_5)\right) - \pi^*(\text{R})\left(N(k_2) + N(k_3)\right)\right)^2}{\pi^*(\text{R})(N(k_2) + N(k_3))} \qquad [\text{R}]$$

$$+ \frac{\left(\left(N(y_{17}, k_7) - \pi^*(\text{A})N(k_7)\right)\right)^2}{\pi^*(\text{A})N(k_7)} + \frac{\left(\left(N(y_{19}, k_9) - \pi^*(\text{C})N(k_9)\right)\right)^2}{\pi^*(\text{C})N(k_9)}. \qquad [\text{A},\text{C}]$$

Tables 7.30 to 7.37 contain the results of a search for ciphertext fragments that have the same vowel/consonant patterns as the cribs in cipherEx7.8. The top row of Table 7.30 contains

- The ciphertext fragment vcesfafrxee,
- The position of the ciphertext fragment,

TABLE 7.30   Ciphertext Fragments In `cipherEx7.8` for the Crib PERFORMANCE

vcesfafrxee	10	11 E c	12 R e	15 R a	17 A r	19 C e	20 E e	27.0828	√
wddxfdpdwud	231	7 E d	8 R d	11 R d	13 A d	15 C u	16 E d	40.1840	√
xceyjawrkee	960	11 E c	12 R e	15 R a	17 A r	19 C e	20 E e	27.0828	√
gedhfaleqau	1059	10 E e	11 R d	14 R a	16 A e	18 C a	19 E u	7.4899	√
hddzpdpdoud	1131	7 E d	8 R d	11 R d	13 A d	15 C u	16 E d	40.1840	√
jeriscyuxdc	1319	20 E e	21 R r	24 R c	1 A u	3 C d	4 E c	4.5806	√
oddxqdbdnud	1631	7 E d	8 R d	11 R d	13 A d	15 C u	16 E d	40.1840	√
muasbrnewuc	1676	2 E u	3 R a	6 R r	8 A e	10 C u	11 E c	22.0248	√
kacshemejae	1825	1 E a	2 R c	5 R e	7 A e	9 C a	10 E e	8.9805	√
icryjekdsaa	1857	8 E c	9 R r	12 R e	14 A d	16 C a	17 E a	20.4440	√
iurbxuxroee	1968	19 E u	20 R r	23 R u	0 A r	2 C e	3 E e	11.9077	√

TABLE 7.31   Ciphertext Fragments in `cipherEx7.8` for the Crib PREDICTION

kacdwrybsi	34	10 R a	11 E c	12 D d	14 C r	5.6051	√
frduxupoif	480	6 R r	7 E d	8 D u	10 C u	21.3161	√
mccrndkwoy	748	24 R c	0 E c	1 D r	3 C d	8.8003	√
qaccxetvzw	880	6 R a	7 E c	8 D c	10 C e	21.3161	√
fuedwdbqgi	996	22 R u	23 E e	24 D d	1 C d	8.2689	√
hrduvuhqpx	1330	6 R r	7 E d	8 D u	10 C u	21.3161	√
meuuvdbznf	1700	1 R e	2 E u	3 D u	5 C d	8.5911	√
peacfaonty	1979	5 R e	6 E a	7 D C	9 C a	51.1305	√
yrueodlmlv	2036	12 R r	13 E u	14 D e	16 C d	14.8865	

- Triples $(11, E, c)\,(12, R, e) \cdots (20, E, e)$ for each VOW-letter in the plaintext, consisting of
  - the position of the vowel,
  - the plaintext vowel at the that position, and
  - The ciphertext vowel at that position,
- The χ^2-score of the ciphertext fragment, and
- The information *un*known to us as to whether the entry is correct (√) or not.

Tables 7.38 to 7.42 contain the results of a search for ciphertext fragments that have the same vowel/consonant patterns as the cribs in `cipherEx7.9`.

Tables 7.43 to 7.46 contain the results of a search for ciphertext fragments that have the same vowel/consonant patterns as the cribs in `cipherEx7.10`.

TABLE 7.32   Ciphertext Fragments in `cipherEx7.8` for the Crib EVALUATION

etazeufjqy	21	21 E e	23 A a	0 U e	1 A u	7.4816	√
uyaodalnzw	1343	18 E u	20 A a	22 U d	23 A a	9.2809	√
rydjcrbzvz	1687	12 E r	14 A d	16 U c	17 A r	7.0681	√
emejaeskww	1830	5 E e	7 A e	9 U a	10 A e	12.7854	
afcxarslgy	1992	17 E a	19 A c	21 u a	22 A r	24.7920	√
cfrpucvibg	2014	14 E c	16 A r	18 u u	19 A c	69.7911	√

TABLE 7.33 Ciphertext Fragments in `cipherEx7.8` Corresponding to the Crib PROCESSOR

ldzudinnu	590	16 R d	18 C u	10 E d	23 R u	7.9992
ocsedyqgr	820	21 R c	23 C e	24 E d	3 R r	7.4952
wuvaehkxa	1556	7 R u	9 C a	10 E e	14 R a	5.2006 ✓
kdsaamffe	1863	14 R d	16 C a	17 E a	21 R e	11.3083

TABLE 7.34 Ciphertext Fragments in `cipherEx7.8` for the Crib PROGRAMMING

jaixeezklhl	315	16 R a	19 R e	20 A e	2.4987
tukserjnqft	1922	23 R u	1 R e	2 A r	8.8106 ✓

7.9.1 Does the Ciphertext Uniquely Determine the V-Stepper and Plugboard?

The combined action of the vowel-plugboard and V-stepper in position i is given by the equation

$$\widetilde{VS}_i(x) = y = PL_V^{-1}(VS_{VP(i)}(PL_V(x))), \qquad x \in VOW, \qquad i = 0, 1, \ldots. \qquad (7.56)$$

The combined vowel-plugboard/V-stepper for the parameters in *Example 7.7* and Table 7.25 is shown in Table 7.47. Does Equation (7.56) uniquely determine PL_V for a given VS? If vowel-plugboards PL_{V_1} and PL_{V_2} exist satisfying Equation (7.56) for given VS, then

$$\widetilde{VS}_{1,i}(x) = \widetilde{VS}_{2,i}(x), \qquad x \in VOW, \qquad i = 0, 1, \ldots \qquad (7.57)$$

$$\widetilde{VS}_{1,i}(x) = PL_{V_1}^{-1}(VS_{VP(i)}(PL_{V_1}(x))), \qquad x \in VOW, \qquad i = 0, 1, \ldots \qquad (7.58)$$

$$\widetilde{VS}_{2,i}(x) = PL_{V_2}^{-1}(VS_{VP(i)}(PL_{V_2}(x))), \qquad x \in VOW, \qquad i = 0, 1, \ldots, \qquad (7.59)$$

TABLE 7.35 Ciphertext Fragments in `cipherEx7.8` for the Crib WORKLOAD

wmukvmdd	0	2 R u	6 A d	7 D d	43.7902
kqusovcu	142	19 R u	23 A c	24 D u	4.6232
ttezbgau	193	20 R e	24 A a	0 D u	6.7812
nyrvhjdu	557	9 R r	13 A d	14 D u	18.8191 ✓
nnukohru	596	23 R u	2 A r	3 D u	10.2210 ✓
xiafhocc	688	15 R a	19 A c	20 D c	8.6394 ✓
ytelsmcc	743	20 R e	24 A c	0 D c	6.7812
zwcysqur	888	15 R c	19 A u	20 D r	8.6394
qydhvjer	1314	16 R d	20 A e	21 D r	3.5226
mtclftec	1356	8 R c	12 A e	13 D c	19.1043
vvumhlrc	1383	10 R u	14 A r	15 D c	4.3270
myewbmca	1482	9 R e	13 A c	14 D a	18.8191
qgakhbcc	1594	21 R a	0 A c	1 D c	2.2286
wtupjner	1802	4 R u	8 A e	9 D r	9.5336
shcqmtur	2062	14 R c	18 A u	19 D r	3.5246

TABLE 7.36 Ciphertext Fragments in `cipherEx7.8` for the Crib OPERATINGSYSTEM

fwecrpqhxzxhkej 1421	23 E e	24 R c	0 A r	9 E e	4.3457 √
kvdddqglqhbqzub 1505	7 E d	8 R d	9 A d	18 E u	9.7915

TABLE 7.37 Ciphertext Fragments in `cipherEx7.8` for the Crib PERFORMANCEEVALUATION

vcesfafrxeeetazeufjqy (10)

11 E c	12 R e	15 R a	17 A r	19 C e
20 E e	21 E e	23 A a	0 U e	1 A u	34.5645 √

muasbrnewucrydj crbzvz (1676)

2 E u	3 R a	6 R r	8 A e	10 C u
11 E c	12 E r	14 A d	16 U c	17 A r	29.0929 √

TABLE 7.38 Ciphertext Fragments in `cipherEx7.9` for the Crib COMPUTERSCIENCE

elxzcpurjagezac (24)

24 C e	3 U c	5 E u	6 R r
8 C a	10 E e	12 C a	13 E c	23.3246 √

cnvqabecqdwekda (367)

17 C c	21 U a	23 E e	24 R c
1 C d	3 E e	5 C d	6 E a	13.8825 √

uqlheiuasdsdbae (546)

21 C u	0 U e	2 E u	3 R a
5 C d	7 E d	9 C a	10 E e	23.9789 √

uxqjabeuqepaldc (1240)

15 C u	19 U a	21 E e	22 R u
24 C e	1 E a	3 C d	4 E c	78.6649 √

aspgavcujaneoee (1309)

9 C a	13 U a	15 E c	16 R u
18 C a	20 E e	22 C e	23 E e	-30.0182 √

egjjcqurfamehac (1399)

24 C e	3 U c	5 E u	6 R r
8 C a	10 E e	12 C a	13 E c	23.3246 √

digjabacxupagae (1520)

20 C d	24 U a	1 E a	2 R c
4 C u	6 E a	8 C a	9 E e	60.7500 √

**TABLE 7.39   Ciphertext Fragments in `cipherEx7.9` for the Crib
`COMPUTERENGINEERING`**

		cfthdlrrewgowuerbsq (107)			
6 C c	10 U d	12 E r	13 R r		
14 E e	19 E u	20 E e	21 R r	17.6025	✓
		agjtepcaczkizeeukqb (382)			
7 C a	11 U e	13 E c	14 R a		
15 E c	20 E e	21 E e	22 R u	23.9663	✓
		rjslrhaeulxzfuceiwi (561)			
11 C r	15 U r	17 E a	18 R e		
19 E u	24 E u	0 E c	1 R e	58.3495	✓
		ajwhcweadsbvxecutot (1258)			
8 C a	12 U c	14 E e	15 R a		
16 E d	21 E e	22 E c	23 R u	23.9022	✓
		ekqvcmceujyvidcrznf (1444)			
19 C e	23 U c	0 E c	1 R e		
2 E u	7 E d	8 E c	9 R r	38.2905	

which implies

$$VS_{VP(i)}(x) = PL_{V_*}^{-1}(VS_{VP(i)}(PL_{V_*}(x))), \qquad x \in VOW, \qquad i = 0, 1, \ldots, \qquad (7.60)$$

where $PL_{V_*}, = PL_{V_2} PL_{V_1}^{-1}$. Equation (7.59) may be rewritten as

$$PL_{V_*}(VS_{VP(i)}(x)) = VS_{VP(i)}(PL_{V_*}(x)), \qquad x \in VOW, \qquad i = 0, 1, \ldots, \qquad (7.61)$$

which implies that

$$VS_{VP(i)}(x) = x \Rightarrow (PL_{V_*}(x)) = x, \qquad x \in VOW, \qquad i = 0, 1, \ldots, \qquad (7.62)$$

From Table 7.25

$$PL_{V_*}(A) \xrightarrow{VS_{VP(0)}} PL_{V_*}(A) \qquad PL_{V_*}(C) \xrightarrow{VS_{VP(3)}} PL_{V_*}(C) \qquad PL_{V_*}(D) \xrightarrow{VS_{VP(6)}} PL_{V_*}(D)$$

$$PL_{V_*}(E) \xrightarrow{VS_{VP(4)}} PL_{V_*}(E) \qquad PL_{V_*}(R) \xrightarrow{VS_{VP(6)}} PL_{V_*}(R) \qquad PL_{V_*}(U) \xrightarrow{VS_{VP(9)}} PL_{V_*}(U),$$

which shows that PL_{V_*} is the identity connection for the PURPLE parameters in *Example 7.7* and Table 7.25. More generally

TABLE 7.40   Ciphertext Fragments in `cipherEx7.9` for the Crib `DEPARTMENT`

dcpuuvquqs 12	12 D d	13 E c	15 A u	16 R u	19 E u	15.1413	
dctdubkuvt 1387	12 D d	13 E c	15 A d	16 R u	19 E u	15.1413	✓
rexruyjaoz 1419	19 D r	20 E e	22 A r	23 R u	1 E a	6.6907	✓

TABLE 7.41 Ciphertext Fragments in `cipherEx7.9` for the Crib GRADUATE

ircacdqc	308	9 R r	19 A c	11 D a	12 U c	13 A d	15 E c	17.6702 √
wuadeuwe	496	22 R u	23 A a	24 D d	9 U e	1 A u	3 E e	8.6661 √
gudrucbe	791	17 R u	18 A d	19 D r	29 U u	21 A c	23 E e	8.2767 √
jurdcrgc	872	23 R u	24 A r	9 D d	1 U c	2 A r	4 E c	33.3329 √
wrdecriu	887	13 R r	14 A d	15 D e	16 U c	17 A r	19 E u	13.4968 √
bdacuama	1012	13 R d	14 A a	15 D c	16 U a	17 A a	19 E a	13.4968
nuecduvc	1106	7 R u	8 A e	9 D c	19 U d	11 A u	13 E c	13.7687 √
zaardeve	1127	3 R a	4 A a	5 D r	6 U d	7 A e	9 E e	10.2515 √
nddreule	1182	8 R d	9 A d	19 D r	11 U e	12 A u	14 E e	9.3103 √
badrddpe	1338	14 R a	15 A d	16 D r	17 U d	18 A d	29 E e	27.7128 √
badrddte	1463	14 R a	15 A d	16 D r	17 U d	18 A d	29 E e	27.7128 √
oedructr	1559	19 R e	11 A d	12 D r	13 U u	14 A c	16 E r	10.5894

Proposition 7.2: If every vowel $x \in \text{VOW}$ is a fixed point of $\text{VS}_{\text{VP}(i)}(x)$ for some position i, then

$$\text{VS}_{\text{VP}(i)}(x) = \text{PL}_{V_*}^{-1}(\text{VS}_{\text{VP}(i)}(\text{PL}_{V_*}(x))), \qquad x \in \text{VOW}, \qquad i = 0, 1, \ldots, \Rightarrow \text{PL}_{V_*}(x) = x,$$

$$x \in \text{VOW}$$

7.9.2 Does the Ciphertext Uniquely Determine the Initial Setting of the V-Stepper?

If $i_0(V) = j$ and

$$\widetilde{\text{VS}}_{1,i}(x) = \widetilde{\text{VS}}_{2,i}(x), \qquad x \in \text{VOW}, \qquad i = 0, 1, \ldots \tag{7.63}$$

$$\widetilde{\text{VS}}_{1,i}(x) = \text{PL}_V^{-1}(\text{VS}_{\text{VP}(i)}(\text{PL}_V(x))), \qquad x \in \text{VOW}, \qquad i = 0, 1, \ldots \tag{7.64}$$

$$\widetilde{\text{VS}}_{2,i}(x) = \text{PL}_V^{-1}(\text{VS}_{\text{VP}(i+j)}(\text{PL}_V(x))), \qquad x \in \text{VOW}, \qquad i = 0, 1, \ldots, \tag{7.65}$$

then

$$\text{VS}_{\text{VP}(i)}(x) = \text{VS}_{\text{VP}(i+j)}(x), \qquad x \in \text{VOW}, \qquad i = 0, 1, \ldots \tag{7.66}$$

and by induction

$$\text{VS}_{\text{VP}(i)}(x) = \text{VS}_{\text{VP}(i+kj)}(x), \qquad x \in \text{VOW}, \qquad i = 0, 1, \ldots, \qquad k = 1, 2, \ldots. \tag{7.67}$$

TABLE 7.42 Ciphertext Fragments in `cipherEx7.9` for the Crib ELECTRICAL

uieuousaup	93	18 E u	20 E e	21 C u	23 R u	0 C a	1 A u	23.4340 √
usauprzrcf	98	23 E u	0 E a	1 C u	3 R r	5 C r	6 A c	5.2248
ateuhrkado	401	1 E a	3 E e	4 C u	6 R r	8 C a	9 A d	33.2915 √
apcawdqedp	1431	6 E a	8 E c	9 C a	11 R d	13 C e	14 A d	33.5265 √
dqedpeycek	1436	11 E d	13 E e	14 c d	16 R e	18 C c	19 A e	11.0298
ayacbaxadz	1583	8 E a	10 E a	11 C c	13 R a	15 C a	16 A d	39.4222
axadzaiurk	1588	13 E a	15 E a	16 C d	18 R a	20 C u	21 A r	21.4107
ejeufrbrdf	1624	24 E e	1 E e	2 C u	4 R r	6 C r	7 A d	13.3951
rbrdfaqeep	1629	4 E r	6 E r	7 C d	9 R a	11 C e	12 A e	39.5229

TABLE 7.43   Ciphertext Fragments in `cipherEx7.10` for the Crib COMMUNICATION

dgsirhfuuplfk	3	3	C	d	7	U	r	10	C	u	11	A	u	33.3797 √
uhxmatgeaqomz	540	15	C	u	19	U	a	22	C	e	23	A	a	73.7981 √
evglckyuaokfq	597	22	C	e	1	U	c	4	C	u	5	A	a	93.7950 √
evwzdlbdcbmbz	788	13	C	e	17	U	d	20	C	d	21	A	c	58.0507 √
atwvukkdrpwyb	1041	16	C	a	20	U	u	23	C	d	24	A	r	5.0862 √
ulsvrmbruzqyf	1154	4	C	u	8	U	r	11	C	r	12	A	u	60.9707 √
ugfpctxcdxqxo	1310	10	C	u	14	U	c	17	C	c	18	A	d	27.9789 √
amzxuwkdrkzjh	1416	16	C	a	20	U	u	23	C	d	24	A	r	5.0862 √

TABLE 7.44   Ciphertext Fragments in `cipherEx7.10` for the Crib COMPUTER

uolzcvdu	385	10	C	u	14	U	c	16	E	d	17	R	u	17.8559
ahfvcyud	718	18	C	a	22	U	c	24	E	u	0	R	d	8.4388
uzljrved	1079	4	C	u	8	U	r	10	E	e	11	R	d	59.2350 √

If j is relatively prime to 25, the rows of the combined vowel-plugboard/V-stepper are generated by a single row. This is not the case for the combined vowel-plugboard/V-stepper in *Example 7.7* and Table 7.25.

Table 7.48 lists the number of vowels in each V-stepper position for `cipherEx7.8-10`. A careful examination of the columns in which the maximum counts appear suggests that the vowel-plugboards and V-stepper initial positions are the same.

Step 3:   Resolve contradictions of potential ciphertext fragments of cribs by a pruning algorithm and recover as much of the vowel-stepper ciphertext alphabet as possible.

From a collective crib table $\mathcal{C}$ using the entries in Table 7.30–7.37, 7.38–7.42, and 7.43–7.46, and from the set $\mathcal{T}$ of all triples (i, s, t) from $\mathcal{C}$ with s, $t \in$ VOW and $0 \leq i < 25$. For example, the first row in Table 7.30 includes the six triples

11	E	c	12	R	e	15	R	a	17	A	r	19	C	e	20	E	e

TABLE 7.45   Ciphertext Fragments in `cipherEx7.10` for the Crib INFORMATION

logtavegooy	127	6	R	a	8	A	e	5.3985	
pfxvdvcgofv	404	8	R	d	10	A	c	1.0107	√
gqvseoefxgn	476	5	R	e	7	A	e	2.2519	
mgtmuzdlwjx	703	7	R	u	9	A	d	3.5908	√
klvnrmuzzoq	855	9	R	r	11	A	u	2.9362	√

TABLE 7.46   Ciphertext Fragments in `cipherEx7.10` for the Crib COMMUNICATIONSYSTEMS

atwvukkdrpwybsfstciz	1041	16	C	a	20	U	u	23	C	d	24	A	r	8	E	c	8.7730	√
ulsvrmbruzqyfzsyxepm	1154	4	C	u	8	U	r	11	C	r	12	A	u	21	E	e	61.0924	
ugfpctxcdxqxohpzvuzz	1310	10	C	u	14	U	c	17	C	c	18	A	d	2	E	u	28.1070	√

TABLE 7.47 Combined Plugboard/Vowel-Stepper for Table 7.25 Parameters

	A	C	D	E	R	U
0	r	a	d	c	u	e
1	u	d	r	a	e	c
2	r	e	d	u	c	a
3	r	d	u	e	a	c
4	a	u	d	c	e	r
5	a	d	r	u	e	c
6	c	e	a	r	d	u
7	e	a	c	d	u	r
8	e	a	u	c	d	r
9	d	a	c	e	r	u
10	c	u	r	e	a	d
11	u	r	a	c	d	e
12	u	a	d	r	e	c
13	d	e	u	c	r	a
14	d	r	u	e	a	c
15	d	u	e	c	a	r
16	e	a	r	d	u	c
17	r	c	e	a	u	d
18	d	a	c	u	e	r
19	c	e	r	u	d	a
20	a	d	c	e	r	u
21	c	u	d	e	r	a
22	r	e	a	c	u	d
23	d	r	e	u	c	a
24	r	e	d	u	c	a

Next, count the number $N(i, s, t)$ of entries in $\mathcal{T}$ with $s, t \in$ VOW and $0 \le i < 25$, and

$$N(i) = \sum_{s,\, t \in \text{VOW}} N(i, s, t).$$

If *no* errors occurred in the cribbing tables, the matrix of frequencies $F_i = (f(i, s, t))$

$$f(i, s, t) = \frac{N(i, s, t)}{N(i)}$$

would be a 6×6 permutation matrix of 0's and 1's and if $f(i, s, t) = 1$, then

$$t = \text{PL}_V^{-1}(\text{VS}_{\text{VP}(i)}(\text{PL}_V(s))).$$

We *prune* entries from $\mathcal{C}$ and thereafter from $\mathcal{T}$ in order to maximize

$$V = \frac{1}{25} \sum_{i=0}^{24} \sum_{t \in \text{VOW}} \frac{N^2(i, s, t)}{N^2(i)}. \tag{7.68}$$

TABLE 7.48 Vowel Counts in `cipherEx7.8-10`

	cipherEx7.8							cipherEx7.9					
i	$N(a)$	$N(c)$	$N(d)$	$N(e)$	$N(r)$	$N(u)$	i	$N(a)$	$N(c)$	$N(d)$	$N(e)$	$N(r)$	$N(u)$
0	4	11	2	2	11	5	0	1	5	5	3	3	3
1	11	3	3	6	3	3	1	14	3	1	7	2	9
2	1	4	5	4	6	8	2	4	4	0	2	6	8
3	7	2	6	9	5	3	3	5	3	3	8	8	6
4	4	9	3	9	0	9	4	3	9	8	1	3	3
5	2	0	7	4	3	9	5	4	2	3	8	4	10
6	11	1	5	3	8	9	6	10	5	2	2	6	6
7	1	2	15	8	1	5	7	5	4	9	2	4	5
8	3	10	9	4	2	5	8	10	6	6	6	1	3
9	5	2	1	16	10	2	9	7	1	7	11	6	0
10	2	8	4	9	5	8	10	2	9	2	11	5	0
11	1	13	7	3	2	3	11	3	8	2	4	2	4
12	5	2	3	9	9	6	12	5	3	6	2	6	5
13	0	8	9	5	2	2	13	4	10	5	4	7	4
14	4	3	9	8	5	2	14	6	1	8	13	0	1
15	8	10	6	1	2	4	15	9	7	3	2	2	7
16	6	1	14	5	4	1	16	2	5	10	4	4	6
17	14	5	2	1	8	5	17	8	3	4	1	5	4
18	2	2	7	3	2	13	18	2	2	8	7	2	6
19	2	9	3	6	6	13	19	3	4	3	4	6	13
20	5	1	6	18	6	4	20	4	1	6	13	3	3
21	5	6	1	7	4	5	21	2	7	2	9	7	5
22	2	9	3	4	10	4	22	2	8	3	3	4	6
23	11	4	4	9	2	7	23	5	4	5	9	4	9
24	1	7	7	3	5	11	24	4	6	4	5	6	9

	cipherEx7.10					
i	$N(a)$	$N(c)$	$N(d)$	$N(e)$	$N(r)$	$N(u)$
0	2	4	6	2	6	5
1	10	5	5	1	1	3
2	0	4	5	7	4	3
3	2	2	2	9	9	2
4	3	14	2	5	1	7
5	4	1	4	5	3	9
6	10	3	5	5	2	5
7	2	0	5	6	2	6
8	2	10	5	4	6	2
9	3	3	9	15	3	0
10	4	8	1	5	5	5
11	3	4	4	5	6	4
12	2	4	1	3	6	8
13	0	10	4	3	2	1
14	4	3	5	11	2	2
15	4	8	5	0	5	6
16	3	2	10	6	0	3
17	8	6	1	1	3	5
18	3	1	7	5	2	7
19	3	4	4	2	2	7
20	3	3	2	17	3	3
21	2	8	1	9	1	2
22	3	10	1	3	5	3
23	7	3	6	4	3	0
24	1	7	0	1	4	11

TABLE 7.49   Trace of Hill Climbing

k	Crib		$V \to V + \nabla V$
1	ejeufrbrdf	0	$0.710185 \to 0.725374$
2	usauprzrcf	0	$0.725374 \to 0.739352$
3	axadzaiurk	0	$0.739352 \to 0.752729$
4	oedructr	0	$0.752729 \to 0.764782$
5	rbrdfaqeep	0	$0.764782 \to 0.775823$
6	ayacbaxadz	0	$0.775823 \to 0.786081$
7	dqedpeycek	0	$0.786081 \to 0.795142$
8	bdacuama	0	$0.795142 \to 0.804019$
9	vvumhlrc	0	$0.804019 \to 0.812537$
10	ocsedyqgr	0	$0.812537 \to 0.820767$
11	kqusovcu	0	$0.820767 \to 0.828915$
12	zwcysqur	0	$0.828915 \to 0.836600$
13	qgakhbcc	0	$0.836600 \to 0.844100$
14	yrueodlmlv	0	$0.844100 \to 0.850829$
15	myewbmca	0	$0.850829 \to 0.857866$
16	qaccxetvzw	0	$0.857866 \to 0.864309$
17	uyaodalnzw	1	$0.864309 \to 0.870606$
18	ldzudinnu	0	$0.870606 \to 0.874905$
19	kdsaamffe	0	$0.874905 \to 0.879009$
20	shcqmtur	0	$0.879009 \to 0.882713$
21	gedhfaleqau	1	$0.882713 \to 0.886046$
22	peacfaonty	1	$0.886046 \to 0.889379$
23	nuecduvc	1	$0.889379 \to 0.892713$
24	dcpuuvquqs	0	$0.892713 \to 0.894779$
25	ttezbgau	0	$0.894779 \to 0.896720$
26	ytelsmcc	0	$0.896720 \to 0.905520$
27	logtavegooy	0	$0.905520 \to 0.906978$

7.9.3   Hill Climbing Algorithm

1. Choose $\epsilon > 0$; set $T_0 = T$ and $C_0 = C$.
2. Step $k = 0, 1, 2, \ldots$

    (a) Test *every* entry in T_k by computing $V + \nabla V$ with the entry removed from T_k and all corresponding triples from C_k;

    (b) Remove that entry from T_k and all corresponding triples from C_k that maximize $V + \nabla V$;

    (c) Terminate when $V > 1 - \epsilon$.

Table 7.49 shows the changes ∇V in the hill climbing algorithm; the format of the entries are

Column 0: step number;

Columns 1–2: the crib removed and the *un*known indication of whether the crib entry was valid (1) or *in*valid (0);

Column 3: the change $V \to V + \nabla V$.

TABLE 7.50   V-Stepper Counts After Pruning

$VS_{VP(0)}$	A	C	D	E	R	U
a	0	1	0	0	0	0
c	0	0	0	3	0	0
d	0	0	1	0	1	0
e	0	0	0	0	0	4
r	2	0	0	0	0	0
u	0	0	0	0	0	0

$VS_{VP(1)}$	A	C	D	E	R	U
a	0	0	0	5	0	0
c	0	0	0	0	0	2
d	0	2	0	0	0	0
e	0	0	0	0	4	0
r	0	0	1	0	0	0
u	5	0	0	0	0	0

$VS_{VP(2)}$	A	C	D	E	R	U
a	0	0	0	0	0	0
c	0	0	0	0	2	0
d	0	0	0	0	0	0
e	0	1	0	0	0	0
r	3	0	0	0	0	0
u	0	0	0	6	1	0

$VS_{VP(3)}$	A	C	D	E	R	U
a	0	0	0	0	4	0
c	0	0	0	0	0	2
d	0	4	0	0	0	0
e	0	0	0	4	0	0
r	0	0	0	0	0	0
u	0	0	2	0	0	0

$VS_{VP(4)}$	A	C	D	E	R	U
a	1	0	0	0	0	0
c	0	0	0	3	0	0
d	0	0	0	0	0	0
e	0	0	0	0	0	0
r	0	0	0	0	0	0
u	0	6	0	0	1	0

$VS_{VP(5)}$	A	C	D	E	R	U
a	1	0	0	0	0	0
c	0	0	0	0	0	0
d	0	3	0	0	0	0
e	0	0	0	1	2	0
r	0	0	1	0	0	0
u	0	0	0	2	0	0

$VS_{VP(6)}$	A	C	D	E	R	U
a	0	0	0	3	0	0
c	0	1	0	0	0	0
d	1	0	0	0	0	1
e	0	0	0	0	0	0
r	0	0	0	0	7	0
u	0	0	0	0	0	0

$VS_{VP(7)}$	A	C	D	E	R	U
a	0	1	0	0	0	0
c	0	0	0	0	0	0
d	0	0	1	8	0	0
e	4	0	0	0	0	0
r	0	0	0	0	0	1
u	0	0	0	0	2	0

$VS_{VP(8)}$	A	C	D	E	R	U
a	0	5	0	0	0	0
c	0	0	0	4	1	0
d	0	0	0	0	6	0
e	3	0	0	0	0	0
r	0	0	0	0	0	3
u	0	0	2	0	0	0

$VS_{VP(9)}$	A	C	D	E	R	U
a	0	5	0	0	0	1
c	0	0	0	0	0	0
d	4	0	0	0	0	0
e	0	0	0	3	0	0
r	0	0	1	0	5	0
u	0	0	0	0	0	0

$VS_{VP(10)}$	A	C	D	E	R	U
a	0	0	0	0	1	0
c	2	0	0	0	0	0
d	0	0	0	0	0	1
e	1	0	0	6	0	0
r	0	0	1	0	0	0
u	0	8	0	0	0	0

(Continued)

TABLE 7.50 *Continued*

VS$_{VP(11)}$	A	C	D	E	R	U
a	0	0	1	0	0	0
c	0	0	0	6	0	0
d	0	0	0	0	5	0
e	0	0	0	0	0	2
r	0	3	0	0	0	0
u	2	0	0	0	0	0

VS$_{VP(12)}$	A	C	D	E	R	U
a	0	2	0	0	0	0
c	0	0	0	0	0	2
d	0	0	2	0	0	0
e	1	0	0	0	4	0
r	0	0	0	3	0	0
u	3	0	0	0	0	0

VS$_{VP(13)}$	A	C	D	E	R	U
a	0	0	0	0	0	1
c	0	0	1	4	0	0
d	5	0	0	0	0	0
e	0	2	0	0	0	0
r	0	0	0	0	2	0
u	0	0	0	0	0	0

VS$_{VP(14)}$	A	C	D	E	R	U
a	0	0	0	0	4	0
c	0	0	0	1	0	3
d	5	0	0	0	0	0
e	0	0	0	3	0	0
r	0	1	0	0	0	0
u	0	0	1	0	0	0

VS$_{VP(15)}$	A	C	D	E	R	U
a	0	0	0	0	5	0
c	0	0	0	3	0	0
d	3	0	0	0	0	0
e	0	0	1	0	0	0
r	0	0	0	0	0	1
u	0	5	0	0	0	0

VS$_{VP(16)}$	A	C	D	E	R	U
a	0	4	0	0	1	0
c	0	0	0	0	0	3
d	0	0	0	5	1	0
e	0	0	0	0	0	0
r	1	0	2	0	0	0
u	0	0	0	0	2	0

VS$_{VP(17)}$	A	C	D	E	R	U
a	0	0	0	3	0	0
c	0	3	0	0	0	0
d	0	0	0	0	0	3
e	0	0	0	0	0	0
r	6	0	0	0	0	0
u	0	0	0	0	2	0

VS$_{VP(18)}$	A	C	D	E	R	U
a	0	2	0	0	0	0
c	0	0	0	0	0	0
d	5	0	0	0	0	0
e	0	0	0	0	1	0
r	0	0	0	0	0	0
u	0	0	0	2	0	1

VS$_{VP(19)}$	A	C	D	E	R	U
a	0	0	0	0	0	2
c	3	0	0	0	0	0
d	0	0	0	0	0	0
e	0	4	0	0	1	0
r	0	0	2	0	0	0
u	0	0	0	5	0	0

VS$_{VP(20)}$	A	C	D	E	R	U
a	0	0	0	0	0	0
c	0	0	1	0	0	0
d	0	2	0	0	0	0
e	2	0	0	11	0	0
r	0	0	0	0	1	0
u	0	0	0	0	0	4

VS$_{VP(21)}$	A	C	D	E	R	U
a	0	0	0	0	0	2
c	2	0	0	0	0	0
d	0	0	0	0	0	0
e	0	0	0	6	0	0
r	0	0	1	0	2	0
u	0	2	0	0	0	0

(Continued)

TABLE 7.50   *Continued*

	$VS_{VP(22)}$							$VS_{VP(23)}$							$VS_{VP(24)}$					
	A	C	D	E	R	U		A	C	D	E	R	U		A	C	D	E	R	U
a	0	0	0	0	0	0	a	4	0	0	0	0	0	a	0	0	0	0	0	1
c	0	0	0	1	0	1	c	0	0	0	0	0	1	c	0	0	0	0	4	0
d	0	0	0	0	0	0	d	0	3	0	0	0	0	d	0	0	2	0	0	0
e	0	3	0	0	0	0	e	0	0	0	5	0	0	e	0	3	0	0	0	0
r	2	0	0	0	0	0	r	0	0	0	0	0	0	r	4	0	0	0	0	0
u	0	0	0	0	4	0	u	0	0	0	0	7	0	u	0	0	0	2	0	0

The V-stepper in each position can be recovered from the residual set of triples $\mathcal{T}$ after pruning. The first step is to enter the data for all triples in each V-stepper position. The entries in Table 7.50 pertain to the combined V-stepper; for example, entry 3 in row c, column E of the first subtable means that there were three surviving triples (E,c,0). By reference to Table 7.47, we see that this is the correct value. Not all rows in the V-stepper recovered; Table 7.51 lists our results.

TABLE 7.51   **Partial Recovery of V-Stepper**

i	A	C	D	E	R	U
0	a	r	u	d	e	c
1	d	e	c	u	a	r
2	*	u	r	d	c	*
3	u	c	e	d	a	r
4	*	r	*	e	u	*
5	d	u	c	e	a	r
6	*	e	d	*	r	a
7	r	a	u	c	e	d
8	u	r	a	c	e	d
9	r	c	d	a	e	c
10	d	c	e	r	u	a
11	e	r	a	u	d	c
12	a	d	c	u	e	r
13	u	r	d	a	c	e
14	u	c	e	a	d	r
15	c	r	e	a	u	d
16	d	a	u	d	e	r
17	c	e	u	d	r	a
18	d	u	c	a	e	u
19	d	u	c	r	c	a
20	r	c	d	e	a	u
21	a	c	d	r	u	e
22	c	r	u	d	c	a
23	d	c	u	e	a	r
24	a	u	r	d	c	e

7.10 CRIBBING PURPLE: FINDING THE C-STEPPERS

Recovery of the C-steppers is considerably more complicated, because the consonant substitution has the very large period of 25^3. Rowlett [1998, p. 151] describes the excitement when Genevieve Feinstein (née Grotjan) discovered the characteristic property of the C-stepper alphabets that was crucial in the success of Magic, the United States codename for intelligence derived from the cryptanalysis of PURPLE.

Table 7.52 lists the positions of the three banks of C-steppers for $0 \leq i < 78$.

7.10.1 First Characteristic Property of C-Steppers

If

- The speed of the C-stepper banks is (S, M, F).
- The permutations $\prod (i, i+1)$ $(i = 0, 1)$ are factored into the C-stepper substitutions, and
- The initial positions of the V-stepper and all C-steppers are 0, then

the ciphertext alphabets in positions [0, 23] and [26, 49] are related as follows:

$$x \to \begin{cases} \mathrm{PL}_V^{-1}\left(\mathrm{CS}^{(2)}_{\mathrm{CP}^{(2)}(i)}\left(\mathrm{CS}^{(1)}_{\mathrm{CP}^{(1)}(i)}\left(\mathrm{CS}^{(0)}_{\mathrm{CP}^{(0)}(l)}(\mathrm{PL}_V(x))\right)\right)\right) \\ \mathrm{PL}_V^{-1}\left(\mathrm{CS}^{(2)}_{\mathrm{CP}^{(2)}(i+26)}\left(\mathrm{CS}^{(1)}_{\mathrm{CP}^{(1)}(i+26)}\left(\mathrm{CS}^{(0)}_{\mathrm{CP}^{(0)}(i+26)}(\mathrm{PL}_V(x))\right)\right)\right). \end{cases} \tag{7.69}$$

Table 7.52 shows

$$\begin{cases} \mathrm{CS}^{(j)}_{\mathrm{CP}^{(j)}(i)} \\ \mathrm{CS}^{(j)}_{\mathrm{CP}^{(j)}(i+26)} \end{cases} = \begin{cases} \mathrm{CS}^{(j)}_{\mathrm{CP}^{(j)}(0)} \\ \mathrm{CS}^{(j)}_{\mathrm{CP}^{(j)}(26)} \end{cases}, \qquad 0 \leq i \leq 23, \qquad j = 0, 1 \tag{7.70}$$

$$\mathrm{CS}^{(2)}_{\mathrm{CP}^{(2)}(i)} = \mathrm{CS}^{(2)}_{\mathrm{CP}^{(2)}(i+26)}, \qquad 0 \leq i \leq 23. \tag{7.71}$$

If $x_2, x_2 \in \mathrm{CON}$ and

$$\mathrm{CS}^{(1)}_{\mathrm{CP}^{(1)}(0)}\left(\mathrm{CS}^{(0)}_{\mathrm{CP}^{(0)}(0)}(\mathrm{PL}_V(x_1))\right) = \mathrm{CS}^{(1)}_{\mathrm{CP}^{(1)}(26)}\left(\mathrm{CS}^{(0)}_{\mathrm{CP}^{(0)}(26)}(\mathrm{PL}_V(x_2))\right)$$

implies

$$\mathrm{PL}_V^{-1}\left(\mathrm{CS}^{(2)}_{\mathrm{CP}^{(2)}(i)}\left(\mathrm{CS}^{(1)}_{\mathrm{CP}^{(1)}(i)}\left(\mathrm{CS}^{(0)}_{\mathrm{CP}^{(0)}(i)}\left(\mathrm{PL}_V(x_1)\right)\right)\right)\right)$$

$$= \mathrm{PL}_V^{-1}\left(\mathrm{CS}^{(2)}_{\mathrm{CP}^{(2)}(i+26)}\left(\mathrm{CS}^{(1)}_{\mathrm{CP}^{(1)}(i+26)}\left(\mathrm{CS}^{(0)}_{\mathrm{CP}^{(0)}(i+26)}(\mathrm{PL}_V(x_2))\right)\right)\right) \tag{7.72}$$

for $0 \leq i \leq 23$. That is, when

- the consonant x_1 is enciphered in position 0 to the same letter as the consonant x_2 is enciphered in position 26, then
- x_1 is enciphered to the same letter in position i to the same letter as the consonant x_2 is enciphered in position $i + 26$.

For example,

- B in position 0 and 0 in position 26 are both enciphered to t;
- B in position 1 and 0 in position 27 are both enciphered to s;

TABLE 7.52 Positions of the C-Steppers for $0 \leq i < 78$

i:	0	1	2	3	4	5	6	7	8	9	10	11	12	13	14	15	16	17	18	19	20	21	22	23	24	25	26	27	28	29	30	31	32	33	34	35	36	37	38
F:	0	1	2	3	4	5	6	7	8	9	10	11	12	13	14	15	16	17	18	19	20	21	22	23	24	24	0	1	2	3	4	5	6	7	8	9	10	11	12
M:	0	0	0	0	0	0	0	0	0	0	0	0	0	0	0	0	0	0	0	0	0	0	0	0	0	1	1	1	1	1	1	1	1	1	1	1	1	1	1
S:	0	0	0	0	0	0	0	0	0	0	0	0	0	0	0	0	0	0	0	0	0	0	0	0	0	0	0	0	0	0	0	0	0	0	0	0	0	0	0
V:	0	1	2	3	4	5	6	7	8	9	10	11	12	13	14	15	16	17	18	19	20	21	22	23	24	0	1	2	3	4	5	6	7	8	9	10	11	12	13

i:	39	40	41	42	43	44	45	46	47	48	49	50	51	52	53	54	55	56	57	58	59	60	61	62	63	64	65	66	67	68	69	70	71	72	73	74	75	76	77
F:	13	14	15	16	17	18	19	20	21	22	23	23	24	0	1	2	3	4	5	6	7	8	9	10	11	12	13	14	15	16	17	18	19	20	21	22	22	23	24
M:	1	1	1	1	1	1	1	1	1	1	1	2	2	2	2	2	2	2	2	2	2	2	2	2	2	2	2	2	2	2	2	2	2	2	2	2	3	3	3
S:	0	0	0	0	0	0	0	0	0	0	0	0	0	0	0	0	0	0	0	0	0	0	0	0	0	0	0	0	0	0	0	0	0	0	0	0	0	0	0
V:	14	15	16	17	18	19	20	21	22	23	24	0	1	2	3	4	5	6	7	8	9	10	11	12	13	14	15	16	17	18	19	20	21	22	23	24	0	1	2

TABLE 7.53 (S, M, F) PURPLE Encipherment of CON for $0 \leq i < 52$

	B	F	G	H	I	J	K	L	M	N	O	P	Q	S	T	V	W	X	Y	Z
0	t	y	i	x	h	j	q	l	b	o	k	n	z	g	w	s	f	p	m	v
1	s	j	z	x	k	p	f	b	t	n	i	l	h	w	q	g	y	v	m	o
2	f	p	o	x	y	b	n	g	m	l	s	h	i	q	j	w	t	z	k	v
3	i	l	y	v	f	p	b	s	m	k	j	q	z	x	h	o	t	g	n	w
4	j	v	w	i	m	o	x	h	f	q	l	k	s	p	n	y	z	t	g	b
5	h	w	k	p	n	g	b	y	t	i	s	x	j	m	o	l	q	z	f	v
6	i	m	o	b	s	q	g	v	p	z	x	n	w	k	y	t	j	l	h	f
7	n	m	o	t	v	w	j	b	g	h	z	l	x	y	p	f	i	q	k	s
8	t	s	y	n	z	g	o	h	x	l	b	q	j	m	k	v	f	w	p	i
9	n	x	g	z	b	s	h	v	t	i	f	k	l	m	j	q	p	o	w	y
10	m	j	s	x	g	q	o	i	v	w	y	f	t	h	z	n	l	k	p	b
11	n	m	i	y	o	j	w	t	b	h	v	l	k	f	g	s	x	p	z	q
12	w	y	t	z	o	h	m	v	l	n	j	s	p	f	b	k	g	q	i	x
13	i	j	z	q	t	v	m	p	o	x	k	h	s	g	y	w	n	l	f	b
14	k	m	v	g	x	t	i	l	q	z	p	w	o	h	j	f	s	b	y	n
15	v	s	w	g	h	z	x	m	o	f	y	j	l	k	q	i	n	p	b	t
16	g	w	m	v	l	o	b	t	i	q	f	p	k	j	s	h	x	z	n	y
17	y	s	l	k	t	x	i	m	z	j	f	n	w	p	h	o	v	q	g	b
18	k	j	g	y	b	l	f	z	v	t	i	p	x	m	o	s	w	h	n	q
19	g	z	f	o	y	b	h	w	j	l	n	m	p	q	t	i	s	k	x	v
20	f	i	t	o	n	j	l	v	h	s	y	q	k	b	p	g	m	x	w	z
21	x	j	m	n	t	w	i	s	p	q	l	b	y	f	g	h	o	z	v	k
22	q	g	w	x	z	i	o	p	j	v	k	b	n	h	t	m	y	s	l	
23	k	v	m	z	l	q	h	b	i	f	n	t	p	w	j	x	s	o	g	y
24	y	q	i	l	k	m	n	o	x	v	p	z	b	s	t	f	j	h	w	g
25	s	x	g	w	i	o	l	n	j	m	y	v	q	p	f	t	h	k	b	z
26	g	b	v	m	i	l	x	q	f	j	t	o	y	k	s	w	p	h	z	n
27	w	t	o	m	z	b	x	f	y	p	s	n	j	i	g	q	v	k	h	l
28	q	m	v	k	o	g	x	n	t	b	f	l	p	s	w	j	z	y	i	h
29	x	m	w	n	y	s	v	b	t	p	i	k	l	j	o	h	g	f	z	q
30	p	f	b	g	w	h	i	x	z	o	j	q	v	l	y	n	t	m	s	k
31	m	t	v	f	k	y	p	b	q	g	h	i	w	s	l	o	z	n	j	x
32	k	p	f	h	o	v	b	g	j	q	i	z	m	x	t	y	l	s	w	n
33	y	g	s	k	o	b	t	j	i	w	n	h	m	z	f	p	q	v	x	l
34	m	x	i	p	y	h	n	o	f	g	t	l	s	b	v	k	w	z	j	q
35	m	t	y	w	g	v	z	h	p	s	n	i	x	f	q	j	o	b	l	k
36	h	v	b	p	s	i	x	o	l	q	m	w	j	y	n	z	k	g	t	f
37	f	b	q	z	i	t	y	w	x	j	n	h	m	v	s	g	p	o	k	l
38	f	l	x	i	t	v	z	m	g	h	w	n	y	j	k	b	q	o	p	s
39	g	o	b	f	z	p	q	m	n	v	i	x	j	k	w	y	l	t	s	h
40	h	q	n	y	v	l	g	i	s	t	k	z	m	p	f	j	b	x	o	w
41	k	o	t	b	w	m	g	x	n	z	v	f	s	y	i	q	p	h	l	j
42	j	i	y	n	m	t	v	b	x	o	g	q	w	f	h	s	z	l	k	p
43	p	z	b	g	l	m	k	i	v	x	y	j	s	f	o	h	q	t	w	n
44	m	v	q	n	g	z	y	f	w	l	k	t	j	i	s	o	h	b	x	p
45	q	j	v	x	f	w	o	h	s	b	g	l	z	n	i	t	k	y	p	m
46	b	h	z	w	t	v	o	l	m	j	f	s	i	y	g	p	x	n	k	q
47	f	p	k	v	m	s	n	i	o	w	x	q	j	l	h	g	z	t	y	b
48	n	j	l	s	w	p	x	o	m	i	q	f	g	v	t	h	y	z	b	k
49	w	i	y	g	m	b	z	h	s	q	k	f	v	n	x	j	o	l	p	t
50	i	k	p	v	y	t	x	m	b	l	j	w	h	z	n	g	o	s	f	q
51	x	y	b	q	g	z	f	i	o	k	t	s	n	l	p	w	h	j	v	m

In other words, pairs of columns in rows [0,23] and [26,49] shown with a vertical rule on-the-right are isomorphs.

Table 7.53 illustrates that

- Column B in rows 0-23 is *identical* to column 0 in rows 26-49.
- Column F in rows 0-23 is *identical* to column Q in rows 26-49.

$$\cdot \cdot \cdot$$

- Column Z in rows 0-23 is *identical* to column G in rows 26-49.

The First Characteristic Property of the C-Stepper allows the consonant alphabets (Table 7.53) to be filled in by partial data when their motion is (S,M,F).

When cribbing identifies the V-stepper as in Section 7.8, entries in the C-stepper ciphertext alphabets (Table 7.53) are also determined. The characteristic property of the C-steppers expressed in Equations (7.69) to (7.72) fills in additional entries.

7.10.2   Second Characteristic Property of C-Steppers

If

- The speed of the C-stepper banks is (F,M,S),
- The permutations $\prod(i, i+1)$ $(i = 0, 1)$ are factored into the C-stepper substitutions, and
- The initial positions of the V-stepper and all C-steppers are 0, then Equations (7.70) and (7.71) are replaced by

$$\begin{cases} CS^{(j)}_{CP^{(j)}(i)} \\ CS^{(j)}_{CP^{(j)}(i+26)} \end{cases} = \begin{cases} CS^{(j)}_{CP^{(j)}0} \\ CS^{(j)}_{CP^{(j)}(26)} \end{cases}, \quad 0 \le i \le 23, \quad j = 1, 2 \quad (7.73)$$

$$CS^{(0)}_{CP^{(0)}(i)} = CS^{(0)}_{CP^{(0)}(i+26)}, \quad 0 \le i \le 23 \quad (7.74)$$

If $x \in$ CON, then

$$CS^{(1)}_{CP^{(1)}(i)}\left(CS^{(0)}_{CP^{(0)}(i)}\left(PL_V(x)\right)\right) = CS^{(1)}_{CP^{(1)}(j)}\left(CS^{(0)}_{CP^{(0)}(j)}\left(PL_V(x)\right)\right)$$

if and only if

$$CS^{(1)}_{CP^{(1)}(i+26)}\left(CS^{(0)}_{CP^{(0)}(i+26)}\left(PL_V(x)\right)\right) = CS^{(1)}_{CP^{(1)}(j+26)}\left(CS^{(0)}_{CP^{(0)}(j+26)}\left(PL_V(x)\right)\right) \quad (7.75)$$

for $0 \le i \le 23$. That is, when

- the consonant x is enciphered to the same (or different *resp.*) letter in positions i and j, then
- the consonant x is enciphered to the same (or different *resp.*) letter in positions $i + 26$ and $j + 26$ for $0 \le i \le j \le 23$.

For example

- B in rows [0,23] is enciphered to `tgbwqyjmlm ... qnxiqk`
- B in rows [26,49] is enciphered to `plxkvnyomo ... vwibvh` which are *isomorphs* of one another.

TABLE 7.54 (S, M, F) PURPLE Encipherment of CON for $0 \leq i < 52$

	B	F	G	H	I	J	K	L	M	N	O	P	Q	S	T	V	W	X	Y	Z
0	t	y	i	x	h	j	q	l	b	o	k	n	z	g	w	s	f	p	m	v
1	g	b	v	m	i	l	x	q	f	j	t	o	y	k	s	w	p	h	z	n
2	b	t	z	y	v	n	s	i	l	h	w	g	q	x	k	m	p	f	o	j
3	w	x	o	s	k	g	j	i	v	z	f	m	n	l	t	h	q	p	y	b
4	q	x	m	t	s	o	h	w	y	j	g	b	z	v	l	n	i	f	k	p
5	y	v	n	q	j	x	o	b	s	h	f	i	w	m	t	g	k	z	p	l
6	j	f	s	z	o	b	t	m	i	g	q	y	x	v	n	k	l	w	p	h
7	m	n	k	i	p	l	b	v	y	h	w	j	z	f	q	x	o	s	g	t
8	l	f	g	n	z	t	m	v	s	h	j	w	i	y	p	k	o	x	b	q
9	m	w	k	q	f	o	l	s	y	x	i	n	g	b	p	j	v	z	t	h
10	k	f	z	j	p	h	l	q	w	o	t	v	b	x	m	g	n	i	y	s
11	t	m	k	b	h	n	l	y	g	z	q	j	o	p	s	i	x	v	f	w
12	g	h	x	y	n	b	w	f	k	s	v	t	i	l	p	o	z	j	m	q
13	o	s	t	z	l	j	i	x	m	k	h	g	w	p	y	n	b	q	f	v
14	w	m	i	y	t	q	o	v	n	z	f	k	x	p	j	l	s	g	b	h
15	f	h	t	w	i	g	o	s	q	k	m	p	b	z	n	j	y	l	x	v
16	m	s	j	v	t	b	i	y	f	h	p	k	w	o	q	n	l	x	g	z
17	f	y	i	l	v	g	b	z	t	x	n	p	j	k	m	q	s	w	h	o
18	q	v	h	l	k	m	w	z	p	x	f	s	y	g	n	b	j	o	t	i
19	n	g	f	j	w	y	s	o	l	t	q	p	i	h	v	b	k	m	z	x
20	x	z	w	v	b	i	n	p	l	j	m	o	g	q	f	h	t	s	y	k
21	i	m	f	x	o	h	z	y	p	t	b	w	l	v	s	k	q	g	n	j
22	q	v	n	j	f	b	p	g	s	x	z	h	m	l	i	t	y	k	w	o
23	k	b	s	o	y	w	f	m	q	p	i	j	n	t	v	z	g	h	x	l
24	l	b	x	v	w	t	i	z	k	y	g	p	o	h	q	s	n	m	j	f
25	m	x	i	j	k	p	b	g	h	n	l	s	z	t	v	f	w	o	y	q
26	p	n	b	i	t	y	v	m	x	z	h	w	g	l	k	f	q	s	o	j
27	l	x	j	o	b	m	i	v	q	y	p	z	n	h	f	k	s	t	g	w
28	x	p	g	n	j	w	f	b	m	t	k	l	v	i	h	o	s	q	z	y
29	k	i	z	f	h	l	y	b	j	g	q	o	w	m	p	t	v	s	n	x
30	v	i	o	p	f	z	t	k	n	y	l	x	g	j	m	w	b	q	h	s
31	n	j	w	v	y	i	z	x	f	t	q	b	k	o	p	l	h	g	s	m
32	y	p	f	g	z	x	p	o	b	l	v	n	i	j	w	h	m	k	s	t
33	o	w	h	b	s	m	x	j	n	t	k	y	g	q	v	i	z	f	l	p
34	m	q	l	w	g	p	o	j	f	t	y	k	b	n	s	h	z	i	x	v
35	o	k	h	v	q	z	m	f	n	i	b	w	l	x	s	y	j	g	p	t
36	h	q	g	y	s	t	m	v	k	z	p	j	x	i	o	l	w	b	n	f
37	p	o	h	x	t	w	m	n	l	g	v	y	z	s	f	b	i	j	q	k
38	l	t	i	n	w	x	k	q	h	f	j	p	b	m	s	z	g	y	o	v
39	z	f	p	g	m	y	b	i	o	h	t	l	k	s	n	w	x	v	q	j
40	k	o	b	n	p	v	z	j	w	g	q	h	i	s	y	m	f	l	x	t
41	q	t	p	k	b	l	z	f	v	h	o	s	x	g	w	y	n	m	i	j
42	o	f	y	j	p	x	b	n	q	t	s	h	k	z	v	w	m	i	l	g
43	q	n	b	m	j	l	x	g	p	i	w	s	y	h	o	v	f	k	t	z
44	v	j	t	m	h	o	k	g	s	i	q	f	n	l	w	x	y	z	p	b
45	w	l	q	y	k	n	f	z	m	p	v	s	b	t	j	x	h	o	g	i
46	i	g	k	j	x	b	w	s	m	y	o	z	l	v	q	t	p	f	n	h
47	b	o	q	i	z	t	g	n	s	p	x	k	m	j	f	h	v	l	w	y
48	v	j	w	y	q	x	s	l	f	i	g	t	o	m	b	p	n	h	k	z
49	h	x	f	z	n	k	q	o	v	s	b	y	w	p	j	g	l	t	i	m
50	m	o	t	b	y	l	j	v	k	w	q	h	x	g	z	f	p	n	i	s
51	s	o	i	z	l	g	q	f	m	y	p	w	b	n	k	t	x	v	h	j

- C in rows [0,23] is enciphered to `ybtxxvfn...vgzmvb`
- C in rows [26,49] is enciphered to `nxpiijqw...jlqojx`
  which are *isomorphs* of one another.

In other words, corresponding pairs of columns in rows [0,23] and [26,49] shown with a vertical rule on-the-right are isomorphs of one another.

Table 7.54 illustrates that

- Column B in rows 0-23 is an *isomorph* of column B in rows 26-49.
- Column C in rows 0-23 is an *isomorph* of column C in rows 26-49.

  .·.

- Column Z in rows 0-23 is an *isomorph* of column Z in rows 26-49.

The Second Characteristic Property of the C-Stepper allows the consonant alphabets (Table 7.54) to be filled in by partial data when their motion is (F,M,S).

When cribbing identifies the V-stepper as in Section 7.8, entries in the C-stepper ciphertext alphabets (Table 7.54) are also determined. The second characteristic property of the C-steppers expressed in Equations (7.73) to (7.75) fills in additional entries.

Deavours and Kruh (1985) write that Rowlett discovered the pattern used by the Japanese to select the daily keys thus making the process more efficient. Even so, the cryptanalysis of PURPLE represented a monumental achievement.

REFERENCES

C. A. DEAVOURS, AND L. KRUH, *Machine Cryptography and Modern Cryptanalysis*, Artech House, Norwood, Massachusetts, 1985.

L. FARAGO, *The Broken Seal*, Random House, 1967.

D. KAHN, *The Codebreakers*, MacMillan, 1967.

F. B. ROWLETT and D. KAHN, *The Story of Magic*, Aegean Park Press, 1998.

J. SEBERRY and J. PIEPRZYK, *Cryptography: An Introduction to Computer Security*, Prentice-Hall, 1989.

CHAPTER 8

STREAM CIPHERS

THE INVENTION of the transistor in the 1940s led to the development of solid-state devices capable of generating (0, 1)-sequences with very large periods enjoying many properties of randomly generated sequences. The resulting key stream would then be combined character by character with plaintext. This chapter describes the properties of linear feedback shift registers and their output sequences and illustrates the cribbing of ciphertext resulting from the stream encipherment of ASCII character plaintext. Various nonlinear extensions and their application to cell phone encipherment are discussed.

8.1 STREAM CIPHERS

Stream encipherment combines the plaintext $x_0, x_1, \ldots, x_{n-1}$ letter-by-letter with a *key stream* of 0's and 1's. For ASCII plaintext, each letter x_i might first be coded into its 7-bit ASCII ordinal value $\underline{x_i}$

$$x_0, x_1, \ldots, x_{n-1} \quad \longrightarrow \quad \underline{x}_0, \underline{x}_1, \underline{x}_2, \ldots, \underline{x}_{n-1}$$

and then enciphered by the exclusive-OR (XOR) with the key stream.

Several methods of generating the key stream are described in this chapter. Good references for this material include Beker and Piper [1982] and Lidl and Niederrieter [1997]. The original research on linear recurring (periodic) sequences is contained in Selmer [1966] and Zierler [1959].

8.2 FEEDBACK SHIFT REGISTERS

A *finite state machine* (FSM) [Mealy, 1955] consists of finite sets of (internal) *states* $\{s\}$, *input* and *output* alphabets $\{a\}$ and $\{b\}$, an *output* function T determining the output

$$T : (s, a) \to b,$$

and a *state* function Σ determining the *successor* state.

$$\Sigma : (s, a) \to s^* = \Sigma(s, a).$$

Given an *initial* internal state s_0, and sequence of input states $a_0, a_1, \ldots$, the functions T and Σ determine the output sequence $b_0, b_1, \ldots$, according to the recursion

$$b_i = T(s_i, a_i) \qquad s_{i+1} = \Sigma(s_i, a_i), \qquad i = 0, 1, \ldots.$$

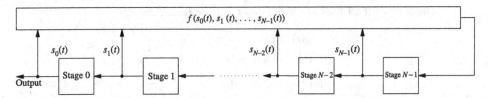

Figure 8.1   Feedback shift register.

Figure 8.1 depicts a *feedback shift register* (FSR) with *feedback function f*, an FSM with *null* input consisting of *N stages* (each capable of storing one bit), a feedback register, and a single output port, where

- The content of Stage i at time t is $s_i(t) = 0$ or 1,
- The output $s_0(t)$ is the content of Stage 0 at time t,
- The state of the FSR at time t is the N-vector $\underline{s}(t) = (s_0(t), s_1(t), \ldots, s_{N-1}(t)) \in \mathcal{Z}_{N,2}$ (where $\mathcal{Z}_{N,2}$ is the set of 2^N vectors of length N with components 0 or 1), and
- The feedback value at time t is $f(s_0(t), s_1(t), \ldots, s_{N-1}(t))$.

The states of the FSR change only when a *clocking* signal is applied and then as follows:

- The content $s_i(t)$ of Stage $i + 1$ at time t is shifted to the left, meaning it becomes the new content of Stage i at time $t + 1$; $s_i(t + 1) = s_{i+1}(t)$ for $0 \le i < N - 1$, and
- The value $f(s_0(t), s_1(t), \ldots, s_{N-1}(t))$ in the feedback register at time t becomes the new content of Stage $N - 1$ at time $t + 1$; $s_{N-1}(t + 1) = f(s_0(t), s_1(t), \ldots, s_{N-1}(t))$.

Figure 8.2 depicts a *linear feedback shift register* (LFSR), the special case of a feedback shift register with linear feedback function f

$$f(s_0(t), s_1(t), \ldots, s_{N-1}(t)) = \sum_{n=0}^{N-1} c_{N-n} s_n(t),$$

where

- $c_0, c_1, \ldots, c_N$ are the *feedback coefficients* or *taps* [$c_0 = 1$],
- The output of the AND-gate $A[j]$ is the (current) content of Stage j if $c_{N-j} = 1$, and 0, otherwise, and
- The feedback bit entering Stage $N - 1$ when a clock pulse is applied is the exclusive-OR (XOR) of the current outputs of the N AND-gates.

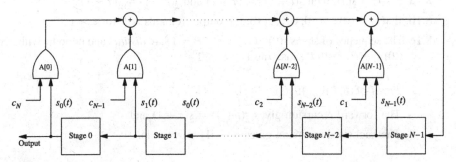

Figure 8.2   Linear feedback shift register.

The state of the LFSR at times t and $t + 1$ are related by

$$\underline{s}(t) = (s_0(t), s_1(t), \ldots, s_{N-1}(t))$$
$$\underline{s}(t + 1) = (s_0(t + 1), s_1(t + 1), \ldots, s_{N-1}(t + 1)). \tag{8.1}$$

As $s_i(t + 1) = s_{i+1}(t)$ for $0 \le i < N - 1$

$$\underline{s}(t + 1) = (s_1(t), s_2(t), \ldots, s_{N-2}(t), s_{N-1}(t)), s_{N-1}(t + 1)) \tag{8.2}$$

where

$$s_{N-1}(t + 1) = \sum_{n=0}^{N-1} c_{N-n} s_n(t), \tag{8.3}$$

the addition in Equation (8.3) being modulo 2. As $s_0(t + k) = s_k(t)$ for $0 \le k < N$, Equations (8.2) and (8.3) give

$$s_0(t + N) = \sum_{n=0}^{N-1} c_{N-n} s_0(t + n), \qquad 0 \le t < \infty. \tag{8.4}$$

Equation (8.4) is a *forward recursion*, because the *future* output $s_0(t + N)$ is determined by the most recent N outputs $(s_0(t), s_0(t+1), \ldots, s_0(t + N - 1))$. When $c_N = 1$, Equation (8.4) may be rearranged such that

$$s_0(t) = \sum_{n=1}^{N} c_{N-n} s_0(t + n). \tag{8.5}$$

Equation (8.5) is a *backward recursion*, because the N outputs $(s_0(t + 1), s_0(t + 2), \ldots, s_0(t + N))$ from time $t + 1$ on determine the *past* output $s_0(t)$.

Remark: We may always assume that $c_N = 1$, for if $c_N = c_{N-1} = \cdots = c_{N-(k-1)} = 0$, $c_{N-k} = 1$, the LFSR essentially contains $N - k$ active stages and the output sequence

$$\underbrace{s_0(0), s_0(1), \ldots, s_0(k - 1)}_{\text{prefix}} s_0(k), s_0(k + 1), \ldots$$

consists of the k-bit prefix determined by the contents of the leftmost k-stages concatenated with the output of a $(N - k)$-stage LFSR.

Proposition 8.1: An N-stage LFSR with feedback coefficients $(c_0, c_1, \ldots, c_N)$ enjoys the following properties:

8.1a If $\underline{s}(t) = \underline{s}(\tau)$, then $\underline{s}(t + 1) = \underline{s}(\tau + 1)$ and $\underline{s}(t - 1) = \underline{s}(\tau - 1)$;

8.1b If $\underline{s}(\tau) = (0)_N \equiv (0, 0, \ldots, 0)$, the output remains *null* for $t > \tau$;

8.1c The sequence of states $\underline{s}(0), \underline{s}(1), \ldots, \underline{s}(P - 1)$ are *distinct* and periodic with period P; $\underline{s}(0) = \underline{s}(P)$, with P satisfying $1 \le P \le 2^N - 1$.

*Proof of (**8.1a**):* If $\underline{s}(t) = \underline{s}(\tau)$,

- The forward recursion gives $\underline{s}(t + 1) = \underline{s}(\tau + 1)$ and
- The backward recursion gives $\underline{s}(t - 1) = \underline{s}(\tau - 1)$.

*Proof of (**8.1b**):* This follows immediately from (**8.1a**).

TABLE 8.1 The States of the Example 8.1 LFSR

t	$\underline{s}(t)$			$s_0(t)$
0	1	0	0	1
1	0	0	1	0
2	0	1	1	0
3	1	1	1	1
4	1	1	0	1
5	1	0	1	1
6	0	1	0	0
7	1	0	0	1
0	0	0	0	0
1	0	0	0	0

Proof of (**8.1c**): If $\underline{s}(0) = (0)_N$, then $P = 1$; otherwise, the transformation of states $\underline{s}(t) \to \underline{s}(t+1)$ is invertible and as $\underline{s}(t) \neq (0)_N$, there are only $2^N - 1$ possible states, and there exists a largest value P such that $\underline{s}(0), \underline{s}(1), \ldots, \underline{s}(P-1)$ are distinct. (**8.1a**) proves that $\underline{s}(0) = \underline{s}(P)$ and $P \leq 2^N - 1$. ∎

Example 8.1
The output $s_0(t)$ of the LFSR with $N = 3$ and $f(s_0(t), s_0(t+1), s_0(t+2)) = s_0(t) + s_0(t+2)$ is listed in Table 8.1. The LFSR output is periodic with period 7 for *every* initial state other than $s(0) = (0)_3$.

8.3 THE ALGEBRA OF POLYNOMIALS OVER $\mathbb{Z}_2$

$\mathcal{P}[z]$ will denote the set of polynomials in the variable z whose coefficients $\{p_i\}$ are in $\mathbb{Z}_2 = \{0, 1\}$:

$$p(z) = p_0 + p_1 z + p_2 z^2 + \cdots + p_n z^n.$$

Arithmetic operations on polynomials are the usual, except that the addition and multiplication of coefficients is performed modulo 2. We write $\deg(p)$ for the degree of $p \in \mathcal{P}[z]$ The subset of $\mathcal{P}[z]$ consisting of polynomials with $\deg(p) \leq n$ will be denoted by $\mathcal{P}_n[z]$. We next summarize several basic properties of $\mathcal{P}[z]$.

8.3.1 Properties of $\mathcal{P}[z]$

1. $f \in \mathcal{P}[z]$ has a *factorization*, if $f(z) = g(z)h(z)$ with $g, h \in \mathcal{P}[z]$. If $f(z) = g(z)h(z)$, then $g(z)$ and $h(z)$ are *factors* of $f(z)$
   (a) $f(z) = g(z)h(z)$ is a *non-trivial* factorization of $f(z)$ if both $g(z) \neq 1$ and $\neq f(z)$
   (b) $f(z) = g(z)h(z)$ is a *trivial* factorization of $f(z)$ otherwise.
2. $f(z)$ is *reducible* if $f(z)$ has a nontrivial factorization $f(z) = g(z)h(z)$.
3. $f(z)$ is *irreducible* if every factorization of $f(z) = g(z)h(z)$ is trivial; $f(z) = g(z)h(z)$ implies either $g(z) = f(z)$ or $h(z) = f(z)$.
4. *Division algorithm for polynomials*: If $f(z), g(z) \in \mathcal{P}[z]$, there exist polynomials $q(z)$ and $r(z)$ such that $f(z) = q(z)g(z) + r(z)$ with $0 \leq \deg(r) < \deg(g)$; $q(z)$ is the *quotient* and $r(z)$ is the *remainder* of the division of $f(z)$ by $g(z)$.

Remarks

1. (a) If $p(1) = 0 \Leftrightarrow (z + 1)$ is a factor of $p(z)$; $p(0) = 0 \Leftrightarrow z$ is a factor of $p(z)$.
   (b) If $p(1) = 0$, the division algorithm gives $p(z) = (z + 1)q(z) + r(z)$, where the remainder $r(z)$ is a polynomial of degree 0, that is, a constant (0 or 1), As $p(1) = 0$, it follows that $r(z) = 0$.

2. The factorization $p(z) = 1 + z^n = (1 + z)(1 + z + z^2 + \cdots + z^{n-1})$ shows that $p(z) = 1 + z^n$ is reducible for every $n > 1$.

3. The polynomial $p(z) = 1 + z + z^3$ is irreducible. If $p(z)$ is reducible, it must have a factor of degree 1. As $p(0) = p(1) = 1$ and neither z or $z + 1$ are factors of $p(z)$, so we conclude that $p(z)$ is irreducible.

8.3.2   Modular Arithmetic for Polynomials

If $f(z) \in \mathcal{P}[z]$ and $p(z) \in \mathcal{P}_n[z]$ with $p(0) = 1$, then by the division algorithm

$$f(z) = q(z)p(z) + r(z), \qquad \deg(r) < \deg(p).$$

Analogous to integer modular arithmetic, we write

$$f(z) \equiv r(z) \ (\text{modulo } p(z)).$$

Again by analogy with modular integer arithmetic, $r(z)$ is referred to as the *residue* of $f(z)$ modulo $p(z)$.

Remark: If $p(0) = 1$, the residue of z^i (modulo $p(z)$) cannot be the zero polynomial for $i \geq 1$; otherwise, $z^i = q(z)(1 + p_1 z + p_2 z^2 + \cdots)$, which requires $q(z) = z^i + \cdots$, leading to $i = \deg(q) + \deg(p) > i$, a contradiction.

Example 8.2

Table 8.2 expresses $z^i = q_i(z)p(z) + r_i(z)$ using the division algorithm and the residues $z^i(\text{modulo } p(z))$ with $p(z) = 1 + z + z^3$ and $0 \leq i \leq 7$. Table 8.2 illustrates two important properties of polynomial modular arithmetic:

- If $p(z)$ is of degree r, the residue z^k (modulo $p(z)$) is a polynomial of degree $\leq r - 1$ for *every* value of k, and

- If $p(1) = 0$, then $p(z)$ divides $1 + z^m$ for *some* integer m.

The following three statements are easily seen to be equivalent:

$$p(z) \text{ divides } 1 + z^m \qquad 0 = (1 + z^m) \ (\text{modulo } p(z)) \qquad 1 = z^m \ (\text{modulo } p(z))$$

TABLE 8.2   The Residues z^i (modulo $p(z)$), $p(z) = 1 + z + z^2$

	$1 = 1$ (modulo $p(z)$)	
	$z = z$ (modulo $p(z)$)	
	$z^2 = z^2$ (modulo $p(z)$)	
$z^3 = p(z) + (1 + z)$	$\Longleftrightarrow$	$1 + z = z^3$ (modulo $p(z)$)
$z^4 = zp(z) + (z + z^2)$	$\Longleftrightarrow$	$z + z^2 = z^4$ (modulo $p(z)$)
$z^5 = (1 + z^2)p(z) + (1 + z + z^2)$	$\Longleftrightarrow$	$1 + z + z^2 = z^5$ (modulo $p(z)$)
$z^6 = (1 + z + z^3)p(z) + (1 + z^2)$	$\Longleftrightarrow$	$1 + z^2 = z^6$ (modulo $p(z)$)
$z^7 = (1 + z + z^2 + z^4)p(z) + 1$	$\Longleftrightarrow$	$1 = z^7$ (modulo $p(z)$)

From Table 8.2

$$p(z) = 1 + z + z^3 \text{ divides } (1 + z^7) \qquad 0 = (1 + z^7) \text{ (modulo } p(z)) \qquad 1 = z^7 \text{(modulo } p(z))$$

Proposition 8.2: If $p(z)$ is of degree N and $p(0) = 1$, then

8.2a The residue z^i (modulo $p(z)$) is a polynomial of degree at most $N - 1$,

8.2b There exists an integer m, the *exponent* of $p(z)$, such that $p(z)$ divides $1 + z^m$,

8.2c The sequence of residues z^0 (modulo $p(z)$), z^1 (modulo $p(z)$), z^2 (modulo $p(z)$),... is periodic with period m, and

8.2d The exponent m of $p(z)$ satisfies $1 \leq m \leq 2^N - 1$.

Proof of (8.2a):   This follows directly from the division algorithm.

Proof of (8.2b–d):   If $p(0) = 1$, then since z^i (modulo $p(z)$) $\neq 0$, it follows that there are only $2^N - 1$ different values for the residues z^i (modulo $p(z)$). The sequence of residues

$$z^0 \text{ (modulo } p(z)), \ z^1 \text{ (modulo } p(z)), \ z^2 \text{ (modulo } p(z)),\ldots$$

must therefore contain a repetition.

Suppose the *first* repetition occurs for the pair (i, j) with $0 \leq i < j \leq 2^N - 1$,

$$z^i \text{ (modulo } p(z)) = z^j \text{ (modulo } p(z))$$

TABLE 8.3   Irreducible and Primitive Polynomials of Degree $n = 2(1)9$

Degree 2					
7*					
Degree 3					
13*					
Degree 4					
23*	37				
Degree 5					
45*	75*	67*			
Degree 6					
103*	127	147*	111	155*	
Degree 7					
211*	217*	235*	367*	277*	325*
203*	313*	345*			
Degree 8					
435*	567	763	551*	675	747*
453*	727	545*	613	545*	613
543*	433	477	537*	703*	471
Degree 9					
1021*	1131*	1461*	1231	1423*	1055*
1167*	1541*	1333*	1605*	1027*	1751*
1743*	1617*	1553*	1401	1157*	1715*
1563*	1713*	1175*	1725*	1225*	1275*
1773*	1511	1425*	1267*		

so that

$$0 = (z^i + z^j) \text{ (modulo } p(z)).$$

If

$$(z^i + z^j) = q(z)p(z),$$

then z^i divides $q(z)$ as $p(0) = 1$ and therefore

$$0 = (1 + z^{j-i}) \text{ (modulo } p(z)).$$

This shows $i = 0$ and $m = j$ and completes the proof.   ∎

Table 8.3 [Marsh, 1957] lists irreducible polynomials of degree n for $n = 2(1)9$. (Note, the table-maker's notation $n = 2(1)9$ indicates that n ranges from 2 to 9 steps of 1.) The entries in Table 8.3 are in octal; for example; $217^* = 010\ 001\ 111$ corresponds to the polynomial $p(z) = 1 + z + z^2 + z^3 + z^7$. An asterisk (*) signals the entry is a primitive polynomial. The *reciprocal* of the polynomial

$$p(z) = p_0 + p_1 z + \cdots + p_{N-1} z^{N-1} + p_N z^N$$

is the polynomial with the coefficients written in the reverse order,

$$p^*(z) \equiv z^N p\left(\frac{1}{z}\right) = p_N + p_{N-1} z^{N-1} + \cdots + p_1 z + p_0 z^N.$$

$p(z)$ is irreducible (*resp.* primitive) if and only if the same property holds for $p^*(z)$ and Table 8.3 lists only one of the pair $p(z)$, $p^*(z)$.

Table 8.4 gives the number $N(n)$ of irreducible and the number $N^*(n)$ of primitive polynomials of degree n for $n = 1(1)12$.

TABLE 8.4   The Number of Irreducible and Primitive Polynomials of Degree $n = 1(1)12$

n	$N(n)$	$N^*(n)$
1	2	1
2	1	1
3	2	2
4	3	2
5	6	6
6	9	6
7	18	18
8	30	16
9	56	48
10	99	60
11	186	176
12	335	144

8.4 THE CHARACTERISTIC POLYNOMIAL OF A LINEAR FEEDBACK SHIFT REGISTER

The *characteristic polynomial* of the N-stage LFSR with recursion

$$s_0(t + N) = \sum_{n=0}^{N-1} c_{N-n} s_0(t + n), \qquad 0 \le t < \infty,$$

and feedback coefficients $\{c_i\}$ is

$$p(z) = c_N + c_{N-1}z + \cdots + c_1 z^{N-1} + c_0 z^N.$$

We will always assume $c_0 = c_N = 1$.

Example 8.3
The LFSR with characteristic polynomial $p(z) = 1 + z + z^2 + z^3$ is shown in Figure 8.3. As $p(z)$ does not divide $1 + z^k$ for $k = 1, 2, 3$ and $(1 + z)p(z) = 1 + z^4$, the exponent of $p(z)$ is 4. Table 8.5 gives the output and states of this LFSR for three different initial states. Table 8.5 illustrates that the period of the sequence $s_0(0), s_0(1), s_0(2), \ldots$ depends on the initial state $\underline{s}(0)$:

- $\underline{s}(0) = (0, 0, 1)$ produces a sequence of period 3,
- $\underline{s}(0) = (1, 0, 1)$ produces a sequence of period 2, and
- $\underline{s}(0) = (1, 1, 1)$ produces a sequence of period 1.

Proposition 8.3: [Beker and Piper, 1982, pp. 192–193] If $p(z) = c_N + c_{N-1}z + \cdots + c_1 z^{N-1} + c_0 z^N$ is the characteristic polynomial of the LFSR, then

8.3a The period of the output sequence $s_0(0), s_0(1), s_0(2), \ldots$ is a divisor of the exponent of $p(z)$, and

8.3b If the initial state $\underline{s}(0) \ne (0)_N$, the period of the output sequence $s_0(0), s_0(1), s_0(2), \ldots$ is $2^N - 1$ if and only if $p(z)$ is primitive.

Example 8.4
The LFSR with characteristic polynomial $p(z) = 1 + z + z^3$ is shown in Figure 8.4. The exponent of $p(z)$ was shown to be 7 in *Example 8.2*. Table 8.6 gives the output states of

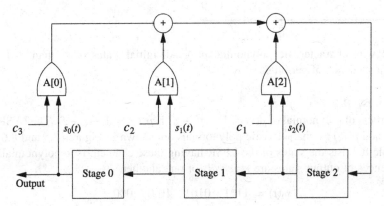

Figure 8.3 The LFSR with characteristic polynomial $p(z) = 1 + z + z^2 + z^3$.

TABLE 8.5 The States and Output of the LFSR with Characteristic Polynomial $p(z) = 1 + z + z^2 + z^3$

	$\underline{s}(0)$					
	0 0 1		1 0 1		1 1 1	
t	$\underline{s}_0(t)$	$\underline{s}(t)$	$\underline{s}_0(t)$	$\underline{s}(t)$	$\underline{s}_0(t)$	$\underline{s}(t)$
0	1	1 0 0	1	1 0 1	1	1 1 1
1	0	0 1 1	0	0 1 0	1	1 1 1
2	0	0 1 1	1	1 0 1	1	1 1 1
3	1	1 1 0	0	0 1 0	1	1 1 1
4	1	1 0 0	1	1 0 1	1	1 1 1

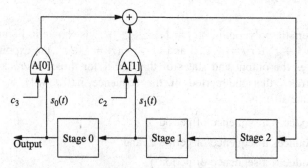

Figure 8.4 The LFSR with characteristic polynomial $p(z) = 1 + z + z^3$.

TABLE 8.6 The States and Output of the LFSR with Characteristic Polynomial $p(z) = 1 + z + z^3$

t	$s_0(t)$	$\underline{s}(t)$
0	1	1 0 0
1	0	0 0 1
2	0	0 1 0
3	1	1 0 1
4	0	0 1 1
5	1	1 1 1
6	1	1 1 0
7	1	1 0 0

the LFSR with characteristic polynomial $p(z)$. All initial states other than $\underline{s}(0) = (0)_3$ produces a sequence of period 7.

Example 8.5

The reciprocal of polynomial of $p(z) = 1 + z^3 + z^4$ is $p^*(z) = 1 + z + z^4$. The LFSRs that have $p(z)$ and $p^*(z)$ as characteristic polynomials are shown in Figures 8.5 and 8.6.

Table 8.7 lists the states of the LFSR having these characteristic polynomials. The two sequences of output states are *reversals* of one another.

$$s_0(t) = 1111 \quad 0101 \quad 1001 \quad 000$$
$$s_0^*(t) = 0001 \quad 0011 \quad 0101 \quad 111$$

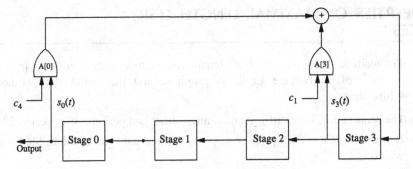

Figure 8.5   The LFSR with characteristic polynomial $p(z) = 1 + z^3 + z^4$.

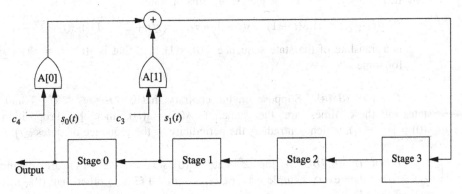

Figure 8.6   The LFSR with characteristic polynomial $p^*(z) = 1 + z + z^4$.

TABLE 8.7   States of the LFSR with $p(z) = 1 + z + z^4$ and $p^*(z) = 1 + z^3 + z^4$

$p(z) = 1 + z + z^4$		$p^*(z) = 1 + z^3 + z^4$	
t	$\underline{s}(t)$	t	$\underline{s}^*(t)$
0	1 1 1 1	0	0 0 0 1
1	1 1 1 0	1	0 0 1 1
2	1 1 0 1	2	0 1 1 1
3	1 0 1 0	3	1 1 1 1
4	0 1 0 1	4	1 1 1 0
5	1 0 1 1	5	1 1 0 1
6	0 1 1 0	6	1 0 1 0
7	1 1 0 0	7	0 1 0 1
8	1 0 0 1	8	1 0 1 1
9	0 0 1 0	9	0 1 1 0
10	0 1 0 0	10	1 1 0 0
11	1 0 0 0	11	1 0 0 1
12	0 0 0 1	12	0 0 1 0
13	0 0 1 1	13	0 1 0 0
14	0 1 1 1	14	1 0 0 0
15	1 1 1 1	15	0 0 0 1

8.5   PROPERTIES OF MAXIMAL LENGTH LFSR SEQUENCES

Proposition 8.4: If the characteristic polynomial $p(z) = c_N + c_{N-1}z + \cdots + c_1 z^{N-1} + c_0 z^N$ of an N-stage LFSR is primitive and the initial state is not null $\underline{s}(0) \neq (0)_N$, then

8.4a The sequence of states $s(0), s(1), \ldots$ are distinct and periodic with period $2^N - 1$,

8.4b Every N-tuple $v = (v_0, v_1, \ldots, v_{N-1}) \neq (0)_N$ is a state $\underline{s}(t)$ of the LFSR for some t with $0 \leq t < 2^N - 1$,

8.4c The sum of two states $\underline{s}(t_1)$ and $\underline{s}(t_2)$ of the LFSR with $0 \leq t_1 < t_2 < 2^N - 1$ is another state of the LFSR, and

8.4d If $0 < \tau < 2^N - 1$, the sequence of sums of states

$$\underline{s}(t) + \underline{s}(t + \tau), \underline{s}(t+1) + \underline{s}(t+1+\tau), \ldots, \underline{s}(t+2^N - 1) + \underline{s}(t+2^N - 1 + \tau)$$

is a translate of the state sequence $\underline{s}(0), \underline{s}(1), \ldots$, that is $\underline{s}(t+s) = \underline{s}(t) + \underline{s}(t+\tau)$ for some s.

Proof of (8.4a): Suppose on the contrary that $0 \leq t_1 < t_2 < 2^N - 1$ and LFSR states at these times are the same. If $\underline{s}(t_1) = \underline{s}(t_2)$, then by Proposition **8.1b** $\underline{s}(0) = \underline{s}(t_2 - t_1)$, which contradicts the periodicity of the sequence of states $\underline{s}(t)$.

Proof of (8.4b): If the 2^N-states $\underline{s}(0), s(1), \ldots, s(2^N - 1)$ are distinct and $\underline{s}(t) \neq (0)_N$, then every N-tuple $\underline{v} = (v_0, v_1, \ldots, v_{N-1}) \in \mathcal{Z}_{N,2}$ other than $(0)_N$ must be a state of the LFSR.

Proof of (8.4c): If

$$\underline{s}(t_1) = (s_0(t_1), s_0(t_1 + 1), \ldots, s_0(t_1 + N - 1))$$
$$\underline{s}(t_2) = (s_0(t_2), s_0(t_2 + 1), \ldots, s_0(t_2 + N - 1))$$

with $0 \leq t_1 < t_2 < 2^N - 1$, then

$$\underline{s}(t_1) \neq \underline{s}(t_2) \Rightarrow (t_1) + \underline{s}(t_2) \neq (0)_N,$$

which implies $\underline{s}(t_1) + \underline{s}(t_2)$ is a state of the LFSR by Proposition **8.4b.**

Proof of (8.4d): This is a direct consequence of the forward recursion and 8.4c. ∎

We described *Bernoulli* trials in Chapter 4 as a random process consisting of a sequence of independent and identically distributed $(0, 1)$-valued random variables $K_0, K_1, \ldots$. Bernoulli trials are a mathematical model of the repeated and independent trials of tossing a fair coin.

$$\Pr\{K_i = 0\} = \Pr\{K_i = 1\} = \frac{1}{2} \tag{8.6}$$

$$E\{K_i\} = \frac{1}{2} \tag{8.7}$$

More generally, for every k-tuple $(u_0, u_1, \ldots, u_{k-1})$ of 0's and 1's with $1 \leq k \leq N$

$$\Pr\{K_i = u_0, K_{i+1} = u_1, \ldots, K_{i+k-1} = u_{k-1}\} = \frac{1}{2^k}, \qquad i = 0, 1, \ldots, \quad 1 \leq k \leq N. \tag{8.8}$$

Finally, the *autocorrelation* function of a Bernoulli process in the difference between the probabilities of an *agreement* and *disagreement* in the ith and $(i + \tau)$th outcomes of the toss of the coin:

$$\rho(\tau) = \Pr\{K_i = K_{i+\tau}\} - \Pr\{K_i \neq K_{+\tau}\} = 0, \qquad 0 < \tau < 2^N - 1. \qquad (8.9)$$

Chapter 4 described the *one-time* encipherment system, in which the outcomes of Bernoulli trials were exclusive-ORed (XOR) to a sequence of $(0, 1)$-valued plaintext. The resulting ciphertext statistically resembles the Bernoulli trials and therefore encryption completely hides the plaintext. The need to generate the output of Bernoulli limits the one-time system. Can the output of a LFSR $s_0(0), s_0(1), s_0(2), \ldots$ serve as the outcomes of Bernoulli trials?

The renowned mathematician John von Neumann once wrote

Anyone, who considers arithmetical methods of producing random digits is, of course, in a state of sin.

D. H. Lehmer, a pioneer in random number generation methodology, wrote in 1951

A random sequence is a vague notion embodying the idea of a sequence in which each term is unpredictable to the uninitiated and whose digits pass a certain number of tests, traditional with statisticians and depending on the uses to which the sequence is to be put.

How closely does the output of an LFSR whose characteristic polynomial is $p(z) = c_N + c_{N-1}z + \cdots + c_1 z^{N-1} + c_0 z^N$ with initial state $\underline{s}(0) \neq (0)_N$ resemble a "random" sequence?

A *run* of 0's (*resp.* of 1's) of length k occurs in the LFSR output sequence $s_0(0)$, $s_0(1), s_0(2), \ldots$ starting at time t if

$$(s_0(t-1), \underbrace{s_0(t), s_0(t+1), \ldots, s_0(t+k-1)}_{0\text{-run}}), \qquad s_0(t+k) = 1(0)_k 1$$

$$(s_0(t-1), \underbrace{s_0(t), s_0(t+1), \ldots, s_0(t+k-1)}_{1\text{-run}}), \qquad s_0(t+k) = 0(1)_k 0$$

Proposition 8.5: If the polynomial $p(z) = c_N + c_{N-1}z + \cdots + c_1 z^{N-1} + c_0 z^N$ of an N-stage LFSR is primitive and the initial state satisfies $\underline{s}(0) \neq (0)_N$, the following properties hold in every period of $2^N - 1$ output states

$$\ldots \underbrace{s_0(t), s_0(t+1), s_0(t+2), \ldots, s_0(t+2^N - 1)}_{\text{cycle}} \ldots$$

8.5a It contains 2^{N-1} 1's and $2^{N-1} - 1$ 0's;

8.5b It has one run of 1's of length N and no runs of 0's of length N;

8.5c It has one run of 0's of length $N - 1$;

8.5d It does *not* have a run of 1's of length $N - 1$;

8.5e It contains 2^{N-r-2} runs of 1's of length r and 2^{N-r-2} runs of 0's of length r for every $r, 1 \leq r < N - 1$.

Proof of (8.5): [Beker and Piper, 1982, p. 196] For each k-tuple $\underline{u} = (u_0, u_1, \ldots, u_{k-1})$ of 0's and 1's, with $1 \leq k \leq N$, Proposition **8.5b** implies

• There are 2^{N-k} states $\underline{s}(t)$ with $0 \leq t < 2^N - 1$ such that

$$(s_0(t), s_0(t+1), \ldots, s_0(t+(k-1))) = \underline{u} = (u_0, u_1, \ldots, u_{k-1})$$

if $1 \leq k \leq N$ and $\underline{u} \neq (0)_k$, and

- There are $2^{N-k} - 1$ states $\underline{s}(t)$ with $0 \le t < 2^N - 1$ such that

$$(s_0(t), s_0(t+1), \ldots, s_0(t+(k-1))) = \underline{u} = (u_0, u_1, \ldots, u_{k-1})$$

if $1 \le k < N$ and $\underline{u} = (0)_k$.

In terms of the indicator function $\chi_{\{\cdots\}}$

$$\sum_{t=0}^{2^N-2} \chi_{\{(s_0(t),\, s_0(t+1),\, \ldots,\, s_0(t+(k-1)))=\underline{u}\}} = \begin{cases} 2^{N-k}, & \text{if } 1 \le k \le N \text{ and } \underline{u} \ne (0)_k \\ 2^{N-k} - 1, & \text{if } 1 \le k \le N \text{ and } \underline{ub} \ne (0)_k \end{cases}$$

The probability that k bits of an LFSR state satisfy $(s_0(t), s_0(t+1), \ldots, s_0(t+(k-1))) = \underline{u}$ is the fraction of times t that this condition holds. Thus

$$\Pr\{(s_0(t), s_0(t+1), \ldots, s_0(t+(k-1))) = \underline{u}\}$$

$$= \frac{1}{2^N - 1} \sum_{t=0}^{2^N-2} \chi_{\{(s_0(t),\, s_0(t+1),\, \ldots,\, s_0(t+(k-1)))=\underline{u}\}}$$

$$= \begin{cases} \dfrac{2^{N-k}}{2^N - 1}, & \text{if } \underline{u} \ne (0)_k \quad \text{and} \quad 1 \le k \le N \\[2mm] \dfrac{2^{N-k} - 1}{2^N - 1}, & \text{if } \underline{u} = (0)_k \quad \text{and} \quad 1 \le k < N \end{cases} \approx \frac{1}{2^k}, \quad \text{as } N \to \infty,$$

properties that are analogous to those in Equations (8.6) to (8.8).

The *autocorrelation function* of the output states of the LFSR is the average number of agreements *minus* disagreements between $s_0(t)$ and $s_0(t+\tau)$ computed over a cycle:

$$\rho_s(\tau) = \frac{1}{2^N - 1} \sum_{t=0}^{2^N-2} \left(\chi_{\{s_0(t)=s_0(t+\tau)\}} - \chi_{\{s_0(t) \ne s_0(t+\tau)\}} \right).$$

To make the computation of $\rho_{\underline{s}}(\tau)$, we need a connection between modulo 2 integer and ordinary integer arithmetic. If u, v are 0 or 1, then

$$(2u - 1)(2v - 1) = \begin{cases} 1, & \text{if } u = v \\ -1, & \text{if } u \ne v \end{cases}$$

so that

$$\chi_{\{s_0(t)=s_0(t+\tau)\}} - \chi_{\{s_0(t) \ne s_0(t+\tau)\}} = (2s_0(t) - 1)(2s_0(t+\tau) - 1),$$

leading to the formula

$$\rho_{\underline{s}}(\tau) = \frac{1}{2^N - 1} \sum_{t=0}^{2^N-2} (2s_0(t) - 1)(2s_0(t+\tau) - 1)$$

$$= \frac{4}{2^N - 1} \sum_{t=0}^{2^N-2} s_0(t)s_0(t+\tau) - \underbrace{\frac{2}{2^N - 1} \sum_{t=0}^{2^N-2} s_0(t)}_{\text{Term\#1}} - \underbrace{\frac{2}{2^N - 1} \sum_{t=0}^{2^N-2} s_0(t+\tau)}_{\text{Term\#2}} + \frac{1}{2^N - 1} \sum_{t=0}^{2^N-2} 1.$$

Terms #1 and #2 are equal by Proposition 8.5b, so that

$$\rho_{\underline{s}}(\tau) = \frac{4}{2^N - 1} \sum_{t=0}^{2^N-2} s_0(t)s_0(t+\tau) - \frac{4}{2^N - 1} \sum_{t=0}^{2^N-2} s_0(t) + \frac{1}{2^N - 1} \sum_{t=0}^{2^N-2} 1.$$

If $\tau = 0$, then

$$\sum_{t=0}^{2^N-2} s_0(t)s_0(t+\tau) = \sum_{t=0}^{2^N-2} s_0^2(t) = \sum_{t=0}^{2^N-2} s_0(t),$$

so that the first two summands above cancel, giving $\rho_s(0) = 1$.

If $\tau \neq 0$, then $\underline{s}(t) + \underline{s}(t+\tau) \neq (0)_N$; Proposition **8.5d** shows a value of s exists such that

$$\underline{s}(t+s) = \underline{s}(t) + \underline{s}(t+\tau), \qquad t = 0, 1, \ldots,$$

which gives

$$s_0(t+s) = s_0(t) + s_0(t+\tau), \qquad t = 0, 1, \ldots.$$

Next, if $u, v = 0, 1$, then $(u+v)$ (modulo 2) is equal to the real number $u + v - 2uv$, so that

$$2s_0(t)s_0(t+\tau) = s_0(t) + s_0(t+\tau) - s_0(t+s) \quad \text{[real]}.$$

Replacing the term $s_0(t)s_0(t+\tau)$ and summing over t gives

$$\sum_{t=0}^{2^N-2} s_0(t+s) = \sum_{t=0}^{2^N-2} s_0(t) + s_0(t+\tau) - 2s_0(t)s_0(t+\tau) \quad \text{[real]}.$$

But

$$\frac{2^N - 1}{2} = \sum_{t=0}^{2^N-2} s_0(t+s) = \sum_{t=0}^{2^N-2} s_0(t) = \sum_{t=0}^{2^N-2} s_0(t+\tau),$$

so we conclude

$$\frac{2^N}{4} = \sum_{r=0}^{2^N-2} s_0(t)s_0(t+\tau),$$

proving Proposition **8.6**.

Proposition 8.6:   The autocorrelation function of the sequence $s_0(t), s_0(t+1), \ldots,$ $s_0(t+2^N-2)$ of an N-stage LFSR generated by the primitive polynomial $p(z) = c_N + c_{N-1}z + \cdots + c_1 z^{N-1} + c_0 z^N$ whose initial state is not $(0)_N$ is the real number

$$\rho_s(\tau) = \begin{cases} 1, & \text{if } \tau = 0 \\ -\dfrac{1}{2^N - 1}, & \text{if } \tau \neq 0. \end{cases}$$

Propositions **8.4** to **8.6** indicate that the output of an LFSR exhibits some characteristics of a Bernoulli process; the output of an LFSR is an example of a *pseudorandom* sequence.

Menezes et al. [1996] define the *next bit* test on a binary sequence $x_0, x_1, \ldots, x_{\ell-1}$ as an algorithm for which

Given: $x_0, x_1, \ldots, x_{\ell-1}$

Determine: x_ℓ

They define a *pseudorandom number generator* (PRG) as a *deterministic* algorithm, which starts with the *seed*, a sample of random binary values $X_0, X_1, \ldots, X_{k-1}$ and outputs for which it can be proved that *no* polynomial-time algorithm exists to solve the *next bit* test.

8.6   LINEAR EQUIVALENCE

The output of an LFSR $s_0(0), s_0(1), \ldots$ may be generated by more than one characteristic polynomial and initial state.

Example 8.6

The LFSRs with characteristic polynomials and initial states

$$p_1(z) = 1 + z + z^3 + z^4, \qquad \underline{s}(0) = (1, 1, 0, 1)$$
$$p_2(z) = (1 + z + z^3)(1 + z + z^3 + z^4), \qquad \underline{s}(0) = (1, 1, 0, 1, 1, 0, 1)$$

both generate the sequence $\underline{s} = (1, 1, 0, 1, 1, 0, \ldots)$. Note that an LFSR to generate a given *n*-sequence of 0's and 1's $\underline{\sigma} = (\sigma(0), \sigma(1), \ldots, \sigma(n - 1))$ always exists as $\underline{\sigma}$ could be used as the initial state of the *n*-stage LFSR with any coefficient vector.

More relevant are the questions

Q1.   What is the minimum number of stages needed by an LFSR to generate $\underline{\sigma}$?

Q2.   What is the *minimal polynomial* of $\underline{\sigma}$, the characteristic polynomial of the minimal-length LFSR that generates $\underline{\sigma}$?

The *linear equivalence* $L(\underline{\sigma})$ of the *n*-sequence $\underline{\sigma} = (\sigma(0), \sigma(1), \ldots, \sigma(n - 1))$ is the length of the shortest LFSR that generates $\underline{\sigma}$.

The principal properties of linear equivalence are summarized in the next proposition.

Proposition 8.7:   [Beker and Piper, 1982, p. 200; Menezes et al., 1996, p. 198][1] the *n*-sequence $\underline{\sigma} = (\sigma(0), \sigma(1), \ldots, \sigma(n - 1))$

8.7a   If $\underline{\sigma}$ is of length *n*, then[1]
$$\begin{cases} 0 \leq L(\underline{s}) \leq n \\ L(\underline{\sigma}) = 0, & \text{if and only if } \underline{\sigma} = (0)_n \\ L(\underline{\sigma}) = n, & \text{if and only if } \underline{\sigma} = (0)_{n-1}, \end{cases}$$[1]

(Note, in analogy with the convention for a summation or product with an empty index set, a 0-stage LFSR always outputs 0.)

8.7b   The linear equivalence of $\underline{\sigma}$ and $\underline{v}$, possibly of different lengths, satisfies $L(\underline{\sigma} + \underline{v}) \leq L(\underline{\sigma}) + L(\underline{v})$.

8.7c   If $L(\underline{\sigma}) = N$, the characteristic polynomial $p(z)$ of the LFSR that generates $\underline{\sigma}$ has degree N. If $\underline{\sigma}$ is also generated by the LFSR with characteristic polynomial $q(z)$, then $p(z)$ divides $q(z)$.

The Berlekamp–Massey algorithm [Massey, 1969] solves the problem

Given: $\sigma = (\sigma_0, \sigma_1, \ldots, \sigma_{N-1})$

Find: the minimal-length LFSR that generates $\underline{\sigma}$

---

[1]The linear equivalence $L(\underline{\sigma})$ satisfies Menezes et al. use the term *linear complexity* instead of linear equivalence.

8.7   COMBINING MULTIPLE LINEAR FEEDBACK SHIFT REGISTERS

Figure 8.7 shows how linear feedback shift registers can be combined by XORing their outputs. The XOR of periodic sequence with periods $\{P_i\}$ is periodic with period equal to the *least common multiple* $P = \text{lcm}\{P_i\}$ of the individual periods. (Note, the least common multiple of integers $\{n_i\}$ is the *smallest* integer n divisible by each of the $\{n_i\}$.)

When the characteristic polynomials are primitive, and their exponents $2^{N_i} - 1$ $(0 \leq i < k)$ which are relatively prime in pairs

$$1 = \gcd\{2^{N_i} - 1, 2^{N_j} - 1\}, \qquad 0 \leq i < j < k$$

the period of the combined generator is $\prod_{i=0}^{k-1}(2^{N_i} - 1)$. (Note, the greatest common divisor $\gcd\{n_1, n_2\}$ is the *largest* integer n that divides both the n_1 and n_2; if $1 = \gcd\{n_1, n_2\}$, the integers are *relatively prime*.) Just as Vernam additively combined tapes of relatively prime lengths to produce a tape with a much longer period, the same result is achieved by additively combining LFSRs of suitable total lengths $\sum_{i=1}^{k} N_i$ to produce a LFSR with a much larger period.

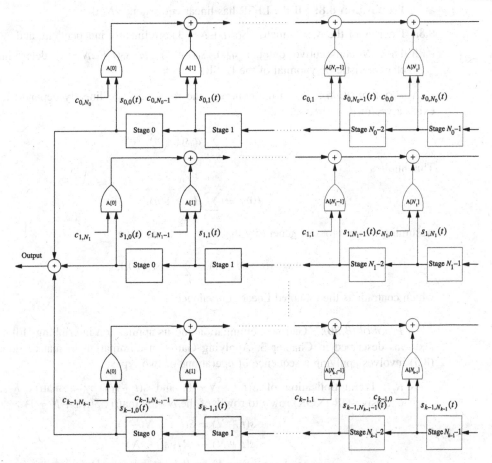

Figure 8.7   The XOR of k linear feedback shift registers.

8.8 MATRIX REPRESENTATION OF THE LFSR

In addition to the Berlekamp–Massey algorithm, there is another approach that will be useful to calculate the minimal polynomial $p(z) = c_N + c_{N-1}z + \cdots + c_1z^{N-n} + c_0z^N$ of an LFSR output sequence $s_0(0)$, $s_0(1)$, ... when the length N of the LFSR is known. The forward recursion $s_0(t + N) = \sum_{n=0}^{N-1} c_{N-n}s_0(t + n)$ provides a relationship between consecutive N-blocks of LFSR output values:

$$\underline{s}(t + N) = S(t, t + N - 1)\underline{c}$$

$$\underline{s}(t + N) = \begin{pmatrix} s_0(t + N) \\ s_0(t + N + 1) \\ \vdots \\ s_0(t + 2N - 1) \end{pmatrix}, \qquad \underline{c} = \begin{pmatrix} c_N \\ c_{N-1} \\ \vdots \\ c_1 \end{pmatrix}$$

$$S(t, t + N - 1) = \begin{pmatrix} s_0(t) & s_0(t + 1) & \cdots & s_0(t + N - 1) \\ s_0(t + 1) & s_0(t + 2) & \cdots & s_0(t + N) \\ \vdots & \vdots & \ddots & \vdots \\ s_0(t + N - 1) & s_0(t + N) & \cdots & s_0(t + 2N - 2) \end{pmatrix}$$

Proposition 8.8:   If the LFSR has linear equivalence N, then

8.8a The row of the $N \times N$ matrix $S(t, t + N - 1)$ are linearly independent, and

8.8b The $2N$ consecutive outputs $s_0(t)$, $s_0(t + 1)$, ..., $s_0(t + 2N - 1)$ determine the characteristic polynomial of the LFSR.

Proof of (8.8a):   If on the contrary, the rows of S are linearly dependent, there exists a vector $\underline{d} \neq (0)_N$ such that

$$(0)_N = \sum_{n=0}^{N-1} d_n\underline{s}(t + n).$$

This implies

$$(0)_N = \sum_{n=0}^{N-1} d_n s(t + n).$$

Assuming without loss of generality that $d_{N-1} = 1$, we have

$$s_{N-1}(t + N - 1) = \sum_{n=0}^{N-2} d_n s(t + n),$$

which contradicts the assumed linear equivalence.

Proof of (8.8b):   Gaussian elimination and its application in cribbing Hill ciphertext was described in Chapter 3. Applying Gaussian elimination to matrix Equations (8.5) involves applying a sequence of operations of two types:

- $R_{j,k}$: Premultiplication of $S(t, t + N - 1)$ and $\underline{s}(t + N)$ by a matrix $R_{j,k}$. The exclusive-OR (XOR) row j to row k of the $N \times N$ matrix $S(t, t + N - 1)$

$$\underline{s}(t + N) = S(t, t + N - 1)\underline{c}$$
$$\underline{s}(t + N) \to R_{j,k}\,\underline{s}(t + N)$$
$$S(t, t + N - 1) \to R_{j,k}\,S(t, t + N - 1)$$
$$R_{j,k}s(t + N) = R_{j,k}\,S(t, t + N - 1)\underline{c}.$$

- $E_{j,k}$:   Postmultiplication of $S(t, t+N-1)$ and premultiplication of $\underline{s}(t+N)$ by a matrix $E_{j,k}$. Interchanging rows j and row k of the $N \times N$ matrix $S(t, t+N-1)$

$$\underline{s}(t+N) = S(t, t+N-1)\underline{c}$$
$$\underline{d} \to E_{j,k}\,\underline{d}$$
$$S(t, t+N-1) \to S(t, t+N-1)E_{j,k}$$
$$\underline{s}(t+N) = S(t, t+N-1)\underline{c},$$

where the last equations use $E_{j,k} = E_{j,k}^{-1}$.

The intent of a sequence of these operations is to transform $S(t, t+N-1)$ into a matrix with 1's only on or above the diagonal. The coefficients of the LFSR's characteristic polynomial are determined when this is achieved.   ■

8.9   CRIBBING OF STREAM ENCIPHERED ASCII PLAINTEXT

The stream encipherment of ASCII character plaintext is performed in three steps:

Step 1:   Each letter of the character plaintext $x_0, x_1, \ldots, x_{n-1}$ is replaced by its ordinal value of x_i in the ASCII character set, which is coded into 7 bits; for example

$$x_i = \text{A} \to \text{ord(A)} = 65 \to \underline{x}_i = (1, 0, 0, 0, 0, 0, 1)$$
$$x_i = \text{a} \to \text{ord(a)} = 97 \to \underline{x}_i = (1, 1, 0, 0, 0, 0, 1).$$

The ASCII character plaintext $x_0, x_1, \ldots, x_{n-1}$ of n characters is transformed into a sequence of n 7-bit vectors, the $(0, 1)$-plaintext

$$T : x_0, x_1, \ldots, x_{n-1} \to \underline{x}_0, \underline{x}_1, \ldots, \underline{x}_{n-1}.$$

Step 2:   The LFSR with initial state $\underline{s}(0) = (s_0(0), s_0(1), \ldots, s_0(N-1))$ generates the key stream, a sequence of $7n$-bits $(s_0(0), s_0(1), \ldots, s_0(7n-1))$, which are grouped into n 7-bit blocks:

$$\underline{s}_0 = (s_0(0), s_0(1), \ldots, s_0(6))$$
$$\underline{s}_1 = (s_0(7), s_0(8), \ldots, s_0(13))$$
$$\vdots$$
$$\underline{s}_{n-1} = (s_0(7(n-1)), s_0(7(n-1)+1), \ldots, s_0(7n-1))$$

Step 3:   The ciphertext $\underline{y} = (\underline{y}_0, \underline{y}_1, \ldots, \underline{y}_{n-1})$ consists of n 7-bit vectors where $\underline{y}_i$ is the XOR of the ith plaintext block $\underline{x}_i$ and the block of key $\underline{s}_i$

$$\underline{y}_i = \underline{x}_i + \underline{s}_i, \qquad 0 \le i < n.$$

The key of an LFSR encipherment system has three components:

1. The number of stages N of the LFSR,
2. The characteristic polynomial $p(z) = c_N + c_{N-1}z + \cdots + c_1 z^{N-1} + c_0 z^N$, and
3. The initial state $\underline{s}(0) = (s_0(0), s_0(1), \ldots, s_0(N-1))$.

We formulate the cribbing of ASCII character plaintext as:

> *Given*: A plaintext crib of M characters, the ciphertext $\underline{y}$ and integers N, i;
>
> *Test*: If $\underline{y}$ was generated by an LFSR of width N and if the crib starts as the tth character in the plaintext.

If

- N is the correct width of the LFSR that has enciphered the plaintext crib of length M, and
- The crib starts as the tth character in the plaintext, then

$$\underbrace{x(t), x(t+1), \ldots, x(t+M-1)}_{\text{crib}} \to \underbrace{\underline{x}_t, \underline{x}_{t+1}, \ldots, \underline{x}_{t+M-1}}_{(0,1)-\text{plaintext of crib}}$$

$$(\underline{x}_t, \underline{x}_{t+1}, \ldots, \underline{x}_{t+M-1})$$
$$+ (\underline{s}_t, \underline{s}_{t+1}, \ldots, \underline{s}_{t+M-1})$$
$$= (\underline{y}_t, \underline{y}_{t+1}, \ldots, \underline{y}_{t+M-1})$$

Or equivalently

$$(\underline{y}_t, \underline{y}_{t+1}, \ldots, \underline{y}_{t+M-1})$$
$$+ (\underline{x}_t, \underline{x}_{t+1}, \ldots, \underline{x}_{t+M-1})$$
$$= (\underline{s}_t, \underline{s}_{t+1}, \ldots, \underline{s}_{t+M-1}).$$

If $7M \geq 2N$, the leftmost $2N$ bits of the output $(\underline{s}_t, \underline{s}_{t+1}, \ldots, \underline{s}_{t+M-11})$

$$
\begin{array}{cccc}
s_0(7t) & s_0(7t+1) & \cdots & s_0(7t+N-1) \\
s_0(7t+N) & s_0(7t+N+1) & \cdots & s_0(7t+2N-1) \\
\ddots & \ddots & \ddots & \ddots \\
s_0(7t+N) & s_0(7t+N+1) & \cdots & s_0(7t+2N-1)
\end{array}
$$

satisfy

$$\underline{s}(7t+N) = S(7t, 7t+N-1)\underline{c}$$

where

$$\underline{s}(7t+N) = \begin{pmatrix} sx_0(7t+N) \\ s_0(7t+N+1) \\ \vdots \\ s_0(7t+2N+1) \end{pmatrix}$$

$$S(7t, 7t+N-1) = \begin{pmatrix} s_0(7t) & s_0(7t+1) & \cdots & s_0(7t+N-1) \\ s_0(7t+1) & s_0(7t+2) & \cdots & s_0(7t+N) \\ \vdots & \vdots & \ddots & \vdots \\ s_0(7t+N-1) & s_0(7t+N) & \cdots & s_0(7t+2N-2) \end{pmatrix}$$

$$\underline{c} = (c_N, c_{N-1}, \ldots, c_1)$$

Proposition **8.8** asserts that the matrix $S(7t, 7t + N - 1)$ has an inverse and Gaussian elimination determines the taps $(c_1, c_2, \ldots, c_{N-1}, c_N)$.

Cribbing stream enciphered ASCII plaintext *tests* a value of N and a position t in the plaintext with two possible outcomes:

1. If N is correct and the crib starts as the tth character in the plaintext, then
   (a) The matrix $S(t, t + N - 1)$ is invertible determining taps $(c_1, c_2, \ldots, c_{N-1}, c_N)$ and
   (b) Backward and forward recursion will determine the entire key stream and plaintext.

2. If N is *in*correct or if the crib does *not* start as the tth character in the plaintext, then
   (a) The matrix $S(t, t + N - 1)$ may *fail* to be invertible, or
   (b) The matrix $(t, t + N - 1)$ may be invertible determining taps $(c_1, c_2, \ldots, c_{N-1}, c_N)$, but backward and forward recursion will determine a large percentage of non-printable plaintext ASCII characters.

The cribbing strategy is to test if $S(7t, 7t + N - 1)$ has an inverse for some interval of N, t-values

Test [widths] for $N := N_1$ to N_2;

Test [positions] for $t := t_1$ to t_2;

If $S(7t, 7t + N - 1)$ has an inverse

If **YES**, compute $\underline{c}$ and use the forward or backward recursions to compute a segment of the key stream and plaintext

$$\underbrace{\underline{s}(7(t + N - k)), \underline{s}(7(t + N - k + 1)), \ldots, \underline{s}(7(t + N - 1))}_{\text{backward segment}}$$

$$\underbrace{\underline{s}(7(t + N + 1)), \ldots, \underline{s}(7(t + N + 2)), \ldots, \underline{s}(7(t + N + k))}_{\text{forward segment}}$$

and plaintext

$$\underbrace{\underline{x}(7(t + N - k)), \underline{x}(7(t + N - k + 1)), \ldots, \underline{x}(7(t + N - 1))}_{\text{backward segment}}$$

$$\underbrace{\underline{x}(7(t + N + 1)), \ldots, \underline{x}(7(t + N + 2)), \ldots, \underline{x}(7(t + N + k))}_{\text{forward segment}}$$

for some k, and test if these 7-bit plaintext vectors above correspond to printable ASCII characters;

for example, upper/lower-case letters, numerals, punctuation, blank space.

Example 8.7
The LFSR with (primitive) characteristic polynomial $p(z) = 1 + z^4 + z^5 + z^6 + z^8$ enciphers

---

plainEx8.7

The pre-major requirements for the B.A. and the B.S. degrees
in computer science are the same. Students intending to
major in computer science should declare a pre-major when
applying for admission to the university.

---

to the ciphertext of 214 7-grams.

---

cipherEx8.7

0	1	1	0	0	0	1
0	0	1	0	1	0	1
0	0	1	0	1	1	0
0	0	1	1	0	1	1
0	1	1	1	0	1	0
⋮	⋮	⋮	⋮	⋮	⋮	⋮
0	1	1	0	0	0	1
0	0	0	0	1	1	1

We use the crib pre-major testing the widths $5 \leq N \leq 12$ and positions $0 \leq t \leq 4$:

	$N = 5, t = 0$		
	Plaintext	Ciphertext	Key
p	1110000	0110001	1000001
r	1110010	0010101	1100111
e	1100101	0010110	1110011
–	0101101	0011011	0110110
m	1101101	0111010	1010111
a	1100001	0111000	1011001
j	1101010	1110111	0011101
o	1101111	1000101	0101010
r	1110010	0001010	1111000

$$
S(0,4) = \begin{pmatrix}
s_0(0) & s_0(1) & s_0(2) & s_0(3) & s_0(4) \\
s_0(1) & s_0(2) & s_0(3) & s_0(4) & s_0(5) \\
s_0(2) & s_0(3) & s_0(4) & s_0(5) & s_0(6) \\
s_0(3) & s_0(4) & s_0(5) & s_0(6) & s_0(7) \\
s_0(4) & s_0(5) & s_0(6) & s_0(7) & s_0(8)
\end{pmatrix}
$$

$$
\begin{pmatrix}
s_0(5) \\
s_0(6) \\
s_0(7) \\
s_0(8) \\
s_0(9)
\end{pmatrix} = S(0,4) \begin{pmatrix}
c_5 \\
c_4 \\
c_3 \\
c_2 \\
c_1
\end{pmatrix}
\begin{pmatrix}
0 \\
1 \\
1 \\
1 \\
0
\end{pmatrix} = \begin{pmatrix}
1 & 0 & 0 & 0 & 0 \\
0 & 0 & 0 & 0 & 0 \\
0 & 0 & 0 & 0 & 1 \\
0 & 0 & 0 & 1 & 1 \\
0 & 0 & 1 & 1 & 1
\end{pmatrix} \begin{pmatrix}
c_5 \\
c_4 \\
c_3 \\
c_2 \\
c_1
\end{pmatrix}
$$

Gaussian Elimination: <5 linearly independent vectors!

| | $N = 5, t = 1$ | | |
	Plaintext	Ciphertext	Key
p	1110000	0010101	1100101
r	1110010	0010110	1100100
e	1100101	0011011	1111110
–	0101101	0111010	0010111
m	1101101	0111000	1010101
a	1100001	1110111	0010110
j	1101010	1000101	0101111
o	1101111	0001010	1100101
r	1110010	1111111	0001101

Input: $S(7, 11)$ to Gaussian elimination.

$$S(7, 11) = \begin{pmatrix} s_0(7) & s_0(8) & s_0(9) & s_0(10) & s_0(11) \\ s_0(8) & s_0(9) & s_0(10) & s_0(11) & s_0(12) \\ s_0(9) & s_0(10) & s_0(11) & s_0(12) & s_0(13) \\ s_0(10) & s_0(11) & s_0(12) & s_0(13) & s_0(14) \\ s_0(11) & s_0(12) & s_0(13) & s_0(14) & s_0(15) \end{pmatrix}$$

$$\begin{pmatrix} s_0(13) \\ s_0(13) \\ s_0(14) \\ s_0(15) \\ s_0(16) \end{pmatrix} = S(7, 11) \begin{pmatrix} c_5 \\ c_4 \\ c_3 \\ c_2 \\ c_1 \end{pmatrix} \qquad \begin{pmatrix} 0 \\ 1 \\ 1 \\ 1 \\ 0 \end{pmatrix} = \begin{pmatrix} 1 & 1 & 0 & 0 & 1 \\ 1 & 0 & 0 & 1 & 0 \\ 0 & 0 & 1 & 0 & 1 \\ 0 & 1 & 0 & 1 & 1 \\ 1 & 0 & 1 & 1 & 1 \end{pmatrix} \begin{pmatrix} c_5 \\ c_4 \\ c_3 \\ c_2 \\ c_1 \end{pmatrix}$$

Gaussian Elimination:

$$\begin{pmatrix} 0 \\ 1 \\ 1 \\ 1 \\ 0 \end{pmatrix} \quad \underbrace{\begin{pmatrix} 1 & 1 & 0 & 0 & 1 \\ 1 & 0 & 0 & 1 & 0 \\ 0 & 0 & 1 & 0 & 1 \\ 0 & 1 & 0 & 1 & 1 \\ 1 & 0 & 1 & 1 & 1 \end{pmatrix}}_{S_0(1, 5)} \quad \begin{pmatrix} c_5 \\ c_4 \\ c_3 \\ c_2 \\ c_1 \end{pmatrix}$$

XOR row 0 with rows 1 and 4 of $\underline{S}_0(7, 11)$

$$\begin{pmatrix} 0 \\ 1 \\ 1 \\ 1 \\ 0 \end{pmatrix} = \underbrace{\begin{pmatrix} 1 & 1 & 0 & 0 & 1 \\ 0 & 1 & 0 & 1 & 1 \\ 0 & 0 & 1 & 0 & 1 \\ 0 & 1 & 0 & 1 & 1 \\ 0 & 1 & 1 & 1 & 0 \end{pmatrix}}_{S_1(7, 11)} \begin{pmatrix} c_5 \\ c_4 \\ c_3 \\ c_2 \\ c_1 \end{pmatrix}$$

XOR row 1 with rows 3 and 4 of $S_1(7, 11)$

$$\begin{pmatrix} 0 \\ 1 \\ 1 \\ 1 \\ 0 \end{pmatrix} = \underbrace{\begin{pmatrix} 1 & 1 & 0 & 0 & 1 \\ 0 & 1 & 0 & 1 & 1 \\ 0 & 0 & 1 & 0 & 1 \\ 0 & 0 & 0 & 0 & 0 \\ 0 & 0 & 1 & 0 & 1 \end{pmatrix}}_{S_2(7, 11)} \begin{pmatrix} c_5 \\ c_4 \\ c_3 \\ c_2 \\ c_1 \end{pmatrix}$$

<5 linearly independent vectors.

		$N = 5, t = 2$	
	Plaintext	Ciphertext	Key
p	1110000	0010110	1100110
r	1110010	0011011	1101001
e	1100101	0111010	1011111
–	0101101	0111000	0010101
m	1101101	1110111	0011010
a	1100001	1000101	0100100
j	1101010	0001010	1100000
o	1101111	1111111	0010000
r	1110010	1110001	0000011

$$S(14, 18) = \begin{pmatrix} s_0(14) & s_0(15) & s_0(16) & s_0(17) & s_0(18) \\ s_0(15) & s_0(16) & s_0(17) & s_0(18) & s_0(19) \\ s_0(16) & s_0(17) & s_0(18) & s_0(19) & s_0(20) \\ s_0(17) & s_0(18) & s_0(19) & s_0(20) & s_0(21) \\ s_0(18) & s_0(19) & s_0(20) & s_0(21) & s_0(22) \end{pmatrix}$$

$$\begin{pmatrix} s_0(19) \\ s_0(20) \\ s_0(21) \\ s_0(22) \\ s_0(23) \end{pmatrix} = S(14, 18) \begin{pmatrix} c_5 \\ c_4 \\ c_3 \\ c_2 \\ c_1 \end{pmatrix} \quad \begin{pmatrix} 0 \\ 1 \\ 1 \\ 1 \\ 0 \end{pmatrix} = \begin{pmatrix} 1 & 1 & 0 & 0 & 1 \\ 1 & 0 & 0 & 1 & 1 \\ 0 & 0 & 1 & 1 & 0 \\ 0 & 1 & 1 & 0 & 1 \\ 1 & 1 & 0 & 1 & 1 \end{pmatrix} \begin{pmatrix} c_5 \\ c_4 \\ c_3 \\ c_2 \\ c_1 \end{pmatrix}$$

Gaussian Elimination:

$$\begin{pmatrix} 1 \\ 0 \\ 1 \\ 1 \\ 0 \end{pmatrix} = \underbrace{\begin{pmatrix} 1 & 1 & 0 & 0 & 1 \\ 1 & 0 & 0 & 1 & 1 \\ 0 & 0 & 1 & 1 & 0 \\ 0 & 1 & 1 & 0 & 1 \\ 1 & 1 & 0 & 1 & 1 \end{pmatrix}}_{S_0(14, 18)} \begin{pmatrix} c_5 \\ c_4 \\ c_3 \\ c_2 \\ c_1 \end{pmatrix}$$

XOR row 0 to rows 1, 4 of $S_0(14, 18)$

$$\begin{pmatrix} 1 \\ 1 \\ 1 \\ 1 \\ 1 \end{pmatrix} = \underbrace{\begin{pmatrix} 1 & 1 & 0 & 0 & 1 \\ 0 & 1 & 0 & 1 & 0 \\ 0 & 0 & 1 & 1 & 0 \\ 0 & 1 & 1 & 0 & 1 \\ 0 & 0 & 0 & 1 & 0 \end{pmatrix}}_{S_1(14, 18)} \begin{pmatrix} c_5 \\ c_4 \\ c_3 \\ c_2 \\ c_1 \end{pmatrix}$$

XOR row 1 to row 3 of $S_1(14, 18)$

$$\begin{pmatrix} 1 \\ 1 \\ 1 \\ 0 \\ 1 \end{pmatrix} = \underbrace{\begin{pmatrix} 1 & 1 & 0 & 0 & 1 \\ 0 & 1 & 0 & 1 & 0 \\ 0 & 0 & 1 & 1 & 0 \\ 0 & 0 & 0 & 0 & 1 \\ 0 & 0 & 0 & 1 & 0 \end{pmatrix}}_{S_2(14, 18)} \begin{pmatrix} c_5 \\ c_4 \\ c_3 \\ c_2 \\ c_1 \end{pmatrix}$$

XOR row 2 to row 3 of $S_2(14, 18)$

$$\begin{pmatrix} 1 \\ 1 \\ 1 \\ 1 \\ 1 \end{pmatrix} = \underbrace{\begin{pmatrix} 1 & 1 & 0 & 0 & 1 \\ 0 & 1 & 0 & 1 & 0 \\ 0 & 0 & 1 & 1 & 0 \\ 0 & 0 & 0 & 0 & 1 \\ 0 & 0 & 0 & 1 & 0 \end{pmatrix}}_{S_3(14, 18)} \begin{pmatrix} c_5 \\ c_4 \\ c_3 \\ c_2 \\ c_1 \end{pmatrix}$$

Interchange rows 3 and 4 of $S_3(14, 18)$

$$\begin{pmatrix} 1 \\ 1 \\ 1 \\ 1 \\ 1 \end{pmatrix} = \underbrace{\begin{pmatrix} 1 & 1 & 0 & 0 & 1 \\ 0 & 1 & 0 & 1 & 0 \\ 0 & 0 & 1 & 1 & 0 \\ 0 & 0 & 0 & 1 & 0 \\ 0 & 0 & 0 & 0 & 1 \end{pmatrix}}_{S_4(14, 18)} \begin{pmatrix} c_5 \\ c_4 \\ c_3 \\ c_1 \\ c_2 \end{pmatrix}$$

$c_2 = 1$, $c_1 = 1$, $c_3 + c_1 = 1$, $c_4 + c_1 = 1$, $c_5 + c_4 + c_2 = 1$.

Decipherment Test: Six nonprintable characters among the first nine deciphered characters:

	N = 8, t = 4		
	Plaintext	Ciphertext	Key
p	1110000	0111010	1001010
r	1110010	0111000	1001010
e	1100101	1110111	0010010
–	0101101	1000101	1101000
m	1101101	0001010	1100111
a	1100001	1111111	0011110
j	1101010	1110001	0011011
o	1101111	1101011	0000100
r	1110010	1011100	0101110

Input: $S(4, 5)$ to Gaussian elimination:

$$S(28, 35) = \begin{pmatrix} s_0(28) & s_0(29) & s_0(30) & s_0(31) & s_0(32) & s_0(33) & s_0(34) & s_0(35) \\ s_0(29) & s_0(30) & s_0(31) & s_0(32) & s_0(33) & s_0(34) & s_0(35) & s_0(36) \\ s_0(30) & s_0(31) & s_0(32) & s_0(33) & s_0(34) & s_0(35) & s_0(36) & s_0(37) \\ s_0(31) & s_0(32) & s_0(33) & s_0(34) & s_0(35) & s_0(36) & s_0(37) & s_0(38) \\ s_0(32) & s_0(33) & s_0(34) & s_0(35) & s_0(36) & s_0(37) & s_0(38) & s_0(39) \\ s_0(33) & s_0(34) & s_0(35) & s_0(36) & s_0(37) & s_0(38) & s_0(39) & s_0(40) \\ s_0(34) & s_0(35) & s_0(36) & s_0(37) & s_0(38) & s_0(39) & s_0(40) & s_0(41) \\ s_0(35) & s_0(36) & s_0(37) & s_0(38) & s_0(39) & s_0(40) & s_0(41) & s_0(42) \end{pmatrix}$$

$$\begin{pmatrix} s_0(36) \\ s_0(37) \\ s_0(38) \\ s_0(39) \\ s_0(40) \\ s_0(41) \\ s_0(42) \\ s_0(43) \end{pmatrix} = S(28, 35) \begin{pmatrix} c_8 \\ c_7 \\ c_6 \\ c_5 \\ c_4 \\ c_3 \\ c_2 \\ c_1 \end{pmatrix} \quad \begin{pmatrix} 0 \\ 0 \\ 1 \\ 0 \\ 1 \\ 0 \\ 0 \\ 0 \end{pmatrix} = \begin{pmatrix} 1 & 0 & 0 & 1 & 0 & 1 & 0 & 1 \\ 0 & 0 & 1 & 0 & 1 & 0 & 1 & 0 \\ 0 & 1 & 0 & 1 & 0 & 1 & 0 & 0 \\ 1 & 0 & 1 & 0 & 1 & 0 & 0 & 1 \\ 0 & 1 & 0 & 1 & 0 & 0 & 1 & 0 \\ 1 & 0 & 1 & 0 & 0 & 1 & 0 & 1 \\ 0 & 1 & 0 & 0 & 1 & 0 & 1 & 0 \\ 1 & 0 & 0 & 1 & 0 & 1 & 0 & 0 \end{pmatrix} \begin{pmatrix} c_8 \\ c_7 \\ c_6 \\ c_5 \\ c_4 \\ c_3 \\ c_2 \\ c_1 \end{pmatrix}$$

Gaussian Elimination:

$$\begin{pmatrix} 0 \\ 0 \\ 1 \\ 0 \\ 1 \\ 0 \\ 0 \\ 0 \end{pmatrix} = \underbrace{\begin{pmatrix} 1 & 0 & 0 & 1 & 0 & 1 & 0 & 1 \\ 0 & 0 & 1 & 0 & 1 & 0 & 1 & 0 \\ 0 & 1 & 0 & 1 & 0 & 1 & 0 & 0 \\ 1 & 0 & 1 & 0 & 1 & 0 & 0 & 1 \\ 0 & 1 & 0 & 1 & 0 & 0 & 1 & 0 \\ 1 & 0 & 1 & 0 & 0 & 1 & 0 & 1 \\ 0 & 1 & 0 & 0 & 1 & 0 & 1 & 0 \\ 1 & 0 & 0 & 1 & 0 & 1 & 0 & 0 \end{pmatrix}}_{S_0(28, 35)} \begin{pmatrix} c_8 \\ c_7 \\ c_6 \\ c_5 \\ c_4 \\ c_3 \\ c_2 \\ c_1 \end{pmatrix}$$

XOR row 0 to rows 3, 5, and 7 of $S_0(28, 35)$

$$\begin{pmatrix} 0 \\ 0 \\ 1 \\ 0 \\ 1 \\ 0 \\ 0 \\ 0 \end{pmatrix} = \underbrace{\begin{pmatrix} 1 & 0 & 0 & 1 & 0 & 1 & 0 & 1 \\ 0 & 0 & 1 & 0 & 1 & 0 & 1 & 0 \\ 0 & 1 & 0 & 1 & 0 & 1 & 0 & 0 \\ 0 & 0 & 1 & 1 & 1 & 1 & 0 & 0 \\ 0 & 1 & 0 & 1 & 0 & 0 & 1 & 0 \\ 0 & 0 & 1 & 1 & 0 & 0 & 0 & 0 \\ 0 & 1 & 0 & 0 & 1 & 0 & 1 & 0 \\ 0 & 0 & 0 & 0 & 0 & 0 & 0 & 1 \end{pmatrix}}_{S_1(28, 35)} \begin{pmatrix} c_8 \\ c_7 \\ c_6 \\ c_5 \\ c_4 \\ c_3 \\ c_2 \\ c_1 \end{pmatrix}$$

XOR row 2 to rows 4 and 6 of $S_1(28, 35)$

$$
\begin{pmatrix} 0 \\ 0 \\ 1 \\ 0 \\ 1 \\ 0 \\ 0 \\ 0 \end{pmatrix} =
\underbrace{\begin{pmatrix}
1 & 0 & 0 & 1 & 0 & 1 & 0 & 1 \\
0 & 1 & 0 & 1 & 0 & 1 & 0 & 0 \\
0 & 0 & 1 & 0 & 1 & 0 & 1 & 0 \\
0 & 0 & 1 & 1 & 1 & 1 & 0 & 0 \\
0 & 1 & 0 & 1 & 0 & 0 & 1 & 0 \\
0 & 0 & 1 & 1 & 0 & 0 & 0 & 0 \\
0 & 1 & 0 & 0 & 1 & 0 & 1 & 0 \\
0 & 0 & 0 & 0 & 0 & 0 & 0 & 1
\end{pmatrix}}_{S_2(28,\,35)}
\begin{pmatrix} c_8 \\ c_6 \\ c_7 \\ c_5 \\ c_4 \\ c_3 \\ c_2 \\ c_1 \end{pmatrix}
$$

Interchange rows 1 and 2 of $S_2(28, 35)$

$$
\begin{pmatrix} 0 \\ 1 \\ 0 \\ 0 \\ 1 \\ 0 \\ 0 \\ 0 \end{pmatrix} =
\underbrace{\begin{pmatrix}
1 & 0 & 0 & 1 & 0 & 1 & 0 & 1 \\
0 & 1 & 0 & 1 & 0 & 1 & 0 & 0 \\
0 & 0 & 1 & 0 & 1 & 0 & 1 & 0 \\
0 & 0 & 1 & 1 & 1 & 1 & 0 & 0 \\
0 & 0 & 0 & 0 & 0 & 1 & 1 & 0 \\
0 & 0 & 1 & 1 & 0 & 0 & 0 & 0 \\
0 & 0 & 0 & 1 & 1 & 1 & 1 & 0 \\
0 & 0 & 0 & 0 & 0 & 0 & 0 & 1
\end{pmatrix}}_{S_3(28,\,35)}
\begin{pmatrix} c_8 \\ c_6 \\ c_7 \\ c_5 \\ c_4 \\ c_3 \\ c_2 \\ c_1 \end{pmatrix}
$$

XOR row 2 to rows 3 and 5 of $S_3(28, 35)$

$$
\begin{pmatrix} 0 \\ 1 \\ 0 \\ 0 \\ 0 \\ 0 \\ 1 \\ 0 \end{pmatrix} =
\underbrace{\begin{pmatrix}
1 & 0 & 0 & 1 & 0 & 1 & 0 & 1 \\
0 & 1 & 0 & 1 & 0 & 1 & 0 & 0 \\
0 & 0 & 1 & 0 & 1 & 0 & 1 & 0 \\
0 & 0 & 0 & 1 & 0 & 1 & 1 & 0 \\
0 & 0 & 0 & 0 & 0 & 1 & 1 & 0 \\
0 & 0 & 0 & 1 & 1 & 0 & 1 & 0 \\
0 & 0 & 0 & 1 & 1 & 1 & 1 & 0 \\
0 & 0 & 0 & 0 & 0 & 0 & 0 & 1
\end{pmatrix}}_{S_4(28,\,35)}
\begin{pmatrix} c_8 \\ c_6 \\ c_7 \\ c_5 \\ c_4 \\ c_3 \\ c_2 \\ c_1 \end{pmatrix}
$$

XOR row 3 to rows 5 and 6 of $S_4(28, 35)$

$$
\begin{pmatrix} 0 \\ 1 \\ 0 \\ 0 \\ 0 \\ 0 \\ 1 \\ 0 \end{pmatrix} =
\underbrace{\begin{pmatrix}
1 & 0 & 0 & 1 & 0 & 1 & 0 & 1 \\
0 & 1 & 0 & 1 & 0 & 1 & 0 & 0 \\
0 & 0 & 1 & 0 & 1 & 0 & 1 & 0 \\
0 & 0 & 0 & 1 & 0 & 1 & 1 & 0 \\
0 & 0 & 0 & 0 & 0 & 1 & 1 & 0 \\
0 & 0 & 0 & 0 & 1 & 1 & 0 & 0 \\
0 & 0 & 0 & 0 & 1 & 0 & 0 & 0 \\
0 & 0 & 0 & 0 & 0 & 0 & 0 & 1
\end{pmatrix}}_{S_5(28,\,35)}
\begin{pmatrix} c_8 \\ c_6 \\ c_7 \\ c_5 \\ c_4 \\ c_3 \\ c_2 \\ c_1 \end{pmatrix}
$$

XOR row 5 to rows 6 of $S_5(28, 35)$

$$\begin{pmatrix} 0 \\ 1 \\ 0 \\ 0 \\ 0 \\ 0 \\ 1 \\ 0 \end{pmatrix} = \underbrace{\begin{pmatrix} 1 & 0 & 0 & 1 & 0 & 1 & 0 & 1 \\ 0 & 1 & 0 & 1 & 0 & 1 & 0 & 0 \\ 0 & 0 & 1 & 0 & 1 & 0 & 1 & 0 \\ 0 & 0 & 0 & 1 & 0 & 1 & 1 & 0 \\ 0 & 0 & 0 & 0 & 0 & 1 & 1 & 0 \\ 0 & 0 & 0 & 0 & 1 & 1 & 0 & 0 \\ 0 & 0 & 0 & 0 & 0 & 1 & 0 & 0 \\ 0 & 0 & 0 & 0 & 0 & 0 & 0 & 1 \end{pmatrix}}_{S_6(28,\,35)} \begin{pmatrix} c_8 \\ c_6 \\ c_7 \\ c_5 \\ c_4 \\ c_3 \\ c_2 \\ c_1 \end{pmatrix}$$

Interchange rows 5 and 6 of $S_6(28, 35)$

$$\begin{pmatrix} 0 \\ 1 \\ 0 \\ 0 \\ 0 \\ 0 \\ 1 \\ 0 \end{pmatrix} = \underbrace{\begin{pmatrix} 1 & 0 & 0 & 1 & 0 & 1 & 0 & 1 \\ 0 & 1 & 0 & 1 & 0 & 1 & 0 & 0 \\ 0 & 0 & 1 & 0 & 1 & 0 & 1 & 0 \\ 0 & 0 & 0 & 1 & 0 & 1 & 1 & 0 \\ 0 & 0 & 0 & 0 & 1 & 1 & 0 & 0 \\ 0 & 0 & 0 & 0 & 0 & 1 & 1 & 0 \\ 0 & 0 & 0 & 0 & 0 & 1 & 0 & 0 \\ 0 & 0 & 0 & 0 & 0 & 0 & 0 & 1 \end{pmatrix}}_{S_7(28,\,35)} \begin{pmatrix} c_8 \\ c_6 \\ c_7 \\ c_5 \\ c_3 \\ c_4 \\ c_2 \\ c_1 \end{pmatrix}$$

XOR row 5 to row 6 of $S_5(28, 35)$

$$\begin{pmatrix} 0 \\ 1 \\ 0 \\ 0 \\ 0 \\ 0 \\ 1 \\ 0 \end{pmatrix} = \underbrace{\begin{pmatrix} 1 & 0 & 0 & 1 & 0 & 1 & 0 & 1 \\ 0 & 1 & 0 & 1 & 0 & 1 & 0 & 0 \\ 0 & 0 & 1 & 0 & 1 & 0 & 1 & 0 \\ 0 & 0 & 0 & 1 & 0 & 1 & 1 & 0 \\ 0 & 0 & 0 & 0 & 1 & 1 & 0 & 0 \\ 0 & 0 & 0 & 0 & 0 & 1 & 1 & 0 \\ 0 & 0 & 0 & 0 & 0 & 0 & 1 & 0 \\ 0 & 0 & 0 & 0 & 0 & 0 & 0 & 1 \end{pmatrix}}_{S_8(28,\,35)} \begin{pmatrix} c_8 \\ c_6 \\ c_7 \\ c_5 \\ c_3 \\ c_4 \\ c_2 \\ c_1 \end{pmatrix} \quad \begin{aligned} 0 &= c_8 + c_5 + c_4 + c_1 \\ 1 &= c_6 + c_5 + c_4 \\ 0 &= c_7 + c_3 + c_2 \\ 0 &= c_5 + c_4 + c_2 \\ 0 &= c_3 + c_4 \\ 0 &= c_4 + c_2 \\ 1 &= c_2 \\ 0 &= c_1 \end{aligned}$$

with solution $c_8 = 1$, $c_7 = c_6 = c_5 = 0$, $c_4 = c_3 = c_2 = 1$ $c_1 = 0$, $c_0 = 1$. Equation (8.4) determines the key stream for all positions and the 8-stage LFSR shown Figure 8.8:

$$s_0(t + 8) = c_8 s_0(t) + c_7 s_0(t + 1) + c_6 s_0(t + 2) + c_5 s_0(t + 3) + c_4 s_0(t + 4) + c_3 s_0(t + 5)$$
$$+ c_2 s_0(t + 6) + c_1 s_0(t + 7).$$

As $c_8 = 1$, the backward recursion determines the states before time t as shown in Figure 8.9. Why has this form of stream encipherment failed to provide secrecy?

> The culprit is linearity!

In order that stream encipherment truly hides the plaintext, the generation of the key stream must involve some form of nonlinearity.

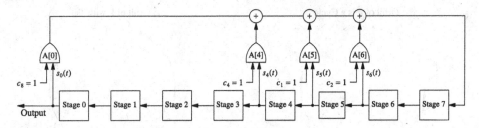

Figure 8.8   The LFSR determined in *Example 8.7* cribbing.

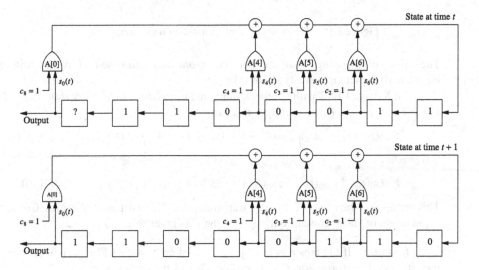

Figure 8.9   Backward recursion in *Example 8.7* cribbing.

8.10   NONLINEAR FEEDBACK SHIFT REGISTERS

There are m^m mappings F of $\mathcal{Z}_m \equiv \{0, 1, 2 \ldots, m-1\}$ into itself. The *orbit* of F for an element $z \in \mathcal{Z}_m$ is the sequence of images of z under F

$$\text{orbit(z)} : z \to F^{(1)}(z) \to F^{(2)}(z) \to \cdots$$

where

$$F^{(j)}(z) = \begin{cases} z, & \text{if } j = 0 \\ F(F^{(j-1)}(z)), & \text{if } 1 \leq j < \infty. \end{cases}$$

There are m^m different mappings from $\mathcal{Z}_m$ to $\mathcal{Z}_m$; of these, $m!$ mappings are permutations (one-to-one/invertible). The orbit of z under a permutation F is a *cycle*; z belongs to an N-cycle if

$$z_0 \to z_1 \to z_2 \to \cdots \to z_{N-1} \to z_0$$

where

$$z_j = \begin{cases} z, & \text{if } j = 0 \\ F(z_{j-1}), & \text{if } 1 \leq j \leq N-1 \\ z, & \text{if } j = N. \end{cases}$$

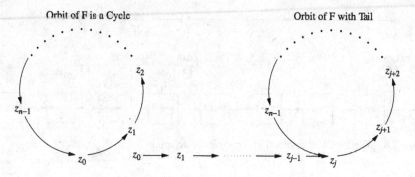

Figure 8.10   The orbits of a transformation under iteration.

The orbits of mappings that are not one-to-one are composed of cycles with *tails*. Figure 8.10 depicts the two types of orbits.

An N-stage LFSR with feedback function f is *nonsingular* if every state $s(t) = (s_0(t), s_0(t+1), \ldots, s_{N+t-1})$ has a unique *successor*

$$F : (s_0(t), s_0(t+1), \ldots, s_0(N+t-1)) \rightarrow (s_0(t+1), s_0(t+2), \ldots, s_0(N+t))$$

and *predecessor*

$$F : (s_0(t-1), s_0(t), \ldots, s_0(N+t-2)) \rightarrow (s_0(t), s_0(t+1), \ldots, s_0(N+t)).$$

This means that the orbits of the state transformation F consist only of cycles. Conversely, if the orbits of states contain only cycles, the F is invertible.

Remark: If the taps $\underline{c} = (c_0, c_1, \ldots, c_N)$ of an N-stage LFSR satisfy $c_N = c_0 = 1$, then its state transformation F is invertible. One of the cycles is

$$F : (0)_N \rightarrow (0)_N.$$

- If the characteristic function $p(z)$ of the LFSR is primitive, there is one additional cycle containing $2^N - 1$ states, and

- If the characteristic function $p(z)$ of the LFSR is *not* primitive, every cycle has length that is a divisor of the exponent of $p(z)$.

These results generalize for the FSR with feedback function f.

Proposition 8.9:   [Golomb, 1982] The state function of an N-stage FSR $F(s_0(t), s_0(t+1), \ldots, s_0(t+N-1))$ with feedback function $f(s_0(t), s_0(t+1), \ldots, s_0(t+N-1))$ is nonsingular if and only if there exists a function $g(s_0(t), s_0(t+1), \ldots, s_0(t+N-1))$ such that

$$f(s_0(t), s_0(t+1), \ldots, s_0(t+N-1)) = g(s_0(t+1), s_0(t+2), \ldots, s_0(t+N-1)) + s_0(t).$$

$$(8.10)$$

Proof: If F is nonsingular and $s_N = 0$ and

$$f(0, s_0(t+1), \ldots, s_0(t+N-1)) = f(1, s_0(t+1), \ldots, s_0(t+N-1))$$

the successor states of $(0, \ s_0(t+1), \ldots, s_0(t+N-1))$ and $(1, \ s_0(t+1), \ldots, s_0(t+N-1))$ are the same.

Therefore

$$f(0, s_0(t+1), \ldots, s_0(t+N-1)) = 1 + f(1, s_0(t+1), \ldots, s_0(t+N-1)),$$

which is equivalent to

$$f(s_0(t), s_0(t+1), \ldots, s_0(t+N-1)) = s_0(t) + g(s_0(t+1), s_0(t+2), \ldots, s_0(t+N-1))$$

with

$$g(s_0(t+1), s_0(t+2), \ldots, s_0(t+N-1)) = f(0, s_0(t+1), s_0(t+2), \ldots, s_0(t+N-1)).$$

Conversely, suppose Equation (8.10) holds but not every orbit of F is a cycle. Thus, there is some state $(s_0(t), \ldots, s_0(t+N-2), s_0(t+N-1))$ that has two predecessors

$$\left. \begin{array}{l} (0, s_0(t), \ldots, s_0(t+N-2)) \\ (1, s_0(t), \ldots, s_0(t+N-2)) \end{array} \right\} \rightarrow (s_0(t), \ldots, s_0(t+N-2), s_0(t+N-1))$$

which is a contradiction. ∎

8.11 NONLINEAR KEY STREAM GENERATION

We illustrate two ways for nonlinear key stream generation, using a *read-only memory* ROM to implement a nonlinear mapping. A k-bit ROM is a table with k-bit input $\underline{x} = (x_0, x_1, \ldots, x_{k-1})$ and output $\underline{y} = (y_0, y_1, \ldots, y_{k-1})$

Figure 8.11 uses the outputs of k-LFSRs as the input of a k-bit ROM from which either a single or k-bit output can be read:

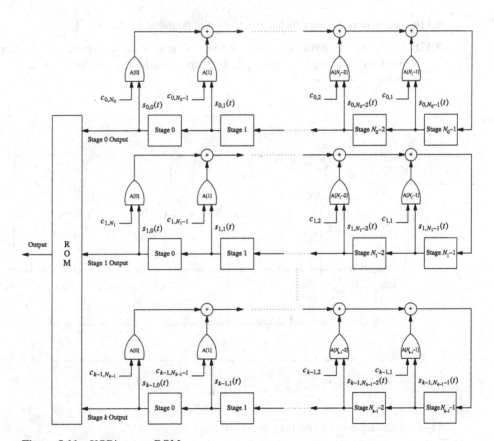

Figure 8.11 XORing to a ROM.

- A *min-term* for n Boolean variable $s_0, s_1, \ldots, s_{n-1}$ is a product in which either s_i or its complement s_i' occurs;

- An *mth order product* a product of m distinct Boolean variables;

- The *algebraic normal form* for a Boolean function $f(s_0, s_1, \ldots, s_{n-1})$ is the (modulo 2) sum of different mth products; and

- The *nonlinear order* of f is the maximum order of the terms appearing in its algebraic normal form.

Example 8.8

1. $s_0 s_1' s_2' s_3 s_4$ is a min-term in the Boolean variables $s_0, s_1, \ldots, s_{n-1}$,

2. The Boolean function $f(s_0, s_1, \ldots, s_{n-1}) = s_1 + s_2 + s_{n-1}$ and has nonlinear order 1,

3. The Boolean function $f(s_0, s_1, \ldots, s_{n-1}) = s_1 + s_1 s_2 + s_0 s_1 s_3$ has nonlinear order 3.

Proposition 8.10: [Menezes et al., 1996, p. 205]   If the lengths $N_0, N_1, \ldots, N_{k-1}$ of the k LFSRs are pairwise distinct and >2, the nonlinear order of the output is ROM$(N_0, N_1, \ldots, N_{k-1}!)$ evaluated as a function over the integers.

Nonlinearity can also be introduce by using the states $s = (s_0(t), s_1(t), \ldots, s_0(t + N - 1))$ of an N-stage LPSR to address the ROM.

Proposition 8.11: [Key, 1976]   If the ROM's function f is nonlinear of order m, then

8.11a The nonlinear order of the key stream is bounded by $L_m = \sum_{i=1}^{m} \binom{N}{i}$;

8.11b For a fixed maximum-length LFSR of length L, a prime, the fraction of Boolean functions f that produce the maximum nonlinear order L_m is $\approx \exp^{-L_{m/(L2^L)}} > e^{-1/L}$.

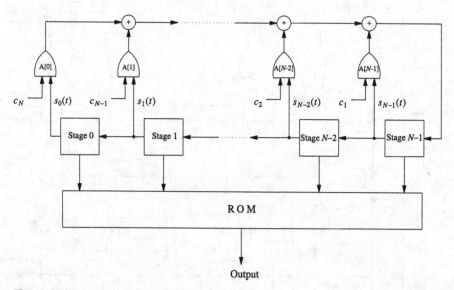

Figure 8.12   Input to a ROM from the LFSR stages.

8.12   IRREGULAR CLOCKING

Nonlinearity may also be introduced by *irregular clocking*, XORing several LFSRs but shifting the LFSRs in a state- and key-dependent manner. One such scheme is described by Günther [1987]. The Global System for Mobile Communication (GSM) Users Association is a consortium providing mobile communication services. GSM has established an elaborate key exchange and encryption protocol to provide both secrecy (privacy) and authentication. Each *mobile* (telephone) contains a *SIM* (Subscriber Identity Module) card, and a processor with memory containing

- The caller's telephone number, International Mobile Subscribers Identification Number (MISDN) of up to 15 (BCD) coded decimal digits
  - MCC, Mobile Country Code;
  - MNC, Mobile Network Code;
  - MSIN, Mobile Subscriber Number.
- Implementation of two algorithms – **A38** and **A5**.
- A user-unique 128-bit secret key K_U.

It is *assumed* that the SIM may not be probed to reveal K_U and that cloning is very difficult.

When a user wants to make a call, the mobile requests service from the network providing its MISDN. The authentication process consists of several steps (Fig. 8.13).

8.12.1   Authentication

A1. The GSM Mobile Services Switching Center (MSC) generates and transmits to the mobile a 128-bit random number RAND.

A2. The mobile's SIM uses RAND and K_U with the **A38** one-way function to derive a 32-bit response SRES = **A38**$\{K_U$, RAND$\}$[0...3], which is returned to MSC. (Note, the GSM standard allows GSM networks to implement different choices for **A38**. One reference claims all networks use **COMP128**, which is described at the Web site www.iol.ie/char126kooltek/ae8.txt. **A38** uses arithmetic operations and the input values K_U; a table of 990 bytes is accessed to construct SRES and K_S.)

A3. The MSC looks up the mobile's MISDN and repeats the computation in Step A2, comparing the result of its computation with the SRES returned by the mobile. If there is agreement, the call is completed.

A4. Both the MSC and the mobile's SIM use RAND and K_U with the same **A38** one-way function to derive a 64-bit *session key* K_S = **A8**$\{K_U$, RAND$\}$[4..11] (Fig. 8.14). K_S is used to initialize three LFSRs, which move irregularly.

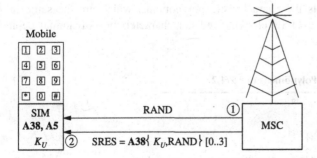

Figure 8.13 GSM authentication process: challenge and response.

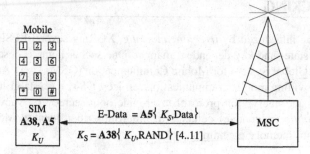

Figure 8.14 Delivery of the session key to the mobile.

8.12.2 Secrecy

S1. Voice data are sampled and formatted in 114-bit TDMA-frames. (Time division multiple access (TDMA) allocates a transmission channel by dividing into *time slots* and allocating them to users.) The GSM frames are stream-enciphered using the output of the **A5**, nonlinear feedback shift-register algorithm.

S2. A GSM conversation is transmitted in TDMA frames one every 4.6 ms; a 114-bit frame *from* the mobile and a 114-bit frame *to* the mobile. Frame #n is identified by an accompanying *frame counter Fn*. The A5/1 registers are loaded with the 64-bit XOR of the session key K_S and frame counter. There are additional initialization steps about which we do not elaborate.

8.12.3 A5/1 and A5/2

GSM originally did not release the details of their encipherment algorithms, which were reverse-engineered. There are four **A5** algorithms:

- The true vanilla **A5**/0 with no provided encryption,
- The original **A5**/1 used by $\approx 130 \times 10^6$ GSM customers in the United States and Europe, but *not* exportable to the Middle East,
- **A5**/2 used by $\approx 100 \times 10^6$ GSM customers in other markets, and
- **A5**/3 algorithm, whose details can be found at gsmworld.com/using/algorithms/index.shtml.

The A5/1 and A5/2 algorithms generate a key stream as the output of three irregularly clocked linear feedback shift registers; A5/2 uses a 17-stage LFSR to control clocking. Table 8.8 lists the characteristic polynomials, which are the same in A5/1 and A5/2 and the A5/2 LFSR clocking register characteristic polynomial depicted in Figure 8.15.

TABLE 8.8 Characteristic Polynomials of A5/1,2

$\text{LFSR}_0(z) = 1 + z + z^2 + z^5 + x^{19}$
$\text{LFSR}_1(z) = 1 + z + z^{22}$
$\text{LFSR}_2(z) = 1 + z + z^2 + z^{15} + z^{23}$

$\text{LFSR}_4(z) = 1 + z^5 + z^{17}$ [**A5**/2 Clocking/Register]

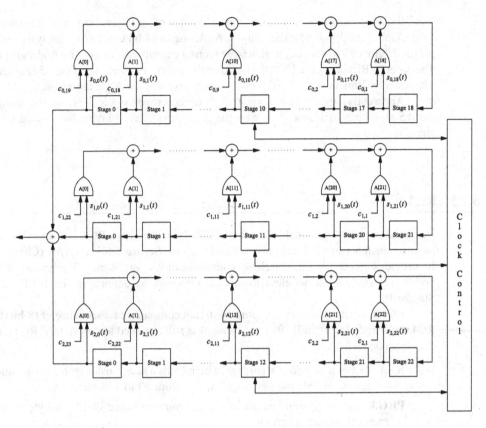

Figure 8.15   A5/1.

The middle bit of each of the registers is the *clock control bit* determining if the registers shift to the next state according to Table 8.9:

- Compute the majority of the three clocking bits shown in Figure 8.15;
- If the clocked bit of a register agrees with the majority bit, then this register is shifed.

If the bits in the middle cells of $LFSR_i$ ($i = 0, 1, 2$) are equally distributed and independent, the registers are *clocked* (shifted) with probability $3/4$.

TABLE 8.9   Clocking of A5/1 Registers

Clock control bit			Next clock state?		
$LFSR_0$	$LFSR_1$	$LFSR_2$	$LFSR_0$	$LFSR_1$	$LFSR_2$
0	0	0	ON	ON	ON
0	0	1	ON	ON	OFF
0	1	0	ON	OFF	ON
0	1	1	OFF	ON	ON
1	0	0	OFF	ON	ON
1	0	1	ON	OFF	ON
1	1	0	ON	ON	OFF
1	1	1	ON	ON	ON

Even before an officially sanctioned description of the internal structure of A5 was published, Golić [1997] published an analysis. As A5 uses a 64-bit key, Golić's analysis is of complexity 2^{40}, much less than key trial. It is also consistent with earlier work by Anderson [1995]. The paper by Biryukor et al. [2000] is based on the reverse-engineering of the A5/2 alogrithm. The paper by Barkan et al. [2003] contains an analysis of the A5/2 algorithm.

Apparently, there was a great deal of controversy surrounding the design of the **A5** algorithm; it is not clear who the *good guys* were. Maybe, there were no good guys.

8.13 RC4

Designed in 1987 by Ronald Rivest of RSA Data Security, RC4 is a member of the suite of encipherment algorithms available in the Secure Socket Layer (Chapter 18). It provides security for wireless communications in Wired Equivalent Privacy (WEP), a protocol for wireless local area networks as defined in the IEEE 802.11b Standard.

RC4 generates a pseudorandom key stream consisting of a sequence of (8-bit) bytes. RC4 was a trade secret until 1994 and its *name* is still regarded as proprietary. RC4 has two components:

KSA – a *key scheduling algorithm*, which loads a key register with a permutation on integers 0 to 255; the key length varies from 40 to 128 bits;

PRGA – a *pseudorandom number generator* producing one 8-bit byte of key on each call of the generator.

8.13.1 The RC4 Algorithm

Key Scheduling Algorithm (KSA)

1. *Input*

   L bytes of key

   $\underline{k}(1) = (k(0), \ldots, k(L-1))$ with $k_i \in \mathcal{Z}_{256} = \{0, 1, \ldots, 255\}$.

2. *Initialization*

   for $i := 0$ *to* 255 do

   $S[i] := i$;

3. *Generation*

   $j := 0$

   for $i := 0$ *to* 255 do

   $j := (j + S[i] + k(i(\text{modulo } L))) \ (\text{modulo } 256)$;

   swap $(S[j], S[j])$;

TABLE 8.10 Key Register Cell Swapping in RC4

Entering					Exiting			
j	i	k_i	$S[j]$	$S[i]$	j	i	$S[j]$	$S[i]$
0	0	4	4	0	4	0	0	4
4	1	11	4	1	16	1	16	1
16	2	18	16	2	36	2	36	2
36	3	25	36	3	64	3	64	3
64	4	32	64	4	100	4	100	4
100	5	39	100	5	144	5	144	5

Example 8.9

If $\underline{k} = (4, 11, 18, 25, 32, \ldots)$, the first six steps in KSA are given in Table 8.10. The contents of cells in the key register change; for example, the contents of $S[4]$ undergo three changes during the KSA program execution.

$$\begin{pmatrix} S[0] = 0 \\ S[4] = 4 \end{pmatrix} \xrightarrow{i=0} \begin{pmatrix} S[0] = 4 \\ S[4] = 0 \end{pmatrix} \xrightarrow{i=4} \begin{pmatrix} S[96] = 0 \\ S[4] = 96 \end{pmatrix} \xrightarrow{i=186} \begin{pmatrix} S[186] = 96 \\ S[4] = 186 \end{pmatrix}.$$

Table 8.11 lists the complete values in the key register.

Pseudorandom Number Generator (PRGA)

1. *Input*

N: Number of bytes of key stream to be generated

S: Key Register.

2. *Generation*

$j := 0$

TABLE 8.11 Key Register in *Example 8.9*

Key register															
4	16	36	64	186	140	255	86	144	12	55	43	13	160	128	155
246	34	145	46	235	18	31	191	92	101	81	190	142	50	241	115
30	29	28	118	230	127	217	102	75	170	175	60	72	20	24	90
106	137	17	198	93	5	80	121	95	53	221	176	76	200	71	67
251	19	212	62	107	14	180	232	77	120	204	132	225	248	11	44
78	193	85	214	122	27	215	206	135	82	103	161	245	111	179	153
231	119	15	48	218	210	205	216	22	104	59	116	167	162	49	117
211	239	131	23	73	63	89	74	236	254	172	136	189	244	97	228
150	109	182	26	123	171	253	147	38	201	188	99	100	168	134	196
129	125	138	152	70	39	45	207	57	159	242	151	54	41	112	61
87	158	3	84	208	98	177	124	199	213	37	126	10	9	6	183
149	69	194	184	65	40	157	202	234	166	96	197	169	203	2	237
58	185	146	238	229	163	42	249	83	21	130	141	56	165	88	8
243	35	105	178	148	174	219	252	247	143	250	223	222	33	227	79
68	173	220	156	91	240	47	164	139	94	108	209	195	110	181	154
7	192	114	226	51	133	113	66	52	25	233	187	0	1	224	32

TABLE 8.12 Key Register in *Example 8.9*

						Key generation									
255	109	201	105	195	98	192	165	188	46	141	179	53	118	235	225
13	64	228	20	129	59	48	242	72	5	113	20	237	242	165	251
135	199	89	141	113	157	203	46	227	110	1	160	196	246	234	220
82	169	11	65	134	26	106	207	237	178	167	87	56	19	217	16

for $i := 0$ *to* $N - 1$ do

$i := (i + 1)$ (modulo 256);

swap $(S[i], S[j])$;

Output $S[(S[i] + S[j])$ (modulo 256)];

Example 8.9 (continued)

The first 64 bytes generated by PRGA are given in Table 8.12. Encryption of wireless communications is a much greater security problem than transmission over other media; electromagnetic radiation allows a third party to possibly monitor communications without detection. The design of a wireless protocol involves an important tradeoff; either users have a secret key as in GSM, or the keys are managed by the service provider. The IEEE 802.11b protocol opted for the second approach. Until recently, export controls limited the key length of cryptographic devices to 56 bits.

IEEE 802.11b employs various "enhancements" to RC4, including

- A 24-bit *initialization vector* (IV) and
- A 24-bit *integrity check value* (ICV).

The only secret is the 4-bit key.

Figure 8.16 shows the format of the IEEE 802.11b data packet. The steps of the encipherment process depicted in Figure 8.17 are as follows:

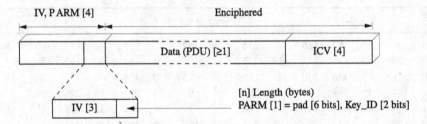

Figure 8.16   IEEE 802.11b enciphered protocol data unit (PDU).

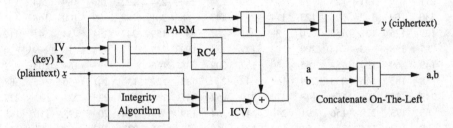

Figure 8.17   IEEE 802.11b encipherment.

1. The key $\underline{K}$ concatenated on the left by IV is input to RC4, which generates a key stream $\underline{s}$;

2. The integrity check value ICV is the 32-bit checksum of the plaintext x computed (using an LFSR) with characteristic function CRC-32

$$\text{CRC-32} = 1 + z + z^2 + z^4 + + z^5 + z^7 + + z^8 + z^{10} + z^{11} + z^{12} + z^{16} + z^{22} + z^{23}$$
$$+ z^{26} + z^{32};$$

3. The plaintext $\underline{x}$ is concatenated on the right by the ICV and then XO Red with the key stream to produce the ciphertext $\underline{y} = \underline{x} + \underline{s}$; and

4. The transmitted packet consisting of the ciphertext is concatenated on the left by IV.

Various researchers have studied RC4; in 2004, Fluhrer and McGrew [2000] announced a weakness in KSA; refinements were given in the subsequent paper Fluhrer et al., 2001

8.14 STREAM ENCIPHERMENT PROBLEMS

I have always included one cribbing problem each time I have taught. Until Spring 2005, the plaintext was the Class_List in the format

Class_List	
0.	Bostrom, Eric
1.	Isaac, Joshua
2.	Piasecki, David
3.	Bautista, Maria
	$\vdots$
57.	Chang, Yao-Yin
58.	Julian, Vincenzo
59.	Riggs, David

with some permutation of the alphabetical order of the names. A N-stage LFSR ($7 \leq N \leq 9$), a primitive characteristic generating polynomial $p(z)$, and an initial state have been used to stream encipher the concatenated variable length records in Class_List. In Spring 2005, I enciphered one of the 10 amendments forming the *Bill of Rights* and challenged the students to identify which one.

REFERENCES

R. ANDERSON, "Searching for the Optimum Correlation Attack," in *Fast Software Encryption*, 2nd International Workshop, December 14–16, 1994, Springer-Verlag, 1995, 137–143.

E. BARKAN, E. BIHAM, AND N. KELLER, "Instant Ciphertext-Only Cryptanalysis is GSM Encrypted Communication," *Proceedings of Crypto 2003*, pp. 600–616.

H. BEKER AND F. PIPER, *Cipher Systems: The Protection of Communications*, John Wiley & Sons, New York, NY, 1982.

A. BIRYUKOV, A. SHAMIR, AND D. SHAMIR, "Weaknesses in the Key Scheduling Algorithm of RC4," *Selected Areas in Cryptography*, 2001, pp. 1–24.

S. R. FLUHRER AND D. A. MCGREW, "Statistical Analysis of the Alleged RC4 Keystream Generator," in *Fast Software Encryption*, 2000, p. 1930.

J. GOLIĆ, "Cryptanalysis of the Alleged A5 Stream Cipher," In *Advances in Cryptology, EUROCRYPT'97*, Springer-Verlag, New York, NY, pp. 239–255.

S. W. GOLOMB, *Shift Register Sequences*, Aegean Park Press, Lagune Beach, CA, 1982.

G. GÜNTHER, "Alternating Step Generators Controlled by de Bruijn Sequences," in *Advances in Cryptography-EUROCRYPT'87*, Springer-Verlag, New York, NY, 1988, 99. 5–14.

E. KEY, "An Analysis of the Structure and Complexity of Nonlinear Binary Sequence Generators," *IEEE Transactions on Information Theory*, **22**, 732–736 (1976).

R. LIDL AND H. NIEDERRIETER, *Finite Fields*, Cambridge University Press, Cambridge, United Kingdom, 1997.

J. J. MASSEY, "Shift-Register Synthesis of BCH Decoding," *IEEE Transactions on Information Theory*, **IT-15**, 1122–1127 (1969).

G. H. MEALY, "A Method for Synthesizing Sequential Circuits," *Bell System Technical Journal*, **34**, 1045–1079 (1955).

A. J. MENEZES, P. C. VAN OORSCHOT AND S. A. VANSTONE, *Handbook of Applied Cryptography* CRC Press, Boca Raton, FL, 1996, Chapter 6.

E. S. SELMER, *Linear Recurrence Relations Over Finite Fields*, Department of Mathematics, University of Bergen (Norway), 1966.

N. ZIERLER, "Linear Recurring Sequences," *Journal of the Society of Industrial and Applied Mathematics*, **7**, 31–38 (1959).

S. R. FLUHRER, I. MANTIN AND A. SHAMIR, "Weakness in the Key Scheduling Algorithm of RC4", *Selected Areas in Cryptography*, 2001, pp. 1–24.

J. GOLIĆ, "Cryptanalysis of the Alleged A5 Stream Cipher" in *Advances in Cryptology, EUROCRYPT '97*, Springer-Verlag, New York, NY, pp 239–255.

S. W. GOLOMB, *Shift Register Sequences*, Aegean Park Press, Lagune Beach, CA, 1982.

C. G. GÜNTHER, "Alternating Step Generators Controlled by de Bruijn Sequences", in *Advances in Cryptography EUROCRYPT '87*, Springer-Verlag, New York, NY, 1988, pp. 5–14.

R. LIDL AND H. NIEDERRIETER, *Finite Fields*, Cambridge University Press, Cambridge, United Kingdom, 1997.

A. J. MENEZES, P. C. VAN OORSCHOT AND S. A. VANSTONE, Handbook of Applied Cryptography [Chapter 6], CRS Press, Boca Raton, Florida, 1986.

CHAPTER 9

BLOCK-CIPHERS: LUCIFER, DES, AND AES

THE **IBM** Corporation decided to offer data security functionality using encryption for its customers in 1966. Horst Feistel (Fig. 9.1), who had previously worked in the cryptographic area, had developed a block cipher that was implemented in the IBM product for the Lloyd's bank. LUCIFER and its successor DES, had a profound effect on cryptography; it led to public-key cryptography, the active involvement of the university community, and changes in NSA. We review this development, the controversy surrounding DES, the replacement of DES by Rijndael, and the design of block ciphers.

9.1 LUCIFER

Horst Feistel's paper [Feistel, 1973] described the role cryptography might play in providing privacy in computer systems. The importance of this paper cannot be underestimated; first, it suggested a template for the design of cryptographic algorithms and second, it challenged the Government's undisputed role as master in the area of cryptology. It initiated a new era in cryptography that would lead to public-key cryptography. It was also of benefit to NSA, forcing it to re-examine its relationship with universities and business organizations.

Feistel's paper described LUCIFER, a *product block-cipher* enciphering plaintext data in blocks of M bits:

$$\underline{x} = (x_0, x_1, \ldots, x_{n-1}) \rightarrow \begin{pmatrix} x_0 & x_1 & \cdots & x_{M-1} \\ x_M & x_{M+1} & \cdots & x_{2M-1} \\ \vdots & \vdots & \ddots & \vdots \\ x_{(n-1)M} & x_{(n-1)M+1} & \cdots & x_{nM-1} \end{pmatrix}.$$

Feistel used the APL programming language to experiment with and test LUCIFER. The program was stored in an APL-workspace, the analogue of a PC/MAC-folder and a UNIX-*directory*. The APL implementation, available at this time, imposed a limit on the number of letters in a workspace name. Feistel's original choice of DEMONSTRATION for the workspace name had to be shortened to DEMON; ultimately, someone suggested the sexier name LUCIFER.

A description of one version of LUCIFER may be found in Sorkin's paper [1984]. Outerbridge [1986] referred to LUCIFER as a Feistel-like block product cipher.

Computer Security and Cryptography. By Alan G. Konheim

Figure 9.1 Horst Feistel (Courtesy of IBM).

In 1966, Lloyd's Banking contracted with IBM to design a remote-terminal-oriented banking system. The role of encipherment in ATM (Automated Teller Machine) transactions will be described in greater detail in Chapter 18, but it was clear that some sort of cryptographic capability would be needed. An algorithm proposed by another IBM division was rejected when it was recognized to be a variant of the Hill encipherment system (see Chapter 3). A group in the Mathematical Sciences Department at the IBM Yorktown Research Center including Roy Adler, Don Coppersmith, Horst Feistel, Edna Grossman, Alan Hoffman, Bryant Tuckerman, and myself had started in the 1960s to investigate encipherment. Feistel's LUCIFER was in the right place at the right time. Although IBM Research traditionally did *not* participate in product development, a good working relationship was established with a development group at the IBM division in Kingston, New York.

There are several versions of LUCIFER; for example Sorkin [1984] describes LUCIFER as it appears in a paper by Lynn Smith [1977]. I will describe the only commercial implementation of LUCIFER, contained in the IBM 2984 Cash Issuing Terminal.

Plaintext data of length $M = 32$ bits was enciphered following the paradigm proposed by Feistel, in which the plaintext $\underline{x}$ was viewed as consisting of equal length left (L) and right (R) blocks

$$\underline{x} = (x_0, x_1, \ldots, x_{M-1}) = (L, R).$$

LUCIFER enciphered plaintext $\underline{x}$ in 16 *rounds*, each round using a key-dependent transformation:

1. The two message halves (L, R) were transformed to $\mathcal{T} : (L, R) \rightarrow (F(R) + L, R)$, where $F(R)$ is a 16-bit to 16-bit mapping applied to the message right block R composed of

   L1. Modulo 16 addition of 16 bits of key to the block R,

   L2. Transformation then of the 16 bits by a nonlinear substitution *S-box*,

   L3. Transformation then of the 16 bits by a *P-box*,

   L4. Finally the addition of the result $F(R)$ to the 32-bit left block L.

2. The two halves $F(R) + L$ and R were interchanged $\vartheta : (F(R) + L, R) \rightarrow (R, F(R) + L)$.

$\mathcal{T}$ and ϑ are involutions

$$\mathcal{T}^{-1} = \mathcal{T}$$

$$(L, R) \xrightarrow{\mathcal{T}} (F(R) + L, R) \xrightarrow{\mathcal{T}} (F(R) + F(R) + L, R) = (L, R)$$

$$\vartheta^{-1} = \vartheta$$

$$(L, R) \xrightarrow{\vartheta} (L, R) \xrightarrow{\vartheta} (R, L)$$

where the *round transformation* $\mathcal{R} = \vartheta\mathcal{T}$ is invertible for every possible function F and

$$\mathcal{R}^{-1} = \mathcal{T}\vartheta.$$

F is a nonlinear transformation on 32-bit data strings in the IBM 2984 Cash Issuing Terminal.

The parameters of the 2984 implementation of LUCIFER [IBM, 1971] are:

2984-1: The block length $M = 32$ bits;

2984-2: Key length 64 bits; and

2984-3: 16 rounds in an encipherment.

A total of 36 bits are used on each round; each key bit is used $9 = \dfrac{16 \times 36}{64}$ times:

K1. 16 bits in Step L1;

K2. 4 bits in Step L2; and

K3. 16 bits in Step L3.

The 2984 LUCIFER-*schedule* specifies the 36 bits used in each round as follows:

KS0. The 64-bit LUCIFER-key is loaded into a *key register* and cyclically left-shifted 28 bit-positions;

KS1. The leftmost 36 bits used in a round are labeled as 4-bit *nibbles* a, b, c, ... , i,

KS2. The 4 bits in nibble a are used in the S-box transformation;

KS3. The 16 bits in nibbles b, d, f, and h are used in key-dependent L1 addition with carry;

KS4. The 16 bits in nibbles c, e, g, and i are used in the P-box transformation;

KS5. The key register is cyclically left-shifted 28 positions after each round.

The nibbles used in each round are shown in Table 9.1.

There are two different S-box mappings S_0 and S_1:

S_0 If $a_i = 0$, then S-box $\mathbf{S}_0$ transforms the input 4-bit data $\underline{d}$;

S_1 If $a_i = 1$, then S-box $\mathbf{S}_1$ transforms the input 4-bit data $\underline{d}$.

The nibble a $= (a_0, a_1, a_2, a_3)$ determines which of the $2^4 = 16$ possible S-box combinations is used to transform the 16 bits of data $\underline{r}$ in Step L2 as specified by the next equation and Table 9.2.

$$\underline{d} = (d_0, d_1, d_2, d_3) \rightarrow (\mathbf{S}_{a_0}(\underline{d}), \mathbf{S}_{a_1}(\underline{d}), \mathbf{S}_{a_2}(\underline{d}), \mathbf{S}_{a_3}(\underline{d}))$$

TABLE 9.1 IBM 2904 Key Register Schedule

Round r	Nibbles Used in Round r								
	a	b	c	d	e	f	g	h	i
1	7	8	9	10	11	12	13	14	15
2	14	15	0	1	2	3	4	5	6
3	5	6	7	8	9	10	11	12	13
4	12	13	14	15	0	1	2	3	4
5	3	4	5	6	7	8	9	10	11
6	10	11	12	13	14	15	0	1	2
7	1	2	3	4	5	6	7	8	9
8	8	9	10	11	12	13	14	15	0
9	15	0	1	2	3	4	5	6	7
10	6	7	8	9	10	11	12	13	14
11	13	14	15	0	1	2	3	4	5
12	4	5	6	7	8	9	10	11	12
13	11	12	13	14	15	0	1	2	3
14	2	3	4	5	6	7	8	9	10
15	9	10	11	12	13	14	15	0	1
15	0	1	2	3	4	5	6	7	8

TABLE 9.2 IBM 2984 S-Box Output

$\underline{d}$	0	1	2	3	4	5	6	7	8	9	A	B	C	D	E	F
$S_0(\underline{d})$	3	0	8	5	1	2	4	F	D	9	C	E	6	B	A	7
$S_1(\underline{d})$	8	D	1	6	c	4	F	B	3	2	5	4	9	0	7	A

The 2984 `LUCIFER` P-box is a key-dependent mapping of 32 bits to 32 bits;The 2984 `LUCIFER` P-box is a key-dependent mapping of 32 bits to 32 bits; Table 9.3 specifies how the nibbles c, e, g, and i are used in the P-box transformation where $'$ denotes the complement operation:

$$(\underline{T}_0, \underline{T}_1, \underline{T}_2, \underline{T}_3) \xrightarrow{P} (\underline{P}_0, \underline{P}_1, \underline{P}_2, \underline{P}_3)$$

$$T_i = (T_{i,0}, T_{i,1}, T_{i,2}, T_{i,3}) \qquad \underline{P}_i = (P_{i,0}, P_{i,1}, P_{i,2}, P_{i,3}), \qquad 0 \le i < 4$$

The input and output vectors to the P-box vectors,

$$\underline{T} = (T_{0,0}, T_{0,1}, T_{0,2}, T_{0,3}, \ldots, T_{3,0}, T_{3,1}, T_{3,2}, T_{3,3})$$

$$\underline{P} = (P_{0,0}, P_{0,1}, P_{0,2}, P_{0,3}, \ldots, P_{3,0}, P_{3,1}, P_{3,2}, P_{3,3})$$

TABLE 9.3 IBM 2984 P-Box Transformation

$P_{0,0} = T_{0,0}i_0' + T_{1,0}g_0$	$P_{0,1} = T_{3,1}c_1' + T_{2,1}e_1$	$P_{0,2} = T_{2,2}e_2'T_{3,2}c_2$	$P_{0,3} = T_{1,3}g_3' + T_{0,3}i_3$
$P_{1,0} = T_{1,0}g_0' + T_{2,0}e_0$	$P_{1,1} = T_{0,1}i_1' + T_{3,1}c_1$	$P_{1,2} = T_{3,2}c_2' + T_{0,2}i_2$	$P_{1,3} = T_{2,3}e_3' + T_{1,3}g_3$
$P_{2,0} = T_{2,0}e_0' + T_{3,0}c_0$	$P_{2,1} = T_{1,1}g_1' + T_{0,1}i_1$	$P_{2,2} = T_{0,2}i_2' + T_{1,2}g_2$	$P_{2,3} = T_{3,3}c_3' + T_{2,3}e_3$
$P_{3,0} = T_{3,0}c_0' + T_{0,0}i_0$	$P_{3,1} = T_{2,1}e_1' + T_{1,1}g_1$	$P_{3,2} = T_{1,2}g_2' + T_{2,2}e_2$	$P_{3,3} = T_{0,3}i_3' + T_{3,3}c_3$

are related by

$$P = \begin{pmatrix} i'_0 & 0 & 0 & 0 & g_0 & 0 & 0 & 0 & 0 & 0 & 0 & 0 & 0 & 0 & 0 & 0 \\ 0 & 0 & 0 & 0 & 0 & 0 & 0 & 0 & 0 & e_1 & 0 & 0 & 0 & c'_1 & 0 & 0 \\ 0 & 0 & 0 & 0 & 0 & 0 & 0 & 0 & 0 & 0 & e'_2 & 0 & 0 & 0 & c_2 & 0 \\ 0 & 0 & 0 & i_3 & 0 & 0 & 0 & 0 & g'_3 & 0 & 0 & 0 & 0 & 0 & 0 & 0 \\ 0 & 0 & 0 & 0 & g'_0 & 0 & 0 & 0 & e_0 & 0 & 0 & 0 & 0 & 0 & 0 & 0 \\ 0 & i'_1 & 0 & 0 & 0 & 0 & 0 & 0 & 0 & 0 & 0 & 0 & 0 & c_1 & 0 & 0 \\ 0 & 0 & i_2 & 0 & 0 & 0 & 0 & 0 & 0 & 0 & 0 & 0 & 0 & c'_2 & 0 \\ 0 & 0 & 0 & 0 & 0 & 0 & 0 & g_3 & 0 & 0 & 0 & e'_3 & 0 & 0 & 0 & 0 \\ 0 & 0 & 0 & 0 & 0 & 0 & 0 & 0 & e'_0 & 0 & 0 & 0 & c_0 & 0 & 0 & 0 \\ 0 & i_1 & 0 & 0 & 0 & g'_1 & 0 & 0 & 0 & 0 & 0 & 0 & 0 & 0 & 0 & 0 \\ 0 & 0 & i'_2 & 0 & 0 & 0 & g_2 & 0 & 0 & 0 & 0 & 0 & 0 & 0 & 0 & 0 \\ 0 & 0 & 0 & 0 & 0 & 0 & 0 & 0 & 0 & 0 & 0 & e_3 & 0 & 0 & 0 & c'_3 \\ i_0 & 0 & 0 & 0 & 0 & 0 & 0 & 0 & 0 & 0 & 0 & 0 & c'_0 & 0 & 0 & 0 \\ 0 & 0 & 0 & 0 & 0 & g_1 & 0 & 0 & 0 & e'_1 & 0 & 0 & 0 & 0 & 0 & 0 \\ 0 & 0 & 0 & 0 & 0 & 0 & g'_2 & 0 & 0 & 0 & e_2 & 0 & 0 & 0 & 0 & 0 \\ 0 & 0 & 0 & i'_3 & 0 & 0 & 0 & 0 & 0 & 0 & 0 & 0 & 0 & 0 & 0 & c_3 \end{pmatrix} T$$

The IBM 2984 P-box is an invertible key-dependent linear transformation but *not* a permutation. Figure 9.2 is a block diagram of $\mathcal{T}: (L, R) \to (L + F(R), R)$.

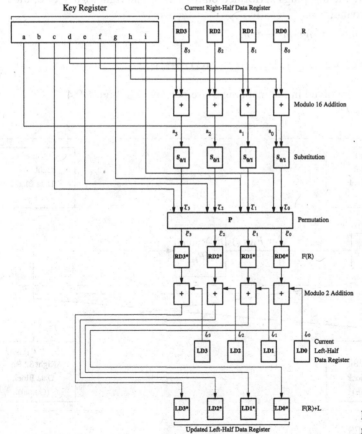

Figure 9.2 IBM 2984 round transformation $\mathcal{T}$.

9.2   DES

DES (Fig. 9.3) is a block cipher where

- plaintext $\underline{x} = (x_0, x_1, \ldots, x_{63}) \in \mathcal{Z}_{64,2}$;
- ciphertext $\underline{y} = (y_0, y_1, \ldots, y_{63}) \in \mathcal{Z}_{64,2}$;
- key $\underline{k} = (k_0, k_1, \ldots, k_{55}) \in \mathcal{Z}_{56,2}$.

$$\mathbf{DES} : \underline{x} \to \underline{y} = \mathrm{DES}_{\underline{k}}\{\underline{x}\}$$

DES is the product (composition) of mappings

$$\mathrm{DES} = \mathrm{IP}^{-1} \times \mathcal{T}_{16} \times \theta \times \mathcal{T}_{15} \times \cdots \times \theta \times \mathcal{T}_2 \times \theta \times \mathcal{T}_1 \times \mathrm{IP}$$
$$\mathcal{T}_i : (\underline{x}_L, \underline{x}_R) \to (\underline{x}_L + F_i(\underline{x}_R), \underline{x}_R)$$

with inverse

$$\mathrm{DES}^{-1} = \mathrm{IP}^{-1} \times \mathcal{T}_1 \times \theta \times \mathcal{T}_2 \times \cdots \times \theta \times \mathcal{T}_{15} \times \theta \times \mathcal{T}_{16} \times \mathrm{IP}.$$

- IP is the *initial permutation* (or wire-crossing, plugboard);
- $\pi_{\mathcal{T}_i}, F_i$ are the mappings performed on the left-x_L and right-x_R halves of the input on the ith round;
- θ is the *interchange involution*

$$\theta : (x_0, x_1, \ldots, x_{31}, x_{32}, x_{33}, \ldots, x_{63}) \to (x_{32}, x_{33}, \ldots, x_{63}, x_0, x_1, \ldots, x_{31})$$

The operations involved in the mapping $\mathcal{T}$ are portrayed in Figure 9.4.

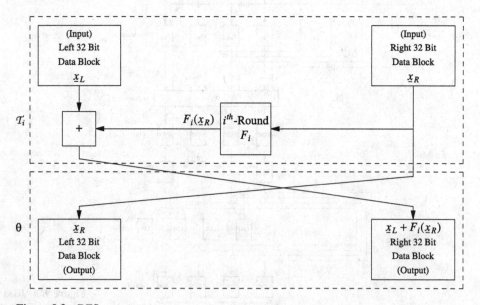

Figure 9.3   DES.

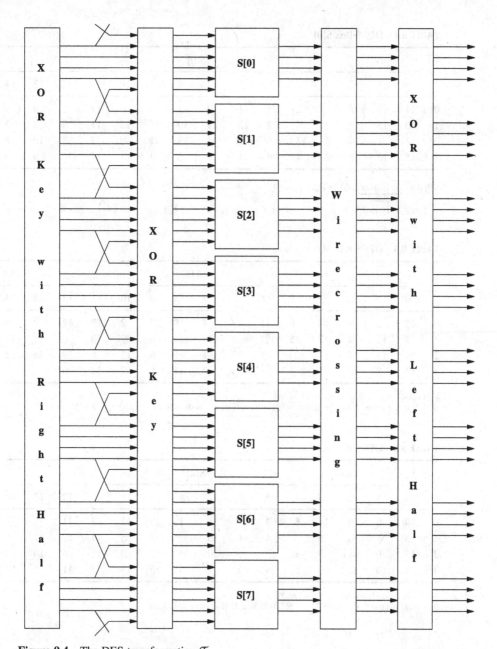

Figure 9.4 The DES transformation T.

9.3 THE DES S-BOXES, P-BOX, AND INITIAL PERMUTATION (IP)

Tables 9.4 to 9.11 specify the seven DES S-boxes, each with a 6-bit input $(x_0, x_1, x_2, x_3, x_4, x_5, x_6)$ and a 4-bit output (y_0, y_1, y_2, y_3); each table contains 4 rows and 15 columns, where

- Bits (x_0, x_6) identify a row in the table, and
- bits (x_1, x_2, x_3, x_4) identify a column in the table.

TABLE 9.4   DES S-Box S[0]

	\$S[0]\$															
	0	1	2	3	4	5	6	7	8	9	10	11	12	13	14	15
0	14	4	13	1	2	15	11	8	3	10	6	12	5	9	0	7
1	0	15	7	4	14	2	13	1	10	6	12	11	9	5	3	8
2	4	1	14	8	13	6	2.	11	15	12	9	7	3	10	5	0
3	15	12	8	2	4	9	1	7	5	11	3	14	10	0	6	13

$S[0] : (x_0, \underset{\text{column}}{\underline{x_1, x_2, x_3, x_4}}, x_5) \rightarrow (y_0, y_1, y_2, y_3)$

$(1, 1, 0, 0, 1, 1)$: row 3, column 9, $S[0](1, 1, 0, 0, 1, 1) = 11 = (1, 0, 1, 1)$

TABLE 9.5   DES S-Box S[1]

	\$S[1]\$															
	0	1	2	3	4	5	6	7	8	9	10	11	12	13	14	15
0	15	1	8	14	6	11	3	4	9	7	2	13	12	0	5	10
1	3	13	4	7	15	2	8	14	12	0	1	10	6	9	11	5
2	0	14	7	11	10	4	13	1	5	8	12	6	9	3	2	15
3	13	8	10	1	3	15	4	2	11	6	7	12	0	5	14	9

$S[1] : (x_0, x_1, x_2, x_3, x_4, x_5) \rightarrow (y_0, y_1, y_2, y_3)$
$(1, 1, 0, 0, 0, 0)$: row 2, column 8, $S[1](1, 1, 0, 0, 0, 0) = 5 = (0, 1, 0, 1)$

TABLE 9.6   DES S-Box S[2]

	\$S[2]\$															
	0	1	2	3	4	5	6	7	8	9	10	11	12	13	14	15
0	10	0	9	14	6	3	15	5	1	13	12	7	11	4	2	8
1	13	7	0	9	3	4	6	10	2	8	5	14	12	11	15	1
2	13	6	4	9	8	15	3	0	11	1	2	12	5	10	14	7
3	1	10	13	0	6	9	8	7	4	15	14	3	11	5	2	12

$S[2] : (x_0, x_1, x_2, x_3, x_4, x_5) \rightarrow (y_0, y_1, y_2, y_3)$
$(0, 0, 1, 1, 1, 1)$: row 1, column 7, $S[2](0, 0, 1, 1, 1, 1) = 10 = (1, 0, 1, 0)$

TABLE 9.7   DES S-Box S[3]

	\$S[3]\$															
	0	1	2	3	4	5	6	7	8	9	10	11	12	13	14	15
0	7	13	14	3	0	6	9	10	1	2	8	5	11	12	4	15
1	13	8	11	5	6	15	0	3	4	7	2	12	1	10	14	9
2	10	6	9	0	12	11	7	13	15	1	3	14	5	2	8	4
3	3	15	0	6	10	1	13	8	9	4	5	11	12	7	2	14

$S[3] : (x_0, x_1, x_2, x_3, x_4, x_5) \rightarrow (y_0, y_1, y_2, y_3)$
$(0, 0, 1, 1, 0, 0)$: row 0, column 6, $S[3](0, 0, 1, 1, 0, 0) = 9 = (1, 0, 0, 1)$

TABLE 9.8   DES S-Box S[4]

								S[4]							
	0	**1**	**2**	**3**	**4**	**5**	**6**	**7**	**8**	**9**	**10**	**11**	**12**	**13**	**14**	**15**
0	2	12	4	1	7	10	11	6	8	5	3	15	13	0	14	9
1	14	11	2	12	4	7	13	1	5	0	15	10	3	9	8	6
2	4	2	1	11	10	13	7	8	15	9	12	5	6	3	0	14
3	11	8	12	7	1	14	2	13	6	15	0	9	10	4	5	3

$S[4] : (x_0, x_1, x_2, x_3, x_4, x_5) \rightarrow (y_0, y_1, y_2, y_3)$
$(1, 0, 1, 0, 1, 1)$: row 3, column 5, $S[4](1, 0, 1, 0, 1, 1) = 14 = (1, 1, 1, 0)$

TABLE 9.9   DES S-Box S[5]

								S[5]							
	0	**1**	**2**	**3**	**4**	**5**	**6**	**7**	**8**	**9**	**10**	**11**	**12**	**13**	**14**	**15**
0	12	1	10	15	9	2	6	8	0	13	3	4	14	7	5	11
1	10	15	4	2	7	12	9	5	6	1	13	14	0	11	3	8
2	9	14	15	5	2	8	12	3	7	0	4	10	1	13	11	6
3	4	3	2	12	9	5	15	10	11	14	1	7	6	0	8	13

$S[5] : (x_0, x_1, x_2, x_3, x_4, x_5) \rightarrow (y_0, y_1, y_2, y_3)$
$(1, 0, 1, 0, 0, 0)$: row 2, column 4, $S[5](1, 0, 1, 0, 0, 0) = 2 = (0, 0, 1, 0)$

TABLE 9.10   DES S-Box S[6]

								S[6]							
	0	**1**	**2**	**3**	**4**	**5**	**6**	**7**	**8**	**9**	**10**	**11**	**12**	**13**	**14**	**15**
0	4	11	2	14	15	0	8	13	3	12	9	7	5	10	6	1
1	13	0	11	7	4	9	1	10	14	3	5	12	2	15	8	6
2	1	4	11	13	12	3	7	14	10	15	6	8	0	5	9	2
3	6	11	13	8	1	4	10	7	9	5	0	15	14	2	3	12

$S[6] : (x_0, x_1, x_2, x_3, x_4, x_5) \rightarrow (y_0, y_1, y_2, y_3)$
$(0, 0, 0, 1, 1, 1)$: row 1, column 3, $S[6](0, 0, 0, 1, 1, 1) = 7 = (0, 1, 1, 1)$

TABLE 9.11   DES S-Box S[7]

								S[7]							
	0	**1**	**2**	**3**	**4**	**5**	**6**	**7**	**8**	**9**	**10**	**11**	**12**	**13**	**14**	**15**
0	13	2	8	4	6	15	11	1	10	9	3	14	5	0	12	7
1	1	15	13	8	10	3	7	4	12	5	6	11	0	14	9	2
2	7	11	4	1	9	12	14	2	0	6	10	13	15	3	5	8
3	2	1	14	7	4	10	8	13	15	12	9	0	3	5	6	11

$S[7] : (x_0, x_1, x_2, x_3, x_4, x_5) \rightarrow (y_0, y_1, y_2, y_3)$
$(1, 0, 0, 1, 0, 0)$: row 2, column 2, $S[7](1, 0, 0, 1, 0, 0) = 4 = (0, 1, 0, 0)$

My description of DES differs slightly from that given in [FIPS, 1988] in two respects:

- I use 0-index origin labeling; for example, a 64-bit plaintext block is $(x_0, x_1, \ldots, x_{63})$ instead of $(x_1, x_2, \ldots, x_{64})$.

TABLE 9.12 DES P-Box

15	6	19	20	28	11	27	16	0	14	22	25	4	17	30	9
1	7	23	13	31	26	2	8	18	12	29	5	21	10	3	24

TABLE 9.13 DES IP

57	49	41	33	25	17	9	1
59	51	43	35	27	19	11	3
61	53	45	37	29	21	13	5
63	55	47	39	31	23	15	7
56	48	40	32	24	16	8	0
58	50	42	34	26	18	10	2
60	52	44	36	28	20	12	4
62	54	46	38	30	22	14	6

- FIPS 46 speaks of a 64-bit key, although only the first 7 bits in each byte play a role in the encipherment process.

The P-box (Table 9.12) is a permutation of the 32-bit permutation $(x_0, x_1, \ldots, x_{31}) \rightarrow (x_{15}, x_6, \ldots, x_3, x_{24})$ DES plaintext $\underline{x}$ is first permuted by the *initial permutation* **IP** (Table 9.13) before the 16 round operations start:

$$\textbf{IP} : (x_0, x_1, \ldots, x_{63}) \rightarrow (x_{57}, x_{49}, \ldots, x_{14}, x_6)$$

9.4 DES KEY SCHEDULE

Three arrays **PC-1**, **PC-2**, and **KS** specify the 48 key bits that are used on each round (Tables 9.14–9.16). The DES *key schedule* starts with the 56-bit *user key* $\underline{k} = (k_0, k_1, \ldots, k_{55})$ and derives 16 *internal keys* $\underline{k}_i = (k_{i,0}, k_{i,1}, \ldots, k_{i,47})$ with $0 \le i < 16$, as shown in Figure 9.5. The 48-bit internal key $\underline{k}_i$ used on the ith round is derived as follows:

- **KS-1:** The user key $\underline{k}$ is inserted in two 28-bit registers $[C, D]$ according to (**PC-1**).

Input Key Register C_0 D_0

$$\boxed{k_0, k_1, \ldots, k_{27}, k_{28}, k_{29}, k_{30}, \ldots, k_{55}} \xrightarrow{\textbf{PC-1}} \boxed{k_{49}, k_{42}, \ldots, k_{38}, k_{31}} \boxed{k_{55}, k_{48}, \ldots, k_{10}, k_3}$$

- **KS-2:** $[C_0, D_0]$ is the initial state of the registers $[C, D]$.
- **KS-3:** At the start of the ith round, the combined register-pair $[C_{i-1}, D_{i-1}]$ is left-circular shifted by $KS[i]$ positions, producing $[C_i, D_i]$. For example,

$[C_0, D_0]$ C_1 D_1

$$\boxed{k_{49}, k_{42}, \ldots, k_{38}, k_{31}, k_{55}, k_{48}, \ldots, k_{10}, k_3} \xrightarrow{\textbf{KS[1]}} \boxed{k_{42}, k_{35}, \ldots, k_{31}, k_{55}} \boxed{k_{48}, k_{41}, \ldots, k_3, k_{49}}$$

- **KS-4:** $\underline{k}_i$ is derived from the 28 bits of the concatenation of $[C_i, D_i]$ according to (**PC-2**).

$[C_{16}, D_{16}]$ $\underline{k}_0$

$$\boxed{k_{42}, k_{35}, \ldots, k_{31}, k_{55}, k_{48}, k_{41}, \ldots, k_3, k_{49}} \xrightarrow{\textbf{PC-2}} \boxed{k_8, k_{44}, \ldots, k_{12}, k_{15}, k_{19}, k_4, \ldots, k_{48}, k_{34}}$$

Each bit of the user key is used about 13.7 times in a DES-encipherment. The key schedule is designed to use the key bits of k in as uniform a manner as possible.

TABLE 9.14   PC-1

			pc-1			
49	42	35	28	21	14	7
0	50	43	36	29	22	15
8	1	51	44	37	30	23
16	9	2	52	45	38	31
55	48	41	34	27	20	13
6	54	47	40	33	26	19
12	5	53	46	39	32	25
18	11	4	24	17	10	3

TABLE 9.15   PC-2

		pc-2			
13	16	10	23	0	4
2	27	14	5	20	9
22	18	11	3	25	7
15	6	26	19	12	1
40	51	30	36	46	54
29	39	50	44	32	47
43	48	38	55	33	52
45	41	49	35	28	31

TABLE 9.16   DES Key Shifts

i	1	2	3	4	5	6	7	8	9	10	11	12	13	14	15	16
KS[i]	1	1	2	2	2	2	2	2	1	2	2	2	2	2	2	1

It is intended that the key be *randomly* chosen. If $\underline{k}$ has special characteristics, the derived internal keys may fail to sufficiently disguise the plaintext. Of the 2^{56} possible keys, there are a few with this property.

9.4.1   Weak Keys

It was observed quite early in 1973 that certain user keys will produce internal keys with special regularity.

Example 9.1

The contents of the registers C_i and D_i contain a *constant* value so that DES is the 16th power of a transformation. For such a key $\underline{k}$

$$\underline{y} = \mathrm{DES}\{\underline{k}, \underline{x}\} \longleftrightarrow \underline{x} = \mathrm{DES}_{\underline{k}}^{-1}\{\underline{y}\}$$

There are four weak keys corresponding to the register contents $C, D \in \{(0)_{28}, (1)_{28}\}$, where $(0)_{28} \equiv \underbrace{(0, 0, \ldots, 0)}_{28 \text{ bits}}$ and $(1)_{28} \equiv \underbrace{(1, 1, \ldots, 1)}_{28 \text{ bits}}$.

Table 9.17 lists the weak keys written in hexadecimal notation, appending an odd parity check bit on the right. (Note, NIST (formerly NBS) often describes the DES key as a 64-bit key by appending a parity check bit on the right of each 7-bit block. Needless to say, this bit plays *no* role in the encipherment process.)

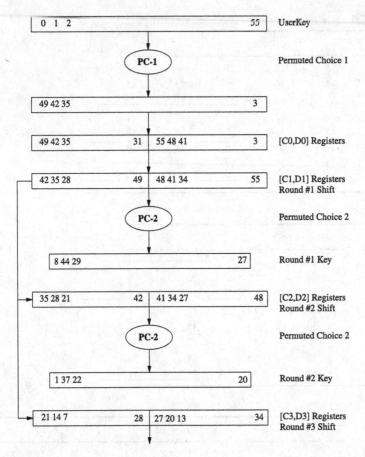

Figure 9.5 DES key schedule.

Example 9.2
A *semi-weak key* results when the contents of the registers C_i and D_i result in *at most* two internal keys. As the vector of key shifts in $KS = (1, 1, (2)_6, 1, (2)_6, 1)$, the only possible register values for C and D are in the set $\{(0,1)_{14}, (1,0)_{14}, (0)_{28}, (1)_{28}\}$.

Table 9.18 lists the six pairs of semi-weak keys in hex (with an odd parity check digit appended on the right).

9.5 SAMPLE DES ENCIPHERMENT

A trace of DES is shown next in Table 9.19 including

- The initialization, including the user key $\underline{k}$, the contents of the registers $[C_0, D_0]$, the plaintext $\underline{x}$, the result of the initial permutation IP[$\underline{x}$], and the left and right data registers ($L[0]$, $R[0]$);

TABLE 9.17 Weak DES Keys

01	01	01	01	01	01	01	01	$C = (0)_{28}$	$D = (2)_{28}$
1F	1F	1F	1F	1F	1F	1F	1F	$C = (0)_{28}$	$D = (1)_{28}$
E0	E0	E0	E0	E0	E0	E0	E0	$C = (1)_{28}$	$D = (0)_{28}$
FE	FE	FE	FE	FE	FE	FE	FE	$C = (1)_{28}$	$D = (1)_{28}$

TABLE 9.18 Semi-Weak DES Keys

01	FE	01	FE	01	FE	01	FE	$C = (0, 1)_{14}$	$D = (0, 1)_{14}$
FE	01	FE	01	FE	01	FE	01	$C = (1, 0)_{14}$	$D = (1, 0)_{14}$
1F	E0	1F	E0	1F	E0	1F	E0	$C = (0, 1)_{14}$	$D = (1, 0)_{14}$
E0	1F	E0	1F	E0	1F	E0	1F	$C = (1, 0)_{14}$	$D = (0, 1)_{14}$
01	E0	01	E0	01	E0	01	E0	$C = (0, 1)_{14}$	$D = (0)_{28}$
E0	01	E0	01	E0	01	E0	01	$C = (1, 0)_{14}$	$D = (0)_{28}$
1F	FE	1F	FE	1F	FE	1F	FE	$C = (0, 1)_{14}$	$D = (1)_{28}$
FE	1F	FE	1F	FE	1F	FE	1F	$C = (1, 0)_{14}$	$D = (1)_{28}$
01	1F	01	1F	01	1F	01	1F	$C = (0)_{28}$	$D = (0, 1)_{14}$
1F	01	1F	01	1F	01	1F	01	$C = (0)_{28}$	$D = (1, 0)_{14}$
E0	FE	E0	FE	E0	FE	E0	FE	$C = (1)_{28}$	$D = (0, 1)_{14}$
FE	E0	FE	E0	FE	E0	FE	E0	$C = (1)_{28}$	$D = (1, 0)_{14}$

- The transformations on rounds 1, 2, and 16 displaying
  - The entering contents of the left- and right-half-data registers ($L[i-1]$, $R[i-1]$),
  - The entering contents of the registers [C_{i-1}, D_{i-1}],
  - The updated contents of the registers [C_i, D_i],
  - The key KEY[i] used on Round i,
  - The expanded right data block $E[R[i-1]]$,
  - The XOR of KEY[i] and $E[R[i]]$,
  - The output of the S-boxes with input KEY[i] + $E[R[i]]$,
  - The output of the P-box,
  - The entering left-half data register $L[i-1]$,
  - The XOR of the P-box output and the contents of $L[i-1]$,
  - The concatenation on the right of the P-BOX output + $L[i-1]$ with $R[i-1]$,
  - The updated ($L[i]$, $R[i]$), and
- The output.

9.6 CHAINING

The DES only specifies the encipherment a block of 64 bits. DES can be extended to encipher plaintext of arbitrary length in two ways.

The *Standard Extension of DES* divides the plaintext $\underline{x} = (x_0, x_1, \ldots, x_{N-1}) \in \mathcal{Z}_{N,2}$ into 8-byte blocks

$$\underline{x}^{(0)} = (x_0, x_1, \ldots, x_{63})$$

$$\underline{x}^{(1)} = x_{64}, x_{65}, \ldots, x_{127}$$

$$\vdots$$

$$\underline{x}^{(n-1)} = (x_{64(n-1)}, x_{64(n-1)+1}, \ldots, x_{64(n-1)})$$

and enciphers each block separately

$$\text{DES} : \underline{x}^{(i)} \rightarrow \underline{y}^{(i)} = \text{DES}_{\underline{k}}\{\underline{x}^{(i)}\}.$$

TABLE 9.19 Trace of DES

	Initialization
$\underline{k}$	0001 0011 0011 0100 0101 0011 0111 1001 1001 1011 1011 1100 1101 1111 1111 0001
$[C_0, D_0]$	1111000011001100101010101111 * 0101010101100010011110001111
$\underline{x}$	01010101 01010101 01010101 01010101 01010101 01010101 01010101 01010101
IP$[\underline{x}]$	11111111 11111111 11111111 11111111 00000000 00000000 00000000 00000000
$(L[0], R[0])$	11111111 11111111 11111111 11111111 * 00000000 00000000 00000000 00000000
	Round 1
$(L[0], R[0])$	11111111 11111111 11111111 11111111 * 00000000 00000000 00000000 00000000
$[C_0, D_0]$	1111000011001100101010101111 * 0101010101100010011110001111
$[C_1, D_1]$	1110000110011001010101011111 * 1010101011000100111100011110
KEY[1]	000110 110000 001011 101111 011111 000111 000001 110010
$E[R[0]]$	000000 000000 000000 000000 000000 000000 000000 000000
$E[R[0]] +$ KEY[1]	000110 110000 001011 101111 011111 000111 000001 110010
S-BOX	0001 0101 0100 1000 0110 0010 1101 0110
P-BOX	0000 0010 0011 0111 0100 0000 1111 0011
$L[0]$	1111 1111 1111 1111 1111 1111 1111 1111
P-BOX $+ L[0]$	1111 1101 1100 1000 1011 1111 0000 1100
(P-BOX $+ L[0], R[0])$	11111101 11001000 10111111 00001100 * 00000000 00000000 00000000 00000000
$(L[1], R[1])$	00000000 00000000 00000000 00000000 * 11111101 11001000 10111111 00001100
	Round 2
$(L[1], R[1])$	00000000 00000000 00000000 00000000 * 11111101 11001000 10111111 0001100
$[C_1, D_1]$	1110000110011001010101011111 * 1010101011000100111100011110
$[C_2, D_2]$	1100001100110010101010111111 * 0101010110001001111000111101
KEY[2]	011110 011010 111011 011001 110110 101100 100111 100101
$E[R[1]]$	011111 111011 111001 010001 010111 111110 100001 011001
$E[R[1]] +$ KEY[2]	000001 100001 000010 001000 100001 010010 000110 111100
S-BOX	0000 1101 0000 0000 1011 1101 1110 0101
P-BOX	0011 0001 0001 1000 0110 1100 1011 1001
$L[1]$	0000 0000 0000 0000 0000 0000 0000 0000
P-BOX $+ L[1]$	0011 0001 0001 1000 0110 1100 1011 1001
(P-BOX $+ L[1], R[1])$	00110001 00011000 01101100 10111001 * 11111101 11001000 10111111 00001100
$(L[2], R[2])$	11111101 11001000 10111111 00001100 * 00110001 00011000 01101100 10111001
	Round 16
$(L[15], R[15])$	00110101 10010111 11000000 00101100 * 11001110 10010001 00110001 01100100
$[C_{15}, D_{15}]$	1111000011001100101010101111 * 1010101010110001001111000111
$[C_{16}, D_{16}]$	1111000011001100101010101111 * 0101010101100010011110001111
KEY[16]	110010 110011 110110 001011 000011 100001 011111 100101
$E[R[15]]$	011001 011101 010010 100010 100110 100010 101100 001001
$E[R[15]] +$ KEY[16]	101011 101110 100100 101001 100101 000011 110011 101100
S-BOX	1001 0001 0100 1010 1100 1111 0101 1110
P-BOX	0001 1011 1111 0111 0110 0000 0110 1010
$L[15]$	0011 0101 1001 0111 1100 0000 0010 1100
P-BOX $+ L[15]$	0010 1110 0110 0000 1010 0000 0100 0110
(P-BOX $+ L[15]$, $R[15]$)	00101110 01100000 10100000 01000110 * 11001110 10010001 00110001 01100100
$(L[16], R[16])$	00101110 01100000 10100000 01000110 * 11001110 10010001 00110001 01100100
	Output
$\underline{y}$	00101000 11000001 11000011 11000000 00101000 01011110 10010011 10100100

There remains the question of how to handle the encipherment of plaintext whose length is not a multiple of $8n$ bytes. More importantly, there are instances in which the encipherment as defined above reveals structure in the plaintext. For example, when we encipher a file containing a picture, the outline of the picture might be detectable in the ciphertext. Also, stereotyped preambles of plaintext messages, like `Dear Mr./Ms.` or `To :` may be visible in the ciphertext. In order to hide the repetitive nature of plaintext and stereotyped preambles, *chaining* was introduced.

The *record chained* encipherment of plaintext $\underline{x} = (\underline{x}^{(0)}, \underline{x}^{(1)}, \ldots, \underline{x}^{(n-1)}, \underline{x}^{(n)})$ of length $8n + k$ bytes with $0 \leq k < 8$ by DES is defined as follows:

1. A nonsecret and randomly chosen 8-byte $\underline{y}^{(-1)}$ *initial chaining value* (ICV) prefixes the ciphertext.

2. The XOR of the ith block of plaintext $\underline{x}^{(i)}$, $0 \leq i < n$, with the $(i-1)$st block of ciphertext $\underline{y}^{(i-1)}$, enciphered by DES, becomes the ith block of ciphertext:

$$\text{Block Chained DES} : \underline{x}^{(i)} \rightarrow \underline{y}^{(i)} = \text{DES}_{\underline{k}}\{\underline{x}^{(i)} + \underline{y}^{(i-1)}\}, \qquad 0 \leq i < n.$$

3. If the length $8n + k$ of the plaintext is a multiple of 8 bytes ($k = 0$), the encipherment is complete; otherwise, the *final block* $\underline{x}^{(n)}$ of k-bytes is enciphered by first re-enciphering the $(n-1)$st block of ciphertext

$$\underline{z}^{(n-1)} = \text{DES}_{\underline{k}}\{\underline{y}^{(n-1)}\}$$

and thereafter XORing the leftmost k bytes of the result with $\underline{x}^{(n-1)}$

$$\underline{y}^{(n)} = \underline{x}^{(n)} + \text{Left}_k[\underline{z}^{(n-1)}]$$

where

$$\text{Left}_k[w_0, w_1, \ldots, w_{63}] = (w_0, w_1, \ldots, w_{8k-1})$$

On pages 275–277 of Konheim [1981] it is verified that record chaining is reversible and examples of chaining are given.

9.7 IS DES A RANDOM MAPPING?

In Section 10 of Chapter 8 the mappings of the set $\mathcal{Z}_m = \{0, 1, \ldots, m-1\}$ were described.

Proposition 9.1: If F is a randomly chosen one-to-one mapping of $\mathcal{Z}_m$ and Z is a randomly chosen element of $\mathcal{Z}_m$, then

9.1a The probability that Z belongs to an n-cycle in $\dfrac{1}{m}$ and

9.1b The average length of the cycle containing Z is $(m+1)/2$.

Proof: First an explanation of what is meant by "random"; there are $m!$ permutations of the elements of $\mathcal{Z}_m$. By the phrase "choose a mapping F randomly", we mean that the permutation F is selected with probability $1/m!$. Similarly, by the phrase "choose $Z \in \mathcal{Z}_m$ randomly", we mean that a particular $Z \in \mathcal{Z}_m$ is selected with probability $1/m$.

Let L denote the length of the cycle of F containing Z. As Z is to be any of m values, there are $(m - 1)!$ permutations of the remaining $m - 1$ elements so that

- The probability that $F(Z) = Z$ (meaning Z belongs to a 1-cycle) is $\Pr\{L = 1\} = (m - 1)!/m! = 1/m$.
- The probability that the nth iterate of F satisfies $F^n(Z) \begin{cases} \neq Z, & \text{if } n = 1 \\ = Z & \text{if } n = 2 \end{cases}$ is

$$\Pr\{L = 2\} = \frac{(m - 1)(m - 2)!}{m!} = \frac{1}{m}.$$

This argument can be extended yielding $\Pr\{L = r\} = \dfrac{1}{m}$.

Next, we consider the analog of **Proposition 9.1** when F is not necessarily a one-to-one mapping of the elements of $\mathcal{Z}_m$.

As observed in Chapter 8, the orbits of mappings that are not one-to-one are composed of cycles with *tails* (Fig. 9.6). As the orbit of z must contain some repetition, we have $F^{(n)}(z) = F^{(j)}(z)$ with $0 \leq j < n$, where n is the first such repetition.

Proposition 9.2: If F is a randomly chosen mapping of $\mathcal{Z}_m$ and Z is a randomly chosen element of $\mathcal{Z}_m$, then

9.2a The probability that the first repeated element in the orbit $Z \to F(Z) \to F^{(2)}(Z) \to \cdots$ occurs at position $L = n$, $F^{(n)}(Z) = F^{(j)}(Z)$ for $0 \leq j < n$ is

$$\Pr\{L = n\} = \frac{n}{m} \prod_{i=0}^{n-1} \left(1 - \frac{i}{m}\right)$$

$$\Pr\{L > n\} = \prod_{i=0}^{n-1} \left(1 - \frac{i}{m}\right)$$

9.2b The expected value of L is asymptotically $\sqrt{0.5\pi m}$ as $m \to \infty$.

Proof: If $L = n$ then $Z, F^{(1)}(Z), \ldots, F^{(n-1)}(Z)$ are all distinct elements of $\mathcal{Z}_m$:

- There are $m(m - 1)(m - 2) \cdots (m - (n - 1))$ possible choices for these elements;
- As $F^{(n)}(z) \in \{Z, F^{(1)}(Z), \ldots, F^{(n-1)}(Z)\}$, it must be one of n values;
- Each of the values of $F(Z)$ with $Z \notin \{Z, F^{(1)}(Z), \ldots, F^{(n-1)}(Z)\}$ may be chosen in m ways;

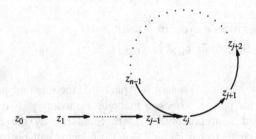

Figure 9.6 An orbit with a tail.

which gives

$$\Pr\{L = n\} = \frac{1}{m^m}[m \times (m-1) \times \cdots \times (m-(n-1)) \times n \times m^{m-n}],$$

proving **Proposition 9.2a**. The expectation of L is

$$E\{L\} = \sum_{n=1}^{m-1} \Pr\{L > n\} = \sum_{n=1}^{m-1} \prod_{n=0}^{m-1} \left(1 - \frac{i}{m}\right).$$

If $\frac{i}{m}$ is small, so that the approximation $1 - \frac{i}{m} \approx e^{-\frac{i}{m}}$.

$$\prod_{i=1}^{n-1}\left(1 - \frac{i}{m}\right) \approx c^{\frac{n^2}{2m}}.$$

This suggests that as $m \to \infty$

$$E\{L\} \approx \sum_{n=1}^{m-1} e^{-\frac{n^2}{2m}} \approx \sqrt{m} \sum_{s \in \{\sqrt{m}, \sqrt{2m}...\}} m^{-\frac{1}{2}} e^{\frac{s^2}{2}}.$$

The last summation approximates the Riemann integral $\int_0^\infty e^{-\frac{x^2}{2}} dx$, which gives Proposition **9.2b**. To prove that the approximation of the product by the exponential is valid, the summation for $E\{L\}$ is divided into two parts Σ_1 and Σ_2; the terms with $n \le B$ are included in Σ_1 and tail terms with $n < B$ in Σ_2.

The approximation is valid for the terms in Σ_1; the second sum Σ_2 converges to 0.

9.8 DES IN THE OUTPUT-FEEDBACK MODE (OFB)

DES may be used to generate a key stream to be XORed to plaintext. DES is the *output feedback mode* (OFB) (Fig. 9.7) and starts with

1. A *nonsecret initial seed* $\underline{z}^{(0)} = (z_0^{(0)}, z_1^{(0)}, \ldots, z_{63}^{(0)}) \in \mathcal{Z}_{64,2}$;
2. A key $\underline{k} = (k_0, k_1, \ldots, k_{55}) \in \mathcal{Z}_{56,2}$; and
3. A *feedback parameter* m with $1 \le m \le 64$.

The key stream $\{\underline{z}^{(i)} : 1 \le i < \infty\}$ is defined by

$$\underline{z}^{(i)} = \text{Right}_{64-m}(\underline{z}^{(i-1)}), \text{Left}_m \text{DES}_{\underline{k}}\{\underline{z}^{(i-1)}\}$$

where Right_m and Left_m take the *rightmost* and *leftmost* m bits of $\underline{w}$:

$$\text{Right}_m(w_0, w_1, \ldots, w_{63}) = (w_{64-m}, w_{65-m}, \ldots, w_{63}) \in \mathcal{Z}_{m,2}$$

$$\text{Left}_m(w_0, w_1, \ldots, w_{63}) = (w_0, w_1, \ldots, w_{m-1}) \in \mathcal{Z}_{m,2}$$

is XORed to plaintext to create the ciphertext.

When $m = 64$, the output-feedback mode mapping depicted in Fig. 9.7 is a one-to-one mapping of $\mathcal{Z}_{64,2}$ onto itself. The average cycle length is 2^{63}.

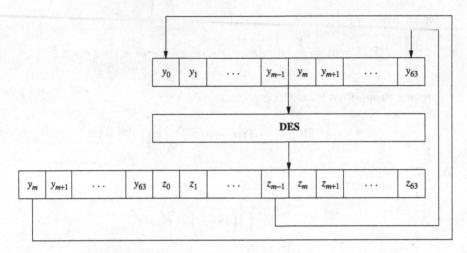

Figure 9.7   Output feedback mode.

When $m < 64$, the OFB mapping is not one to one and its cycle length is $O(2^{32})$, an observation first made by Davies and Parkin [1982]. This means that in a large ciphertext file with $m = 1$, we are likely to see the same key bit used to encipher different bits of the plaintext. And why should any value of $m < 64$ be used?

9.9   CRYPTANALYSIS OF DES

The exportation of American technology is regulated by the Bureau of Export Administration: Office of Strategic Trade and Foreign Policy, an agency within the U.S. Department of Commerce. A list of products covered by 15 CFR chapter VII, subchapter C may be found on the Web page www.bxa.gov; included are commercial encryption devices.

The LUCIFER cryptographic facility was incorporated into the IBM Liberty Banking System and a patent application protecting the technology was filed by IBM. United States Patent Office rules require a patent to be first filed in the United States and reviewed by the Patent Office before foreign patent coverage can be sought. In cases where the publication of an application or the granting of a patent would be detrimental to national security, the Commissioner of Patents may issue a *secrecy order* to stop the patent process. This

1. Requires that the invention be kept secret,
2. Withholds the publication of the application or the grant of the patent for such period as the national interest requires,
3. Forbids the dissemination of material related to the patent by all parties, and
4. Restricts filing of foreign patent applications.

The owner of an application that has been placed under a secrecy order has a right to appeal the order to the Secretary of Commerce, 35 U.S.C. 181. If no secrecy order is issued in the six months after the submission of a U.S. patent application, patent applications may be filed outside the United States.

IBM's patent application did not result, in a secrecy order, probably because it dealt with a "banking system" and did not describe the encryption process in the terms NSA is familiar with. IBM filed in France six months later and was granted a patent.

Up to this point, NSA had been the undisputed center of cryptographic competence in the United States. As the cat was out of the bag, so to speak, NSA decided that it would have to "influence" the direction of commercial cryptography rather than forbid it. The IBM Corporation developed a follow-on to LUCIFER in response to encouragement from NSA, and submitted the "improved" algorithm to NBS for certification as a national standard.

During the design of DES, certain desirable properties of S-boxes were formulated. With the exception of three criteria fisted below, they have never been made public at the request of NSA.

C1. No S-box is either a linear or affine[1] function.

C2. S-box constraints

    C2a. Changing one bit in the input of an S-box resulting in at least two output bits changing;

    C2b. If two inputs to an S-box differ in the middle two bits, their outputs must be different by at least two bits [Coppersmith, 1993];

    C2c. If two inputs to an S-box differ in their first two bits and agree on their last two, their two outputs must differ;

    C2d. For any nonzero 6-bit difference between S-box inputs, no more than 32 pairs of inputs exhibiting that difference may result in the same output difference.

A *twiddle* of a vector $\underline{x}$ is a vector $\underline{x} + \underline{y}$ that differs from $\underline{x}$ in at least one component. If the length of the XOR is small, say $|\text{ROM}[\underline{x}] + \text{ROM}[\underline{x} + \underline{y}]| < 2$, a twiddle could conceivably propagate in many rounds so that $|T(\underline{x}) + T(\underline{x} + \underline{y})|$ might also be small. If many different twiddles are present, they might lead to a determination of several key bits. During design of DES, twiddles were *not* excluded until it was discovered that they could be used as indicated above.

Searching the block cipher parameters for good *differential changes* – the new term for twiddles – and using them for cryptanalysis is the basic idea of Bilham's and Shamir's *differential* cryptanalysis [Bilham and Shamir, 1993], the closely related *linear cryptanalysis* of Matsui [1994], which searches for good linear approximations to the ROMs, and the recent paper by Bilham [1995].

---

[1]An S-box $F(x)$ is *linear* in $\underline{x} = (x_0, x_1, x_2, x_3, x_4, x_5)$ if

$$F(\underline{x}) = \begin{pmatrix} y_0 \\ y_1 \\ y_2 \\ y_3 \end{pmatrix} = \begin{pmatrix} c_{0,0} & c_{0,1} & c_{0,2} & c_{0,3} & c_{0,4} & c_{0,5} \\ c_{1,0} & c_{1,1} & c_{1,2} & c_{1,3} & c_{1,4} & c_{1,5} \\ c_{2,0} & c_{2,1} & c_{2,2} & c_{2,3} & c_{2,4} & c_{2,5} \\ c_{3,0} & c_{3,1} & c_{3,2} & c_{3,3} & c_{3,4} & c_{3,5} \end{pmatrix} \begin{pmatrix} x_0 \\ x_1 \\ x_2 \\ x_3 \\ x_4 \\ x_5 \end{pmatrix}$$

F is *affine* if

$$F(\underline{x}) = \begin{pmatrix} y_0 \\ y_1 \\ y_2 \\ y_3 \end{pmatrix} = \begin{pmatrix} b_0 \\ b_1 \\ b_2 \\ b_3 \end{pmatrix} + \begin{pmatrix} c_{0,0} & c_{0,1} & c_{0,2} & c_{0,3} & c_{0,4} & c_{0,5} \\ c_{1,0} & c_{1,1} & c_{1,2} & c_{1,3} & c_{1,4} & c_{1,5} \\ c_{2,0} & c_{2,1} & c_{2,2} & c_{2,3} & c_{2,4} & c_{2,5} \\ c_{3,0} & c_{3,1} & c_{3,2} & c_{3,3} & c_{3,4} & c_{3,5} \end{pmatrix} \begin{pmatrix} x_0 \\ x_1 \\ x_2 \\ x_3 \\ x_4 \\ x_5 \end{pmatrix}$$

C3. The S-boxes were chosen to minimize the differences between the number of 1's and 0's when any single bit is held constant.

This is essentially the criterion discovered by Matsui and the basis for the measure of nonlinearity.

As IBM did not reveal the design principles, there was the suspicion that Big-Blue and NSA had conspired to put a trap into the system. DES has been analyzed over the past 25 years and no *systemic* weakness has been found [Schneier, 1996]. Biham and Shamir [1992, 1993] wrote

> The replacement of the order of the eight DES S-boxes (without changing their values) also makes DBS much weaker: DES with 16 rounds of a particular order is breakable in about 2^{38} steps. DES with random S-boxes is shown very easy to break. Even a minimal change of one entry of one of the DES S-boxes can make DES easier to break.

Of course, Bilham and Shamir may be wrong and, in retrospect, the key length of 56 bits seems to be inappropriate.

DES and the controversy stimulated a significant amount of research in the academic community on cryptography. It has produced an extensive literature dealing with the design of S-boxes, in particular with regarding the *nonlinearity* of an S-box [Nyberg, 1992; Seberry and Zheng, 1993; Charnes and Piepzryk, 1993; Detombe and Tavares, 1993; Seberry et al., 1994, 1995; O'Connor, 1995a, b].

9.10   DIFFERENTIAL CRYPTANALYSIS

Suppose two plaintexts are enciphered by S-box S[0] with the same key.

$$\underline{y}_1 = S[0](\underline{x}_1 + \underline{k}), \qquad \underline{y}_2 = S[0](\underline{x}_2 + \underline{k}).$$

We conclude that

$$\underline{y}_1 + \underline{y}_2 = S[0](\underline{x}_1 + \underline{k}) + S[0](\underline{x}_2 + \underline{k})$$

and write this last relationship as

$$S[0] : \Delta \underline{x} \rightarrow \Delta \underline{y}$$

where

$$\text{(Input XOR)} \quad \Delta x \equiv \underline{x}_1 + \underline{x}_2 = (\underline{x}_1 + \underline{k}) + (\underline{x}_2 + \underline{k})$$
$$\text{(Output XOR)} \quad \Delta \underline{y} \equiv \underline{y}_1 + \underline{y}_2$$

How much of the 6-bit key is revealed by corresponding pairs of plain- and cipher-text $(\underline{x}_i, \underline{y}_i)$ $(i = 1, 2)$ enciphered by S-box S[0] with the same *un*known key? That is, how many solutions are there to

$$\underline{y}_1 = S[0](\underline{x}_1 + \underline{k}), \qquad \underline{y}_2 = S[0](\underline{x}_2 + \underline{k})$$

given

$$\Delta \underline{x} \equiv \underline{x}_1 + \underline{x}_2, \qquad \Delta \underline{y} \equiv \underline{y}_1 + \underline{y}_2.$$

Define

$$\mathcal{D}(\Delta \underline{x}, \Delta \underline{y}) \equiv \{(\underline{z}_1, \underline{z}_2) : \Delta \underline{x} = \underline{z}_1 + \underline{z}_2, \Delta \underline{y} = S[0](\underline{z}_1) + S[0](\underline{z}_2)\}.$$

A pair (z_1, z_2) in $\mathcal{D}(\Delta x, \Delta y)$ determines a possible unknown key by setting

$$\underline{k} = \underline{x}_1 + \underline{z}_1$$

If the size of $\mathcal{D}(\Delta x, \Delta y)$ is much smaller than $64 = 2^6$, then the *differentials* $(\Delta x, \Delta y)$ reveal a great deal of the key. Of course, the encipherment process described above uses only one S-box and it will be necessary to extend this to the full DES encipherment process. This is the principle of *differential cryptanalysis*, a *known corresponding plain/ciphertext* attack whose objective is to attempt to identify the *un*known key from corresponding plain/ciphertext differentials $(\Delta x, \Delta y)$ enciphered with the same key.

Tables 9.20 and 9.21 list the size of the set $|\mathcal{D}(\Delta x, \Delta y)|$ for all pairs of Input/Output XOR $(\Delta x, \Delta y)$. A row is labeled by the 6-bit Input XOR $\Delta(x)$ (as two hex digits), a column

TABLE 9.20 $|\mathcal{D}(\Delta x, \Delta y)|$ for S-Box S[0]

Input XOR						Output XOR of S[0]										
	0	1	2	3	4	5	6	7	8	9	A	B	C	D	E	F
00	64	0	0	0	0	0	0	0	0	0	0	0	0	0	0	0
01	0	0	0	6	0	2	4	4	0	10	12	4	10	6	2	4
02	0	0	0	8	0	4	4	4	0	6	8	6	12	6	4	2
03	14	4	2	2	10	6	4	2	6	4	4	0	2	2	2	0
04	0	0	0	6	0	10	10	6	0	4	6	4	2	8	6	2
05	4	8	6	2	2	4	4	2	0	4	4	0	12	2	4	6
06	0	4	2	4	8	2	6	2	8	4	4	2	4	2	0	12
07	2	4	10	4	0	4	8	4	2	4	8	2	2	2	4	4
08	0	0	0	12	0	8	8	4	0	6	2	8	8	2	2	4
09	10	2	4	0	2	4	6	0	2	2	8	0	10	0	2	12
0A	0	8	6	2	2	8	6	0	6	4	6	0	4	0	2	10
0B	2	4	0	10	2	2	4	0	2	6	2	6	6	4	2	12
0C	0	0	0	8	0	6	6	0	0	6	6	4	6	6	14	2
0D	6	6	4	8	4	8	2	6	0	6	4	6	0	2	0	2
0E	0	4	8	8	6	6	4	0	6	6	4	0	0	4	0	8
0F	2	0	2	4	4	6	4	2	4	8	2	2	2	6	8	8
10	0	0	0	0	0	0	2	14	0	6	6	12	4	6	8	6
11	6	8	2	4	6	4	8	6	4	0	6	6	0	4	0	0
12	0	8	4	2	6	6	4	6	6	4	2	6	6	0	4	0
13	2	4	4	6	2	0	4	6	2	0	6	8	4	6	4	0
14	0	8	8	0	10	0	4	2	8	2	2	4	4	8	4	0
15	0	4	6	4	2	2	4	10	6	2	0	10	0	4	6	4
16	0	8	10	8	0	2	2	6	10	2	0	2	0	6	2	6
17	4	4	6	0	10	6	0	2	4	4	4	6	6	6	2	0
18	0	6	6	0	8	4	2	2	2	4	6	8	6	6	2	2
19	2	6	2	4	0	8	4	6	10	4	0	4	2	8	4	0
1A	0	6	4	0	4	6	6	6	6	2	2	0	4	4	6	8
1B	4	4	2	4	10	6	6	4	6	2	2	4	2	2	4	2
1C	0	10	10	6	6	0	0	12	6	4	0	0	2	4	4	0
1D	4	2	4	0	8	0	0	2	10	0	2	6	6	6	14	0
1E	0	2	6	0	14	2	0	0	6	4	10	8	2	2	6	2
1F	2	4	10	6	2	2	2	8	6	8	0	0	0	4	6	4

by the Output XOR $\Delta(y)$ (as two hex digits) for the S-box $S[0]$; for example, the entry in row $1A = (01\ 1010)$ and column $C = (1100)$ is 4.

Note that

- The sum of the entries in a row is 64, the average is 4;
- The distribution of values in a row is *not* uniform; and
- If $\Delta\underline{x} \neq \underline{0}$; then if $(\underline{z}_1, \underline{z}_2)$ is in $\mathcal{D}(\Delta\underline{x}, \Delta\underline{y})$, then so is the pair $(\underline{z}_2, \underline{z}_1)$.

Example 9.3

Table 9.22 is derived from the row 34 data in Table 9.21 and the S-box description of $S[0]$ in Table 9.4; it lists the input pairs $(\underline{z}_1, \underline{z}_2)$ (as two hex digits) that satisfy

$$\Delta\underline{x} = \underline{z}_1 + \underline{z}_2 = (1, 1, 0, 1, 0, 0) = 34 \qquad \text{(Input XOR)}$$

TABLE 9.21 $\ |\mathcal{D}(\Delta\underline{x}, \Delta\underline{y})|$ **for S-Box S[0]**

Input XOR	Output XOR of S[0]															
	0	1	2	3	4	5	6	7	8	9	A	B	C	D	E	F
20	0	0	0	10	0	12	8	2	0	6	4	4	4	2	0	12
21	0	4	2	4	4	8	10	0	4	4	10	0	4	0	2	8
22	10	4	6	2	2	8	2	2	2	2	6	0	4	0	4	10
23	0	4	4	8	0	2	6	0	6	6	2	10	2	4	0	10
24	10	0	0	2	2	2	2	0	14	14	2	0	2	6	2	4
25	6	4	4	12	4	4	4	10	2	2	2	0	4	2	2	2
26	0	0	4	10	10	10	2	4	0	4	6	4	4	4	2	0
27	0	4	2	0	2	4	2	0	4	8	0	4	8	8	4	4
28	12	2	2	8	2	6	12	0	0	2	6	0	4	0	6	2
29	4	2	2	10	0	2	4	0	0	14	10	2	4	6	0	4
2A	4	2	4	6	0	2	8	2	2	14	2	6	2	6	2	2
2B	12	2	2	2	4	6	6	2	0	2	6	2	6	0	8	4
2C	4	2	2	4	0	2	10	4	2	2	4	8	8	4	2	6
2D	6	2	6	2	8	4	4	4	2	4	6	0	8	2	0	6
2E	6	6	2	2	0	2	4	6	4	0	6	2	12	2	6	4
2F	2	2	2	2	2	6	8	8	2	4	4	6	8	2	4	2
30	0	4	6	0	12	6	2	2	8	2	4	4	6	2	2	4
31	4	8	2	10	2	2	2	2	6	0	0	2	2	4	10	8
32	4	2	6	4	4	2	2	4	6	6	4	8	2	2	8	0
33	4	4	6	2	10	8	4	2	4	0	2	2	4	6	2	4
34	0	8	16	6	2	0	0	12	6	0	0	0	0	8	0	6
35	2	2	4	0	8	0	0	0	14	4	6	8	0	2	14	0
36	2	6	2	2	8	0	2	2	4	2	6	8	6	4	10	0
37	2	2	12	4	2	4	4	10	4	4	2	6	0	2	2	4
38	0	6	2	2	2	0	2	2	4	6	4	4	4	6	10	10
39	6	2	2	4	12	6	4	8	4	0	2	4	2	4	4	0
3A	6	4	6	4	6	8	0	6	2	2	6	2	2	6	4	0
3B	2	6	4	0	0	2	4	6	4	6	8	6	4	4	6	2
3C	0	10	4	0	12	0	4	2	6	0	4	12	4	4	2	0
3D	0	8	6	2	2	6	0	8	4	4	0	4	0	12	4	4
3E	4	8	2	2	2	4	4	14	4	2	0	2	0	8	4	4
3F	4	8	4	2	4	0	2	4	4	2	4	8	8	6	2	2

for all S-box S[0] Output XORs $\Delta y \neq (0, 0, 0, 0)$ (as two hex digits) and is constructed as follows:

- For each pair of input values to S-box S[0], $(z_0, z_1, z_2, z_3, z_4, z_5)$ and $(z'_0, z'_1, z'_2, z'_3, z'_4, z'_5)$ for which $\underline{z}_1 + \underline{z}_2 = (1, 1, 0, 1, 0, 0) = (z_0 + z'_0, z_1 + z'_1, z_2 + z'_2, z_3 + z'_3, z_4 + z'_4, z_5 + z'_5)$, compute
- $\underline{y}_1 = S[0](z_0, z_1, z_2, z_3, z_4, z_5)$ and $\underline{y}_2 = S[0] (z'_0, z'_1, z'_2, z'_3, z'_4, z'_5)$.

There is an entry (in hex)

$$\begin{pmatrix} z_0, z_1, z_2, z_3, z_4, z_5 \\ z'_0, z'_1, z'_2, z'_3, z'_4, z'_5 \end{pmatrix}$$

in Table 9.13C provided $\Delta y = \underline{y}_1 + \underline{y}_2$. For example,

- Table 9.21 shows that there are 8 pairs $(\underline{z}_1 + \underline{z}_2)$ if $\Delta \underline{y} = (0, 0, 0, 1) = 1$;
- The entry $\begin{pmatrix} 03 \\ 37 \end{pmatrix}$ in Table 9.22 corresponds to

$$\underline{z}_1 = (0, 0, 0, 0, 1, 1), \underline{z}_2 = (1, 1, 0, 1, 1, 1) \text{ with sum } (1, 1, 0, 1, 0, 0);$$

- Table 9.4 shows the (row 1, column 1) S-box S[0] entry for $\underline{z}_1 = (0, 0, 0, 0, 1, 1)$ is $15 = (1, 1, 1, 1)$;
- Table 9.4 shows the (row 3, column 11) S-box S[0] entry for $\underline{z}_2 = (1, 1, 0, 1, 1, 1)$ is $14 = (1, 1, 1, 0)$;
- The sum of these two S-box S[0]-entries is $1 = (1, 1, 1, 1) + (1, 1, 1, 0)$.

leading to the entry $\begin{pmatrix} 03 \\ 37 \end{pmatrix}$ in the row corresponding to $\Delta y = 1$.

TABLE 9.22 Input Pairs $(\underline{z}_1, \underline{z}_2)$ Satisfying $\underline{z}_1 + \underline{z}_2 = (1, 1, 0, 1, 0, 0)$

$\Delta \underline{y}$					$\underline{z}_1 + \underline{z}_2 = (1, 1, 0, 1, 0, 0)$											
1	03	0F	1E	1F	2A	2B	37	3B								
	37	3B	2A	2B	1E	1F	03	0F								
2	04	05	0E	11	12	14	1A	1B	20	25	26	2E	2F	30	31	3A
	30	31	3A	25	26	20	2E	2F	14	11	12	1A	1B	04	05	0E
3	01	02	15	21	35	36										
	35	36	25	15	11	10										
4	13	27														
	27	13														
7	00	08	0D	17	18	1D	23	29	2C	34	39	3C				
	34	3C	39	23	2C	29	17	1D	18	00	0D	08				
8	09	0C	19	2D	38	3D										
	3D	38	2D	19	0C	09										
D	06	10	16	1C	22	24	28	32								
	32	24	22	28	16	12	1C	06								
F	07	0A	0B	33	3E	3F										
	33	3E	3F	07	0A	0B										

Example 9.3 (continued)

Suppose we have

- $\underline{x}_1 = (1, 1, 1, 1, 1, 1)$, $\underline{x}_2 = (0, 0, 1, 0, 1, 0)$, $\Delta\underline{x} = (1, 1, 0, 1, 0, 0)$ and
- $\underline{y}_1 = S[0](\underline{x}_1 + \underline{k}) = (0, 1, 1, 0)$, $\underline{y}_2 = S[0](\underline{x}_2 + \underline{k}) = (0, 0, 1, 0)$.

There is essentially one entry in Table 9.22 and it shows that

- $\underline{z}_1 = (0, 1, 0, 0, 1, 1) = 13$, $\underline{z}_2 = (1, 0, 0, 1, 1, 1) = 27$ satisfies $\underline{z}_1 + \underline{z}_2 = (1, 1, 0, 1, 0, 0) = 34$ and
- There are *only* two possible keys $\underline{k} = (1, 0, 1, 1, 0, 0) = 2C$ and $\underline{k} = (0, 1, 1, 0, 0, 0) = 18$.

The inference of the key in *Example 9.3* can be generalized to a one-round characteristic of DES as shown in Figure 9.8 where

$$\mathbf{L}(\underline{y}_i) = \mathbf{R}(\underline{x}_i) \qquad \mathbf{R}(\underline{y}_i) = \mathbf{L}(\underline{x}_i) + \mathbf{F}[\mathbf{R}(\underline{x}_i)], \quad i = 1, 2$$

$$\Delta\underline{x} = \underline{x}_1 + \underline{x}_2 \qquad \Delta\underline{y} = \underline{y}_1 + \underline{y}_2$$

$$\mathbf{L}(\Delta\underline{x}) = \mathbf{L}(\underline{x}_1) + \mathbf{L}(\underline{x}_2) \qquad \mathbf{R}(\Delta\underline{x}) = \mathbf{R}(\underline{x}_1) + \mathbf{R}(\underline{x}_2)$$

$$\mathbf{L}(\Delta\underline{y}) = \mathbf{L}(\underline{y}_1) + \mathbf{L}(\underline{y}_2) \qquad \mathbf{R}(\Delta\underline{y}) = \mathbf{R}(\underline{y}_1) + \mathbf{R}(\underline{y}_2).$$

The inputs to the one-round DES characteristic are

- The XOR $\Delta\underline{x}$ of plaintext $\underline{x}_1$ and $\underline{x}_2$ and
- The XOR $\Delta\underline{y}$ of the ciphertext $\underline{y}_1 = DES_{\underline{k}}\{\underline{x}_1\}$ and $\underline{y}_2 = DES_{\underline{k}}\{\underline{x}_2\}$.

The probability of the one-round DES characteristic is the conditional probability

$$\Pr\{\underline{x}_1, \underline{x}_2, \underline{y}_1, \underline{y}_2 / \Delta\underline{x}, \Delta\underline{y}\}$$

computed assuming a uniform distribution on plaintext and key.

Note that the difference $\mathbf{R}(\Delta\underline{y})$ depends on

- The key,
- The plaintext $(\mathbf{R}(\underline{x}_1), \mathbf{R}(\underline{x}_2))$ and
- The plaintext difference $\mathbf{L}(\Delta\underline{x})$.

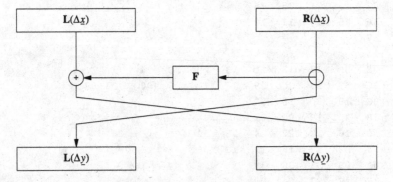

Figure 9.8 One-round DES generic characteristic.

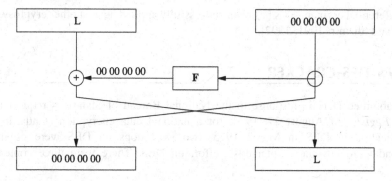

Figure 9.9   A one-round DES characteristic of probability 1.

Differential cryptanalysis infers the key by computing the probability of a specified pair of XORs (Δx, Δy) assuming the undetermined variables are chosen independently with the distribution.

Example 9.4
A one-round DES characteristic of probability 1 is shown in Figure 9.9. Table 9.20 shows that if the input XOR is c, then the output XOR is E for 14 of the 64 possible keys.

Example 9.5
A one-round DES characteristic of probability 14/64 is shown in Figure 9.10. By combining the one-round characteristics in *Examples 9.4* and *9.5*, we obtain *Example 9.6*.

Example 9.6
A two-round DES characteristic of probability 14/64 is shown in Figure 9.11.

Example 9.7
A three-round DES characteristic of probability $(14/64)^2$ is shown in Figure 9.12. This is as far as we will go in the exposition. The complete details are to be found in Bilham and Shamir [1993]. Differential cryptanalysis would offer a significant improvement over exhaustive key search for DES if there were fewer than 16 rounds. With 16 rounds, a time complexity of 2^{37} uses 2^{36} plain/ciphertext pairs pruned from larger pool of 2^{47} pairs. Nevertheless, differential cryptanalysis is the first and only attack on DES with complexity less than 2^{55}.

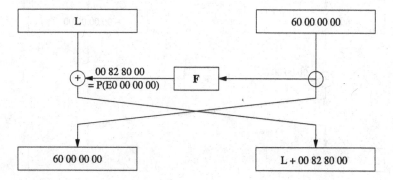

Figure 9.10   A one-round DES characteristic of probability 14/64.

Differential cryptanalysis has been successfully applied against other cryptosystems [Bilham and Shamir, 1991, 1992].

9.11 THE EFS DES-CRACKER

IBM's submitted DES in response to the National Bureau of Standards request in the *Federal Register* of August 27, 1974, for a national data encryption standard. After the publication in DES in March 1975, two workshops on DES were organized, the second to review the cryptanalysis effort on DES. There were three contentious areas:

1. Did DES contain any hidden *trap doors* whose knowledge might permit the decipherment of DES ciphertext without the key?

2. What design principles were used in DES?

3. Why was the key length chosen to be 56 bits?

Very few answers were forthcoming. IBM does business throughout the world and feels itself required to abide by the wishes of the U.S. Government. In any event $2^{56} = 72,057,594,037,927,936$ seemed like to large a number of key trial and the cost of building a machine required to perform key trial seemed to make the possibility remote.

A practical architecture for a *DES-cracker* with custom chips was proposed in 1993 by Michael Wiener of Bell Northern Research [Wiener, 1993]. The *Electronic Frontier Foundation* (EFF) founded in 1990 is a nonprofit public-interest group of "passionate people lawyers, technologists, volunteers, and visionaries working to protect your digital rights." The EFF seeks to educate individuals, organizations, companies, and governments about the issues that arise when computer and communications technologies change. The EFF sponsored the design and assembling of a DES-cracker [EFF, 1998].

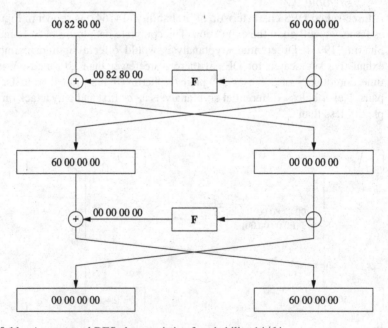

Figure 9.11 A two-round DES characteristic of probability 14/64.

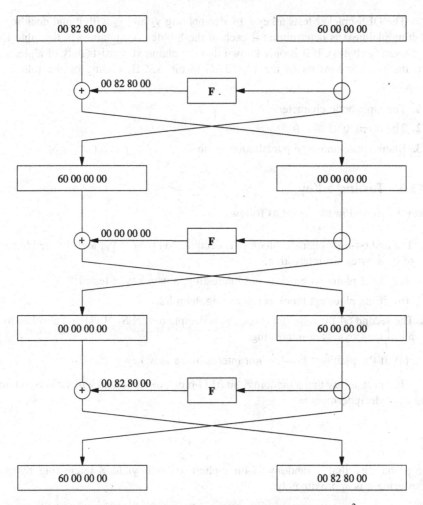

Figure 9.12 A three-round DES characteristic of probability $(14/64)^2$.

9.11.1 The Architecture

The basic component of the DES-cracker is the *search unit*, which has hardware including two 64-bit ciphertext registers and a 56-bit key register. The DES-cracker contains

1. 24 search units contained within a *custom chip*;
2. 64 customer chips mounted on a *board*;
3. 64 boards in each *chassis*; and
4. two chassis.

9.11.2 Key Search Algorithm

The ciphertext registers contain two 64-bit ciphertext blocks

$$\underline{y}_1 = \text{DES}_{\underline{k}^{(*)}}\{\underline{x}_1\} \qquad \underline{y}_2 = \text{DES}_{\underline{k}^{(*)}}\{\underline{x}_2\},$$

whose plaintexts $\underline{x}_1$, $\underline{x}_2$ and key $\underline{k}^{(*)}$ are unknown.

The DES-cracker tests a key $\underline{k}$ by deciphering $\underline{y}_1$ and $\underline{y}_2$ with it and deciding if the resulting plaintext is determining if each of the 8 bytes is contained in the table INTER of *interesting* (bytes). If it is only known that the plaintext consists only of alphanumeric text, the INTER consists of the EBCIDIC (8-bit ASCII) coding of the following 69 characters:

1. The alphabetic characters a b $\cdots$ z A B $\cdots$ Z
2. The digits 0 1 $\cdots$ 9
3. Blank space and nine punctuation symbols . , ? ; : ( )] [.

9.11.3   Testing a Key

A key $\underline{k}$ is tested in two steps as follows.

S1. The first 64-bit ciphertext block $\underline{y}_1$ is deciphered $\mathrm{DES}_{\underline{k}}^{-1}\{\underline{y}_1\}$ and checked to see if all of its 8 bytes are interesting:

(a) If the plaintext block is *not* interesting, a new key is tested;

(b) If the plaintext block is interesting, then S2.

S2. The second 64-bit ciphertext block $\underline{y}_2$ is deciphered $\mathrm{DES}_{\underline{k}}^{-1}\{\underline{y}_2\}$ and checked to see if all of its 8 bytes are interesting:

(a) If the plaintext block is *not* interesting, a new key is tested.

The probability that a random 8-bit (0,1)-block of ciphertext will yield an interesting byte upon decipherment is

$$\frac{69}{256} \approx \frac{1}{4}.$$

The probability that a random 64-bit ciphertexts will yield 8 interesting bytes upon decipherment is approximately

$$\frac{1}{4^8} = \frac{1}{2^{16}}.$$

The probability that two random 64-bit ciphertexts will yield 16 interesting bytes upon decipherment is approximately

$$\frac{1}{4^{16}} = \frac{1}{2^{32}}.$$

If we assume that only one of the 2^{56} keys will give the true plaintext; the number of keys that will pass both steps S1 and S2 is about 2^{40}. These keys will require further testing using additional ciphertext.

A search unit performs one decipherment in 16 clock cycles. Since the clock runs at 40 MHz (40 million cycles/second) a search unit can test 2.5 million keys/second. A board therefore tests 4.8 billion keys/second and the DES-cracker tests 92,160,000,000 keys/second. On the average only half of the $2^{56} = 72,057,594,037,927,936$ keys need to be tested before a match is discovered.

The cost to build of the DES-cracker was $220,000. Its proud parents announced on July 17, 1998, that it had found a DES key in 3 days.

9.12   WHAT NOW?

If the key length were 2^{64} it would have taken the DES-cracker 768 days; if the key length were 2×56, the DES-cracker would have to work a *very* long time to find the key. This points out the power of exponentiation and the advantage enjoyed by the designer of a cryptosystem over the cryptanalyst. Adding one bit to the key doubles the time for exhaustive search. If the designers of DES had been careless and there was some intrinsic weakness, or a trap-door, such a statement would not necessarily be true.

Walter Tuchman of IBM's Kingston Facility was a designer and implementor of DES. He also proposed *triple DES* [FIPS PUB 46-3, 1999] defined by[2]

$$DES3 : \underline{x} \to \underline{y} = DES_{\underline{k_1}}\{DES_{\underline{k_2}}^{-1}\{DES_{\underline{k_3}}\{\underline{x}\}\}\}.$$

If $\underline{k_1} = \underline{k_2}$, DES3 reduces to ordinary DES.

The U.S. Munitions List is part of the secondary regulations (the International Traffic in Arms Regulations or ITAR) that defines which defence articles and services are subject to licensing. Cryptographic products are included in the products (Category XIII – Auxiliary Military Equipment) regulated by ITAR.

Current export rules do not permit the export of DES3 to certain countries. An article in the *Wall Street Journal* (September 17, 1998) entitled "Encryption Export Rules Relaxed" claims that the current 56-bit limitation will be relaxed, asserting

> *U.S. vendors also won more freedom to export network-encryption products used primarily by Internet-service provides and communication carriers.*

In "Draft Encryption Export Regulations" (dated November 23, 1999) changes in the rules were proposed. Included are:

1. Encryption commodities, software and technology for U.S. subsidiaries. You may export and re-export any encryption item of any key length under ECCNs 5A002, 5D002, and 5E002 to foreign subsidiaries of U.S. firms (as defined in part 772).[3] This includes source code and technology for internal company proprietary use, including the development of new products. U.S. firms may also transfer encryption technology (5E002) to a foreign national in the United States (except foreign nationals from Cuba, Iran, Iraq, Libya, North Korea, Sudan, and Syria) for internal company proprietary use, including the development of new products. All items developed with U.S. encryption commodities, software, and technology are subject to the EAR.

2. Encryption commodities and software. You may export and re-export any encryption commodities and software including components of any key length under ECCNs 5A002 and 5D002 to individuals, commercial firms, and other nongovernment endusers.

Export controls were transferred from the Department of Commerce to the State Department and a new policy was announced on December 9, 2004. It provides for a review for cryptographic products with key length larger than 64 bits. Details can be found at www.bis.doc.gov/encryption/default.htm.

---

[2]FIPS PUB 46-3, October 25, 1999, specifies what I refer to as DES3. It is also described in ANSI X9.52-1998, "Triple Data Encryption Algorithm Modes of Operation".

[3]ECCN is the the Export Control Classification Number.

9.13   THE FUTURE ADVANCED DATA ENCRYPTION STANDARD

DES was first approved as FIPS Standard 46-1 in 1977. It has been (reluctantly) reaffirmed as a standard several times, most recently in 1993, and then *only* until December 1998. At that time, the affirmation included the statement

> *At the next review (1998), the algorithm specified in this standard will be over twenty years old. NIST will consider alternatives which offer a higher level of security. One of these alternatives, may be proposed as a replacement standard at the 1998 review.*

The National Institute of Standards (NIST) solicited proposals in the *Federal Register* (January 1, 1997) for an *Advanced Encryption Standard* (AES). The rules included

R1. AES shall be publicly defined.

R2. AES shall be a symmetric block cipher.

R3. AES shall be designed so that its key length may be increased as needed.

R4. AES shall be implementable in both hardware and software.

R5. AES shall either be

  (a) freely available, or

  (b) available under terms consistent with the ANSI Patent Policy.

R6. Algorithms which meet the above requirements will be judged based on the following factors:

  (a) security (resistance to cryptanalysis),

  (b) computational efficiency,

  (c) memory requirements,

  (d) hardware and software suitability,

  (e) simplicity,

  (f) flexibility, and

  (g) licensing requirements.

A subsequent announcement in the *Federal Register* (September 12, 1997) specified the (key, block) sizes to be supported by the AES; (128, 128) (192, 128) (256, 128). The statistical tests to be applied to evaluate the strength of the AES standard are described in Chapter 5 and specified in [FIPS, 1994, FIPS 140-1]. The selection process has involved two rounds; 15 submissions were made in Round 1. Of these, five survived in Round 2.

9.14   AND THE WINNER IS!

Rijndael was announced as the winning algorithm in October 2000 [Daemen and Rijmen, 1999] and is specified in [FIPS, 2001, FIPS-197]. Susan Landau [2004] wrote

> *Daemen and Rijmen sought simplicity – simplicity of specification and simplicity of analysis. Not every cryptographer sees simplicity as an important goal – two AES finalists, MARS and Twofish, have far more complex designs. Some observers felt that this complexity was part of the reason the two algorithms were not chosen as the Advanced Encryption Standard, as their round functions were simply too difficult to analyze fully.*

Too difficult to analyze! Indeed!

Rijndael is a block cipher supporting a variety of plaintext block sizes and cipher key lengths. The cipher key k is an array of dimension $4 \times Nk$ (a total of Nk 4-byte *words*)

$$\underline{k} = \begin{pmatrix} k_{0,0} & k_{0,1} & \cdots & k_{0,Nk-1} \\ k_{1,0} & k_{1,1} & \cdots & k_{1,Nk-1} \\ k_{2,0} & k_{2,1} & \cdots & k_{2,Nk-1} \\ k_{3,0} & k_{3,1} & \cdots & k_{3,Nk-1} \end{pmatrix}.$$

Each $\{k_{i,j}\}$ is regarded as both

- An 8-bit byte, that is, an element in the set $\mathcal{Z}_{2,8}$, and
- An integer in the set $\mathcal{Z}_{256}$.

Rijndael supports the Nk values of 4, 6, and 8 words (128, 192, and 256 bits).

The cipher key $\underline{k}$ is read into and from the array by columns from left to right

$$\underline{k} = (k_{0,1}, k_{1,0}, k_{2,0}, k_{3,0}, \ldots, k_{0,Nk-1}, k_{1,Nk-1}, k_{2,Nk-1}, k_{3,Nk-1}).$$

Plaintext $\underline{x}$ is an array of dimension $4 \times Nb$ (a total of Nb words)

$$\underline{x} = \begin{pmatrix} x_{0,0} & x_{0,1} & \cdots & x_{0,Nb-1} \\ x_{1,0} & x_{1,1} & \cdots & x_{1,Nb-1} \\ x_{2,0} & x_{2,1} & \cdots & x_{2,Nb-1} \\ x_{3,0} & x_{3,1} & \cdots & x_{3,Nb-1} \end{pmatrix}.$$

Each $\{x_{i,j}\}$ is regarded as both

- An 8-bit byte, that is, an element in the set $\mathcal{Z}_{2,8}$, and
- An integer in the set $\mathcal{Z}_{256}$.

Rijndael supports the Nb values of 4, 6, and 8 words (128, 192, and 256 bits).

The plaintext x is read into and from the array by columns from left to right

$$\underline{x} = (x_{0,1}, x_{1,0}, x_{2,0}, x_{3,0}, \ldots, x_{0,Nb-1}, x_{1,Nb-1}, x_{2,Nb-1}, x_{3,Nb-1})$$

A Rijndael *state* $\omega = (\omega_{i,j})$ is an array

$$\underline{\omega} = \begin{pmatrix} \omega_{0,0} & \omega_{0,1} & \cdots & \omega_{0,Nb-1} \\ \omega_{1,0} & \omega_{1,1} & \cdots & \omega_{1,Nb-1} \\ \omega_{2,0} & \omega_{2,1} & \cdots & \omega_{2,Nb-1} \\ \omega_{3,0} & \omega_{3,1} & \cdots & \omega_{3,Nb-1} \end{pmatrix}$$

of dimension $4 \times Nb$ whose entries are integers in $\mathcal{Z}_{256}$.

Like DES, the Rijndael encipherment process is the composition of transformations on the state, also referred to as *rounds* by Rijndael:

$$RIJ(\underline{x}) = \underline{y} = (T_{Nr} * T_{Nr-1} * \ldots * T_1 * T_0)(\underline{x}).$$

where the * (asterisk) denotes composition of mappings.

The number of rounds Nr depends on the values of Nb and Nk as shown in Table 9.23. The domain and range of a round T_i is a state $\underline{\omega}$ with data type `array [0..3,0..Nb]` of $\mathcal{Z}_{256}$.

The initial round T_0 is an exclusive XOR of $4Nb$ bytes of *round key* (R-key) to the state (plaintext). As in DES, subsequent rounds modify the state ω as a result of several transformations, referred to by Rijndael as *layers*:

L1. Linear Mixing Layer – the transformations `ShiftRow` and `MixColumn`;

L2. Nonlinear Layer – the transformation `ByteSub`;

L3. Key Addition Layer – the transformation `AddRoundKey`.

In order to simplify the decipherment process, DES employed a *Fiestel structure*, each round only modifying part of the data.

As π_{T_i} and θ are involutions in the Feistel structure, the inverse of the transformation $\theta * \pi_{T_i}$ on 64-bit blocks is $\pi_{T_i} * \theta$. The Feistel structure was introduced to simplify computation of the inverse transformation.

Rijndael does not follow this paradigm; each round modifies all of the bits in the data. The inverse to Rijndael is the composition

$$RIJ^{-1}(\underline{y}) = \underline{x} = (T_0^{-1} * T_1^{-1} * \cdots * T_{Nr-1}^1 * T_{Nr}^{-1})(\underline{y})$$

of the necessarily invertible round transformations $\{T_i\}$.

9.15 THE RIJNDAEL OPERATIONS

Rijndael uses a second interpretation for the components in a byte $\underline{x} = (x_0, x_1, \ldots, x_6, x_7) \in \mathcal{Z}_{2,8}$, namely, as the coefficients of a polynomial of degree 7

$$x(\zeta) \equiv x_0\zeta^7 + x_1\zeta^6 + \cdots + x_6\zeta + x_0 \leftrightarrow \underline{x} = (x_0, x_1, \ldots, x_6, x_7).$$

The addition of bytes $\underline{x} + \underline{y}$ is according to the usual rules for the addition of polynomials, Rijndael refers to addition as EXOR rather than XOR.

Associating a byte with a polynomial provides a way to define the multiplication; if

$$x(\zeta) \equiv x_0\zeta^7 + x_1\zeta^6 + \cdots + x_6\zeta + x_7 \leftrightarrow \underline{x} = (x_0, x_1, \ldots, x_6, x_7)$$

$$y(\zeta) \equiv y_0\zeta^7 + y_1\zeta^6 + \cdots + y_6\zeta + y_7 \leftrightarrow \underline{y} = (y_0, y_1, \ldots, y_6, y_7)$$

then

$$z(\zeta) \equiv z_0\zeta^7 + z_1\zeta^6 + \cdots + z_6\zeta + z_7 \leftrightarrow \underline{z} = (z_0, z_1, \ldots, z_6, z_7) \equiv x \cdot y,$$

TABLE 9.23 Number of Rijndael Rounds *Nr*

	$Nb = 4$	$Nb = 6$	$Nb = 8$
$Nk = 4$	10	12	14
$Nk = 6$	12	12	14
$Nk = 8$	14	14	14

where

$$z(\zeta) = x(\zeta)\, y(\zeta)(\text{modulo } m(\zeta))$$

and

$$m(\zeta) = 1 + \zeta + \zeta^3 + \zeta^4 + \zeta^8$$

where $m(\zeta)$ is a primitive (see Table 8.3) but *not* irreducible polynomial.

For fixed $x = (x_1, x_1, \ldots, x_6, x_7) \in \mathcal{Z}_{2,8}$, the transformation

$$z(\zeta) = x(\zeta)\, y(\zeta)(\text{modulo } m(\zeta)) \tag{9.1}$$

with

$$\underline{y} = (y_0, y_1, \ldots, y_6, y_7) \neq (0)_8$$

is a transformation on $\mathcal{Z}_{256} - \{0\}$.

Proposition 9.3: The transformation in Equation (9.1) is invertible; given $\underline{w} = (w_0, w_1, \ldots, w_6, w_7) \neq (0)_8$, there exists a unique $\underline{y} = (y_0, y_1, \ldots, y_6, y_7) \neq (0)_8$ such that

$$w(\zeta) = x(\zeta)\, y(\zeta)\, (\text{modulo } m(\zeta)).$$

Proof: If $y_1(\zeta)$ and $y_2(\zeta)$ satisfy

$$x(\zeta) = y_1(\zeta)\, (\text{modulo } m(\zeta)) = x(\zeta)\, y_2(\zeta)\, (\text{modulo } m(\zeta))$$

then

$$0 = x(\zeta) = (y_1(\zeta) + y_2(\zeta))\, (\text{modulo } m(\zeta))$$

which contradicts the irreducibility of $m(\zeta)$ unless $y_1(\zeta) = y_2(\zeta)$.

It follows that $y(\zeta) \to x(\zeta)\, y(\zeta)\, (\text{modulo } m(\zeta))$ is a 1-to-1 mapping on $\mathcal{Z}_{256} - \{0\}$ for each fixed x.

Proposition 9.3 implies that for each $x \neq (0)_8$, there must be a unique byte x^{-1} such that

$$x \cdot x^{-1} = (1, (0)_7)$$

or equivalently, for each polynomial $x(\zeta) \neq 0$, there exists a polynomial $x^{-1}(\zeta)$ such that

$$x(\zeta) x^{-1}(\zeta) = 1\ (\text{modulo } m(\zeta)).$$

The computation of the (multiplicative) inverse of $\underline{x}$ uses the extended Euclidean algorithm, which we will now describe.

Using the notation in Chapter 8,

- The polynomial $r(\zeta)$ in $\mathcal{P}[z]$ is a *divisor* of polynomials $p(\zeta)$ and $p(\zeta)$ *in* $\mathcal{P}[z]$ if $r(\zeta)$ is a factor of both polynomials;
- $r(\zeta)$ is the *greatest common divisor* of $p(\zeta)$ and $q(\zeta)$ if it is a divisor and has the maximum degree of all common divisors.

$\gcd\{p(\zeta), q(\zeta)\}$ denotes the greatest common divisor of $p(\zeta)$ and $q(\zeta)$.

Proposition 9.4 (Extended Euclidean Algorithm for Polynomials with Coefficients in $\mathcal{Z}_2$):

9.4a If $p(\zeta)$ and $q(\zeta)$ are polynomials in $\mathcal{P}[z]$, the sequence of remainders $\{r_j(\zeta) : j \geq 2\}$

$$r_0(\zeta) = p(\zeta)$$
$$r_1(\zeta) = q(\zeta)$$
$$r_0(\zeta) = c_1(\zeta)r_1(\zeta) + r_2(\zeta); \qquad 0 \leq \deg(r_2) < \deg(r_1)$$
$$r_1(\zeta) = c_2(\zeta)r_2(\zeta) + r_3(\zeta); \qquad 0 \leq \deg(r_3) < \deg(r_2)$$

$$\vdots \qquad\qquad \vdots \qquad\qquad \vdots$$

$$r_{s-2}(\zeta) = c_{s-1}(\zeta)r_{s-1}(\zeta) + r_s(\zeta); \qquad 0 \leq \deg(r_s) < \deg(r_{s-1})$$
$$r_{s-1}(\zeta) = c_s(\zeta)r_s(\zeta) + r_{s+1}(\zeta); \qquad 0 \leq \deg(r_{s+1}) < \deg(r_s)$$

is ultimately identically 0.

9.4b If s is the first index for which $r_{s+1}(\zeta) = 0$, then $r_s(\zeta) = \gcd\{p(\zeta), q(\zeta)\}$.

9.4c If $\deg(p) > \deg(q)$, the time to compute $\gcd\{p(\zeta), q(\zeta)\}$ is $O((\log_2 \deg(p))^3)$.

Example 9.8

$$p(\zeta) = 1 + \zeta^4 + \zeta^5 + \zeta^6 + \zeta^8 + \zeta^9 + \zeta^{10}$$
$$q(\zeta) = 1 + \zeta^2 + \zeta^3 + \zeta^5 + \zeta^6 + \zeta^9$$
$$r_0(\zeta) = p(\zeta)$$
$$r_1(\zeta) = q(\zeta)$$

$$r_0(\zeta) = (1 + z)r_1(\zeta) + r_2(\zeta) \qquad\qquad r_2(\zeta) = z + z^2 + z^6 + z^7 + z^8$$
$$r_1(\zeta) = (z + 1)r_2(\zeta) + r_3(\zeta) \qquad\qquad r_3(\zeta) = 1 + z + z^2 + z^5$$
$$r_2(\zeta) = (z^3 + z^2 + z + 1)r_3(\zeta) + r_4(\zeta) \qquad r_4(\zeta) = 1 + z + z^3$$
$$r_3(\zeta) = (z^2 + 1)r_4(\zeta) + r_5(\zeta) \qquad\qquad r_5(\zeta) = 0$$
$$\gcd\{p(\zeta), q(\zeta)\} = 1 + z + z^3$$

The Operations ByteSub *and* InvByteSub *are defined first for bytes* $\underline{x}$ *as* follows:

$$BS_1(\underline{x}) = \underline{z} \equiv \begin{cases} 0, & \text{if } \underline{x} = (0)_8 \\ \underline{x}^{-1}, & \text{if } \underline{x} \neq (0)_8 \end{cases}$$

$$BS_2(\underline{z}) = A\underline{z} + B$$

$$A = \begin{pmatrix} 1 & 0 & 0 & 0 & 1 & 1 & 1 & 1 \\ 1 & 1 & 0 & 0 & 0 & 1 & 1 & 1 \\ 1 & 1 & 1 & 0 & 0 & 0 & 1 & 1 \\ 1 & 1 & 1 & 1 & 0 & 0 & 0 & 1 \\ 1 & 1 & 1 & 1 & 1 & 0 & 0 & 0 \\ 0 & 1 & 1 & 1 & 1 & 1 & 0 & 0 \\ 0 & 0 & 1 & 1 & 1 & 1 & 1 & 0 \\ 0 & 0 & 0 & 1 & 1 & 1 & 1 & 1 \end{pmatrix} \qquad B = (1, 1, 0, 0, 1, 1, 0)$$

$$BS(\underline{x}) = BS_2(BS_1(\underline{x}))$$

Remarks:

1. $BS_1^{-1} = BS_1$.
2. A simple computation shows that the transpose A^t of A is equal to A^{-1} so that $BS_2^{-1} = BS_2$.

The operation ByteSub is defined for a state

$$\underline{\omega} = \begin{pmatrix} \omega_{0,0} & \omega_{0,1} & \cdots & \omega_{0,Nb-1} \\ \omega_{1,0} & \omega_{1,1} & \cdots & \omega_{1,Nb-1} \\ \omega_{2,0} & \omega_{2,1} & \cdots & \omega_{2,Nb-1} \\ \omega_{3,0} & \omega_{3,1} & \cdots & \omega_{3,Nb-1} \end{pmatrix}$$

by

$$BS(\underline{\omega}) = \begin{pmatrix} BS(\omega_{0,0}) & BS(\omega_{0,1}) & \cdots & BS(\omega_{0,Nb-1}) \\ BS(\omega_{1,0}) & BS(\omega_{1,1}) & \cdots & BS(\omega_{1,Nb-1}) \\ BS(\omega_{2,0}) & BS(\omega_{2,1}) & \cdots & BS(\omega_{2,Nb-1}) \\ BS(\omega_{3,0}) & BS(\omega_{3,1}) & \cdots & BS(\omega_{3,Nb-1}) \end{pmatrix}.$$

ByteSub plays the role of the S-box in DES and is the *only* nonlinear element in Rijndael.

The Operations ShiftRow *and* InvShiftRow are cyclic left and right shifts of the rows of a state $\underline{\omega}$. SR cyclically left-shifts row $\underline{i}$ of $\underline{\omega}$ by C_i bytes as listed in Table 9.24. For example, when $Nb = 4$

$$SR: \underline{\omega} = \begin{pmatrix} \omega_{0,0} & \omega_{0,1} & \omega_{0,2} & \omega_{0,3} \\ \omega_{1,0} & \omega_{1,1} & \omega_{1,2} & \omega_{1,3} \\ \omega_{2,0} & \omega_{2,1} & \omega_{2,2} & \omega_{2,3} \\ \omega_{3,0} & \omega_{3,1} & \omega_{3,2} & \omega_{3,3} \end{pmatrix} \rightarrow \begin{pmatrix} \omega_{0,0} & \omega_{0,1} & \omega_{0,2} & \omega_{0,3} \\ \omega_{1,1} & \omega_{1,2} & \omega_{1,3} & \omega_{1,0} \\ \omega_{2,2} & \omega_{2,3} & \omega_{2,0} & \omega_{2,1} \\ \omega_{3,3} & \omega_{3,0} & \omega_{3,1} & \omega_{3,2} \end{pmatrix}.$$

The inverse InvShiftRow is a cyclic right shift of the row i of a state $\underline{\omega}$ by C_i bytes.

TABLE 9.24   Rijndael Row Shift Parameters

Nb	C_0	C_1	C_2	C_3
4	0	1	2	3
6	0	1	2	3
8	0	1	3	4

The Operations MixColumn *and* InvMixColumn are defined in terms of multiplication of polynomials whose coefficients are bytes. We write $x = \langle ab \rangle$ to show that the byte x is composed of the two hexadecimal digits a and b. Table 9.25 shows a coding between x and $\langle ab \rangle$. To compute the product

$$c(\zeta) = a(\zeta) \times b(\zeta) \ (\text{modulo } (1 + \zeta^4)) \tag{9.2}$$

$$c(\zeta) = c_3\zeta^3 + c_2\zeta^2 + c_1\zeta + c_0$$

with

$$a(\zeta) = a_3\zeta^3 + a_2\zeta^2 + a_1\zeta + a_0$$

$$b(\zeta) = b_3\zeta^3 + b_2\zeta^2 + b_1\zeta + b_0$$

the sum of the products of the coefficient of z^i in $a(\zeta)$ and the coefficient of z^j in $b(\zeta)$ with $i + j = k$ (modulo 4) for fixed k with $k = 0, 1, 2, 3$ is computed. This may be written as

$$\begin{pmatrix} c_0 \\ c_1 \\ c_2 \\ c_3 \end{pmatrix} = \begin{pmatrix} a_0 & a_3 & a_2 & a_1 \\ a_1 & a_0 & a_3 & a_2 \\ a_2 & a_1 & a_0 & a_3 \\ a_3 & a_2 & a_1 & a_0 \end{pmatrix} \begin{pmatrix} b_0 \\ b_1 \\ b_2 \\ b_3 \end{pmatrix} \tag{9.3}$$

$$c_0 = (a_0 \cdot b_0) + (a_3 \cdot b_1) + (a_2 \cdot b_2) + (a_1 \cdot b_3)$$
$$c_1 = (a_1 \cdot b_0) + (a_0 \cdot b_1) + (a_3 \cdot b_2) + (a_2 \cdot b_2)$$
$$c_2 = (a_2 \cdot b_0) + (a_1 \cdot b_1) + (a_0 \cdot b_2) + (a_3 \cdot b_3)$$
$$c_3 = (a_3 \cdot b_0) + (a_2 \cdot b_1) + (a_1 \cdot b_2) + (a_0 \cdot b_3) \tag{9.4}$$

Example 9.9

We compute $c(\zeta) = a(\zeta) \times b(\zeta) \ (\text{modulo } (1 + \zeta^4))$ with

$$a(\zeta) = \langle 02 \rangle + \langle 01 \rangle \zeta + \langle 01 \rangle \zeta^2 + \langle 03 \rangle \zeta^3$$

$$b(\zeta) = \langle 0E \rangle + \langle 09 \rangle \zeta + \langle 0D \rangle \zeta^2 + \langle 0B \rangle \zeta^3$$

TABLE 9.25   Byte-to-Hex Coding Table

Bits	Hex	Bits	Hex	Bits	Hex	Bits	Hex
0000	0	0100	4	1000	8	1100	C
0001	1	0101	5	1001	9	1101	D
0010	2	0110	6	1010	A	1110	E
0011	3	0111	7	1011	B	1111	F

by adding the products of the coefficient of z^i in a (ζ) and the coefficient of z^j in $b(\zeta)$ with $i + j = k$ (modulo 4) for fixed k with $k = 0, 1, 2, 3$.

1. The coefficient of ζ^0 in $c(\zeta)$ is the sum of the products of
   (a) the coefficient of ζ^i in $a(\zeta)$ and
   (b) the coefficient of ζ^j in $b(\zeta)$ with $i + j = 0$ (modulo 4); that is,

$$\langle 02 \rangle \cdot \langle 0E \rangle \leftrightarrow \zeta(\zeta + \zeta^2 + \zeta^3) = \zeta^2 + \zeta^3 + \zeta^4$$

$$\langle 01 \rangle \cdot \langle 0B \rangle \leftrightarrow 1(1 + \zeta + \zeta^3) = 1 + \zeta + \zeta^3$$

$$\langle 01 \rangle \cdot \langle D, 0 \rangle \leftrightarrow 1(1 + \zeta^2 + \zeta^3) = 1 + \zeta^2 + \zeta^3$$

$$\langle 03 \rangle \cdot \langle 09 \rangle \leftrightarrow (1 + \zeta)(1 + \zeta^3) = 1 + \zeta + \zeta^3 + \zeta^4$$

with value 1.

2. The coefficient of ζ^1 in $c(\zeta)$ is the sum of the products of
   (a) the coefficient of ζ^i in $a(\zeta)$ and
   (b) the coefficient of ζ^j in $b(\zeta)$ with $i + j = 1$ (modulo 4); that is,

$$\langle 02 \rangle \cdot \langle 09 \rangle \leftrightarrow \zeta(1 + \zeta^3) = \zeta + \zeta^4$$

$$\langle 01 \rangle \cdot \langle 0E \rangle \leftrightarrow 1(\zeta + \zeta^2 + \zeta^3) = \zeta + \zeta^2 + \zeta^3$$

$$\langle 01 \rangle \cdot \langle 0B \rangle \leftrightarrow 1(1 + \zeta + \zeta^3) = 1 + \zeta + \zeta^3$$

$$\langle 03 \rangle \cdot \langle 0D \rangle \leftrightarrow (1 + \zeta)(1 + \zeta^2 + \zeta^3) = 1 + \zeta + \zeta^2 + \zeta^4$$

with value 0.

3. The coefficient of ζ^2 in $c(\zeta)$ is the sum of the products of
   (a) the coefficient of ζ^i in $a(\zeta)$ and
   (b) the coefficient of ζ^j in $b(\zeta)$ with $i + j = 2$ (modulo 4); that is,

$$\langle 02 \rangle \cdot \langle 0D \rangle \leftrightarrow \zeta(1 + \zeta^2 + \zeta^3) = \zeta + \zeta^3 + \zeta^4$$

$$\langle 01 \rangle \cdot \langle 09 \rangle \leftrightarrow 1(1 + \zeta^3) = 1 + \zeta^3$$

$$\langle 01 \rangle \cdot \langle 0E \rangle \leftrightarrow 1(\zeta + \zeta^2 + \zeta^3) = \zeta + \zeta^2 + \zeta^3$$

$$\langle 03 \rangle \cdot \langle 0B \rangle \leftrightarrow (1 + \zeta)(1 + \zeta + \zeta^3) = 1 + \zeta^2 + \zeta^3 + \zeta^4$$

with value 0.

4. The coefficient of ζ^3 in $c(\zeta)$ is the sum of the products of
   (a) the coefficient of ζ^i in $a(\zeta)$ and
   (b) the coefficient of ζ^j in $b(\zeta)$ with $i + j = 3$ (modulo 4); that is,

$$\langle 02 \rangle \cdot \langle 0B \rangle \leftrightarrow \zeta(1 + \zeta + \zeta^3) = \zeta + \zeta^2 + \zeta^4$$

$$\langle 01 \rangle \cdot \langle 0D \rangle \leftrightarrow 1(1 + \zeta^2 + \zeta^3) = 1 + \zeta^2 + \zeta^3$$

$$\langle 01 \rangle \cdot \langle 09 \rangle \leftrightarrow 1(1 + \zeta^3) = 1 + \zeta^3$$

$$\langle 03 \rangle \cdot \langle 0E \rangle \leftrightarrow (1 + \zeta)(\zeta + \zeta^2 + \zeta^3) = \zeta + \zeta^4$$

with value 0.

Example 9.9 shows that

$$c(\zeta) = a(\zeta) \times b(\zeta) \ (\text{modulo}(1 + \zeta^4)) = 1$$

when

$$a(\zeta) = \langle 02 \rangle + \langle 01 \rangle \zeta + \langle 01 \rangle \zeta^2 + \langle 03 \rangle \zeta^3 \quad b(\zeta) = \langle 0E \rangle + \langle 09 \rangle \zeta + \langle 0D \rangle \zeta^2 + \langle 0B \rangle \zeta^3.$$

This computation proves Proposition 9.5.

Proposition 9.5: If $a(\zeta) = \langle 02 \rangle + \langle 01 \rangle \zeta + \langle 01 \rangle \zeta^2 + \langle 03 \rangle \zeta^3$, then the transformation

$$T_a : b(\zeta) \to a(\zeta) \ b(\zeta) \ (\text{modulo}(1 + \zeta^4))$$

is invertible with inverse

$$T_a^{-1} : b(\zeta) \to a^{-1}(\zeta) \ b(\zeta) \ (\text{modulo}(1 + \zeta^4))$$

with

$$a^{-1}(\zeta) = \langle 0E \rangle + \langle 09 \rangle \zeta + \langle 0D \rangle \zeta^2 + \langle 0B \rangle \zeta^3.$$

A column in the state

$$\underline{\omega} = \begin{pmatrix} \omega_{0,0} & \omega_{0,1} & \cdots & \omega_{0,Nb-1} \\ \omega_{1,0} & \omega_{1,1} & \cdots & \omega_{1,Nb-1} \\ \omega_{2,0} & \omega_{2,1} & \cdots & \omega_{2,Nb-1} \\ \omega_{3,0} & \omega_{3,1} & \cdots & \omega_{3,Nb-1} \end{pmatrix}$$

is identified with a polynomial of degree (at most) three, whose coefficients are bytes. The linear transformation MixColumn (MC) consists of the application of MC to each of the Nb columns of a state $\underline{\omega}$ (Fig. 9.13):

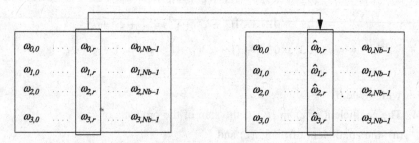

Figure 9.13 MixColumn applied to the rth column of the state.

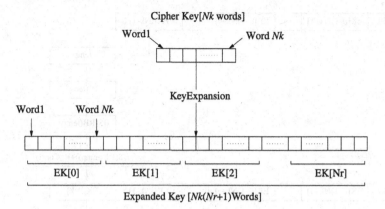

Figure 9.14 Rijndael key expansion.

$$(\hat{\omega}_{0,r}, \hat{\omega}_{1,r}, \hat{\omega}_{2,r}, \hat{\omega}_{3,r}) = \text{MC}(\omega_{0,r}, \omega_{1,r}, \omega_{2,r}, \omega_{3,r})$$

$$\begin{pmatrix} \hat{\omega}_{0,r} \\ \hat{\omega}_{1,r} \\ \hat{\omega}_{2,r} \\ \hat{\omega}_{3,r} \end{pmatrix} = \begin{pmatrix} \langle 02 \rangle & \langle 03 \rangle & \langle 01 \rangle & \langle 01 \rangle \\ \langle 01 \rangle & \langle 02 \rangle & \langle 03 \rangle & \langle 01 \rangle \\ \langle 01 \rangle & \langle 01 \rangle & \langle 02 \rangle & \langle 03 \rangle \\ \langle 03 \rangle & \langle 01 \rangle & \langle 01 \rangle & \langle 02 \rangle \end{pmatrix} \begin{pmatrix} \omega_{0,r} \\ \omega_{1,r} \\ \omega_{2,r} \\ \omega_{3,r} \end{pmatrix}$$

The Operation AddRoundKey is the exclusive-OR of Nb words of R-key to a state $\underline{\omega}$. The Nb words of the R-key used in each round are derived from expanding the Nk words of cipher key into $Nb(Nr + 1)$ words of R-key (Fig. 9.14):

$$\underline{EK} = (EK[0], EK[1], EK[2], \ldots, EK[Nr]).$$

The algorithm for key expansion is different for $Nk \le 6$ and $Nk > 6$.

Key Expansion Algorithm (Nk $\le$ 6)

1. for $i := 0$ to $Nk - 1$

$EK[i] = (k_{0,i}, k_{1,i}, k_{2,i}, k_{3,i})$ $k_{j,i}$ is a word;

2. for $i := Nk$ to $NkNr - 1$

temp $= EK[i - 1]$

if $0 \ne (i \bmod Nk)$, then $EK[i] = \text{temp} + EK[i - Nk]$;

if $0 = (i \bmod Nk)$, then temp $= \text{BS}(\text{RB}(\text{temp})) + \text{R\_Con}(\lfloor i/Nk \rfloor)$

where

- The transformation RotByte (RB) is the left-cyclic shift fay one byte of a word $(\omega_0, \omega_1, \omega_2, \omega_3)$

$$\text{RB} : (\omega_0, \omega_1, \omega_2, \omega_3) \rightarrow (\omega_1, \omega_2, \omega_3, \omega_0).$$

- ByteSub (BS) is applied to each of bytes of $\text{RB}(\omega_0, \omega_1, \omega_2, \omega_3)$

$$\text{BS}(\text{RB}) : (\omega_0, \omega_1, \omega_2, \omega_3) \rightarrow (\text{BS}(\omega_1), \text{BS}(\omega_2), \text{BS}(\omega_3), \text{BS}(\omega_0)).$$

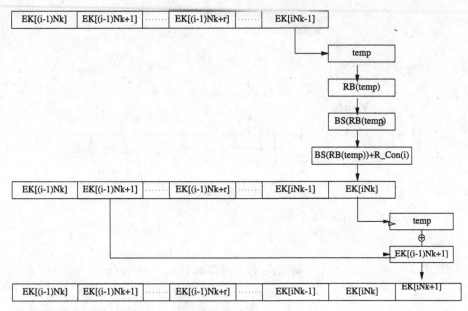

Figure 9.15   Two intermediate steps in Rijndael key expansion.

- The *round constants* {R_Con(j)} of type `array [0..3]` of $\mathcal{Z}_{256}$ are defined by

$$R\_Con(,j) = (RC[j], \langle 00 \rangle, \langle 00 \rangle, \langle 00 \rangle)$$
$$RC[1] = \langle 01 \rangle$$
$$RC[2] = x = \langle 02 \rangle$$
$$RC[i] = x \cdot RC[i-1]$$

Key Expansion Algorithm (Nk > 6)

1. for $i := 0$ to $Nk - 1$

EK[i] = ($k_{0,i}$, $k_{1,i}$, $k_{2,i}$, $k_{3,i}$) $k_{j,i}$ is a word;

2. for $i := Nk$ to $NkNr - 1$

temp = EK[$i - 1$]
    if $0 \neq (i \bmod Nk)$, then EK[i] = temp $+$ EK[$i - Nk$];
    if $4 = (i \bmod Nk)$, then temp = BS(temp);

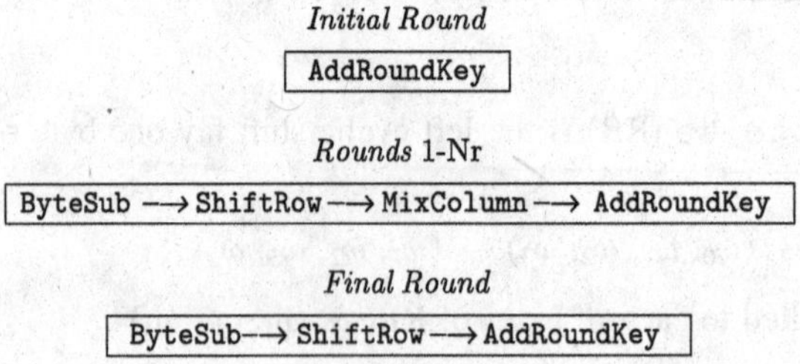

Initial Round

```
AddRoundKey
```

Rounds 1-Nr

```
ByteSub ⟶ ShiftRow ⟶ MixColumn ⟶ AddRoundKey
```

Final Round

```
ByteSub ⟶ ShiftRow ⟶ AddRoundKey
```

Figure 9.16   The order of operations in the Rijndael Cipher.

Two intermediate steps in the Rijndael expansion for $Nk \leq 6$ are shown in Figure 9.15. Any Nk consecutive word of R-key determine the complete R-key.

9.16 THE RIJNDAEL CIPHER

The order in which the transformations `ByteSub`, `ShiftRow`, `MixColumn`, and `AddRoundKey` are to be applied is as shown in Figure 9.16.

9.17 RIJNDAEL'S STRENGTH: PROPAGATION OF PATTERNS

Although there is no proof that Rijndael can resist all cryptographic attacks

- The authors have tested whether several existing cryptanalytic techniques when applied to Rijndael can recover die key with a work factor less than exhaustive key trial, and
- Rijndael has been exposed to a careful scrutiny by outside cryptanalysts.

We summarize some of the unsuccessful attacks on Rijndael.

9.17.1 Differential Cryptanalysis

Define the *byte weight* of two states $\underline{\omega}_1$ and $\underline{\omega}_2$ as the number of nonzero bytes in $\underline{\omega}_1 \oplus \underline{\omega}_2$. Differential cryptanalysis has two phases:

1. A search for pairs of states $(\underline{\omega}_1, \underline{\omega}_2)$ whose byte weight does not change significantly over several rounds when the states $\underline{\omega}_i$ are enciphered with the same key, and

2. An attempt to use such pairs to infer key bits.

The Rijndael round transformation on a state

$$T : \underline{\omega} \rightarrow \text{AddRoundKey}(\text{MixColumn}(\text{ShiftRow}(\text{ByteSub}(\omega))))$$

is a permutation on the states in $\mathcal{Z}_{4Nb,8}$.

Nyberg [1993] and Beth and Ding [1993] introduced a measure of nonlinearity for permutations F on $\mathcal{Z}_{n,2}$ defining

$$N_F = \max_{b \in \mathcal{Z}_{n,2}} N_F(a)$$

$$N_F(a) = |\{z \in \mathcal{Z}_{n,2} : F(z+a) - F(z) = b\}|, \quad a \neq 0,$$

where $|\cdots|$ is the size of the set $\cdots$. Note that if F is a linear transformation, then $F(z+a) - F(z) = b$ has either 0 or 2 solution.

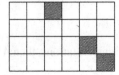

Figure 9.17 An $Nk = 6$ Rijndael Activity Pattern.

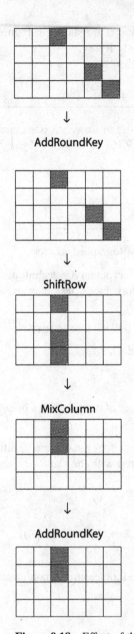

Figure 9.18 Effect of the round transformation the $Nk = 6$ Rijndael activity pattern.

Nyberg calls F *differentially δ-uniform* if $N_F \leq \delta$ and proves Proposition 9.6.

Proposition 9.6:

9.6a $N_F \leq 2$.

9.6b If F is differentially δ-uniform and A and B are linear transformations, then $A * F * B$ is differentially δ-uniform.

9.6c The permutation ByteSub is differentially 4-uniform.

An *active byte* in a state is a nonzero byte. An *activity pattern* is a description of the active bytes in a pair of states $(\underline{\omega}_1, \underline{\omega}_2)$.

Example 9.10

An activity pattern for $Nk = 6$ is illustrated in Figure 9.17; bytes (0,2), (2,4), and (3,5) are active. The effect of a Rijndael round transformation on an activity pattern uses the following observations:

- An activity pattern remains *un*changed under `AddRoundKey`, `ByteSub`, and `ShiftRow`;
- `MixColumn` only alters the columns containing an active byte.

A possible effect of the Rijndael round transformation on the activity pattern in *Example 9.10* is shown in Figure 9.18.

Example 9.10 shows that the number of active bytes depends on the number of *active columns*; that is, columns with an active byte.

Daemen and Rijmen define an m-round differential trail as a sequence of state-pairs

$$\begin{array}{ccccccc} \underline{\omega}_1 & \xrightarrow{T_1} & \underline{\omega}_2 & \xrightarrow{T_2} & \cdots \xrightarrow{T_{m-1}} & \underline{\omega}_m \\ \underline{\omega}_1 + \underline{a}_1 & & \underline{\omega}_2 + \underline{a}_2 & & & \underline{\omega}_m + \underline{a}_m \end{array}$$

related by chaining

$$\begin{array}{ccc} \underline{\omega}_i & \xrightarrow{T_1} & \underline{\omega}_{i+1} \\ \underline{\omega}_i + \underline{a}_i & & \underline{\omega}_{i+1} + \underline{a}_{i+1} \end{array}, \quad i = 1, 2, \ldots m - 1.$$

The fraction of key values that are consistent for the ith segment is denoted by

$$R\left(\begin{array}{ccc} \underline{\omega}_i & \xrightarrow{T_1} & \underline{\omega}_{i+1} \\ r\underline{\omega}_i + i & & \underline{\omega}_{i+1} + \underline{a}_{i+1} \end{array} \right)$$

Daemen and Rijmen argue in Daemen [1995] and in the supplementary annex [Daemen and Rijmen, 1999a] that when the fractions of consistent keys

$$R\left(\begin{array}{ccc} \underline{\omega}_i & \xrightarrow{T_i} & \underline{\omega}_{i+1} \\ \underline{\omega}_i + \underline{a}_i & & \underline{\omega}_{i+1} + \underline{a}_{i+1} \end{array} \right), \quad i = 1, 2, \ldots, m - 1$$

are small, the keys act *independently* and the fractions may be multiplied to give

$$R\left(\begin{array}{ccccc} \underline{\omega}_1 & \xrightarrow{T_1} & \underline{\omega}_2 & \xrightarrow{T_2} \cdots \xrightarrow{T_{m-1}} & \underline{\omega}_m \\ \underline{\omega}_1 + \underline{a}_1 & & \underline{\omega}_2 + \underline{a}_2 & & \underline{\omega}_m + \underline{a}_m \end{array} \right)$$

$$\approx \prod_{i=1}^{m-1} R\left(\begin{array}{ccc} \underline{\omega}_i & \xrightarrow{T_i} & \underline{\omega}_{i+1} \\ \underline{\omega}_i + \underline{a}_i & & \underline{\omega}_{i+1} + \underline{a}_{i+1} \end{array} \right).$$

In Daemen and Rijmen [1999b], the authors state Proposition 9.7.

Proposition 9.7

9.7a The number of active bytes after two rounds is at least 5.

9.7b The number of active bytes after four rounds is at least 25.

Combining **Proposition 9.7b** with Nyberg's result shows 2^{-150} to be the probability that a four-round differential attack will be successful.

9.18   WHEN IS A PRODUCT BLOCK-CIPHER SECURE?

In LUCIFER, DES, and Rijndael, the substitution (S-box) provides the only nonlinear element in the encipherment transformation. In the 16 years various authors have studied the general design principles of strong product block-ciphers, which have been investigated since the beginning of the 1980s. Susan Landau's paper [Landau, 2004] is a very fine summary of the concepts.

$\mathcal{Z}_{2,n}$ will continue to denote the set of all binary n-vectors. The *Hamming distance* $d(\underline{x}, \underline{y})$ between two n-vectors $\underline{x} = (x_0, x_1, \ldots, x_{n-1})$ and $\underline{y} = (y_0, y_1, \ldots, y_{n-1})$ is the number of coordinates in which they differ.

If

$$\underline{0} = \underbrace{0, 0, \ldots, 0}_{n \text{ copies}} \quad \underline{1} = \underbrace{1, 1, \ldots, 1}_{n \text{ copies}}$$

$$\underline{u}_i = \begin{cases} (1, (0)_{n-1}), & \text{if } i = 0 \\ (\underbrace{0, 0, \ldots, 0}_{(i-1) \text{ terms}}, 1, \underbrace{0, 0, \ldots, 0}_{(n-i) \text{ terms}}), & \text{if } 0 < i < n-1 \\ ((0)_{n-1}, 1), & \text{if } i = n-1 \end{cases}$$

$$\underline{x} = (x_0', x_1', \ldots, x_{n-1}')$$

where, indicates complementation, then

$$\begin{aligned} n &= d(\underline{0}, \underline{1}) & 2 &= d(\underline{u}_i, \underline{u}_j), & 0 \le i < j < n \\ n &= d(\underline{x}, \underline{x}') & 1 &= d(\underline{0}, \underline{u}_i), & 0 \le i < n \end{aligned}$$

An S-box is *Boolean function*; that is, a mapping

$$f : \mathcal{Z}_{2,n} \to \mathcal{Z}_{2,m}.$$

We use the notations

- $\mathcal{B}_n$ for the set of all Boolean functions on $\mathcal{Z}_{2,n}$ with values in $\mathcal{Z}_2$,
- $\mathcal{L}_n$ for the set of all *linear Boolean functions* $f(\underline{x}) = a_0 x_0 + a_1 x_1 + \cdots + a_{n-1} x_{n-1}$ where the coefficient vector $\underline{a} = (a_0, a_1, \ldots, a_{n-1})$ is in $\mathcal{Z}_{2,n}$, and
- $\mathcal{A}_n$ for the set of all affine Boolean functions $f(\underline{x}) = b + a_0 x_0 + a_1 x_1 + \cdots + a_{n-1} x_{n-1}$ where the coefficient vector $\underline{a} = (a_0, a_1, \ldots, a_{n-1})$ is in $\mathcal{Z}_{2,n}$, and $b \in \mathcal{Z}_2$.

Although Feistel's paradigm

$$\mathcal{T} : (L, R) \to (F(R) + L, R)$$

does *not* require F to be invertible, some form of nonlinearity must be part of the design. Pierpryzk's paper [1990] proposed measuring the *nonlinearity* of $f \in \mathcal{B}$ by

$$\mathcal{N}(f) = d(f, \mathcal{B}_n) \equiv \min_{g \in \mathcal{L}_n} d(f, g)$$

where the Hamming distance between two functions $f(\underline{x})$ and $g(\underline{x})$ is

$$d(f, g) = \#\{\underline{x} : f(\underline{x}) \ne g(\underline{x})\}$$

and $\#\{\cdots\}$ is the cardinality of $\{\cdots\}$.

The nonlinearity $\mathcal{N}(f)$ of a permutation $f = (f_0, f_0, \ldots, f_{n-1})$ of $\mathcal{Z}_{2,\,n}$ is

$$\mathcal{N}(f) \equiv \lim_{0 \le i < n} \mathcal{N}(f_i).$$

Another interpretation is possible where an element $\underline{x} = (x_0, x_1, \ldots, x_{n-2}, x_{n-1})$ of $\mathcal{Z}_{2,n}$ may be interpreted as the coefficient of the polynomial of degree at most $n-1$

$$p_{\underline{x}}(z) \equiv x_{n-1} + x_{n-2}z + \cdots + x_1 z^{n-2} + x_0 z^{n-1} \Leftrightarrow \underline{x} = (x_0, x_1, \ldots, x_{n-2}, x_{n-1}).$$

The vector space $\mathcal{Z}_{2,n}$ is then identified with the space of polynomials $\mathcal{P}_{n-1}[z]$ of degree at most $n - 1$.

The addition and multiplication of integers in $\mathcal{Z}_2$ is trivial; similarly, the addition and multiplication of n-vectors in $\mathcal{Z}_{2,n}$ may be defined. The idea is central to understanding Rijndael.

This identification of vectors with polynomials is fruitful; Pierpryzk proved that $p(z) = z^{2^k} + 1$ for $k > 2$ has maximum nonlinearity.

Nyberg [1993] argues that a better definition of $\mathcal{N}_f$ is to find the *best* affine approximation

$$\mathcal{N}_f = d(f, \mathcal{B}_n) \equiv \min_{g \in \mathcal{L}_n} d(f, g)$$

as he proves that, with his definition, the nonlinearity of an *invertible* f is the same as f^{-1}. That is, the measure of the nonlinearity of f is the closest distance to it by a line or affine approximation.

The Boolean functions with Nyberg's maximum nonlinearity have been studied previously in cryptography by Rothhaus [1976]. He called a Boolean function f on $\mathcal{Z}_{2,n}$ *bent* if its distance to the space of affine functions is a maximum. Various equivalent definitions have been found. First, the *discrete Fourier* (*Hadamard*) or *Walsh transform* of a Boolean function $f(\underline{x})$ is defined by

$$\widehat{F}(\underline{x}) = \sum_{\underline{x} \in \mathcal{Z}_{2,n}} (-1)^{f(\underline{x}) + (\underline{x} \cdot \underline{y})}.$$

The transform operator $f \to \widehat{F}$ satisfies the *Parseval's formula*

$$\sum_{\underline{y} \in \mathcal{Z}_{2,n}} (\widehat{F}(\underline{y}))^2 = 2^{2n}.$$

Rothhaus proved that f is bent for $n = 2m$ provided

$$\widehat{F}(y) = \pm 2^m.$$

second, if f is bent and

$$h(\underline{x}) = (\underline{a} \cdot \underline{x}) + b$$

if affine, then

$$(-1)^b \widehat{F}(\underline{y}) = 2^n - 2d(f, h).$$

9.19   GENERATING THE SYMMETRIC GROUP

Product block ciphers acting on plaintext on $\mathcal{Z}_{2,n}$ are often constructed from certain primitives; for example, XOR, addition-with-carry, and circular-shift. DES, LUCIFER, and IDEA (defined in Chapter 17) are examples. The *symmetric group* of $\mathcal{Z}_{2,n}$ is the group containing the $2^n!$ permutations of the elements of $\mathcal{Z}_{2,n}$. It is the richest possible cryptographic family; to specify an element of this symmetric group requires $\log_2 2^n! \approx n2^n$ bits

In the design of a product block cipher it seems reasonable to ask if the components of the cipher generate the symmetric group or as large as possible group.

Proposition 9.8: The group generated by the following two operators acting on the *n*-vectors in $\mathcal{Z}_{2,n}$

9.8a α: addition (with carry) on elements of $\mathcal{Z}_{2,n}$ and

9.8a $\rho\,[\rho^{-1}]$: shift-left [-right] circular

is the symmetric group of permutations of $\mathcal{Z}_{2,n}$.

Proof: This result does *not* state that a particular group of operators generated by α and ρ is the symmetric group. It does imply, however, that when sufficiently long "strings" of these operations are allowed, then the group "approximates" the symmetric group.

To prove Proposition **9.8** we show that every two-element transposition

$$(i,j), \quad i \equiv \underline{x} \quad j \equiv \underline{y},$$

can be constructed by a suitable composition of $\{\alpha, \rho\}$. The notation $i \equiv \underline{x}$ above means that the integer i is the decimal value of the *n*-vector in $\underline{x} \in \mathcal{Z}_{2,n}$.

1. The operator $\beta \equiv \rho^{-1}\alpha^2\rho\,\alpha^{-1}$ interchanges the *n*-vectors $\underbrace{(1,0,0,\cdots,0)}_{n \text{ copies}}$ and $\underline{0} = \underbrace{(0,0,\ldots,0)}_{(n-1) \text{ copies}}$.

$$\underbrace{(1,0,0,\ldots,0)}_{(n-1)\text{ copies}} \overset{\alpha^{-1}}{\to} \underbrace{(0,1,1,\ldots,1)}_{(n-1)\text{ copies}} \overset{\rho}{\to} \underbrace{(1,1,\ldots,1,0)}_{(n-1)\text{ copies}} \overset{\alpha^2}{\to} \underbrace{(0,0,\ldots,0)}_{n\text{ copies}} \overset{\rho^{-1}}{\to} \underbrace{(0,0,\ldots,0)}_{\text{copies}}$$

$$\underbrace{(0,0,\ldots,0)}_{n\text{ copies}} \overset{\alpha^{-1}}{\to} \underbrace{(1,1,\ldots,1)}_{n\text{ copies}} \overset{\rho}{\to} \underbrace{(1,1,\ldots,1)}_{n\text{ copies}} \overset{\alpha^2}{\to} \underbrace{(0,0,\ldots,0,1)}_{(n-1)\text{ copies}} \overset{\rho^{-1}}{\to} \underbrace{(1,0,0,\ldots,0)}_{(n-1)\text{ copies}}.$$

Furthermore, as we show next, *all* other *n*-vectors in $\mathcal{Z}_2$ are fixed points under β:

$$(0,\underline{u},1,\underbrace{0,0,\ldots,0}_{k\text{ copies}}) \overset{\alpha^{-1}}{\to} (0,\underline{u},0,\underbrace{1,1,\ldots,1}_{k\text{ copies}}) \overset{\rho}{\to} (\underline{u},0,\underbrace{1,1,\ldots,1,0}_{k\text{ copies}})$$

$$\overset{\alpha^2}{\to} (\underline{u},1,\underbrace{1,1,\ldots,1}_{k+1\text{ copies}}) \overset{\rho^{-1}}{\to} (0,\underline{u},1,\underbrace{0,0,\ldots,0}_{k\text{ copies}})$$

$$(1,\underline{u},1,\underbrace{0,0,\ldots,0}_{k\text{ copies}}) \overset{\alpha^{-1}}{\to} (1,\underline{u},0,\underbrace{1,1,\ldots,1}_{k\text{ copies}}) \overset{\rho}{\to} (\underline{u},0,\underbrace{1,1,\ldots,1}_{(k+1)\text{ copies}})$$

$$\overset{\alpha^2}{\to} (\underline{u},1,\underbrace{0,0,\ldots,1}_{k\text{ copies}}) \overset{\rho^{-1}}{\to} (1,\underline{u},1,\underbrace{0,0,\ldots,0}_{k\text{ copies}}).$$

2. Next, we observe that $\gamma \equiv \rho\beta\rho^{-1}$ interchanges the n-vectors $(0, \underbrace{0, 0, \ldots, 0}_{(n-1) \text{ copies}})$ and $(0, 0, \ldots, 0, 1)$:
$\underbrace{}_{(n-1) \text{ copies}}$

$$(\underbrace{0, 0, \ldots, 0, 1}_{(n-1) \text{ copies}}) \xrightarrow{\rho^{-1}} (1, \underbrace{0, 0, \ldots, 0}_{(n-1) \text{ copies}}) \xrightarrow{\beta} (0, \underbrace{0, 0, \ldots, 0}_{(n-1) \text{ copies}}) \xrightarrow{\rho} (0, \underbrace{0, 0, \ldots, 0}_{(n-1) \text{ copies}})$$

$$(0, \underbrace{0, 0, \ldots, 0}_{(n-1) \text{ copies}}) \xrightarrow{\rho^{-1}} (0, \underbrace{0, 0, \ldots, 0}_{(n-1) \text{ copies}}) \xrightarrow{\beta} (1, \underbrace{0, 0, \ldots, 0}_{(n-1) \text{ copies}}) \xrightarrow{\rho} (\underbrace{0, 0, \ldots, 0, 1}_{(n-1) \text{ copies}})$$

and an identical argument as in **1.** above shows that *all* other n-vectors in $\mathcal{Z}_{2,n}$ are fixed points of $\rho^{-1}\beta\rho$.

3. Finally, the operation $\alpha^\tau \gamma \alpha^{-x}$ produces the two-element transposition $(r, r+1)$.

It follows that all two-element transpositions (i, j) may be produced by a *word* involving α, its inverse α^{-1}, together with ρ and its inverse ρ^{-1}. This proves that the group generated is the symmetric group of (invertible) transformations on $\mathcal{Z}_n$.

Every permutation on a finite set S can be written as a product of 2-element transpositions. While this representation is not unique, the parity of a representation is always either even, meaning an even number of 2-element transpositions, or odd. The *alternating group* is composed of those permutations whose transpositions have even parity. Coppersmith and Grossman [1975] show that the *round* transformations of DES and LUCIFER can potentially generate the *alternating group* composed of the elements of the symmetric group of (invertible) transformations with even parity.

9.20   A CLASS OF BLOCK CIPHERS

A "Cryptographic Device" designed by my former colleague Dr. Roy L. Adler is described in IBM [1974] and in U.S. Patent #4.255,811 "Key Control Block Cipher System", issued to Adler on March 10, 1981. This algorithm provides the cryptographic feature in a key-card entry system to be described in Chapter 18.

128-bit plaintext blocks are enciphered to 128-bit ciphertext blocks under ,the control of a 128-bit key:

$$\underline{x} = (x_0, x_1, \ldots, x_{127}) \rightarrow y = (y_0, y_1, \ldots, y_{127}).$$

Like LUCIFER and DES, encipherment is the result of r rounds; the $(3 \times 128) + 7$ bits of key used in a round are derived from the user-supplied 128-bit key in a manner to be described shortly.

First, a 128-bit key $\underline{a}_0 = (a_{0,0}, a_{0,1}, \ldots, a_{0,127})$ derived by the *key processor* from the user-supplied key is added modulo 2^{128} to the 128-bit plaintext block $\underline{x} = (x_0, x_1, \ldots, x_{127})$:

$$\underline{x} \rightarrow \underline{y} \equiv \underline{x} + \underline{a}_0$$

Using the key supplied by the processing device, the steps in the ith round are:

Ri-1 Modulo 2^{128}-addition of 128-bit key $\underline{b}_i = (b_{i,0}, b_{i,1}, \ldots, b_{i,127})$

$$\underline{y}_0 \rightarrow \underline{y} + \underline{b}_i.$$

Ri-2 128-to-128 wire-crossing $\underline{\theta} = (\theta_0, \theta_1, \ldots, \theta_{127})$

$$\underline{y}_0 \rightarrow \underline{\theta}(\underline{y} + \underline{b}_i).$$

Ri-3 7- or 8-bit shift-left-circular ρ_i determined by key $\underline{\beta}_i = (\beta_{i,0}, \beta_{i,1}, \ldots, \beta_{i,7})$

$$\underline{y}_0 \rightarrow \rho_{\underline{\beta}}(\underline{\theta}(\underline{y} + \underline{b}_i)).$$

Ri-4 128-to-128 inverse wire-crossing $\underline{\theta}_i^{-1} = (\theta_{i,0}^{-1}, \theta_{i,1}^{-1}, \ldots, \theta_{i,7}^{-1})$

$$\underline{y}_0 \rightarrow \underline{\theta}^{-1}(\rho_{\underline{\beta}}(\underline{\theta}(\underline{y} + \underline{b}_i))).$$

Ri-5 Exclusive-OR of 128-bit key $\underline{c}_i = (c_{i,0}, c_{i,1}, \ldots, c_{i,127})$

$$\underline{y}_0 \rightarrow (\theta^{-1}(\rho_{\underline{\beta}}(\underline{\theta}(\underline{y} + \underline{b}_i)))) + \underline{c}_i.$$

The derivation of the internal key by the key processor is depicted in Figure 9.19. The steps in the generation, of the internal key are:

KP-0 The user-supplied key resides in a 128-bit key register **K**;

KP-1 The content of **K** is loaded into registers **R1**, **R2**, **R3**, and **R4** of sizes 35, 33, 31, and 29 bits;

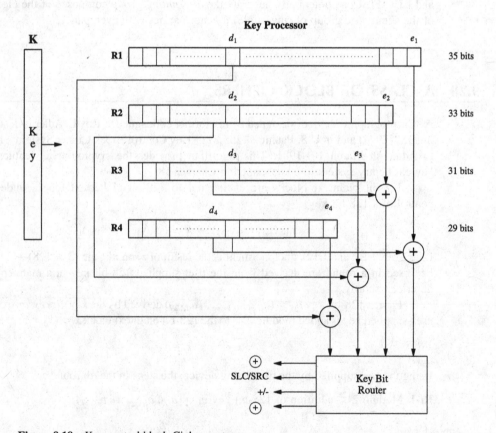

Figure 9.19 Key control block Cipher system.

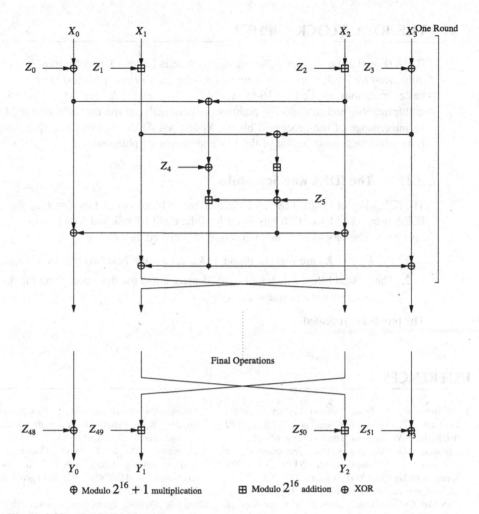

Figure 9.20   The IDEA algorithm.

KP-2 Bits are tapped from register **Ri** at positions d_i and e_i for $i = 1, 2, 3, 4$ in each cycle – the choice tap positions is dependent on the number of rounds r;

KP-3 The XORs

$d_1 \oplus e_4$	$d_2 \oplus e_3$	$d_3 \oplus e_2$	$d_4 \oplus e_1$

are computed at four modulo 2 adders to generate the 4-bit input to tbe *key bit router*;

KP-4   The registers are left-shifted one position after the read operation;

KP-5a Each round takes 32 cycles to generate the required 128 bits for the vector a_0;

KP-5b Each round takes 98 cycles to generate the required $392 = (3 \times 128) + 8$ bits.

As since the lengths of the shift registers. **Rl, R2, R3**, and **R4** are relatively prime, the key generation process is periodic with period $P = 1,038,345 = 35 \times 33 \times 31 \times 29$

9.21 THE IDEA BLOCK CIPHER

IDEA (Fig. 9.20) is a block cipher design by Xuejia Lai and James Massey. Its design was influenced by DES; it uses eight rounds to mix the key and plaintext. In each round the basic operations applied to 16-bit variables X_1, X_1, X_2, X_3 are XOR, modulo $2^{16}+1$ multiplication, and modulo 2^{16} addition. Additionally, at the end of each round there is an interchange of the processed blocks X_1 and X_2. At the end of the eighth round there is an additional combination of the key and processed plaintext.

9.21.1 The IDEA Key Schedule

The IDEA key of length 128-bits is divided into 8 blocks of 16 bits $\underline{K} = (K_0, K_i, \ldots, K_7)$. IDEA uses six blocks of 16 bits in each of the eight rounds and four blocks for the final operation. The blocks used in each round are derived as follows:

1. $K_0, K_1, \ldots, K_5$ are used in round 1; K_6, K_7 are the first two blocks in round 2.
2. The 128-bit block $\underline{K}$ is left-shifted 25 places, and the first four 16-bit blocks K_8, K_9, K_{10}, K_{12} are used in round 2.

The process is repeated.

REFERENCES

T. J. Beth and C. Ding, "Almost Perfect Nonlinear Permutations", *Advances in Cryptology – EUROCRYPT '93*, Springer-Verlag (New York, NY), pp. 65–76.

E. Bilham, "On Matsui's Linear Cryptanalysis", in *Advances in Cryptology, EUROCRYPT '94*, 1995, Springer-Verlag (New York, NY), pp. 341–355.

E. Bilham and A. Shamir, "Differential Cryptanalysis of DES-like Cryptosystems", *Journal of Cryptology*, **4**, 3–72 (1991).

E. Bilham and A. Shamir, "Differential cryptanalysis of Snefru, Khafre, REDOC II, LOKI and LUCIFER", in *Advances in Cryptology – CRYPTO '91*, Springer-Verlag (New York, NY), 1992. pp. 156–171.

E. Bilham and A. Shamir, *Differential Cryptanalysis of the Data Encryption Standard*, Springer-Verlag (New York, NY), 1993.

C. Charnes and J. Piepzryk, "Linear Nonequivalence Versus Nonlinearity", in *Advances in Cryptology–AUSCRYPT '92*, Springer-Verlag (New York, NY), 1993, pp. 156–164.

D. Coppersmith, "The Data Encryption Standard (DES) and its Strength Against Attacks", *IBM Journal of Research and Development*, **30**, 243–250 (1993).

D. Coppersmith and E. Grossman, "Generators for Certain Alternating Groups with Applications to Cryptography", *SIAM Journal of Applied Mathematics*, **29**, 624–627 (1975).

J. Daemen, "Cipher and Hash Function Design Strategies Based on Linear and Differential Cryptanalysis." Doctoral Dissertation, K. U. Leuven. March 1995.

D. W. Davies and G. I. P. Parkin, "The Average Cycle Size of the Key Stream in Output Feedback Encipherment", *Cryptography, Proceedings of the Workshop on Cryptography*, Berg Feuerstein, Germany, March 1992, Springer-Verlag (New York, NY), pp. 263–279.

J. Detombe and S. Tavares, "Constructing Large Cryptographically Strong S-Boxes", in *Advances in Cryptology – AUSCRYP '92*, Springer-Verlag (New York, NY), 1993, pp. 165–181.

Electronic Frontier Foundation, *Secrets of Encryption Research: Wiretap Politics & Chip Design*, Electronic Frontier Foundation, O'Reilly & Associates (Cambridge, Massachusetts), 1998.

H. Feistel "Cryptography and Computer Privacy", *Scientific American*, **228**, 15–23 (1993).

National Bureau of Standards, Federal Information Processing Standards Publication 46-1, "Data Encryption Standard (DES)", National Bureau of Standards, January 22, 1988; superseded by Federal Information Processing Standards Publication 46-2, December 30, 1993, and reaffirmed as FIPS PUB 46-2, October 25, 1999.

National Bureau of Standards, Federal Information Processing Standards Publication 140-1, "Security Requirements for Cryptographic Modules", January 11, 1994.

National Bureau of Standards, Federal information Processing Standards Publication 197, "Advanced Encryption Standard (AES)", November 26, 2001.

"IBM, 2984-1 Data Protection Programming and Procedure Guide". IBM Corporation, November 22, 1971.

IBM, *IBM Technical Disclosure Bulletin*, **16**(10), 3406–3409 (1974).

A. G. Konheim, *Cryptography: A Prime*, Wiley, 1981.

S. LANDAU, "Polynomials in the Nation's Service: Using Algebra to Design the Advanced Encryption Standard", *American Mathematical Monthly*, February, 89–117 (2004).

M. MATSUI, "Linear Cryptanalysis Method for DES Cipher", in *Advances in Cryptology – EUROCRYPT '93*, Springer-Verlag (New York, NY), 1994, pp. 386–397.

K. NYBERG, "On the Construction of Highly Nonlinear Permutations", in *Advances in Cryptology – EUROCRYPT '92*, Springer-Verlag (New York, NY), pp. 92–98, 1993.

K. NYBERG, "Differentially Uniform Mappings for Cryptology", *Advances in Cryptology – EUROCRYPT '93*, Springer-Verlag (New York, NY), pp. 55–64.

L. O'CONNOR, "Convergence in Differential Distributions", in *Advances in Cryptology – EUROCRYPT '94*, Springer-Verlag (New York, NY), 1995a, pp. 13–23.

L. O'CONNOR, "S-boxes and Round Functions with Controllable Linearity and Differentials Uniformity", in *Fast Software Encryption*, Springer-Verlag (New York, NY), 1995b, pp. 111–130.

R. OUTERBRIDGE, "Some Design Criteria for Feistel-Cipher Key Schedules, *Cryptologia*, **10**, 142–156 (1986).

J. P. PIERPRYZK, "Nonlinearity of Exponent Polynomials", in *Advances in Cryptology: EUROCRYPT '89*, J.-J. QUISQUATER AND J. VANDEWALLE (eds), Springer-Verlag (New York, NY), 1990, pp. 89–92.

J. DAEMEN AND V. RIJMEN, "AES Proposal: Rijndael" (1999b). Available at http://crsc.nist.gov.encryption/aes/rijndael/.

J. DAEMEN AND V. RIJMEN, "Annex to AES Proposal: Chapter 5, Propagation and Correlation" (1999a). Available at http://crsc.nist.gov.encryption/aes/rijndael/.

O. S. ROTHHAUS. "On Bent Functions", *Journal of Combinatorial Theory*, **20A**, pp. 300–305 (1976).

J. SEBERRY AND XIAN-MO ZHENG, "Highly Nonlinear 0-1 Balanced Boolean Functions Satisfying Strict Avalanche Criterion", in *Advances in Cryptology – AUSCRYPT '92*, Springer-Verlag (New York, NY), 1993, pp. 145–155.

J. SEBERRY, XIAN-MO ZHANG, AND Y. ZHENG, "Improving the Strict Avalanche Characteristics of Cryptographic Functions", *Information Processing Letters*, **50**, 1994, pp. 37–41.

J. SEBERRY, XIAN-MO ZHANG, AND Y. ZHENG, Relationships Among Nonlinearity Criteria", in *Advances in Cryptology – EUROCRYPT '94*, Springer-Verlag (New York, NY), 1995, pp. 376–386.

J. L. SMITH, "The Design of Lucifer, A Cryptographic Device for Data Communications", IBM Research Report RC3326, Yorktown Heights, New York, 1971.

A. SORKIN, "Lucifer, A Cryptographic Algorithm", *Cryptologia*, **8**, pp. 22–41 (1984); with addendum *Cryptologia*, **84**, 260–261 (1984).

M. WIENER, "Efficient DES Key Search", reprinted in *Practical Cryptography for Data Internetworks*, William Stallings (ed.), IEEE Computer Society Press (New York, NY), 1996, pp. 31–79.

Bruce Schneier Applied Cryptography (2nd edn), John Wiley, 1993, p. 296.

CHAPTER 10

THE PARADIGM OF PUBLIC KEY CRYPTOGRAPHY

THE ENLARGED role of information processing in non-governmental applications, the emergence of the Internet and its potential for commercial transactions over public data networks (E-commerce) became the stimulus for the development of a new type of cryptographic system. While governments have couriers capable of distributing keys between users by an alternative secure path, commercial users needed a new approach to securely connect two users over a potentially *insecure networks*. The solution was *public key* cryptography in which the capability to encipher data was separated from the capability to decipher it. This chapter introduces the concepts and implications of public key cryptographic systems.

10.1   IN THE BEGINNING. . .

For centuries, encipherment was provided exclusively by *conventional* or *single key* cryptosystems. A class of transformations $\mathcal{K} = \{T_k : k \in \mathcal{K}\}$ was defined with $y = T_k(x)$ denoting the ciphertext resulting from the encipherment of x using the key k. Knowledge of k permitted the computation of T_k^{-1} and the recovery of the plaintext $x = T_k^{-1}(y)$. Each party to an enciphered communication *either* agreed in advance to key k or a third party delivered the key over an alternative *secure path*. The secrecy proffered by the encipherment data depended on whether the cryptosystem T would resist cryptanalysis. Could the key k or plaintext be recovered from $\{y_i = T_k(x_i)\}$ under suitable conditions?

All of this changed in 1976 with the appearance of papers by Whitfield Diffie (then a graduate student) and Martin Hellman [Diffie and Hellman 1976a,b]. They invented *public key cryptography* (PKC) in response to the expanded role of information processing technology in our society, coupled with access to public data networks. Encipherment would not only be needed by governments, but also to protect

- The confidentiality of medical record, and
- That of participants in commercial transactions carried out over a public data network.

The first customers were banks and large corporations. In the mid-1960s, the International Business Machines Corporation decided to provide its customers with the capability to protect communications and files. The LUCIFER algorithm was incorporated in an IBM product for a banking customer. Lloyd's Bank (London) requested the IBM Corporation to design a banking system incorporating automated teller machines (ATMs) to facilitate 24-hour banking services (deposits, withdrawals). The transactions between the ATM and the bank's processor would be over public networks and require protection. Cryptography was incorporated into the authentication protocol in IBM's Liberty Banking System.

In response to the need for secure methods of processor-to-processor communication and the related problem of file security, the National Bureau of Standards (NBS) solicited proposals for a National Encryption Standard in the *Federal Register* in 1972. An IBM product division modified LUCIFER and submitted the algorithm, now referred to as the *data encryption standard* (DES).

The debate about DES awakened the need for research in cryptography by the academic and commercial sectors. The past twenty years has witnessed the development of a technical competence in cryptography in the academic and commercial sectors.

10.2 KEY DISTRIBUTION

The traditional role of cryptography is to hide the data in communications. The availability of public data networks meant that large amounts of data might be transmitted over potentially insecure channels. Methods were needed to protect the privacy of such information while at the same time providing relatively open access for users with a need to obtain the information. When the government uses cryptography it provides a secure path using couriers for the distribution of keys.

If N users are connected by a computer network as shown in Figure 10.1, where the network links are insecure, then they might be wiretapped by an *opponent*. If a single-key cryptosystem is used to encipher data, it is necessary that a key $k_{i,j}$ ($i \neq j$) be specified and available for each pair of networked users. It is not feasible in a network of N users for each user to maintain a table of $\approx N^2$ keys $\{k_{i,j}\}$. The problem of *key exchange* or *key distribution* is to implement a secure mechanism to make the keys available for each pair of users.

One simple solution uses a *trusted authority* or *key server* as proposed by Needham and Schroeder [1978]. Each user has a network-unique (user) *identifier* and secret key; ID[i] is the identifier of User_ID[i] and K(ID[i]) is User_ID[i]'s secret key. The key server maintains a table with entries (ID[i], K(ID[i])) of the N keys of the users. The key server is responsible for securely maintain this table.

User_ID[i] communicates with the key server an intention to securely communicate with User_ID[j]; the key server performs the following services:

1. The key server generates a random *session key* k_{SK};
2. (a) The key server retrieves the secret key K(ID[i]) of User_ID[i], enciphers and transmits to User_ID[i] the session key k_{SK} enciphered using User_ID[i]'s private key $E_{K(ID[i])}\{ID[i], ID[j], k_{SK}\}$.
   (b) The key server retrieves the secret key K(ID[j]) of User_ID[j], enciphers and transmits to User_ID[j] the session key k_{SK} enciphered using User_ID[j]'s private key $E_{K(ID[j])}\{ID[i], ID[j], k_{SK}\}$.
3. (a) User_ID[i] deciphers $E_{K(ID[i])}\{ID[i], ID[j], k_{SK}\}$ and obtains the session key k_{SK}.
   (b) User_ID[j] deciphers $E_{K(ID[j])}\{ID[i], ID[j], k_{SK}\}$ and obtains the session key k_{SK}.

A solution using a key server suffers from the need to maintain a table, adding users as they join the network. This might have been feasible when the Internet consisted of a few thousand users, but it is very difficult to manage networks with several million users. Moreover, many independent public networks with different operating systems need to be connected

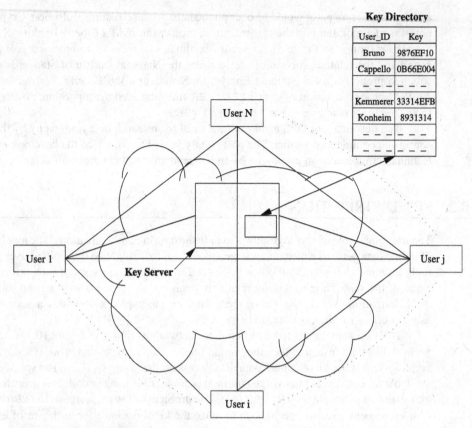

Figure 10.1 Network Key Server.

and it is not feasible for a single key server to provide network-wide serve. There must be a hierarchy of key servers with different domains and keys used to exchange information between the key servers if User_ID[i] and User_ID[j] are in different domains.

10.3 E-COMMERCE

The use of networks for *electronic commerce* (E-commerce) to be examined in Chapter 18 provides a second application of cryptography.

- Customer_ID[A] might want to buy 100 shares of IBM at \$151/share from Broker_ID[B];
- Customer_ID[A] might want to buy a book from Seller_ID[B] (www.amazon.com);
- Customer_ID[A] might want to buy airplane tickets from Seller_ID[C] (www.orbitz.com).

There are several issues in these examples of E-commerce;

- If payment is made by direct debit of the purchaser's bank account, Customer_ID[A] is concerned about the secrecy of the bank account number and authorization traveling over the network;

- If payment is made with a credit card, Customer_ID[A] is concerned about the secrecy of the credit card number traveling over the network to Server_ID[B] and Server_ID[C];

- User_ID[A] wants proof that a purchase was made and the terms of the transaction; and

- The network servers Server_ID[B] and Server_ID[C] want proof that an order was received from Customer_ID[A].

In normal commercial transactions, the parties meet and sign in each other's presence a document (contract) specifying the rules of their transaction. In E-commerce, an electronic transaction requires a *digital signature* to be appended to the transaction data. We return to this problem in Chapter 17.

10.4 PUBLIC-KEY CRYPTOSYSTEMS: EASY AND HARD COMPUTATIONAL PROBLEMS

Diffie and Hellman proposed a new type of cryptosystem that would alleviate but *not* eliminate the problem of key distribution *and* also provide a mechanism for digital signatures. The characteristic property of conventional cryptosystems $T = \{T_k : k \in \mathcal{K}\}$ is that T_k determines the inverse transformation T_k^{-1}. Normally, the key k determines a second key k^{-1} so that $T_k^{-1} = T_{k-1}$. Diffie and Hellman proposed (public-key) cryptosystems that used two keys: a *public key* PuK for encipherment and a *private key* PrK for decipherment.

$$\text{Encipher} : \underline{x} \rightarrow \underline{y} = E_{\text{PuK}}\{\underline{x}\}$$
$$\text{Decipher} : \underline{y} \rightarrow \underline{x} = E_{\text{PrK}}\{\underline{x}\}.$$

In addition to the usual properties required of a *strong* cryptosystem, it was crucial that the computation of PrK with knowledge of PuK would be infeasible. User_ID[A] would publish the public key PuK(ID[A]) and thereby enable every user to encipher information intended only for User_ID[A]. Knowledge of PrK(ID[A]), known only by User_ID[A], would permit User_ID[A] to decipher such messages. How can such pairs (PuK(ID[A]), (PrK(ID[A])) be found?

Diffie and Hellman argued that there are complex mathematical functions $f(x)$ for which the problem

> *Given*: x
>
> *Find*: $y = f(x)$

is easy to solve, but for which the problem

> *Given*: $y = f(x)$
>
> *Find*: x

is hard to solve.

A solution to the easy problem would be computation of the ciphertext, the encipherment $y = E_{\text{PuK(ID[A])}}\{x\}$ of the plaintext x using User_ID[A]'s public key PuK(ID[A]). A solution to the hard problem would be computation of the plaintext, the decipherment $x = E_{\text{PrK(ID[A])}}\{y\}$ of the ciphertext y using User_ID[A]'s private key PrK(ID[A]).

Easy and hard refer to the complexity class of the problem. A problem is considered *computationally infeasible* if the cost of finding a solution, as measured by either the amount of memory used or the computing time, while finite is extraordinarily large, much greater than the value of the solution. The *execution time* of an algorithm A with n inputs is the number of times some basic operation is performed. Algorithm A with n inputs executes in *polynomial time* or is an $O(n^d)$-algorithm if there is a constant C such that the execution time is no larger than Cn^d.

Many problems admit such a description; two examples are

1. *Addition*
   - *Given* n-bits $(x_0, x_1, \ldots, x_{n-1})$ and n integers $(b_0, b_1, \ldots, b_{n-1})$ each expressed with n bits
   - *Compute* the sum $S = \sum_{i=0}^{n-1} b_i x_i$.

   The sum may be computed by an $O(n^2)$-algorithm.

2. *Modular Exponentiation*
   - *Given* M, e, and N, each an n-bit integer
   - *Compute* $C = M^e$ (modulo N).

   C may be computed using a $O(n^3)$-algorithm.

For some problems; either a polynomial time algorithm $O(n^d)$ for the solution is *unknown* or the running time of the best *known* algorithm is exponential-like.

1. *Knapsack Problem*
   - *Given* the sum S
   - *Compute* n-bits $(x_0, x_1, \ldots, x_{n-1})$ to satisfy $S = \sum_{i=0}^{n-1} b_i x_i$. $(x_0, x_1, \ldots, x_{n-1})$ may be computed by a $O(2^{n/2})$-algorithm.
   No polynomial time algorithm is *known*.

2. *Logarithm Problem* (modulo N)
   - *Given* $C = M^e$ (modulo N), M, and N where C, M, and N are each n-bit integers.
   - *Calculate* the (discrete) logarithm $e = \log_M C$ (modulo N)
   $\log_M C$ (modulo N) may be calculated using a $O(2^{\beta\sqrt{\log n \log \log n}})$-algorithm.

No $O(n^d)$-algorithm to compute $\log_M C$ (modulo N) is *known*.
Generally speaking, a problem is

- *Easy*, if a $O(n^c)$-algorithm is *known* to find a solution, and
- *Hard*, if no $O(n^d)$-algoithm to find a solution is *known*.

Complexity theory stemming from the work of Alan Turing classifies algorithms (or problems) depending on their execution times.

P Polynomial-time problems with n inputs. An $O(n^d)$-algorithm to solve the problem exists.

NP Nondeterministic polynomial-time problems with n inputs. An $O(n^d)$-algorithm to check a possible solution to the problem exists.

Complexity theory identifies a distinguished subclass of **NP** consisting of problems that are *equivalent*, in the sense that a solution to any one **NP-Complete** problem can be transformed to a solution to another problem in this class.

The relationship between the classes is not known; in particular, the truth of the equality $\mathbf{P} = \mathbf{NP}$ or proper inclusion $\mathbf{P} \subset \mathbf{NP}$ remains unsettled. If the second statement $\mathbf{P} \subset \mathbf{NP}$ is true, there are some problems for which *no* $O(n^d)$ solution algorithm exists. Examples of corresponding easy (f) and hard (f^{-1}) problems include:

E   *Addition (of knapsack weights)*

  – *Given* a knapsack vector $\underline{b} = (b_0,\ b_1, \ldots, b_n)$ and a selection vector $\underline{x} = (x_0, x_1, \ldots, x_{n-1}); \quad (x_i = 0,\ 1)$

  – *Compute* $S = b_0 x_0 + b_1 x_1 + \cdots + b_{n-1} x_{n-1}$; Addition (of knapsack weights) is in the complexity call $\mathbf{P}$.

H   *Knapsack Problem (Subset Sum Problem)*

  – *Given a* knapsack vector $\underline{b} = (b_0, b_1, \ldots, b_{n-1})$ and a sum S

  – *Determine* a vector $\underline{x} = (x_0, x_1, \ldots, x_{n-1})$ with components 0 and 1 such that

$$S = b_0 x_0 + b_1 x_1 + \cdots + b_{n-1} x_{n-1}.$$

The knapsack problem is in the complexity class **NP-Complete**. No **P**-algorithm to solve the knapsack problem is *known*. The fastest algorithm to solve the knapsack problem runs in time $O(2^{\pi/2})$

E   *Multiplication of Integers*

  – *Given* integers p and q whose lengths are each n-bits.

  – *Calculate the product* $N = pq$.

Multiplication of integers is in the complexity class $\mathbf{P}$.

H   *Factorization of Integers*

  – *Given* an n-bit integer that is the product of two primes p, q.

  – *Calculate* the factors p and q.

Factorization is in the complexity class **NP**; it is not believed to be **NP-Complete**. No **P**-algorithm to factor is *known*. There is a $O(2^{\alpha\sqrt{\log n \log \log n}})$-algorithm to factor.

E   *Modular Exponentiation* (Modulo p)

  – *Given* p a prime, q a primitive root of p and e an exponent each number requiring n-bits. Note, q is a *primitive root* of p if the powers q^i (modulo p) are distinct for $0 \le i < p - 1$ and therefore a rearrangement (permutation) of the integers $1, 2, 3, \ldots, p - 1$

  – *Calculate* $N = q^e$ (modulo p).

Exponentiation modulo p is in the complexity class $\mathbf{P}$. Exponentiation modulo p is an $O(n^3)$-algorithm.

H   *Logarithm Problem* (modulo p)

  – *Given* p a prime, q a primitive root of p and $N = q^e$ (modulo p).

  – *Calculate ithe exponent* e $= \log_q N$ (modulo p).

Taking logarithms modulo p is in the complexity class **NP**; it is not believed to be **NP-Complete**. No **P**-algorithm to calculate logarithms modulo p is *known*. There is a $O(2^{\beta\sqrt{\log n \log \log n}})$-algorithm to calculate logarithms modulo p.

Diffie and Hellman suggested that encipherment be based on an *easy* problem while decipherment requires the solution of the corresponding *hard* problem. But there is a detect! If computing $y = f(x)$ is easy, but computing $x = f^{-1}(y)$ is infeasible for a third party, it must also be so for the creator of the (easy, hard)-pair. Diffie and Hellman called f a *trap-door* one-way function if it satisfies the following three properties:

1. *Given*:

    A description of $f(x)$ and x;

    It is computationally feasible to compute $y = f(x)$.

2. *Given*:

    A description of $f(x)$ and $y = f(x)$;

    It is computationally *in*feasible to compute $x = f^{-1}(x)$.

3. *Given*:

    A description of $f(x)$ and $y = f(x)$ and parameters z;

    It is computationally feasible to compute $x = f^{-1}(y)$.

In problem 3

1. The computation of $y = f(x)$ is the encipherment $E_{PuK}\{x\} \rightarrow y$ of the plaintext with the public key PuK, and

2. The computation of $x = f^{-1}(y)$ is the decipherment $E_{PrK}\{y\} \rightarrow x$ of the ciphertext with the private key PrK, then

knowledge of the trap-door z for a trap-door one-way function f, permits the construction of a pair (PuK, PrK) of public-key cryptosystem keys. Without the trap-door z, a user is not in a position to find PrK from PuK.

    What functions f are one-way and which of them have trap-doors? Diffie and Hellman [1976a,b] were unable to provide any example of a trap-door one-way function. Merkle and Hellman [1978] described a PKS that satisfied *some* but not *all* of the requirements of a trap-door PKS. Shortly thereafter, Ronald Rivest, Adi Shamir, and Len Adelman [1978] provided the first example of a public-key cryptosystem, which, to the best of out current knowledge, meets all of the desiderata of a PKS system.

    In terms of easy and hard problems, the Merkle-Hellman and RSA Systems are compared in Table 10.1. Chapter 11 discusses the Merkle–Hellman knapsack encipherment, Chapter 12 RSA encipherment. The strength of the RSA cryptosystem appears to

TABLE 10.1 Comparison of the Merkle–Hellman and RSA Systems

Easy			Hard		
Merkle–Hellman					
Given	plaintext	$\underline{x}$	*Given*	ciphertext	$S = \sum_{i=0}^{n-1} b_i x_i$
	key	$\underline{b}$		key	$\underline{b}$
Compute	ciphertext	$S = \sum_{i=0}^{m-1} b_i x_i$	*Compute*	plaintext	$\underline{x}$
RSA					
Given	plaintext	M	*Given*	ciphertext	$C = M^e$ (modulo N)
	key	e, N		key	e, N
Compute	ciphertext	$C = M^e$ (modulo N)	*Compute*	plaintext	M

depend on the difficulty of factoring large numbers. The generation of prime numbers and factorization are reviewed in Chapter 13. Remarkably, elliptic groups provide a framework in which integer factorization may be carried out efficiently. Chapter 15 describes elliptic groups and a public-key system based on (discrete) elliptic groups published in 1993.

10.5 DO PKCs SOLVE THE PROBLEM OF KEY DISTRIBUTION?

In a PKC system, User_ID[A] enciphers data for User_ID[B] using User_ID[B]'s public key PuK(ID[B]). How does User_ID[A] learn the value of PuK(ID[B])? There is either

1. A network-wide table of pairs (ID[. . .],PuK(ID[. . .])) maintained by some entity that User_ID[A] accesses, or

2. User_ID[B] delivers PuK(ID[B]) to User_ID[A] on demand, or

3. User_ID[A] receives PuK(ID[B]) at the time of a transaction from some entity.

We seem to be faced with the same problem considered in Section 10.2. Of course, if User_ID[A] asks User_ID[B] to transmit a copy of PuK(ID[B]), then communications enciphered with PuK(ID[B]) would then be able to be read only by someone with knowledge of PrK(ID[B]), but who might the party supplying PuK(ID[B]) be? It is necessary for User_ID[A] to have some way of verifying the link ID[B] $\longleftrightarrow$ PuK(ID[B]).

The need for a *certificate* to authenticate link the public key and identifier of a user was conceived in 1978 by Adelman's student Kohnfelder [1978]. In Part I, Section D, *Weaknesses in Public-Key Cryptosystems* of Kohnfelder [1978], Kohnfelder writes

> *Although the enemy may eavesdrop on the key transmission system, the key must be sent via a channel in such a way that the originator of the transmission is reliably known.*

Kohnfelder observed that *all* public-key cryptosystems are vulnerable to a *spoofing* attack if the public keys are not certified; User_ID[C] pretending to be User_ID[A] *to* User_ID[B] by providing User_ID[C]'s public key (in place of User_ID[A]'s public key) *to* User_ID[B]. Unless User_ID[B] has some way of checking the correspondence between ID[A] and PuK(ID[K]), this type of spoofing attack is possible.

Kohnfelder said that

> *. . . each user who wishes to receive private communications must place his enciphering algorithm (his public key) in the public file.*

Kohnfelder proposed a method to make spoofing more difficult in Part III of Kohnfelder [1978]. He postulates the existence of a *public file* $\mathcal{F}$ which contains (in my notation) pairs {ID[A], PuK(ID[A])} for each user in the system. While it might be possible for User_ID[A] to contact $\mathcal{F}$ to ask for a copy of User_ID[B]'s public key, this solution suffers from the same operational defect as a network-wide key server:

- What entity will maintain and certify a large database that is continually changing?
- The public file will need to be replicated to prevent severe access times to obtain information.

Kohnfelder defines a *certificate* as a dataset consisting of an *authenticator* ($A_{ID[A]}$) and an *identifier* (ID[A]), which are related by

$$A_{ID[A]} = E_{PrK([\mathcal{F}])}\{ID[A], \ PuK(ID[A])\},$$

where $PrK([\mathcal{F}])$ is the private key of $\mathcal{F}$.

Any user can check the correspondence $AU_{ID} \Longleftrightarrow ID$ by making the comparison

$$ID[A], PuK(ID[A]) \overset{?}{=} E_{PrK([\mathcal{F}])}\{AU_{ID[A]}\},$$

where $PuK([\mathcal{F}])$ is the well-known public key of $\mathcal{F}$. However, if the public-key cryptosystem is *strong*, then it will not be computationally feasible for a user to determine $PrK([\mathcal{F}])$ from $PuK([\mathcal{F}])$.

10.6 P.S.

Although Diffie and Hellman are acknowledged as the inventors of public-key cryptography, the idea was apparently discovered before their papers appeared. GCHQ is responsible for communications intelligence in the United Kingdom, much as NSA is in the United States. And like NSA, its discoveries are often not shared with the scientific community. James H. Eillis, Clifford C. Cocks, and Malcolm J. Williamson were employed at GCHQ in the 1960s. They published internal Computer Electronics Security Group (CESG) reports in the 1970–1976 period [Ellis, 1970; Cocks, 1973; Williamson, 1974, 1976]. There is also a paper [Ellis, 1987] reviewing GCHQ activity in this area. This paper claims they invented the concept of public-key cryptography, motivated as Diffie and Hellman. One system proposed by Cocks was a variant of the RSA system.

The secret environment of the government intelligence agencies worked against the inventors and it remained a secret until its discovery in 1976. To be fair to Cocks, Ellis and Williamson,

1. The issue of key distribution would not really be a natural problem for cryptographers in the employ of GCHQ to study, and

2. The need for digital signatures to support E-commerce is also not a likely subject for study.

The real contribution of Diffie–Hellman is *not* only the invention of asymmetric two-key cryptography, but the realization that there was a real need for it.

The url www.cesg.gov.uk contains links to papers describing the invention by Cocks et al.

REFERENCES

C. C. Cocks, "A Note on Non-Secret Encryption", CESG Report, 20 November 1973.

J. H. Ellis, "The Possibility of Secure Non-Secret Digital Encryption", CESG Report, January 1970.

J. H. Ellis, "The Story of Non-Secret Encryption", available on the web at www.cesg.gov.uk/site/publications/media/ellis.pdf, 1987.

W. Diffie and M. Hellman, "Multiuser Cryptographic Techniques", *National Computer Conference*, New York, 1976a, pp. 109–112.

W. Diffie and M. Hellman, "New Directions in Cryptography", *IEEE Transactions on Information Theory*, **IT-22**, 644–654 (1976b).

L. M. Kohnfelder, "Towards a Practical Public-Key Cryptosystem", M.I.T Bachelor's Thesis, May 1978.

R. C. Merkle and M. E. Hellman, "Hiding Information and Signatures in Trapdoor Knapsacks", *IEEE Transactions on Information Theory*, **IT-24**, 525–530 (1978).

R. M. Needham and M. D. Schroeder, "Using Authentication for Authentication in Large Networks of Computers", *Communications of the ACM*, **21**, 993–999 (1978).

R. L. Rivest, A. Shamir, and L. Adelman, "A Method for Obtaining Digital Signatures and Public-Key Cryptosystems", *Communications of the ACM*, **21**, 120–126 (1998).

M. J. Williamson, "Non-Secret Encryption Using a Finite Field", CESG Report, 21 January 1974.

M. J. Williamson, "Thoughts on Cheaper Non-Secret Encryption", CESG Report, 10 August 1976.

CHAPTER 11

THE KNAPSACK CRYPTOSYSTEM

THE MERKLE-HELLMAN knapsack system was the first example of a public key cryptographic system. Although the trap-door knapsack problem did not live up to its promises of being "computationally infeasible" to solve, it was a major cryptographic achievement. This chapter examines the contribution and the remarkably elegant cryptanalysis of the Merkle–Hellman system by Adi Shamir.

11.1 SUBSET SUM AND KNAPSACK PROBLEMS

The original (one-dimensional) knapsack problem is a problem of combinatorial optimization; items of different weights are to be packed into a knapsack (container) of total capacity S.

> *Given*: An integer S and a *knapsack vector* $a = (a_0, a_1, \ldots, a_{n-1})$ of knapsack lengths $\{a_i\}$,
>
> *Find*: All solutions of $\sum_{i=0}^{n-1} x_i a_i \leq S$ with $x_i \in \{0,1\}$ $(0 \leq i < n)$.

Different variants of the knapsack problem exist, including

- *Bin packing*, in which the number or total length of the items to be packed into $N > 1$ *bins* (containers) each of capacity b is to be maximized;
- *Stock cutting*, in which several (one-dimensional) items (e.g., rolls of paper or perhaps extraordinarily long kosher sausages) each of length b are to be cut into pieces of possible lengths $\{a_i\}$ with minimal wastage;
- The $(0,1)$-knapsack problem in dimension $M > 1$ where items of specified shapes of areas (volumes) $\{a_i\}$ can be packed into an M-dimensional knapsack of total area (volume).

Solutions of these knapsack problems are in general, difficult to obtain and therefore they are candidates for problems that might lead to strong public key cryptosystems as described in Chapter 10. We formulate a $(0, 1)$-knapsack problem in two guises as shown in **Table 11.1**. Note that S-SUM$\{\underline{a}, b\}$ and $K\{\underline{a}, b\}$ are NP-complete.

Proposition 11.1: S-SUM$\{\underline{a}, b\}$ and $K\{\underline{a}, b\}$ are equivalent.

Proof: Suppose ALG$\{\underline{a}, b\}$ is an algorithm whose output is YES if there is a solution to the subset sum problem S-SUM$\{\underline{a}, b\}$ and NO otherwise. By evaluating

---

TABLE 11.1 Two Subset Sum Problems

Subset Sum Problem **S-SUM{$\underline{a}$, b}**

Given: $\underline{a} = (a_0, a_1, \ldots, a_{n-1}) \in \mathcal{Z}_n^+, b \in \mathcal{Z}^+$
Determine: The existence of a $(0, 1)$-vector $\underline{x} = (x_0, x_1, \ldots, x_{n-1}) \in \mathcal{Z}_{2,n}$, a solution of $b = \sum_{i=0}^{n-1} a_i x_i$.
(0,1)-Knapsack Problem **K{$\underline{a}$, b}**
Given: $\underline{a} = (a_0, a_1, \ldots, a_{n-1}) \in \mathcal{R}_n^+, b \in \mathcal{R}^+$
Find: Any $(0,1)$-vector $\underline{x} = (x_0, x_1, \ldots, x_{n-1}) \in \mathcal{Z}_{2,n}$, which is a solution of $b = \sum_{i=0}^{n-1} a_i x_i$.

ALG$\{(a_0, a_1, \ldots, a_{i-1}, a_{i+1}, \ldots, a_{n-1}), b - a_i \varepsilon\}$ for $i = 0, 1, \ldots$, with $\varepsilon = 0, 1$, a solution to the knapsack problem $K\{\underline{a}, b\}$ is found.

The statement, that S-SUM$\{\underline{a}, b\}$ and $K\{\underline{a}, b\}$ are NP-complete is an assertion about the *general* instance of the $(0,1)$-knapsack problem, without conditions on $\underline{a}$. For some special knapsack vectors, a solution of the problem $K\{\underline{a}, b\}$ poses no difficulty.

Example 11.1

If $\underline{a} = (1, 2, 4, 8, 16, 32, 64, 128)$ and $b = 71$, a solution of $K\{\underline{a}, b\}$ asks for the base-2 representation of b, so that it has the unique solution $\underline{x} = (1, 1, 1, 0, 0, 0, 1, 0)$.

There are other simple knapsack problem, like the base-2 coding in *Example 11.1*. For example, call a knapsack vector $\underline{s} = (s_0, s_1, \ldots, s_{n-1}$ a *super-increasing knapsack vector* and write $\underline{s} \in \text{SUP}_n$, if

$$0 < s_0 < s_1 < \cdots < s_{n-1} \quad \text{and} \quad \sum_{i=0}^{j-1} s_i < s_j, \quad 1 \le j < n.$$

The components of $\underline{s} \in \text{SUP}_n$ increase exponentially like the powers $1, 2, 2^2, 2^4, \ldots$.

If $\underline{s}$ is a super-increasing knapsack vector, the solution of $K\{\underline{s}, t\}$, if it exists, is unique and is easy to determine.

11.1.1 Algorithm 11A: Solution of K{s, t}, with s ∈ SUP$_n$

Set $t^{(0)} = t$ and $\underline{s}^{(0)} = (s_0, s_1, \ldots, s_{n-1})$;
For $j = 0$ to $n-1$ do Steps 1 and 2a or 2b.

1. Evaluate

$$\Delta_j \equiv t_j - \sum_{i=0}^{n-j-2} s_i.$$

2a. If $\Delta_j > 0$, then set
   $$x_{n-j-1} = 1 \quad \underline{s}^{(j+1)} = (s_0, s_1, \ldots, s_{n-j-2}) \quad t_{j+1} = t_j - s_{n-j-1} \quad \text{and} \quad j \to j+1.$$

   Return to Step 1 and solve the reduced knapsack problem $K\{\underline{s}^{(j+1)}, t_{j+1}\}$.

2b. If $\Delta_j \le 0$, then set
   $$x_{n-j-1} = 0 \quad \underline{s}^{(j+1)} = (s_0, s_1, \ldots, s_{n-j-2}) \quad t_{j+1} = t_j \quad \text{and} \quad j \to j+1.$$

   Return to Step 1 and solve the reduced knapsack problem $K\{\underline{s}^{(j+1)}, t_{j+1}\}$.

3. If $\begin{cases} t_n = 0, & \text{a solution to } K\{\underline{s}, t\} \text{ exists and has been found.} \\ t_n \ne 0, & \text{no solution to } K\{\underline{s}, t\} \text{ exists.} \end{cases}$

   END.

Example 11.2

When $n = 4$, $\underline{s} = (2, 3, 9, 16)$, and $t = 1, 12, 15$, the steps in the execution of the above algorithm are

j	t_j	Δ_j	$\underline{x}$	j	t_j	Δ_j	$\underline{x}$	j	t_j	Δ_j	$\underline{x}$
	1		(?,?,?,?)		12		(?,?,?,?)		15		(?,?,?,?)
0	1	-13	(?,?,?,0)	0	12	-2	(?,?,?,0)	0	15	1	(?,?,?,1)
1	-1	-4	(?,?,0,0)	1	12	7	(?,?,1,0)	0	1	-6	(?,?,0,1)
2	1	-1	(?,0,0,0)	2	3	0	(?,1,1,0)	2	-1	-1	(?,0,0,1)
3	1	-1	(0,0,0,0)	3	0	0	(0,1,1,0)	3	-1	-1	(0,0,0,1)

One reason solutions of the knapsack problem are difficult to obtain is that some parameter sets $(\underline{a}, b)$ may yield *no* solution $\underline{x}$, but others may yield *more* than one solution.

Example 11.3

If $\underline{a} = (1, 4, 6, 11, 25)$, then $K\{\underline{a}, b\}$ has

- *Two* solutions $\underline{x} = (1, 1, 1, 0, 1)$ and $\underline{x} = (0, 0, 0, 1, 1)$ if $b = 36$;
- *One* solution $\underline{x} = (0, 1, 1, 0, 1)$ if $b = 35$;
- *No* solution if $b = 34$.

Proposition 11.2: If a solution to $K\{\underline{s}, t\}$ with $\underline{s} \in \text{SUP}_n$ exists, it is unique.

11.2 MODULAR ARITHMETIC AND THE EUCLIDEAN ALGORITHM

The starting point for our study of modular arithmetic is Proposition **11.3**.

Proposition 11.3: (The Division Algorithm for Integers): If $a, b \in \mathcal{Z}$, with $b > 0$, there exist unique integers $q, r \in \mathcal{Z}$ such that $a = qb + r$ with $0 \leq r < b$ and we write $a = r$ (modulo b).

Proof: If b divides a, then $a = qb$ and the algorithm is true with $r = 0$. Otherwise, let $S = \{a - qb : q \in \mathcal{Z}, a - qb > 0\}$.

11.3a If $A > 0$, $q = 0$ is in S so that $S \neq \emptyset$;

11.3b If $a \leq 0$, let $q = a - 1$ so that $q < 0$. If $b \geq 1$, then $a - qb = a(1 - b) + b > 0$ so again $S \neq \emptyset$.

By the well-ordering principle, S has a minimum element, say r. If $r = a - qb$, then $0 \leq r < b$ or otherwise $r - b = a - (q + 1)b$, contradicting the minimality of r. ∎

For every integer $n \geq 2$, addition, subtraction, and multiplication can be defined on the set of *residues modulo n*, that is, on the set of integers $\mathcal{Z}_n = \{0, 1, 2, \ldots, n - 1\}$. If $a, b \in \mathcal{Z}_n$, the division algorithm can be used to define addition, subtraction, and multiplication as follows:

$$+: a + b = qn + r; \ 0 \leq r < n \qquad r = (a + b) \text{ (modulo } n)$$
$$-: a - b = sn + t; \ 0 \leq t < n \qquad t = (a - b) \text{ (modulo } n)$$
$$\times: a \times b = un + v; \ 0 \leq v < n \qquad v = (a \times b) \text{ (modulo } n)$$

Example 11.4

The addition and multiplication tables for modulo n arithmetic with $n = 2, 3$ and 6 are

$a + b$ (modulo 2)		
$a \downarrow b \rightarrow$	0	1
0	0	1
1	1	0

$a \times b$ (modulo 2)		
$a \downarrow b \rightarrow$	0	1
0	0	0
1	0	1

$a + b$ (modulo 3)			
$a \downarrow b \rightarrow$	0	1	2
0	0	1	2
1	1	2	0
2	2	0	1

$a \times b$ (modulo 3)			
$a \downarrow b \rightarrow$	0	1	2
0	0	0	0
1	0	1	2
2	0	2	1

$a + b$ (modulo 6)						
$a \downarrow b \rightarrow$	0	1	2	3	4	5
0	0	1	2	3	4	5
1	1	2	3	4	5	0
2	2	3	4	5	0	1
3	3	4	5	0	1	2
4	4	5	0	1	2	3
5	5	0	1	2	3	4

$a \times b$ (modulo 6)						
$a \downarrow b \rightarrow$	0	1	2	3	4	5
0	0	0	0	0	0	0
1	0	1	2	3	4	5
2	0	2	4	0	2	4
3	0	3	0	3	0	3
4	0	4	2	0	4	2
5	0	5	4	3	2	1

$\mathcal{Z}_n$, with the arithmetic operations $+, \times$, is an example of a *ring*; the sum (difference) and product of integers in $\mathcal{Z}_n$ are integers in $\mathcal{Z}_n$ and both an *additive* and *multiplicative identity* exist. For example,

- The additive identity element 0 satisfies $x + 0 = 0 + x = x$ (modulo n), and
- The multiplicative identity element 1 satisfies $x \times 1 = 1 \times x = x$ (modulo n).

It is not always possible to-solve the equation $ax = b$ (modulo n) for x given a, b. For example, if $n = 6$, a solution exists for $a = 1, 5$, and all b; for $a = 4, 5$, a solution exists only for $b = 0, 2$, and 4. The formal solution $x = a^{-1}b$ (modulo n) requires a to have a *multiplicative inverse* (modulo n); that is, an integer $c \equiv a^{-1}$ exists in $\mathcal{Z}_n$ such that $1 = (a \times c)$ (modulo n) $= (c \times a)$ (modulo n). When n is a prime, *every* $a \neq 0$ has a multiplicative inverse and $\mathcal{Z}_n$ is a *field*.

If $a, b \in \mathcal{Z}^+$, the greatest common divisor of a and b, denoted by $d = \gcd\{a, b\}$, is the unique integer d satisfying

1. d divides *both* a and b and
2. If c divides *both* a and b, then c divides d.

Proposition 11.4: $d = \gcd\{a, b\}$ is uniquely determined.

Proof: Let $S = \{sa + tb : s, t \in \mathcal{Z}, sa + tb > 0\}$. As $a + b > 0$, $S \neq \emptyset$ and therefore it contains a minimal positive element, say $d = xa + yb$. If d does *not* divide a, then

$a = qd + r$ $(0 < r < d)$ by the Division Algorithm of arithmetic. But then $r = a - qd = (1 - qx)a + (-qy)b > 0$ is in S and smaller than d, a contradiction, proving that d divides a; similarly, d divides b so that d is a common divisor of a and b.

$a, b \in \mathcal{Z}^+$ are *relatively prime* if $1 = \gcd\{a, b\}$. According to the proof of Proposition **11.4**, if $1 = \gcd\{a, b\}$, there exist integers x, y such that

$$1 = ax + by$$

if $x > 0$, then $y < 0$ and

$$xa = 1 + (-y \times b) \Rightarrow xa = 1(\text{modulo } b) \Rightarrow a^{-1} = x(\text{modulo } b)$$

$x < 0$, then $y > 0$; if r is such that $rb + x > 0$, then $ra - y > 0$ and

$$(rb + x)a = 1 + (-y + ra)b \Rightarrow (rb + x)a = 1(\text{modulo } b) \Rightarrow a^{-1} = (rb + x)(\text{modulo } b)$$

so that if $1 = \gcd\{a, b\}$ and $0 < a < b$, the multiplicative inverse of a modulo b, denoted by a^{-1}, exists and it satisfies $1 = (a \times a^{-1} (\text{modulo } b)) = (a^{-1} \times a) (\text{modulo } b)$.

The computation of x and y is provided by Proposition **11.5**.

Proposition 11.5   (Euclidean Algorithm): If $a, b \in \mathcal{Z}^+$, the sequence r_0, $r_1, \ldots, r_s, r_{s+1}$ defined by:

$a, b \in \mathcal{Z}^+; r_0 = a; r_1 = b$		
$r_0 = c_1 r_1 + r_2$	$0 < r_2 < r_1$	$r_2 = r_0 \ (\text{modulo } r_1)$
$r_1 = c_2 r_2 + r_3$	$0 < r_3 < r_2$	$r_3 = r_1 \ (\text{modulo } r_2)$
$r_2 = c_3 r_3 + r_4$	$0 < r_4 < r_3$	$r_4 = r_2 \ (\text{modulo } r_3)$
$\vdots$	$\vdots$	$\vdots$
$r_{s-2} = c_{s-1} r_{s-1} + r_s$	$0 < r_s < r_{s-1}$	$r_s = r_{s-2} \ (\text{modulo } r_{s-1})$
$r_{s-1} = c_s r_s + r_{s+1}$	$0 < r_{s+1} < r_s$	$r_{s+1} = r_{s-1} \ (\text{modulo } r_s)$

satisfies

11.4a   For some value of s,

$$r_j \begin{cases} \neq 0, & \text{if } 0 \leq j \leq s \\ = 0, & \text{if } j = s + 1 \end{cases},$$

11.4b $r_s = \gcd\{a, b\}$;

11.4c $\exists x, y \in \mathcal{Z}, r_s = xa + yb$.

Example 11.5
$a = 560, b = 1547, ??? = \gcd\{560, 1547\}$

$\quad 1547 = 2 \times 560 + 427$
$\quad\quad 427 = 1547 - (2 \times 560)$

$\quad 560 = 1 \times 427 + 133$
$\quad\quad 133 = 560 - 427 = -1547 + (3 \times 560)$

$\quad 427 = 3 \times 133 + 28$
$\quad\quad 28 = 427 - (3 \times 133) = (4 \times 1547) - (11 \times 560)$

$\quad 133 = 4 \times 28 + 21$
$\quad\quad 21 = 133 - (4 \times 28) = (-17 \times 1547) + (47 \times 560)$

$$28 = 1 \times 21 + 7$$
$$7 = 28 - 21 = (21 \times 1547) - (58 \times 560)$$
$$21 = 3 \times 7 + 0$$

Therefore

$$7 = \gcd\{560, 1547\} = (21 \times 1547) - (58 \times 560), \quad x = -58, y = 21$$

Example 11.6
$a = 654, b = 1807, ??? = \gcd\{645, 1807\}$

$$1807 = 2 \times 654 + 499$$
$$499 = 1807 - (2 \times 654)$$

$$654 = 1 \times 499 + 155$$
$$155 = 654 - 499 = -1807 + (3 \times 654)$$

$$499 = 3 \times 155 + 34$$
$$34 = 499 - (3 \times 155) = (4 \times 1807) - (11 \times 654)$$

$$155 = 4 \times 34 + 19$$
$$19 = 155 - (4 \times 34) = (-17 \times 1807) + (47 \times 654)$$

$$34 = 1 \times 19 + 15$$
$$15 = 34 - 19 = (21 \times 1807) - (58 \times 654)$$

$$19 = 1 \times 15 + 4$$
$$4 = 19 - 15 = (-38 \times 1807) + (105 \times 654)$$

$$15 = 3 \times 4 + 3$$
$$3 = 15 - (3 \times 4) = (135 \times 1807) - (373 \times 654)$$

$$4 = 1 \times 3 + 1$$
$$1 = 4 - 3 = (-173 \times 1807) + (478 \times 654)$$

$$3 = 3 \times 1 + 0$$

Therefore

$$1 = \gcd\{560, 1547\} = (-173 \times 1807) + (478 \times 654), \quad x = 478, \ y = 173$$

$$477 = 654^{-1} \ (\text{modulo } 1807) \Leftrightarrow 1 = (478 \times 654) \ (\text{modulo } 1807)$$

Example 11.7
$a = 123, b = 277, ??? = \gcd\{123, 277\}$

$$277 = 2 \times 123 + 31$$
$$31 = 277 - (2 \times 123)$$

$$123 = 3 \times 31 + 30$$
$$30 = 123 - (3 \times 31) = (7 \times 123) - (3 \times 277)$$

$$31 = 1 \times 30 + 1$$
$$1 = 31 - (1 \times 30) = (-9 \times 123) + (4 \times 277)$$

$$30 = 30 \times 1$$

Therefore,

$$1 = \gcd\{277, 123\} = (-9 \times 123) + (4 \times 277)$$

$$9 = 123^{-1}(\text{modulo } 277) \Leftrightarrow 1 = (9 \times 123)(\text{modulo } 277)$$

TABLE 11.2 The Euler Totient Function $\phi(n)$ for $n = 2(1)13$

n	2	3	4	5	6	7	8	9	10	11	12	13
$\phi(n)$	1	2	2	4	2	6	4	6	4	10	4	12

The *Euler totient function* $\phi(n)$ for the positive integer n is the number of positive integers less than n that are relatively prime to n. The values of $\phi(n)$ for $n = 2(1)13$ are listed in Table 11.2.

Proposition 11.6: If the prime factorization of $n = p_1^{n1} p_2^{n2}, \ldots, p_k^{nk}$, then $\phi(n) = \prod_{i=1}^{k} p_i^{n_i-1} (p_i - 1)$.

Proof: See Problem 11.1.

11.3 A MODULAR ARITHMETIC KNAPSACK PROBLEM

The first example of a public-key cryptosystem used a variant of the knapsack problem that results when integer arithmetic is replaced by modular arithmetic.

(0,1)-Knapsack problem Modulo m $K\{\underline{a}, b, m\}$

Given: $\underline{a} = (a_0, a_1, \ldots, a_{n-1}) \in \mathcal{Z}_n^+, b, m \in \mathcal{Z}^+$
Find: A solution $\underline{x} \in \mathcal{Z}_{2,n}$ of $b \sum_{i=0}^{n-1} a_i x_i$ (modulo m)

The *knapsack problem* modulo m in NP-complete.

11.4 TRAP-DOOR KNAPSACKS

In their important paper. Merkle and Hellman [1978] published the first example of a trap-door public-key cryptosystem. They define a transformation relating

- A knapsack problem $K\{\underline{s}, t\}$ with a knapsack vector $\underline{s}$ that is super-increasing and
- A knapsack problem $K\{\underline{a}, b, m\}$ modulo m with a seemingly *general* knapsack vector $\underline{a}$.

It was intended that the transformation $K\{\underline{s}, t\} \rightarrow K\{\underline{a}, b, m\}$ satisfy three properties:

1. $K\{\underline{a}, b, m\}$ and $K\{\underline{s}, t\}$ are equivalent, meaning they have a common solution;
2. It is computationally infeasible to find a solution to $K\{\underline{a}, b, m\}$;
3. It is easy to find a solution to $K\{\underline{s}, t\}$.

We develop their ideas in this section.

Let $\text{SUP}_n[m]$ be the subset of SUP_n that satisfies the *size condition*

$$\sum_{i=0}^{n-1} s_i < m.$$

TABLE 11.3   The Knapsack Multipliers for $m = 14$

$\Omega_{14} = \{1, 3, 5, 9, 11, 13\}$						
ω	1	3	5	9	11	13
ω^{-1}	1	5	3	11	9	13

Let $\Omega_m = \{\omega \in \mathcal{Z}_m : \gcd\{\omega, m\} = 1\}$ denote the set of integers, referred to as *knapsack multipliers*, which are relatively prime to the modulus m. Each $\omega \in \Omega_m$ has a multiplicative inverse $\omega^{-1} \in \Omega_m$; that is, $1 = \omega\omega^{-1}$ (modulo m).

Note that the modulus m is *not* required to be a prime number.

Example 11.8

Table 11.3 lists the knapsack multipliers from $m = 14$.

Example 11.9

Table 11.4 lists the knapsack multipliers for $m = 13$. When ω is relatively prime to m, the transformation

$$T_{\omega,m} : z \to \omega z \text{ (modulo } m)$$

is a one-to-one mapping on $\mathcal{Z}_m$ to $\mathcal{Z}_m$ with inverse

$$T_{\omega^{-1}, m} : z \to \omega^{-1} z \text{ (modulo } m).$$

$T_{\omega^{-1}, m}$ maps a super-increasing knapsack vector $\underline{s}$ into the knapsack vector $\underline{a}$ according to the formula

$$\underline{a} = T_{\omega^{-1},m}(\underline{s}) = (T_{\omega^{-1},m}(s_0), T_{\omega^{-1},m}(s_1), \ldots, T_{\omega^{-1},m}(s_{n-1})).$$

Example 11.10

$m = 14$, $\underline{s} = (1, 3, 5)$, $\omega = 9 \in \Omega_m$, and $\omega^{-1} = 11$:

$$T_{11,14} : \underline{s} = (1, 3, 5) \to \underline{a} = (11, 5, 13)$$
$$T_{9,14} : \underline{a} = (11, 5, 13) \to \underline{s} = (1, 3, 5).$$

Proposition 11.7:   If $\underline{a} = T_{\omega^{-1},m}(\underline{s})$ and $b = \omega^{-1} t$ (modulo m), the knapsack problems

$K\{\underline{s}, t\}$	$K\{\underline{a}, b, m\}$
Given: $\underline{s} = (s_0, s_1, \ldots, s_{n-1}) \in \mathrm{SUP}_n[m]$, $t \in \mathcal{Z}_m$	*Given*: $\underline{a} = (a_0, a_1, \ldots, a_{n-1}) \in \mathcal{Z}_n^+$, $b, m \in \mathcal{Z}_m$
Find: $\underline{x} \in \mathcal{Z}_{2,n}$ satisfying $t = \sum_{i=0}^{n-1} s_i x_i$	*Find*: $\underline{x} \in \mathcal{Z}_{2,n}$ satisfying $b = \sum_{i=0}^{n-1} s_i x_i$ (modulo m)

TABLE 11.4   The Knapsack Multipliers for $m = 13$

$\Omega_{13} = \{1, 2, 3, 4, 5, 6, 7, 8, 9, 10, 11, 12\}$												
ω	1	2	3	4	5	6	7	8	9	10	11	12
ω^{-1}	1	7	9	10	8	11	2	5	3	4	6	12

are equivalent, in the sense that they share a common solution, if a solution to either problem exists.

Proof: Suppose $K\{\underline{a}, b, m\}$ has a solution, $\underline{x} \in \mathcal{Z}_{2,n}$

$$b = \sum_{i=0}^{n-1} a_i x_i \text{ (modulo } m).$$

If $t = \omega b$ (modulo m), then $\omega b = t + Jm$. As $\omega^{-1} s_i$ (modulo m) $= a_i \Longleftrightarrow \omega a_i$ (modulo m) $= s_i$, multiplying by ω gives

$$t + Jm = \omega b = \sum_{i=0}^{n-1} \omega a_i x_i, \quad 0 \le t < m$$

$$= \sum_{i=0}^{n-1} (s_i x_i + k_i m) = Km + \sum_{i=0}^{n-1} s_i x_i.$$

The size condition $\sum_{i=0}^{n-1} s_i < m$ implies $J = K$ and

$$t = \sum_{i=0}^{n-1} s_i x_i,$$

which shows that $\underline{x}$ is a solution to $K\{\underline{s}, t\}$.

Conversely, suppose the knapsack problem $K\{\underline{s}, t\}$ has a solution $\underline{x} \in \mathcal{Z}_2^n$

$$t = \sum_{i=0}^{n-1} s_i x_i.$$

If $b = \omega^{-1} t$ (modulo m), then $\omega^{-1} t = b + Hm$. As ωa_i (modulo m) $= a_i \Leftrightarrow \omega^{-1} s_i$ (modulo m) $= a_i$, multiplying by ω^{-1} gives

$$\omega^{-1} t = b + Hm = \sum_{i=0}^{n-1} (\omega^{-1} s_i) x_i$$

$$= \sum_{i=0}^{n-1} (a_i + j_i m) x_i = Lm + \sum_{i=0}^{n-1} a_i x_i,$$

from which it follows that $\underline{x} \in \mathcal{Z}_2^n$ is a solution to $K\{\underline{a}, b, m\}$

$$b = \sum_{i=0}^{n-1} a_i x_i \text{ (modulo } m) \qquad \blacksquare$$

To determine if the transformation $T_{\omega^{-1}, m}(\underline{s})$ has really replaced an *easy* problem by a *hard* problem, Merkle and Hellman studied the properties of the transformation. They began with Proposition **11.8**.

Proposition 11.8: If $\underline{s} \in \text{SUP}_n[m]$, then

$$2^j(s_0 + s_1 + \cdots + s_{n-j-1}) < m \qquad \text{for } 0 \le j < n$$

and the weaker bound

$$2^j s_{n-j-1} < m \qquad \text{for } 0 \le j < n.$$

Proof: The proof is by induction on j; when $j = 0$, the inequality above is the size condition. If we suppose

$$2^j(s_0 + s_1 + \cdots + s_{n-j-1}) < m,$$

the super-increasing property

$$s_0 + s_1 + \cdots + s_{n-j-2} < s_{n-j-1}$$

gives

$$2^{j+1}(s_0 + s_1 + \cdots + s_{n-j-2}) = 2^j[(s_0 + s_1 + \cdots + s_{n-j-2}) + (s_0 + s_1 + \cdots + s_{n-j-2})]$$
$$< 2^j(s_0 + s_1 + \cdots + s_{n-j-2} + s_{n-j-1})$$
$$< m,$$

completing the induction. ∎

How small can the knapsack lengths $\{a_i\}$ be if $\underline{a} = T_{\omega^{-1}, m}(\underline{s})$ when $\omega \in \Omega_m$? To answer this, we use a *model problem* in which the multiplier ω, or equivalently its inverse ω^{-1}, is chosen by a chance experiment.

Fix $\underline{s} = (s_0, s_1, \ldots, s_{n-1}) \in \mathrm{SUP}_n[m]$. Choose ω as the result of tossing a d-sided fair coin where $d = \gcd\{\omega, m\}$; that is

$$\Pr\{\Omega^{-1} = \omega^{-1}\} = \frac{d}{m}, \qquad \omega^{-1} \in \Omega_m.$$

Problems 11.2 to 11.4 ask you to show that

$$\left\lceil \frac{m}{d} \right\rceil = |\omega^{-1}s : \omega^{-1} \in \Omega_m|.$$

Fix a value $0 < \alpha < 1$; it follows that the cardinality of the set

$$C_i \equiv \{\omega^{-1} \in \Omega_m : a_i = (\omega^{-1} \times s_i)(\text{modulo } m) \leq \alpha m\}$$

is

$$|C_i| = \left\lceil \frac{\alpha m}{d} \right\rceil.$$

If m is very large, then

$$|\{\omega^{-1} : T_{\omega^{-1}, m}(s_i) < \alpha m\} \approx \alpha \frac{m}{d},$$

so that

$$\Pr\{\omega^{-1} : T_{\omega^{-1}, m}(s_i) < \alpha m\} \approx \alpha$$

From this computation, we conclude that if

- ω is chosen from ω_m according to the uniform distribution

then

- a_i is uniformly distributed over $\mathcal{Z}_m$.

Applying DeMorgan's Law $\overline{\cap_i E_i} = \cup_i \overline{E_i}$, with $E_i = \{\omega^{-1} : T_{\omega^{-1},m}(s_i) \geq \alpha m\}$, gives

$$\left| \overline{\bigcap_{i=0}^{n-1} \{\omega^{-1} : T_{\omega^{-1},m}(s_i) \geq \alpha m\}} \right| = \left| \bigcup_{i=0}^{n-1} \{\omega^{-1} : T_{\omega^{-1},m}(s_i) < \alpha m\} \right|$$

$$\leq \sum_{i=0}^{n-1} \left| \{\omega^{-1} : T_{\omega^{-1},m}(s_i) < \alpha m\} \right| \approx n\alpha \frac{m}{d}.$$

The choice $\alpha = \dfrac{1}{n^2}$ leads to Proposition **11.9**.

Proposition 11.9:

$$\Pr\{T_{\omega^{-1},m}(s_i) \geq \frac{m}{n^2} \text{ for } 0 \leq i < n\} = 1 - O(n^{-1}).$$

We conclude that for *large* n and m, it is likely that *all* of the knapsack lengths of $a = T_{\omega^{-1},m}(\underline{s})$ will be larger than $\dfrac{m}{n^2}$.

Any data stored on or transmitted between computer systems is represented by a $(0,1)$-sequence. As the Merkle–Hellman knapsack encipherment system enciphers a $(0,1)$-vector into an integer, it is necessary to specify how the ciphertext is to be encoded into a $(0,1)$-sequence. If the plaintext $\underline{x} = (x_0, x_1, \ldots, x_{n-1})$ is enciphered to

$$b = \sum_{i=0}^{n-1} a_i x_i \text{ (modulo } m),$$

a ciphertext b is coded into *fixed* length $(0,1)$-vectors, and the length μ must be

$$\mu = \log_2 \left\{ \sum_{i=0}^{n-1} a_i \right\} \text{ [bits].}$$

Clearly $\mu > n$, so that encipherment produces an expansion of the text by a factor

$$R \equiv R(\underline{a}) = \frac{n}{\log_2 \sum_{i=0}^{n-1} a_i} < 1,$$

referred to as the *information rate* of the encipherment.

Merkle and Hellman suggested $n = 100$ and

- Selecting the $\{s_i\}$ such that $\log_2 s_i \approx 100 + i$ [bits];
- $\log_2 m \approx 200$ [bits].

In this case, the knapsack lengths of $\underline{a} = T_{\omega^{-1},m}(\underline{s})$ are all likely to require approximately

$$100 + n - 2\log_2 n \approx 100 + n \text{ [bits];}$$

that is

$$1 \approx \frac{m}{a_i}.$$

Merkle and Hellman offered the knapsack system as the first example of a public-key cryptographic system with a trap-door:

- The *private key* consisting of the modulus m, the multiplier $\omega \in \Omega_m$ and a knapsack vector $\underline{s} \in \text{SUP}_n[m]$.
- The *public key* consisting of the knapsack vector $\underline{a} = T_{\omega^{-1},m}(\underline{s})$.

The ciphertext corresponding to plaintext $\underline{x}$ for the user with public key $\underline{a}$ is the sum $B = \sum_{i=0}^{n-1} a_i x_i$ causing an expansion of data under encipherment; n bits of plaintext $\underline{x}$ are enciphered into approximately $\log_2 \sum_{i=0}^{n-1} a_i$ bits of ciphertext.

Implicit is their assumption that it would be difficult to solve the knapsack problem $K\{\underline{a}, b, m\}$.

11.5 KNAPSACK ENCIPHERMENT AND DECIPHERMENT OF ASCII-PLAINTEXT

Knapsack encipherment derives a μ-bit ciphertext integer $B^{(i)}$ from each plaintext $(0,1\}$-vector $\underline{x} = (x_0^{(i)}, x_1^{(i)}, \ldots, x_{n-1}^{(i)})$. Then Internet standard [Linn, 1989] specifies the translation from ASCII text for Merkle–Hellman encipherment. I use a similar coding translation scheme illustrated in *Example 11.11*, which follows.

11.5.1 Knapsack Encipherment of ASCII-Plaintext

Plaintext: $x^{(0)} x^{(1)} \cdots x^{(N-1)}$ (ASCII characters)

Knapsack Public Parameter: $\underline{a} = (a_0, a_1, \ldots, a_{n-1})$

Ciphertext: $\underline{y} = (\underline{y}^{(0)}, \underline{y}^{(1)}, \ldots, \underline{y}^{(M-1)})$

$\underline{y}^{(i)} = (y_0^{(i)}, y_1^{(i)}, \ldots, y_\mu^{(i)})$ $(0 \le i \le M)$ (0, 1)-vectors.

E1. Each of the N ASCII plaintext characters $x^{(i)}$ in first coded into the 7-bit binary representation of its ordinal position in the ASCII character set

$$x^{(i)} \to (x_0^{(i)}, x_1^{(i)}, \ldots, x_6^{(i)});$$

E2. The vectors $\{\underline{x}^{(i)}\}$ are concatenated to form the binary plaintext

$$\underline{x}_0^{(0)}, \underline{x}_0^{(1)}, \ldots, \underline{x}^{(N-1)} \to \underline{z} = (z_0, z_1, \ldots, z_{7N-1});$$

E3. The binary plaintext $\underline{z}$ is divided into equal length blocks of n bits, padding $\underline{z}$ on the right by 0's if necessary. By this process $M = \left\lceil \frac{7N}{n} \right\rceil$ blocks of n bits are obtained

$$\underline{z} = (z_0, z_1, \ldots, z_{Mn-1}) \to (\underline{z}^{(0)}, \underline{z}^{(1)}, \ldots, \underline{z}^{(M-1)});$$

E4. For each bit-vector $(\underline{z}^{(i)})$, the integer $B^{(i)} = \sum_{j=0}^{n-1} a_j z_j^{(i)}$ is computed;

E5. If μ is the smallest integer satisfying $\mu > \sum_{j=0}^{n-1} a_j$, the ciphertext is the concatenation of the M μ-bit vectors

$$\underline{y} = \left(\underline{y}^{(0)}, \underline{y}^{(1)}, \ldots, \underline{y}^{(M-1)}\right) \quad \text{where} \quad B^{(i)} = \sum_{j=0}^{n-1} a_j y_j^{(i)}$$

Example 11.11

Plaintext: `Demonstration of knapsack encipherment.`

Knapsack Public Parameter: $\underline{a} = (1318, 3954, 3282, 2597, 2428, 898, 2455, 284)$, $n = 8$, $\mu = 15$.

My rendition of Merkle–Hellman knapsack encipherment, shown in Table 11.5, processes one ASCII character of plaintext at a time to obtain the ith block of n bits of plaintext

$$\underline{z}^{(i)} \equiv (z_{i,0}, z_{i,1}, \ldots, z_{i,n-1})$$

TABLE 11.5 Merkle–Hellman Knapsack Encipherment in *Example 11.11*

		Plaintext			Ciphertext
$x^{(i)}$	$\text{ord}(x^{(i)})$	$\underline{x}^{(i)}$	$\underline{z}^{(i)}$	$B^{(i)}$	$\underline{y}^{(i)}$
D	68	1000100			
e	101	1100101	10001001	4030	000111110111110
m	109	1101101	10010111	7552	001110110000000
o	111	1101111	01101110	13017	011001011011001
n	110	1101110	11111101	14761	011100110101001
s	115	1110011	11011100	11195	010101110111011
t	116	1110100	11111010	16034	011111010100010
r	114	1110010	01110010	12288	011000000000000
a	97	1100001			
t	116	1110100	11000011	8011	001111101001011
i	105	1101001	11010011	10608	010100101110000
o	111	1101111	01001110	9735	010011000000111
n	110	1101110	11111101	14761	011100110101001
	32	0100000	11001000	7700	001111000010100
o	111	1101111	00110111	9516	010010100101100
f	102	1100110	11100110	11907	010111010000011
	32	0100000			
k	107	1101011	01000001	4238	001000010001110
n	110	1101110	10101111	10665	010100110101001
a	97	1100001	01110110	13186	011001110000010
p	112	1110000	00011110	8378	010000010111010
s	115	1110011	00011100	5923	001011100100011
a	97	1100001	11110000	11151	010101110001111
c	99	1100011	11100011	11293	010110000011101
k	107	1101011			
	32	0100000	11010110	11222	010101111010110
e	101	1100101	10000011	4057	000111111011001
n	110	1101110	00101110	9063	010001101100111
c	99	1100011	11101100	11880	010111001101000
i	105	1101001	01111010	14716	011100101111100
p	112	1110000	01111000	12261	010111111100101
h	104	1101000	01101000	9664	010010111000000
e	101	1100101			
r	114	1110010	11001011	10439	010100011000111
m	109	1101101	11001011	10439	010100011000111
e	101	1100101	01101110	13017	011001011011001
n	110	1101110	01011101	10161	010011110110001
t	116	1110100	11011101	11479	010110011010111
.	46	0101110	00010111	6234	001100001011010
			00000000	0	000000000000000

which is thereupon enciphered by the Merkle–Hellman transformation

$$z^{(i)} \to B^{(i)} \equiv \sum_{k=0}^{n-1} a_k z_{i,k}$$

and finally encoded into a $\mu = 15$-bit $(0, 1)$-vector.

$$B^{(i)} \to y^{(i)}.$$

11.5.2   Decipherment of Knapsack-Enciphered ASCII-Plaintext

Ciphertext: $\underline{y} = (\underline{y}^{(0)}, \underline{y}^{(1)}, \ldots, \underline{y}^{(M-1)})$

$\underline{y}^{(i)} = (y_0^{(i)}, y_1^{(i)}, \ldots, y_\mu^{(i)})$ $(0 \le i < n)$ $(0, 1)$-vectors.

Knapsack Private Parameters: $m, \omega, \underline{s} = (s_0, s_1, \ldots, s_{n-1})$

Plaintext: $x^{(0)} x^{(1)} \ldots x^{(N-1)}$ (ASCII characters).

TABLE 11.6   Merkle–Hellman Knapsack Encipherment in *Example 11.11*

Ciphertext				Plaintext			
$\underline{y}^{(i)}$	$B^{(i)}$	$B_m^{(i)}$	$\underline{w}^{(i)}$	$\underline{z}^{(i)}$	$\underline{x}^{(i)}$	ord($x^{(i)}$)	$x^{(i)}$
000111110111110	4030	2107	10001001	10001001	1000100	68	D
001110110000000	7552	3533	10010111	110010111	1100101	101	e
011001011011001	13017	1621	01101110	1101101110	1101101	109	m
011100110101001	14761	2647	11111101	11011111101	1101111	111	o
010101110111011	11195	631	11011100	110111011100	1101110	110	n
011111010100010	16034	1144	11111010	1110011111010	1110011	115	s
011000000000000	12288	1042	01110010	11101001110010	1110100	116	t
					1110010	114	r
001111101001011	8011	3016	11000011	11000011	1100001	97	a
010100101110000	10608	3038	11010011	111010011	1110100	116	t
010011000000111	9735	1610	01001110	1101001110	1101001	105	i
011100110101001	14761	2647	11111101	11011111101	1101111	111	o
001111000010100	7700	108	11001000	110111001000	1101110	110	n
010010100101100	9516	3542	00110111	010000110111	0100000	32	
010111010000011	11907	1523	11100110	11011111100110	1101111	111	o
					1100110	102	f
001000010001110	4238	2011	01000001	01000001	0100000	32	
010100110101001	10665	3622	10101111	110101111	1101011	107	k
011001110000010	13186	1543	01110110	1101110110	1101110	110	n
010000010111010	8378	1626	00011110	11000011110	1100001	97	a
001011100100011	5923	623	00011100	111000011100	1110000	112	p
010101110001111	11151	41	11110000	1110011110000	1110011	115	s
010110000011101	11293	3027	11100011	11000011100011	1100001	97	a
					1100011	99	c
010101111010110	11222	1534	11010110	11010110	1101011	107	k
000111111011001	4057	3010	10000011	010000011	0100000	32	
010001101100111	9063	1615	00101110	1100101110	1100101	101	e
010111001101000	11880	620	11101100	11011101100	1101110	110	n
011100101111100	14716	1142	01111010	110001111010	1100011	99	c
010111111100101	12261	139	01111000	1101001111000	1101001	105	i
010010111000000	9664	117	01101000	11100001101000	1110000	112	p
					1101000	104	h
010100011000111	10439	3116	11001011	11001011	1100101	101	e
010100011000111	10139	3116	11001011	111001011	1110010	114	r
011001011011001	13017	1621	01101110	1101101110	1101101	109	m
010011110110001	10161	2634	01011101	11001011101	1100101	101	e
010110011010111	11479	2636	11011101	110111011101	1101110	110	n
001100001011010	6234	3531	00010111	1110100010111	1110100	116	t
000000000000000	0	0	00000000	01011100000000	0101110	46	.

D1. From each of the M ciphertext vectors $\underline{y}^{(i)} = (y_0^{(i)}, y_1^{(i)}, \ldots, y_\mu^{(i)})$ of length μ bits, calculate the integers

$$B^{(i)} = \sum_{j=0}^{\mu-1} a_j y_j^{(i)} \quad \text{and} \quad B_m^{(i)} = (\omega B^{(i)}) \text{ (modulo } m);$$

D2. Find the n-vector $\underline{w}^{(i)}$ solution of the easy knapsack problem for each of the M knapsack values $B_m^{(i)}$ with $0 \le i < M$

$$B_m^{(i)} = \sum_{j=0}^{n-1} s_j w_j^{(i)};$$

D3. Adjoin the solution on the right $\underline{w}^{(i)}$ to the vector $\underline{z}^{(i)}$; and

D4. Determine the ASCII plaintext character from the leftmost 7 bits of $\underline{z}^{(i)}$.

My rendition of Merkle–Hellman decipherment shown in Table 11.6 serially processes the ith block of μ bits of ciphertext $\underline{y}^{(i)} = (y_{i,0}, y_{i,1}, \ldots, y_{i,\mu-1})$, evaluates $B^{(i)}$, $B_m^{(i)}$, and then solves the easy superincreasing knapsack problem $B_m^{(i)} = \sum_{j=0}^{n-1} s_j w_j^{(i)}$. The n bits of the solution vector are accumulated as the vector $\underline{z}^{(i)}$. Blocks of 7 bits are removed (from the left) to obtain the plaintext.

Example 11.11 (continued)

Ciphertext: 0 0 0 1 1 1 1 1 0 0 ... 0 0 0

Knapsack Private Parameters: $m = 3967$, $\omega^{-1} = 649$, $\omega = 915$, $\underline{s} = (2, 6, 11, 22, 100, 501, 1003, 2005)$

11.6 CRYPTANALYSIS OF THE MERKLE–HELLMAN KNAPSACK SYSTEM (MODULAR MAPPING) [SHAMIR, 1982]

UCSB has been the site of a meeting dealing with current topics in cryptography starting with CRYPTO '81 in 1981. Adi Shamir electrified the attendees at CRYFTO '82 by presenting an analysis of the Merkle–Hellman cryptosystem. A program running on an *Apple* during his lecture illustrated the solution technique that we now describe.

The mapping $T_{\omega^{-1}, m}: \underline{s} = (s_0, s_1, \ldots, s_{n-1}) \to \underline{a} = (a_0, a_1, \ldots, a_{n-1})$ from the superincreasing to the public knapsack vector is nonlinear and this was the basis for believing that the Merkle–Hellman scheme provided a secure public-key encipherment scheme.

For $a \in \mathcal{Z}_m$ define the *modular mapping* (function) $\phi_{a,m}(w)$ for $0 \le a$, $w < m$ (Fig. 11.1) by

$$\phi_{a,m}(w) : w \to \phi_{a,m}(w) = aw \text{ (modulo } m),$$

- The continuous representation of the discrete-valued function $\phi_{a,m}(w)$ consists of straight-line segments with slope $\dfrac{1}{a}$;
- $\phi_{a,m}(w)$ has minima *nearly* equal to 0 at the points $i\dfrac{m}{a}$ with $i = 0, 1, \ldots, a-1$; the distance between consecutive minima is larger than 1.

Write

$$s_j = \phi_{a_j, m}(\omega), \qquad a_j \omega = k_j m + s_j,$$

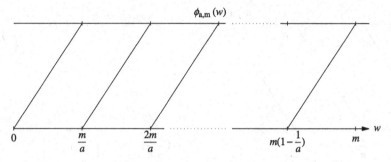

Figure 11.1   The modular mapping function.

where k_j is an integer $<m$. According to Proposition **11.8**, $s_j \le m/(2^{n-(j+1)})$, which implies that for $j \le 4$ and *large n*, the rational number $\frac{s_j}{m}$ is very small.

Rewriting the relationship $a_j\omega = k_km + s_j$,

$$\omega = \frac{k_jm}{a_j} + \frac{s_j}{a_j} \in I_{j,n}(k_j), \quad I_{j,n}(k_j) = \frac{m}{a_j}\left[k_j, \; k_j + \frac{1}{2^{n-(j+1)}}\right] \tag{11.1}$$

As $\frac{m}{a_j} \approx 1$, the integer ω is an element in an interval of relatively small length $1/(2^{n-(j+1)})$ whose length endpoint mk_j/a_j is one of the minima of $\phi_{a,m}(w)$.

However k_j is *un*known and hence Equation (11.1) is replaced by the following weaker assertion:

$$\omega \in \bigcup_{i=0}^{m-1} I_{j,n}(i), \quad I_{j,n}(i) = \frac{m}{a_j}\left[i, \; i + \frac{1}{2^{n-(j+1)}}\right]. \tag{11.2}$$

But the membership statement for ω in Equation (11.2) holds for *every* a_j with $0 < j < n$, so that

$$\omega \in \bigcup_{i=0}^{m-1} I_{1,n}(i) \cap \bigcup_{i=0}^{m-1} I_{2,n}(i) \cdots \cap \bigcup_{i=0}^{m-1} I_{k,n}(i)$$

$$= \bigcup_{i_1, i_2, \ldots, i_k} I_{1,n}(i_1) \cap I_{2,n}(i_2) \cap I_{k,n}(i_k) \tag{11.3}$$

for every integer k with $1 \le k \le n$.

For any fixed j, it is quite likely that there are many point y that are closer than $O(2^{-(n-(j+1))})$ to a minimum of $\phi_{a_{j,m}}(w)$. However, the number of poins y that are close to a minima of *all* the k functions $\{\phi_{a_{j,m}}(w) : 0 \le j < k\}$ decreases as k increases. Adi Shamir argued that the likelihood of having a point y simultaneously close to say $k = 4$ minima is very small *unless* $y = \omega$.

Unfortunately m is unknown; to rectify this, replace the integer-valued function $\phi_{a,m}(w)$ with $w \in \mathcal{Z}_m$ by the *sawtooth modular* function (Fig. 11.2).

$$\Phi_{a_j} : w \longrightarrow a_jw \; (\text{modulo } 1), \quad 0 \le w < 1,$$

which scales the interval $[0, m)$ to $[0, 1)$.

- The graph of $\Phi_a(w)$ consists of straight-line segments with slope $\frac{1}{a}$.
- $\Phi_a(w)$ has minima *exactly* equal to 0 at the points $\frac{i}{a}$ with $i = 0, 1, \ldots, a - 1$; the distance between consecutive minima is larger than 1.

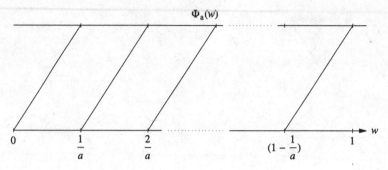

Figure 11.2 The sawtooth mapping function.

The statement

$$s_j = \phi_{a_j, m}(\omega)$$

translates to

$$s_j = \phi_{a_j}(\omega),$$

which may be written as

$$w = \frac{k_j}{a_j} + \frac{s_j}{a_j} \in I_{j,n}(k_j), \quad I_{j,n}(k_j) = \frac{1}{a_j}\left[k_j, \ k_j + \frac{1}{2^{n-(j+1)}}\right],$$

$$s_j = \phi_{a_j}(w)$$

$$(11.4)$$

where k_j is an integer $<a_j$

The argument just given for the functions $\{\phi_{a_{j,m}}\}$ carries over and we conclude that the unknown rational $w \equiv \frac{\omega}{m}$ will be *close* to a minimum of each of the functions $\Phi_{a_j}(w)$. To calculate the set containing possible values of the rational number $w \equiv \frac{\omega}{m}$, it is necessary to calculate the intersection of pairs of intervals $I_{j_1,n}(k_{j_1}) \cap I_{j_1,n}(k_{j_1})$. The four possible intersections of two intervals A, B and their intersection $C = A \cap B$ are shown in Figure 11.3.

Example 11.12

Tables 11.7 and 11.8 list the intervals determined by Equation (11.4) for $k = 2$, 3 and

Knapsack Public Parameters: $n = 9$, $\underline{s} = (2, 13, 30, 50, 121, 254, 480, 1000, 2000)$

Knapsack Private Parameters: $m = 5879$, $\omega^{-1} = 4610$, $\omega = 2233$, $\underline{a} = (3341, 1140, 3083, 1219, 5184, 1019, 2296, 864, 1728)$

In the general case with $m \approx 100$, the intervals are determined by a *merge-sort*.

Having determined a set of possible intervals, say $\{\mathfrak{I}_k^{(s)} = (e_s, f_s)\}$, it is necessary to find the rational numbers $w \equiv \frac{\Omega}{M} \in \mathfrak{I}_k^{(s)}$ that satisfy the conditions

```
A ├──────────┤              A ├──────────┤
    B ├──────────┤              B ├──────────┤
C = A∩B ├──────────┤        C = A∩B ├──────────┤

    A ├──────────┤              A ├──────┤
B ├──────────┤                         B ├──────┤
C = A∩B ├──────────┤        C = A∩B = ∅
```

Figure 11.3 The possible intersections of intervals A and B.

TABLE 11.7   Two-Way Intersections in *Example 11.12*

$k = 2$	
[0.0254385964912281,0.0254426537713260]	[0.0508829691709069,0.0508840460526316]
[0.0885964912280702,0.0885973978599222]	[0.1140350877192982,0.1140388824453756]
[0.1394736842105263,0.1394803670308291]	[0.1771929824561404,0.1771936265339719]
[0.2026315789473684,0.2026351111194253]	[0.2280701754385965,0.2280765957048788]
[0.2657894736842105,0.2657898552080215]	[0.2912280701754386,0.2912313397934750]
[0.3166666666666667,0.3166728243789285]	[0.3543859649122807,0.3543860838820712]
[0.3798245614035088,0.3798275684675247]	[0.4052631578947368,0.4052690530529781]
[0.4684210526315789,0.4684237971415744]	[0.4938596491228070,0.4938652817270278]
[0.5570175438596491,0.5570200258156241]	[0.5824561403508772,0.5824615104010775]
[0.6456140350877193,0.6456162544896737]	[0.6710526315789474,0.6710577390751272]
[0.6964980544747082,0.6964980811403509]	[0.7342105263157895,0.7342124831637234]
[0.7596491228070175,0.7596539677491769]	[0.7850942831487579,0.7850945723684210]
[0.8228070175438597,0.8228087118377731]	[0.8482456140350877,0.8482501964232266]
[0.8736905118228075,0.8736910635964912]	[0.9114035087719298,0.9114049405118228]
[0.9368421052631579,0.9368464250972763]	[0.9622867404968572,0.9622875548245614]

TABLE 11.8   Three-Way Intersections in *Example 11.12*

$k = 3$
[0.1394745377878690,0.1394796059033409]
[0.3798248459292897,0.3798275684675247]
[0.7596496918585793,0.7596539677491769]

- $\dfrac{\Omega}{M} \in \Im_k^{(s)} = (e_s, f_s]$ for some s;

- $\underline{\sigma} = (\sigma_0, \sigma_1, \ldots, \sigma_{n-1})$ is superincreasing with $\sigma_i = a_i \Omega$ (modulo M) for $0 \le i < n$, and

- $\underline{\sigma} = (\sigma_0, \sigma_1, \ldots, \sigma_{n-1})$ satisfies the size condition $\sum_{l=0}^{n-1} \sigma_l < M$.

As $a_i < m$, the value of M is certainly larger than $\text{Max\_}A = \max_i a_i$. For some unknown multiplier $\Xi > 1$ and $M \in [\text{Max\_}A, \Xi \, \text{Max\_}A]$ and interval $\Im_k^{(s)}$, each integer Ω in the interval $M \times (e_s, \ell_R]$ is tested as a possible value for Ω. We accept a pair (Ω, M) provided there are affirmative answers to the question

- Is the vector $(\Omega a_0, \Omega a_1, \ldots, \Omega a_{n-1})$ (modulo M) superincreasing?
- Is the size condition $M < \sum_{i=0}^{n-1} \Omega a_i$ (modulo m) satisfied?
- Does Ω have a multiplicative inverse modulo M?

The *true* pair (ω, m) and corresponding rational ω/m will be found along with other rational numbers Ω/M. Knapsack encipherment in general has several *equivalent* private keys $(m, \Omega, \underline{s})$ corresponding to a public key $\underline{a}$; that is, different values that yield the same public key.

Example 11.12 (continued)
Table 11.9 lists the equivalent keys for where $\text{Max\_}A = 5184$ and $\Xi = 2$. An $*$ indicates that Ω does not have a multiplicative inverse.

TABLE 11.9 Solution Space in *Example 11.12*

$\mathfrak{I}_3^{(s)}$	M	Ω	Ω^{-1}	$\dfrac{\Omega}{M}$	σ
Searching for $m \in$ [Max_A, ΞMax_A], $\Xi = 2$					
[0.37982484592929, 0.37982756846752)	5879	2233	4610	0.37982650110563	2 13 30 50 121 254 480 1000 2000
[0.37982484592929, 0.37982756846752)	7148	2715	5879	0.37982652490207	3 16 37 61 148 309 584 1216 2432
[0.37982484592929, 0.37982756846752)	7951	3020	3341	0.37982643692617	1 17 39 67 161 343 648 1352 2704
[0.37982484592929, 0.37982756846752)	8417	3197	7148	0.37982654152311	4 19 44 72 175 364 688 1432 2864
[0.37982484592929, 0.37982756846752)	9220	3502	*	0.37982646420824	2 20 46 78 188 398 752 1568 3136
[0.37982484592929, 0.37982756846752)	9686	3679	8417	0.37982655378897	5 22 51 83 202 419 792 1648 3296
[0.37982484592929, 0.37982756846752)	10489	3984	4610	0.37982648488893	3 23 53 89 215 453 856 1784 3568
[0.37982484592929, 0.37982756846752)	10955	4161	9686	0.37982656321314	6 25 58 94 229 474 896 1864 3728
[0.37982484592929, 0.37982756846752)	11292	4289	3341	0.37982642578817	1 24 55 95 228 487 920 1920 3840
[0.37982484592929, 0.37982756846752)	11758	4466	*	0.37982650110563	4 26 60 100 242 508 960 2000 4000

If the larger interval $M \in$ [5184, 51840] is searched, 192 equivalent private keys are found.

The merge-sort I described With $n = 100$, $k = 4$, and $m \approx 2^{200}$ requires an examination of 2^{800} cases and is computationally intractable. There is another formulation whose solution is computationally feasible.

Integer Programming Problem A

Find: integers c_0, c_1, c_2, c_3
Such That: a rational x exists satisfying $0 \leq x = \dfrac{c_j}{a_j} < 2^{-(n+(j-1))}$

Integer Programming Problem B

Find: integer c_0, c_1, c_2, c_3
Such That:

$$0 \leq \frac{c_0}{a_0} - \frac{c_1}{a_1} < 2^{-(n-2)}, \quad 1 \leq c_1 < a_1$$

$$0 \leq \frac{c_0}{a_0} - \frac{c_2}{a_2} < 2^{-(n-3)}, \quad 1 \leq c_2 < a_2$$

$$0 \leq \frac{c_0}{a_0} - \frac{c_3}{a_3} < 2^{-(n-4)}, \quad 1 \leq c_3 < a_3$$

$x = \dfrac{\omega}{m}$ is a solution to this integer programming problem. A polynomial time algorithm appears in a paper by Lenstra et al. [1982a].

As the rational ω/m is contained in the interval $\left(\dfrac{c_0}{a_0}, \dfrac{c_0}{a_0}+2^{-n+1}\right)$, by choosing $\varepsilon > 0$ sufficiently small, it is possible to guarantee that any rational

$$\frac{p}{q} \in \Im = \left(\frac{c_0}{a_0}, \frac{c_0}{a_0}+2^{-n+1}+\epsilon\right)$$

will satisfy the size condition

$$\sum_{i=0}^{n-1} pa_i \,(\text{modulo } q) < q.$$

However, the rational p/q may not produce superincreasing lengths under the transformation

$$a_i \rightarrow pa_i \,(\text{modulo } q), \qquad 0 \le i < n.$$

As $\omega/m \in \Im$, there are rationals in $\Im$ that satisfy both the size condition and produce superincreasing knapsack lengths. To find such a rational solution, note that the functions $\{\Phi_{aj} : 0 \le j < n\}$ are free of discontinuities on the interval $\Im$. On $\Im$ these n straight-line segments can have at most $k + O(n^2)$ points of intersection. The k points of intersection partition $\Im$ into $k + 1$ subintervals

$$\Im_0, \Im_1, \ldots, \Im_k$$

such that on each subinterval the line segments are linearly ordered. On $\Im_j$ we write

$$a_{\pi_j(0)} > a_{\pi_j(1)} > \cdots > a_{\pi_j(n-1)}$$

to indicate that the line segment of $\Phi a_{\pi_j(i)}$ is above line segment of $\Phi a_{\pi_j(i+1)}$ for $0 \le i < n-1$.

If the system of linear inequalities

$$xa_{\pi_j(i)} - c_{\pi_j(i)} > \sum_{k=0}^{i-1} (xa_{\pi_j(k)} - c_{\pi_j(k)}), \qquad 0 \le i < n$$

has a rational solution $x = p/q$ on $\Im_j$, then

$$pa_{\pi_j(i)} - qc_{\pi_j(i)} > \sum_{k=0}^{i-1} (pa_{\pi_j(k)} - qc_{\pi_j(k)}), \qquad 0 \le i < n,$$

so that

$$pa_{\pi_j(i)} \,(\text{modulo } q) > \sum_{k=0}^{i-1} pa_{\pi_j(k)}(\text{modulo } q), \qquad 0 \le i < n,$$

which means that the transformed knapsack lengths

$$T_{p,q} : a_i \rightarrow pa_i \,(\text{modulo } q)$$

are superincreasing. To verify if the system

$$xa_{\pi_j(i)} - c_{\pi_j(i)} > \sum_{k=0}^{i-1} (xa_{\pi_j(k)} - c_{\pi_j(k)}), \qquad 0 \le i < n$$

has a solution, we need only look at the function

$$x\left[a_{\pi_j(i)} - \sum_{k=0}^{i-1} a_{\pi_k(k)}\right] - \left[c_{\pi_j(i)} - \sum_{k=0}^{i-1} c_{\pi_k(k)}\right]$$

at the endpoints of $\Im_j$.

11.7   DIOPHANTINE APPROXIMATION

Diophantus was a Greek geometer who developed the theory of equations with integer solutions, a subject now referred to as *diophantine equations*.[1] Diophantus determined all the integer *Pythagorean triples* (x, y, z), solutions of $x^2 + y^2 = z^2$. He proved that if x and y are relatively prime and $x - y$ is positive and odd, then $(x, y, z) = (x^2 - y^2, 2xy, x^2 + y^2)$ is a Pythagorean triple $x^2 + y^2 = z^2$, and conversely all primitive Pythagorean triples arise in this manner.

A standard reference on diophantine approximation is Cassels [1957].

Diophantine approximation studies the accuracy with which a real number x can be approximated by a rational number p/q. The accuracy of the approximation is measured by $\|x - p/q\|$, where

$$\|x\| = \min[\{x\}, 1 - \{x\}], \quad \{x\} = x - \lfloor x \rfloor.$$

It should be obvious that an approximation by rational numbers p/q of a real number, say $\pi = 3.1415927\ldots$, is improved by increasing q. A basic result is

Proposition 11.10:   [Cassels, 1957]:

11.10a   Given x and $Q > 1$, there exists an integer q with $0 < q < Q$ such that $\|qx\| \leq Q^{-1}$.

11.10b   There are infinitely many integers q such that $\|qx\| < q^{-1}$.

11.10c   For every $\epsilon > 0$ and real number x there are only finitely many integers q such that $\|qx\| < q^{-1-\epsilon}$.

11.10d   If $\|qx\| < 1$, there exists an integer p such that $\|qx\| = |qx - p| < 1$. Equivalently, $|z - p/q| < 1$, which asserts that p is the best choice for the numerator for the rational number p/q for fixed denominator q.

A rational number p/q is a *best rational approximation* to x if $\|q^*x\| > \|qx\|$ for $q^* < q$.

The following algorithm computes the sequence of best rational approximations to x.

---

[1] Although it is known that Diophantus lived around 250 A.D., much of his life is a mystery. The following epigram gives his age at death:

Diophantus' boyhood lasted 1/6th of his life span; his beard grew an additional 1/12th of his life span; after still a further 1/7th of his life span, he married. His son was born 5 years later. The son lived to half his father's age. Diophantus died 4 years after his son died.

What what his age at death?

11.7.1   Continued Fraction Algorithm

If x is a positive real number, define

1. $x = x_0$; $z_0 = \lfloor x_0 \rfloor$ where $\lfloor \ldots \rfloor$ is the *floor* or *integer part of* $\cdots$ and

2. while $z_n \neq \lfloor x_n \rfloor$ do

$$x_{n-1} = \frac{1}{x_n + z_n}; \quad z_{n+1} = \lfloor x_{n+1} \rfloor.$$

$$x = z_0 + \frac{1}{x_1}$$

$$x = z_0 + \cfrac{1}{z_1 + \cfrac{1}{x_2}}$$

$$x = z_0 + \cfrac{1}{z_1 + \cfrac{1}{z_2 + \cfrac{1}{x_3}}}$$

$$\vdots$$

$$x = z_0 + \cfrac{1}{z_1 + \cfrac{1}{z_2 + \cdots + \cfrac{1}{z_{n-1} + \cfrac{1}{x_n}}}}.$$

Stopping the continued fraction recursion after the nth step yields the nth *convergent*

$$\{x_0 : z_0, \, z_1, \, \ldots, z_n\} = z_0 + \cfrac{1}{z_1 + \cfrac{1}{z_2 + \cdots + \cfrac{1}{z_n}}} = \frac{p_n}{q_n}.$$

Example 11.13

If $\pi \simeq 3.141592653588$, the continued fraction recursion produces the convergents

$$\pi \simeq 3.0 = \frac{3}{1}$$

$$\pi \simeq 3 + \frac{1}{7} = 3.142857142857\ldots = \frac{22}{7}$$

$$\pi \simeq 3 + \cfrac{1}{7 + \cfrac{1}{15}} = 3.141509433962\ldots = \frac{333}{106}$$

$$\pi \simeq 3 + \cfrac{1}{7 + \cfrac{1}{15 + \cfrac{1}{1}}} = 3.141592920354\ldots = \frac{355}{113}.$$

Table 11.10 lists the convergents and their errors

$$Error = x - \{x : z_0, z_1, \ldots, x_n\}.$$

Note that the convergents successively *under* and *over* approximate π, a very desirable property of a numerical algorithm that permits error estimates.

TABLE 11.10   Continued Fraction Expansion of π

n	zn	$\{z : z_0, z_1, \ldots, x_n\}$	Error
0	3	3.0000000000000	0.141592653588
1	7	3.142857142857	−0.001264489269
2	15	3.141509433962	0.000083219626
3	1	3.141592920354	−0.000000266766
4	292	3.141592653012	0.000000000576
5	1	3.141592653921	−0.000000000334
6	1	3.141592653467	0.000000000120
7	1	3.141592653619	−0.000000000031
8	2	3.141592653581	0.000000000007
9	1	3.141592653591	−0.000000000004
10	1	3.141592653587	0.000000000001
11	2	3.141592653588	−0.000000000000

Simultaneous diophantine approximation is concerned with the accuracy by which a vector of real numbers $\underline{x} = (x_1, x_2, \ldots, x_n)$ can be approximated by a vector of rational numbers with the same denominator $\underline{q} = \left(\dfrac{q_1}{q}, \dfrac{q_2}{q}, \ldots, \dfrac{q_n}{q} \right)$.

The degree of approximation is measured by

$$\{\{\underline{q}x\}\} = \max_{1 \leq i \leq n} \lim_{q_1, q_2, \ldots, q_n} |qx_i - q_i|.$$

The following generalization of Proposition **11.10** describes the degree of simultaneous approximation of a real vector by a vector of rational numbers.

Proposition 11.11:

11.11a   For every n-dimensional vector $\underline{\theta} = (\theta_1, \theta_2, \ldots, \theta_n)$, there are infinitely positive integers p such that $\{\{p\underline{\theta}\}\} < p^{-\frac{1}{n}}$.

11.11b   For any fixed positive number ϵ, the set of n-dimensional vectors $\underline{\theta} = (\theta_1, \theta_2, \ldots, \theta_n)$ for which $\{\{p\underline{\theta}\}\} < p^{-\frac{1}{n} - \epsilon}$ has n-dimensional "volume". (Note, this result requires some technical results from *measure theory*.)

To show the relation of simultaneous diophantine approximation to the analysis of the Merkle–Hellman knapsack cryptosystem, start with

$$s_i = wa_i \text{ (modulo } m) \rightarrow s_i = wa_i - j_i m$$

$$\frac{w}{m} = \frac{j_i}{a_i} - \frac{s_i}{a_i m}.$$

By subtracting the equation with $i = 1$ from the ith equation and using the estimate

$$\frac{s_i}{a_i m} = O(n^2 2^{-n+i} m^{-1}),$$

we obtain

$$\frac{j_i}{a_i} - \frac{j_i}{a_1} = O(n^2 2^{-n+i+1} m^{-1}).$$

As the multiplier ω is chosen randomly, we expect $a_i \approx m$ and $j_i \approx m$ so that

$$\frac{j_i}{j_1} - \frac{a_i}{a_1} = O(n^2 2^{-n+i+1} m^{-1}).$$

As $O(n^2 2^{-n+i+1} m^{-1})$ is *very* small for $i \le 5$ and n large, the (known) d-dimensional vector

$$\left(\frac{a_2}{a_1}, \frac{a_3}{a_1}, \ldots, \frac{a_{d+1}}{a_1}\right)$$

is a simultaneous approximation to the (unknown) d-dimensional vector

$$\left(\frac{j_2}{j_1}, \frac{j_3}{j_1}, \ldots, \frac{j_{d+1}}{j_1}\right).$$

How good is the approximation? If

$$R = \frac{n}{\log_2 \sum_{i=0}^{n-1} a_i},$$

simple algebra gives

$$m^{-1} \approx 2^{-n^{R-1}}, \quad a^{-1} \approx 2^{-n^{R-1}}, \quad n^2 \approx a_i^{-R \frac{\log_2 n}{n}}, \quad 2^{j+1} \approx a_i^{-R \frac{j+1}{n}},$$

so that

$$\left| \left(\frac{a_2}{a_1}, \frac{a_3}{a_1}, \ldots, \frac{a_{d+1}}{a_1}\right) - \left(\frac{j_2}{j_1}, \frac{j_3}{j_1}, \ldots, \frac{j_{d+1}}{j_1}\right) \right| = O\left(a_1^{-1-R\left[1-\frac{d+\log_2 n}{\log_2 n}\right]}\right).$$

The approximation by

$$\underline{a} = \left(\frac{a_2}{a_1}, \frac{a_3}{a_1}, \ldots, \frac{a_{d+1}}{a_1}\right)$$

to the vector

$$\underline{j} = \left(\frac{j_2}{j_1}, \frac{j_3}{j_1}, \ldots, \frac{j_{d+1}}{j_1}\right)$$

is called

1. δ-*quality* when

$$\|a_1 j\| = \max_{1 \le i \le n} \left(\min_{a_i \in \mathbb{Z}} \left| a_1 \frac{j_i}{j} - a_i \right| \right) < a_1^{-\delta};$$

2. An *unusually good simultaneous diophantine approximation* (UGSDA) if it is a δ-quality approximation with $\delta < \frac{1}{d}$.

The term unusually good is used because such approximations are rare.

Proposition 11.12:

For $n \geq 2$, the set

$$\mathcal{S}^*(b) = \left\{ \{ \underline{b} = \left(\frac{b_1}{b}, \frac{b_2}{b}, \ldots, \frac{b_n}{b} \right) : 0 \leq b_i < b, \ 1 = \gcd\{b, b_i\} \right\}$$

contains at least $\frac{1}{2} b^n$ vectors. Of these, at most $O(b^{n(1-\delta)+1})$ are UGSDA.

We conclude that for fixed $\delta > \frac{1}{n}$, the fraction of vectors $\underline{b}$ with a δ-quality approximation is infinitesimal. There exists a UGSDA approximation to

$$\left(\frac{j_2}{j_1}, \frac{j_3}{j_1}, \ldots, \frac{j_n}{j_1} \right)$$

if

$$R\left(1 - \frac{d + \log_2 n}{n} \right) > \frac{1}{n}.$$

Shamir's startling announcement at CRYPTO '82 stimulated cryptologic research. Almost immediately, other methods of analysis of the knapsack cryptosystem (and variants) were announced – [Largias, 1982, 1984; Lagarias and Odlyzko, 1983; Brickell, 1983].

11.8   SHORT VECTORS IN A LATTICE

A *lattice* as depicted in Figure 11.4 is "a framework or structure of crossed wood or metal strips" — definition from standard dictionary "The Merriam-Webster Dictionary (Pocket Book) NY, 1974. A lattice is determined by a sequence of vectors $b_0, b_i, \ldots, b_{n-1}$ (in real n-dimensional $\mathfrak{R}^n$, which are linearly independent over $\mathcal{Z}^n$); that is

$$\underline{0} = u_0 \underline{b}_0 + u_1 \underline{b}_1 + \cdots + u_{n-1} \underline{b}_{n-1} \quad (u_0, u_1, \ldots, u_{n-1}) \in \mathcal{Z}^n \Rightarrow (u_0, b_1, \ldots, b_{n-1)} = \underline{0}.$$

The lattice $\mathcal{L}$ consists of all points $\underline{u} \in \mathfrak{R}^n$, which may be written as a linear combination of the basis vectors $\{\underline{b}_i\}$ with integer coefficients.

$$\underline{u} = u_1 \underline{b}_1 + u_2 \underline{b}_2 + \cdots + u_n \underline{b}_n.$$

The vectors $\{\underline{b}_i\}$ are the *basis* for the lattice $\mathcal{L}$.

Example 11.14

The lattice in Figure 11.5 consists of all points that are *integer* linear combinations of the *basis vectors* $\underline{b}_1 = (0.125, 0.25)$, and $\underline{b}_1 = (-0.125, 0.2)$. The simultaneous diophantine approximation problem is

$$\text{Given}: \ \underline{a} = \left(\frac{a_2}{a_1}, \frac{a_3}{a_1}, \ldots, \frac{a_n}{a_1} \right)$$

$$\text{Find}: \ \underline{j} = \left(\frac{j_2}{j_1}, \frac{j_3}{j_1}, \ldots, \frac{j_n}{j_1} \right) \text{ a UGSDA approximation to } \underline{a}.$$

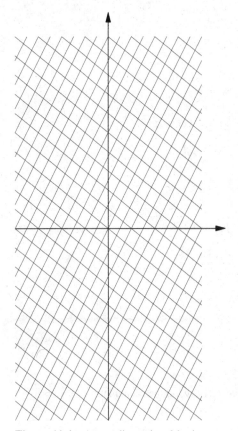

Figure 11.4 A two-dimensional lattice.

Associate the lattice $\mathcal{L}$ whose basis vectors are

$$\underline{b}_1 = (\lambda, a_2, a_3, \ldots, a_{n-1}, a_n)$$
$$\underline{b}_2 = (0, -a_1, 0, \ldots, 0, 0)$$

$$\vdots$$

$$\underline{b}_{n-1} = (0, 0, 0, \ldots, -a_1, 0)$$
$$\underline{b}_n = (0, 0, 0, \ldots, 0, -a_1).$$

Setting $u_1 = j_1$ and $u_i = j_i (2 \leq i \leq n)$, the length (in $\mathfrak{R}^n$) of the point $u = u_1 b_1 + u_2 b_2 + \cdots + u_n b_n$ is

$$||u|| = \sqrt{\lambda^2 + \sum_{i=2}^{n} (j_1 a_i - j_i a_1)^2}.$$

$\underline{j}$ is a UGSDA to $\underline{a}$ occurs when the length of the vector $\underline{u}$ is *small*. The problem of finding *short* vectors may be solved by an algorithm (L^3) of Lenstra et al. [1982b]. Applying the L^3-algorithm to analyze the knapsack cryptosystem was first suggested by

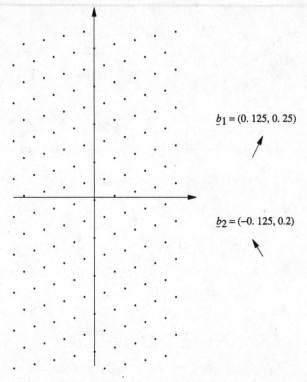

$\underline{b}_1 = (0.\,125, 0.\,25)$

$\underline{b}_2 = (-0.\,125, 0.2)$

Figure 11.5 Integer points in the *Example 11.14* two-dimensional lattice.

Len Adelman [1983]. The connection to diophantine approximation was then developed by Lagarias and Odlyzko [1983], Lagaris [1982, 1984] and Brickell [1983].

The application by Brickell, Lagarias, and Odlyzko of the L³-algorithm does not attack the Merkle–Hellman trap-door as Shamir did by finding, a weakness in the trap-door mapping $\underline{s} \to \underline{a}$. Instead, it finds a direct attack on the knapsack problem. It is successful when the density of public knapsack weights

$$R \equiv R(\underline{a}) = \frac{n}{\log_2 \sum\limits_{i=0}^{n-1} a_i}$$

is small enough. For example, Lagarias and Odlyzko prove that when $R(\underline{a}) < 0.645$, then the solution to the knapsack problem is the shortest nonzero vector in the lattice with basic vectors

$$\underline{b}_1 = (1,\, 0, \ldots,\, 0,\, -a_1)$$
$$\underline{b}_2 = (0,\, 1, \ldots,\, 0,\, -a_2)$$
$$\vdots$$
$$\underline{b}_n = (1,\, 0, \ldots,\, 1,\, -a_n)$$
$$\underline{b}_{n+1} = (1,\, 0, \ldots,\, 1,\, -M).$$

11.9 KNAPSACK-LIKE CRYPTOSYSTEMS

Although the Merkle–Hellman trap-door knapsack system can be analyzed, it provided the first example of the paradigm of public-key cryptography. It encouraged many other inventors to try their luck in devising other knapsack-like cryptosystems. A partial list of such systems is given in Lu and Lee [1979], Goethals and Couvrers [1980], Adiga and Shankar [1985], Niederreiter [1986], Goodman and McAuley [1984], and Piepryzk [1985].

I believe that with only two exceptions [McEliece, 1978; Chor and Rivest, 1988], all of these variants of the knapsack system have been analyzed.

11.10 KNAPSACK CRYPTOSYSTEM PROBLEMS

Problems 11.1 to 11.4 provide technical details used in Chapter 11. In each example, the integer m has the factorization into primes $m = p_1^{n_1} p_2^{n_2} \ldots p_k^{n_k}$.

The ciphertext files `cipherPr11.1-cipherPr11.12` may be downloaded from the following ftp address: ftp://ftp.wiley.com/public/sci_tech_med/computer_security.

PROBLEMS

11.1 Show how the principle of inclusion–exclusion can be used to derive the formula of Proposition 11.6 for the Euler totient function.

11.2 Prove that $\Omega_m = \{\omega : 1 = \gcd\{\omega, m\}\}$ is a *group*; that is,

    11.2a $\omega_1, \omega_2 \in \Omega_m \Rightarrow \omega_1 \omega_2 \in \Omega_m$;

    11.2b $1 \in \Omega_m$;

    11.2c If $\omega \in \Omega_m$, then $\omega^{-1} \in \Omega_m$.

11.3 Prove that the cardinality of $|\Omega_m|$ is the value of the Euler totient function $\phi(m)$.

11.4 Calculate the cardinality of $\Gamma_m(s) = \{\omega s : \omega \in \Omega_m\}$.

Problems 11.5 to 11.8 provide examples of Merkle–Hellman knapsack encipherment. They require two programs: the first to encipher ASCII character plaintext, and the second to decipher ciphertext.

The Merkle–Hellman encipherment program takes as parameters

- The number of knapsack lengths n,
- The vector of public knapsack lengths $\underline{a} = (a_0, a_1, \ldots, a_{n-1})$, and
- A string of N ASCII characters $x = (x^{0)}, x^{1)}, \ldots, x^{(N-1)})$,

and returns ciphertext formatted as in Section 11.5.

The Merkle–Hellman decipherment program ciphertext takes as parameters

- The number of knapsack lengths n,
- The secret modulus m,
- The secret multiplier ω,
- The vector of public knapsack lengths $\underline{a} = (a_0, a_1, \ldots, a_{n-1})$, and
- The ciphertext $\underline{y} = (y_0, y_1, \ldots)$ written as a sequence of μ-bit integers where μ is the smallest integer satisfying $2^\mu > \sum_{j=0}^{n-1} a_j$,

and returns the tabular output formatted as in Section 11.5, whose columns contain

1. The ciphertext integer B_i, which is the base-2 encoding of $\sum_{j=0}^{n-1} a_j x_j^{(i)}$,

2. The integer $B_m^{(i)} = (\omega \times B_i)$ (modulo m),

3. The solution of the easy knapsack problem, the μ-bit vector $\underline{w} = (w_0, w_1, \ldots, w_{n-1})$ satisfying $B_m^{(i)} = \sum_{j=0}^{n-1} s_j w_j^{(i)}$,

4. The concatenation on the left of $\underline{w}$ to the string $\underline{z}$,

5. $\underline{x}^{(i)}$, the leftmost 7 bits of the string $\underline{z}$,

6. The ordinal number of ith plaintext character $\underline{x}^{(i)}$ in the ASCII character set, and

7. The ith plaintext character.

11.5

11.5a Using the parameters $n = 6$ and the public knapsack lengths $\underline{a} = (a_0, a_1, \ldots, a_5) = (228, 325, 346, 485, 556, 525)$, encipher the plaintext $\underline{x} = \text{We are nearly at the end of the quarter.}$

11.5b Decipher the Merkle–Hellman ciphertext

				cipherPr11.5					
694	599	722	939	722	131	1175	814	620	620
131	970	755	620	1132	131	621	722	131	825
599	939	722	722	131	835	970	939	722	131
599	970	835	722	1175	970	939	949	1154	346

that results from a knapsack encipherment with the parameters

$n = 7, m = 523, \omega = 28$

$\underline{a} = (355, 131, 318, 113, 21, 135, 215)$.

11.6

11.6a Using the parameters $n = 7$ and the public knapsack lengths $a = (a_0, a_1, \ldots, a_{n-1}) = (102, 238, 3400, 284, 1044, 2122, 425)$, encipher the plaintext $\underline{x} = \text{This is an example of knapsack encipherment.}$

11.6b Decipher the Merkle–Hellman ciphertext

				cipherPr11.6					
386	1809	5862	1809	238	1049	6287	238	765	3790
4215	4784	624	1809	5862	238	1809	4024	765	2093
3740	1668	1809	238	4215	3506	238	3171	3790	765
3740	6287	765	2887	3171	238	1809	3790	2887	1049
3740	624	1809	5862	2093	1809	3790	4784	3688	

that results from a knapsack encipherment with the parameters

$n = 7, m = 3989, \omega = 352$

$\underline{a} = (a_0, a_1, \ldots, a_{n-1}) = (102, 238, 3400, 284, 1044, 2122, 425)$.

11.7

11.7a Using the parameters $n = 7$ and public knapsack lengths $\underline{a} = (a_0, a_1, \ldots, a_{n-1}) = (2244, 599, 2245, 1649, 1205, 1364, 1980, 669)$, encipher the plaintext $\underline{x} = \text{This is the plaintext for homework \#7.}$

11.7b Decipher the Merkle-Hellman ciphertext

cipherPr11.7									
694	599	722	939	722	131	1175	814	620	131
970	755	620	1132	131	621	722	131	825	599
939	131	722	835	970	939	722	131	599	970
835	722	1175	970	939	949	1154	346		

that results from a knapsack encipherment with the parameters

$n = 7$, $m = 523$, $\omega = 28$

$\underline{a} = (a_0, a_1, \ldots, a_{n-1}) = (355, 131, 318, 113, 21, 135, 215)$.

11.8

11.8a Using the parameters $n = 7$ and public knapsack lengths $a = (a_0, a_1, \ldots, a_{n-1}) = (102, 238, 3400, 284, 1044, 2122, 425)$, encipher the plaintext $x = $ `Test of knapsack encipherment.`

11.8b Decipher the Merkle–Hellman ciphertext

cipherPr11.8									
4546	624	1049	6287	238	1049	6287	238	765	238
624	4215	2093	1809	7331	4215	5862	3171	238	3740
5862	4215	2462	1668	1809	2093	238	4215	3790	238
3171	3790	765	3740	6287	765	2887	3171	238	1809
3790	2887	1049	3740	624	1809	5862	2093	1809	3790
4784	3688								

that results from a knapsack encipherment with the parameters

$n = 7$, $m = 3989$, $\omega = 34$

$\underline{a} = (a_0, a_1, \ldots, a_{n-1}) = (102, 238, 3400, 284, 1044, 2122, 425)$.

Problems 11.9 to 11.15 provide examples of Shamir's cryptanalysis of the Merkle–Hellman knapsack cryptosystem. In each example, a public key

$$\underline{a} = (a_0, a_1, \ldots, a_{n-1})$$

and ciphertext are specified. The private key

$$\underline{s} = (s_0, s_1, \ldots, s_{n-1})$$

satisfies the conditions

$$1 \leq s_0 < s_1 < \cdots < s_{n-1}, \quad \sum_{i=0}^{j-1} s_i < s_j, \quad 1 \leq j < n. \qquad (*)$$

The public key $\underline{a} = (a_0, a_1, \ldots, a_{n-1})$ and private key $\underline{s} = (s_0, s_1, \ldots, s_{n-1})$ are related by

$$a_i = \omega^{-1} s_i \ (\text{modulo } m), \quad s_i = \omega a_i \ (\text{modulo } m), \quad 0 \leq i < n.$$

The private key $\underline{s}$, modulus m, and multiplier ω are all secret.

A solution requires you to write three programs to find the private knapsack parameters ($\underline{d}$, m, ω) and plaintext.

- *Program A*
  - Write a program to find the set of intervals $I^{(s)} = [L^{(s)}, R^{(s)}$ of $[0, 1)$ that might contain the ratio ω/m using the first k values $a_0, a_1, \ldots, a_{n-1}$ for $k = 2, 3, 4$ and 5.
  - Display the results in a table like that shown in Section 11.6.
- *Program B*
  - Write a program to find all ratios Ω/M that satisfy the three conditions
  - $(\Omega/M) \in I^{(s)}$ for some s;
  - Ω having a multiplicative inverse modulo M;
  - $\underline{s} = (s_0, s_1, \ldots, s_{n-1})$ defined by $s_i = a_i \Omega$ (modulo M) satisfying Equation (*) and the size condition $\sum_{i=0}^{n-1} s_i < M$.

Display the results found by the program in **B** using the tabular form as in Section 11.6.

- *Program C*
  - Write a program to decipher using any *two* solutions Ω, M, s found by *Program B*. Display the plaintext in the tabular form as in Section 11.6.

The data in Problems 11.9 to 11.12 will consist of

- A vector of public knapsack lengths $\underline{a} = (a_0, a_1, \ldots, a_{n-1})$, and
- Ciphertext $\underline{y} = y_0, y_1, \ldots)$ written as a sequence of μ-bit integers, where μ is the smallest integer satisfying $2^\mu > \sum_{j=0}^{n-1} a_j$.

11.9 Public key $\underline{a} = (a_0, a_1, \ldots, a_7) = (638, 2108, 1914, 472, 1277, 2138, 505, 1039)$:

cipherPr11.9									
2149	4320	5667	4718	4392	8176	8309	3147	3459	5834
7034	4023	4702	8309	6428	5597	6873	6306	6810	4806
8075	8414								

11.10 Public key $\underline{a} = (a_0, a_1, \ldots, a_8) = (418, 3362, 4198, 509, 5743, 5180, 2855, 4802, 536)$:

cipherPr11.10									
2149	4320	5667	4718	4392	8176	8309	3147	3459	5834
7034	4023	4702	8309	6428	5597	6873	6306	6810	4806
8075	8414								

11.11 Public key $\underline{a} = (a_0, a_1, \ldots, a_7) = (638, 3578, 971, 1942, 1388, 141, 89, 1123)$:

cipherPr11.11									
1991	1991	6580	2741	5513	8606	1609	6868	2962	6721
3719	4594	3054	5813	4701	5428	2810	4198	7546	7968
5813	4701	4350	3712	3933	5187				

11.12 Public key $\underline{a} = (a_0, a_1, \ldots, a_8) = (575, 436, 1586, 1030, 1921, 569, 721, 1183, 1570)$:

cipherPr11.12									
4358	4394	5145	3731	5070	8408	1466	6254	7446	8586
2591	4049	4109	4907	3189	4816	6682	5918	5648	1005
5938	6406	6406	2597						

REFERENCES

Len Adelman, "On Breaking Generalized Knapsack Public Key Cryptosystems," *Proceedings of the 15th ACM Symposium on The Theory of Computing*, New York, NY, 1983, pp. 402–412.

B. S. Adiga and P. Shankar, "Modified Lu-Lee Cryptosystem," *Electronic Letters*, **21**, 794–795 (1985).

E. Brickell, "Are Most Low Density Knapsacks Solvable in Polynomial Time?," *Proceedings of the 14th Southeastern Conference on Combinatorics, Graph Theory and Computing*, 1983.

J. W. S. Cassels, *An Introduction to Diophantine Approximation*, Cambridge Tracts in Mathematics, Number 45, 1957.

B. Chor and R. L. Rivest "A Knapsack-Type Public Key Cryptosystem Based on Arithmetic in Finite Fields," *IEEE Transactions on Information Theory*, **34**, pp. 901–990 (1988).

J. M. Goethals and C. Couvrer, "A New Trapdoor Knapsack Public Key Cryptosystem," *Philips Journal of Research*, **35**, 301–306 (1980).

R. M. Goodman and A. J. McAuley. "A New Trapdoor Knapsack Public Key Cryptosystem," *Proceedings of Eurocrypt 84* Springer Verlag, New York, 1984.

J. C. Lagarias, "The Computational Complexity of Simultaneous, Diophantine Approximation Problems," *SIAM Journal of Computing*, **14**, 1985, pp. 196–209; [Preliminary version in *Proceedings of the 23rd Annual Symposium on Foundations of Computer Science*, IEEE Press, New York, November 1982, pp. 32–39.]

J. C. Lagarias, "Knapsack Public Key Cryptosystems and Diophantine Approximation," *Advances in Cryptography*, Plenum Publishing Company (New York), 1984.

J. C. Lagarias and A. M. Odlyzko, "Solving Low-Density Subset Sum Problems," *Journal of the Association for Computing Machinery*, 32 (1985), pp. 229–246. [Preliminary version in *Proceedings of the 24th Annual Symposium on Foundations of Computer Science* IEEE Press, New York, 1983, pp. 1–10.]

A. K. Lenstra, H. W. Lenstra Jr., and L. Lovász, "Factoring Multivariate Polynomials over Finite Fields," *Journals of Computer and System Science*, **30**, 235–248 (1982).

A. K. Lenstra, H. W. Lenstra Jr., and L. Lovász, "Integer Programming with a Fixed Number of Variables," *Mathematische Annalen*, **261**, 515–534 (1982).

J. Linn, "Privacy Enhancement for Internet Electronic Mail," RFC1113, August 1989.

S. C. Lu and L. N. Lee, "A Simple and Effective Public-Key Cryptosystem," *COMSAT Technical Review*, 1979, pp. 15–24.

R. Merkle and M. Hellman, "Hiding Information and Signatures in Trapdoor Knapsacks," *IEEE Transactions on Information Theory*, **IT-24**, 525–530 (1978).

R. J. McEliece, "A Public-Key Cryptosystem Based on Algebraic Coding Theory," *Deep Space Network Progress Report 42-44*, Jet Propulsion Laboratory, California Institute of Technology, 1978, pp. 42–44. A more accessible reference to this paper is W. Patterson, *Mathematical Cryptology for Computer Scientists and Mathematicians*, Rowman & Littefield, New York, 1987.

H. Niederreiter, "Knapsack-Type Cryptosystem and Algebraic Condition," *Problems of Control and Information*, **15**, 159–166 (1986).

J. P. Piepryzk, "On Public-Key Cryptosystems Built Using Polynomial Rings," *Proceedings of EUROCRYPT 85*, Linz, Austria, 1985.

A. Shamir, "A Polynomial Time Algorithm for Breaking the Basic Merkle–Hellman Cryptosystem," *IEEE Transactions on Information Theory*, **IT-30**, 699–704 (1984).

CHAPTER 12

THE RSA CRYPTOSYSTEM

WHILE THE Merkle–Hellman knapsack system was the first example of a public-key cryptographic system, it did not provide the required security. Shortly thereafter, the RSA cryptosystem was published. It has withstood scrutiny for nearly thirty years; no viable analysis has been published. It appears that finding the private key is equivalent to factorization, so that even as the size of integers that can be factored increases, it will only require an adjustment to the RSA parameter sizes. This chapter defines the RSA cryptosystem and reviews what is known.

12.1 A SHORT NUMBER-THEORETIC DIGRESSION [KOBLITZ, 1987]

Proposition 12.1: If a, k, n are positive integers, the complexity of *modular exponentiation* a^k (modulo n) is $O((\log_2 k)(\log_2 n)^2)$.

Proof: The complexity of the multiplication two s-bit numbers in $O(s^2)$. If we write

$$k = k_0 + k_1 2 + k_2 2^2 + \cdots + k_{s-1} 2^{s-1}$$

each of the $O(\log_2 k)$ powers a^{2^j} (modulo n) ($j = 1, 2, \ldots$) can be computed in time $O((\log_2 n)^2)$. ∎

MOD (a, k, n)

---

d := 1;
aa := a;
while (k > 0) do begin
if (1 = (k mod 2)) then
   d := (d*a) mod n;
k := (k − (k mod 2)) div 2;
aa := (aa*aa) mod n;
end;

Example 12.1
Evaluate $y = 1311^{134}$ (modulo 39,979). First, the base-2 expansion of the exponent 134 is determined:

$$134 = 128 + 4 + 2 = 2^7 + 2^2 + 2^1.$$

Computer Security and Cryptography. By Alan G. Konheim
Copyright © 2007 John Wiley & Sons, Inc.

Next, $T_j = 1311^{2^j}$ (modulo 39,979) for $1 \le j \le 7$ is computed by repeated squaring

$$T_1 = T_0^2 \text{ (modulo 39,979)} = [1311^2 \text{ (modulo 39,979)}]$$

$$T_2 = T_1^2 \text{ (modulo 39,979)} = [1311^4 \text{ (modulo 39,979)}]$$

$$\cdot \cdot \cdot$$

$$T_7 = T_6^2 \text{ (modulo 39,979)} = [1311^{128} \text{ (modulo 39,979)}]$$

Finally, y is expressed as a product

$$y = 1311^{134} \text{ (modulo 39,979)}$$

$$= [1311^2 \text{ (modulo 39,979)}] \times [1311^4 \text{ (modulo 39,979)}]$$

$$\times [1311^{128} \text{ (modulo 39,979)}]$$

multiplying all of the terms $\{T_j\}$ for which 2^j appears in the base-2 expansion of 134 to obtain the value of y, $y = 17,236$.

Proposition 12.2: (Fermat's Little Theorem):   If p is a prime number

12.2a $a^p = a$ (modulo p) for any integer, and

12.2b $a^{p-1} = 1$ (modulo p) if a is not divisible by p.

Proof: Expand $(x + 1)^p$ by the Binomial Theorem $(x + 1)^p = x^p + 1 + \sum_{i=1}^{p-1} \binom{p}{i} x^i$ and note that the binomial coefficient $\binom{p}{i}$ is divisible by p for $1 \le i \le p - 1$. This proves $(x + 1)^p = (1 + x^p)$ (modulo p) so that Proposition **12.2a** follows by induction. Writing $a^p - a = a(a^{p-1} - 1) = 0$ (modulo p) and assuming $\gcd\{a, p\} = 1$, both sides may be divided by a (equivalently multiplied by a^{-1}) to obtain $a^{p-1} = 1$ (modulo p).   ∎

Remark: Is there a converse to Fermat's Theorem? For example, suppose $a^{n-1} = 1$ (modulo n) for every integer a with $1 = \gcd\{a, n\}$. Does it follow that n is a prime? The answer is no; for example, $561 = 3 \times 11 \times 17$, and although it is not obvious, $a^{560} = 1$ (modulo 561). Moreover, there are infinite numbers of such *Carmichael numbers*. We return to the "false" converse of Fermat's Theorem later in this chapter when we examine the testing of numbers to determine if they are prime.

The Euler totient function $\phi(n)$ of an integer n was defined in Section 11.2 as the number of intergers *less* than n that are relative prime to n. Proposition 11.6 gave the formula $\phi(n) = \prod_{i=1}^{k} p_i^{n_i - 1}(p_i - 1)$ when the prime factorization of n is $n = p_1^{n_1} p_2^{n_2} \cdots p_k^{n_k}$. Here we need only the special case where n is the product of two (distinct) primes $n = p_1 p_2$; in this case, $\phi(n) = (p_1 - 1)(p_2 - 1)$.

We need an important generalization of Fermat's Little Theorem.

Proposition 12.3: (Euler's Theorem):   If integers n and m are *relatively prime*, meaning their greatest common divisor is 1, $1 = \gcd\{m, n\}$, then $m^{\phi(n)} = 1$ (modulo n).

Proposition 12.4:   If $1 = \gcd\{m, n\}$, then m has a multiplicative inverse in $\mathcal{Z}_n$ that may be computed in time $O((\log_2 n)^2)$.

Proof: Using the Euclidean Algorithm, find a, b such that if $1 = an + bm$; then $1 = bm$ (modulo n). ∎

The numbers used in *Example 12.1* and those which follow will be *small* in the sense that they are expressible as 4-byte words. On the other hand, to achieve cryptographic strength of the encipherment systems to be described in this chapter and later in Chapters 14–18, this size limitation must be considerably relaxed. We need to perform arithmetic operations modulo m with very *large* integers m, requiring perhaps thousands of digits. The necessary size may in fact increase as more refined cryptanalytic techniques are introduced. We provide a short introduction to *multiprecision modular arithmetic* in Section 12.6.

12.2   RSA [RIVEST ET AL., 1978]

A four-tuple (p, q, e, d) is an *RSA parameter set* if

RSA-a p and q are prime numbers and $N = pq$;

RSA-b   The *RSA enciphering* exponent e satisfies $1 = \gcd\{e, \phi(N)\}$;

RSA-c   The *RSA deciphering* exponent d satisfies $1 = \gcd\{d, \phi(N)\}$; and

RSA-d e and d are multiplicative inverses modulo $\phi(N)$ of one another, $e\,d = 1$ (modulo $\phi(N)$).

Proposition 12.5:   When (p, q, e, d) is an RSA parameter set, the *RSA encipherment transformation* $\mathbf{E}_e$ is *modular exponentiation*, defined for integers n in $\mathcal{Z}_N$ by

$$\mathbf{E}_e : n \rightarrow \mathbf{E}_e(n) = n^e \text{ (modulo } N) \tag{12.1}$$

$\mathbf{E}_e$ is a one-to-one mapping on $\mathcal{Z}_N$ onto $\mathcal{Z}_N$. Its inverse *RSA decipherment transformation* $\mathbf{D}_d$ is also modular exponentiation, defined for integers n in $\mathcal{Z}_N$ by

$$\mathbf{D}_d : n \rightarrow \mathbf{D}_d(n) = n^d \text{ (modulo } N) \tag{12.2}$$

$$I = \mathbf{E}_e \mathbf{D}_d = \mathbf{D}_d \mathbf{E}_e \tag{12.3}$$

Proof: The second assertion clearly implies the first; if (p, q, e, d) is an RSA parameter set, then

$$(n^e)^d = n^{1 + C\phi(N)}$$

as $e\,d = 1$ (modulo $\phi(N)$). If $n = pm$ with $1 = \gcd\{m, q\}$, then p divides n ad q does not divide n, so that

$$(n^e)^d - n = n[(n^{p-1})^{C(q-1)} - 1]$$

The factor within the brackets $[\cdots]$ is congruent to 0 modulo q by Fermat's Little Theorem and hence the left-hand-side above is congruent to 0 modulo N.

A similar argument shows that if $n = qm$ with $1 = \gcd\{n, m\}$ then $(n^e)^d - n = 0$ (modulo N). Finally, if n is relatively prime to both p and q

$$(n^e)^d - n = n[(n^{p-1})^{C(q-1)} - 1]$$

$$(n^e)^d - n = n[(n^{q-1})^{C(p-1)} - 1]$$

∎

Remark: The Diffie–Hellman public-key cryptosystem paradigm only required that operations of encipherment $x \to y = E_{\text{PuK}}\{x\}$ and decipherment $y \to y = E_{\text{PrK}}\{y\}$ be inverses of one another. In the RSA system, Equations (12.1) and (12.2) state that *both* are modular exponentiation, differing only by the exponent.

Example 12.2
$p = 31, q = 5, e = 7, d = 103$

$$N = 155 = 31 \times 5$$

$$\phi(N) = 120 \ (31 - 1) \times (5 - 1)$$

$$ed = 721 = 1 \ (\text{modulo } 120)$$

$$67 = 98^7 \ (\text{modulo } 155)$$

$$98 = 67^{103} \ (\text{modulo } 155)$$

Proposition 12.6: If e, p, and q are given, d can be computed in time $O(\log_2 \phi(N))$.

12.3 THE RSA ENCIPHERMENT AND DECIPHERMENT OF ASCII-PLAINTEXT

RSA enciphers and deciphers integers in $\mathcal{Z}_N$. To encipher data, RSA needs to be extended to encipher n-grams of ASCII characters $\underline{x} = (x^{(0)}, x^{(1)}, \ldots, x^{(n-1)})$. An Internet standard is described in [Linn, 1989]; I describe a slightly modified version, using 7 bits for each ASCII character rather than 8 bits.

The extension replaces ASCII text by a binary sequence, which is segmented into bit-vectors of length $N_2 - 1$ where $2^{N_2-1} - 1 \le N < 2^{N_2}$. Each such bit-vector corresponds to an integer k in $\mathcal{Z}_N$ to which RSA-exponentiation $\mathbf{E}_e$ can be applied. The resulting integer $j = \mathbf{E}_e(k)$ in general requires N_2 bits in its base-2 representation so that there is an expansion under RSA encipherment.

12.3.1 RSA Encipherment of ASCII Plaintext

E1. Replace each character $x^{(i)}$ of ASCII plaintext $\underline{x} = (x^{(0)}, x^{(1)}, \ldots, x^{(n-1)})$ by the 7-bit binary encoding of its ordinal value in the ASCII character code $\underline{x}^{(i)} = (x_0^{(i)}, x_1^{(i)}, \ldots, x_6^{(i)})$ (Table 12.1).

E2. Concatenate to form the (0,1)-plaintext $\underline{z} \ (\underline{x}^{(0)}, \underline{x}^{(1)}, \ldots, \underline{x}^{(n-1)}) \to \underline{z} = (z_0, z_1, \ldots, z_{7n-1})$.

E3. Assume integers in $\mathcal{Z}_N$ require N_2 bits in their base-2 representation, $2^{N_2-1} - 1 \le N < 2^{N_2} - 1$. The plaintext $\underline{z}$ is expanded $\underline{z} \to E\langle\underline{z}\rangle = (z_0, z_1, \ldots, z_{nP-1})$ by padding with 0's on the right (if necessary) to make the length n_P of $E\langle\underline{z}\rangle$ a multiple of $N_2 - 1$, say $n_P = (N_2 - 1)B$.

$$B \equiv B(n, N_2) = \begin{cases} \left\lfloor \dfrac{7n}{N_2 - 1} \right\rfloor + 1, & \text{if } 7n = r \ (\text{modulo } (N_2 - 1)) \text{ with } 0 < r < N_2 - 1 \\[3mm] \dfrac{7n}{N_2 - 1}, & \text{if } 7n = 0 \ (\text{modulo } (N_2 - 1)). \end{cases}$$

TABLE 12.1   Step E1 in RSA Encipherment

$x^{(i)}$	$\underline{x}^{(i)}$	$x^{(i)}$	$\underline{x}^{(i)}$	$x^{(i)}$	$\underline{x}^{(i)}$	$x^{(i)}$	$\underline{x}^{(i)}$
E	1000101	x	1111000	a	1100001	m	1101101
p	1110000	l	1101100	e	1100101		0100000
o	1101111	f	1100110		0100000	R	1010010
S	1010011	A	1000001		0100000	e	1100101
n	1101110	c	1100011	i	1101001	p	1110000
h	1101000	e	1100101	r	1110010	m	1101101
e	1100101	n	1101110	t	1110100	.	0101110

E4. The expanded plaintext $E\langle \underline{z} \rangle$ is divided into $E(n, N_2 - 1)$ bit vectors each of length $N_2 - 1$ (Table 12.2):

$$E(\underline{z}) = (\underline{z}^{(0)}, \underline{z}^{(1)}, \ldots, \underline{z}^{(E-1)})$$

$$\underline{z}^{(i)} = (z_0^{(i)}, z_1^{(i)}, \ldots, z_{N_2-2}^{(i)}), \qquad 0 \le i < E \equiv E(n, N_2).$$

E5. The $(0,1)$-vector $\underline{z}^{(i)}$ of length $N_2 - 1$ corresponds to the integer $k^{(i)} = \sum_{j=0}^{N_2-2} 2^{N_2-j-2} z_j^{(i)}$ in $\mathcal{Z}_N$ (Table 12.2).

E6. RSA enciphers $E_e: k^{(i)} \rightarrow j^{(i)} = (k^{(i)})^e$ (modulo N) each of the E integers $\{k^{(i)}\}$ (Table 12.2).

TABLE 12.2   Steps E4–E7 in RSA Encipherment

$\underline{z}^{(i)}$	$k^{(i)}$	$j^{(i)}$	$\underline{y}^{(i)}$
1000101111	559	258	00100000010
1000110000	560	44	00000101100
1110110111	951	894	01101111110
1000011011	539	971	01111001011
0011001010	202	1654	11001110110
1000001101	525	1115	10001011011
1111100110	998	1760	11011100000
0100000101	261	890	01101111010
0010101001	169	1389	10101101101
1100000101	773	300	00100101100
0000011001	25	640	01010000000
0111011101	477	299	00100101011
1000111101	573	655	01010001111
0011110000	240	382	00101111110
1101000110	838	551	01000100111
0101111001	377	1017	01111111001
0110110111	439	384	00110000000
0010111011	187	1622	11001010110
1011101000	744	1012	01111110100
1011100000	736	1109	10001010101

TABLE 12.3   Step E8 in RSA Encipherment

0010000001000000101100011011111110
0111100101111001110110100010101011
1101110000001101111010101011101101
0010010110001010000000000100101011
0101000111001011111100100010100111
0111111100100110000000011001010110

E7. Each integer $j^{(i)}$ in $\mathcal{Z}_N$ is replaced by its N_2-bit base-2 representation $j^{(i)} \rightarrow \underline{y}^{(i)} = (y_0^{(i)}, y_1^{(i)}, \ldots, y_{N_2-1}^{(i)})$ (Table 12.2).

E8. The B (0,1)-vectors $\{\underline{y}^{(i)}\}$ are concatenated to form ciphertext $\underline{y} = (\underline{y}^{(0)}, \underline{y}^{(1)}, \ldots, \underline{y}^{(B-1)})$ of length $n_C = N_2 B$.

Example 12.3
RSA parameters $(p, q, e, d) = (41, 43, 11, 6112)$

- $N = 1763$, $\phi(N) = 40 \times 42 = 1680$, $N_2 = 11$
- *Plaintext*: Example of RSA encipherment.

12.3.2   Decipherment of RSA Ciphertext to ASCII Plaintext

D1. Divide the ciphertext $\underline{y} = (y_0, y_1, \ldots, y_{nC-1})$ of length $nC = N_2 B$ into bit-vectors of length N_2 $\underline{y} \rightarrow (\underline{y}^{(0)}, \underline{y}^{(1)}, \ldots, \underline{y}^{(B-1)})$ (Table 12.4).

D2. The (0,1)-vector $\underline{y}^{(i)}$ of length N_2 is the binary representation of the integer $j^{(i)} = \sum_{t=0}^{N_2-1} 2^{N_2-t} y_t^{(i)}$ in $\mathcal{Z}_n$ (Table 12.4).

D3. RSA deciphers each of the integers $\{j^{(i)}\}$ according to $\mathbf{D}_d$: $j^{(i)} \rightarrow k^{(i)} = (j^{(i)})^d$ (modulo N) (Table 12.5).

D4. The integer $k^{(i)} = \sum_{t=0}^{N_2-2} z_t^{(i)} 2^{(N_2-t-2)}$ is replaced by its binary representation $\underline{z}^{(i)} = (z_0^{(i)}, z_1^{(i)}, \ldots, z_{N_2-2}^{(i)})$ of length $N_2 - 1$ (Table 12.5).

D5. The (0,1)-vectors $\underline{z}^{(i)} = (z_0^{(i)}, z_1^{(i)}, \ldots, z_{N_2-2}^{(i)})$ are concatenated $\underline{z} = (z_0, z_1, \ldots, z_{7n-1})$ where $n = B(N_2 - 1)$ (modulo 7), discarding any padding bits on the right (Table 12.5).

D6. Each 7-bit vector is replaced by its corresponding ASCII character (Table 12.5).

The ciphertext determined by the parameters in *Example 12.2* written in blocks of $N_2 = 11$ bits are derived according to the rules D1–D7.

TABLE 12.4   Steps D1–D2 in RSA Decipherment

$j^{(i)}$	$\underline{y}^{(i)}$	$j^{(i)}$	$\underline{y}^{(i)}$	$j^{(i)}$	$\underline{y}^{(i)}$
258	00100000010	44	00000101100	894	01101111110
971	01111001011	1654	11001110110	1115	10001011011
1760	11011100000	890	01101111010	1389	10101101101
300	00100101100	640	01010000000	299	00100101011
655	01010001111	382	00101111110	551	01000100111
1017	01111111001	384	00110000000	1622	11001010110
1012	01111110100	1109	10001010101		

TABLE 12.5 Steps D3–D6 in RSA Decipherment

Ciphertext		Plaintext					
$\underline{y}^{(i)}$	$j^{(i)}$	$k^{(i)}$	$\underline{z}^{(i)}$		$\underline{x}^{(i)}$	ord($x^{(i)}$)	$x^{(i)}$
00100000010	258	559	1000101111	111	1000101	69	E
00000101100	44	560	1000110000	110000	1111000	120	x
01101111110	894	951	1110110111	110110111	1100001	97	a
			110011011	11	1101101	109	m
01111001011	971	539	1000011011	11011	1110000	112	p
11001110110	1654	202	0011001010	11001010	1101100	108	l
			11001010	0	1100101	101	e
10001011011	1115	525	1000001101	1101	0100000	32	
11011100000	1760	998	1111100110	1100110	1101111	111	o
			1100110		1100110	102	f
01101111010	890	261	0100000101	101	0100000	32	
10101101101	1389	169	0010101001	101001	1010010	82	R
00100101100	300	773	1100000101	100000101	1010011	83	S
			1000001	01	1000001	65	A
01010000000	640	25	0000011001	11001	0100000	32	
00100101011	299	477	0111011101	11011101	1100101	101	e
			1101110	1	1101110	110	n
01010001111	655	573	1000111101	1101	1100011	99	c
00101111110	382	240	0011110000	1110000	1101001	105	i
			1110000		1110000	112	p
01000100111	551	838	1101000110	110	1101000	104	h
01111111001	1017	377	0101111001	111001	1100101	101	e
00110000000	384	439	0110110111	110110111	1110010	114	r
			11		1101101	109	m
11001010110	1622	187	0010111011	11011	1100101	101	e
01111110100	1012	744	1011101000	11101000	1101110	110	n
			0		1110100	116	t
10001010101	1109	736	1011100000	0000	0101110	46	.

12.4 ATTACK ON RSA [SIMMONS, 1983; DELAURENTIS, 1984]

A conceivable network implementation of the RSA algorithm uses a *system public key table* as in Figure 12.1.

$$N_i = p_i q_i \quad \text{and} \quad e_i \text{ with } 1 = \gcd\{e_i, (p_i - 1)(q_i - 1)\}.$$

The maintenance of the table, in particular certifying that it is free from malicious entries, is the responsibility of the system manager. It was even suggested that a simplification would result if a single pair of primes p, q could be used throughout the network.

⋮	⋮	⋮
ID[i]	$N_{\text{ID}[i]}$	PuK(ID[i])
⋮	⋮	⋮
ID[j]	$N_{\text{ID}[j]}$	PuK(ID[j])
⋮	⋮	⋮

Figure 12.1   A system's RSA parameter table.

Proposition 12.7: [Simmons, 1983]:   If $p_i = p$, $q_i = q$, $N = pq$ for all i, knowledge of two public keys e_i and e_j with $1 = \gcd\{e_i, e_j\}$ permits the decipherment of *all* messages of *every* user.

Proof: Suppose a single common pair of primes (p, q) is used, then

$$C_i = M^{e_i} \text{ (modulo } N)$$

and

$$C_j = M^{e_i} \text{ (modulo } N).$$

As $1 = \gcd\{e_i, e_j\}$, there exist integers a, b (by the Euclidean algorithm) such that

$$1 = ae_i + be_j.$$

One of the two integers a, b must be negative (the other positive). Suppose $b < 0$. If $\gcd\{C_j, N\} \neq 1$, C_j has a factor in common with N, which must equal p or q. In this case many messages may not only be deciphered M, but each user's private (deciphering) key d_i can be found. If $\gcd\{C_j, N\} = 1$, the Euclidean algorithm finds C_j^{-1}, satisfying

$$C_j C_j^{-1} = 1 \text{ (modulo } N),$$

which gives

$$C_i^a (C_j^{-1})^{|b|} = M^{aei} M^{-e_j|b|} \text{ (modulo } N)$$

$$= M^{(ae_i + be_j)} \text{ (modulo } N) = M.$$

If the factors of $N = pq$ can be found, then $e\,d$ is found using the Euclidean algorithm. It is *not* known if this is the *only* way in which d can be recovered from e, N and examples of corresponding plaintext and ciphertext.

12.5   WILLIAMS VARIATION OF RSA

$e = 2$ is not a permissible exponent in RSA, as the mapping $\mathbf{E}_e$ is *not* one-to-one. The ambiguity in decipherment might be resolved by using a standard format for the plaintext x. It is unlikely, but *not* proved that only one of the (four) square roots would be in the standard format.

Hugh Williams [1980] found a very clever way around this difficulty. He transforms the plaintext x into $\mathbf{E}_1[x]$ where $\mathbf{E}_1$ is an invertible mapping with inverse $\mathbf{D}_1$. For primes with appropriate restrictions, there exist transformations $\mathbf{E}_2$ and $\mathbf{D}_2$ that correspond to encipherment and encipherment such that

$$x \to \mathbf{E}_1[x] \to \mathbf{E}_2[\mathbf{E}_1[x]] \to \mathbf{D}_2[\mathbf{E}_2[\mathbf{E}_1[x]]] \to \mathbf{D}_1[\mathbf{D}_2[\mathbf{E}_2[\mathbf{E}_1[x]]]] = x$$
$$x \to \mathbf{E}_1[x] \to \mathbf{D}_2[\mathbf{E}_1[x]] \to \mathbf{E}_2[\mathbf{D}_2[\mathbf{E}_1[x]]] \to \mathbf{E}_1[\mathbf{E}_2[\mathbf{D}_2[\mathbf{E}_1[x]]]] = x.$$

The *Jacobi symbol* $J(p/q)$ when q is a prime is defined by

$$J(p/q) = \begin{cases} 0, & \text{if } q \text{ divides } p \\ 1, & \text{if } p^{\frac{q-1}{2}} = 1 \text{ (modulo } q) \\ -1, & \text{if } p^{\frac{q-1}{2}} = -1 \text{ (modulo } q). \end{cases}$$

$J(p/q)$ can be extended for q not being a prime.

Proposition 12.8: (Properties of the Jacobi Symbol):

12.8a If $p_1 = p_2$ (modulo q), then $J(p_1/q) = J(p_2/q)$;

12.8b $J(p_1 p_2/q) = J(p_1/q)J(p_2/q)$;

12.8c $J(p/q_1 q_2) = J(p/q_2)J(p/q_2)$;

12.8d $J(p/q)J(q/p) = (-1)^{\frac{(p-1)(q-1)}{4}}$ if p, q are odd; and

12.8e If q is a prime, then $J(2/q) = (-1)^{q^{\frac{2-1}{8}}}$.

Proposition 12.9: If p, q are primes such that $3 = p$ (modulo 4) $= q$ (modulo 4) and $J(x/pq) = 1$, then

$$x^{\frac{(p-1)(q-1)}{4}} = \pm 1.$$

Proof: Using Proposition **12.8c** and the hypothesis $J(x/pq) = 1$, we conclude that either $J(x/p) = J(x/q) = 1$ or $J(x/p) = J(x/q) = -1$.

Case 1

$$J(x/p) = J(x/q) = 1 \text{ t}$$

Using the definition of $J(\cdots/\cdots)$

$$x^{\frac{p-1}{2}} = 1 \text{ (modulo } p) \quad \text{and} \quad x^{\frac{q-1}{2}} = 1 \text{ (modulo } q).$$

Therefore

$$x^{\frac{(p-1)(q-1)}{4}} = \pm 1 \text{ (modulo } p) \quad \text{and} \quad x^{\frac{(p-1)(q-1)}{4}} = \pm 1 \text{ (modulo } q),$$

which implies $x^{\frac{(p-1)(q-1)}{4}} = \pm 1$ (modulo pq).

Case 2

$$J(x/p) = J(x/q) = -1$$

This is treated exactly as in *Case 1*. ∎

12.5.1 Williams Quadratic Encipherment

Let the parameters p, q, e, d be selected to satisfy

RSA*-a $N = pq$ where p and q are primes such that $p = 3$ (modulo 4) and $q = 7$ (modulo 8);

RSA*-b e is relatively prime to $\lambda(N) = \text{lcm} \{p - 1, q - 1\}$ (note, $\text{lcm}\{a, b\}$ is the *least common multiple* of a, b; that is, the smallest integer m divisible by *both* a and b);

RSA*-c Let d satisfy $de = m$ (modulo $\lambda(N)$) where

$$m = \frac{\frac{(p-1)(q-1)}{4} + 1}{2};$$

RSA*-d

$$\mathcal{X} = \left\{ x \in \mathcal{Z}_N^+ : \begin{cases} 4(2x + 1), & \text{if } J(2x + 1/N) = 1 \\ 2(2x + 1), & \text{if } J(2x + 1/N) = -1 \end{cases} \right\}.$$

The operators $\mathbf{E}_1$, $\mathbf{E}_2$, $\mathbf{D}_1$, and $\mathbf{D}_2$ on $\mathcal{Z}_N$ are given by

$$\mathbf{E}_1 : x \to \begin{cases} 4(2x + 1), & \text{if } J(2x + 1/N) = 1 \\ 2(2x + 1), & \text{if } J(2x + 1/N) = -1 \end{cases}$$

$$\mathbf{E}_2 : x \to x^{2e} \text{ (modulo } N)$$

$$\mathbf{D}_2 : x \to x^d \text{ (modulo } N)$$

$$\mathbf{D}_1 : x \to \begin{cases} (x/4 - 1)/2, & \text{if } 0 = x \text{ (modulo 4)} \\ (N - x/4 - 1)/2, & \text{if } 1 = x \text{ (modulo 4)} \\ (x/2 - 1)/2, & \text{if } 2 = x \text{ (modulo 4)} \\ (N - x/2 - 1)/2, & \text{if } 3 = x \text{ (modulo 4)}. \end{cases}$$

$\mathbf{E}_1[x]$ is not defined if $J(2x + 1/N) = 0$; that is, if either $J(2x + 1/p) = 0$, $J(2x + 1/q) = 0$. The fraction of integers in $\mathcal{Z}_N^+$ that meet this condition is $p + q/N$; if $O(p) \approx O(q)$, the fraction becomes infinitesimally small as $N \to \infty$.

Proposition 12.10: If p, q, e, and d are Williams Quadratic Encipherment parameters, then

$$x \to \mathbf{E}_1[x] \to \mathbf{E}_2[\mathbf{E}_1[x]] \to \mathbf{D}_2[\mathbf{E}_2[\mathbf{E}_1[x]]] \to \mathbf{D}_1[\mathbf{D}_2[\mathbf{E}_2[\mathbf{E}_1[x]]]] = x$$
$$x \to \mathbf{E}_1[x] \to \mathbf{D}_2[\mathbf{E}_1[x]] \to \mathbf{E}_2[\mathbf{D}_2[\mathbf{E}_1[x]]] \to \mathbf{E}_1[\mathbf{E}_2[\mathbf{D}_2[\mathbf{E}_1[x]]]] = x$$

Proof: Let $x_1 = \mathbf{E}_1[x]$; then

$$J(x_1/N) = \begin{cases} J(2/N)J(2/N)J(2x + 1/N), & \text{if } J(2x + 1/N) = 1 \\ J(2/N)J(2x + 1/N), & \text{if } J(2x + 1/N) = -1. \end{cases}$$

Using the conditions on p and q we have $N = 5$ (modulo 8) and hence by Proposition **12.8e** $J(x_1/N) = 1$. Next

$$x_2 = \mathbf{D}_2[\mathbf{E}_2[x_1]]$$
$$= x_1^{2ed} \text{ (modulo } N)$$
$$= x_1^{2m} \text{ (modulo } N)$$
$$= \pm x_1 \text{ (modulo } N).$$

Note that

- x_1^{2ed} (modulo N) $= x_1^{2m}$ (modulo N) uses Euler's Theorem (Proposition **11.6**);
- x_1^{2e} (modulo $N = \pm x_1$ (modulo N) uses Proposition **12.9**.

If x_2 is even, then $x_2 = x_1$; if x_2 is odd, then $x_2 = R - x_1$, completing the proof of

$$x \to \mathbf{E}_1[x] \to \mathbf{E}_2[\mathbf{E}_1[x]] \to \mathbf{D}_2[\mathbf{E}_2[\mathbf{E}_1[x]]] \to \mathbf{D}_1[\mathbf{D}_2[\mathbf{E}_2[\mathbf{E}_1[x]]]] = x.$$

For the second assertion, we use the definitions of $\mathbf{E}_2$ and $\mathbf{D}_2$ to conclude $\mathbf{E}_2[\mathbf{D}_2] = \mathbf{D}_2[\mathbf{E}_2]$. ∎

With the parameters p, q, e, and d as in Williams Quadratic encipherment, define the operators

$$\mathbf{E} : x \to \mathbf{E}[x] = \mathbf{E}_2[\mathbf{E}_1[x]], \quad x \in \mathcal{X}$$
$$\mathbf{D} : x \to \mathbf{D}[x] = \mathbf{D}_1[\mathbf{D}_2[x]], \quad x \in \mathcal{X}$$

Proposition 12.11:

12.11a $\mathbf{E}[\mathbf{D}[x]] = \mathbf{D}[\mathbf{E}[x]]$ for $x \in \mathcal{X}$;

12.11b $\mathbf{E}$ and $\mathbf{D}$ are easy to compute;

12.11c Knowledge of $\mathbf{E}$ does not provide a computationally feasible method to determine $\mathbf{D}$.

Proposition 12.12: If there exists an algorithm to solve the problem

Given: $y = \mathbf{E}[x]$.

Find: For *every* $x \in \mathcal{X}$,

then N may be factored.

Example 12.4

Table 12.6 lists the plaintext x and the all of the intermediate values

$$x \to \mathbf{E}_1[x] \to \mathbf{E}_2[\mathbf{E}_1[x]] \to \mathbf{D}_2[\mathbf{E}_2[\mathbf{E}_1[x]]] \to \mathbf{D}_1[\mathbf{D}_2[\mathbf{E}_2[\mathbf{E}_1[x]]]]$$

for the parameter values

TABLE 12.6 $x \to \mathsf{E}_1[x] \to \mathsf{E}_2[\mathsf{E}_1[x]] \to \mathsf{D}_2[\mathsf{E}_2[\mathsf{E}_1[x]]] \to \mathsf{D}_1[\mathsf{D}_2\mathsf{E}_2[\mathsf{E}_1[x]]]$

x	$\mathbf{E}_1[x]$	$\mathbf{E}_2[\mathbf{E}_1[x]]$	$\mathbf{D}_2[\mathbf{E}_2[\mathbf{E}_1[x]]]$	$\mathbf{D}_1[\mathbf{D}_2[\mathbf{E}_2[\mathbf{E}_1[x]]]]$
130	1,044	42,926	1,044	130
131	1,052	17,201	1,052	131
132	1,060	36,896	53,193	132
133	534	34,245	53,719	133
134	538	2,771	538	134
135	1,084	29,613	1,084	135
136	546	14,765	546	136
137	1,100	32,968	1,100	137
138	1,108	5,905	53,145	138
139	558	19,689	558	139
140	1,124	54,020	53,129	140
141	566	9,227	566	141
142	1,140	10,067	53,113	142
143	574	46,598	574	143
144	1,156	13,371	1,156	144
145	582	36,657	53,671	145
146	586	4,942	586	146
147	1,180	4,151	53,073	147
148	1,118	1,937	1,188	148
149	598	27,189	598	149

$$p = 239, q = 227, N = 54{,}253, m = 6724$$
$$\gcd\{p - 1, q - 1\} = \gcd\{238, 226\} = 2$$
$$\lambda(N) = \text{lcm}\{p - 1, q - 1\} = \text{lcm}\{238, 226\} = 26{,}894$$
$$e = 19, d = 21{,}586$$

One final word: even with the small primes as in this example, some care must be taken with the exponentiation to detect (and correct) the single-precision overflow.

12.6 MULTIPRECISION MODULAR ARITHMETIC

The basic modular operations *addition*, *multiplication*, and *division* on numbers with a *large* number of digits is an extension of the pencil-and-paper technique learned in elementary school. Excellent descriptions of the concepts of multiprecision arithmetic are given in Riesel [1994] and Menezes et al. [1996].

12.6.1 Internal Representation of Numbers

The internal base-b representation of a number x

$$\underline{x} : \text{sgn}(x), n, x_0 \, x_1 \ldots x_{n-2} x_{n-1}$$

contains

- The *sign* of x

$$\text{sgn}(x) = 0 \text{ if } x \geq 0,$$
$$\text{sgn}(x) = b - 1 \text{ if } x \leq 0;$$

- The number n of base-b digits in the *magnitude* of x;
- A string of n base-b digits $x_0 \, x_1 \ldots x_{n-2} x_{n-1}$ determining the magnitude of x where x_i is a base-b *digit* of the magnitude of x.[1] If $x \geq 0$

$$x = x_0 + x_1 b + \cdots + x_{n-2} b^{n-2} + x_{n-1} b^{n-1}, \qquad 0 \leq x_i < b \quad (0 \leq i < n).$$

The two n-bit base b representations of $x = 0$ are $(0)_n$ and $(b - 1)_n$. The usual choices for b are 2, 10, 16, and 256.

Remarks:

1. Base-b negative integers can also be represented using the b's *complement* notation. If $x < 0$ and the digits of $-x$ are $x_0 \, x_1 \ldots x_{n-2} \, x_{n-1}$, then the digits of $-x$ are $\bar{x}_0 \, \bar{x}_1 \ldots \bar{x}_{n-2} \, \bar{x}_{n-1}$ with $\bar{x}_i = b - 1 - \bar{x}_i$.

2. The complement notation has as advantage in simplifying subtraction of signed integers.

3. If $\underline{x} : \text{sgn}(x), n, x_0 \, x_1 \ldots x_{n-2} \, x_{n-1}$, then x_0 is the *least* significant digit of x and x_{n-1} is the *most* significant digit of x.

4. When $x_{n-1} = 0$, the integer x requires fewer than n digits in its internal representation and hence we may assume that the most significant digit of x is positive.

---

[1]The GNU Multiple Precision Arithmetic Library, which is described at www.swox.comb/gmp, refers to the digits as *limbs*. A number x referred to as mpz_t has a sign, a number of limbs _mp_size, and, if this last number is positive, a pointer to a dynamically allocated array for _mp_d data.

12.6.2   Multiprecision Addition, Subtraction, and Multiplication

Addition, subtraction, and multiplication are performed using digit-by-digit operations. For example, addition of two positive integers of the same length n

$$
\begin{array}{r}
x_{n-1}\, x_{n-2} \ldots x_1\, x_0 \\
+ \quad y_{n-1}\, y_{n-2} \cdots y_1\, y_0 \\
\hline
z_n\ z_{n-1}\ z_{n-2} \cdots z_1\, z_0
\end{array}
$$

requires one DO-loop.

> *Algorithm A1*
>
> *Input*:   Two n-digit base-b positive integers.
>
> $$\underline{x} : 0, n, x_0 x_1 \ldots x_{n-2} x_{n-1}$$
> $$\underline{y} : 0, n, y_0 y_1 \ldots y_{n-2} y_{n-1}$$
>
> *Output*: z, the $n + 1$-digit base-b positive integer which is the sum $x + y$ and a carry
>
> $$c. \ \underline{z} : 0, n + !1, z_0\, z_1 \ldots\ z_{n-1} z_n$$

1. $c_i \leftarrow 0$ (input *carry digit*).
2. For i from 0 to $n - 1$ do
   2.1 $z_i \leftarrow (x_i + y_i + c_i)$ (modulo b)
   2.2 if $(x_i + y_i + c_i) < b$, then $c_{i+1} \leftarrow 0$; otherwise, $c_{i+1} \leftarrow 1$.
3. $z_n \leftarrow c_n$
4. End.

> *Remarks*:

1. if $z_n = 0$, the length parameter is adjusted.
2. If the lengths of inputs are different, the strings may be padded (on the right) to make their lengths equal.

When the signed magnitude representation is used, the addition of *signed* integers, which is equivalent to subtraction, requires a consideration of several cases.

> *Algorithm A2*
>
> *Input*:   Two n-digit base-b positive integers x and y with $x \geq y$.
>
> $$\underline{x} : 0, n, x_0\, x_1 \ldots x_{n-2} x_{n-1}$$
> $$\underline{y} : 0, n, y_0\, y_1 \ldots y_{n-2} y_{n-1}$$
>
> *Output*: z, the $n + 1$-digit base-b positive integer which is the sum $x - y$.
>
> $$\underline{z} : 0, n + !1, z_0\, z_1 \ldots n_{n-1} z_n$$

1. $c_i \leftarrow 0$ (input *carry digit*).
2. For i from 0 to $n - 1$ do
   2.1 $z_i \leftarrow (x_i - y_i + c_i)$ (modulo b)
   2.2 If $(x_i - y_i + c_i) < b$, then $c_{i+1} \leftarrow 0$; otherwise, $c_{i+1} \leftarrow -1$.

3. $z_n \leftarrow c_n$

4. End.

Remarks:

1. If $x \geq y$, then $c_n = 0$.

2. If $x < y$, then $c_n = -1$ and the output $\underline{z} : 0, n + !1, z_0 \, z_1 \ldots z_{n-1} z_n$ is *in*correct. To mimic the correct result, Algorithm A2 is repeated with $\underline{x} : 0, n, \underbrace{0, 0, \ldots, 0}_{n \text{ copies}}$ and $\underline{y} = \underline{z}$.

REFERENCES

J. DeLaurentis, "A Further Weakness in the Common Modulus Protocol for the RSA Cryptoalgorithm," *Cryptologia*, **8**, 253–259 (1984).

N. Koblitz, *A Course in Number Theory and Cryptography*, Springer-Verlag, New York, 1987.

J. Linn, "Privacy Enhancement for Internet Electronic Mail,", RFC 1113, *Internet Engineering Task Force* (IETE), August 1989.

R. L. Rivest, A. Shamir, and L. Adelman, "A Method for Obtaining Digital Signatures and Public-Key Cryptosystems," *Communications of the ACM*, **21**, 120–126 (1978).

G. J. Simmons, "A Weak Privacy Protocol Using the RSA Algorithm," *Cryptologia*, **7**, 180–182 (1983).

H. C. Williams "A Modification of the RSA Public-Key Encryption," *IEEE Transactions on Information Theory*, **IT-26**, 726–729 (1980).

H. Riesel, *Prime Numbers and Compute Methods for Factorization* (2nd edn), Birhäuser, Cambridge, Massachusetts, 1985.

A. J. Menezes, P. C. van Dorschot, and S. A. Vanstone, *Handbook of Applied Cryptography*, CRC Press, Boca Raton, Florida, 1996.

CHAPTER 13

PRIME NUMBERS AND FACTORIZATION

BEFORE MICROSOFT AND DELL enlarged our computational horizons, mathematicians explored the mysteries of numbers. The publication in 1978 of the RSA algorithm, whose strength appears to depend on infeasibility factoring very large numbers, stimulated research in number theory. This chapter describes the dual number theoretic issues of factorization and primality testing.

13.1 NUMBER THEORY AND CRYPTOGRAPHY

The distinguished number theorist Carl Pomerance begins the Preface to a 1990 collection of papers [Pomerance, 1990] on number theory and cryptography writing

> *Although they are both ancient and noble subjects, it is only a phenomena of the past dozen years or so that cryptology and computational number theory have become so intertwined.*

The strength of several public-key cryptosystems is related to problems in classical number theory, including the prime-factorization of integers, testing if an integer is a prime, and the generation of prime numbers. A brief discussion of these three problems will be given. Additional material can be found in Koblitz [1987], Riesel [1994], and Pomerance [1990].

13.2 PRIME NUMBERS AND THE SIEVE OF ERATOSTHENES

Eratosthenes (276–194 B.C.E) born in Syene (now Libya) was a Greek geometer. By measuring the sun's angle θ cast by the obelisk at Alexandria and the distance d between Alexandria and Syene, he calculated the circumference of the Earth to be 24,901 miles, as compared to the now accepted value of 29,000 miles, an error of only 17% (Fig. 13.1).

Eratosthenes also invented a *sieving*[1] algorithm to determine all primes $\leq N$. Begin with the set ODD of odd integers $\leq N$; for every integer m, remove from ODD the integer m^2 and every mth integer following.

---

[1]Pastry chefs *sift* flour by passing it through a wire mesh or *sieve*; sieving flour breaks up clumps in the flour for a lighter cake. The number theorist's sieve retains some numbers, allowing the others to be discarded.

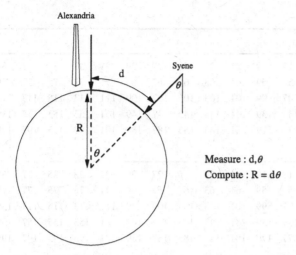

Measure : d,θ

Compute : R = dθ

Figure 13.1 Eratosthenes' measurement of Earth's circumference.

Example 13.1

$N = 201$ (Tables 13.1 and 13.2); the numbers removed are *underlined* in Table 13.1. The time needed for sieving is exponential in the number of bits in N, so that Eratosthenes' sieve is not a viable computational method except for small N.

Although there are infinitely many primes, they are *rare*, in the sense that their density in the set of integers is 0.

Proposition 13.1 (The Prime Number Theorem):   The number $\pi(n)$ of primes less than or equal to n is asymptotic to $n/\ln n$ as $n \to \infty$; that is, $1 = \lim_{n \to \infty}(\pi(n))/(n/\ln n)$. This distance between consecutive primes increases much faster than n as $n \to \infty$ so that the density of primes is 0.

There are two central number-theoretic issues in its application to cryptography:

- efficient methods for finding the prime factors of an integer n, and
- efficient methods for generating prime numbers.

Although these two problems have always existed in number theory before RSA, it is the scale of the numbers involved that sets these problems apart from those in "classical" number theory and has invigorated this ancient branch of mathematics.

13.3 POLLARD'S $p - 1$ METHOD [POLLARD, 1974]

Find the prime factors of n

1. Choose an integer k that is a multiple of all integers less than some bound B; for example, $k = B!$ or $k = \text{lcm}\{1, 2, \ldots, B\}$.

2. Randomly choose an integer a between 2 and $n - 2$.

3. Compute $b = a^k$ (modulo n) and $d = \gcd\{n, b - 1\}$.

4. If d is a trivial divisor of n, start over again with another choice of a and/or k.

TABLE 13.1 *Example 13.1*

ODD

3	5	7	9	11	13	15	17	19	21	23	25	27	29	31	33	35	37	39	41
43	45	47	49	51	53	55	57	59	61	63	65	67	69	71	73	75	77	79	81
83	85	87	89	91	93	95	97	99	101	103	105	107	109	111	113	115	117	119	121
123	125	127	129	131	133	135	137	139	141	143	145	147	149	151	153	155	157	159	161
163	165	167	169	171	173	175	177	179	181	183	185	187	189	191	193	195	197	199	201

$m = 3$

3	5	7	9	11	13	15	17	19	21	23	25	27	29	31	33	35	37	39	41
43	45	47	49	51	53	55	57	59	61	63	65	67	69	71	73	75	77	79	81
83	85	87	89	91	93	95	97	99	101	103	105	107	109	111	113	115	117	119	121
123	125	127	129	131	133	135	137	139	141	143	145	147	149	151	153	155	157	159	161
163	165	167	169	171	173	175	177	179	181	183	185	187	189	191	193	195	197	199	201

$m = 5$

3	5	7	9	11	13	15	17	19	21	23	25	27	29	31	33	35	37	39	41
43	45	47	49	51	53	55	57	59	61	63	65	67	69	71	73	75	77	79	81
83	85	87	89	91	93	95	97	99	101	103	105	107	109	111	113	115	117	119	121
123	125	127	129	131	133	135	137	139	141	143	145	147	149	151	153	155	157	159	161
163	165	167	169	171	173	175	177	179	181	183	185	187	189	191	193	195	197	199	201

$m = 7$

3	5	7	9	11	13	15	17	19	21	23	25	27	29	31	33	35	37	39	41
43	45	47	49	51	53	55	57	59	61	63	65	67	69	71	73	75	77	79	81
83	85	87	89	91	93	95	97	99	101	103	105	107	109	111	113	115	117	119	121
123	125	127	129	131	133	135	137	139	141	143	145	147	149	151	153	155	157	159	161
163	165	167	169	171	173	175	177	179	181	183	185	187	189	191	193	195	197	199	201

$m = 9$

3	5	7	9	11	13	15	17	19	21	23	25	27	29	31	33	35	37	39	41
43	45	47	49	51	53	55	57	59	61	63	65	67	69	71	73	75	77	79	81
83	85	87	89	91	93	95	97	99	101	103	105	107	109	111	113	115	117	119	121
123	125	127	129	131	133	135	137	139	141	143	145	147	149	151	153	155	157	159	161
163	165	167	169	171	173	175	177	179	181	183	185	187	189	191	193	195	197	199	201

$m = 11$

3	5	7	9	11	13	15	17	19	21	23	25	27	29	31	33	35	37	39	41
43	45	47	49	51	53	55	57	59	61	63	65	67	69	71	73	75	77	79	81
83	85	87	89	91	93	95	97	99	101	103	105	107	109	111	113	115	117	119	121
123	125	127	129	131	133	135	137	139	141	143	145	147	149	151	153	155	157	159	161
163	165	167	169	171	173	175	177	179	181	183	185	187	189	191	193	195	197	199	201

$m = 13$

3	5	7	9	11	13	15	17	19	21	23	25	27	29	31	33	35	37	39	41
43	45	47	49	51	53	55	57	59	61	63	65	67	69	71	73	75	77	79	81
83	85	87	89	91	93	95	97	99	101	103	105	107	109	111	113	115	117	119	121
123	125	127	129	131	133	135	137	139	141	143	145	147	149	151	153	155	157	159	161
163	165	167	169	171	173	175	177	179	181	183	185	187	189	191	193	195	197	199	201

TABLE 13.2   List of Primes ≤ 201

3	5	7	11	13	17	19	23	29	31	37	41	43	47	53	59	61	67	71	73
79	83	8997	101	103	107	109	113	127	131	137	139	149	151	157	163	167	173	179	181
191	193	197	199																

Example 13.2

$n = 53{,}467$, $a = 3$, $k = 840 = \text{lcm}\{i : 1 \leq i \leq 8\}$. See Tables 13.3 and 13.4.

Example 13.3

$n = 34{,}163$, $a = 2$, $k = 840 = \text{lcm}\{i : 1 \leq i \leq 8\}$. See Tables 13.5 and 13.6.

13.3.1   Explanation of Pollard's $p - 1$ Method

Let B be larger than any prime factor of $p - 1$ where p is a prime factor of n. If k is the least common multiple of all integers i with $1 \leq i \leq B$, then by Fermat's Little Theorem, $a^k = a^{C(p-1)} = 1$ (modulo p). This implies p divides both $b - 1 = (a^k - 1)$ (modulo n) and n, ensuring that $d = \gcd\{b - 1, n\}$ is a nontrivial divisor of n.

Improved methods to factor require a diversion to review some number theory.

TABLE 13.3   Computing $34{,}944 = 3^{840}$ (modulo 53,467)

j	k	$(k \bmod 2)$	$k \leftarrow \dfrac{k - (k \bmod 2)}{2}$	d	3^{2^j} (mod 53,467)
1	840	0	420	1	9
2	420	0	210	1	81
3	210	0	105	1	6,561
4	105	1	52	6,561	5,786
5	52	0	26	6,561	7,454
6	26	0	13	6,561	9,903
7	13	1	6	11,178	10,931
8	6	0	3	11,178	41,483
9	3	1	1	31,150	3,894
10	1	1	0	34,944	32,075

TABLE 13.4   Computing $421 = \gcd\{34{,}943, 53{,}467\}$

j	r_j	r_{j+1}	r_{j+2}
0	53,467	34,943	18,524
1	34,943	18,524	16,419
2	18,524	16,419	2,105
3	16,419	2,105	1,684
4	2,105	1,684	421
5	1,684	421	0

TABLE 13.5 Computing $16,892 = 2^{840}$ (modulo 34,163)

j	k	$(k \bmod 2)$	$k \leftarrow \dfrac{k - (k \bmod 2)}{2}$	d	3^{2^j} (mod 53,467)
1	840	0	420	1	4
2	420	0	210	1	16
3	210	0	105	1	256
4	105	1	52	256	31,373
5	52	0	26	256	29,099
6	26	0	13	256	21,846
7	13	1	6	24,007	24,769
8	6	0	3	24,007	4,207
9	3	1	1	11,621	2,415
10	1	1	0	16,892	24,515

TABLE 13.6 Computing $127 = \gcd\{16,891, 34,163\}$

j	r_j	r_{j+1}	r_{j+2}
0	34,163	16,891	381
1	16,891	381	127
2	381	127	0

13.4 POLLARD'S ρ-ALGORITHM [POLLARD, 1978]

If positive integers x and y in $\mathcal{Z}_N$ can be found so that $1 < d = \gcd\{x - y, N\} < N$, then d is a factor of N.

Pairs (x, y) can be found by random trials, hence the name *Monte Carlo*; accordingly, a random function f mapping the integers in $\mathcal{Z}_N - \{0\}$ into themselves is selected. The sequence $x_1, x_2, \ldots$ is determined by the rule

$$\begin{cases} x_1 = 1 \\ x_i = f(x_{i-1}), \quad \text{for } 2 \le i < n. \end{cases}$$

As we observed in Chapter 9, the $f(n)$ must repeat before $N - 1$ iterations and the sequence

$$x_1 \rightarrow x_2 = f(x_1) \rightarrow x_3 = f(x_2) \rightarrow \cdots$$

has

- A *tail* $x_1 \rightarrow x_2 = f(x_1) \rightarrow \cdots \rightarrow x_k = f(x_{k-1})$, and
- Then enters a *loop* or *cycle* $x_k = f(x_{k-1}) \rightarrow \cdots \rightarrow x_{j+k} = f(x_{j+k-1}) = x_k$.

The name ρ chosen by Pollard for his algorithm is perfectly clear; the iterates of the mapping f appear like the Greek letter ρ.

Unfortunately $N = O(2^{100})$ so that $j + k$ could be very large and we cannot wait $\cdots$ and we do not have to, because of the *Birthday Paradox*.

13.4.1 The Birthday Paradox

What is the probability $\Pr\{E_n\}$ that in a class of n students, that *no* day is the birthday of two or more students?

Answer: Assuming that a year contains 365 days, the probability that no two students in a class of n have the same birthday is

$$\Pr\{E_n\} = P_n = \frac{365 \times 364 \times \cdots \times (365 - (n-1))}{365^n}$$

$$= -\left(1 - \frac{1}{365}\right)\left(1 - \frac{2}{365}\right)\cdots\left(1 - \frac{n-1}{365}\right)$$

Using the approximation

$$1 - x \approx e^{-x}, \quad x \text{ small},$$

gives

$$P_n \approx \tilde{P}_n \approx e^{-\frac{n(n-1)}{2\times365}}.$$

Equivalently, $1 - P_n$ (or $1 - \tilde{P}_n$) is the probability that two (or more) students in a class of n have the same birthday. The values of P_n and $\tilde{P}_n$ are tabulated in Table 13.7 for $10 \le n \le 53$.

Using the approximation, $\tilde{P}_n = 0.5$ requires $n \approx \sqrt{2 \ln 2d}$ so that $1 - P_{23} \ge 0.5$. If there were d instead of 365 birthdays in a year, $\tilde{P}_n = 0.5$ requires $n \approx 1.7741\sqrt{d}$. However, there is another complication; if the Monte Carlo algorithm computes and stores x_i and then tests if $x_i \in \{x_0, x_1, \ldots, x_{i-1}\}$, then both the storage required and the number of comparison operations will be onerous.

Robert Floyd [1967] published a *cycle detecting algorithm* that reasons as follows; if the loop begins with x_k and $x_{j+k} = x_k$, then j must be a multiple of the cycle length. Therefore, if two indices $i_1 < i_2$ are found such that $x_{i_1} = x_{i_2}$, then $i_2 - i_2$ must be a multiple of the cycle length. We can test for the *first repeat* by

1. Run two executions of the random function f evaluation in parallel computing x_m and x_{2m}, and

2. Test $x_m \stackrel{?}{=} x_{2m}$.

TABLE 13.7 Probability of Distinct Birthdays in a Class of n Students

n	P_n	$\tilde{P}_n$	n	P_n	$\tilde{P}_n$	n	P_n	$\tilde{P}_n$	n	P_n	$\tilde{P}_n$
10	0.883052	0.884009	11	0.858859	0.860119	12	0.832975	0.834584	13	0.805590	0.807592
14	0.776897	0.779334	15	0.747099	0.750008	16	0.716396	0.719811	17	0.684992	0.688939
18	0.653089	0.657587	19	0.620881	0.625945	20	0.588562	0.594195	21	0.556312	0.562512
22	0.524305	0.531062	23	0.492703	0.499998	24	0.461656	0.469464	25	0.431300	0.439588
26	0.401759	0.410487	27	0.373141	0.382264	28	0.345539	0.355007	29	0.319031	0.328792
30	0.293684	0.303680	31	0.269545	0.279718	32	0.246652	0.256942	33	0.225028	0.235375
34	0.204683	0.215028	35	0.185617	0.195903	36	0.167818	0.177990	37	0.151266	0.161273
38	0.135932	0.145726	39	0.121780	0.131318	40	0.108768	0.118010	41	0.096848	0.105761
42	0.085970	0.094524	43	0.076077	0.084250	44	0.067115	0.074887	45	0.059024	0.066382
46	0.051747	0.058682	47	0.045226	0.051734	48	0.039402	0.045483	49	0.034220	0.039879
50	0.029626	0.034869	51	0.025568	0.030405	52	0.021992	0.026440	53	0.018862	0.022929

TABLE 13.8 Evaluations and Comparisons in Floyd's Cycle Detecting Algorithm

Step #	Evaluate	Compare
1	$x_2 = f(x_1)$	x_1, x_2
2	$x_3 = f(x_2), x_4 = f(x_3)$	x_2, x_4
3	$x_5 = f(x_4), x_6 = f(x_5)$	x_3, x_6
4	$x_7 = f(x_6), x_8 = f(x_7)$	x_4, x_8

TABLE 13.9 $\gcd\{N, |x_{2m} - x_m|\}$ in *Example 13.4*

m	x_m	$\gcd\{N, |x_{2m} - X_m|\}$
1	33,791	1
2	10,832,340	1
3	12,473,782	1
4	4,239,855	1
5	309,274	0
6	11,965,503	1
7	15,903,688	1
8	3,345,998	1
9	2,476,108	0
10	11,948,879	1
11	9,350,010	1
12	4,540,646	1
13	858,249	0
14	1,424,664	1
15	4,073,290	0
16	4,451,768	1
17	14,770,419	257

A word about "evaluation in parallel"; Table 13.8 shows what we do at each step of the Floyd algorithm. Only two evaluations and one comparison are made at each step.

The speed-up in Floyd's algorithm depends on the size of the tail and, of course, the time until the first $x_m \overset{?}{=} x_{2m}$ thereafter.

Pollard suggested the use of the polynomial functions $f(x) = (ax^2 + b)$ (modulo N). The following example appears in several Web sites, including www.csh.rit.edu/pat/math/quickies/rho.

Example 13.4

$x_{n+1} = (1024x_n^2 + 3767)$ (modulo 16,843,009) (Table 13.9). Some care must be taken in finding the values in Table 13.9 if you do not have multiprecision modular arithmetic.

13.5 QUADRATIC RESIDUES

An integer $x \in Z_N$ is a *quadratic residue* of N if x has a square root modulo N; that is, if there exists a value $y \equiv \sqrt{x}$ (modulo n) $\in \mathcal{Z}_n$ that satisfies

$$y^2 = x \text{ (modulo } n).$$

The case of interest in cryptography is where N is the product of two prime numbers $N = pq$. The Chinese Remainder Theorem (Proposition **13.6**) allows $N = pq$ to be reduced to the study of each of the prime factors p and q of N. We now develop the theory in this special case $N = p$, a prime.

Proposition 13.2:   If p is an odd prime:

13.2a For every positive integer $x \in \mathcal{Z}_p$, the equation $y^2 - x = 0$ (modulo p) has either 0 or 2 solutions.

13.2b The set QUAD[p] of nonzero quadratic residues modulo p consists of the $(p - 1)/2$ integers in $\mathcal{Z}_p$ that are the values $1^2, 2^2, \ldots, (p - 1/2)^2$ modulo p.

13.2c $x \in$ QUAD[p] if and only if $x^{\frac{p-1}{2}} = 1$(modulo p).

13.2d $x \notin$ QUAD[p] if and only if $x^{\frac{p-1}{2}} = -1$ (modulo p) $= (p - 1)$ (modulo p).

Proof: If $y^2 = x$ (modulo p), then $(y - p)^2 = x$ (modulo p), proving Proposition **13.2a**; the assertion of Proposition **13.2b** is obvious. By Fermat's Little Theorem

$$y^{p-1} - 1 = 0 \text{ (modulo } p)$$

for $1 \le y < p$. Writing

$$y^{p-1} - 1 = \left(y^{\frac{p-1}{2}} - 1\right)\left(y^{\frac{p-1}{2}} + 1\right)(\text{modulo } p),$$

we see that *every* nonzero $y \in \mathcal{Z}_p$ satisfies one of the two equations

$$y^{\frac{p-1}{2}} - 1 = 0 \text{ (modulo } p) \quad \text{or} \quad y^{\frac{p-1}{2}} + 1 = 0 \text{ (modulo } p).$$

If x is a quadratic residue, then $y^2 = x$ (modulo p), which implies $y^{\frac{p-1}{2}} = x^{p-1} = 1$(modulo p).

Example 13.5

The quadratic residues of $p = 17$ are given in Table 13.10

Remark: If p is an odd prime and q is primitive, then $q^{\frac{p-1}{2}} = -1$ (modulo p); that is, q is *not* a quadratic residue of p.

Proof: As q is primitive, $q^k = 1$ (modulo p) with $0 < k < p$ implies $k = p - 1$.

Propositions **12.1** and **13.2b** show that there is a polynomial time algorithm to *test* if x is a quadratic residue modulo p. Finding quadratic residues is another matter. Although there is no polynomial time algorithm to *find* elements of QUAD[p], there is

TABLE 13.10   The Quadratic Residues of $p = 17$

x	1	2	4	8	9	13	15	16
$\sqrt{x}$	1,16	6,11	2,15	5,12	3,14	8,9	7,10	4,13

a random search algorithm with acceptable search time and we now turn to an exposition of it.

In Chapter 11, we discussed the Euclidean algorithm to compute $d = \gcd\{a, b\}$, the greatest common divisor d of integers a and b. If $a(z)$ and $b(z)$ are polynomials whose coefficients are integers in $\mathcal{Z}_p$, then $d(z)$ is the greatest common division of $a(z)$ and $b(z)$

- If the polynomial $d(z)$ divides both $a(z)$ and $b(z)$; that is, polynomials $A(z)$ and $B(z)$ exist so that $a(z) = A(z)d(z)$ (modulo p) and $b(z) = B(z)d(z)$ (modulo p), and
- If the polynomial $e(z)$ is also a divisor of $a(z)$ and $b(z)$, then $d(z)$ divides $e(z)$.

Although the greatest common divisor of integers a and b is unique, this is *not* the case for the greatest common divisor of polynomials $a(z)$ and $b(z)$.

Example 13.6

If $p = 3$, $a(z) = 2(z^3 + z^2 + z + 1)$, and $b(z) = 2z^2 + z + 2$, then

$$a(z) = (z^2 + 1)d(z), \qquad b(z) = (z + 1)d(z), \qquad d(z) = 2(z + 1),$$

and

$$a(z) = 2(z^2 + 1)d(z), \qquad b(z) = 2(z + 1)d(z), \qquad d(z) = (z + 1).$$

Uniqueness is restored if $d(z)$ is required to be a *monic polynomial*, one whose leading coefficient is 1.

The Euclidean algorithm as defined in Chapter 11 (Proposition **11.5**) is directly extended for polynomial operations.

Proposition 13.3 (Euclidean Algorithm for Polynomials with Coefficients in $\mathcal{Z}_p$): If $a(z)$ and $b(z)$ are two polynomials in z whose coefficients are in $\mathcal{Z}_p$, for the sequence

$$r_0(z) = a(z)$$
$$r_1(r) = b(z)$$
$$r_0(z) = c_1(z)r_1(z) + r_2(z); \qquad 0 \leq \deg(r_2) < \deg(r_1)$$
$$r_1(z) = c_2(z)r_2(z) + r_3(z); \qquad 0 \leq \deg(r_3) < \deg(r_2)$$
$$\vdots$$
$$r_{s-2}(z) = c_{s-1}(z)r_{s-1}(z) + r_s(z); \qquad 0 \leq \deg(r_s) < \deg(r_{s-1})$$
$$r_{s-1}(z) = c_s(z)r_s(z) + r_{s+1}(z); \qquad 0 \leq \deg(r_{s+1}) < \deg(r_s)$$

13.3a The sequence is ultimately identically 0;

13.3b If s is the first index for which $r_{s+1}(z) = 0$, then $r_s(z) = \gcd\{a(z), b(z)\}$;

13.3c If $\deg(a(z)) > \deg(b(z))$, the time to compute $\gcd\{a(z), b(z)\}$ is $O((\log_2 \deg(a(z)))^3)$.

Example 13.7

$p = 2$, $a(z) = 1 + z^4 + z^5 + z^6 + z^8 + z^9 + z^{10}$, $b(z) = 1 + z^2 + z^3 + z^5 + z^6 + z^9$.

$$r_0(z) = a(z)$$

$$r_1(z) = b(z)$$

$$r_0(z) = (1 + z)r_1(z) + r_2(z); \qquad r_2(z) = z + z^2 + z^6 + z^7 + z^8$$

$$r_1(z) = (z + 1)r_2(z) + r_3(z); \qquad r_3(z) = 1 + z + z^2 + z^5$$

$$r_2(z) = (z^3 + z^2 + z + 1)r_3(z) + r_4(z); \qquad r_4(z) = 1 + z + z^3$$

$$r_3(z) = (z^2 + 1)r_4(z) + r_5(z); \qquad r_5(z) = 0$$

$$\gcd\{a(z), b(z)\} = 1 + z + z^3$$

The following algorithm finds $\sqrt{x}$ (modulo p) in randomized expected time 2.

Proposition 13.4   (Berlekamp's Algorithm [Berlekamp, 1970]): Let p be an odd prime and $x \in \text{QUAD}[p] \subset \mathcal{Z}_p^+$. Define

$$a(z) = z^2 - x$$

$$a_k(z) = a(z - k)$$

$$b(z) = z^{\frac{p-1}{2}} - 1.$$

To compute the square root of x

13.4a Choose k randomly in $\mathcal{Z}_p^+$.

13.4b Compute $d_k(z) = \gcd\{a_k(z), b(z)\}$.

As the degree of $a_k(z)$ is two, the result is either

13.4b-1 $d_k(z) = 1$;

13.4b-2 $d_k(z) = a_k(z)$; or

13.4b-3 $d_k(z) \neq 1$, $a_k(z)$ and $\deg(d_k) = 1$.

13.4c In cases 13.4b-1 and 13.4b-2, choose another value for k and repeat steps 13.4a and b.

If $d_k(z)$ has degree one, $z^{\frac{p-1}{2}} - 1 = (z - k - \eta)R(z)$ and $(k + \eta)^{\frac{p-1}{2}} - 1 = 0$, so that $k + \eta$ is a quadratic residue of x.

Proposition 13.5:   The probability that Steps 13.4a and b determine the square root of x is approximately $\frac{1}{2}$. Therefore, the expected number of values of k that need to be tested before success is ≈ 2.

Proof: When will Step 13.4b be successful? There are four cases to be examined.

		$d_k(z)$
$(k + x) \in \text{QUAD}[p]$	$(k - x) \in \text{QUAD}[p]$	$a_k(z)$
$(k + x) \notin \text{QUAD}[p]$	$(k - x) \notin \text{QUAD}[p]$	1
$(k + x) \in \text{QUAD}[p]$	$(k - x) \notin \text{QUAD}[p]$	$(z - k + x)$
$(k + x) \notin \text{QUAD}[p]$	$(k - x) \in \text{QUAD}[p]$	$(z - k - x)$

If k is such that *exactly one* of the two numbers $k + x$ or $k - x$ is a nonquadratic residue modulo p, the Berlekamp algorithm will succeed. How likely is it to choose such a k?

Consider the mapping for integers $k \in \mathcal{Z}_p$

$$T : k \rightarrow T(k) = \frac{k + x}{k - x} \equiv (k + x)(k - x)^{-1}, \quad k \neq x,$$

is a one-to-one mapping because

$$
\begin{aligned}
T(k) = T(k') &\Leftrightarrow \frac{k + x}{k - x} = \frac{k' + x}{k' - x} \\
&\Leftrightarrow x(k - k') = -x(k - k') \\
&\Leftrightarrow k = k'.
\end{aligned}
$$

$T(k) = 1$ because this requires $x = -x = p - x$, implying $p = 2x$. Thus, T maps the integers $\neq x$ into all of $\mathcal{Z}_p$ except for the single value 1 so that

$$\Pr\left\{ \frac{K + x}{K - x} \in \mathrm{QUAD}[p] \right\} \approx \frac{1}{2},$$

where K denotes the random choice in Step 13.4a.

Finally, $\frac{k+x}{k-x}$ is a quadratic residue modulo p if and only if both or neither $k + x$ and $k - x$ are quadratic residues modulo p, which completes the proof of Proposition **13.4**.

Berlekamp's Algorithm can be applied to compute quadratic residues modulo $N = pq$, where p and q are odd primes. If N is the product of two primes, there are four solutions. Why four?

Proposition 13.6 (The Chinese Remainder Theorem)[2]:

13.6a $m_1, m_2, \ldots, m_k$ are relatively prime integers;

13.6b $a_1, a_2, \ldots, a_k$ are residues $0 \leq a_i < m_i$ for $1 \leq i \leq k$.

There exists a unique integer x with $0 \leq x < M \equiv m_1, m_2, \ldots, m_k$ such that $a_i = x$ (modulo m_i) for $1 \leq i \leq k$.

Proof: If $x - y = 0$ (modulo m_i) for $1 \leq i \leq k$, then x is a positive multiple of M, proving that there is *at most* one solution.

Let $M_i = \frac{M}{m_i}$; use the Euclidean algorithm to find the multiplicative inverse $M_i N_i = 1$ (modulo m_i) of M_i.

Then

$$
M_i N_i \text{ (modulo } m_j) = \begin{cases} 1, & \text{if } j = i \\ 0, & \text{if } j \neq i. \end{cases}
$$

If

$$x = \sum_{i=1}^{k} a_i M_i N_i \text{ (modulo } M)$$

then

$$
a_i M_i N_i \text{ (modulo } m_j) = \begin{cases} x \text{ (modulo } m_i), & \text{if } j = i \\ 0, & \text{if } j \neq i, \end{cases}
$$

[2]A special case of the Chinese Remainder Theorem was stated by Sun-Tsŭ sometime between 200 B.C.E. and 200 A.D.

so that

$$x = \sum_{i=1}^{k} a_i M_i N_i \text{ (modulo } M)$$

satisfies $a_i = x$ (modulo m_i) for $1 \leq i \leq k$.

The Chinese Remainder Theorem explains why there are four solutions to $y^2 = x$ (modulo N) when $N = pq$. If x_1 is a quadratic residue of p, and x_2 a quadratic residue of q,

- There are two solutions y_1 and $p - y_1$ to $y^2 = x_1$ (modulo p), and
- There are two solutions y_2 and $q - y_2$ to $y^2 = x_2$ (modulo q).

Each of the four pairs

1. (y_1, y_2) $x = y_1$ (modulo p) $x = y_2$ (modulo q)
2. $(p - y_1, y_2)$ $x = p - y_1$ (modulo p) $x = y_2$ (modulo q)
3. $(y_1, p - y_2)$ $x = y_1$ (modulo p) $x = q - y_2$ (modulo q)
4. $(p - y_1, p - y_2)$ $x = p - y_1$ (modulo p) $x = q - y_2$ (modulo q)

provides a solution to $y^2 = x$ (modulo pq).

Proposition 13.7:   The factors of $N = pq$ are determined by any two *distinct* solutions to the congruence $y^2 = u$ (modulo N).

Proof: If $z^2 = u$ (modulo N) and $x^2 = u$ (modulo N), then

$$0 = (z^2 - x^2) \text{ (modulo } N) = (z - x)(z + x) \text{ (modulo } N).$$

As two distinct solutions were assumed, neither of the factors $(z - x)$ or $(z + x)$ equal 0. It follows that one factor must be divisible by p and the other by q.

13.6   RANDOM FACTORIZATION

We assume that N is both composite and odd. Several factorization methods are based on a simple idea attributed to Dixon [1981]; if integers x and y can be found so that $x^2 = y^2$ (modulo N), then $(x - y)(x + y) = 0$ (modulo N). If $x \neq \pm y$ (modulo N), then either gcd$\{N, x - y\}$ or gcd$\{N, x + y\}$ is a nontrivial factor of n. In fact, the factorizations $N = ab$ are in 1–1 correspondence with pairs of integers s, t such that $0 = (t^2 - s^2)$ (modulo N) in the sense that $t = \frac{a+b}{2}$ and $s = \frac{a-b}{2}$ [Koblitz, 1987, Proposition V.3.1].

Example 13.8
$37^2 = 7^2$ (modulo 55).

$$(37 - 7) \times (37 + 7) = 30 \times 44 = 0 \text{ (modulo 55)}$$
$$5 = \text{gcd}\{55, 30\}, \qquad 11 = \text{gcd}\{55, 44\}.$$

To find pairs (x, y), random values of s in $\mathcal{Z}_n$ are chosen, and $u = s^2$ (modulo N) is computed. If u is a perfect square (modulo N), say $u = t^2$ (modulo N), and both $0 \neq (s - t)$ (modulo N) and $0 \neq (s + t)$ (modulo N), then we find a factor of N.
For example, if $N = 55$ and $s = 13$, then

$$13^2 \text{(modulo 55)} = 4 = 2^2 \text{ (modulo 55)}$$

leading to the factorization

$$11 = \gcd\{55, 13 - 2\}, \qquad 5 = \gcd\{55, 13 + 2\}.$$

Of course, if we have chosen $s = 12$, then

$$12^2 \text{ (modulo 55)} = 34,$$

which is not a perfect square. However, we may lessen the effect of bad choice of s as follows; randomly choose r integers $\{s_i\}$ and compute their squares (modulo N):

$$u_i = s_i^2 \text{ (modulo } N), \qquad 1 \le i \le r.$$

Write the prime factorizations of the $\{u_i\}$

$$u_1 = \prod_k p_k^{e_{1,k}} \qquad u_2 = \prod_k p_k^{e_{2,k}} \qquad \cdots \qquad u_r = \prod_k p_k^{e_{r,k}}$$

The strategy is to combine my multiplication for *some* of the $\{u_i\}$ so that the total exponent of the terms included is even. In this way, the product of the terms included is a perfect square.

Example 13.9 $N = 77$

$$15 = 13^2 \text{(modulo 77)}, \qquad 15 = 3 \times 5$$
$$56 = 21^2 \text{(modulo 77)}, \qquad 56 = 2^3 \times 7$$
$$60 = 37^2 \text{(modulo 77)}, \qquad 60 = 2^2 \times 3 \times 5$$
$$70 = 42^2 \text{(modulo 77)}, \qquad 2 \times 5 \times 7$$

yielding

$$15 \times 60 = 2^2 \times 3^3 \times 5^2 = 30^2 = (13 \times 37)^2 \text{ (modulo 77)}$$

leading to the factorization

$$11 = \gcd\{77, 481 - 30\}, \qquad 7 = \gcd\{77, 481 + 30\}.$$

Combining the $\{s_i : 1 \le i \le r\}$ can be performed systematically as follows:

1. Find the prime factorization of $u_i = s_i^2 \text{ (modulo } n) = \prod_j p_j^{e_{j,i}}$;
2. If $p_1 < p_2 < \cdots < p_m$ denote the set of primes arising in the factorization of the $\{u_i\}$, form the $r \times m$ array of exponents

$$\Gamma = \begin{pmatrix} e_{1,1} & e_{1,2} & \cdots & e_{1,m} \\ e_{2,1} & e_{2,2} & \cdots & e_{2,m} \\ \cdots & \cdots & \ddots & \cdots \\ e_{r,1} & e_{r,2} & \cdots & e_{r,m} \end{pmatrix}$$

and try to find an r-vector $\underline{x} = (x_1, x_2, \ldots, x_r) \in \mathcal{Z}_{r,2}$ such that

$$\underbrace{(0, 0, 0, \ldots, 0)}_{\text{length } m} = (x_1, x_2, \ldots, x_r)\Gamma \text{ (modulo 2)}.$$

Using Gaussian elimination, calculate

$$v^2 \equiv (s_{i_1} \times s_{i_2} \cdots s_{i_M}) \text{ (modulo } N), \quad u^2 \equiv (u_{i_1}^2 \times u_{i_2}^2 \cdots u_{i_M}^2) \text{ (modulo } N)$$

$$u^2 = v^2 \text{ (modulo } N)$$

The process is successful if $u \neq \pm v$ (modulo N); if not, choose another set $\{u_i\}$.

13.7 THE QUADRATIC SIEVE (QS)

Dixon's method may be inefficient, often requiring a large number of random terms $\{u_i\}$ in order to construct a pair of integers x, y such that $x^2 = y^2$ (modulo N). The *quadratic sieve* refines Dixon's idea of searching only for pairs (x, y) close to $m \approx \sqrt{N}$. When $m = \lfloor \sqrt{N} \rfloor$ and x is *small* compared to m, then

$$q(x) = (x + m)^2 - N = x^2 + 2mx + m^2 - N \approx x^2 + 2mx$$

is of the order $\sqrt{N}$ and it is *reasonable* to expect the prime factors of $q(x)$ to be *small*. The following observation will be used; if a prime p divides $q(x)$ so that

$$q(x) = 0 \text{ (modulo } p)$$

then

$$q(x) = (x + m)^2 - N = 0 \text{ (modulo } p)$$

so that N is a quadratic residue of p and *only* these primes occur in the factorization of $q(x)$. The quadratic sieve consists of the following steps:

QS0. *Select a Factor Base*: The *factor base* $S = \{ p_0, p_1, p_2, \ldots, p_t \}$ contains $p_0 = -1$ and $p_1 = 2$; the remaining terms are the next $t - 1$ primes $p_2, p_3, \ldots, p_t$ satisfying n is a quadratic residue modulo p_i.

QS1. *Find Smooth x-Values*: An integer x is *smooth* relative to the factor base S provided the factorization of $q(x) = (x + m)^2 - N$ involves only primes in S. $p_0 = -1$ is included in S as $q(x)$ may be negative.

QS2. For $x = 0, 1, -1, 2, -2, \ldots, r, -r$ with $r \approx 40 - 60$ compute $q(x)$. Construct a table whose ith row for $i = 1, 2, \ldots$ contains the ith smooth value of x denoted by x_i and

$$q_i = (x_i + m)^2 - N = \prod_{j=0}^{t} p_j^{e_{i,j}}, \quad b_i = (x_i + m)^2 (\text{modulo } N), \quad a_i = (x_i + m),$$

$$\underline{e}_i = (e_{i, 0}, e_{i, 1}, \ldots, e_{i, r}).$$

Example 13.10
See Table 13.11.

QS3. *Find Dependency Sets T*: Use Gaussian elimination to determine subsets $T = \{i_1, i_2, \ldots, i_k\}$ for which the exponent of each of the t primes in the product

$$b_T \equiv \prod_{s=1}^{r} b_{i_s} = \prod_{s=1}^{r} \prod_{j=1}^{t} p_j^{e_{i_s, j}}$$

TABLE 13.11 Step QS2 in *Example 13.10*. ($N = 24{,}961$, $m = 157$, $S = \{-1, 2, 3, 5, 13, 23, 41, 43, 47,$ $59, 61, 67, 71, 79, 83, 97\}$)

i	x_i	q_i	a_i	$\underline{e}_i$ (mod 2)
1	0	$-312 = -2^3 \times 3 \times 13$	157	(1, 1, 1, 0, 1, 0, 0, 0, 0, 0, 0, 0, 0, 0, 0, 0)
2	1	$3 = 3$	158	(0, 0, 1, 0, 0, 0, 0, 0, 0, 0, 0, 0, 0, 0, 0, 0)
3	-1	$-625 = -5^4$	156	(1, 0, 0, 0, 0, 0, 0, 0, 0, 0, 0, 0, 0, 0, 0, 0)
4	2	$320 = 2^6 \times 5$	159	(0, 0, 0, 1, 0, 0, 0, 0, 0, 0, 0, 0, 0, 0, 0, 0)
5	-2	$-936 = -2^3 \times 3^2 \times 13$	155	(1, 1, 0, 0, 1, 0, 0, 0, 0, 0, 0, 0, 0, 0, 0, 0)
6	3	$639 = 3^2 \times 71$	160	(0, 0, 0, 0, 0, 0, 0, 0, 0, 0, 0, 1, 0, 0, 0, 0)
7	-3	$-1245 = -3 \times 5 \times 83$	154	(1, 0, 1, 1, 0, 0, 0, 0, 0, 0, 0, 0, 0, 0, 1, 0)
8	4	$960 = 2^6 \times 3 \times 5$	161	(0, 0, 1, 1, 0, 0, 0, 0, 0, 0, 0, 0, 0, 0, 0, 0)
9	-4	$-1552 = -2^4 \times 97$	153	(1, 0, 0, 0, 0, 0, 0, 0, 0, 0, 0, 0, 0, 0, 0, 1)
10	6	$1608 = 2^3 \times 3 \times 67$	163	(0, 1, 1, 0, 0, 0, 0, 0, 0, 0, 1, 0, 0, 0, 0)
11	-6	$-2160 = -2^4 \times 3^3 \times 5$	151	(1, 0, 1, 1, 0, 0, 0, 0, 0, 0, 0, 0, 0, 0, 0, 0)
12	7	$1935 = 3^2 \times 5 \times 43$	164	(0, 0, 0, 1, 0, 0, 0, 1, 0, 0, 0, 0, 0, 0, 0, 0)
13	-8	$-2760 = -2^3 \times 3 \times 5 \times 23$	149	(1, 1, 1, 1, 0, 1, 0, 0, 0, 0, 0, 0, 0, 0, 0, 0)
14	10	$2928 = 2^4 \times 3 \times 61$	167	(0, 0, 1, 0, 0, 0, 0, 0, 0, 0, 1, 0, 0, 0, 0)

is even

$$\underbrace{(0, 0, 0, \ldots, 0)}_{r} = (\underline{e}_{i_1} + \underline{e}_{i_2} + \cdots + \underline{e}_{i_r}) \;(\text{modulo } 2).$$

Defining

$$a_T = \prod_{s=1}^{r} a_{i_s}, \qquad \sqrt{b_T} = \prod_{j=1}^{t} p_j^{\ell_j}, \qquad \ell_j = \frac{1}{2}\sum_{s=1}^{r} e_{i_s, j}, \qquad 1 \le j \le t,$$

we have

$$b_i \;(\text{modulo } n) = (x_i + m)^2 (\text{modulo } n) = a_i^2 \;(\text{modulo } n).$$

This implies

$$a_T^2 \;(\text{modulo } N) = b_T \;(\text{modulo } n).$$

QS4. *Has a NonTrivial Factor Been Found?* Use the Euclidean algorithm to compute $\gcd\{a_T \pm \sqrt{b_T}\}$. If $a_T \ne \pm\sqrt{b_T}$ (modulo N), then either $\gcd\{a_T - \sqrt{b_T}, n\}$ or $\gcd\{a_T + \sqrt{b_T}, n\}$ is a nontrivial factor of n. If $a_T = \pm\sqrt{b_T}$ (modulo N), then test another linear dependency T.

TABLE 13.12 Step QS3 in *Example 13.10*

T	$\sqrt{b_T}$ (modulo n)	a_T (modulo n)
$\{1, 2, 5\}$	$2^3 \times 3^2 \times 13 = 936$	$157 \times 158 \times 155 = 936$
$\{2, 4, 8\}$	$2^6 \times 3 \times 5 = 960$	$158 \times 159 \times 161 = 960$
$\{3, 8, 11\}$	$2^5 \times 3^2 \times 5^3 = 11{,}039$	$156 \times 161 \times 151 = 23{,}405$

Example 13.10 (Continued)
See Table 13.12. Only the set $T = \{3, 6, 7\}$ gives nontrivial factors

$$229 = \gcd\{23{,}405 - 11{,}039, 24{,}961\} = \gcd\{12{,}366, 24{,}961\}$$
$$109 = \gcd\{23{,}405 + 11{,}039, 24{,}961\} = \gcd\{9483, 24{,}961\}.$$

13.8 TESTING IF AN INTEGER IS A PRIME

RSA encipherment requires prime numbers for its implementation. Fermat's Little Theorem is the basis for testing if n is a prime; if it is, then $a^{n-1} = 1$ (modulo N) for every a for which $1 = \gcd\{a, n\}$.

- If n is an odd composite number and $1 \leq a < n$ such that $a^{n-1} \neq 1$ (modulo N), then a is a *Fermat witness* to the compositeness of n.

- If n is an odd composite number and $1 \leq a < n$ such that $a^{n-1} = 1$ (modulo N), then n is a *pseudoprime to base a* and a is a *Fermat liar* to the primality of n.

13.8.1 Fermat's Primality Test

n is an odd integer and $t \geq 1$.
For $i = 1$ to t do

(a) Choose a random integer a with $2 \leq a \leq n - 2$

(b) Compute $r = a^{n-1}$ (modulo n)

(c) If $r \neq 1$, Return ("Composite").

Return("Prime")
Fermat's Primality Test may *falsely* conclude n is a prime. A composite integer n is a *Carmichael number* (discovered by R. D. Carmichael in 1910) if $a^{n-1} = 1$ (modulo N) for every a for which $1 \leq a \leq n - 1$.

Proposition 13.8:

13.8a n is a Carmichael number if and only if
  - n is square-free and
  - $p - 1$ divides $n - 1$ for every prime divisor of n;

13.8b   Each Carmichael number has at least three distinct prime factors;

13.8c   There are an infinite number of Carmichael numbers;

13.8d   The smallest Carmichael number is $n = 561 = 3 \times 11 \times 17$ and $\cdots$ for *Triple Jeopardy*; there are only 105,212 Carmichael numbers $\leq 10^{15}$.

Suppose n is composite; a primality test that computes the value a^{n-1} (modulo N) until an a is found yielding a residue $\neq 1$ may fail for two reasons:

- n might be a Carmichael number, or
- The computation could be infeasible if the first a for which computing a^{n-1} (modulo N) is *not* satisfied is too large.

Proposition 13.9 (Miller–Rabin) [Rabin, 1976]: Let N be an odd prime, $n - 1 = 2^r s$ where r is odd and a is any integer such that $1 = \gcd\{a, n\}$. Then either $a^r = 1$ (modulo N) or $a^{2^j r} = -1$ (modulo N) for *some* j with $0 \leq j \leq s - 1$.

Let N be an odd composite number, $N - 1 = 2^r s$ where r is odd and a is integer in $[1, N - 1]$.

- If $a^r \neq 1$ (modulo N) or $a^{2^{jr}} \neq -1$ (modulo N) for *every* j with $0 \leq j \leq s - 1$, then a is a *strong witness* to the compositeness of N.
- Otherwise, if $a^r = 1$ (modulo N) or $a^{2^{jr}} = -1$ (modulo N) for *some* j with $0 \leq j \leq s - 1$, then N is a *strong pseudoprime to the base a* to the compositeness of a.

13.8.2 Miller–Rabin Primality Test

MR1. Write $n - 1 = 2^s r$, where r is odd.

MR2. Choose a random integer a with $2 \leq a \leq N - 2$.

MR3. Compute $b = a^r$ (modulo N).

MR4. If $b = 1$ (modulo N), then RETURN("prime") and END.

MR5. For $i = 0$ to $s - 1$ do

MR6a. If $b = -1$ (modulo N), then RETURN("prime") and END.

MR6b. Else, compute b^2 (modulo N).

MR7. RETURN("composite").

END.

Proposition 13.10:

13.10a. If N is an odd prime, the output of the Miller–Rabin test is RETURN ("prime").

13.10b. If N is an odd composite number, the probability that the Miller–Rabin test fails RETURN("prime") for t independent values of a is less than $(\frac{1}{4})^t$.

Proof of 13.10a: Assume the contrary is true, meaning that the squaring operation $b^2 \to b$ (modulo N) in Step MR6b is performed $s - 1$ times producing the sequence of values

$$a^r (\text{modulo } N) \; a^{2r}(\text{modulo } N) \cdots a^{2^{s-1}r}(\text{modulo } N),$$

none of which equal -1. By Fermat's Little Theorem, $1 = a^{2^s}r$ (modulo N) $= a^{n-1}$ (modulo N) so that $a^{2^{s-1}}r$ (modulo N) $\neq -1 \Rightarrow 1 = a^{2^{s-1}}r$ (modulo N). Repeating this argument, we conclude that each of the numbers

$$a^r (\text{modulo } N) \; a^{2r} (\text{modulo } N) \cdots a^{2^{s-1}r} (\text{modulo } N).$$

must be equal to 1, which means the Miller–Rabin test would have ended after Step MR4.

Example 13.11
Miller–Rabin test for $N = 229$, $N - 1 = 2^2 \times 57$

$a = 225$	$y = a^r$ (modulo N) $= 1$	prime
$a = 47$	$y = a^r$ (modulo N) $= 107$	prime
$a = 151$	$y = a^r$ (modulo N) $= 1$	prime
$a = 101$	$y = a^r$ (modulo N) $= 122$	prime
$a = 52$	$y = a^r$ (modulo N) $= 107$	prime
$a = 21$	$y = a^r$ (modulo N) $= 107$	prime

$a = 180$	$y = a^r$ (modulo N) = 1	prime
$a = 189$	$y = a^r$ (modulo N) = 107	prime
$a = 79$	$y = a^r$ (modulo N) = 107	prime
$a = 126$	$y = a^r$ (modulo N) = 1	prime

Example 13.12
Miller–Rabin test for $231 = 3 \times 77$; $n = 231$, $n - 1 = 2^1 \times 115$.

$a = 227$	$y = a^r$ (modulo N) = 164	composite
$a = 47$	$y = a^r$ (modulo N) = 89	composite
$a = 152$	$y = a^r$ (modulo N) = 89	composite
$a = 101$	$y = a^r$ (modulo N) = 164	composite
$a = 53$	$y = a^r$ (modulo N) = 221	composite
$a = 21$	$y = a^r$ (modulo N) = 21	composite
$a = 182$	$y = a^r$ (modulo N) = 98	composite
$a = 190$	$y = a^r$ (modulo N) = 1	prime
$a = 79$	$y = a^r$ (modulo N) = 142	composite
$a = 127$	$y = a^r$ (modulo N) = 43	composite

Let n be odd and $n - 1 = 2^s r$ with r odd. An integer a with $2 \leq a \leq n-2$ is a *witness* to the compositeness of n if the Miller–Rabin test fails to RETURN("prime"); that is,

1. a^r (modulo N) $\neq 1$, and
2. $a^{2^j r}$ (modulo N) $\neq 1$ for all j with $1 \leq j < s$.

Proposition 13.11 (Gary Miller) [Mil76]: If n is composite and the Generalized Riemann Hypothesis holds, there exists a constant c such that there exists an a that is a witness to the compositeness of n with $1 < a \leq c(\log_2 n)^2$.[3]

It has been shown that c may be taken to be 2, but more is true; Agrawal, Kayal and Saxena [2004] have published a polynomial-time algorithm to test primality with *no* assumptions.

13.9 THE RSA CHALLENGE

RSA Data Security Incorporated (Redwood City) supplies encryption protocols using the RSA algorithm. As the strength of RSA *appears* to depend upon the intractability of factoring $n = pq$ for suitably large prime numbers, the *RSA Factoring Challenge* was set up in March 1991; it consists of a list of numbers, each the product of two primes of roughly comparable size. There are 42 numbers in the challenge; the smallest length is 100 digits and they increase in steps of 10 digits to 500 digits.

[3]The *Riemann zeta function* is denned for complex z by $\zeta(z) = \sum_{n=1}^{\infty} n^{-z}$. The series converges when $\mathrm{Re}(z) > 1$. The zeta function may be continued analytically to a domain in the complex plane including the region $0 < \mathrm{Re}(z) < 1$.
  The Riemann Hypothesis: All zeros of $\zeta(z)$ lie on the line $\mathrm{Re}(z) = \frac{1}{2}$.
  The *Generalized Riemann Hypothesis* replaces $\zeta(z)$ by the Dirichlet L-series and makes the same assertion about zeros.

TABLE 13.13   The RSA Challenge

Number	Date Factored
RSA-100	April 1991
RSA-110	April 1992
RSA-120	June 1993
RSA-129	April 1994
RSA-130	April 1996
RSA-140	February 1999
RSA-155	August 1999

```
RSA-129 = 114381625757888867669235779976146612010218296721242362562561842935706935245573389783059712356395870505898990751475992900268795435 41
N = pq
p = 3490529510847650949147849619903898133417764638493387843990820577
q = 32769132993266709549961988190834461413177642967992942539798288533
```

Figure 13.2   RSA-129.

Table 13.13 gives some of the results in the RSA Challenge. RSA-129 (Fig. 13.2) appears in Martin Gardner's article [Gardner, 1977] in *Scientific American*; the factorization of RSA-129 was posed as the first RSA Challenge with a prize of $100 for the solution.

The message THE MAGIC WORDS ARE SQUEAMISH OSSIFRAGE[4] was enciphered with RSA-129 using the public key $e = 9007$ and private key

```
d = 10669861436857802444286877132892015478070990663393786280122622449663106312591177447087334016859746230655396854451327710905360 6095
```

The factorization of RSA-129 used the double large prime variation of the multiple polynomial quadratic sieve factoring method. The sieving step took approximately 5000 mips years, and was carried out in 8 months by about 600 volunteers from more than 20 countries, on all continents except Antarctica. Combining the partial relations produced a sparse matrix of 569,466 rows and 524,338 columns. This matrix was reduced to a dense matrix of 188,614 rows and 188,160 columns using structured Gaussian elimination. Ordinary Gaussian elimination on this matrix, consisting of 35,489,610,240 bits (4.13 gigabyte), took 45 hours on a 16K MasPar MP-1 massively parallel computer. The first three dependencies all turned out to be "unlucky" and produced the trivial factor RSA-129. The fourth dependency produced the above factorization.

13.10   PERFECT NUMBERS AND THE MERSENNE PRIMES

The integer n is *perfect* if the sum of all of its divisors is equal to $2n$. Mystical interpretations were given to perfect numbers.[5] The first four perfect numbers are

$$6 = 2 \times (2^2 - 1)$$
$$28 = 2^2 \times (2^3 - 1)$$

---

[4]ossifrage *n.*, bone-breaking.

[5]The Christian theologian Saint Augustine (354–430) described the perfection of the number 6, writing "Six is a number perfect in itself, and not because God created all things in six days; rather, the the inverse is true, that God created all things in six days, because this number is perfect."

TABLE 13.14   Mersenne Primes

#	p	Year	$D(M_p)$	#	p	Year	$D(M_p)$	#	p	Year	$D(M_p)$
1	2		2	1	3		3	1	5		2
4	7		3	5	13	1456	6	6	17	1588	6
7	19	1588	6	8	31	1772	10	9	61	1883	19
10	89	1911	27	11	107	1914	33	12	127	1876	39
13	521	1952	157	14	607	1952	183	15	1,279	1952	386
16	2,203	1952	684	17	2,281	1952	687	18	3,217	1957	969
19	4,253	1961	1,281	20	4,423	1961	1,332	21	9,689	1963	2,917
22	9,941	1963	2,993	23	11,213	1963	3,376	24	19,937	1971	6,002
25	21,701	1978	6,533	26	23,209	1979	6,987	27	44,497	1979	13,395
28	86,243	1982	25,962	29	110,503	1988	33,265	30	132,049	1983	39,751
31	216,091	1985	65,050	32	756,839	1992	227,832	33	859,433	1994	258,716
34	1,257,787	1996	378,632	35	1,398,269	1996	420,921	36	2,976,221	1997	895,932
37	3,021,377	1998	909,526	38	6,972,593	1999	2,098,960	39	13,466,917	2001	4,053,946
40	20,996,011	2003	6,320,430	41	24,036,583	2004	25,964,951	42	25,964,951	2005	7,816,230
43	30,402,457	2005	9,152,052								

$$496 = 2^4 \times (2^5 - 1)$$
$$8128 = 2^6 \times (2^7 - 1).$$

The perfect numbers listed above are all *even*; it is not known if odd perfect numbers exist. In the third century B.C., Euclid proved that if p and $2^p - 1$ are prime, then $2^{p-1}(2^p - 1)$ is perfect. Euler proved in the eighteenth century that every even perfect number was of this form.

Marin Mersenne (1588–1648) was a monk in the *Order of Minims* near Paris. He taught philosophy and was interested in science and mathematics. If $2^n - 1$ ($n > 2$) is a prime, then n must be a prime; for if $N = st$, then $2^{st} - 1 = (2^s - 1)(2^{s(t-1)} + 2^{s(t-2)} + \cdots + 1)$. In 1644 Mersenne conjectured that $2^p - 1$ is a prime for $p = 2, 3, 5, 7, 13, 17, 19, 31, 67, 127, 257$ *and* these were the only solutions for $p \leq 257$. It is unlikely that Mersenne could have tested all of these numbers in 1644 and his conjecture is not completely correct.

Table 13.14 lists 43 known Mersenne numbers, the last discovered on December 15, 2005, by Dr Curtis Cooper and Dr Steven Boone, professors at Central Missouri State University. The table includes the value of $p(M_p = 2^p - 1)$, the year of the discovery of M_p, and the number of digits $D(M_p)$ in M_p.

13.11 MULTIPRECISION ARITHMETIC

The 43rd Mersenne prime contains 9,152,052 digits, not the kind of number we are used to writing out, much less manipulating. Although such numbers usually do not arise in day-to-day computations, some public-key cryptosystems require numbers with several hundred digits. Floating-point computations arising in navigational calculation also require great precision. The basic modular operations *addition*, *multiplication*, and *division* on numbers with a *very* large number of digits use a pencil and paper, a technique learned in elementary school.

Each n-digit base-b number is represented as a string of *characters* $x : x_{n-1}, x_{n-2} \cdots x_1 x_0$ where x_i is a base-b digit. Addition (multiplication and divison) is performed using

TABLE 13.15 Multiprecision Parameters and Operations

Name	Parameters	Operation
M_ADD	m, Na, Nb, Nc; a, b, c	$a = b + c$
M_SUB	sign, m Na, Nb, Nc, a, b, c	$a = (sign)(a - b)$
M_MUL	m, Na, Nb, Nc, a, b, c	$a = b \times c$
M_DIV	m, Na, Nb, Nq, Nr, a, b, q, r	$a = (q \times b) + r$
M_COMPARE	Na, Nb, cresult, a, b	$cresult = \begin{cases} 1 & \text{if } a \geq b \\ 0 & \text{if } a < b \end{cases}$
M_toBIN	Na, Nb, a, b	translation of a in (base-m) to be (base-2)
M_MODEXP	m, Na, Nb, Nc, Nd, a, b, c, d	$d = a^{\wedge} b \pmod c$

digit-by-digit operations. For example, addition

$$
\begin{array}{r}
x_{n-1}x_{n-2}\cdots x_1 x_0 \\
+ \quad y_{n-1}y_{n-2}\cdots y_1 y_0 \\
\hline
z_n z_{n-1} z_{n-2}\cdots z_1 z_0
\end{array}
$$

is carried out in a single DO-loop.

Subtraction, multiplication, and division are implemented similarly. Division is the most tedious, producing a *quotient* and a *remainder*. The *Montgomery reduction* is used to make the computation of a^m (modulo N) more efficient.

Multiprecision modular arithmetic is needed in cryptography, for example, to implement RSA encipherment. Modular operations combine an addition/multiplication and division step. The parameters of the multiple-precision procedures include

m: the base of the operation;

$\underline{a}$: a multiple-precision integer as a string of integers (*itype*);

Na: the length parameter of the string $\underline{a}$.

Multiple-precision procedures expect a multiprecision base-m *itype* parameter a *in reverse order* $\underline{a} = (a_0, a_1, \ldots, a_{Na})$, with the least-significant digit on the left. The calling program must therefore read character strings $x : x_{n-1}x_{n-2}\ldots x_1 x_0$ (without intervening separators between the characters) with the most-significant digit on the left, translate each character to an integer variable, and reverse the order of the integers.

The syntax of multiprecision procedures is M_FUNCTION(var : m, Na,$\cdots$ integer; var : a, $\cdots$ itype) (Table 13.15).

13.12 PRIME NUMBER TESTING AND FACTORIZATION PROBLEMS

Problem 13.1 requires a program to implement the Miller–Rabin Primality Test.[6] Your implementation should use *at least* $T = 10$ random a-values. Your solution should include a trace of your Miller–Rabin primality test as in Section 13.7; my trace for the composite number 42,091 is given in Table 13.16.

Problems 13.2 to 13.12 are examples of factorization of the integer $N = pq$ using the quadratic residue sieve to find the two prime factors p, q. Factorization using the quadratic residue sieve involves four phases:

---

[6]You may write your own random number generator to use in the Rabin–Miller test to supply the required random a-values. I use the random number generator described in the paper by L'Ecuyer (1988).

TABLE 13.16 Trace for Composite Number 42,091

$N = 42{,}091 \quad 42{,}090 = 2 \times 21{,}045$	

$a = 42{,}087$	$y = a^r$ (Modulo 42091)= 25073	composite
$a = 8{,}564$	$y = a^r$ (Modulo 42091)= 22434	composite
$a = 28{,}115$	$y = a^r$ (Modulo 42091)= 41152	composite
$a = 18{,}617$	$y = a^r$ (Modulo 42091)= 30353	composite
$a = 9{,}503$	$y = a^r$ (Modulo 42091)= 28148	composite
$a = 3{,}657$	$y = a^r$ (Modulo 42091)= 35965	composite
$a = 33{,}571$	$y = a^r$ (Modulo 42091)= 40788	composite
$a = 35{,}144$	$y = a^r$ (Modulo 42091)= 4124	composite
$a = 14{,}510$	$y = a^r$ (Modulo 42091)= 5900	composite
$a = 23{,}374$	$y = a^r$ (Modulo 42091)= 23031	composite

QS1. Select a factor base $S = \{p_0,\ p_1,\ p_2,\ p_3, \ldots,\ p_t\}$ with $p_0 = -1$ and $p_1 = 2$; the next $t - 1$ odd primes $p_2,\ p_3,\ \ldots,\ p_t$ are those primes $\{p_i\}$ for which n is a quadratic residue modulo p_i. Section 13.1 provides as list of the primes ≤ 199.

> *Query:* How do you test if N is a quadratic residue modulo a prime p?

> *Answer:* By checking if $1 = N^{\frac{p-1}{2}}$ (modulo p).

QS2. For $x = 0, 1, -1, 2, -2, \ldots, r, -r$ with $r \approx 400$, compute

$$q(x) = (x + m)^2 - n, \qquad b(x) = (x + m)^2 \text{ (modulo } N),$$
$$a(x) = (x + m) \text{ (modulo } N)$$

with $m = \lfloor \sqrt{N} \rfloor$. Make a table whose ith row $(i = 1, 2, \ldots)$ contains i, x_i and

$$q_i \equiv (x_i + m)^2 - N = \prod_{s=0}^{t} p_s^{e_{i,s}}, \qquad a_i \equiv x_i + m, \qquad \underline{e}_i \equiv (e_{i,0}, e_{i,1}, \ldots, e_{i,t}).$$

$N = \quad m = \quad S = \{-1, 2, \ldots\}$			

i	x_i	q_i	a_i	$\underline{e}_i$ (modulo 2)

x_i is the ith value of x for which $q(x)$ is *smooth* relative to the factor base S; that is, the factorization of $q(x)$ only involves primes in S.

QS3. Search for sets $T = \{i_1, i_2, \ldots, i_m\}$ for a linear dependency; that is, a collection of rows in the table for which the exponent in each of the t primes in the product

$$b_T \equiv \prod_{s=1}^{r} b_{i_s}, \qquad b_{i_s} \equiv (x_{i_s} + m)^2 \text{ (modulo } N) = \prod_{j=1}^{t} p_j^{e_{i_s,j}}$$

is even

$$\underbrace{(0, 0, 0, \ldots, 0)}_{r} = (\underline{e}_{i_1} + \underline{e}_{i_2} + \cdots + \underline{e}_{i_r}) \text{ (modulo 2)}.$$

Defining

$$a_T = \prod_{s=1}^{r} a_{i_s}, \quad \sqrt{b_T} = \prod_{j=1}^{t} p_j^{\ell_j}, \quad \ell_j = \frac{1}{2}\sum_{s=1}^{r} e_{i_s, j}, \quad 1 \le j \le t$$

we have

$$b_i \,(\text{modulo } N) = (x_i + m)^2 \,(\text{modulo } N) = a_i^2 \,(\text{modulo } N)$$

so that

$$a_T^2 \,(\text{modulo } N) = b_T \,(\text{modulo } N).$$

Display your results in a tabular form.

T	$\sqrt{b_T}$ (modulo N)	a_T (modulo N)

QS4. If $a_T \ne \pm\sqrt{b_T}$ (modulo N), then $d = \gcd\{a_T - \sqrt{b_T}, N_e = 9007\}$ or $d = \gcd\{a_T + \sqrt{b_T}, N\}$ is a nontrivial factor of N, the algorithm ends.

Otherwise, if $a_T = \pm\sqrt{b_T}$ (modulo N), then return to QS2 and test another linear dependency T.

13.2 Write a program to implement the quadratic sieve and use it to factor $N = 4601$.

13.3 Write a program to implement the quadratic sieve and use it to factor $N = 8633$.

13.4 Write a program to implement the quadratic sieve and use it to factor $N = 66,887$.

13.5 Write a program to implement the quadratic sieve and use it to factor $N = 141,467$.

13.6 Write a program to implement the quadratic sieve and use it to factor $N = 200,819$.

13.7 Write a program to implement the quadratic sieve and use it to factor $N = 809,009$.

13.8 Write a program to implement the quadratic sieve and use it to factor $N = 2,043,221$.

13.9 Write a program to implement the quadratic sieve and use it to factor $N = 4,472,529$.

13.10 Write a program to implement the quadratic sieve and use it to factor $N = 16,843,009$.

13.11 Write a program to implement the quadratic sieve and use it to factor $N = 19,578,079$.

13.12 Write a program to implement the quadratic sieve and use it to factor $N = 92,296,873$.

REFERENCES

M. AGRAWAL, N. KAYAL, AND N. SAXENA, "PRIMES in P", *Annals of Mathematics*, **160**: 2, 781–793 (2004).

E. BERLEKAMP, "Factoring Polynomials over Large Finite Fields", *Mathematics of Computation*, **24**, 713–735 (1970).

J. D. DIXON, "Asymptotically Fast Factorization of Integers", *Mathematics of Computation*, **36**, 255–260 (1981).

R. FLOYD, "Non-Deterministic Algorithms", *Journal of the Association for Computing Machinery*, **14**, 636–644 (1967).

M. GARDNER, "A New Kind of Cipher That Would Take Millions of Years to Break", *Scientific American*, **237**, 120–124 (1977).

N. KOBLITZ, *A Course in Number Theory and Cryptography*, Springer-Verlag, New York, NY, 1987.

P. L'ECUYER, "Efficient and Portable Combined Random Number Generators", *Communications of the ACM*, **31**, 742–769 (1988).

G. L. MILLER, "Riemann's Hypothesis and Tests for Primality", *Journal of Computer and System Sciences*, **13**, 300–317 (1976).

J. M. POLLARD, "Propositions on Factorization and Primality Testing", *Proceedings of the Cambridge Philosophical Society*, **76**, 243–264 (1974).

J. M. POLLARD, "Monte Carlo Methods for Factorization", *Nordisk Tidskroft for Informationsbehandlung (BIT)*, **15**, 331–334 (1975).

C. POMERANCE, "Cryptology and Computational Number Theory", *Proceedings of Symposia in Applied Mathematics*, Vol. 142, Carl Pomerance (Ed.) American Mathematical Society, Boston, Massachusetts, 1980.

M. RABIN, "Probabilistic Algorithms", in J. F. Traub, ed., *Algorithms and Complexity*, Academic Press, San Diego, California, 1976, pp. 21–38.

H. RIESEL, *Prime Numbers and Computer Methods for Factorization* (2nd edn.), Birhaüser, Cambridge, Massachusetts, 1994.

CHAPTER 14

THE DISCRETE LOGARITHM PROBLEM

THE CRYPTOGRAPHIC strength of the RSA algorithm appears to depend on the computational infeasibility of factoring very large numbers. This chapter describes the discrete logarithm problem (DLP), which is intimately related to both factoring and the problem of key exchange. Several solution methods will be described.

14.1 THE DISCRETE LOGARITHM PROBLEM MODULO *p*

If p is a prime, the set $\mathcal{Z}_p = \{0, 1, 2, \ldots, p - 1\}$ is a *field*. The nonzero elements $\mathcal{Z}_p^+ \equiv \mathcal{Z}_p - \{0\}$ form a *cyclic group*, meaning there exists a $q \in \mathcal{Z}_p^+$ called a *primitive root* of p or a *generator* of $\mathcal{Z}_p^+$ such that every nonzero element of the field is a power q^k (modulo p). The sequence of powers $q, q^2, \ldots, q^{p-1}$ computed modulo p are a permutation of the integers $1, 2, \ldots, p - 1$.

> *Example 14.1*
> $p = 11$; $q = 2, 6, 7$, and 8 are the only primitive roots of 11 (Table 14.1).
> The *discrete logarithm problem* (modulo p) (DLP) is

> *Given*: A prime p, q a primitive root of p and $y = q^x$ (modulo p);

> *Find*: $x \equiv \log_q y$ (modulo p).

A solution to the DLP modulo p can be found by *exhaustive trial*; that is, computing q^x (modulo p) for $x = 1, 2, \ldots$ *until* an x is found for which $y = q^x$ (modulo p). This solution, which requires $O(p)$ steps, is not computationally practical for $p > 10^{10}$. A *feasible* solution technique is one for which a solution is found in $O(\log_2^k p)$ steps.

> The generalized *discrete logarithm problem in a group* $\mathcal{G}$ is

> *Given*: $\mathcal{G}$ a cyclic group of order n, q a generator of $\mathcal{G}$, and $y = q^x$;

> *Find*: $x = \log_q y \langle \mathcal{G} \rangle$.

We need a slightly more elaborate version of Fermat's Little Theorem than that given as Proposition **12.2**.

TABLE 14.1 q^k (modulo p), $1 \leq k < p$

q	1	2	3	4	5	6	7	8	9	10
2	2	4	8	5	10	9	7	3	6	1
3	3	9	5	4	1	3	9	5	4	1
4	4	5	9	3	1	4	5	9	3	1
5	5	3	4	9	1	5	3	4	9	1
6	6	3	7	9	10	5	8	4	2	1
7	7	5	2	3	10	4	6	9	8	1
8	8	9	6	4	10	3	2	5	7	1
9	9	4	3	5	1	9	4	3	5	1
10	10	1	10	1	10	1	10	1	10	1

Proposition 14.1   (Fermat's Little Theorem):   If p is a prime

14.1a $a^{p-1} = 1$ (modulo p) for every a for which $1 = \gcd\{a, p\}$;

14.1b $a^p = a$ (modulo p) for every (integer) a;

14.1c If $r = s$ (modulo $p - 1$) and $1 = \gcd\{a, p\}$, then $a^r = a^s$ (modulo p);

14.1d If $a^r = a^s$ (modulo p) and a is a primitive root of p, then $r = s$ (modulo $p - 1$).

Proof: The binomial coefficient $\binom{p}{k}$ is divisible by p for $0 < k < p$ so that the binomial theorem

$$x^p = (x - 1 + 1)^p = \sum_{k=0}^{p} \binom{p}{k}(x - 1)^k$$

leads to the recurrence

$$x^p = [(x - 1)^p + 1] \, (\text{modulo } p),$$

which may be written

$$(x - 1)^p = x - 1 \, (\text{modulo } p).$$

Induction then proves Proposition **14.1a**.

If $a^{p-1} = 1$ (modulo p), then $a^p = a$ (modulo p) without the condition $1 = \gcd\{a, p\}$-proving Proposition **14.1b**.

If $r = s$ (modulo $p - 1$) and $1 = \gcd\{a, p\}$, then

$$a^{r-s} = a^{C(p-1)} = 1(\text{modulo } p)$$

by Proposition **14.1a**, proving Proposition **14.1c**. Conversely, if $a^r = a^s$ (modulo p), then

$$a^{r-s} = a^{C(p-1)+t} = a^t(\text{modulo } p).$$

If a is primitive, a^t (modulo p) $\Rightarrow t = 0$, completing the proof.

14.2   SOLUTION OF THE DLP MODULO p GIVEN A FACTORIZATION OF $p-1$

The Pohlig–Hellman Algorithm [Pohlig and Hellman, 1978] for solving the discrete logarithm problem modulo p assumes the factorisation of $p - 1$ is known:

Given: $p - 1 = p_1^{n_1} p_2^{n_2} \dots p_k^{n_k}$, q a primitive root of p, and $y = q^x$ (modulo p);

Find: $x = \log_p y$ (modulo p).

The important observation is that it suffices to solve the DLP if x is replaced by its residues modulo $p_i^{n_i}$ for each prime factor. Write the base-$p_i^{n_i}$ representation of x for the prime factor $p_i^{n_i}$ of $p - 1$:

$$x = x(p_i^{n_i}) + Cp_i^{n_i}$$

$x(p_i^{n_i}) \equiv x \ (\text{modulo } p_i^{n_i})$

$$= x_{i,0} + x_{i,1}p_i + x_{i,2}p_i^2 + \dots + x_{i,n_i-1}p_i^{n_i-1}, \qquad 0 \le x_{i,j} < p_i; \qquad 0 \le j < n_i - 1,$$

where C is some (positive) integer. Then, for $1 \le i \le k$

$$y^{\frac{p-1}{p_i}} \ (\text{modulo } p) = q^{x\frac{p-1}{p_i}} \ (\text{modulo } p)$$

$$= q^{[x(p_i^{n_i}) + Cp_i^{n_i}]\frac{p-1}{p_i}} \ (\text{modulo } p)$$

$$= q^{x(p_i^{n_i})\frac{p-1}{p_i}} \ (\text{modulo } p) \times q^{Cp_i^{n_i}(p-1)} \ (\text{modulo } p).$$

As $n_i - m > 0$, $Cp_i^{n_i - m}$ is an integer, Fermat's Little Theorem gives $1 = q^{Cp_i^{n_i} \ (p-1)}$ (modulo p) so that

$$y^{\frac{p-1}{p_i}} \ (\text{modulo } p) = q^{x(p_i^{n_i})\frac{p-1}{p_i}} \ (\text{modulo } p).$$

The Pohlig–Hellman Algorithm determines the base-p_i digits $\{x_{i,j}\}$ for each prime factor p_i and combines them using the Chinese Remainder Theorem to find x.

14.2.1   Pohlig–Hellman Algorithm Precomputation

Evaluate $\gamma_{i,j} = q^{j\frac{p-1}{p_i}}$ (modulo p) for $0 \le j < n_i$ and $1 \le i \le k$.

The Pohlig–Hellman Algorithm Calculation for the Factor $p_i^{n_i}$

For $1 \le i \le k$ and $m = 0$ to $n_i - 1$ do

S1. Calculation of $x_{i,m}$; write

$$y = q^{[x_{i,m}p_i^m + x_{i,m+1}p_i^{m+1} + \dots + x_{i,n_i-1}p_i^{n_i-1}]} \ (\text{modulo } p)$$

$$y^{\frac{p-1}{p_i^{m+1}}} \ (\text{modulo } p) = q^{x_{i,m}p_i^m \frac{p-1}{p_i^{m+1}}} \ (\text{modulo } p) \times q^{D(p-1)} \ (\text{modulo } p)$$

where $D = \dfrac{x_{i,m+1}p_i^{m+1} + \dots + x_{i,n_i-1}p_i^{n_i-1}}{p_i^{m+1}}$. But, D is an integer, so that

$$1 = q^{D(p-1)} (\text{modulo } p)$$

by Fermat's Little Theorem, yielding

$$y^{\frac{p-1}{p_i^{m+1}}} \ (\text{modulo } p) = q^{x_{i,m}\frac{p-1}{p_i}} \ (\text{modulo } p).$$

TABLE 14.2

j	$p_1 = 2$	$p_2 = 3$	$p_3 = 5$
0	1	1	1
1	-1	5883	3547
2		2217	356
3			7077
4			5221

The p_i possible values for $q^{x_{i,m} \frac{p-1}{p_i}}$ (modulo p) corresponds to the p_i possible values of $x_{i,m}$; the precomputation of a table containing $\gamma_{i,j} = q^{j\frac{p-1}{p_i}}$ for $0 \le j < p_i$ and $1 \le i \le k$ is now used to determine $x_{i,m}$.

S2. Replace y by $yq^{-x_{i,m}p_i^m}$ (modulo p), m by $m+1$, and return to S1.

   Example 14.2
$p = 8101$, $q = 6$. Find $x = \log_q 7531$ (modulo p).

$$p - 1 = 8100 = 2^2 \times 3^4 \times 5^2$$

$$\frac{p-1}{q^{-1}} = 6751$$
$$\gamma_{i,j} = q^{j\frac{p-1}{p_i}} \text{ (modulo } p), \quad 0 \le j < p_i; 1 \le i \le 3.$$

Table 14.2 shows the results of the Pohlig-Hellman solution in Example 14.2.

The Pohlig–Hellman Calculation for the First Prime Factor 2^2 of $p-1$ in Example 14.2

$$x(p_1^{n_1}) = x \text{ (modulo } 2^2) = x_{1,0} + x_{1,1}2$$
$$m = 0$$

S1. $y^{\frac{p-1}{2}}$(modulo p) = 7531^{4050}(modulo 8101) = $-1 \Rightarrow x_{1,0} = 1$
S2. $y = 7531 \to y = (7531 \times q^{-1})$ (modulo 8101) = 8060
   $m = 1$

S1. $y^{\frac{p-1}{2}}$(modulo p) = 8060^{2025} (modulo 8101) = $1 \Rightarrow x_{1,1} = 0$
   $x_1 = 1 + (0 \times 2)$

The Pohlig–Hellman Calculation for the Second Prime Factor 3^4 of $p-1$ in Example 14.2

$$x(p_2^{n_2}) = x(\text{modulo } 3^4) = x_{2,0} + x_{2,1}3 + x_{2,3}3^2 + x_{2,2}3^3$$
$$m = 0$$

S1. $y^{\frac{p-1}{3}}$(modulo p) = 7531^{2700} (modulo 8101) = $2271 \Rightarrow x_{2,0} = 2$
S2. $y = 7531 \to y = (7531 \times q^{-2})$ (modulo 8101) = 6735
   $m = 1$

S1. $y^{\frac{p-1}{3^2}}$ (modulo p) = 6735^{900}(modulo 8101) = 1 $\Rightarrow$ $x_{2,1} = 0$

S2. $y = 6735$ $\rightarrow$ $y = (6735 \times q^{-0})$ (modulo 8101) = 6735

$m = 2$

S1. $y^{\frac{p-1}{3^3}}$ (modulo p) = 6735^{300}(modulo 8101) = 2271 $\Rightarrow$ $x_{2,2} = 2$

S2. $y = 6735$ $\rightarrow$ $y = (6735 \times q^{-18})$ (modulo 8101) = 6992

$m = 3$

S1. $y^{\frac{p-1}{3^4}}$ (modulo p) = 6992^{100}(modulo 8101) = 5883 $\Rightarrow$ $x_{2,3} = 1$

$$x_2 = 47 = 2 + (0 \times 3) + (2 \times 3^2) + (1 \times 3^3)$$

The Pohlig–Hellman Calculation for the Third Prime Factor 5^2 of $p - 1$ in Example 14.2

$$x(p_3^{n_3}) = x \,(\text{modulo } 5^2) = x_{3,0} + x_{3,1}5$$
$$m = 0$$

S1. $y^{\frac{p-1}{5}}$ (modulo p) = 7531^{1620} (modulo 8101) = 5221 $\Rightarrow$ $x_{3,0} = 4$

S2. $y = 7531 \rightarrow y = (7531 \times q^{-4})$ (modulo 8101) = 7613

$m = 1$

S1. $y^{\frac{p-1}{5^2}}$ (modulo p) = 7613^{900} (modulo 8101) = 356 $\Rightarrow$ $x_{3,1} = 2$

$x_3 = 14 = 4 + (2 \times 5)$

14.2.2 Using the Chinese Remainder Theorem in Example 14.2

$$x = 1 (\text{modulo } 2^2)$$
$$x = 47 (\text{modulo } 3^4)$$
$$x = 14 (\text{modulo } 5^2)$$
$$M_1 = 2025 = 3^4 \times 5^2$$
$$M2 = 100 = 2^2 \times 5^2$$
$$M3 = 324 = 2^2 \times 3^4$$

The Euclidean Algorithm gives

$$N_1 = 1 = M_1^{-1} (\text{modulo } 2^2)$$
$$N_2 = 64 = M_2^{-1} (\text{modulo } 3^4)$$
$$N_3 = 24 = M_3^{-1} (\text{modulo } 5^2)$$
$$x = 6889 = [(1 \times 2025 \times 1) + (47 \times 100 \times 64) + (14 \times 324 \times 24)](\text{modulo } 8100)$$

14.3   ADELMAN'S SUBEXPONENTIAL ALGORITHM FOR THE DISCRETE LOGARITHM PROBLEM [ADELMAN, 1979]

A number x is *smooth* relative to a bound N if the prime factorization of $x = p_1^{n_1} p_2^{n_2} \dots p_s^{n_s}$ involves only prime numbers satisfying $p_i \leq N$.

Proposition 14.2   (Adelman's Algorithm for the Discrete Logarithm Problem):

> *Given*: p a prime, q a primitive root of p, and $x = q^k$ (modulo p),
>   A bound $N(p)$ and primes $p_1 < p_2 < \dots < p_m \leq N(p)$;
>
> *Find*: k.

S1. Find an integer R by random sampling such that B is smooth relative to $N(p)$

$$\underline{B} = (n_1, n_2, \dots, n_m)$$

$$B = x^R (\text{modulo } p) = p_1^{n_1} p_2^{n_2} \dots p_m^{n_m}$$

$$1 = \gcd\{R, p - 1\}$$

S2. Find integers R_i for $1 \leq i \leq m$ by random sampling such that A_i is smooth relative to $N(p)$.

$$A_i = q^{R_i} (\text{modulo } p) = p_1^{n_{i,1}} p_2^{n_{i,2}} \dots p_m^{n_{i,m}}$$

and the vectors

$$A_i = (n_{i,1}, n_{i,2}, \dots, n_{i,m})$$

span the m-dimensional vector space over $\mathcal{Z}_p$.

S3. Use Gaussian elimination to write

$$\underline{B} = \left(\sum_{i=1}^{m} a_i \underline{A}_i \right) (\text{modulo } p - 1).$$

Then

$$B = x^R (\text{modulo } p) = \prod_{j=1}^{m} p_j^{n_j} = \prod_{\text{from } j=1}^{n} p_j^{\left(\sum_{i=1}^{m} a_i n_{i,j} \right) (\text{modulo } p-1)} \quad (\text{modulo } p)$$

$$B = \prod_{i=1}^{m} \left(\prod_{j=1}^{m} p_j^{n_j} \right)^{a_i} (\text{modulo } p)$$

$$B = \prod_{i=1}^{m} A_i^{a_i} (\text{modulo } p)$$

$$B = \prod_{i=1}^{m} q^{R_i a_i} (\text{modulo } p)$$

Raising both sides of the equation $B = x^R$ (modulo p) to the power $S = R^{-1}$ (modulo p) gives

$$x = \prod_{i=1}^{m} q^{R_i S a_i} \ (\text{modulo } p)$$

Adelman proved.

Proposition 14.3:   The running time of the algorithm in Proposition **14.2** is RTIME $= 2^{O\left(\sqrt{\log p \, \log \log p} \right)}$ if $N(p) = 2^{O\left(\sqrt{\log p \, \log \log p} \right)}$.

TABLE 14.3 **Precomputation for Shank's Baby-Step, Giant-Step Algorithm with $p = 127, q = 3$**

j	0	1	2	3	7	12	4	8	6	11	5	10	9
3^j (modulo 127)	1	3	9	27	28	73	81	84	94	109	116	121	125

TABLE 14.4 **Steps 14a−b for Shank's Baby-Step, Giant-Step Algorithm with $p = 127, q = 3$**

i	0	1	2	3	4	5	6	7	8	9	10	11	12
γq^{-12i} (modulo 127)	57	6	14	75	48	112	92	3	7	101	24	56	46

14.4 THE BABY-STEP, GIANT-STEP ALGORITHM

The *baby-step, giant-step algorithm* (Shank's Algorithm) [Shanks, 1962] makes a time/memory tradeoff to solve the DLP in the cyclic group $\mathcal{G}$ of order n.

Suppose q is a generator of $\mathcal{G}$ and $m = \lceil \sqrt{n} \rceil$; the exponent x of $y = q^x$ has a representation $x = im + j$ where $0 \leq i, j < m$. Write $yq^{-im} = q^j$ and construct a table of size $O(\sqrt{n})$ whose entries (j, q^j) are sorted according to the second term. The cost of the sort is $O(\sqrt{n} \log \sqrt{n}) = O(\sqrt{n} \log n)$ comparisons.

Proposition 14.4 (Shank's Baby-Step, Giant-Step Algorithm):
Initialization: Compute q^{-m} and set $\gamma = y$.
    For $i = 0$ to $m - 1$ do

14.4a Check if γ is the second component of some term q^j in the table; if so, return $x = im + j$.

14.4b Replace γ by γq^{-m}.

END

The cost of **14.4a** is $O(\log n)$ comparisons; the cost of **14.4b** is 1 multiplication.

Example 14.3
When $p = 127$, $q = 3$ is a generator of the (multiplicative) group $\mathcal{Z}_{127}^+$ of order 126. Computing $x = \log_{127} 57$, $m = \lceil \sqrt{127} \rceil = 12$. Table 14.3 gives in a sorted table the precomputation results of 3^j (modulo 127) $(0 \leq j < 13)$. Next, $q^{-1} = 3^{-1} = 85$ and $q^{-12} = 85^{12}$ (modulo 127) $= 87$.

Table 14.4 lists the results of Steps 14.4a−b. The entry for $i = 7$ is in the precomputed table for $j = 1$, which gives $x = (7 \times 12) + 1 = 85$ so that $57 = q^{85}$ (modulo 127).

14.5 THE INDEX-CALCULUS METHOD

Let q be a generator of a cyclic group $\mathcal{G} = \{1, 2, \ldots, p - 1\}$ of order $p - 1$ and $y = q^x$ (modulo p).

Proposition 14.5 (The Index-Calculus Algorithm): *Initialization*: Select a *factor base* $\mathcal{S} = \{p_1, p_2, \ldots, p_s\}$ consisting of elements of $\mathcal{G}$. $\mathcal{S}$ is chosen so that a *significant* proportion of the elements of $\mathcal{G}$ can be expressed in the form $p_1^{n_1} p_2^{n_2} \ldots p_s^{n_s}$ with $n_i \geq 0$.

14.5a Select a random k with $0 \leq k < n$ and compute q^k (modulo p).

14.5b Try to write q^k (modulo p) as a product $p_1^{c_1} p_2^{c_2} \ldots p_s^{c_s}$ with $c_i \geq 0$:

- if *un*successful, return to Step 14.5a and choose another value for k;
- if successful, write $k = [c_1 \log_q p_1 + [c_2 \log_q p_2 + \cdots + [c_s \log_q p_s] (\text{modulo } p - 1)$.

14.5c Repeat Steps 14.5a−b until a sufficient number of linear relations as above are found in order to solve the system of equations to determine $\log_q p_i$ for $1 \leq i \leq s$.

14.5d Select a random k with $0 \leq k < n$ and compute yq^k (modulo p).

14.5e Try to write yq^k as a product $p_1^{d_1} p_2^{d_2} \ldots p_s^{d_s}$ with $d_i \geq 0$:

- if *un*successful, return to Step 14.5d and choose another value for k;
- if successful, write $x = [d_1 \log_q p_1 + d_2 \log_q p_2 + \cdots + d_s \log_q p_s - k] (\text{modulo } p - 1)$.

Remark All text (messages/files) in a data processing system are transmitted/ stored as $(0, 1)$-vectors.

When encipherment is a transformation $\mathcal{T}$ on text written in an alphabet $\mathcal{A}$ other than $(0, 1)$-vectors, some translation process (TR and TR^{-1}) between $(0, 1)$-text and text composed in the cryptosystem's alphabet is required:

$$\underbrace{\underline{x}_{(0,1)- \text{plaintext}}}_{} \xrightarrow{\text{TR}} \underbrace{\underline{x}_{\mathcal{A}- \text{plaintext}}}_{} \xrightarrow{\mathcal{T}} \underbrace{\underline{y}_{\mathcal{A}-\text{ciphertext}}}_{} \xrightarrow{\text{TR}^{-1}} \underbrace{\underline{y}_{(0,1)-\text{ciphertext}}}_{}$$

We have already described translation processes, for RSA and Merkle−Hellman knapsack encipherments. Intrinsic to the translation is an overhead; the bit-length of the plaintext increases as a result of translation. The process is simplified if the elements of the $\mathcal{A}$ are $(0, 1)$-vectors; for example, if the alphabet $\mathcal{A}$ consists of the $(0, 1)$-vectors $\mathcal{Z}_{m,2}$ of length m. The elements of $\mathcal{Z}_{m,2}$ form an *extension field* obtained by *adjoining* a root ϑ of some irreducible polynomial $p(x)$ of degree m whose coefficients are in $\mathcal{Z}_2$. The mathematics of extension fields is summarized in Section 14.7.

If $p(x)$ is irreducible and of degree m, the elements of the extension field $\mathcal{Z}_{m,2}$ $\underline{x} = (x_0, x_1, \ldots, x_{m-2}, x_{m-1}) \in \mathcal{Z}_{m,2}$ can be identified with the polynomial $x_0 \vartheta^{m-1} + x_1 \vartheta^{m-2} + \cdots + x_{m-2} \vartheta + x_{m-1}$. Addition is componentwise XOR

$$\begin{array}{c} x_0 x_1 \cdots x_{m-2} x_{m-1} \\ + \quad y_0 y_1 \cdots y_{m-2} y_{m-1} \\ \hline z_0 z_1 \cdots z_{m-2} z_{m-1} \end{array}$$

Multiplication of $f(\vartheta) = x_0 \vartheta^{m-1} + x_1 \vartheta^{m-2} + \cdots + x_{m-2} \vartheta + x_{m-1}$ and $g(\vartheta) = y_0 \vartheta^{m-1} + y_1 \vartheta^{m-2} + \cdots + y_{m-2} \vartheta + y_{m-1}$ is according to the rule

$$f(\vartheta) \times g(\vartheta) = f(\vartheta) g(\vartheta) (\text{modulo } p(\vartheta)).$$

To facilitate computations in the extension field $\mathcal{Z}_{m,2}$, it is helpful to have a library of programs to perform arithmetic on polynomials including those in Table 14.5.

TABLE 14.5 Programs for Performing Arithmetic on Polynomials

PADD	Addition of polynomials with coefficients in $\mathcal{Z}_2$
PMUL	Multiplication of polynomials with coefficients in $\mathcal{Z}_2$
PDIV	Division algorithm for polynomials with coefficients in $\mathcal{Z}_2$
PEUCLID	Euclidean algorithm for polynomials with coefficients in $\mathcal{Z}_2$
PXEUCLID	Extended Euclidean algorithm for polynomials with coefficients in $\mathcal{Z}_2$

Proposition 14.6 (The Index-Calculus Algorithm for $\mathbb{Z}_{m,2}$): $f(x)$ is a primitive polynomial of degree m.

> *Given*: $y = x^r$ (modulo $f(x)$);
> *Find*: r.

Initialization: Select a *factor base* $\mathcal{S} = \{p_1(x), p_2(x), \ldots, p_s(x)\}$ consisting of all irreducible polynomials of degree at most $m - 1$.

14.6a Select a random k with $0 \le k < 2^m$ and compute x^k (modulo $f(x)$).

14.6b Try to express x^k (modulo $f(x)$) as a product $p_1^{c_1}(x)p_2^{c_2}(x) \cdots p_s^{c_s}(x)$ with $c_i \ge 0$:
- if *un*successful, return to Step 14.6a and choose another value for k;
- if successful, write

$$k = c_1 \log_x p_1(x) + c_2 \log_x p_2(x) + \cdots + c_s \log_x p_s(x) \; \langle \mathcal{G} \rangle \qquad (*)$$

14.6c Repeat Steps 14.6a–b until a sufficient number of relations of the type $*$ are found in order to solve the system of equations to determine $\log_x p_i(x)$ $\mathcal{G}$ for $1 \le i \le s$.

14.6d Select a random k with $0 \le k < 2^m$ and compute yx^k (modulo $f(x)$).

14.6e Try to express yx^k (modulo $f(x)$) as a product $p_1^{d_1}(x)\, p_2^{d_2}(x) \ldots p_s^{d_s}(x)$ with $d_i \ge 0$;
- if *un*successful, return to Step 14.6c and choose another value for k;
- if successful, write $x = d_1 \log_x \, p_1(x) + d_2 \log_x \, p_2(x) + \cdots + d_s \log_x \, p_s(x) - k \, \langle \mathcal{G} \rangle$.

Example 14.4

$m = 8$. The polynomial $f(x) = 1 + x + x^7$ is primitive; the vector $u = (u_0, u_1, \ldots, u_7) \in \mathbb{Z}_{8,2}$ is identified with the polynomial $g(x) = u_0 x^7 + u_1 x^6 + \cdots + u_6 x + u_7$. The cyclic group of nonzero elements of $\mathbb{Z}_{8,2}$ is generated by x:

> *Given*: $y = 1 + x + x^2 + x^3 + x^4 = x^r$ (modulo $f(x)$);
> *Find*: r.

The *Factor Base* consists of the five irreducible polynomials

$$p_1(x) = x, \quad p_2(x) = 1 + x, \quad p_3(x) = 1 + x + x^2,$$

$$p_4(x) = 1 + x + x^3, \quad p_5(x) = 1 + x^2 + x^3.$$

The five exponents 18, 105, 72, 45, 121 yield the relations

$$x^{18} \text{ (modulo } f(x)) = x^4 + x^6 = x^4(1 + x)^2$$
$$= p_1^4(x)p_2^2(x)$$
$$x^{105} \text{ (modulo } f(x)) = x + x^4 + x^5 + x^6 = x(1 + x)^2(1 + x^2 + x^3)$$
$$= p_1(x)p_2^2(x)p_5(x)$$
$$x^{72} \text{ (modulo } f(x)) = x^2 + x^3 + x^5 + x^6 = x^2(1 + x)^2(1 + x + x^2)$$
$$= p_1^2(x)p_2^2(x)p_3(x)$$

$$x^{45} \text{ (modulo } f(x)) = 1 + x + x^2 + x^5 = (1+x)^2(1+x+x^3)$$
$$= p_2^2(x)p_4(x)$$
$$x^{121} \text{ (modulo } f(x)) = 1 + x + x^2 + x^3 + x^4 + x^5 + x^6 = (1+x+x^3)(1+x^2+x^3)$$
$$= p_4(x)p_5(x),$$

which may be written

$$18 = 4\log_x p_1(x) + 2\log_x p_2(x) \text{ (modulo 127)} \qquad \text{(E1)}$$

$$105 = \log_x p_1(x) + 2\log_x p_2(x) + \log_x p_5(x) \text{ (modulo 127)} \qquad \text{(E2)}$$

$$72 = 2\log_x p_1(x) + 2\log_x p_2(x) + \log_x p_3(x) \text{ (modulo 127)} \qquad \text{(E3)}$$

$$45 = 2\log_x p_2(x) + \log_x p_4(x) \text{ (modulo 127)} \qquad \text{(E4)}$$

$$121 = \log_x p_4(x) + \log_x p_5(x) \text{ (modulo 127)} \qquad \text{(E5)}$$

S3. To solve the system of relations (E1–E5), compute the differences

$$105 - 18 = 87\log_x p_5(x) - 3\log_x p_1(x) \qquad \text{(E2 – E1)}$$
$$121 - 45 = 76 = \log_x p_5(x) - 2\log_x p_2(x), \qquad \text{(E5 – E4)}$$

subtract these two equations

$$-11 = 3\log_x p_1(x) - 2\log_x p_2(x)$$

and add to (E1)

$$7 = 7\log_x p_1(x).$$

Backward substitution finally gives

$$\log_x p_1(x) = 1, \quad \log_x p_2(x) = 7, \quad \log_x p_3(x) = 56, \quad \log_x p_4(x) = 31, \quad p_5(x) = 90$$

$x^k(1 + x + x^2 + x^3 + x^4)$ (modulo $f(x)$) is computed for four randomly chosen values of k:

$$x^{66} + x^{67} + x^{68} + x^{69} + x^{70} \text{ (modulo } f(x)) = x + x^3 + x^5$$

$$x^{71} + x^{72} + x^{73} + x^{74} + x^{75} \text{ (modulo } f(x)) = x + x^2 + x^3 + x^4 + x^6$$

$$x^{92} + x^{93} + x^{94} + x^{95} + x^{96} \text{ (modulo } f(x)) = x^5 + x^6$$

$$x^{32} + x^{33} + x^{34} + x^{35} + x^{36} \text{ (modulo } f(x)) = 1 + x + x^2 + x^4 + x^5.$$

Only for two of the values is a complete factorization obtained

$$x^{66} + x^{67} + x^{68} + x^{69} + x^{70} \text{ (modulo } f(x)) = x(1 + x + x^2)^2 = p_1(x)p_3^2(x)$$

$$x^{92} + x^{93} + x^{94} + x^{95} + x^{96} \text{ (modulo } f(x)) = (x)^5(1 + x) = p_1^5(x)p_2(x).$$

Either of these factorizations can be used to conclude

$$\log_x(1 + x + x^2 + x^3 + x^4) \text{ (modulo 127)} = \log_x p_1(x) + 2\log_x p_3(x) - 66 \text{(modulo127)}$$
$$= 1 + (2 \times 56) - 66 = 47$$

$$\log_x(1 + x + x^2 + x^3 + x^4) \text{ (modulo 127)} = 5\log_x p_1(x) + \log_x p_2(x) - 92 \text{(modulo 127)}$$
$$= (5 \times 1) + 7 - 92 = -80 = 47 \text{(modulo 127)}$$

14.6 POLLARD'S ρ-ALGORITHM [POLLARD, 1978]

The discrete logarithm problem in a group is

> *Given*: α is a generator in a cyclic group G of order p and β in G;
>
> *Find*: γ is in $\mathcal{Z}_p$, satisfying α^γ.

Pollard extended the ρ-algorithm described in Chapter 13 for factorization to the DLP. Randomly generate the sequence $x_1, x_2, \ldots, x_n$ with $x_i = \alpha^{a_i}\beta^{b_i}$. If

$$x_i = x_j$$

then

$$\alpha^{a_i - a_j} = \beta^{b_j - b_i}$$

If $r = (b_i - b_j)$ and $(b_i - b_j)^{-1}$ exists, then

$$\alpha = \beta^{(b_i - b_j)^{-1}(a_j - a_i)}$$

so that $\gamma = (b_i - b_j)^{-1}(a_i - a_j)$.

The same computational issues that appeared in Pollard's ρ-factorization algorithm occur here and a Monte Carlo method for generating the sequence (x_i, a_i, b_i) together with Floyd's cycling finding algorithm comes to the rescue.

Pollard's ρ-algorithm for the DLP follows these steps:

P1. Partition the group G into three roughly equal subsets $G = G_0 \cup G_1 \cup G_2$. For example, for the cyclic group $G = \{x^n : 0 \leq n < 509\}$ where $x = e^{2\pi\frac{i}{509}}$ is the 509th roots of unity, let $G_i = \{x^n : 0 \leq n < 50, i = (n \bmod 3)\}$.

P2. Let α be a generator of G and $\beta = \alpha^r$; choose $a, b \in G$.

P3. Define the random mappings

$$f(x) : x \to f(x), \qquad x \in G$$
$$g(x, a) : a \to g(x, a), \qquad x \in G$$
$$h(x, b) : b \to h(x, b), \qquad x \in G$$

by

$$f(x) = \begin{cases} bx, & \text{if } x \in G_0 \\ x^2, & \text{if } x \in G_1 \\ ax, & \text{if } x \in G_2 \end{cases}$$

$$g(x, a) = \begin{cases} a, & \text{if } x \in G_0 \\ 2a, & \text{if } x \in G_1 \\ a+1, & \text{if } x \in G_2 \end{cases}$$

$$h(x, b) = \begin{cases} b+1, & \text{if } x \in G_0 \\ 2b, & \text{if } x \in G_1 \\ b, & \text{if } x \in G_2. \end{cases}$$

P4. Floyd's cyclic algorithm is applied to the sequence $x_i = \alpha^{a_i}\beta^{b_i}$ with $i = 1, 2, \ldots$.

P5. If $x_i = x_{2i}$, then $\alpha^{a_i}\beta^{b_i} = \alpha^{a_{2i}}\beta^{b_{2i}}$; if $(b_i - b_{2i})^{-1}$ exists, then $\alpha^{(a_{2i}-a_i)(b_i-b_{2i})^{-1}} = \beta = \alpha^x$.

Example 14.5

G is the cyclic subgroup of $\mathcal{Z}_{383}$ generated by the integer $\alpha = 2$. The steps in Pollard's ρ-algorithm for $\beta = 132$ are given in Table 14.6.

- We have $x_{2i} = x_i = 36$ when $i = 48$.
- This gives $r = 82 = (b_i - b_{2i})$ (modulo 191), $r^{-1} = 7$, and $\gamma = 33 = (r^{-1}(a_{2i} - a_i))$ (modulo 191).

TABLE 14.6 *Example 14.5* **Steps in Pollard's ρ-Algorithm**

i	x_i	a_i	b_i	x_{2i}	a_{2i}	b_{2i}	i	x_i	a_i	b_i	x_{2i}	a_{2i}	b_{2i}
1	132	0	1	189	0	2	2	189	0	2	63	0	8
3	102	0	4	347	0	17	4	63	0	8	239	2	17
5	139	0	16	190	4	17	6	347	0	17	370	5	18
7	311	1	17	224	5	20	8	239	2	17	130	7	20
9	95	3	17	233	8	21	10	190	4	17	166	10	21
11	185	4	18	50	20	44	12	370	5	18	178	21	45
13	199	5	19	321	21	47	14	224	5	20	28	43	94
15	65	6	20	338	86	190	16	130	7	20	203	88	190
17	308	7	21	46	90	190	18	233	8	21	72	180	0
19	83	9	21	250	169	1	20	166	10	21	124	170	2
21	81	10	22	243	149	6	22	50	20	44	35	107	13
23	100	21	44	48	108	14	24	178	21	45	36	50	56
25	133	21	46	161	9	33	26	321	21	47	374	10	34
27	14	42	94	347	12	34	28	28	43	94	239	14	34
29	249	43	95	190	16	34	30	338	86	190	370	17	35
31	293	87	190	224	17	37	32	203	88	190	130	19	37
33	23	89	190	233	20	38	34	46	90	190	166	22	38
35	327	90	0	50	44	78	36	72	180	0	178	45	79
37	205	169	0	321	45	81	38	250	169	1	28	91	162
39	62	169	2	338	182	135	40	124	170	2	203	184	135
41	282	170	3	46	186	135	42	243	149	6	72	181	81
43	67	107	12	250	171	163	44	35	107	13	124	172	164
45	70	108	13	243	153	139	46	48	108	14	35	115	88
47	6	25	28	48	116	89	48	36	50	56	36	82	165

Like other developments in mathematics, Pollard's work led Lenstra and Lenstra [1993] to the very powerful factorization methods in the special and general number field sieve (SNF/GNF).

14.7 EXTENSION FIELDS

Every student of cryptography needs to understand the basic concepts of modern algebra. A reference is the book by Peterson and Weldon [1972].

A *field* $\mathcal{F}$ is a mathematical system in which addition $(+)$ and multiplication $(\times)$ are defined with the following properties:

- $\mathcal{F}$ is a group under the operation addition $+$ with (additive) identity element 0;
- $\mathcal{F}^* \equiv \mathcal{F} - \{0\}$ is a *cyclic group* under the operation multiplication $\times$ with (multiplicative) identity 1.

The real $\mathfrak{R}$ and complex numbers $\mathcal{C}$ systems arc examples of fields.

There are two possibilities in a field $\mathcal{F}$ when repeated copies $1 + 1 + \cdots$ of the (multiplicative) identity element 1 are added:

1. If $1 + 1 + \cdots$ is *never* equal to 0, $\mathcal{F}$ is a field of *characteristic* 0; $\mathfrak{R}$ and $\mathcal{C}$ are examples;

2. $\underbrace{1 + 1 + \cdots + 1}_{n} \begin{cases} \neq 0, & \text{if } 1 \leq n < q \\ = 0, & \text{if } n = q. \end{cases}$

In the second case q must be a prime; for if $q = q_1 q_2, q_1 \neq 0, q_1 \neq 0$ and $q_1 q_2 = 0$ which cannot occur in a field.

When p is a prime number. $\mathcal{Z}p$ is a field of *characteristic* p, and its nonzero elements $\mathcal{Z}_p^* = \{1, 2, \ldots, p - 1\}$ form a cyclic group of order $p - 1$.

$\mathcal{Z}_p$ is not the *only* field of characteristic p. It is easy to prove that a field $\mathcal{F}$ of characteristic p (a prime) must contain p^m elements for some integer m. Morcover, there is a very simple description of such a field, which we now turn to.

The problem:

Given: $a, y \in \mathfrak{R}$;

Find: $x \in \mathfrak{R}$ such that $y = ax$

has a unique solution $x = a^{-1}y$ provided a^{-1} exists.

The same conclusion fails for the equation $y = ax^2 + bx$; it may *not* always have a root (solution) in the field $\mathfrak{R}$. However, if the field $\mathfrak{R}$ is augmented by including complex numbers, the equation $y = ax^2 + bx$ always has two roots. Defining $\iota = \sqrt{-1}$ as a solution of the equation $0 = x^2 + 1$ and *adjoining* $\iota = \sqrt{-1}$ to the field $\mathfrak{R}$ produces the complex number system $\mathcal{C}$.

The complex number system $\mathcal{C}$ consisting of all numbers of the form $x = u + v$ forms a field in which the operations $+, -, \div$ are defined by

Addition: $(u_1 + \iota v_1) + (u_2 + \iota v_2) = (u_1 + u_2) + \iota(v_1 + v_2)$

Multiplication: $(u_1 + \iota v_1) \times (u_2 + \iota v_2) = (u_1 u_2 - v_1 v_2) + \iota(u_1 v_2 + u_2 v_1)$

Division: $(u_1 + \iota v_1) \div (u_2 + i v_2) = \dfrac{(u_1 u_2 + v_1 v_2) + \iota(u_2 v_1 - u_1 v_2)}{D}$ Provided

$$D = (u_2^2 + v_2^2) \neq 0.$$

TABLE 14.7 z^j (modulo $p(z)$), $0 \leq j \leq 5$ for $p(z) = 1 + z + z^2 + z^3 + z^4$

z^0 (modulo $p(z)$) = 1 : (0,0,0,1)

z^1 (modulo $p(z)$) = z : (0,0,1,0)

z^2 (modulo $p(z)$) = z^2 : (0,1,0,0)

z^3 (modulo $p(z)$) = z^3 : (1,0,0,0)

z^4 (modulo $p(z)$) = $z^3 + z^2 + z + 1$: (1,1,1,1)

z^5 (modulo $p(z)$) = 1 : (0,0,0,1)

Moreover, every polynomial $p(x) = p_0 + p_1 x + \cdots + p_n x^n$ with coefficients in C and $p_n \neq 0$ has precisely n roots, and $p(x)$ splits into the product $p(x) = p_n(x - x_1)$ $(x - x_2) \cdots (x - x_n)$ of linear factors where each of the $x_j = u_j + \iota\, v_j$ are roots of $p(x) = 0$.

This same process can be defined in *any* field $\mathcal{F}$; if the polynomial $p(x) = p_0 + p_1 x + \cdots + p_n x^n$ with coefficients $\{ p_j \}$ in $\mathcal{F}$ does *not* have any roots in $\mathcal{F}$, then by adjoining the fictitious root ϑ to $\mathcal{F}$ we obtain an *extension field* of $\mathcal{F}$ in which the polynomial $p(z)$ now has a root.

We focus our discussion to $\mathcal{P}[z]$, polynomials $p(x) = p_0 + p_1 z + \cdots + p_n z^n$ with coefficients in the field $\mathcal{Z}_2$. We write $\underline{P}(x) : \underline{P} = (p_0, p_1, \ldots, p_n)$ to indicate the correspondence of the polynomial $p(z)$ and its coefficient vector $\underline{p}$. In Section 8.3 we summarized the basic properties of the algebra of polynomials $\mathcal{P}[z]$.

Example 14.6

Table 14.7 lists z^j (modulo $p(x)$) together with its 4-bit representation for $0 \leq j \leq 5$ for the irreducible polynomial $p(z) = 1 + z + z^2 + z^3 + z^4$ with exponent $e = 5$. If a root ϑ of an irreducible polynomial $p(z)$ of degree m is adjoined to $\mathcal{Z}_2$, an extension field $\mathcal{Z}_{m,2}$ containing 2^m elements is obtained

When $p(z)$ is primitive, the elements of the extension field $\mathcal{Z}_{m,2}$ are powers 1, ϑ, $\vartheta^2, \ldots, \vartheta^{2^m - 2}$ of the adjoined root ϑ, and the $2^m - 1$ elements in the extension field $\mathcal{Z}_{m,2}$ correspond to the *nonzero* m-bit binary sequences $\underline{z} = (z_0, z_1, \ldots, z_{m-1})$. $\underline{z} = (z_0, z_1, \ldots, z_{m-1}) \neq (0)_m$ is the base-2 representation of some power of ϑ.

TABLE 14.8 Coding of ϑ^j with $0 = 1 + \vartheta + \vartheta$

$p(x) = 1 + x + x^4$				$p(\vartheta) = 0$	
(0,0,0,1)	1	(0,0,1,0)	ϑ	(0,1,0,0)	ϑ^2
(1,0,0,0)	ϑ^3	(0,0,1,1)	ϑ^4	(0,1,1,0)	ϑ^5
(1,1,0,0)	ϑ^6	(1,0,1,1)	ϑ^7	(0,1,0,1)	ϑ^8
(1,0,1,0)	ϑ^9	(0,1,1,1)	ϑ^{10}	(1,1,1,0)	ϑ^{11}
(1,1,1,1)	ϑ^{12}	(1,1,0,1)	ϑ^{13}	(1,0,0,1)	ϑ^{14}

TABLE 14.9 Coding of ϑ^j with $0 = 1 + \vartheta + \vartheta^2 + \vartheta^3 + \vartheta^4$

$p(x) = 1 + x + x^2 + x^3 + x^4$					
(0,1,1,0)	u	(1,0,1,1)	u^2	(0,1,0,0)	u^3
(1,1,0,0)	σu	(1,0,0,1)	σu^2	(1,0,0,0)	σu^3
(0,1,1,1)	$\sigma^2 u$	(1,1,0,1)	$\sigma^2 u^2$	(1,1,1,1)	$\sigma^2 u^3$
(1,1,1,0)	$\sigma^3 u$	(0,1,0,1)	$\sigma^3 u^2$	(0,0,0,1)	$\sigma^3 u^3$
(0,0,1,1)	$\sigma^4 u$	(1,0,1,0)	$\sigma^4 u^2$	(0,0,1,0)	$\sigma^4 u^3$

When $p(x)$ is irreducible but *not* primitive, this correspondence is missing.

The nonzero elements of the field $\mathcal{Z}_{2,2^4}$ form a cyclic group of order $15 = 2^4 - 1$ which contains generators of order 3, 5, and 15. Tables 14.8 and 14.9 below give two coding of the elements of the extension field $\mathcal{Z}_{2,2^4}$:

- The generator in Table 14.8 is ϑ of order 15;
- The element u is of order 3; σ is the left-shift operator,

14.8   THE CURRENT STATE OF DISCRETE LOGARITHM RESEARCH

There has been active research to improve algorithms for integer factorization and the discrete logarithm problems. An excellent survey by Odlyzko [1999] reports on the current state. My only criticism of this paper is with Professor Odlyzko's crystal ball gazing. He writes "The most worrisome long-term threat to discrete log cryptosystems that we can forsee right now comes from quantum computers." Of course, he wrote this in 1999 just after Peter Shor's [1997] remarkable paper on polynomial-time integer factorization had appeared. Nevertheless, it has been nine years since then and . . . well?

It is always risky to predict the future or to criticize those who do so . . . especially in technology. And why should you, the reader, listen to me? The original notes for this book were prepared using a line editor and I do not even own a single cellphone, even the old-fashioned kind that just makes and receives calls.

REFERENCES

L. M. ADELMAN, "A Subexponential Algorithm for the Discrete Logarithm Problem with Applications to Cryptography," *Proceedings of the 20th IEEE Symposium on the Foundations of Computer Science*, New York, 1979, pp. 55–60.

A. K. LENSTRA AND H. W. LENSTRA, JR, *The Development of the Number Field Sieve*, Lecture Notes in Mathematics #1554, Springer-Verlag, New York, NY, 1993.

A. M. ODLYZKO, "Discrete Logarithms: The Past and the Future," *Designs, Codes, and Cryptography*, **19**, 129–145 (1999).

W. WESLEY PETERSON AND E. J. WELDON, *Error-Correcting Codes* Revised 2nd edn., The M.I.T Press, Cambridge, Massachusetts, 1972.

S. POHLIG AND M. HELLMAN, "An Improved Method for Computing Logarithms Over GF(p) and its Cryptographic Significance," *IEEE Transactions on Information Theory*, **IT-24**, 107–110 (1978).

J. M. POLLARD, "Monte Carlo Methods for Index Computation Mod p," *Mathematics of Computation*, **32**, 918–924 (1978).

D. SHANKS, *Solved and Unsolved Problems in Number Theory*, Chealsea Publishing Spartan Books (New York, NY), 1962.

P. W. SHOR, "Polynomial-Time Algorithms for Prime Factorization and Discrete Logarithms on a Quantum Computer," *SIAM Journal of Computing*, **26**, 1484–1509 (1997).

CHAPTER *15*

ELLIPTIC CURVE CRYPTOGRAPHY

JUST TWENTY years ago, Koblitz and Miller suggested the use of elliptic curves to construct cryptographic systems. Using a result from the nineteenth century of Carl Gustav Jacob Jacobi, a group structure can be defined. There is a tremendous cryptographic advantage to encipherment based on elliptic groups. In the ensuing 20 years, a considerable body of results has been published so that there are now elliptic curve encryption, key exchange, and signature algorithms. These are the subjects of this chapter.

15.1 ELLIPTIC CURVES

A *plane curve* is the locus of points (x, y) in the plane which are the solutions of $f(x, y) = 0$ with $f(x, y)$ a polynomial in two variables with rational coefficients. The study of plane curves has occupied mathematics for nearly two millennia; in 250 A.D., Diophantus determined the integer solutions[1] for $f(x, y) = x^2 + y^2 - r^2$; in 1995, Peter Wiles announced the solution to Fermat's famous conjectured theorem,[2] the case

$$f(x, y) = x^n + y^n - r^n.$$

By changing variables, the general cubic equation $y^2 + b_1 xy + b_2 xy = x^3 + a_1 x^2 + a_2 x + a_3$ yields the normal form for an *elliptic curve* $y^2 = x^3 + ax + b$. Although an elliptic curve may have one or three real roots, it does not have multiple roots provided the *discriminant*[3] $D = 4a^3 + 27b^2$ is not 0.

An elliptic curve $y^2 = x^3 + ax + b$ with one real root is shown in Figure 15.1. The relation of an elliptic curve to the ellipse $x^2/A^2 + y^2/B^2 = 1$ is somewhat convoluted. In essence, the connection comes from the quartic in the $\sqrt{\cdots}$ appearing in the denominator of the *elliptic integral*

$$A \int_0^{x/A} \frac{1 - kt^2}{\sqrt{(1 - t^2)(1 - kt^2)}} \, dt, \qquad k^2 = (A^2 - B^2)/A^2,$$

giving the arc length along the ellipse from $(0, B)$ to (x, y). For more details see the work of Markushevich [1965].

If $x^3 + ax + b$ has three (distinct) real roots, the curve consists of two sections, an example of which is shown in Figure 15.2.

---

[1]If n and m are relatively prime and $n - m$ is positive and odd then $(x, y, r) = (n^2 - m^2, 2nm, n^2 + m^2)$ is a Pythagorean triple $m^2 + n^2 = r^2$ and conversely all primitive Pythagorean triples arise in this manner.

[2]There are no nontrivial nonzero integer solutions to $x^n + y^n = r^n$ for $n \geq 3$.

[3]The discriminant of the polynomial $f(x) = \prod_i a(x - r_i)$ of degree n is $D = a^{n-1} \prod_{i<j} (e_i - e_j)^2$. The roots of $f(x)$ are distinct if and only if $D \neq 0$.

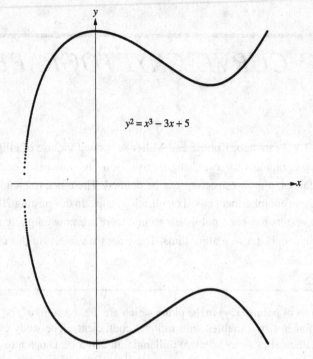

$$y^2 = x^3 - 3x + 5$$

Figure 15.1 Elliptic curve with one real root.

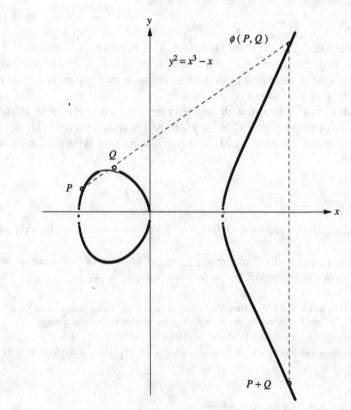

$$y^2 = x^3 - x$$

Figure 15.2 Elliptic curve with three real distinct roots.

15.2 THE ELLIPTIC GROUP OVER THE REALS

The curve $y^2 = x^3 - x = x(x - 1)(x + 1)$ enjoys a property characteristic of all elliptic curves – the *chord-tangent group law* discovered by Carl Gustav Jacob Jacobi (1804–1851) in the nineteenth century.

Proposition 15.1 *(Bezout's Theorem)*: If $P = (x_1, y_1)$ and $Q = (x_2, y_2)$ are two points on the elliptic curve $y^2 = x^3 + ax + b$ with $4a^3 + 27b^2 \neq 0$ and if the line $\underline{PQ}$ joining these points is *not* vertical, then the line $\underline{PQ}$ will intersect the curve in a third place $\phi(P, Q) = R = (x_3, -y_3)$ whose coordinates are given by

$$x_3 = \begin{cases} \left(\dfrac{y_2 - y_1}{x_2 - x_1}\right)^2 - x_1 - x_2, & \text{if } x_1 \neq x_2 \\[2ex] \left(\dfrac{3x_1^2 + a}{2y_1}\right)^2 - 2x_1, & \text{if } x_1 = x_2 \end{cases}$$

and

$$y_3 = \begin{cases} -y_1 + \dfrac{y_2 - y_1}{x_2 - x_1}(x_1 - x_3), & \text{if } x_1 \neq x_2 \\[2ex] -y_1 + \dfrac{3x_1^2 + a}{2y_1}(x_1 - x_3), & \text{if } x_1 = x_2. \end{cases}$$

Proof: Suppose the equation of the line $\underline{PQ}$ is

$$\underline{PQ} : y = \lambda x + \mu.$$

There are two cases to consider; if $x_1 \neq x_2$, then

$$y_1 = \lambda x_1 + \mu, \qquad y_2 = \lambda x_2 + \mu.$$

Square y and substitute into the equation $y^2 = x^3 + ax + b$ to obtain

$$\begin{aligned} 0 &= (\lambda^2 x^2 + 2\lambda\mu x + \mu^2) - x^3 - ax - b \\ &= x^3 - \lambda^2 x^2 + (a - 2\lambda\mu)x + (b - \mu^2) \\ &= (x - x_1)(x - x_2)(x - x_3) \\ &= x^3 - (x_1 + x_2 + x_3)x^2 + (x_1 x_2 + x_1 x_3 + x_2 x_3)x - x_1 x_2 x_3 \end{aligned}$$

so that

$$\lambda^2 = x_1 + x_2 + x_3$$

$$a - 2\lambda\mu = x_1 x_2 + x_1 x_3 + x_2 x_3$$

$$b - \mu^2 = -x_1 x_2 x_3$$

which gives

$$\lambda = \frac{y_2 - y_1}{x_2 - x_1}$$

$$x_3 = \lambda^2 - x_1 - x_2 = \left(\frac{y_2 - y_1}{x_2 - x_1}\right)^2 - x_1 - x_2$$

$$y_3 = -y_1 + \lambda(x_1 - x_3) = -y_1 + \frac{y_2 - y_1}{x_2 - x_1}(x_1 - x_3).$$

The case $x_1 = x_2$ is the limiting case $x_2 = x_1 + \delta$ as $\delta \to 0$ and λ is the slope of the curve $y^2 = x^3 + ax + b$ at the point of intersection.

$$\lambda = \frac{3x_1^2 + a}{2y_1},$$

which completes the proof.

Bezout's Theorem provides a way to define a group for the points on an elliptic curve. Let $\phi(P, Q)$ denote the point at the intersection of the line $\underline{PQ}$ and the elliptic curve:

1. If the line $\underline{PQ}$ is vertical ($x_1 = x_2$), the vertical line *meets* the curve at ∞ so that $\phi(P, Q) = \infty$.

2. The value of $\phi(\infty, P)$ is the reflection about the x-axis of P so that $\phi(\infty, Q) = P$ if $Q = \phi(\infty, P)$.

Define the *sum* of P and Q by

$$P + Q \equiv \phi(\infty, \phi(P, Q)).$$

The third point on the line $\underline{PQ}$ is determined and reflected about the x-axis.

3. The point at ∞ satisfies $\phi(P, \infty) = \phi(\infty, P) = P$ so that $\mathcal{O} = \infty$ acts as an *identity* element under $+$.

4. The point $\phi(\infty, P)$ satisfies $\phi(P, \phi(\infty, P)) = \infty$ so that $\phi(\infty, P)$ is the *inverse* of P under $+$ satisfying $P + \phi(\infty, P) = \mathcal{O}$.

Although surprisingly difficult, it can be proved that addition $+$ satisfies the associativity law [Husemoller, 1987]:

$$P + (Q + R) = (P + Q) + R.$$

Proposition 15.2: $\mathcal{O}$ together with the points on the elliptic curve $y^2 = x^3 + ax + b$ $(4a^3 + 27b^2 \neq 0)$ form the Abelian elliptic group $\mathcal{E}(a, b)$ with group operation $+$ and identity element $\mathcal{O}$.

Figure 15.3 presents an elliptic curve with $a = -3$, $b = 2$. The resolvent $D = 4a^3 + 27b^2 = 0$ and the cubic $y^2 = x^3 + ax + b$ has a double root at $x = 1$. The chord-tangent for $P = (-1, 0)$ and $Q = (0, 0)$ yields $(-1, 0) + (0, 0) = (0, 0)$.

15.3 LENSTRA'S FACTORIZATION ALGORITHM [LENSTRA, 1986]

One of the first cryptographic applications of elliptic curves was a factoring algorithm due to H. W. Lenstra.

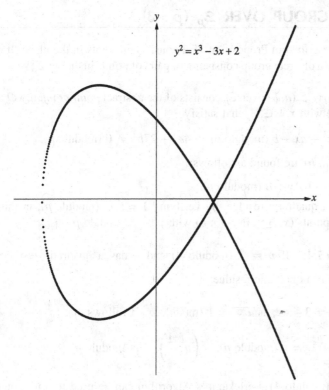

Figure 15.3 Elliptic curve with three real roots.

Let (x, y) be a *rational point* on $y^2 = x^3 + ax + b$ where a and b are rational numbers. Lenstra writes $x_2 = x_1$ (modulo m) if m is a factor of $x_2 - x_1$ after common factors are cancelled, with $x_1 = (a_1/b_1)$ and $\dot{x}_2 = (a_2/b_2)$. The factors of N will be found in the elliptic curve modulo N.

15.3.1 Lenstra's Factorization Algorithm

1. Randomly choose $x, y \in \mathcal{Z}_N$.
2. Randomly choose a and b subject to $y^2 = x^3 + ax + b$ (modulo N).
3. Test if $D = 4a^3 + 27b^2 = 0$ (modulo N); return to (2) if $D = 0$.
4. Choose a bound M and define

$$E = \prod_{\substack{q \leq M \\ q \, a \, prime}} q^{[\log_q N]}.$$

5. Let $P = (x, y)$ and compute P^E by repeated squaring. Before multiplying (x_1, y_1) by (x_2, y_2) compute $g = \gcd\{x_1 - x_2, N\}$. If $1 < g < N$, return g and END.

Proposition 15.3: If p is the smallest prime divisor of N (which is not divisible by 2 or 3), then the running time of Lenstra's Algorithm is $RT = O\left(e^{\sqrt{(2+\epsilon)\log p \log\log p}}\right)$. Koblitz's book [1987a] discusses why the algorithm works and how the running time estimate is derived.

15.4 THE ELLIPTIC GROUP OVER $\mathcal{Z}_p$ ($p > 3$)

The elliptic group described in Proposition 15.2 consists of points in the plane. It can be generalized to obtain a discrete group consisting of pairs of points in the set $\mathcal{Z}_p$ when $p > 3$ as follows.

The *elliptic curve* $\mathcal{E}_p(a, b)$ over $\mathcal{Z}_p$ consists of the abstract *point at infinity* $\mathcal{O}$ and all pairs of points (x, y) with $x, y \in \mathcal{Z}_p$ that satisfy

$$y^2 = x^3 + ax + b \text{ (modulo } p), \quad 4a^3 + 27b^2 \neq 0 \text{ (modulo } p).$$

The elements of $\mathcal{E}_p(a, b)$ are found as follows:

1. Compute $z = x^3 + Ax + B$ (modulo p).
2. Check if z is a quadratic residue, by verifying $1 = z^{\frac{p-1}{2}}$ (modulo p); in this case, there are two points $(x, \pm y)$ in $\mathcal{E}_p(a, b)$ with $y^2 = z$ (modulo p).

Proposition 15.4: If $p = 3$ (modulo 4) and u has a quadratic residue, then $v = u^{\frac{p+1}{4}}$ (modulo p) is a quadratic residue of u.

Proof: Let $p = 3 + 4d$; as $u^{\frac{p-1}{2}} = 1$ (modulo p), it follows that

$$u^{\frac{p+1}{2}} = u \text{ (modulo } p), \quad \left(u^{\frac{p+1}{4}}\right)^2 = u \text{ (modulo } p)$$

When $p = 1$ (modulo 4), Berlekamp's Algorithm can be used to find a quadratic residue; another method is described in Koblitz [1987a].

The following examples list the elements of $\mathcal{E}_{23}(a, b)$ for three choices of (a, b) and the *order* of the (discrete) elliptic group $|\mathcal{E}_{23}(a, b)|$.

Examples 15.1–15.3
Tables 15.1 to 15.3 lists the elements of three discrete elliptic groups with $p = 23$.

Proposition 15.5 (Hasse): The *order* of the elliptic group $\mathcal{E}_p(a, b)$ satisfies

$$1 + p - 2\sqrt{p} \leq |\mathcal{E}_p(a, b)| \leq 1 + p + 2\sqrt{p}, \quad |\mathcal{E}_p(a, b) - (1 + p)| \leq 2\sqrt{p}.$$

The elliptic curve $\mathcal{E}_p(a, b)$ is *supersingular* if $((1 + p) - |\mathcal{E}_p(a, b)|)^2 \in \{0, p, 2p, 3p, 4p\}$.

TABLE 15.1 The Elliptic Group $\mathcal{E}_{23}(1, 1)$, $p = 23$, $a = b = 1$

$|\mathcal{E}_{23}(1, 1)| = 28$			
(0,1)	(0,22)	(1,7)	(1,16)
(3,10)	(3,13)	(4,0)	
(5,4)	(5,19)	(6,4)	(6,19)
(7,11)	(7,12)	(9,7)	(9,16)
(11,3)	(11,20)	(12,4)	(12,19)
(13,7)	(13,16)	(17,3)	(17,20)
(18,3)	(18,20)	(19,5)	(19,18)

TABLE 15.2 The Elliptic Group $\mathcal{E}_{23}(1,2)$, $p = 23$, $a = 1$, $b = 2$

$|\mathcal{E}_{23}(1, 2)| = 23$			
(0,5)	(0,18)	(1,2)	(1,21)
(2,9)	(2,14)	(3,3)	(3,20)
(4,1)	(4,22)	(8,4)	(8,19)
(9,2)	(9,21)	(10,0)	
(13,2)	(13,21)	(14,0)	
(19,7)	(19,16)	(20,8)	(20,15)
(22,0)			

TABLE 15.3   The Elliptic Group $\mathcal{E}_{23}(1, 3)$, $p = 23$, $a = 1$, $b = 3$

	$|\mathcal{E}_{23}(1, 3)| = 27$		
(0,7)	(0,16)	(2,6)	(2,17)
(4,5)	(4,18)	(5,8)	(5,15)
(6,8)	(6,15)	(7,10)	(7,13)
(10,1)	(10,22)	(12,8)	(12,15)
(14,1)	(14,22)	(15,9)	(15,14)
(19,2)	(19,21)	(21,4)	(21,19)
(22,1)	(22,22)		

Discussion: $y^2 = 1$ (modulo p) is satisfied for half of the elements of $\mathcal{Z}_p$. If the values $x^3 + ax + b$ were uniformly distributed over $\mathcal{Z}_p$, each of approximately $p/2$ values of x should generate a pair of points $(x, \pm y)$ in $\mathcal{E}_p$.

Proposition 15.6:   If $p > 3$, the addition rule for the elliptic group $\mathcal{E}_p(a, b)$ consisting of $\mathcal{O}$ and all points (x, y) satisfying $y^2 = x^3 + ax + b$ (modulo p) with $4a^3 + 27b^2 \neq 0$ (modulo p) is

$$P = (x_1, y_1), \quad Q = (x_2, y_2) \rightarrow R = P + Q = (x_3, y_3) \in \mathcal{E}_p(a, b)$$

$$x_3 = \lambda^2 - x_1 - x_2, \quad y_3 = \lambda(x_1 - x_3) - y_1$$

$$\lambda = \begin{cases} \dfrac{y_2 - y_1}{x_2 - x_1}, & \text{if } x_1 \neq x_2 \\[2mm] \dfrac{3x^2 + A}{2y_1}, & \text{if } x_1 = x_2. \end{cases}$$

Proof: At the intersection of $\mathcal{E}_p(a, b)$ and the linear form $y = \lambda x + \mu$

$$0 = x^3 - \lambda^2 x^2 + (a - 2\mu)x + b - \mu^2.$$

There are two cases. If the linear form $y = \lambda x + \mu$ has two distinct points of intersection (x_i, y_i) $(i = 1, 2)$ with $y^2 = x^3 + ax + b$, it must have a third, say $R = (x_3, v_3)$

$$0 = (x - x_1)(x - x_2)(x - x_3)$$

so that

$$\lambda^2 = x_1 + x_2 + x_3$$

giving

$$x_3 = \lambda^2 - x_1 - x_2$$
$$v_3 = y_1 + \lambda(x_3 - x_1).$$

The sum $(x_1, y_1) + (x_2, y_3)$ is defined by the *reflection* or inverse of the point (x_3, v_3), namely $(x_3, y_3) = (x_3, -v_3)$

$$x_3 = \lambda^2 - x_1 - x_2$$
$$y_3 = -y_1 + \lambda(x_1 - x_3).$$

In the second case, the linear form $y = \lambda x + \mu$ is tangent to the curve $y^2 = x^3 + ax + b$, which requires (x, y) to be a solution to the pair of equations

$$2y = 3x^2 + a$$
$$y^2 = x^3 + ax + b,$$

which completes the proof.

Example 15.4
$P = (3, 10)$, $Q = (9, 7)$, $\lambda = \dfrac{7 - 10}{9 - 3} = \dfrac{20}{6} = \dfrac{10}{3}$. As the inverse of 3 in $\mathcal{Z}_{23}$ is 8
$$\lambda = 10 \times 8 = 80 = 11 (\text{modulo } 23).$$

Next

$$x_3 = 11^2 - 9 - 3 = 109 = 17 \ (\text{modulo } 23),$$
$$y_3 = 11 \times (3 - (-6)) - 10 = 89 = 20 \ (\text{modulo } 23),$$

which gives

$$P + Q = (17, 20).$$

The *inverse* of $P = (x, y)$ is $-P \equiv (x, -y)$. The *order* of an element $(x, y) \in \mathcal{E}_p(a, b)$ is the smallest integer n such that $nx = \mathcal{O}$.

Example 15.4 (Continued)
The elements $(x, y) \in \mathcal{E}_{23}(1, 1)$ are of order 1, 2, 4, 7, 14, or 28.

15.5 ELLIPTIC GROUPS OVER THE FIELD $\mathcal{Z}_{m,2}$

Let $p(x)$ be a primitive polynomial over $\mathcal{Z}_2$ of degree m. The *elliptic group* $\mathcal{E}_{\mathcal{Z}_{m,2}}(a, b)$ consists of the point at infinity $\mathcal{O}$ together with all pairs $(x, y) \in \mathcal{Z}_{m,2}$ that satisfy the equation

$$y^2 + xy = x^3 + ax^2 + b, \qquad a, b \in \mathcal{Z}_{m,2}, \qquad b \neq 0.$$

As $b \neq 0$, the point $(0, 0)$ is *not* a solution and $(0, 0)$ is used as the representation of $\mathcal{O}$.

Proposition 15.7: If $y \in \mathcal{Z}_{m,2}$ is a solution of $y^2 + xy = x^3 + ax^2 + b$, then $y + x \in \mathcal{Z}_{m,2}$ is also a solution.

Proof: If

$$y^2 + xy = x^3 + ax^2 + b$$

then

$$(y + x)^2 + x(y + x) = y^2 + x^2 + xy + x^2 = y^2 + xy$$

as the field $\mathcal{Z}_{m,2}$ is of characteristic 2.

Proposition 15.8: $\mathcal{E}_{\mathcal{Z}_{m,2}}(a, b)$ is a group under addition $+$ where

15.8a $(x, y) + (0, 0) = (0, 0) + (x, y) = (x, y)$;

15.8b $(x, y) + (x, y + x) = (0, 0)$;

15.8c If $x_1 \neq x_2$, then $(x_1, y_1) + (x_2, y_2) = (x_3, y_3)$, where (x_3, y_3) is the reflection of the y-value $x_3 + y_3$ of the point (x, y) of the linear form $y = \lambda x + \mu$ at x_3

$$\lambda = \frac{y_1 + y_2}{x_1 + x_2}$$

$$x_3 = \lambda^2 + \lambda + x_1 + x_2 + a$$

$$y_3 = \lambda(x_1 + x_3) + x_3 + y_1;$$

15.8d $2(x, y) = (x_2, y_2)$ where

$$\lambda = x + \frac{y}{x}$$

$$x_2 = \lambda^2 + \lambda + a$$

$$y_2 = x_2 + (\lambda + 1)x_2.$$

Proof: There are two cases to be examined; if there are two distinct points of intersection (x_1, y_1) and (x_2, y_2) of the linear form $y = \lambda x + \mu$ and the curve $y^2 + xy + x^3 + ax^2 + b$, then

$$0 = x^3 - (\lambda^2 + \lambda + a) - x\mu + b - \mu^2$$
$$= (x - x_1)(x - x_2)(x_3)$$

and

$$\lambda + \lambda^2 + a = x_1 + x_2 + x_3,$$

which gives

$$x_3 = \lambda^2 + \lambda + x_1 + x_2 + a$$

and

$$y_3 = \lambda(x_1 + x_3) + x_3 + y_1$$

In the second case, the linear form $y = \lambda x + \mu$ is tangent to the curve $y^2 + xy = x^3 + ax^2 + b$, which requires (x, y) to be a solution to the pair of equations

$$x\frac{dy}{dx} + y = x^2 \Leftrightarrow 2y\frac{dy}{dx} + x\frac{dy}{dx} + y = 3x^2 + 2ax$$
$$y^2 + xy = x^3 + ax^2 + b.$$

This gives

$$\lambda = x + \frac{y}{x}$$

$$x_2 = \lambda^2 + \lambda + a$$

$$y_2 = x^2 + (\lambda + 1)x_2.$$

15.6 COMPUTATIONS IN THE ELLIPTIC GROUP $\mathcal{E}_{\mathcal{Z}_{m,2}}(a, b)$

Programs to manipulate polynomials are required to carry out arithmetic in the elliptic group $\mathcal{E}_{\mathcal{Z}_{m,2}}(a, b)$. As described in Section 14.5, these programs include PADD, PMUL, and PDIV, and PXEUCLID; the last program, PXEUCLID, is used to find the inverse of an element in $\mathcal{Z}_{m,2}$. Only one task remains to generate the elements (x, y) of $\mathcal{E}_{\mathcal{Z}_{m,2}}(a, b)$. For this purpose, linear operations in $\mathcal{Z}_{m,2}$ viewed as a vector space need to be performed. An example may make the ideas clear.

Example 15.5

$p(x) = 1 + x + x^4$ is primitive over $\mathcal{Z}_2$. Suppose ϑ is the root of $p(x) = 0$ adjoined to $\mathcal{Z}_2$ to obtain the extension field $\mathcal{Z}_{4,2}$.

Multiplication: $\mathbf{xy}$, $\mathbf{x} = (\mathbf{x_0}, \mathbf{x_1}, \mathbf{x_2}, \mathbf{x_3})$; $\mathbf{y} = (\mathbf{y_0}, \mathbf{y_1}, \mathbf{y_2}, \mathbf{y_3})$

$$x = (x_0, x_1, x_2, x_3) = x_0 \vartheta^3 + x_1 \vartheta^2 + x_2 \vartheta + x_3$$

$$y = (y_0, y_1, y_2, y_3) = y_0 \vartheta^3 + y_1 \vartheta^2 + y_2 \vartheta + y_3$$

$$xy = x_0 y_0 \vartheta^6 + (x_0 y_1 + x_1 y_0) \vartheta^5 + (x_0 y_2 + x_1 y_1 + x_2 y_0) \vartheta^4$$

$$+ (x_0 y_3 + x_1 y_2 + x_2 y_1 + x_3 y_0) \vartheta^3 + (x_1 y_3 + x_2 y_2 + x_3 y_1) \vartheta^2$$

$$+ (x_2 y_3 + x_3 y_2) \vartheta + x_3 y_3.$$

Next, we use the formulas

$$\vartheta^4 = 1 + \vartheta$$

$$\vartheta^5 = \vartheta + \vartheta^2$$

$$\vartheta^6 = \vartheta^2 + \vartheta^3$$

to write

$$xy = (z_0, z_1, z_2, z_3) = z_0 \vartheta^3 + z_1 \vartheta^2 + z_2 \vartheta + z_3,$$

where

$$z_0 = x_0 y_3 + x_1 y_2 + x_2 y_1 + x_3 y_0 + \underbrace{x_0 y_0}_{\vartheta^6 - \text{term}}$$

$$z_1 = x_1 y_3 + x_2 y_2 + x_3 y_1 + \underbrace{x_0 y_0}_{\vartheta^6 - \text{term}} + \underbrace{x_0 y_1 + x_1 y_0}_{\vartheta^5 - \text{term}}$$

$$z_2 = x_2 y_3 + x_3 y_2 + \underbrace{x_0 y_2 + x_1 y_1 + x_2 y_0}_{\vartheta^4 - \text{term}} + \underbrace{x_0 y_1 + x_1 y_0}_{\vartheta^5 - \text{term}}$$

$$z_3 = x_3 y_3 + \underbrace{x_0 y_2 + x_1 y_1 + x_2 y_0}_{\vartheta^4 - \text{term}}$$

or in matrix notation

$$(z_0, z_1, z_2, z_3) = (y_0, y_1, y_2, y_3)M(x)$$

$$M(x) = \begin{pmatrix} x_3 + x_0 & x_1 + x_0 & x_2 + x_1 & x_2 \\ x_2 & x_3 + x_0 & x_1 + x_0 & x_1 \\ x_1 & x_2 & x_3 + x_0 & x_0 \\ x_0 & x_1 & x_2 & x_3 \end{pmatrix}$$

Inverse: $\mathbf{x}^{-1}, \mathbf{x} = (\mathbf{x_0}, \mathbf{x_1}, \mathbf{x_2}, \mathbf{x_3})$

If $y \neq 0, x \neq 0$, then $xy \neq 0$ and $M(x)$ is nonsingular. The inverse of $x = (x_0, x_1, x_2, x_3)$ is the solution $y = (y_0, y_1, y_2, y_3)$ of

$$(y_0, y_1, y_2, y_3) = (0, 0, 0, 1)(M(x))^{-1}$$

If $p(x)$ is primitive degree m, the computation of

$$\vartheta^j = \sum_{k=0}^{m-1} t_{j,k}\vartheta^k = (t_{j,m-1}, \ldots, t_{j,1}, t_{j,0}), \qquad 0 \le j < m,$$

requires m shifts and m-bit XORs.

The inversion of the $m \times m$ matrix $M(x)$ can be effected by Gaussian elimination.

Schroeppel et al. [1995] optimized the code for the elliptic group with $m = 155$ and the irreducible (but not primitive) trinomial $p(x) = x^{155} + x^{62} + 1$.

Example 15.6

The elements $(x, y) \neq (0, 0)$ of the elliptic group $\mathcal{E}_{\mathcal{Z}_{6,4}}(a, b)$ with $p(x) = 1 + x + x^6, a = 0$ and $b = (0, 0, 1, 0)$ are listed in Table 15.4.

Computing Solutions of $y^2 + xy = x^3 + ax^2 + b$: The elements of the elliptic group $\mathcal{E}_{\mathcal{Z}_{4,2}}(a, b)$ with $a, b \in \mathcal{Z}_{4,2}$ and $b \neq (0, 0, 0, 0)$ are the solutions of

$$y^2 + xy = x^3 + ax^2 + b.$$

If

$$y = (y_0, y_1, y_2, y_3) = y_0\vartheta^3 + y_1\vartheta^2 + y_2\vartheta + y_3,$$

then

$$y^2 = y_0\vartheta^6 + y_1\vartheta^4 + y_2\vartheta^2 + y_3 = (y_0, (y_2 + y_0), y_1, (y_3 + y_1)).$$

If

$$z = (z_0, z_1, z_2, z_3) = x^3 + ax^2 + b,$$

then (x, y) is an element of the elliptic group $\mathcal{E}_{16}(a, b)$ if

$$z = (y_0, y_2 + y_0, y_1, y_3 + y_1) + (y_0, y_1, y_2, y_3)M(x) = (y_0, y_1, y_2, y_3)N(x),$$

TABLE 15.4 The Elements of the Elliptic Group $\mathcal{E}_{Z_{6,4}}(a, b)$, $p(x) = 1 + x + x^6$, $a = 0$, and $b = (0, 0, 1, 0)$

	$(x, y_j) \, y_j = \vartheta^{k_j} \, (j = 1, 2)$	
$x = (0, 0, 0, 0, 0, 1) = \vartheta^0$	$y_1 = (1, 1, 1, 0, 1, 1) = \vartheta^{21}$	$y_2 = (1, 1, 1, 0, 1, 0) = \vartheta^{42}$
$x = (0, 0, 0, 0, 1, 0) = \vartheta^1$	$y_1 = (0, 0, 1, 1, 1, 1) = \vartheta^{18}$	$y_2 = (0, 0, 1, 1, 0, 1) = \vartheta^{48}$
$x = (0, 0, 0, 1, 0, 0) = \vartheta^2$	$y_1 = (0, 1, 0, 0, 1, 0) = \vartheta^{33}$	$y_2 = (0, 1, 0, 1, 1, 0) = \vartheta^{36}$
$x = (0, 0, 1, 0, 0, 0) = \vartheta^3$	$y_1 = (1, 0, 0, 1, 1, 0) = \vartheta^{17}$	$y_2 = (1, 0, 1, 1, 1, 0) = \vartheta^{55}$
$x = (0, 1, 0, 0, 0, 0) = \vartheta^4$	$y_1 = (0, 0, 1, 0, 0, 0) = \vartheta^3$	$y_2 = (0, 1, 1, 0, 0, 0) = \vartheta^9$
$x = (0, 0, 0, 0, 1, 1) = \vartheta^6$	$y_1 = (1, 0, 0, 1, 0, 0) = \vartheta^{34}$	$y_2 = (1, 0, 0, 1, 1, 1) = \vartheta^{47}$
$x = (0, 0, 0, 1, 1, 0) = \vartheta^7$	$y_1 = (0, 0, 1, 1, 0, 0) = \vartheta^8$	$y_1 = (0, 0, 1, 0, 1, 0) = \vartheta^{13}$
$x = (0, 0, 1, 1, 0, 0) = \vartheta^8$	$y_1 = (0, 0, 0, 0, 1, 1) = \vartheta^6$	$y_2 = (0, 0, 1, 1, 1, 1) = \vartheta^{18}$
$x = (0, 1, 1, 0, 0, 0) = \vartheta^9$	$y_1 = (1, 0, 0, 1, 0, 1) = \vartheta^{31}$	$y_2 = (1, 1, 1, 1, 0, 1) = \vartheta^{59}$
$x = (0, 0, 0, 1, 0, 1) = \vartheta^{12}$	$y_1 = (1, 0, 0, 0, 0, 0) = \vartheta^5$	$y_2 = (1, 0, 0, 1, 0, 1) = \vartheta^{31}$
$x = (0, 0, 1, 0, 1, 0) = \vartheta^{13}$	$y_1 = (1, 1, 0, 1, 1, 1) = \vartheta^{43}$	$y_2 = (1, 1, 1, 1, 0, 1) = \vartheta^{59}$
$x = (0, 1, 0, 1, 0, 0) = \vartheta^{14}$	$y_1 = (0, 1, 0, 0, 1, 1) = \vartheta^{16}$	$y_2 = (0, 0, 0, 1, 1, 1) = \vartheta^{26}$
$x = (0, 1, 0, 0, 1, 1) = \vartheta^{16}$	$y_1 = (0, 0, 0, 1, 0, 1) = \vartheta^{12}$	$y_2 = (0, 1, 0, 1, 1, 0) = \vartheta^{36}$
$x = (0, 0, 1, 1, 1, 1) = \vartheta^{18}$	$y_1 = (1, 0, 1, 1, 1, 0) = \vartheta^{55}$	$y_2 = (1, 0, 0, 0, 0, 1) = \vartheta^{62}$
$x = (0, 1, 1, 1, 1, 0) = \vartheta^{19}$	$y_1 = (1, 1, 1, 1, 1, 1) = \vartheta^{58}$	$y_2 = (1, 0, 0, 0, 0, 1) = \vartheta^{62}$
$x = (0, 1, 0, 0, 0, 1) = \vartheta^{24}$	$y_1 = (1, 1, 0, 0, 0, 0) = \vartheta^{10}$	$y_2 = (1, 0, 0, 0, 0, 1) = \vartheta^{62}$
$x = (0, 0, 0, 1, 1, 1) = \vartheta^{26}$	$y_1 = (1, 0, 1, 0, 0, 1) = \vartheta^{23}$	$y_2 = (1, 0, 1, 1, 1, 0) = \vartheta^{55}$
$x = (0, 0, 1, 1, 1, 0) = \vartheta^{27}$	$y_1 = (0, 0, 0, 0, 0, 1) = \vartheta^0$	$y_2 = (0, 0, 1, 1, 1, 1) = \vartheta^{18}$
$x = (0, 1, 1, 1, 0, 0) = \vartheta^{28}$	$y_1 = (0, 0, 1, 0, 0, 1) = \vartheta^{32}$	$y_2 = (0, 1, 0, 1, 0, 1) = \vartheta^{52}$
$x = (0, 0, 1, 0, 0, 1) = \vartheta^{32}$	$y_1 = (0, 1, 1, 0, 0, 0) = \vartheta^9$	$y_2 = (0, 1, 0, 0, 0, 1) = \vartheta^{24}$
$x = (0, 1, 0, 0, 1, 0) = \vartheta^{33}$	$y_1 = (1, 0, 1, 1, 1, 1) = \vartheta^{40}$	$y_2 = (1, 1, 1, 1, 0, 1) = \vartheta^{59}$
$x = (0, 0, 1, 0, 1, 1) = \vartheta^{35}$	$y_1 = (0, 1, 0, 0, 0, 0) = \vartheta^4$	$y_2 = (0, 1, 1, 0, 1, 1) = \vartheta^{38}$
$x = (0, 1, 0, 1, 1, 0) = \vartheta^{36}$	$y_1 = (1, 0, 0, 1, 1, 1) = \vartheta^{47}$	$y_2 = (1, 1, 0, 0, 0, 1) = \vartheta^{61}$
$x = (0, 1, 1, 0, 1, 1) = \vartheta^{38}$	$y_1 = (1, 0, 1, 0, 1, 0) = \vartheta^{53}$	$y_2 = (1, 1, 0, 0, 0, 1) = \vartheta^{61}$
$x = (0, 1, 1, 1, 0, 1) = \vartheta^{41}$	$y_1 = (1, 1, 1, 0, 0, 0) = \vartheta^{29}$	$y_2 = (1, 0, 0, 1, 0, 1) = \vartheta^{31}$
$x = (0, 1, 1, 0, 0, 1) = \vartheta^{45}$	$y_1 = (0, 0, 0, 0, 0, 1) = \vartheta^0$	$y_2 = (0, 1, 1, 0, 0, 0) = \vartheta^9$
$x = (0, 0, 1, 1, 0, 1) = \vartheta^{48}$	$y_1 = (1, 1, 1, 1, 0, 0) = \vartheta^{20}$	$y_2 = (1, 1, 0, 0, 0, 1) = \vartheta^{61}$
$x = (0, 1, 1, 0, 1, 0) = \vartheta^{49}$	$y_1 = x(0, 0, 0, 1, 0, 0) = \vartheta^2$	$y_2 = (0, 1, 1, 1, 1, 0) = \vartheta^{19}$
$x = (0, 1, 0, 1, 0, 1) = \vartheta^{52}$	$y_1 = (1, 1, 0, 0, 1, 0) = \vartheta^{46}$	$y_2 = (1, 0, 0, 1, 1, 1) = \vartheta^{47}$
$x = (0, 1, 0, 1, 1, 1) = \vartheta^{54}$	$y_1 = (0, 0, 0, 0, 0, 1) = \vartheta^0$	$y_2 = (0, 1, 0, 1, 1, 0) = \vartheta^{36}$
$x = (0, 1, 1, 1, 1, 1) = \vartheta^{56}$	$y_1 = (0, 0, 0, 0, 1, 0) = \vartheta^1$	$y_2 = (0, 1, 1, 1, 0, 1) = \vartheta^{41}$

where

$$N(x) = \begin{pmatrix} x_3 + x_0 + 1 & x_1 + x_0 & x_2 + x_1 & x_2 \\ x_2 & x_3 + x_0 & x_1 + x_0 + 1 & x_1 + 1 \\ x_1 & x_2 + 1 & x_3 + x_0 & x_0 \\ x_0 & x_1 & x_2 & x_3 + 1 \end{pmatrix}.$$

As

$$(0, 0, 0, 0) = (y_0 + x_0, y_1 + x_1, y_2 + x_2, y_3 + x_3) N(x),$$

$N(x)$ is singular, consistent with Proposition **15.7**.

Suppose $P = (x_1, y_1)$ and $Q = (x_2, y_2)$ are the points of intersection of the straight line

$$\underline{PQ} : y = \lambda x + \mu$$

and the elliptic curve

$$y_1^2 + x_1 y_1 = x_1^3 + ax_1^2 + b$$
$$y_2^2 + x_2 y_2 = x_2^3 + ax_2^2 + b.$$

Substituting $y = \lambda x + \mu$ into $y^2 + xy = x^3 + ax^2 + b$ gives the relation

$$0 = x^3 - x^2(\lambda^2 + \lambda + a) + x\mu + (b - \mu^2).$$

If $(x_3 - y_3)$ is the third root of the cubic above,

$$0 = (x - x_1)(x - x_2)(x - x_3),$$

then by identifying coefficients of powers of x,

$$\lambda^2 + \lambda = x_1 + x_2 + x_3 + a.$$

When $x_1 + x_2 \neq 0$

$$\lambda = \frac{y_2 + y_1}{x_2 + x_1},$$

which gives

$$x_3 = \lambda^2 + \lambda + x_1 + x_2 + a$$

and

$$y_3 = \lambda(x_1 + x_3) + x_3 + y_1.$$

Example 15.6 (continued)
Computation of $(x_3, y_3) = (x_1, y_1) + (x_2, y_2)$.

$x_1 = (0, 1, 0, 0, 0, 0) = \vartheta^4$	$x_2 = (0, 0, 1, 1, 0, 0) = \vartheta^8$	$x_1 + x_2 = (0, 1, 1, 1, 0, 0) = \vartheta^{28}$
$y_1 = (0, 0, 1, 0, 0, 0) = \vartheta^3$	$y_2 = (0, 0, 0, 0, 1, 1) = \vartheta^6$	$y_1 + y_2 = (0, 0, 1, 0, 1, 1) = \vartheta^{35}$
$\lambda = (0, 0, 0, 1, 1, 0) = \vartheta^7$	$x_3 = (0, 0, 1, 1, 1, 0) = \vartheta^{27}$	$y_3 = (0, 0, 0, 0, 0, 1) = \vartheta^0$

15.7 SUPERSINGULAR ELLIPTIC CURVES

The strength that cryptographic systems derive from elliptic curves depends on the difficulty of solving the elliptic curve discrete logarithm problem (ECDLP) and factorization in an elliptic curve: *given* $x = pq$, *find* p *and* q. It is believed that factorization algorithms have exponential execution times.

Are there bad elliptic curves? More precisely, are there some elliptic curves in which the factorization problem is not as hard?

If the order q of $\mathcal{E}_p(a, b)$ were p or a divisor of $p^m - 1$ for some m, then bad news. Menezes et al. [1991] give a subexponential algorithm for the supersingular elliptic curves.

The National Institute of Standards [NIST, 2000, NIST186-2] has given its *Good Crypto* seal of approval to several elliptic groups; in each example, the coordinates (G_x, G_y) of the *base point P* and its order r are given. One of these groups, designated by NIST as P192, is based on the 192-bit prime $p = 2^{192} - 2^{64} + 1$.

$$p = 6277101735386680763835789423207666416083908700390324961279$$

Say you are not satisfied – well, then try P521:

$$p = 6864797660130609714981900799081393217269435300143305409394463459185543183397656052122559640661454554977296311391480858037121987999716643812574028291115057151$$

There are elliptic curves over binary fields; for example

- K163 is generated by the polynomial $p(x) = 1 + x^3 + x^6 + x^7 + x^{163}$, and
- K571 is generated by the polynomial $p(x) = 1 + x^2 + x^5 + x^{10} + x^{571}$.

All text stored in and transmitted between computer systems are strings of 0's and 1's. When elliptic cryptosystems are used, plaintext must be coded into points of the curve $\mathcal{E}_F$ where F is the underlying field. If F is identified with $\mathcal{Z}_{m,2}$ generated by $p(x)$, the translation is easy. If F is identified with $\mathcal{Z}_{m,p}$ with $p \neq 2$, the natural coding

$$\underline{x} = (x_0, x_1, \ldots, x_{n-1}) \to x \equiv \sum_{i=0}^{n-1} x_i 2^{n-i-i}$$

may not map x into a point on the curve of $\mathcal{E}_F$ and some rule has to be specified.

15.8 DIFFIE–HELLMAN KEY EXCHANGE USING AN ELLIPTIC CURVE

The idea of using elliptic curves for cryptosystems is due to Neal Koblitz [1987b] and Victor Miller [1986]. We begin, however, as did the public-key publications, with key exchange. Following tradition, *Alice* or *Bob* want to securely exchange a key.

0. *Alice* or *Bob* choose a point x on an elliptic curve $\mathcal{E}_p(a, b)$ with a very large $p > 3$ and transmit the value of x to the other party.

1. *Alice* and *Bob* each randomly choose integers a and b.

2a. *Alice* computes ax and transmits it to *Bob*.

2b. *Bob* computes bx and transmits it to *Alice*.

3a. *Alice* computes abx.

3b. *Bob* computes bax.

x, ax, and bx are transmitted in the clear; a and b are secret. The secrecy of the Diffie–Hellman elliptic curve key exchange is the complexity of elliptic curve "integer" factorization.

The elliptic curve DH has been blessed by NSA [NIST, 2005, 800-56].

15.9 THE MENEZES–VANSTONE ELLIPTIC CURVE CRYPTOSYSTEM

The system we describe appears in Menezes and Vanstone [1993]. Let $p > 3$ be a prime and $\mathcal{E}_p(a, b)$ the elliptic group generated by $y^2 = x^3 + ax + b$. The Menezes–Vanstone (public-key) elliptic curve cryptosystem is a variant of El Gamal's encipherment system to be described in Chapter 17. Its keys are

Private Key: $K_P \in \mathcal{Z}_p$
Public Keys: $K_1, K_2 \in \mathcal{E}_p(a, b)$, $K_2 = K_P K_1 \in \mathcal{E}_p(a, b)$.

The encipherment and decipherment processes are

Encipherment – Plaintext: $x_1, x_2 \in \mathcal{Z}_p^*$.

1. Choose a secret (session key) $k_S \in \mathcal{Z}_p$.
2. Compute $y_0 = k_S K_1 \in \mathcal{E}_p(a, b)$.
3. Compute $(z_1, z_2) = k_S K_2 \in \mathcal{E}_p(a, b)$.
4. Compute $y_1 = z_1 x_1 \pmod{p} \in \mathcal{Z}_p^*$.
5. Compute $y_2 = z_2 x_2 \pmod{p} \in \mathcal{Z}_p^*$.

Ciphertext: (y_0, y_1, y_2); $y_0 \in \mathcal{E}_p(a, b)$, $y_1, y_2 \in \mathcal{Z}_p^*$.

Decipherment – Ciphertext: (y_0, y_1, y_2); $y_0 \in \mathcal{E}_p(a, b)$, $y_1, y_2 \in \mathcal{Z}_p^*$

1. Compute $K_P y_0 = K_P k_S K_1 = k_S K_P K_1 = k_S K_2 = (z_1, z_2) \in \mathcal{E}_p(a, b)$.
2. Compute $x_1 = z_1^{-1} y_1 \pmod{p} \in \mathcal{Z}_p^*$.
3. Compute $x_2 = z_2^{-1} y_2 \pmod{p} \in \mathcal{Z}_p^*$.

Plaintext: $x_1, x_2 \in \mathcal{Z}_p^*$.

Example 15.7
$p = 23$, $a = b = 1$.
  Private Key: $K_P = 8 \in \mathcal{Z}_{23}$
  Public Keys: $K_1 = (3, 13)$, $K_2 = (13, 7) \in \mathcal{E}_{23}(1, 1)$
      $K_2 = K_P K_1 = 8(3, 13) = (13, 7) \in \mathcal{E}_{23}(1, 1)$.

Encipherment – Plaintext: $(x_1, x_2) = (3, 5) \in \mathcal{Z}_{23}^*$.

1. Choose the secret (session key) $k_S = 5 \in \mathcal{Z}_{23}$.
2. Compute $y_0 = k_S K_1 = 5(3, 13) = (9, 7) \in \mathcal{E}_{23}(1, 1)$.
3. Compute $(z_1, z_2) = k_S K_2 = 5(13, 7) = (9.7) \in \mathcal{E}_{23}(1, 1)$.
4. Compute $y_1 = z_1 x_1 \pmod{23} = 5 \times 3 = 15 \in \mathcal{Z}_{23}^*$.
5. Compute $y_2 = z_2 x_2 \pmod{23} = 19 \times 5 \pmod{23} = 3 \in \mathcal{Z}_{23}^*$.

Ciphertext: (y_0, y_1, y_2); $y_0 = (9, 7) \in \mathcal{E}_{23}(1, 1)$, $y_1 = 15$, $y_2 = 3$

Decipherment – Ciphertext: (y_0, y_1, y_2); $y_0 = (9, 7) \in \mathcal{E}_{23}(1, 1)$, $(y_1, y_2) = (15, 3) \in \mathcal{Z}_{23}^*$.

1. Compute $K_P y_0 = 8(9, 7) = (5, 19) = K_P k_S K_1 = k_S K_P K_1 = k_S K_2 = (z_1, z_2) \in \mathcal{E}_{23}(1, 1)$.

2. Compute $x_1 = z_1^{-1} y_1$ (modulo 23) $= 5^{-1} \times 15$ (modulo 23) $= 14 \times 15$ (modulo 23) $= 3 \in \mathcal{Z}_{23}^*$.

3. Compute $x_2 = z_2^{-1} y_2$ (modulo 23) $= 19^{-1} \times 3$ (modulo 23) $= 17 \times 3$ (modulo 23) $= 5 \in \mathcal{Z}_{23}^*$.

Plaintext $(x_1, x_2) = (3, 5) \in \mathcal{Z}_{23}^*$.

The papers by Okamoto et al. [1999] and Okamoto and Pointcheval [2000] also devise an El-Gamal-like elliptic curve encipherment. The proposed *Elliptic Curve Integrated Encryption Standard* (ECIEC) [Shoup, 2001], is designed to protect against chosen plain- and ciphertext attacks.

15.10 THE ELLIPTIC CURVE DIGITAL SIGNATURE ALGORITHM

The digital signature algorithm ported to elliptic curve cryptosystems is standardized by ANSI [ECDSA, 2005] and the NIST Federal Information Processing Standard 186–2. When *Alice* wants to sign a message m for *Bob*, she chooses a finite field F, an elliptic group $\mathcal{E}_F$ and a base point P of order n. *Alice*'s keys are

- Public key PuK(ID[*Alice*]) $\in \mathcal{E}_F$;
- Private key PrK(ID[*Alice*]), an integer.

15.10.1 Signing the Message *m*

S1. *Alice* chooses a random number k satisfying $1 \le k \le n - 1$;

S2. *Alice* computes $kP = (x_1, y_1)$ and $r = x_1$ (modulo n); If $r = 0$, a bad choice for k was made and *Alice* returns again to Step 1.

S3. *Alice* computes k^{-1}; (modulo n);

S4. If *Alice* uses NIST's SHA-1 and computes SHA[m];

S5. *Alice* computes $s = k^{-1}(\text{SHA}[m] + \text{PrK}(\text{ID}[Alice]r)$ (modulo n); If $s = 0$, another bad choice and *Alice* returns again to Step 1.

Well, we made it! *Alice*'s signature for m is the pair (r, s).

15.10.2 Verifying the Message *m* (*r, s*)

V1. *Bob* verifies that the integers (r, s) satisfy $1 \le r \le n - 1$ and $1 \le s \le n - 1$;

V2. *Bob* uses NIST's SHA-1 and computes SHA[m];

V3. *Bob* computes $w = s^{-1}$ (modulo n);

V4. *Bob* computes $u_1 = \text{SHA}[m]w$ (modulo n) and $u_2 = rw$ (modulo n);

V5. *Bob* computes $x = u_1 P + u_2 \text{PuK}(\text{ID}[Alice])$;

V6a. If $x = \mathcal{O}$ (the identity element of the elliptic group $\mathcal{E}_F$), then the signature is rejected.

V6b. If $x \ne \mathcal{O}$, then *Bob* computes $v = x_1$ (modulo n) where $x = (x_1, y_1)$.

TABLE 15.5 NSA's Key-Length Comparison for Symmetric-Key, RSA and Elliptic Curve Cryptosystems

Key size (in bits)			
Symmetric	RSA	Elliptic	E-Ratio
80	1024	160	3:1
112	2048	224	6:1
128	3072	256	10:1
192	7680	384	32:1
256	15360	521	64:1

Bob accepts (r, s) as the signature of m if and only if $v = r$.

15.11 THE CERTICOM CHALLENGE

The Certicom Corporation markets software products based on Elliptic Curve Cryptography (ECC). According to their Web site www.certicom.com, the Certicom Intellectual Property portfolio includes over 350 patents and patents pending worldwide, covering many key aspects of ECC, including software optimizations, efficient hardware implementations, methods to enhance security, and various cryptographic protocols.

Certicom introduced the ECC challenge in November 1997. The ECC Challenge was introduced "to increase industry understanding and appreciation for the difficulty of the elliptic curve discrete logarithm problem, and to encourage and stimulate further research in the security analysis of elliptic curve cryptosystems."

The challenge is to compute the ECC private keys from the given list of ECC public keys and associated system parameters. There are two levels:

- Level 1: 109-bit and 131-bit challenges;
- Level 2: 163-bit, 191-bit, 239-bit, and 359-bit challenges.

Details can be found on their Web site.

15.12 NSA AND ELLIPTIC CURVE CRYPTOGRAPHY

In their review "The Case for Elliptic Curve Cryptography" (www.nsa.gov/ia/industry/crypto_elliptic_curve.cfm) several points are made by the NSA:

- Elliptic curve cryptosystems seem to offer a considerable efficiency with respect to key size.

In Table 15.5

- The first three columns contain a comparison of NIST-recommended key sizes for symmetric, RSA, and elliptic curve cryptosystems;
- The last column gives the ratio of computational efficiency of RSA to elliptic curve cryptography.

The article also points out that intellectual property rights are a major roadblock to the further adoption of elliptic curve cryptography, citing Certicom, which holds over 130 patents in this area. See my quotations at the start of Chapter 19.

REFERENCES

Accredited Standards Committee X9, American National Standard X9.62-2005, "Public Key Cryptography for the Financial Services Industry, The Elliptic Curve Digital Signature Algorithm (ECDSA)," November 16, 2005.

D. HUSEMOLLER, *Elliptic Curves*, Springer-Verlag, New York, NY, 1986.

N. KOBLITZ, *A Course in Number Theory and Cryptography*, Springer-Verlag, New York, NY, 1987a.

N. KOBLITZ, "Elliptic Curve Cryptosystems," *Mathematics of Computation*, **48**, 203–209 (1987).

H. W. LENSTRA JR, "Factoring Integers with Elliptic Curves," Report 86-16, Mathematisch Institut, Universiteit van Amsterdam, 1986.

A. I. MARKUSHEVICH, *Theory of Functions of a Complex Variables*, Prentice-Hall, Upper Saddle River, New Jersey, 1965.

A. J. MENEZES AND S. A. VANSTONE, "Elliptic Curve Cryptosystems and Their Implementation," *Journal of Cryptology*, **6**, 209–224 (1993).

V. MILLER, "Use of Elliptic Curves in Cryptography," *Advances in Cryptology: Proceedings of CRYPTO'85*, Lecture Notes in Computer Science #218, Springer-Verlag, New York, NY, 1986, pp. 417–426.

A. MENEZES, T. OKAMOTO, AND S. VANSTONE, "Reducing Elliptic Curve Logarithms to Logarithms in a Finite Field," *Proceedings of the 23rd Annual ACM Symposium of Theory of Computing*, Chicago, Illinois, 1991, pp. 80–91.

NIST, Federal Information Processing Standard 186-2, "Digital Signature Standard (DSS)," January 27, 2000.

NIST, Draft Special Publication 800-56, "Recommendation for Pair-Wise Key Establishment Schemes Using Discrete Logarithm Cryptography," July 18, 2005.

T. OKAMOTO, E. FUJISAKI, AND H. MORITA, "PSEC: Provably Secure Elliptic Curve Encryption Scheme," Presented at *IEEE P1363 Meeting on Asymmetric Encryption*, Chicago, Illinois, March 1999.

T. OKAMOTO AND D. POINTCHEVAL, "PSEC-3: Provably Secure Elliptic Curve Encryption Scheme (Version 2)" Submitted to *IEEE P1363 Meeting on Asymmetric Encryption*, Bruges, Belgium, May 23, 2000.

SCHROEPPEL, H. ORMAN, S. O'MALLEY, AND O. SPATSCHECK, "Fast Key Exchange with Elliptic Curve Systems," *Advances in Cryptology, CRYPTO '95*, Springer Lecture Notes in Computer Science #963 New York, NY, 1995.

V. SHOUP, "A Proposal for an ISO Standard for Public Key Encryption," Version 2.1, December 20, International Organization for Standardization, 2001.

KEY EXCHANGE IN A NETWORK

A COMPLICATED mechanism using a hierarchy of keys was provided to exchange a shared key when users in a public data network wanted to encipher their communications using a symmetric-key cryptographic system. Diffie and Hellman invented public-key cryptography to provide a simpler method for key exchange in public data networks. Both methodologies are examined in this chapter.

16.1 KEY DISTRIBUTION IN A NETWORK

Three different schemes have been invented to implement the distribution of keys in an open network (Fig. 16.1):

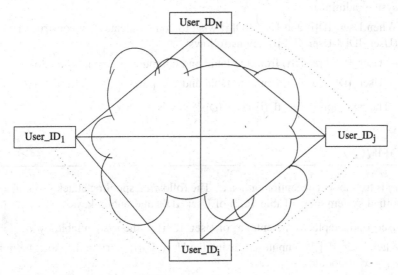

Figure 16.1 Users connected in a network.

- User_ID$_i$ and User_ID$_j$ establish *in advance* a shared key $k_{i,j}$ by some unspecified means.
- A *key server* maintains a list of users keys and constructs a (User_ID$_i$, User_ID$_j$) session key, which is delivered to each user enciphered under the user's secret key.
- The network uses some public-key algorithm to exchange a *shared* key.

TABLE 16.1 The System's Diffie–Hellman Key Exchange Table

User_ID	User public key
$\vdots$	$\vdots$
ID[i]	x_i
$\vdots$	$\vdots$
User_ID[j]	x_j
$\vdots$	$\vdots$
User_ID[k]	x_k
$\vdots$	$\vdots$

16.2 U.S. PATENT '770 [HELLMAN ET AL., 1980; DIFFIE AND HELLMAN, 1976]

The *Diffie–Hellman* key-exchange scheme uses these rules:

DH1. User_ID[i] with identifier ID[i] chooses a secret key k_i and computes $x_i = q^{k_i}$ (modulo p). Table 16.1, containing the pairs (ID[i],x_i), is maintained by the system administrator.

DH2. When User_ID[i] and User_ID[j] wish to communicate they construct a common (User_ID[i]-User_ID[j]) key as follows:

– User_ID[i] reads x_j from the table and computes $x_{i,j} = x_j^{k_i}$ (modulo p).

– User_ID[j] reads x_i from the table and computes $x_{j,i} = x_j^{k_i}$ (modulo p).

The common (User_ID[i]-User-ID[j]) key is $x_{i,j} = x_{j,i}$.

16.3 SPOOFING

To *spoof* is to "cause a deception or hoax." The following spoofing attack is possible using the modified system table (Table 16.2) of User_ID's and public keys.

SP1. User_ID[k] replaces the entry x_i of User_ID[i] in the system table by x_k.

SP2. When User_ID[j] computes $x_{j,i}$ using the User_ID[i] entry in the table, there results $x_{j,k} = x_j^{k_k}$ (modulo p).

TABLE 16.2 User_ID[k] Modifies the System's Diffie–Hellman Key Exchange Table

User_ID	User public key
$\vdots$	$\vdots$
User_ID[i]	x_k
$\vdots$	$\vdots$
User_ID[j]	x_j
$\vdots$	$\vdots$
User_ID[k]	x_k
$\vdots$	$\vdots$

TABLE 16.3 The System's Diffie–Hellman Key Exchange Table with Linked Entries

User_ID	User public key	Link
$\vdots$	$\vdots$	$\vdots$
User_ID[i]	x_i	LINK$\langle$User_ID[i],$x_i\rangle$
User_ID[j]	x_j	LINK$\langle$User_ID[j],$x_j\rangle$
$\vdots$	$\vdots$	$\vdots$
User_ID[k]	x_k	LINK$\langle$User_ID[k],$x_k\rangle$
$\vdots$	$\vdots$	

SP3. User_ID[k] has been successful in masquerading as User_ID[i] because User_ID[j] is securely communicating with an imposter!

SP4. At the conclusion of the communication, User_ID$_k$ replaces User_ID$_i$ correct entry.

To prevent this spoofing attack, the table must either be write-protected or the entries User_ID[i] and x_i must be *linked* in a way that *any* user can detect an alteration in the table. *Public key certificates*, to be discussed in Chapter 18, attempt to do this; alternatively, the system table includes a LINK $\langle$User_ID[i],$x_i\rangle$ in the table, allowing the user to verify that the entries User_ID[i] and x_i are a proper pair (Table 16.3).

   User_ID$_j$ reads the entry

User_ID[i]	x_i	LINK$\langle$User_ID[i],$x_i\rangle$

and uses LINK $\langle$User_ID[i],$x_i\rangle$ to *authenticate* that x_i properly corresponds to User_ID[i], as depicted in Figure 16.2. LINK$\langle$User_IDi,$x_i\rangle$ is a function of User_ID$_i$ and x_i such that

- Any user may compute F(User_ID$_i$, x_i) *given* User_ID$_i$ and x_i;
- It is computational infeasible for *any* user to compute LINK$\langle$User_ID$_i$, $x_i\rangle$ *given* a (valid) User_ID$_i$ and a value x_i.

The paradigm of one-way functions?

16.3.1 Linked Table Implementation

Diffie–Hellman does not require a table. When User_ID$_i$ and User_ID$_j$ want to exchange a secret key, each generates a secret key k_i and computes $x_i = q^{k_i}$ (modulo p), which is

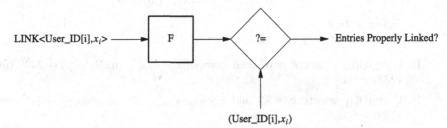

Figure 16.2 Using LINK$\langle$User_ID[i],$x_i\rangle$ to Authenticate (User_ID[i],x_i).

transmitted to User_ID$_j$. The same defect is present; User_ID$_i$ has no proof that x_i originated from the *real* User_ID$_i$.

The security of the Diffie–Hellman key exchange depends on the difficulty of solving the discrete logarithm problem (DLP):

> *Given*: x_i.
>
> *Find*: k_i.

16.4 EL GAMAL'S EXTENSION OF DIFFIE–HELLMAN

Although Diffie–Hellman realized how keys could be exchanged securely if the DLP was infeasible to solve, they did not discover how to modify their idea to encipher data.

The *Secure Electronic Exchange of Keys* (SEEK) is a product of the CYLINK Corporation. It is based on an extension of the Diffie–Hellman scheme discovered by T. El Gamal [1985]

16.4.1 SEEK Cryptosystem

Public Parameters: $p = 2r + 1$ and r primes; q a primitive root of p.

1i. User_ID[i] chooses a random key $k_i \in \mathcal{Z}_p^*$ and computes $x_i = q^{k_i}$ (modulo p).

1j. User_ID$_j$ chooses a random key $k_j \in \mathcal{Z}_p^*$ and computes $x_j = q^{k_i}$ (modulo p).

2. User_ID[i] and User_ID[j] exchange x_i and x_j.

3i. User_ID[i] computes $x_{i,j} = x_j^{k_i}$ (modulo p).

3j. User_ID[j] computes $x_{j,i} = x_i^{k_j}$ (modulo p).

4. $x_{i,j} = x_{i,j}$ is used to derive the common *session key*

$$e_{i,j} = \begin{cases} x_{i,j}, & \text{if } x_{i,j} \text{ is odd} \\ x_{i,j} - 1, & \text{if } x_{i,j} \text{ is even.} \end{cases}$$

5. Each user computes the multiplicative inverse $d_{i,j}$ modulo $p - 1$ of $e_{i,j}$

$$d_{i,j}\, e_{i,j} = 1 \ (\text{modulo } p - 1)$$

by evaluating $d_{i,j} = e_{i,j}^{\frac{p-1}{2} - 2}$ (modulo $p - 1$).

6. Encipherment and decipherment is applied to plaintext M and ciphertext C in $\mathcal{Z}_p$ according to the rules

$$\mathbf{E}: M \longrightarrow C = M^{e_{i,j}} \ (\text{modulo } p)$$

$$\mathbf{D}: C \longrightarrow M = C^{d_{i,j}} \ (\text{modulo } p).$$

Example 16.1
$p = 1283 = 2 \times 641 + 1, q = 24$.

1i. User_ID[i] selects $k_i = 67$ and computes $x_i = q^{k_i}$ (modulo p) $= 24^{67}$ (modulo 1283) $= 98$.

1j. User_ID[j] selects $k_j = 95$ and computes $x_j = q^{k_j}$ (modulo p) $= 24^{95}$ (modulo 1283) $= 933$.

2. User_ID[i] and User_ID[j] exchange x_i and x_j.

3i. User_ID[i] computes $x_{i,j} = x_j^{k_i}$ (modulo p) $= 933^{67}$ (modulo 1283) $= 135$.

3j. User_ID[j] computes $x_{j,i} = x_i^{k_j}$ (modulo p) $= 98^{95}$ (modulo 1283) $= 135$.

4. The common User_ID[i]-User_ID[j] *encipherment* key is $e_{i,j} = 135$.
The common User_ID[i]-User_ID[j] *decipherment* key is $d_{i,j} = 19$.

Proposition 16.1 (The Correctness of the SEEK Protocol):   There are two results to be proved. First, if $d_{i,j} e_{i,j} = 1$ (modulo $p - 1$), then

$$(M^{e_{i,j}} \text{ (modulo } p))^{d_{i,j}} \text{ (modulo } p) = M^{e_{i,j} d_{i,j}} \text{ (modulo } p) = M^{1 + A(p-1)} \text{ (modulo } p) = M,$$

the last equality by Fermat's Little Theorem. This proves the operations **E** and **D** are inverses of one another.

It remains to show that

$$d_{i,j} = e_{i,j}^{\frac{p-1}{2} - 2} \text{ (modulo } p - 1) \Rightarrow d_{i,j} e_{i,j} = 1 \text{ (modulo } p - 1).$$

The proof uses Fermat's Little Theorem:

$$z^{p-1} = 1 \text{ (modulo } p), \qquad z \in \mathcal{Z}_p^+$$

$$z^p = 1 \text{ (modulo } p), \qquad z \in \mathcal{Z}_p.$$

We need to show that if $z \in \mathcal{Z}_p$ is odd, then

$$z^{-1} = z^{\frac{p-1}{2} - 2} \text{ (modulo } p - 1)$$

or equivalently

$$z = z^{\frac{p-1}{2}} \text{ (modulo } p - 1).$$

But $p = 2r + 1$, so $p - 1 = 2r$, and hence

$$z - z^{\frac{p-1}{2}} = 0 \text{ (modulo 2)}$$

$$z - z^{\frac{p-2}{2}} = z - z^r = 0 \text{ (modulo } r).$$

Note that x_i and x_j are available by wiretapping. If the DLP can be solved, then k_i, k_j, and $e_{i,j}$ can be determined from the transmitted x_i and x_j. Furthermore, SEEK as described above suffers from the same defect as Diffie–Hellman; namely, the *identity* of the party claiming to be User_ID[i] needs to be validated by some other information. CYLINK proposed a *certification center* to provide the validation.

16.5   SHAMIR'S AUTONOMOUS KEY EXCHANGE

In unpublished work, Adi Shamir proposed a key exchange protocol that depends on the secure exchange of *no* secret information. The following steps exchange a key between User_ID[i] and User_ID[j]:

0. p is a (known) prime; k_i and k_j are the (secret) keys of User_ID[i] and User_ID[j]. It is assumed that $1 = \gcd\{k_i, p - 1\} = \gcd\{k_j, p - 1\}$ so that both k_i and k_j have multiplicative inverses modulo $p - 1$

$$1 = k_i k_i^{-1} \text{ (modulo } p - 1), \qquad 1 = k_j k_j^{-1} \text{ (modulo } p - 1).$$

By Fermat's Little Theorem

$$x = x^{k_i k_i^{-1}} \text{ (modulo } p), \qquad x = x^{k_j k_j^{-1}} \text{ (modulo } p).$$

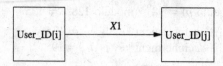

Figure 16.3 Step #1 in Shamir's autonomous key exchange.

1. User_ID[i] (the initiator) selects a session key $X0$ and performs the exponentiation

$$X1 = X0^{k_i} \text{ (modulo } p\text{)}.$$

$X1$ is transmitted to User_ID[j] (Fig. 16.3).

2. User_ID[j] performs the exponentiation

$$X2 = X1^{k_j} \text{ (modulo } p\text{)}.$$

$X2$ is transmitted to User_ID[i] (Fig. 16.4).

3. User_ID[i] performs the exponentiation

$$X3 = X2^{k_i^{-1}} \text{ (modulo } p\text{)}.$$

$X3$ is transmitted to User_ID[j] (Fig. 16.5).

4. User_ID[j] performs the exponentiation

$$X4 = X3^{k_j^{-1}} \text{ (modulo } p\text{)}.$$

Proposition 16.2: $X_4 = X0$.

Proof:

$$X1 = X0^{k_i} \text{ (modulo } p\text{)}$$

$$X2 = X1^{k_i} \text{ (modulo } p\text{)} = X_0^{k_i k_j} \text{ (modulo } p\text{)}$$

$$X3 = X2^{k_i^{-1}} \text{ (modulo } p\text{)} = X_0^{k_i k_j k_i^{-1}} \text{ (modulo } p\text{)} = X_0^{k_j} \text{ (modulo } p\text{)}$$

$$X4 = X3^{k_j^{-1}} \text{ (modulo } p\text{)} = X_0.$$

Example 16.2

Public Parameter: $p = 2543$

Private Parameters: User_ID[i] $k_i = 789, k_i^{-1} = 857$

User_ID[i] $k_j = 715, k_j^{-1} = 1287.$

Step #1

User_ID[i] chooses session key $X0 = 101$;

User_ID[i] computes $X1 = X0^{k_i} = 1163$ (modulo p);

User_ID[i] transmits $X1 = 1163$ to User_ID$_j$.

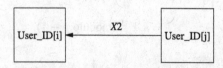

Figure 16.4 Step #2 in Shamir's autonomous key exchange.

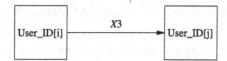

Figure 16.5   Step #3 in Shamir's autonomous key exchange.

Step #2

User_ID[j] computes $X2 = X1^{k_j}$ (modulo p) $= X0^{k_i k_j}$ (modulo p) $= 2447$;

User_ID[j] transmits $X2 = 2447$ to User_ID[i].

Step #3

User_ID[i] computes $X3 = X2^{k_i^{-1}}$ (modulo p) $= X0^{k_i k_j k_i^{-1}}$ (modulo p) $= X0^{k_j}$ (modulo p) $= 515$;

User_ID[i] transmits $X3 = 515$ to User_ID[j].

Step #4

User_ID[j] computes $X4 = X3^{k_j^{-1}}$ (modulo p) $= X0^{k_i k_j k_i^{-1} k_j^{-1}}$ (modulo p) $= 101$; $X4 = 101 = X0$.

What has been achieved?   Let us suppose that the size of the prime p is sufficiently large and that $p - 1$ has large enough prime factors so that any attempt to solve any of the discrete logarithm problems is beyond our enemy's resources. Shamir's protocol exchanges a key without the prior sharing of any *secret* information! Has true cryptographic happiness been achieved?

Look at the exchange Steps 1–4 from User_ID[j]'s perspective; a user on the network contacts User_ID[j] claiming to be User_ID[i]. The two parties agree to exchange information using the protocol outlined above. But who is User_ID[j] communicating with? Perhaps, the *real* User_ID[i] or perhaps, some sinister individual is pretending to be User_ID[i]. Perhaps, a politician ... or even worse, a dean! Can User_ID[j] detect this? For the protocol described above, the answer is no. What is lacking? In order for User_ID[j] to be certain that the party with whom he/she is communicating is User_ID[i], some incontrovertible proof must be offered by User_ID[i], evidence that only the true User_ID[i] can have. The problem is familiar and takes place whenever we identify ourselves with a driver's license or passport (neither of which are really 'proof'). These issues will be examined in more detail in Chapter 17.

16.6   X9.17 KEY EXCHANGE ARCHITECTURE [ANSI, 1985]

X9.17 is a standard of the American National Standards Institute describing the key handling recommendations for the financial industry. It proposes a hierarchy of keys:

- Nodes at the lowest two levels store *data key(s)* (KD) used to encipher transaction data;
- Nodes at all of the levels contain *key encrypting keys* (KK) used to transfer keys between adjacent layers.

X9.17 uses a symmetric key cryptosystem and the following general principle applies.

---

1. Whenever two nodes encipher data using a symmetric key cryptosystem, the key must be available at both nodes.
2. Whenever two nodes compute a message authentication code (MAC) using a symmetric key cryptosystem, the key must be available at both nodes.

Depicted in Figure 16.6 is a three-level hierarchy; in each level, keys are stored in a secure database identified by (NID_xy, key_xy) where #x and #y identify the node and level with which the key will be used.

- A *key distribution center* (CDK) is a facility that manages the distribution of data keys to the nodes. The *key translation center* (CTK) acts for the CDK and *generates* and distributes keys, enciphered under some key encrypting key, to the nodes.
- X9.17 uses the *data encryption algorithm* (DEA), also known as DES, to perform the encipherment of keys and data. The syntax is DEA_{key}{cleartext} where
    - key = KD, cleartext = data message, or
    - key = KK, cleartext = KD.

Triple DEA encipherment with syntax $DEA_{KKM\ell}\{DEA_{KKMr}^{-1}\{DEA_{KKM\ell}\{KK\}\}\}$ may be used to deliver the key KK from a node to an adjacent (lower) level node. The notation $KKM = KKM\ell\|KKMr$ denotes the concatenation ($\|$) of two 56-bit keys $KKM\ell$ and KKMr.

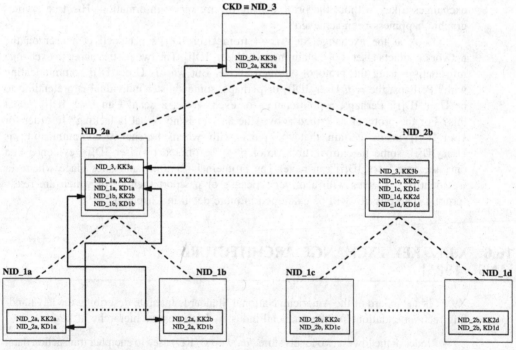

NID_xy : Node Identifier (level #x, identifier #y)

KKxy : Key encrypting key (node level #x, identifier #y)

KDxy : Data key (node level #x, identifier #y)

Figure 16.6 X9-17 key hierarchy.

The idea of using a hierarchy of keys is implicit in the Meyer and Matyas book [1982]. Hierarchy of keys was also implemented in IBM key management in the IBM product 3848 and in the first generation of IBM banking systems (2984) [IBM, 1977, 1985].

16.6.1 X9.17 Distribution of Keys

A key encrypting key is used to encipher a key for delivery (over a network) to an adjacent (lower) level node. They come in several flavors; at level ℓ (and at the adjacent (lower) level $\ell - 1$) resides a key encrypting key (KKℓ), which is placed there manually. A level-ℓ key encrypting key is used to deliver a data key (KD$\ell - 1$) generated by a level-ℓ node to the adjacent level-$\ell - 1$ node. Data keys are used to pass data between adjacent levels. Note that there may be KKs (level 3 → level 2) and many KKs (level 2 → level 1).

16.6.2 X9.17 Protocol Mechanisms

1. The lifetimes of keys are variable; a data key KD may be operational for only a *session* (when a controller in a store is initialized for the day). The key encrypting keys KK may be valid for a longer time period.

2. A *counter* is connected with the distribution of KKs; the counter is incremented whenever a new key encrypting key is distributed.

3. The message authentication code (MAC) is computed as shown in Figure 16.7 using DEA with *cipher block chaining* (CBC). The data in a message is written as the concatenation of k 64-bit blocks $X1\|X2\|\cdots\|Xk$. The final block of 64 bits is the *message authentication block* (MAB); the leftmost 32 bits is the MAC, although its length may be larger.

4. Various types of X9.17 messages are defined:

   – A *cryptographic service message* (CSM) is a message used to transport keys or information to control a keying relationship;

   – A *error service message* (ESM) is a message that reports an error in a previous CSM;

   – An *error recovery service message* (ERS) is a message used to recover from counter or other errors;

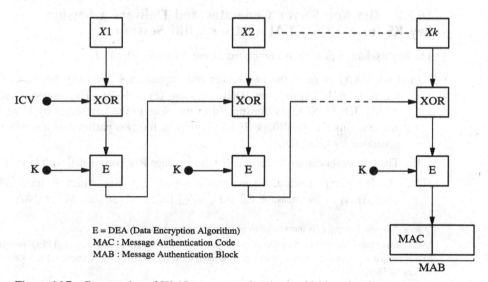

E = DEA (Data Encryption Algorithm)
MAC : Message Authentication Code
MAB : Message Authentication Block

Figure 16.7 Computation of X9.17 message authentication block and code.

– A *request service initiation message* (REI) is a message to request a new keying relationship to be established.

5. If it is desired to detect transmission errors (i.e., when other means, for example, CRC-codes, are not available), the MAC-computation as in (3) above may be used with *fixed* key `0123456789ABCDEF` (in hexadecimal). Error detection is used for ERS, ESM, and RSI messages.

16.7 THE NEEDHAM–SCHROEDER KEY DISTRIBUTION PROTOCOL [NEEDHAM AND SCHROEDER, 1998]

This paper describes a protocol for a *key server* to generate and deliver a *session key* to the pair of users User_ID[A] and User_ID[B]. Two user-authentication issues arise when a common session key is used in a session User_ID[A] $\leftrightarrow$ User_ID[B].

A1. Is User_ID[A] really communicating with User_ID[B]?

A2. Is User_ID$_B$ really communicating with User_ID[A]?

This paper considers two protocols: the first for users enciphering with a symmetric key cryptosystem, the second for users enciphering with a public key cryptosystem (PKC).

16.7.1 Needham–Schroeder Using a Symmetric Key Cryptosystem

The key server is assumed to securely store

- The (secret) key K(ID[A]) of User_ID[A] with identifier ID[A], and
- The (secret) key K(ID[B]) of User_ID[B] with identifier ID[B].

It is assumed that

- *Only* the key server and a user have knowledge of the user's secret key, and
- It is *not* feasible to decipher messages *without* the key.

16.7.2 The Key Server Generates and Delivers a Session Key KS for a User_ID[A] $\leftrightarrow$ User_ID[B] Session

The key exchange process is composed of the following steps:

1a. User_ID[A] contacts the key server and requests a session key KS be generated for a User_ID[A] $\leftrightarrow$ User_ID[B] session (Fig. 16.8). The message REQ = (ID[A], ID[B], N$\langle$A$\rangle$) is transmitted *in the clear* to the key server by User_ID[A] and contains the identifiers (ID[A],ID[B]) of the two parties and a *nonce*[1] N$\langle$A$\rangle$ generated by User_ID[A].

1b. The key server can*not* be certain that the message REQ originated with User_ID[A].[2]

2a. The key server randomly generates a session key KS, which is transmitted to User_ID[A] in the message C2 = $E_{K(ID[A])}${M2}, whose data M2 = (N$\langle$A$\rangle$, ID[B],

---

[1]*Nonce*, for used *only once*, is introduced as part of the authentication process.

[2]An improved Needham–Schroeder protocol modified the request message to (REQ, $E_{K(ID[A])}${REQ}) and included a time-stamp in addition to the nonce. In this case, the request message could only be constructed with knowledge of the key K(ID[A]).

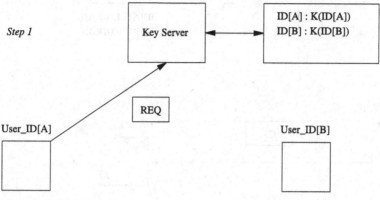

Step 1

REQ = ID[A], ID[B], N<A>

Figure 16.8 Step #1 in the symmetric key Needham–Schroeder protocol.

KS, Auth) is enciphered with User_ID[A]'s key K(ID[A]) (Fig. 16.9). Included within the data M2 is Auth $= E_{K(ID[B])}\{KS, ID[A]\}$, which will be used by User_ID[A] for user-authentication to User_ID[B]. User_ID[A] *cannot* decipher, modify, or construct a valid Auth since K(ID[B]) is secret.

2b. Possession of K[ID[A]] allows User_ID[A] to decipher C2 and recover the data M2, in particular to obtain the session key and the enciphered authentication Auth $= E_{K([ID[B]])}\{KS, ID[A]\}$, which *cannot* be deciphered.

3a. User_ID[A] delivers the session key KS to User_ID[B] in the message Auth $= E_{K(RD[B])}\{KS, ID[A]\}$.

3b. Possession of K[ID[B]] allows User_ID[B] to decipher Auth $= E_{K[ID\_B]}\{KS, ID[A]\}$, in particular to obtain the session key and the identifier ID[A] of the purported sender of C3.

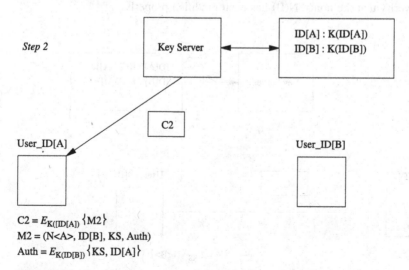

Step 2

C2 $= E_{K([ID[A]])}\{M2\}$
M2 = (N<A>, ID[B], KS, Auth)
Auth $= E_{K(ID[B])}\{KS, ID[A]\}$

Figure 16.9 Step #2 in the symmetric key Needham–Schroeder protocol.

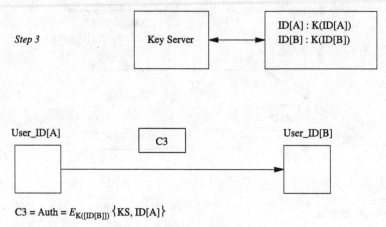

C3 = Auth = $E_{K([ID[B]])}$ {KS, ID[A]}

Figure 16.10 Step #3 in the Needham–Schroeder protocol.

4a. Although the integrity of Auth is assured, the identity of the sender is not; for example, Auth might have been transmitted previously *in the clear* by User_ID[A], recorded by User_ID[?] and *now* replayed to User_ID[B].

4b. It remains for User_ID[B] to authenticate that User_ID[A] was the source of the message C3 containing Auth.

4c. User_ID[B] generates a second nonce $N\langle B \rangle$ and transmits the message C4 = $E_{KS}\{N\langle B \rangle\}$ to User_ID[A] (Fig. 16.11).

5a. Possession of the session key KS allows User_ID[A] to decipher the message C4 and recover the User_ID[B]-generated nonce $N\langle B \rangle$.

5b. User_ID[A] modifies the nonce $N\langle B \rangle$ in some standard manner; for example $N\langle B \rangle \rightarrow N^{*}\langle B \rangle = N\langle B \rangle + 1$.

5c. User_ID[A] transmits the message C5 = $E_{KS}\{N^{*}\langle B \rangle\}$ to User_ID[B] (Fig. 16.12).

6. User_ID[B] completes authentication of the session establishment and key exchange; possession of the session key KS allows User_ID[B] to decipher the message C5 and verify that the nonce $N\langle B \rangle$ has been modified properly.

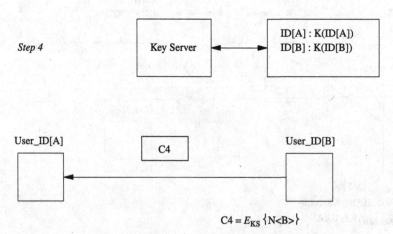

C4 = $E_{KS}\{N<B>\}$

Figure 16.11 Step #4 in the symmetric key Needham–Schroeder protocol.

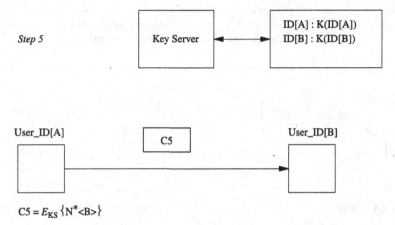

$$C5 = E_{KS}\{N^*<B>\}$$

Figure 16.12   Step #5 in the symmetric key Needham–Schroeder protocol.

16.7.3   Needham–Schroeder Using a Public-Key Cryptosystem

- PuK(ID[A]) and PrK(ID[A]) denote the public and private keys of User_ID[A],
- PuK(ID[B]) and PrK(ID[B]) denote the public and private keys of User_ID[B], and
- PuK(TD[KS]) and PrK(ID[KS]) denote the public and private keys of the key server.

It is assumed that

- The public keys of the key server are known, and
- Knowledge of the public key does not permit the determination of the private key or the decipherment of PuK-enciphered messages.

16.7.4   The Key Generates and Delivers a Session Key KS For a User_ID[A] ↔ User_ID[B] Session

The key exchange process is composed of the following steps:

1a. User_ID[A] contacts the key server and in the message REQ1 requests a session key KS be generated for a User_ID[A] ↔ User_ID[B] session (Fig. 16.13). REQ1 contains the identifiers (ID[A], ID[B]) of the two parties and is transmitted *in the clear* to the key server by User_ID[A].

2a. The key server responds by transmitting the message $C2 = E_{PrK(ID[K])}\{M2\}$ to User_ID[A] enciphered using the private key PrK(ID[KS]) of the key server (Fig. 16.14).

2b. The data M2 consists of the identifier ID[B] and the public key PuK(ID[B]) of User_ID[B].

3a. User_ID[A] generates a nonce N⟨A⟩, which together with the identifier ID[A] is transmitted to User_ID[B] in the message $C3 = E_{PuK(ID[B])}\{N\langle A\rangle, ID[A]\})\}$ enciphered using the public key PuK(ID[B]) of User_ID[B] (Fig. 16.15).

4a. The identity of the sender of C3 must be authenticated, a two-step process.

4b. User_ID_B signals the key server by transmitting the message *in the clear* REQ2 = (ID[B], ID[A]) to the key server (Fig. 16.16).

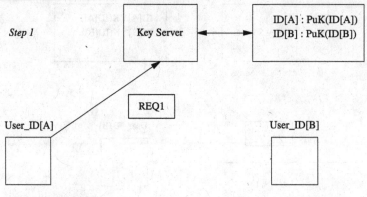

REQ1 = (ID[A], ID[B])

Figure 16.13 Step #1 in the public-key Needham–Schroeder protocol.

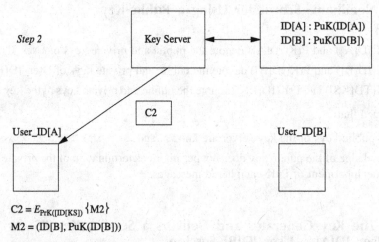

$C2 = E_{PrK((ID[KS]))}\{M2\}$

$M2 = (ID[B], PuK(ID[B]))$

Figure 16.14 Step #2 in the public-key Needham–Schroeder protocol.

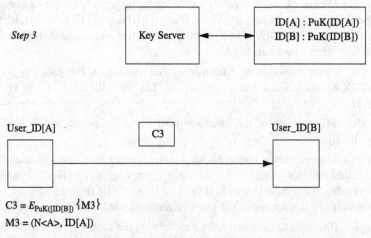

$C3 = E_{PuK((ID[B]))}\{M3\}$

$M3 = (N<A>, ID[A])$

Figure 16.15 Step #3 in the public-key Needham–Schroeder protocol.

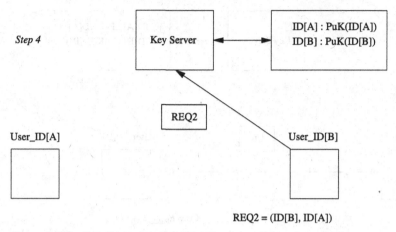

REQ2 = (ID[B], ID[A])

Figure 16.16 Step #4 in the public-key Needham–Schroeder protocol.

5a. The key server responds by transmitting the message $C5 = E_{PrK(ID[KS])}\{M5\}$ (Fig. 16.17).

5b. The data M5 consists of the identifier ID[A] and the public key PuK(ID[A]) of User_ID[A].

5c. Who could have constructed the message $C5 = E_{PrK(ID[KS])}\{M5\}$? Only a party with the secret key PrK[$\mathcal{K}$] of the key server.

At this point, the public keys of the users have been authenticated by messages from the key server. The identity of any communications between User_ID[A] and User_ID[B] must be authenticated, a process composed of two steps:

6a. User_ID[B] transmits the message $C6 = E_{PuK(ID[A])}\{M6\}$ to User_ID[A] enciphered in User_ID[A]'s public key PuK(ID[A]) (Fig. 16.18).

6b. The data M6 consists of a User_ID[B]-generated second nonce N⟨B⟩ along with the nonce N⟨A⟩ received from User_ID[A] in message M2.

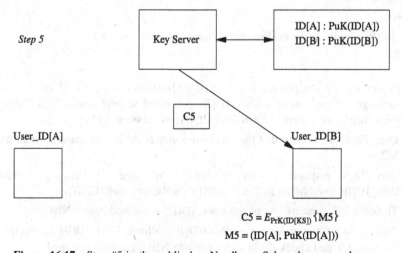

$C5 = E_{PrK(ID[KS])}\{M5\}$

M5 = (ID[A], PuK(ID[A]))

Figure 16.17 Step #5 in the public-key Needham–Schroeder protocol.

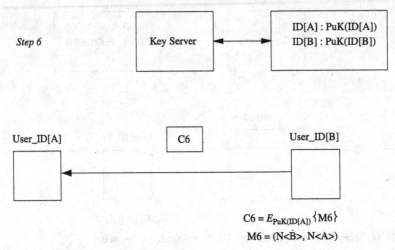

$C6 = E_{PuK(ID[A])}\{M6\}$

$M6 = (N\langle B \rangle, N\langle A \rangle)$

Figure 16.18 Step #6 in the public-key Needham–Schroeder protocol.

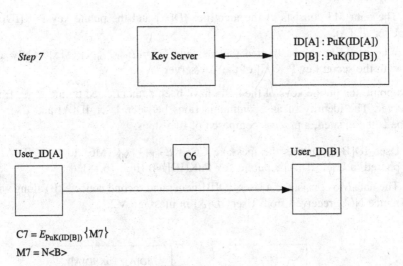

$C7 = E_{PuK(ID[B])}\{M7\}$

$M7 = N\langle B \rangle$

Figure 16.19 Step #7 in the public-key Needham–Schroeder protocol.

7a. Possession of the private key PuK(ID[A]) allows User_ID[A] to decipher the message C6 and recover User_ID[B]-generated second nonce N⟨B⟩ along with the nonce N⟨A⟩ received from User_ID[A] in message M2 (Fig. 16.19).

7b. User_ID[A] can verify that the *received* nonce N⟨A⟩ is that transmitted in message M2.

7c. User_ID[A] responds by transmitting the message $C7 = E_{PuK(ID[B])}\{M7\}$ to User_ID[B] enciphered in User_ID[B]'s public key PuK(ID[B]).

7d. The data M7 consists just of the User_ID[B]-generated nonce N⟨B⟩.

8. Possession of the private key PuK(ID[B]) allows User_ID[B] to decipher the message C7 and check if the correct nonce N⟨B⟩ has been returned.

REFERENCES

W. DIFFIE AND M. HELLMAN, "Multiuser Cryptographic Techniques," *National Computer Conference*, New York, NY, 1976, pp. 109–112.

T. EL GAMAL, "A Public Key Cryptosystem and a Signature System Based on Discrete Logarithms, *IEEE Transactions on Information Theory*, **IT-31**, 469–472 (1985).

IBM, "Data Security Through Cryptography," GC22-906209, IBM Corporation, 1977.

IBM, "IBM Cryptographic Subsystem Concepts and Facilities," GC22-9063-04. IBM Corporation, 1985.

C. H. MEYER AND S. M. MATYAS, "Cryptography: A New Dimension of Data Security," John Wiley & Sons, New York, NY, 1982.

ANSI, *Financial Institution Key Management (Wholesale)*, American National Standards Institute, approved April 4, 1985.

M. E. HELLMAN, B. W. DIFFIE, AND R. C. MERKLE, U.S. Patent 4,200,770, "Cryptographic Apparatus and Method," Filed September 6, 1977; Granted April 29, 1980.

R. M. NEEDHAM AND M. D. SCHROEDER, "Using Authentication for Authentication in Large Networks of Computers," *Communications of the ACM*, **21**, 993–999 (1978).

CHAPTER 17

DIGITAL SIGNATURES AND AUTHENTICATION

TRANSACTIONS BETWEEN users over the Internet require protocols to provide secrecy and authentication of both the sender's identity and the content of the message. We review the elements of digital signatures and message authentication in this chapter, and how cryptographic transformations are able to provide both secrecy and authentication.

17.1 THE NEED FOR SIGNATURES

Protocols exist to govern *transactions* between pairs of *users* of the form

> Customer_ID[A] to Broker_ID[B]: `Purchase for Acct# ... shares of`
> `XYZ Corporation at a price not`
> `exceeding $ ...`
>
> Merchant_ID[A] to Bank_ID[B]: `Credit Acct #04165-02388,`
> `$ 1000; debit Acct #...`

The rules are intended to protect each party against harmful acts by the other or by a third party. Some transactions also require the participation of a lawyer or escrow agent; arbitration procedures are also agreed upon in advance to resolve disputes if they should arise.

The Internet provides mechanisms to support communications like these, but the usual element of personal contact between the parties – physical, visual, or voice – is missing (Fig. 17.1). Ordinary electronic messages are not resistant to forgery or alteration; for example, the sequence of 0's and 1's in the credit/debit message above may be altered, reversing the roles of the credit and debit accounts

> Merchant_ID[A] to Bank_ID[B]: `Debit Acct #······,`
> `$ 1000; credit Acct # 04165-02388`

or the amount could be changed from $1000 to $1,000,000.

The protocols in paper-based commercial transactions, which either prevent or discourage misuse by making detection likely, need to be defined to protect electronic transactions over a network. The Internet requires simple protocols that will be likely to detect or prevent most attempts to modify a transaction. We formulate the requirements of *authentication* and *digital signature* systems and review several proposed solutions in this chapter.

Computer Security and Cryptography. By Alan G. Konheim
Copyright © 2007 John Wiley & Sons, Inc.

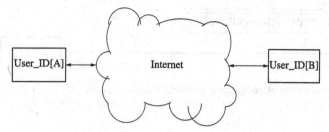

Figure 17.1 User transactions over the Internet.

17.2 THREATS TO NETWORK TRANSACTIONS

A transaction from the *originator* User_ID[A] to the *recipient* User_ID[B] involves the transmission of DATA, committing the users to some course of action. The participants require protection against a variety of harmful acts including:

Reneging: The *originator* subsequently disowns a transaction.

Forgery: The *recipient* fabricates a transaction.

Alteration: The *recipient* alters a previous valid transaction.

Masquerading: A user attempts to masquerade as another.

These actions are often indistinguishable; for example, User_ID[A] might attempt to renege on a transaction with User_ID[B] by claiming that

1. User_ID[B] has altered transaction data or
2. A third party, User_ID[C], has been masquerading as the originator.

Protocols have to be defined that at least detect attempts at alteration and to identify the source of Internet transactions.

17.3 SECRECY, DIGITAL SIGNATURES, AND AUTHENTICATION

Our focus until now has been on *secrecy systems* for hiding information from a surreptitious but passive *wiretapper* who only monitors communications. Cryptography provided a possible solution by altering the form of the message so that only the authorized parties might be able to read the message. Enciphering the electronic fund's transfer message of Figure 17.2 might hide its contents (Fig. 17.3). However, it does not provide proof of the origin of the message. Webster's dictionary defines *authentication* as a "process by which each party to a communication verifies the identity of the other."

Authentication occurs in many day-to-day activities, including using

- A photo-ID when cashing a check,
- A driver's license when making a credit card purchase, and
- A passport when crossing national boundaries.

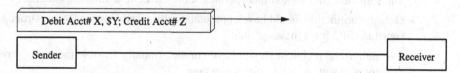

Figure 17.2 Plaintext transaction data.

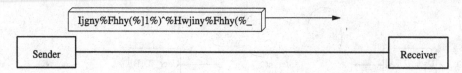

Figure 17.3   Secrecy by means of enciphering plaintext transaction data.

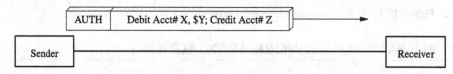

Figure 17.4   Authentication appended to plaintext transaction data.

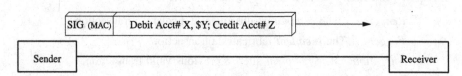

Figure 17.5   A digital signature appended to plaintext transaction data.

Implicit in the authentication of a message MESS from a *Sender* to a *Receiver* is the inclusion of data AUTH, *appended to* or *included within* the message, attesting to the sender's authenticity (Fig. 17.4). The dictionary definition of authentication just given pertains to the identity of the sender but not the content of the message MESS being transmitted.

A *digital signature* SIG is data *appended to* or *included within* a message that attests to *both* the identity of the document's sender and the content of the message (Fig. 17.5). Some authors refer to this process as providing *message integrity* and the signature as a *message authentication code* (MAC). Although their objectives are different, secrecy, authentication, and digital signatures may be combined; encipherment intends to *hide* the content of the message, while the digital signature tries to assure both the integrity of a message and also provide *proof* that a message came from a *specific* sender.

17.4   THE DESIDERATA OF A DIGITAL SIGNATURE

The requirements of a *digital signature* system include:

- The signature SIG should be functionally dependent on every component of the message;
- The signature SIG should incorporates some element of time dependence;
- *Only* the originator should have computationally feasible means to construct a valid signature SIG for a message; and
- *Any* authorized recipient should have computationally feasible means to verify the validity of a signature S1G for a message.

17.5 PUBLIC-KEY CRYPTOGRAPHY AND SIGNATURE SYSTEMS

The structural similarity of these requirements to those of a public-key cryptosystem

- Signing a message corresponding to encipherment E with the private key,
- Verifying the signed transaction corresponding to decipherment D with the public key,

is no coincidence. The papers by Whitfield Diffie and Martin Hellman [1976a, b] clearly indicate that public-key cryptography was invented to implement

- Key exchange in a network and
- Authentication of users and the integrity of the data they exchange.

The landmark paper [Rivest et al., 1978] both announced the first true example of a public-key cryptosystem and suggested a method by which a public-key cryptosystem could be used to *both* authenticate the identity *and* the integrity of data in a transaction. The need for a certificate in authentication to link the public key and identifier of a user was conceived in 1978 by Adelman's student Kohnfelder [1978] who wrote

> . . . *each user who wishes to receive private communications must place his enciphering algorithm (his public key) in the public file.*

We describe certificates, their usage and how the connection PuK(ID[A]) $\leftrightarrow$ ID[A] is established in Chapter 18.

To authenticate their communication, User_ID[A], with public and private keys PuK(ID[A]) and PrK(ID[A]), creates a certificate that

1. Links the public keys PuK(ID[A]) with User_ID[A]'s network identifier ID[A], and
2. Provides a means using the certificate for *any* user to verify the link ID[A] $\leftrightarrow$ PuK(ID[A]).

When User_ID[A] and User_ID[B] engage in a transaction, they first exchange their certificates:

- User_ID[A] uses the certificate to verify that PuK(ID[A]) is the public key of User_ID[A], and
- User_ID[B] uses the certificate to verify that PuK(ID[B]) is the public key of User_ID[B].

User_ID[A] signs the message M to User_ID[B] in two steps:

S1. User_ID[A] first enciphers M using User_ID[B]'s public key PuK(ID[B]):

$$M \rightarrow \tilde{M} \equiv E_{\text{PuK(ID[B])}}\{\text{ID[A], ID[B], M}\}.$$

S2. User_ID[A] next re-enciphers $\tilde{M}$ using User_ID[A]'s private key PrK(ID[A]):

$$\tilde{M} \rightarrow C \equiv E_{\text{PrK(ID[A])}}\{\text{ID[A], ID[B], } \tilde{M}\}.$$

It is assumed that messages M have a certain structure: for example,

- An electronic check M might contain the payor and payee's account number, data, and an amount;

- An *electronic funds transfer* (EFT) message M might contain the payor and payee's account number, data, and an amount.

User_ID[B] authenticates the message C from User_ID[A] in two steps:

A1. User_ID[B] first deciphers C using User_ID[A]'s public key PuK(ID[A]):

$$C \rightarrow \tilde{C} \equiv E_{\text{PuK(ID[A])}}\{ID[A], ID[B], C\}.$$

A2. User_ID[B] next deciphers $\tilde{C}$ using User_ID[B]'s private key KPr(ID[B]):

$$\tilde{C} \rightarrow \hat{M} \equiv E_{\text{PrK(ID[B])}}\{ID[A], ID[B], \tilde{C}\}.$$

If $\hat{M}$ is consistent with the expected plaintext structure in the transaction system, User_ID[B] accepts the received message $M = \hat{M}$ as being properly signed transaction data *from* User_ID[A].

The *signed* message $C \equiv E_{\text{PrK(ID[B])}}\{ID[A], ID[B], \hat{M}\}$ is User_ID[B]'s proof as to the origin and the content of M.

The structural similarity of public-key cryptography and authentication does not require that the latter requires public-key cryptography to be used. Although his protocol is somewhat impractical in light of subsequent developments, Michael Rabin, who made several contributions to the security literature, published a digital signature protocol in Rabin [1978]. His method requires that information for each user-pair (User_ID[A]-User_ID[B]) be exchanged and deposited in advance with a *trusted* third party who participates in the authentication process.

A number of signature protocols have been suggested, whose strength is based on the difficulty of finding solutions for the *integer factorization* and the *discrete logarithm* problems.

17.6 RABIN'S QUADRATIC RESIDUE SIGNATURE PROTOCOL

We begin by considering the important result of Michael Rabin who proved in Rabin [1979] the equivalence of the security of a signature scheme and the difficulty of factorization. We make use of the material on quadratic residues in Section 13.4.

Rabin's Quadratic Residue Signature Protocol depends on the equivalence of three problems:

Problem A

Given: $N = pq$, a product of two primes p, q,

Find: The factors p, q.

Problem B

Given: $N = pq$, a product of two primes p, q and an integer $x = s^2$ (modulo N),

Find: *All* quadratic residues of x, the four solutions y_1, y_2, y_3, y_4 of
$$y^2 - x = 0 \text{ (modulo } N).$$

Problem C

Given: $N = pq$, a product of two primes p, q and an integer $x = s^2$ (modulo N),

Find: *Any* quadratic residue of x, a solution y of $y^2 - x = 0$ (modulo N).

The Chinese Remainder Theorem shows how to find the quadratic residue $y^2 - x = 0$ (modulo N) from the solutions of $y_1^2 - x = 0$ (modulo p) and $y_2^2 - x = 0$ (modulo q). Berlekamp's Algorithm (Proposition **13.4**) shows how to compute quadratic residues if the factors of $N = pq$ are known. Proposition **13.7** concludes that Problems A and B are equivalent. The equivalence of Problem C to Problem B follows from Proposition **17.1**.

Proposition 17.1:   If the algorithm $\mathcal{A}$ solves the problem

Given: $N = pq$, a product of two primes p, q and an integer $x = s^2$ (modulo N),

Find: *Any* quadratic residue of x, a solution y of $y^2 - x = 0$ (modulo N)

with running time $F(N)$, then an algorithm $\mathcal{A}^*$ exists to solve the problem

Given: $N = pq$, a product of two primes p, q,

Find: The factors p, q of N

in randomized time $2F(N)$.

Proof: If $x = k^2$ (modulo N), then x is a quadratic residue of N and the four solutions of

$$y^2 = x \text{ (modulo } N)$$

of y that satisfy

$$
\begin{aligned}
r &= y_1 \text{ (modulo } p), & s &= y_1 \text{ (modulo } q) \\
-r = p - r &= y_2 \text{ (modulo } p), & s &= y_2 \text{ (modulo } q) \\
r &= y_3 \text{ (modulo } p), & -s = p - s &= y_3 \text{ (modulo } q) \\
-r = p - r &= y_4 \text{ (modulo } p), & -s = p - s &= y_4 \text{ (modulo } q)
\end{aligned}
$$

for some pair (r, s). The quadratic residues modulo N are therefore divided into *equivalence classes*, each containing four elements $\{(r, s), (-r, s), (r, -s), (-r, -s)\}$.

Choose k randomly and set $x = k^2$ (modulo N) so that x is a quadratic residue modulo N. Suppose

$$r = k \text{ (modulo } p) \qquad s = k \text{ (modulo } q).$$

Use $\mathcal{A}$ to obtain a solution j of $y^2 = x$ (modulo N). With probability $1/2$, the solution satisfies either

$$-r = p - r = j \text{ (modulo } p), \qquad s = j \text{ (modulo } q)$$

or

$$r = j \text{ (modulo } p), \qquad -s = p - s = j \text{ (modulo } q)$$

so that $\gcd\{k - j, N\}$ is either p or q with probability $1/2$.

Using the equivalence of Problems A and C, Michael Rabin defined a *quadratic residue signature* system and several other authentication protocols [Rabin, 1978]. In Rabin's original solution, let p and q be odd primes and $N = pq$. User_ID[A]'s private key is PrK(ID[A]) = (p, q); User_ID[A]'s public key is PuK(ID[A]) = N.

The message to be signed DATA $= \underline{x} = (x_0, x_1, \ldots, x_{n-1})$ is a string of n bits. The steps in the signing process are as follows.

R1. Concatenate $\underline{x}$ with m random number of bits where $2^{n+m} < N$:

$$\underline{x} \longrightarrow (x_0, x_1, \ldots, x_{n-1}, r_0, r_1, \ldots, r_{m-1}).$$

R2. Associate the integer $\alpha = \sum_{i=0}^{n-1} x_i 2^i + 2^n \sum_{i=0}^{m-1} r_i 2^i < N$ with the extended string.

R3. Using Proposition **13.2**, check if α is a quadratic residue:

–If α is *not* a quadratic residue, then choose another random $\underline{r}$ and repeat steps R1–R2.

–If α is a quadratic residue, then knowledge of the factors of $N = pq$ makes it possible to calculate $\sqrt{\alpha}$; use the Chinese Remainder Theorem (Proposition **13.6**) and Berlekamp's Algorithm (Proposition **13.4**) to calculate the smallest positive quadratic residue of α.

R4. The signature of DATA is SIG $= (\underline{r}, \beta)$.

Approximately $\frac{1}{4}$ of the integers in $\mathcal{Z}_N$ are quadratic residues and an average of four trials will be needed to generate $\underline{r}$.

The *recipient* of the signed message (DATA, SIG) from User_ID[A] verifies the signature by recomputing α and checking that $\alpha = \beta^2$ (modulo N).

17.7 HASH FUNCTIONS

To *hash* is to it chop into small pieces. *Corned beef hash* is the quintessential American food made with left over meat, eggs and whatever is lying around in the refrigerator. A *hashing function h* is a mapping from values x in some finite set $\mathcal{X}$ into a value y contained in another (larger) set $\mathcal{Y}$ that *mixes up* the values x. Hashing is a synonym for a (uniformly distributed) *random mapping* in cryptography (Fig. 17.6).

A hash function h is

- A *one-way hash function* if it is computationally infeasible to determine the *message m given* the *hash-of-message h(m)*.

- A *collision-resistant hash function* if *given* the *hash-of-message h(m)* it is computationally infeasible to determine *any* other message m^* with the same hash value $h(m) = h(m^*)$.

A *message digest* is a hash function that derives a *fixed-length* hash value for every message in some message domain. The processes of computing the message digest with a PKC and verifying the message digest is depicted in Figures 17.7 and 17.8.

Even if a hash function is *not* collision-resistant, knowing the hash $h(m)$ of

$$m : \text{Bank A to Bank:Credit Acct\#04165-02388,}$$
$$\$\,1,000; \text{debit Acct\#} \cdots$$

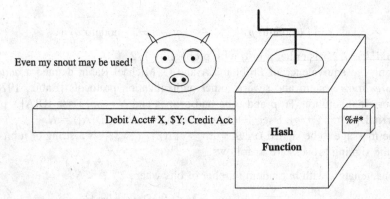

Even my snout may be used!

Debit Acct# X, \$Y; Credit Acc

Hash Function

%#*

Figure 17.6 High-cholesterol hashing.

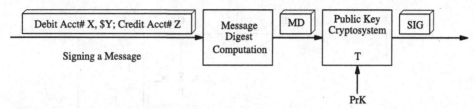

Figure 17.7   Deriving a message digest.

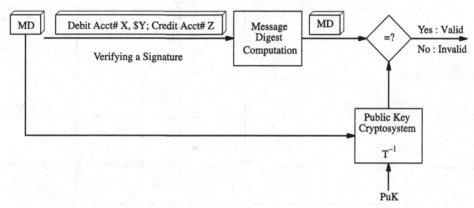

Figure 17.8   Verifying a message digest.

may *not* make it possible to calculate the hash $h(m^*)$ of

$$m^*: \text{Bank A to Bank B}: \text{Credit Acct\#04165-02388,}$$
$$\$1,000,000; \text{ debit Acct\#} \cdots$$

As is the case with cryptograph systems, there is no effective way of testing if a hash function is a one-way hash function or to characterize and easily compute messages that collide with $h(m)$.

17.8 MD5

RSADI has defined several message digests including MD2 [Kaliski, 1992] and MD5, designed by Ronald Rivest in 1991 [Rivest, 1992] to replace the MD4 hash function.

MD5 (Fig. 17.9) begins by *padding* the message to make its length a multiple of 512 bits:

- A 1 is appended (on the right) to signal the start of the padding;
- As many 0's are added so as to make its length a multiple of 512−64; and finally
- The encoding of the original message length is appended to the data.

The message of $512 = 4 \times (4 \times 32)$ bits is processed by the basic MD5 operation, which modifies the contents of four 32-bit registers A, B, C, D.

The MD5 operation is composed of

- A nonlinear operation F;
- A left-circular shift;

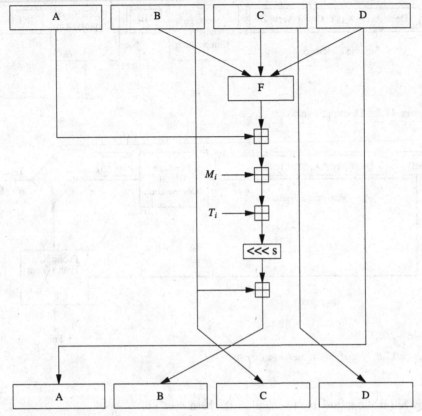

Figure 17.9 Basic MD5 operation.

- Addition (modulo 2^{32}) of constants $\{T_i\}$, and
- Addition (modulo 2^{32}) of a 32-bit word $\{M_i\}$ from the message to (A, B, C, D).

To start the process the registers A, B, C, and D are initialized (in hexadecimal) as follows:

A: 01 23 45 67 B: 89 AB CD EF C: FE DC BA 98 D: 76 54 32 01

The MD5 hash is calculated in four rounds.

It is not possible to determine the set of messages m_1 and m_2 having the same MD5-hash. There *may* not be a serious weakness in MD5 even if MD5[m_1] = MD5[m_2], because hashing is used in applications where messages have very special formats. Various researchers have observed defects in MD5:

- den Boer and Bosselaers [1993] discovered some peculiar "near" collisions.
- Papers by Dobbertin [1996a,b] announced a flaw in the design of MD5 in 1996.
- Recently, Wang and Yu [2005] published a brute force attack to find collisions on a powerful distributed processor.

MD5 processes the message m in just one pass to derive MD5(m); this offers the possibility that collisions for the MD5 hash might be calculated. Collisions are generated by suffixing a message $m \rightarrow m, \sigma$ in such a way to make MD5(m) = MD5(m, σ) likely.

Although not exactly felines, academic cryptographers are a finicky bunch. The ubiquitous phrase *some cryptographers* have even suggested that these "flaws" in MD5 make "further use of the algorithm for security purposes questionable," a judgment that I believe is also questionable.

17.9 THE SECURE HASH ALGORITHM

The *Secure Hash Algorithm* SHA is a family of cryptographic hash functions designed by the NSA and published as a U.S. government standard [NIST, 1994]. The first version published in 1993 is often referred to as SHA-0. SHA-1 is the most commonly used hash function in the family of application protocols including the Transport Layer Security (TLS), Secure Socket Layer (SSL), Pretty Good Privacy (PGP), Secure Shell (SSH), and the Internet Protocol Security (IPSec).

SHA first pads the message data like MD5 to make its length a multiple of 512 bits, but it produces a 160-bit hash value.

The hashing operation involves 80 operations, each of which modifies the contents of five 32-bit registers A, B, C, and D. A SHA operation is shown in Figure 17.10 and consists of

- A nonlinear operation F;
- Left-circular shifts;
- Addition (modulo 2^{32}) of constants $\{K_i\}$; and
- Addition (modulo 2^{32}) of a 32-bit word $\{K_i\}$ derived from the message to (A, B, C, D).

SHA requires an expansion of each message block of $512 = 16 \times 32$ bits, because the 80 operations consume 80 32-bits words. If M_i is the ith 32-bit word of the message

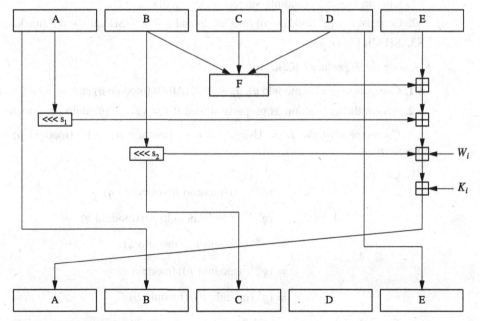

Figure 17.10 A SHA operation.

$(0 \le i < 16)$, then

$$(M_0, M_1, \ldots, M_{15}) \rightarrow (W_0, W_1, \ldots, W_{79})$$

$$W_i = \begin{cases} M_i, & \text{if } 0 \le i < 16 \\ \sigma_i \langle W_{i-3} + W_{i-8} + W_{i-14} + W_{i-16} \rangle, & \text{if } 16 \le i < 80, \end{cases}$$

where σ_i denotes cyclic (left) shift by i places.

The registers A, B, C, D, and E are initialized (in hexadecimal) as follows:

A: 67 45 23 01 B: EF CD AB 89 C: 98 BA DC FE D: 10 32 54 76 E: C3 D2 E1 F0

The first attack on SHA-0 was presented as CRYPTO '98 [Chabqud and Joux, 1998] and E. Bilham and R. Chen [2004] reported *near collisions* in 2004.

17.10 NIST'S DIGITAL SIGNATURE ALGORITHM [NIST, 1991, 1994]

Public Key

$-p$ an L-bit prime: conditions $512 \le L \le 1024$ and L a multiple of 64;

$-q$ a 160-bit prime factor of $p - 1$.

$-h$ (an integer), $1 < h < p - 1$ such that $g = h^{\frac{p-1}{q}}$ (modulo p) > 1.

$-y = g^x$ (modulo p), x (randomly chosen).

Private Key: $x < q$.

Signing the Message: $m \in \mathcal{Z}_p^+ = \{1, 2, \ldots, p - 1\}$.

SHA[m] is the result of the Secure Hash Algorithm applied to the message m.

S1. Choose $k \in \mathcal{Z}_q^+$ randomly subject to $1 = \gcd\{k, q - 1\}$.

S2. Generate $r = (g^k \text{ (modulo } p)) \text{ (modulo } q)$ and $s = (k^{-1}(\text{SHA}[m] + xr)) \text{ (modulo } q)$.

S3. SHA[m] = (r, s).

Verifying the Signature SIG[m] *for* m

V1. Compute $w = s^{-1}$ (modulo q), $u_1 = (w\text{SHA}[m])$ (modulo q) and $u_2 = rw$ (modulo q)

V2. Accept the transaction as properly signed if $r = (g^{u_1}y^{u_2} \text{ (modulo } p)) \text{ (modulo } q)$.

Correctness of the DSS: Using $g = h^{\frac{p-1}{q}}$ (modulo p) $\rightarrow g^q$ (modulo p) $= h^{p-1}$; (modulo p) $= 1$

C1. Compute

$$v = ((g^{u_1}y^{u_2}) \text{ (modulo } p)) \text{ (modulo } q)$$

$$= (g^{w(\text{SHA}[m]+xr)} \text{(modulo } p)) \text{ (modulo } q)$$

$$= (g^{skw} \text{(modulo } p)) \text{ (modulo } q)$$

$$= (g^{sks^{-1}} \text{(modulo } p)) \text{ (modulo } q)$$

$$= (g^k \text{ (modulo } p)) \text{ (modulo } q)$$

A discussion of the validity of this signature protocol is contained in NIST [1991, 1994].

We describe two signature protocols whose strength is based on the difficulty of finding solutions for the factorization and discrete logarithm problems.

17.11 EL GAMAL'S SIGNATURE PROTOCOL [EL GAMAL, 1985a, b]

Parameter : p, a prime

Private Key : x, $1 \le x < p$

Public Key : $y = g^x$ (modulo p) and p, g (randomly chosen)

Signing the Message : $m \in \mathcal{Z}_p^+ = \{1, 2, \dots, p-1\}$

S1. Choose $k \in \mathcal{Z}_p^+$ randomly subject to $1 = \gcd\{k, p-1\}$; the value of k is secret.

S2. Compute $a = g^k$ (modulo p).

S3. Use the Euclidean algorithm to calculate k^{-1}.

S4. Use the Euclidean algorithm to calculate b satisfying $m = (xa + kb)$ (modulo $(p-1)$).

S5. The signature of the message m is the pair $\mathrm{SIG}[m] = (a, b)$.

Verifying the Signature SIG(m) for m

V1. Compute $(y^a a^b)$ (modulo p); and g^m (modulo p).

V2. Accept m as properly signed if $(y^a a^b)$ (modulo p) $= g^m$ (modulo p).

Correctness of the ElGamal Signature Protocol: Using Fermat's Little Theorem

$$y^a \ (\text{modulo } p) = g^{xa} \ (\text{modulo } p)$$

$$a^b \ (\text{modulo } p) = g^{ka} \ (\text{modulo } p)$$

$$y^a a^b \ (\text{modulo } p) = g^{(xa+kb)} \ (\text{modulo } p)$$

$$= g^m \ (\text{modulo } p)$$

Example 17.1

$p = 467$, $x = 127$, $g = 2$, $y = 2^{127}$ (modulo 467) $= 132$.

Signing the Message $m = 100$

S1. Choose $k = 213$ and check that $1 = \gcd\{213, 467\}$; compute $431 = k^{-1}$ (modulo 466).

S2. Compute $a = 2^{213}$ (modulo 467) $= 29$.

S3. Solve the congruence $100 = [(127 \times 29) + (213b)]$ (modulo $(p-1)$); $b = 51$.

The signature for $m = 100$ is $\mathrm{SIG}(100) = (29, 51)$.

Verifying the Signature / SIG(100) = (29, 51)

$$y^a a^b \ (\text{modulo } p) = 132^{29} 29^{51} \ (\text{modulo } 467) = 189$$

$$g^m \ (\text{modulo } p) = 2^{100} \ (\text{modulo } 467) = 189 = 41.$$

17.12 THE FIAT–SHAMIR IDENTIFICATION AND SIGNATURE SCHEMA [FIAT AND SHAMIR, 1986]

User_ID[A] wants to prove *identity* to User_ID[B] by showing possession of some secret information *without* actually revealing this information. The Fiat–Shamir Identification Scheme was the first example of a *zero-knowledge proof*. Its strength and that of the following protocols depends on the computational equivalence of Problems A–C described in Section 17.6.

A trusted signature center chooses secret primes p, q and computes $N = pq$; *only N* is distributed to all users.

- User_ID[A] selects a random s, checks that $1 = \gcd\{s, N\}$ and computes $v^{-1} = s^2$ (modulo N).
- User_ID[A] registers v with the trusted signature center.

Fiat–Shamir Basic Identification Scheme

User_ID[A]: *Private Key*: PrK(ID[A]) $= s \in \mathcal{Z}_N^+$

User_ID[A]: *Public Key*: PuK(ID[A]) $= (N, v)$ with $N = pq$ and $v = s^{-2}$ (modulo N)

---

s^{-1} is a quadratic residue of v. User_ID[A]'s will *prove* identity to User_ID[B] by exhibiting knowledge of the private key PrK(ID[A]) $= s$ *without* actually revealing s.

S1. User_ID[A] chooses a random r in $\mathcal{Z}_N$, computes $x = r^2$ (modulo N) and sends x to User_ID[B].

S2. User_ID[B] chooses a random bit $b = 0$ or 1 (with probability $1/2$) and sends it to User_ID[A].

S3. User_ID[A] returns y to User_ID[B] where

$$y = \begin{cases} r, & \text{if } b = 0 \\ rs, & \text{if } b = 1 \end{cases}.$$

S4. User_ID[B] computes

$$y^2 v^b \text{ (modulo } N) = \begin{cases} r^2 \text{ (modulo } N), & \text{if } b = 0 \\ r^2 s^2 s^{-2} \text{ (modulo } N), & \text{if } b = 1 \end{cases} = r^2 \text{ (modulo } N)$$

and accepts the *identification pass* as valid if $y^2 v^b$ (modulo N) $= x$.

Observe that

O1. It is assumed that p and q are kept secret and sufficiently large so that knowledge of the factors of N is required for s to be determined from v;

O2. If User_ID[A] knows that User_ID[B] will choose $b = 0$, then *any* user will pass the identification pass.

O3. If User_ID[A] knows that User_ID[B] will choose $b = 1$, then

- A random r is chosen but $x = v^{-1} r^2$ (modulo N) is returned to User_ID[B] in **S1** instead of $x = r^2$ (modulo N);

- When User_ID[B] obligingly sends back $b = 1$ in **S2**, User_ID[A] returns $y = v^{-1} r$ (modulo N) to User_ID[B] in **S3**; and

- User_ID[B] computes $y^2 v$ (modulo N) $= v^{-1} r^2$ (modulo N) $= x$.

O4. The probability that the evil User_ID[?] will successfully masquerade as User_ID[A] is thus $1/2$.

If the probability of $1/2$ of escaping detection is too high, the identification steps **S1–S4** may be repeated t times. The probability of User_ID[?] now escaping detection by passing *all* identification passes is 2^{-t}. When repeating steps **S1–S4**, different values of r must be used, as a reuse of r might reveal r and rs.

The original identification scheme can be parallelized [Feige et al., 1988];

Improved Identification Scheme

User_ID[A]: *Private Key*: $\mathrm{PrK}(\mathrm{ID}[A]) = \underline{s} = (s_0, s_1, \ldots, s_{k-1}) \in \mathcal{Z}_{k,N}^+$
User_ID[A]: *Public Key*: $\mathrm{PuK}(\mathrm{ID}[A]) = (N, v)$ with $N = pq$, $v = (v_0, v_1, \ldots, v_{k-1})$
$\in \mathcal{Z}_{k,N}^+$ with $v_i = s_i^{-2}$ (modulo n) for $0 \le i < k$

S1. User_ID[A] chooses a random r in $\mathcal{Z}_N$, computes $x = r^2$ (modulo N) and sends x to User_ID[B].

S2. User_ID[B] chooses a random bit-vector $\underline{b} = (s_0, s_1, \ldots, b_{k-1}) \mathcal{Z}_{k,2}$ using the uniform distribution sends it to User_ID[A].

S3. User_ID[A] returns y to User_ID[B] where $y = r \prod_{i=0}^{k-1} s_i^{b_i}$ (modulo N).

S4. User_ID[B] computes $z = y^2 \prod_{i=0}^{k-1} v_i^{b_i}$ (modulo N) $= r^2 \prod_{i=0}^{k-1} s_i^{2b_i} v_i^{b_i}$ (modulo N) and accepts User_ID[A]'s identity as valid if $z = x$.

The probability of successfully masquerading is now 2^{-k}.

The protocol was modified to derive a signature scheme; suppose h is a hashing function with values in $\mathcal{Z}_{k,2}$ and $x \| y$ denotes the concatenation of x and y.

Digital Signature Scheme

User_ID[A]: *Private Key*: $\mathrm{PrK}(\mathrm{ID}[A]) = \underline{s}$ with $\underline{s} = (s_0, s_1, \ldots, s_{k-1}) \in \mathcal{Z}_{k,N}^+$
User_ID[B]: *Public Key*: $\mathrm{PuK}(\mathrm{ID}[A]) = (N, v)$ with $N = pq$, $v = (v_0, v_1, \ldots, v_{k-1}) \in \mathcal{Z}_{k,N}^+$
with $v_i = s_i^{-2}$ (modulo N) for $0 \le i < k$

Signing the Message m

S1. User_ID[A] randomly chooses t integers $r_0, r_1, \ldots, r_{t-1}$ in Z_N using the uniform distribution and computes $\underline{x} = (x_0, x_1, \ldots, x_{t-1})$ where $x_i = r_i^2$ (modulo n) for $0 \le i < t$.

S2. User_ID[A] computes the hash $(b, \ldots) = h[m \| \underline{x}]$ of the concatenation of the message m and $\underline{x}$.

S3. User_ID[A] computes $\underline{y} = (y_0, y_1, \ldots, y_{t-1})$ where

$$-y_i = r_i \prod_{j=0}^{k-1} s_j^{b_{i,j}} \ (\text{modulo } N) \ \text{for } 0 \le i < t$$

$$-\underline{b} = \begin{pmatrix} b_{0,0} & b_{0,1} & \cdots & b_{0,k-1} \\ b_{1,0} & b_{1,1} & \cdots & b_{1,k-1} \\ \vdots & \vdots & \ddots & \vdots \\ b_{t-1,0} & b_{t-1,1} & \cdots & b_{t-1,k-1} \end{pmatrix} \ \text{is the first } kt \text{ of the hash.}$$

User_ID[A] sends User_ID[B] the signature $\mathrm{SIG}(m) = (\underline{b}, \underline{y})$ for m.

Verifying That SIG(m) is the Signature of m

V1. User_ID[B] obtain's User_ID[A]'s public key $\underline{v} = (v_0, v_1, \ldots, v_{k-1})$ from the certificate of User_ID[A].

V2. User_ID[B] computes $z = (z_0, z_1, \ldots, z_{t-1})$ with $z_i = y_i^2 \prod_{j=0}^{k-1} v_k^{b_{i,j}}$ (modulo N) for $0 \le i < t$.

V3. User_ID[B] verifies that $\underline{b}$ gives the first kt bits of $H[m \parallel \underline{z}]$ and accepts the message as properly signed if this condition is satisfied.

A discussion of the security of the Improved Identification Scheme is given on page 411 of Menezes et al. [1996].

17.13 THE OBLIVIOUS TRANSFER

I attended a lecture by Professor Manuel Blum while at IBM Research in which he described this problem as follows; the Californians *Alice* and *Bob* are contemplating divorce and decide to toss coins to determine which of them receives the car, the child, the house, the dog, and so forth. Although *Alice* and *Bob* are now divorced, their names continue to be used in describing many two-party authentication protocols. I believe the idea first appeared in a report by Michael Rabin [1981]. In another variant [Blum, 1983] *Alice* and *Bob* wish to electronically *fairly toss a coin*.

17.13.1 Oblivious Transfer Protocol: Who Gets the Dog?

Step #1: *Alice* chooses primes p, q and sends *Bob* their product $N = pq$. *Bob*'s task is to factor N:

- If he is successful, the outcome of coin toss is in *Bob*'s favor
- Otherwise, *Alice* wins.

Step #2: *Bob* chooses randomly $x \in \mathcal{Z}_N$, computes $y = x^2$ (modulo N) and sends y to *Alice*.

Step #3: As *Alice* knows the factors of N, she can find all of the solutions of $y^2 = n$ (module N) $x, -x, z, -z$. *Alice* randomly chooses one of the solutions with probability of $\frac{1}{4}$ and returns its value to *Bob*.

Step #4: If the solution returned to *Bob* is x or $-x$, then *Bob* has received no new information. If the solution returned to *Bob* is z or $-z$, then *Bob* computes $\gcd\{x + z, N\}$ (or $\gcd\{x - z, N\}$) and determines the factors of N.
The probability of *Bob's* winning is $\frac{1}{2}$.

REFERENCES

E. BIHAM AND R. CHEN, "Near-Collisions of SHA-0," *Proceedings CRYPTO 2004*, Springer-Verlag, New York, NY, 2004, pp. 290–305.

M. BLUM, "How to Exchange (Secret) Keys," *ACM Transactions on Computer Systems*, **1**, 175–193 (1983).

B. DEN BOER AND A. BOSSELAERS, "Collisions for the Compression Function of MD5," *EUROCRYPT 1993*, Lofthus, Norway, pp. 293–304.

F. CHABAUD AND A. JOUX, "Differential Collisions in SHA-0," *Proceedings of CRYPTO 1998*, Springer-Verlag, New York, NY, 1998, pp. 5671.

W. H. DIFFIE AND M. HELLMAN, "Multiuser Cryptographic Techniques," *National Computer Conference*, New York, NY, 1976a, pp. 109–112.

W. H. DIFFIE AND M. HELLMAN, "New Directions in Cryptography," *IEEE Transactions in Information Theory*, **IT-22**, 644–654 (1976b).

H. Dobbertin, "Cryptanalysis of MD5 Compress," Announcement on Internet, [www.ornl.gov/dunigan/md5crack.ps], May 1996a.

H. Dobbertin, "The Status of MD5 After a Recent Attack," *CryptoBytes*, **2**, 1996b.

"Proposed Federal Information Processing Standard for Digital Signature Standard (DSS)," *Federal Register*, **56**(169), 30.

National Institute of Standards and Technology, NIST FIPS PUB 186, "Digital Signature Standard," U.S. Department of Commerce, US government, May 1994.

T. ElGamal, "A Public-Key Cryptosystem and a Signature Scheme Based on Discrete Logarithms," *Advances in Cryptology – CRYPTO '84*, Berlin, Springer-Verlag, New York, NY, 1985, pp. 101–108.

T. ElGamal, "A Public-Key Cryptosystem and a Signature Scheme Based on Discrete Logarithms," *IEEE Transactions on Information Theory*, **IT-31**, 469–472 (1985).

U. Feige, A. Fiat, and A. Shamir, "Zero-Knowledge Proofs of Identity," *Journal of Cryptology*, **1**, 77–94 (1988).

A. Fiat and A. Shamir, "How to Prove Yourself: Practical Solutions to Identification and Signature Problems," *Proceedings of CRYPTO '86*, Springer-Verlag, New York, NY, 186–194 (1987).

L. M. Kohnfelder, "Towards a Practical Public-Key Cryptosystem," M.I.T Bachelor's Thesis, May 1978.

B. Kaliski, "The MD2 Message Digest," RFC 1319, April 1992a.

R. L. Rivest, "The MD4 Message Digest," RFD 1321, April 1992a.

A. J. Menezes, P. C. van Oorschot, and S. A. Vanstone, *Handbook of Applied Cryptography*, CRC Press, 1996.

National Institute of Standards and Technology, NIST FIPS PUB 180, "Secure Hash Standard," U.S. Department of Commerce, US government, May 1994.

R. L. Rivest, A. Shamir, and L. Adelman, "A Method for Obtaining Digital Signatures and Public-Key Cryptosystems," *Communications of the ACM*, **21**, 120–126 (1978).

M. Rabin, "Signature and certification by Coding," *IBM Technical Disclosure Bulletin*, **20**, 3337–3338 (1978).

M. Rabin, "Digitalized Signatures and Public Key Functions as Intractable as Factorization," Laboratory For Computer Science, Massachusetts Institute of Technology, **MIT/LCS/TR-212**, January 1979.

M. Rabin, "Digital Signatures," in *Foundations of Secure Communication*, Academic Press, Burlington, Massachusetts, 155–168 (1978b).

M. Rabin, "How to Exchange Secrets by Oblivious Transfer," Technical Report TR-81, Aiken Computation Laboratory, Harvard University, 1981.

Xiaoyun Wang and Hongbo Yu, "How to Break MD5 and Other Hash Functions," *EUROCRYPT 2005*, August 1991, pp. 42980–42982.

CHAPTER 18

APPLICATIONS OF CRYPTOGRAPHY

THIS CHAPTER describes several cryptographic applications:

- The UNIX `crypt(3)` password protection;
- Automated teller machine transactions;
- Facility access cards;
- Smart cards;
- The Web's Secure Socket Layer protocol.

18.1 UNIX PASSWORD ENCIPHERMENT

A Log-In to a UNIX system requires the user to provide a password Pass(User_ID), which is hashed to Hass[Pass(User_ID)] and compared with the entries in the UNIX password file consisting of

User_Name	Salt(User_[ID]) [2]	Hash[Pass(User_ID)] [11]	User_[ID]

where the number [n] is the length in characters (bytes). A *cryptographic salt* consists of approximately $4096 = 2^{12}$ randomly chosen bits, which are used to further "mix up" the Hash(UserPass_ID). The UNIX `crypt(3)` command chooses the salt to be a pair of the characters

$$a, b, \ldots, z, A, B, \ldots, Z, 0, 1, \ldots, 9.$$

The original idea is due to George Purdy [1987], who proposed using a one-way function to

1. Recalculate the Pass(User_ID) $\rightarrow$ Hash[Pass(User_ID)] during a log-in, and

2. Compare the result in (1) with a stored value in the file `/etc/passwd.`, which contains (User_Name, Salt(User_ID), Hash[Pass(User_ID)], User_ID)[1] or if a *shadow password* implementation is being used (User_Name, Salt(User_ID), *, User_ID), signalling that Hash[Pass(User_ID)] is stored (encrypted) in another file.

---

[1]The file `/etc/passwd` can be read by any user and certainly presents an exposure. The shadow implementation lessens this threat.

Computer Security and Cryptography. By Alan G. Konheim
Copyright © 2007 John Wiley & Sons, Inc.

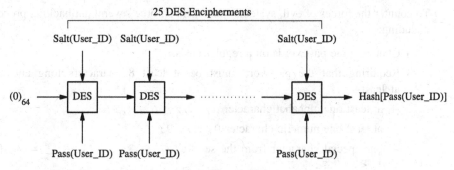

Figure 18.1 `crypt(3)` Computation of Hash[Pass(User_ID)].

Purdy suggested using polynomials over a prime modulus to construct the one-way function. There have been various implementations of the hash function. The `crypt(3)` has several options including MD5; the version that I describe uses a modified DES, depicted in Figure 18.1.

When a User_ID initially chooses a password Pass(User_ID), the following process is followed:

1. A 12-bit salt Salt(User_ID) is chosen for each User_ID and stored in the file `/etc/passwd` as part of User_ID's record.

2. Pass(User_ID) is combined with the 12-bit Salt(User_ID) $= \underline{s} = (s_0, s_1, \ldots, s_{11})$ to modify the 48 bits used by DES on each round as follows:
   - If **E** is the DES (internal) *key expansion function* (Section 9.4) **E**: $(x_0, x_1, \ldots, x_{31}) \rightarrow (y_0, y_1, \ldots, y_{47})$
   - Then bits y_j and y_{j+24} are interchanged if $s_j = 1$ and left unaltered if $s_j = 0$.

3. The modified DES is applied 25 times; the initial ($i = 0$) plaintext is

$$0_{64} \equiv \underbrace{0, 0, \ldots, 0}_{64 \text{ bits}};$$

thereafter the output of the ith use of DES is the input to the $(i + 1)$st use.

4. The 64 bits of DES output is divided into ten 6-bit blocks and a 4-bit block. Associated with each of the 11 DES output blocks is a *printable* ASCII character producing an 11 character Hash[Pass(User_ID)]. The 12-bit salt yields two characters.

18.1.1 Password Cracking

In the usual environment, a *password hacker* has one or more hashed passwords Hash[Pass(User_ID[i_j])] ($j = 1, 2, \ldots$) and wants to recover Pass(User_ID[i_j]). This is made more difficult if the Unix implementation uses a shadow password file. There are several possible attacks:

- A *dictionary attack* makes use of the tendency of users to choose names or words and come with a dictionary to implement the process. The cracking programs try
  - words spelled backwards,
  - alternative upper-case and lower-case lettering, and
  - adding some number to the beginning and/or end of each word.
- *Crack by Alec Muffett* and *John the Ripper* are advertised on the Web.
- A *brute force* attack tries all n-character strings as passwords.

To counter the forces of evil, systems' managers enforce several antihacking procedures, including:

- Changing the passwords on a regular basis.
- Requiring that the password must be at least 8 characters long and contain at least
  - at least one alphabet character a,...,z, A,...,Z;
  - at least one numeric character 0, ... , 9;
  - one special character from the set ' ! © $ % ~& () - _ = + [ ] ; : ' ",<.>/ ?.
- The password must not
  - contain spaces,
  - begin with an exclamation [!] or a question mark [?], or
  - contain your login ID.
- The password must not contain repeated letters and be case sensitive.

18.2 MAGNETIC STRIPE TECHNOLOGY

A *magnetic stripe* is used to store information on plastic bank credit cards, ATM cards, and on paper airline tickets. The use of magnetic stripe technology to record machine-readable information originated over four decades ago:

- The London Transit Authority installed a magnetic stripe system in the London Underground in the early 1960s;
- The San Francisco BART (Bay Area Rapid Transit) system began using magnetic striped fare cards in the late 1960s.

The stripe is made of tiny magnetic particles in a resin. The *coercivity* of the stripe (with units *Oersteds*) is a measure of how difficult it is to encode the information on the card. Higher coercivity increases the difficulty of recording data and diminishes the danger of accidental loss of data. A standard bank card has a coercivity of 300 Oe. The Uniform Industrial Corporation's cards have coercivity from 300 to 4000 Oe. The material used to fabricate the magnetic particles plays a factor in determining the coercivity; low coercivity uses iron oxide, high coercivity uses barium ferrite. The fabricating materials are mixed with a resin to form a *slurry*, which is coated on the substrate (the card) and dried. On paper airline tickets, the magnetic stripe slurry is coated on the card during manufacture. The particles of the stripe are then *aligned* to give a good signal-to-noise ratio. Iron oxide is easy to align; barium ferrite is harder. The end-user defines the requirements, including the signal amplitude needed and the bit density of the recording. The density of the particles in the resin influences the signal amplitude; the more particles, the higher the signal amplitudes.

The polarity of the magnetic particles changes with each bit; together with a coding scheme, this determines the binary data on the card. The magnetic material can be polarized in one of two directions corresponding to 0 and 1. F2F (Two Frequency Recording; Fig. 18.2) is an industry standard coding scheme; it is analogous to a combination of *differential polar* and *Manchester* coding of electrical signals. A "0" does not have a (polarity) transition in the middle of the signal interval *T*; a "1" has a transition. The three card formats

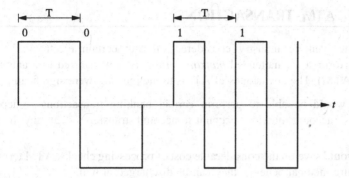

Figure 18.2   F2F (Two frequency recording).

(IATA [Track 1], ABA [Track 2], and Thrift [Track 3]) encode at densities of 210 bits/in., corresponding to 75 bits/in. using either 7- or 5-bit character encoding.

18.2.1   The Case of the Larcenous Laundry (Fig. 18.3)

In the 1970s it became apparent that there were security problems connected with magnetic stripe recoding on BART system cards. According to Michael Harris, a reporter for the *San Francisco Chronicle*, Dr Bill Wattenberg claimed an inexpensive scheme existed to circumvent the value of a BART system ticket. Wattenberg holds a PhD in engineering and was at that time working at a UC Berkeley laboratory. Michael Harris wrote that although IBM (the vendor for the BART system) claimed that "anyone would need at least $500,000 worth of specialized electronic equipment to copy the magnetic stripe and fool their reading machines", Wattenberg asserted that he had devised a simple scheme that any housewife could do in her kitchen. How sexist!! And tut, tut, Wattenberg is from Berkeley. Wattenberg refused to divulge the method to IBM or to the BART system management. For the skeptical, Michael Harris provided a demonstration of Wattenberg's scheme. An article appeared in *Business Week* (August 11, 1973, p. 120) providing detailed instructions on how to duplicate a BART system fare card using an ordinary iron.

Various methods exist today to protect magnetic stripe recording against copying and/ or alteration, including watermarking. For further information, visit the Web site of Watermark Technologies. For those of the opposite inclination, a visit to www.fakeiddexpress.com may prove interesting.

Figure 18.3   Lucky, Number One Son Studied Cryptography at UCSB! (Courtesy of Roger Shimomura and Greg Kucera Gallery, Seattle)

18.3   PROTECTING ATM TRANSACTIONS

In the 1960s, the banking industry considered offering certain electronic banking services to be performed at unattended *banking terminals* now referred to a automated teller machines (ATM). The advantages of ATMs to the industry were significant:

- Customers would be able to perform certain banking transactions – deposits, withdrawals, account queries, account-to-account transfers – at any hour of the day.
- The bank would save on the considerable cost of processing checks; ATM terminals do not require medical benefits, they can be discharged at will.
- Electronic transactions would not require human supervision or intervention, permitting labor savings.

Two conflicting forces have influenced the design of electronic banking systems:

- *Profitability* – the desire by the bank to improve their bottom line;[2]
- *Security* – the fear that individuals might learn how to penetrate the system, for example, to empty the ATM of cash in a largely invisible manner.

The considerable experience of banks with credit card transactions pointed to certain risks, including the use of counterfeit, lost, or stolen banking cards.[3]

It was decided that a valid transaction would therefore require a customer to offer two *bona fides* in establishing a customer's identity:

- The banking card recording the user *primary account number* (PAN) on the card's third stripe;
- A separate identifying element.

Possession of an ATM card alone would not permit a customer to enter into a transaction. The question remained: What should the second identifying element be?

18.3.1   Customer Authentication

If two quantities (Q_1, Q_2) are required for a customer to be authenticated to the system, possible choices of the second *identifier* Q_2 might be

1. The customer's signature;
2. The customer's voiceprint;
3. The customer's fingerprint;
4. A password assigned to the customer.

Signatures and voiceprints vary under stress; indeed, handwriting and voiceprints vary too much under stress to provide a reliable identification method and were too costly to implement in the 1960s. Fingerprints have some connotation of criminality

---

[2]According to Bankrate.com's latest survey (2005) of large banks and thrifts, ATM fees have hit a record high and, despite rising interest rates, interest checking accounts still do not add up. In short, consumers are finding that money sometimes comes out of their checking accounts faster than it goes in.

[3]*Fox News* reported in 2003 that "More than 27 million people have been victims of identity theft in the last five years, costing them $5 billion and businesses and financial institutions almost $48 billion, the Federal Trade Commission said Wednesday."

TABLE 18.1   ATM PAN–PIN Table

User_ID	PAN Q_1	PIN Q_2
Koheim, Alan G.	17894567	8974
Smith, John L.	76654321	7860

that might affect the marketability of ATM systems adversely. The least expensive solution involves a password or *personal identification number* (PIN).

In an ATM transaction, a customer would

- Insert the banking card into the ATM's card reader; the primary account number (PAN $= Q_1$) would be read;
- Enter the PIN ($= Q_2$) at the ATM's keyboard.

To establish the authenticity of a customer, the system must have a mechanism for checking if the offered identifiers (Q_1, Q_2) are properly related. One possible authenticity protocol would reference a table maintained by the bank; the customer's account number (Q_1) is recorded on the banking card and the user enters the PIN (Q_2) at the banking terminal. The ATM terminal transmits the transaction request to the institution's computing system where (Q_1, Q_2) are checked by consulting a table stored somewhere in the system (Table 18.1) whenever authentication is required.

With this protocol, the PIN can be selected either by the customer or institution. The former possibility is attractive for marketing the system as it makes the customer feel that she or he is participating in the security of the system – and, if something goes wrong, the customer can be made to feel at least partially responsible!

There are possible threats to this authentication protocol, including the following.

1. The contents of the table might be compromised by a system's programmer; either information *revealed*, allowing Mr Green to pretend to be Mr Konheim, or information *added* to the system corresponding to a fictitious user.

2. The communications between the ATM and the computing system might be wiretapped so that the signals corresponding to Q_2 might be learned. The manufacture of counterfeit plastic banking cards or the alteration of stolen cards is not technically demanding.

There are remedies:

- The table might be enciphered and/or made write-protected to make it difficult even for a bank's system's programmer to *read* or *modify* its contents.
- Communications between the ATM and computing system might be enciphered to mitigate against wiretapping.

None of these is a complete solution; a portion of the enciphered table has to be logically "in the clear" when the authentication takes place, and during this time, it is exposed. On the other hand, the goal of an authentication protocol is not to make it *impossible* for an opponent to succeed, but to make it very *difficult* and not *cost-effective*. One way, is to limit the amount of cash that can be withdrawn in a 24-hour period.

However, an additional feature was insisted upon by the banking community, which still further complicated the authentication problem.

18.3.2 On-Line/Off-Line Operation

The reliability of computing systems and the need for periodic system maintenance in the 1960s almost mandated the use of banking systems with two modes of operation:

- *On-Line*: identification of a user is performed remotely by the institution's computing system;
- *Off-Line*: identification of a user is performed locally at the banking ATM.

The banks intended to allow both modes of operation to coexist; during normal operation, the authentication would be performed at the institution's computing system. When the system was *down* for repair or maintenance, authentication would be carried out at the ATM.

The limited capability of ATMs and the fact that the list of customers might grow to several millions of customers[4] implies that tables such as those described before *cannot* be stored locally at an ATM. There is a significant logistics problem; the list of customers changes each day. New customers are added and some are dropped. If, say, the 100 Bank of America ATMs in Los Angeles had to be updated daily, the cost advantage of ATMs would be lost. Moreover, banks wanted to cross state boundaries and form networks, like *Interlink*, the *PLUS SYSTEM*, and *CIRRUS*, which would require changes to be made nationally. It might be possible to make these changes by teleprocessing the table changes from the bank's computing system, but this exposes the system to wiretapping.

The solution was to make Q_1 and Q_2 functionally related,

$$Q_2 = f(Q_1),$$

and to check the relationship at the ATM during a customer transaction.

What kind of relationship f? Suppose Q_1 and Q_2 are decimal numbers and are related by

$$Q_2 = f(Q_1) = 1,000,000,000 - Q_1$$

so that Konheim's PIN is

$$Q_2(\text{Konheim}) = 1,000,000,000 - 17,894,567 = 999,982,105,433$$

This relationship f is unacceptable; first, it requires a customer to remember a 12-digit key. It is likely that the customer will write the PIN on the card instead of committing it to memory, thus negating the entire purpose of a separate identifying element. However, more importantly, the relationship f in the equation above is too simple. Customers might learn how Q_1 and Q_2 are related and this would enable them (or others) to counterfeit card–PIN pairs, which would be accepted by an ATM terminal during off-line operation. What is required is a "complicated" relationship f that cannot be easily discovered by the users.

The solution – encipherment!

Suppose Q_2 is some encipherment of the account number (Q_1) $Q_2 = E_K\{Q_1\}$. If the cryptographic algorithm $E_K\{\cdots\}$ is sufficiently strong, then knowledge of the pair (Q_1, Q_2) or even a large number of pairs $(\{Q_1^{(i)}, Q_2^{(i)}\} : 1 \leq i \leq N\}$ might not permit a customer easily to deduce the secret key K.

---

[4]There were 88 million ATM cards in the United Kingdom alone in 2003 according to the Economic & Social Research Council. I cannot find the same number for the United States, but an article at www.atmmarketplace. com claims the number of ATMs worldwide is expected to hit 1.5 million in 2006.

To authenticate a customer, the ATM must check if the relationship $Q_2 = E_K\{Q_1\}$ is satisfied. This means that the *authentication key* K must reside at each ATM. This poses a risk and the bank must be careful to safeguard revealing the key. Each ATM contains a *high-security module* (HSM), a tamper-resistant coprocessor that performs the PIN-validation; the ATM-key resides securely in what is believed to be the tamper-proof HSM.

The IBM Corporation developed an ATM protocol for Lloyd's Banking, initially based on LUCIFER but later retrofitted to the DES algorithm. The authentication protocol used in the IBM LIBERTY banking system is a version of the protocol described in Chapter 9 used by the earlier IBM 3984 Cash Issuing Terminal.

If the PAN(User_ID) is assigned by the bank and PIN(User_ID) = E_K {PAN(User_ID)} is calculated by the card-issuer, it follows that the customer is not able to idependently select the PIN(User_ID). A solution to permit the user to select a U-PIN((User_ID)) was devised in 1957 by Chubb Integrated Systems, a British firm that marketed an early ATM system. Chubb introduced a PINOffset, which is magnetically recorded on the card. The PIN(User_ID), PINOffset(User_ID), and U-PIN(User_ID) in the IBM 3624 system are related by

$$U - PIN(User\_ID) = Left_{16}[E_K\{PAN(User\_ID)\}] + PINOffset(User\_ID)$$

where Left $+ 16[\ldots]$ denotes the leftmost 16 bits of $\ldots.$

In an ATM Transaction,

1. A customer inserts the ATM card into the ATM terminal's card reader,
2. The user keys in U-PIN(User_ID),
3. The PAN(User_ID) and PINOffset(User_ID) are read from the ATM card, and
4. The U-PIN(User_ID) = $Left_{16}[E_K\{PAN(User\_ID)\}]$ + PINOffset(User_ID) computation is made at the terminal and the validity of the relationship U-PIN(User_ID) = $Left_{16}[E_K$ {PAN(User_ID)}] + PINOffset(User_ID) is checked.

One drawback of this scheme is that the 4-hex digit U-PIN(User_ID) may include $0, 1, \ldots, 9, A, B, \ldots, F$ and the characters $A, B, \ldots, F$ are not normally on the ATM keyboard. To solve this problem, a *decimalization table* mapping the U-PIN(User_ID) into the decimal digits is introduced. The default table is presented in Table 18.2. The PIN verification test is performed at the ATM module on an HSM. The IBM "Common Cryptographic Architecture" is an application program interface (API) for HSM with syntax `Encrypted_PIN_Verify(...)`, which returns a YES/NO value. In addition to the PAN, one of the inputs is the decimalization table.

Recently Bond and Zelinski [2003] exploited this to show how ATM U-PIN (User_ID)s could be found by a dishonest system programmer.

TABLE 18.2 Standard Decimalization Table

0	1	2	3	4	5	6	7	8	9	A	B	C	D	E	F
0	1	2	3	4	5	6	7	8	9	0	1	2	3	4	5

18.3.3 The Bond–Zelinski PIN Attack

Programmers with access to the bank's computing system are permitted to perform PIN verification using the HSM, making 60 tests per second. A system programmer tests a (PAN,PIN_Offset)-entry with 10 different User_PINs chosen as follows; the User_PIN$_j$ is selected so that

$$\text{User\_PIN}_j + \text{PIN\_Offset} = (j,j,j,j), \qquad 0 \leq j \leq 9,$$

and the decimalization table is chosen so that the second row contains 1 for the first row entry j. The HSM's output will be YES if some digit of the PIN is j, and 0, otherwise. Thus, 10 tests will determine the digits that appear in the PIN. If the number of distinct digits in the PIN is k, then T_k additional tests are required where

$$T_k = \begin{cases} 1, & \text{if } k = 1 \\ 14, & \text{if } k = 2 \\ 36, & \text{if } k = 3 \\ 24, & \text{if } k = 4. \end{cases}$$

The average number of tests is ~24. If a bank allows a card to withdraw \$200, then during a 30-minute lunch break, a dishonest programmer can discover

$$\frac{30 \times 60 \times 60}{24} \approx 450$$

PINs and withdraw \$90,000.

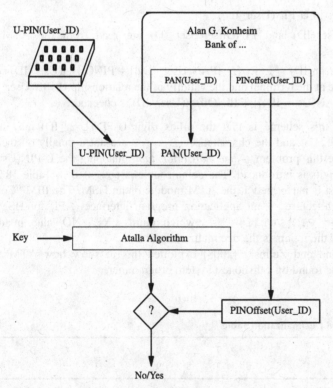

Figure 18.4 Atalla ATM authentication.

This attack on PINs corresponds to a search tree. Bond and Zelinski [2003] developed an improved algorithm that reduces the number of tests. There are several possible remedies; the simplest is to deny the use of a decimalization table as an input. Atalla Technovations introduced a variant of this equation; the customer appears at the issuer's facility and chooses U-PIN(User_ID), which is *not* revealed to the banking institution (Fig. 18.4). The concatenation of the PAN(User_ID) and U-PIN(User_ID), are enciphered by DES to derive the PINOffset(User_ID), which is recorded magnetically on the card:

$$\text{PINOffset(User\_ID)} = DES_K\{\text{PAN(User\_ID)}\|\text{U-PIN(User\_ID)}\}.$$

Off-line authentication consists of repeating the process at the ATM. These is one possible advantage of relating the U-PIN(User_ID) and PINOffset(User_ID) by this relationship. The advantage is that the customer's PIN(User_ID) is not stored at the banking institution.

The National Cash Register Company (NCR) also marketed an ATM product line. An NCR proprietary algorithm $E_{KEY}\{\ldots\}$ was originally implemented, but NCR shifted to DES when it became available.

18.3.4   The ANSI Standard X9.1-1980 ANSI, 1980

The ubiquitous magnetically encoded bankcard contains three stripes (bands) (Fig. 18.5).

- *Track 1*:   International Airlines Transport Association (IATA) Track. Intended for airline-ticket sales from terminals. Read only.
- *Track 2*:   American Bankers Association (ABA) Track. Intended for point-of-sales and credit card transactions; for example, VISA/Mastercard. Read only.
- *Track 3*:   ANSI developed standard for use in electronic funds transfer (EFT). Read and write.

18.3.5   ATM Transactions

The most successful commercial application of cryptography has been in facilitating transactions involving ATMs. Originally intended to be used for transactions at a single banking institution, ATMs have evolved to provide truly international banking. The steps in an ATM transaction are:

1. PAN(User_ID) and PINOffset(User_ID) is read from the ATM card;

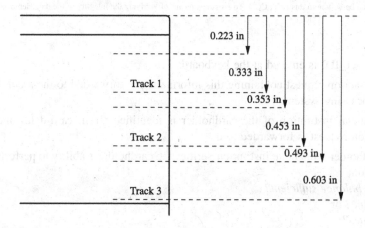

Figure 18.5   ANSI X9.1 Three-track credit/debit card format.

TABLE 18.3   ANSI X9.1 Track 3 Format

Field name	Usage	Status	Length
Start sentinel	M	S	1
Format code	M	S	2
Primary account number (PAN)	M	S	19
Separator (SEP)	M	S	1
Country code or SEP	M	S	3/1
Currency	M	S	3
Currency exponent	M	S	1
Amount authorized per cycle period	M	S	4
Amount remaining this period	M	D	4
Cycle begin	M	D	4
Cycle length	M	S	2
Retry count	M	D	1
PIN control parameters (PINPARM) or SEP	M	S	6/1
Interchange control	M	S	1
Type of account and service restriction (PAN)	M	S	2
Type of account and service restriction (SAN-1)	M	S	2
Type of account and service restriction (SAN-2)	M	S	2
Expiration date or SEP	M	S	4/1
Card sequence number	M	S	1
Card security number or SEP	M	D	9/1
First subsidiary account number (SAN-1)	O	S	Variable
SEP	M	S	1
Secondary subsidiary account number (SAN-2)	O	S	Variable
SEP	M	S	1
Relay marker	M	S	1
Crypto check digits (CCD) or SEP	M	D	6/1
Discretionary data	O	D	Variable
End sentinel	M	S	1
Longitudinal redundancy check (LRS)	M	D	1
			107

M, mandatory field; O, optional field; D, dynamic field (writable); S, static field (read only); PINPARM, Optional security feature; PINOffset can be written in this field; CCD, To provide a means of verifying the integrity of the data elements on Track 3.

2. U-PIN(User_ID) is entered at the keyboard;

3. The transaction request containing this information is forwarded to the *local* ATM bank processing system.

4. The financial institution of the cardholder is identified (from card-data) and the transaction request is forwarded to it.

5. The cardholder's financial institution verifies the cardholder's ability to perform the transaction;
   Account balance sufficient?
   Credit-line? or
   Stolen card?
   and authorization to the local bank to carry out the transaction is forwarded to it.

The same sequence is followed when a credit card is offered as payment at a *point-of-sale* (POS) system.

18.3.6 Track 3 Format

Table 18.3 gives the ANSI X9.1 Track 3 contents.

18.4 KEYED-ACCESS CARDS

The IBM Corporation decided in 1972 to offer customers a *keyed regulated entrance system* to control access into their facilities supported by an IBM Series/1 processing system. The Series/1 Controlled Access System is described in an IBM publication dated March 21, 1978. Each employee would possess a card on which an identifier would be magnetically recorded. The data on the card is the encipherment of the pair (ID,PW) of 5-digit decimal numbers. The ciphertext data on the card would be read at a card reader at an entry door, be deciphered, and (ID,PW) would be verified at the system's database. A single IBM Series/1 processor could handle 31 entry points. The design constraints of the system were these:

1. The data would be read by a card-reader – *no* user-entry of data at a key-pad would be provided;
2. The system database would *not* contain a listing of every valid employee;
3. The database would be able to maintain a list of lost/stolen *and* reported cards;
4. The card-readers would transmit the data read from the card to a shared processor;
5. The verification-processing needed to be simple and fast;
6. The fabrication of bogus cards had to be *in*feasible.

Although the copying of valid access cards existed, it seemed less of a problem for a company who could discharge an employee if it discovered the employee allowed the copying of the keyed-access card.

The keyed-access card of the IBM product contained the encipherment Y of two 16-bit numbers (ID,PW) – approximately two 5-digit decimal numbers

$$Y = E\{C\}$$

$$ID + PW = C(\text{modulo } 10^5)$$

$$0 \leq ID < 2^{16} = 65,636, \qquad 0 < PW < 2^{16}, \qquad 2^{15} < C < 2^{16}.$$

The encipherment algorithm $E\{\cdots\}$ is a variant of that described in Section 9.21.

18.5 SMART CARDS

A *smart card* is a banking card containing an embedded processor; compared to a PC, the smart card's computational power and memory are significantly limited. The ISO standard 7810 specifies the physical details of the smart card designated as ID-1. The dimensions are 85.60 mm (L) × 53.98 mm (W) × 0.80 mm (T). Even the corner radius of 3.18 mm is specified. Leave nothing to chance!

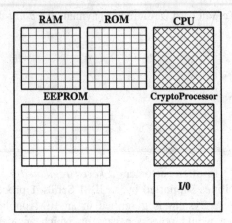

Figure 18.6 Smart card memory.

18.5.1 Smart Card Memory

Figure 18.6 illustrates the different types of memory contained on smart cards.

- ROM (*read-only memory*) – 6–24 Kbytes storing the operating system;
- RAM (*random access memory*) – 256–1024 bytes used as working memory; RAM is *volatile*, meaning that its contents are lost when power to the smart card is removed.
- EEPROM (*electrically erasable programmable memory*) – 1–16 Kbytes of memory that
  - can be written to externally,
  - can be erased externally by an electrical charge, and
  - retains its state when the power is removed.

18.5.2 External Interface of Smart Cards

Most smart cards require an external source of energy. One standard method to transfer data is to use a *card acceptor device* (CAD), which allows for the half-duplex exchange of data at the rate of ≥ 9600 b/s. The ISO standard 7816/3 provides either six or eight connection points for (external) power to the smart card. ISO 7816, Part 1 [ISO, 1998] describes the locations and functions of the contacts on the smart card (Table 18.4).

TABLE 18.4   ISO 7816 Smart Card Contacts

Position		Function
C1	Vcc	Voltage supply
C2	RST	Reset
C3	CLK	Clock frequency
C4	RFU	Reserved for future use
C5	GND	Ground
C6	Vpp	External voltage
C7	I/O	Serial I/O
C8	RLU	Reserved for future use

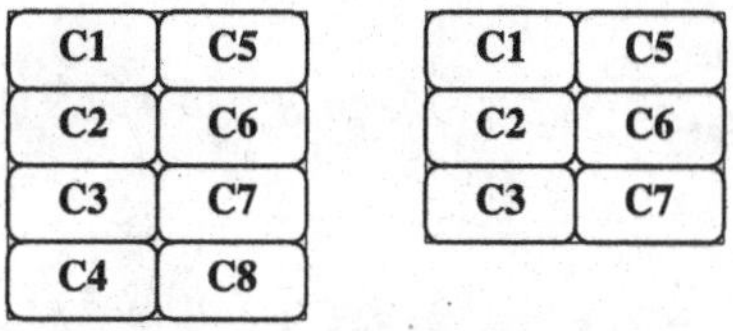

C1	C5
C2	C6
C3	C7
C4	C8

C1	C5
C2	C6
C3	C7

Figure 18.7 Smart card memory interface.

Some newer cards are *contactless* and exchange data over a small distance by inductive or capacitive coupling. The smart card/terminal interface (Fig. 18.7) supports only half-duplex data transmission.

18.5.3 Smart Card Processing

A smart card typically contains an 8-bit microprocessor running at 5 MHz. The operating system is required to handle a small number of tasks, including:

- Half-duplex data transmission;
- Control and execution of instruction sequences;
- Running of management functions;
- Protecting access to data on the card;
- Memory and file management;
- Execution of cryptographic application programs (API).

As a smart card is *not* intended to be a general-purpose processor, it does not supply an interface for users.

18.5.4 Smart Card Functionalities

The cryptographic and related functions on a smart card include

- RSA with 512, 768, or 1024 bit keys;
- The digital signature algorithm (DHA);
- DES and triple-DES;
- Random number generation (RNG).

18.5.5 The Electronic Purse

The advantages of a *cashless society* have been discussed for some time. One application of the smart card is the *electronic wallet* or *electronic purse*. The owner of the smart card deposits at his/her bank a sum. An entry is made (by the bank) on the smart card, which is used as cash. When a purchase is made using the smart card, the amount is debited on the card. What a creative idea for the bank! Perhaps you might even receive interest on the money deposited at the bank, but certainly not at the annual rate of 18%/year. Clearly a pig as in Figure 18.8 is involved, but perhaps it is not used in making the purse.

Although there were high hopes for the viability of electronic purses in the 1990s, according to Leo Van Hove [http://www.firstmonday,dk/.issues/issues/issues5_7/hove/], the public has not been very receptive.

Figure 18.8   *The E-Pig* - Artwork by Carol L. Konheim.

18.5.6   Smart Card Vendors

Several different vendors have introduced smart cards, including

- *PC/SC*:   Microsoft for personal computers;
- *Open Card*:   Java-based standard for POS (point-of-sale), laptops;
- *JavaCard*:   Proposed as a standard by Schlumberger.

18.5.7   The Role of the Smart Card

The smart card will provide *proof of identity* when a user is communicating with a remote server. Secure transactions involving a smart card will require cryptography. If the identification process is based on public-key cryptography, then

- The key will need to be stored in the EEPROM,
- The smart card will need to read-protect the key, and
- The owner of the card will need to use a PIN to *prove* identity to the card.

Various physical attacks on the information stored in a card have been proposed. One is based on the observation that the contents of the EEPROM can be erased or modified by modifying the voltage applied to the card's contacts. Paul Kocher refers to variants of these attacks as *differential power analysis* (DPA) [www.cryptography.com]. Other physical attacks involve heat and UV light.

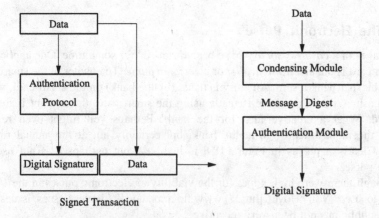

Figure 18.9   TRASEC protocol.

18.5.8 Protocols for Smart Cards

The two articles by Ph. van Heurck [1987, 1989] are among the earliest proposing the application of smart cards. C.I.R.I. is an association of banks in Belgium. These banks created TRASEC in 1987 to develop and maintain a system to develop and implement electronic <u>TRA</u>nsactions in a <u>SEC</u>ure manner.

Several authentication schemes are described; in one scheme, data are suffixed with a digital signature using the protocol in Figure 18.9.

18.6 WHO CAN YOU TRUST?: KOHNFELDER'S CERTIFICATES

Kohnfelder writes in Part I, Section D, *Weaknesses in Public-Key Cryptosystems* of his thesis,

> *Although the enemy may eavesdrop on the key transmission system, the key must be sent via a channel in such a way that the originator of the transmission is reliably known.*

Kohnfelder observed that *all* public-key cryptosystems are vulnerable to a *spoofing* attack if the public keys are not certified; User_ID[C] pretending to be User_ID[A] *to* User_ID[B] by providing User_ID[C]'s public-key (in place of User_ID[A]'s public key) *to* User_ID[B]. Unless User_ID[B] has some way of checking the correspondence between ID[A] and PuK(ID[K]), this type of spoofing attack is possible.

Kohnfelder proposed a method to make spoofing more difficult in Part III of his thesis. He postulates the existence of a *public file* $\mathcal{F}$ that contains (in my notation) pairs {(ID[A]), PuK([ID[A])} for each user in the system. Although it might be possible for User_ID[C] to contact $\mathcal{F}$ to ask for a copy of User_ID[A]'s public key, the public file solution suffers from the same operational defects as a network-wide key server:

- What entity will maintain and certify a large database that is continually changing?
- The public file will need to be replicated to prevent severe access times to obtain information.

Kohnfelder defines a *certificate* as a data set consisting of an *authenticator* ($A_{ID[A]}$) and an *identifier* (ID[A]), which are related by

$$A_{ID[A]} = E_{PrK([\mathcal{F}])}\{ID[A], \; PuK(ID[A])\},$$

where $PrK([\mathcal{F}])$ is the private key of $\mathcal{F}$.

Any user can check the correspondence $AU_{ID} \Leftrightarrow ID$ by making the comparison

$$ID[A], PuK(ID[A]) \stackrel{?}{=} E_{PrK([\mathcal{F}])}\{AU_{ID[A]}\},$$

where $PuK([\mathcal{F}])$ is the well-known public key of $\mathcal{F}$. However, if the public-key cryptosystem is *strong*, then it will not be computationally feasible for a user to determine $PrK([\mathcal{F}])$ from $PuK([\mathcal{F}])$.

18.7 X.509 CERTIFICATES

Until this last quarter century, cryptography needed to be supported in a very limited community. During the Gulf War, secure communications were needed between Washington, U.S. bases in Europe and Japan, and the forces stationed in the Gulf region. Moreover, parties having the capability to monitor and decipher in a timely manner communications between Washington and the Gulf were very limited.

All this has changed because of the Internet; in 1990 there were over 300,000 *hosts* (mainframe machines). Vincent Cerf claimed several years ago that there were over 60 million Internet users then existing. The number of potential user-to-user endpoints is staggering. Public-key cryptography provided a vehicle to replaced the $\left(\frac{N}{2}\right)$-key distribution with N users to one of complexity N. Nevertheless, User_ID[A] must make available the public key PuK(ID[A]) to all users who wish to communicate with User_ID[A]. The thought of a server maintaining a file containing several million keys is absurd. Moreover, even if such a server is contemplated, there is the need to prevent a spoofing attack, wherein User_ID[A]'s public key is temporarily replaced by that of the spoofer.

The proposed solution, based on the user of certificates, provides a link between User_ ID[A]'s network identifier ID[A] and public key PuK(ID[A]). It is planned that various *Certificate Authorities* (CA) will be set up to issue certificates. Such a certificate would

- Need to be issued by a trustworthy party, and
- Be computationally infeasible to forge.

If User_ID[A] wishes to enter into a transaction with User_ID[B], a User_ID[A]-certificate is made delivered (or otherwise made available) to User_ID[B]. The data on the certificate *bind* the pair (ID[A], PuK(ID[A])). User_ID[B] verifies the binding by testing the certificate. Implicit is the assumption that only a valid CA could construct a certificate. Certificates use the same paradigm as public-key cryptography; namely, the signature on the certificate is encipherment of certificate data using the key of the CA.

- User_ID[A] signs DATA using User_ID[A]'s public key appending the certificate.
- User_ID[B] first uses the certificate to verify that PuK(ID[A]) is the public key of the user with identifier ID[A].
- If the agreement is verified, User_ID[B] can then examine the DATA and decide on some action.

What has been gained? The advantage is that *only* the CA's public key must be secured rather than *all* public keys being securely stored. On the other hand, if someone can learn the CA's private key, then all of the certificates become meaningless.

Maintaining worldwide compatibility in communications is the charter of the International Telegraph Union (ITU),[5] an agency of the United Nations. The CCITT (Comité Consultatif Internationale de Télégraphique et Téléphonique) was formed in 1956 by merging the CCIT (Télégraphique) and CCIF (Téléphonique). A reorganization in 1989 divided the ITU into three sectors:

- International Radiocommunications Sector (ITU-R);
- International Telecommunication Development Sector (ITU-D);
- International Telecommunication Standardization Sector (ITU-T).

X-509 [ITU, 1989] is the draft CCITT Recommendation describing the certificate protocol shown in Figure 18.10. X.509 v3.0 [RFC2549] updates the recommendation providing additional functionality.

The fields in an X.509-certificate include:

Serial Number: Unique identifier for the certificate.

Algorithm Identifier: Specifies algorithm used to sign certificate by CA.

Subject: The name of entity *to* whom the certificate is used.

[5]International Telecommunication Union, Telecommunication Standardization Bureau, Place des Nations CH-1211 Geneva 20; tsbdoc@itu.int also www.itu.int/ITU-T

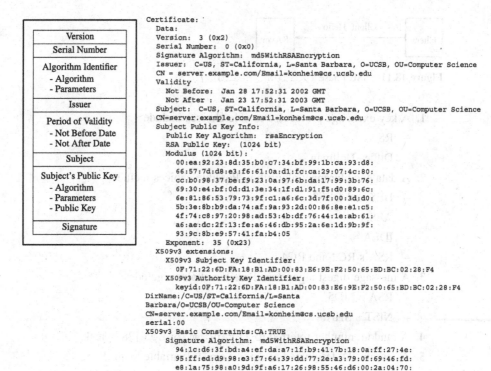

```
Certificate:
  Data:
    Version: 3 (0x2)
    Serial Number: 0 (0x0)
    Signature Algorithm: md5WithRSAEncryption
    Issuer: C=US, ST=California, L=Santa Barbara, O=UCSB, OU=Computer Science
    CN = server.example.com/Email=konheim@cs.ucsb.edu
    Validity
      Not Before: Jan 28 17:52:31 2002 GMT
      Not After : Jan 23 17:52:31 2003 GMT
    Subject: C=US, ST=California, L=Santa Barbara, O=UCSB, OU=Computer Science
    CN=server.example.com/Email=konheim@cs.ucsb.edu
    Subject Public Key Info:
      Public Key Algorithm: rsaEncryption
      RSA Public Key: (1024 bit)
      Modulus (1024 bit):
        00:ea:92:23:8d:35:b0:c7:34:bf:99:1b:ca:93:d8:
        66:57:7d:d8:e3:f6:61:0a:d1:fc:ca:29:07:4c:80:
        cc:b0:98:37:be:f9:23:0a:97:6b:da:17:99:3b:76:
        69:30:e4:bf:0d:d1:3e:34:1f:d1:91:f5:d0:89:6c:
        6e:81:86:53:79:73:9f:c1:a6:6c:3d:7f:00:3d:d0:
        5b:3e:8b:b9:da:74:af:9a:93:2d:00:86:8e:e1:c5:
        4f:74:c8:97:20:98:ad:53:4b:df:76:44:1e:ab:61:
        a6:ae:dc:2f:13:fe:a6:46:db:95:2a:6e:1d:9b:9f:
        93:9c:8b:e9:57:41:fa:b4:05
      Exponent: 35 (0x23)
    X509v3 extensions:
      X509v3 Subject Key Identifier:
        0F:71:22:6D:FA:18:B1:AD:00:83:E6:9E:F2:50:65:BD:BC:02:28:F4
      X509v3 Authority Key Identifier:
        keyid:0F:71:22:6D:FA:18:B1:AD:00:83:E6:9E:F2:50:65:BD:BC:02:28:F4
  DirName:/C=US/ST=California/L=Santa
  Barbara/O=UCSB/OU=Computer Science
  CN=server.example.com/Email=konheim@cs.ucsb.edu
  serial:00
  X509v3 Basic Constraints:CA:TRUE
    Signature Algorithm: md5WithRSAEncryption
      94:1c:d6:3f:bd:a4:ef:da:a7:1f:b9:41:7b:18:0a:ff:27:4e:
      95:ff:ed:d9:98:e3:f7:64:39:dd:77:2e:a3:79:0f:69:46:fd:
      e8:1a:75:98:a0:9d:9f:a6:17:26:98:55:46:d6:00:2a:04:70:
      a8:66:e6:98:0c:8b:35:39:9a:e1:8b:76:d4:b7:9f:b2:3b:22:
      91:c9:61:ef:00:fe:2a:8a:e0:93:67:9f:72:95:36:0b:fc:30:
      ce:ef:b0:8b:d0:d0:5a:49:4f:ab:c0:fd:f2:55:4c:28:81:fc:
      4e:1a:39:e3:e8:00:5a:7c:45:ca:02:39:be:b1:53:ba:c3:18:
      32:39
```

Figure 18.10   X.509 certificate.

Signature: A signature derived by hashing all fields and enciphering using the certificate authority's private key. The hashing functions MD2, MD5, and SHA-1, and the public-key cryptosystems RSA and DSA are supported.

The certificate provides the *link* between the ID[A] and PuK(ID[A]).

18.8   THE SECURE SOCKET LAYER (SSL)

SSL was originated by *Netscape*; it consists of several upper layer protocols[5] by which a pair of users – the *Client* and the *Server* – agree on a key exchange method, an encipherment algorithm, and a message digest.

In what follows we go through the *Handshake Protocol* initiated by a client.

Phase 1 – Client Initiation   The Client proposes the following (Fig. 18.11).

[5]In order for users on two systems to communicate, a common set of rules must be implemented. The International Standards Organization recognized the need in 1977 for the standardization of information-network architectures. ISO's TC97 committee, responsible for information systems, created the Open Systems Interconnection (OSI) model in 1979. Influenced by the earlier network architectures of IBM (SNA 1974) "Systems Network Architecture: Technical Overview" (Third Edition), IBM Corporation, September 1986 and the Digital Equipment Corporation (DNA 1975) "DECnet DIGITAL Network Architecture (Phase V): General Description", Digital Equipment Corporation, September 1987, the ISO Open System Interconnection model divided the services needed to implement computer communication into *layers*.

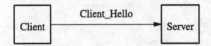

Figure 18.11 SSL Phase 1 (`Client_Hello`).

1. A key exchange protocol. Possible choices include
   - RSA,
   - Diffie–Hellman.
2. A data encipherment algorithm. Possible choices include
   - DES and DES3,
   - AES,
   - IDEA,
   - RSA's RC2 and RC4.
3. A message digest algorithm. Possible choices include
   - RSA's MD5,
   - NIST's SHA.
4. A random number referred to as `random_bytes` [28 bytes].
5. A session ID designated as `SessionID` [variable length].
6. A (lossless) compression method identifier [integer $1 \leq C\_ID < 511$]; a complete specification is not included in the latest SSL-Specification.

Phase 1 – Server Response to `Client_Hello`: The Server accepts one of the choices made in the Client_Hello messages (Fig. 18.12).

Phase 2 – Server Authentication and Key Exchange: The Server delivers its certificate; when authentication/secrecy is enabled there is a key exchange. The Server requests a certificate from the Client (Fig. 18.13).

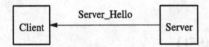

Figure 18.12 Server response to `Client_Hello`.

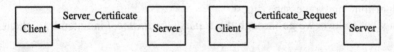

Figure 18.13 SSL Phase 2 – server authentication and key exchange.

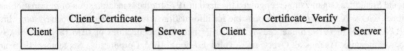

Figure 18.14 SSL phase 2 – client response to server.

Phase 2 – Client Response to Server: The Client delivers its certificate an explicit verification of the Server's certificate (Fig. 18.14).

18.8.1   The SSL Record Protocol

SSL provides for confidentiality (via encryption) and authentication (via a message authentication code, MAC). A block of application data is depicted in Figure 18.15:

1. It may be fragmented into several blocks;
2. Each fragmented block may be *compressed* by a lossless compression algorithm;
3. Each compressed fragment is suffixed by an underbar message authentication code (MAC);
4. Each Compressed_Block + MAC block is enciphered;
5. Each enciphered Compressed_Block + MAC is prefixed by an SSL Header.

18.8.2   The SSL MAC

The SSL MAC results from a hash of the compression of a fragment of the application data. The MAC is a *message digest*, that is, a fixed-length block of 0's and 1's derived from the compressed fragmented data using either RSA's MD5 algorithm or NIST's Secure Hash Algorithm (SHA).

The MAC is defined as

```
hash(MAC_write_secret || pad_2 ||
     hash(MAC_write_secret ||pad_1 ||seq_num ||
SSLCompressed.type ||
     SSLCompressed.length || SSLCompressed.fragment))
```
where

- hash = MD5 or SHA;
- || denotes concatenation;

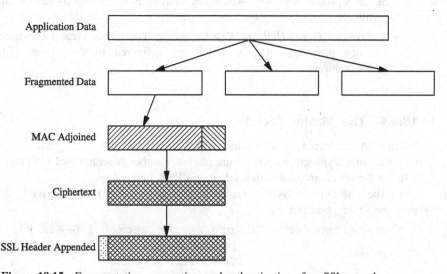

Figure 18.15   Fragmentation, encryption, and authentication of an SSL record.

- MAC_write_secret is a shared secret key;
- pad_1 is the byte (in hex) 36 = 0011 0110 repeated
  - 48 times (348 = 8 × 48 bits) for MD5, and
  - 40 times (320 = 8 × 40 bits) for SHA;
- pad_2 is the byte (in hex) 5C = 0101 1100 repeated
  - 48 times (348 = 8 × 48 bits) for MD5, and
  - 40 times (320 = 8 × 40 bits) for SHA;
- seq_num is the 64-bit sequence number for the SSL Record Protocol Message initialized to 0 and incremented up to $2^{64} - 1$;
- SSLCompressed.type identifies the higher layer protocol to process this fragment;
- SSLCompressed.length is the length of the compressed fragment;
- SSLCompressed.fragment is the compressed fragment of data (or the plaintext, if no compression is used).

18.8.3 The SSL Key Exchange

It remains to make the keys available to both the Client and Server. IF RSA is used for key exchange, the Client generates a pre_master_secret and delivers it to the Server enciphered using the Server's public RSA key, whose authenticity is attested to by the Client's X.509 certificate. The Client and Server process the pre_master_secret, deriving the keys used for the MAC and encipherment.

If Diffie–Hellman is used for key exchange, the Client has three options:

- *Fixed Diffie–Hellman Key Exchange*: Deliver an X.509 certificate to the Server containing (p,q) and attest to the authenticity of the Client's Diffie–Hellman parameters.

- *Ephemeral Diffie–Hellman Key Exchange*: The Client creates one-time Diffie–Hellman parameters (p,q), which are delivered to the Client enciphered using the Server's private RSA key, whose authenticity is attested to by the Client's X.509 certificate.

- *Anonymous Diffie–Hellman Key Exchange*: The Client creates one-time Diffie–Hellman parameters (p, q), which are delivered to the Client without any authentication.

18.8.4 The Master Secret

When RSA is selected for key exchange, the Client generates a pre_master_secret by means of a cryptographically secure random number generator [see §24] and transmits it to the Server enciphered with the Server's RSA public key.

The 48-byte (384-bit) master_secret (MS) is derived from the pre_master_secret by

```
master_secret = MD5(pre_master_secret || SHA(A ||
                    pre_master_secret ||
               ClientHello.random ||
               ServerHello.random))
```

```
         MD5(pre_master_secret || SHA(BB ||
               pre_master_secret ||
               ClientHello.random ||
               ServerHello.random))
         MD5(pre_master_secret || SHA(CCC ||
               pre_master_secret ||
               ClientHello.random ||
               ServerHello.random)) || [···]
```

where A, B, C, ... are hex digits and [···] denotes continued repetition of the MD5 hash until sufficient key is obtained.

The bit sequence ClientHello.random [32 bytes] contained in the ClientHello message is composed of

- gmt_unix_time (4 bytes) current time and date from UNIX internal clock;
- random_bytes (28 bytes) generated by a secure random number generator.

ServerHello.random (32 bytes) is the similar field in the ServerHello message.

SSL derives several keys from the master_secret:

- client_write_MAC_secret (5 bytes);
- server_write_MAC_secret (5 bytes);
- client_write_key (variable number of bytes);
- server_write_key (variable number of bytes).

These keys are derived from a key_block defined in terms of the master_secret as follows:

```
key_bock = MD5(master_secret || SHA(A || master_secret ||
               ServerHello.random ||
               ClientHello.random))
         MD5(master_sercret || SHA(BB ||
               master_secret || ServerHello.random ||
               ClientHello.random))
         MD5(master_secret || SHA(CCC || master_secret ||
               ServerHello.random ||
               ClientHello.random)) || [...]
```

The key_block is partitioned as follows:

```
client_MAC_write_secret(CipherSpec.hash_size)
server_MAC_write-secret(CipherSpec.hash_size)
client_write_key(CipherSpec.key_material)
server_write_key(CipherSpec.key_material)
client_write_IV(CipherSpec.IV_size) /*non-export ciphers */
server_write_IV(CipherSpec.IV_size) /*non-export ciphers */
```

Any additional key material is discarded.

The *write* keys for export ciphers (signaled by the parameter setting CipherSpec.is_exportable is true) are derived as follows:

```
final_client_write_key = MD5(client_write_key +
               ClientHello.random
                   ServerHello.random);
```

```
final_server_write_key = MD5(server_write_key +
                             ServerHello.random +
                             ClientHello.random);
      client_write_IV = MD5(ClientHello.random +
                             ServerHello.random);
      server_write_IV = MD5(ServerHello.random +
                             ClientHello.random);
```

18.8.5 Secure Random Number Generators

A pseudo-random number generator (PRG) is a device (software) whose purpose is to generate a sequence of independent and identically distributed random variables, usually with a uniform distribution on some set. A basic introduction to the properties required for a 'good' random number generator is contained in Golomb [1982]. A more up-to-date presentation of the theory of nonlinear shift register design is given in Rueppel [1986].

A PRG is a *pseudo-random bit generator* (PRBG) if PRG generates a bit stream $x_0, x_1, \ldots$, The PRG passes the *next bit test* if there is *no* polynomial-time algorithm that can solve the problem:

> *Given*: $x_0, x_1, \ldots, x_{\ell-1}$,
>
> *Determine*: x_e,

with probability greater than $1/2$ for all l.

A PRBG is a *cryptographically secure random number bit generator* (CSPRBG) if under some plausible but unproved mathematical assumption, it passes the next bit test.

Algorithm A (RSA PRBG)

1. Let p, q be primes, $n = pq$, $\phi = (p-1)(q-1)$ and e and integers $1 < e < \phi$, which is relatively prime to ϕ;

2. Choose $x - 1 \in [1, n-1]$ (the *seed*);

3. For i: $= 0$ to $\ell - 1$ do

   3.1 $x_i \leftarrow x_{i-1}^e$ (modulo n),

   3.2 z_i is the least significant bit of x_i;

4. $z_0, z_1, \ldots, z_{l-1}$ is the output sequence.

Algorithm A is a cryptographically secure random number generator.

18.9 MAKING A SECURE CREDIT CARD PAYMENT ON THE WEB

The *Secure Socket Layer* (SSL) protocol provides rules for a *Client* (agkonheim@cox.net) to enter into transactions with a *Server* (www.amazon.com). These two parties have different issues:

- The *Server* is concerned about the *Client's* willingness to pay, but can check the credit-worthiness of a *Client* with the issuer of the credit card and receive payment before providing any merchandize or service.

- The *Client* is concerned about revealing a credit card number to a fictitious *Server*, the old fake server as seen in *Get Smart!*

The SSL protocol described in Section 18.7 is modified to accommodate these different viewpoints. The *Server* is required to produce a certificate, but the *Client* is not. The *Client* does *not* normally require a certificate in credit-card transactions on the Web.

X.509 provided the mechanism for dealing with this environment which.

18.9.1 Certificate Hierarchies

To authenticate the link between a user's ID and public key, the user's certificate must be obtained and checked. The size of the potential community of users requiring certificates necessitates that multiple certificate authorities must exist. X.500 v1 uses the term directory information tree (DIT)[6] to describe the "network" of certificate authorities. Three levels are mentioned:

- Level 1: *Internet Policy Registration Authority* (IPRA);
- Level 2: *Policy Certification Authorities* (PCA);
- Level 3: *Certification Authorities* (CA).

A fragment of this tree is shown in Figure 18.16.

In the fragment of the DIT portrayed next

- CA2 has issued a certificate for CA1;
- CA3 has issued certificates for CA2 and CA5;
- CA4 has issued a certificate for CA3;
- CA5 has issued a certificate for CA6;
- CA1 has issued a certificate for User_ID[A] and User_ID[B];
- CA6 has issued a certificate for User_ID[C].

It is assumed that

- User_ID[1] knows the public key of CA1;
- User_ID[2] knows the public key of CA1;
- User_ID[3] knows the public key of CA6.

User_ID[1] Authenticates User_ID[2]'s Public Key: When User_ID[1] requests User_ID[2]'s certificate from User_ID[2], the `issuer` field in the certificate identifies CA1 as the issuing certificate authority. User_ID[1] can therefore check the authenticity of User_ID[2]'s public key.

User_ID[1] Authenticates User_ID[2]'s Public Key: When User_ID[1] requests User_ID[3]'s certificate from User_ID[3], the `issuer` field in the certificate identifies CA6 as the issuing certificate authority. User_ID[1] does *not* have CA6's public key and therefore *cannot* check the authenticity of User_ID[3]'s public key.

The nodes in the DIT contain sufficient information to make CA6's public key available.

---

[6]A tree is a graph consisting of vertices and edges in which there is no simple (traversing an edge at most once) closed path (starting and ending at the same vertex).

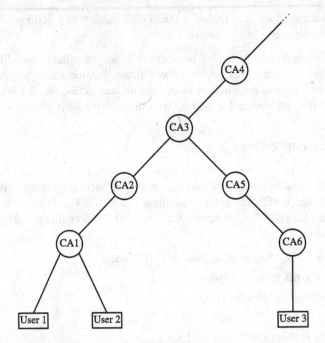

Figure 18.16 Fragment of directory information tree.

1. User_ID[1] requests CA1 to obtain the certificate of User_ID[3] from CA6.
2. CA1, with knowledge of the DIT, initiates the following data transfers:
   - CA5 obtains the certificate of User_ID[3] from CA6,
   - CA5 transmits the certificate of User_ID[3] and CA6 to CA3,
   - CA3 transmits the certificate of User_ID[3], CA5, and CA6 to CA2,
   - CA2 transmits the four certificates of User_ID[3], CA3, CA5, and CA6 to CA1, and finally
   - CA1 transmits the five certificates of User_ID[3], CA3, CA3, CA5, and CA6 to User_ID[1].
3. User_ID[1] can *unwrap* the certificate of User_ID[3] and check the validity of User_ID[3]'s public key.

When I place a credit card order with www.amazon.com, the following modified SSL-steps are followed by my *Netscape Communicator* or *Internet Explorer* browser:

SSL*-1 The browser requests Amazon to send its certificate CERT$_{www.amazon.com}$;

SSL*-2 Amazon's certificate identifies which Certificate Authority (CA) has issued the Amazon certificate and the browser uses the public key of CA, which is resident at the browser to validate the CERT$_{Amazon}$;
Verisign's DER-coded Class-1 certificate, which resides at my PC's *Internet Explorer* browser, is
```
V1
00 cd ba 7f 56 f0 df e4 bc 54 fe 22 ac b3 72 aa 55
md2RSA
OU = Class 1 Public Primary Certification Authority
```

```
O = VeriSign, Inc.
C = US
OU = Class 1 Public Primary Certification Authority
O = VeriSign, Inc.
C = US
Tuesday, August 01, 2028 4:59:59 PM
OU = Class 1 Public Primary Certification Authority
O = VeriSign, Inc.
C =US
30 81 89 02 81 81 00 e5 19 bf 6d a3 56 61 2d 99
48 71 f6 67 de b9 8d eb b7 9e 86 80 0a 91 0e fa 38
25 af 46 88 82 e5 73 a8 a0 9b 24 5d 0d 1f cc 65
6e 0c b0 d0 56 84 18 87 9a 06 9b 10 a1 73 df b4 58 39
6b 6e c1 f6 15 d5 a8 a8 3f aa 12 06 8d 31 ac 7f
b0 34 d7 8f 34 67 88 09 cd 14 11 e2 4e 45 56 69
if 78 02 80 da dc 47 91 29 bb 36 c9 63 5c c5 e0
d7 2d 87 7b a1 b7 32 b0 7b 30 ba 2a 2f 31 aa ee a3 67 da
db 02 03 01 00 01

sha1

90 ae a2 69 85 ff 14 80 4c 43 49 52 ec e9 60 84 77 af 55 6f
VeriSign Class 1 Public Primary CA
Secure Email
Client Authentication
```

SSL*-3 The browser acts for the Client and generates the `mster_secret` and follows the remaining steps to establish a secure connection.

REFERENCES

M. BOND AND P. ZELINSKI, "Decimilisation Table Attacks for PIN Cracking", University of Cambridge, Computer Laboratory, Report 560, February 2003.

DPA, DPA, www.cryptography.com.

ISO/IEC 7816, "ISO 7816 Smart Card Standard", Part 1, 1998.

G. PURDY, "A High Security Log-In Procedure", *Communications of the ACM*, **17**, 442–445 (1984).

RFC, "Internet X.509 Public Key Infrastructure: Certficiate and CRL Prfoile."

PH. VAN HEURCK, "TRASEC: National Security System for EFTSA in Belgium", *Computer Networks and ISDN Systems*, **14**, 389–395 (1987).

PH. VAN HEURCK, "Security and Protection in Information Systems", A. GRISSONMANCHE (ed.), Elsevier Science, 243–251 (1989).

ITU, CCITT, Recommendation X.509, "The Directory – Authentication Framework", Consultation Committee, International Telephone and Telegraph, International Telecommunication Union, Geneva, 1989.

American National Standards Institute, "The ANSI Standard X9.1-1980: Bank Cards – Magnetic Stripe Content for Track 3," 1980).

S. W. GOLOMB, *Shift Register Sequences*, Agean Park Press (Laguna Hills, California), 1982.

R. A. RUEPPEL, *Analysis and Design of Stream Ciphers*, Springer-Verlag, (New York, NY), 1986.

CHAPTER **19**

CRYPTOGRAPHIC PATENTS

"In the end, the only passion is money!", attributed to W. Somerset Maugham
"If Karl, instead of writing about capitalism, had made a lot of money...
    we would all have been much better off!", attributed to Karl Marx's mother
"A class who listens to lectures on law from a computer scientist, has a fool for a teacher,"
Abraham Lincoln

19.1 WHAT IS A PATENT?

A *patent* is a grant of an exclusive property right; the full scope of the right to exclude per
35 U.S.C. §271 is the right to exclude others from making, using, offering for sale, or
selling the invention throughout the United States or importing their invention into the
United States.

The term of a patent now starts on the date the patent issues and continues to the date
20 years after the application date per 35 U.S.C. §154. The change from the seventeen year
term was made in the 1990s to bring U.S. law into line with the patent laws of other
countries.

The federal patent power stems from Article I, §8, Clause 8 of the U.S. Constitution,
which authorizes Congress

*To promote the Progress of Science and useful Arts, by securing for limited Times to Authors and
Inventors the exclusive Right to their respective Writings and Discoveries.*

Different types of patents are defined:

- *Utility Patent*: Granted to anyone who invents or discovers any new and useful
  process, machine, manufacture, or compositions of matter, or any new and useful
  improvement thereof.
- *Design Patent*: Granted to any person who has invented a new, original and
  ornamental design for an article of manufacture.
- *Plant Patent*: Granted to any person who has invented or discovered and asexually
  reproduced any distinct and new variety of plant, including cultivated sports,
  mutants, hybrids, and newly found seedling, other than a tuber-propagated plant
  or a plant found in an uncultivated state.

Computer Security and Cryptography. By Alan G. Konheim
Copyright © 2007 John Wiley & Sons, Inc.

19.2   PATENTABILITY OF IDEAS

Until 1952, a patentable idea required only *novelty* and *utility*. Congress added *nonobviousness* in that year as a further requirement; 35 U.S.C. §103 provides that

> ... *a patent may not be obtained, although the invention is not identically disclosed or described as set forth in 35 U.S.C. §102, if the differences between the subject matter sought to be patented and the prior art are such that the subject matter as a whole would have been obvious at the time the invention was to a person having ordinary skill in the art to which the subject matter pertains.*

The application of 35 U.S.C. §103 involves the consideration of four factors:

1. The scope and content of the *prior art*;[1]
2. Differences between the prior art and the claims at issue;
3. The level of ordinary skill in the pertinent art; and
4. The obviousness or nonobviousness of the subject.

The evaluation of these four factors is not sharply defined.

19.3   THE FORMAT OF A PATENT

1. *Title Page*
   - Title of the invention;
   - Names of inventors and ownership (e.g., assigned to ...);
   - Prior art; papers, prior patents; cross references to related applications, if any;
   - United States Patent Office Classification Code; for example, 380 (Cryptography);
   - Abstract of the patent, without technical details.
2. *Specification*
   - Detailed disclosure of the invention;
   - Must *describe* the claimed invention;
   - Description must be in clear and concise language to *enable* any person of *ordinary skill in the art*[2] to make and use the invention;
   - Provides the *best mode* contemplated by the inventor(s) of carrying out the invention at the time the patent application is written.
3. *Drawings*
   - To simplify the understanding of the invention; to satisfy the *enablement* requirement.
4. *Claims of the Patent*
   - Sets forth the technology that is to be exclusively owned by the patentee;
   - Generally drafted by a patent attorney, often contains the three C's
   - *Comprising*, including these elements but *not* excluding others;
   - *Consisting of*, narrower interpretation than "comprising";
   - *Consisting essentially of*, a compromise between the first two C's.

[1]Prior art refers to the disclosure of the contents of the patent's claims prior to the application date of the patent.

[2]An individual with a reasonably detailed knowledge of the subject matter in the area of the patent.

The specification is a description of a way in which the inventor intends to implement the invention. It need not be the *only* way in which the invention can be practiced. The description must be such that a person of ordinary skill in the art should be able to build it.

The *Claims* section defines what the inventor believes to be his/her invention.

5. *Validity of the Patent*: The following are some general legal principles regarding patents:

   - Claims are interpreted in the light of the specification, the *file history*[3] and the ordinary meaning of the words in the claims.

   - Claims are not limited to the embodiment(s) shown in the specification, *but* a claim written in a *means plus function* form is limited to the structures/acts shown in the specification and their equivalents.

   - A patent claim is *anticipated* under Section 35, U.S.C §102(b), if the invention was patented or described in a printed publication in this or a foreign country or in public use, more than one year prior to the date of application for patent in the United States.

   - A patent claim is *obvious* under Section 35, U.S.C §103, if the claimed matter would have been obvious to one skilled in the art as of the filing date of the patent.

   - A patent claim is *invalid* under the *enablement* requirement of Section 35, U.S.C §112, ¶1, if the specification fails to set forth sufficient information to enable a person skilled in the relevant art to make and use the full scope of the claimed information without undue experimentation.

   - A patent claim is *invalid* under the *written description* requirement of Section 35, U.S.C §112, ¶1, if the specification fails to set forth sufficient information to convey with reasonable clarity to those skilled in the relevant art that the inventor was in possession of the full scope of the claimed invention.

   - A patent claim is *invalid* as *indefinite* under Section 35, U.S.C §112, ¶1, if those skilled in the art would not be able to understand the full scope of the claim when the claim is read in light of the specification.

19.4   PATENTABLE VERSUS NONPATENTABLE SUBJECTS

The patent statue declares that a *process* is patentable; meaning *process*, *art*, or *methods*, including the new use of a known process, machine, manufacture, composition of matter or material. Naked ideas, independent of the means to carry them out, are *not* patentable. A valid patent may *not* be obtained for an abstract principle, idea, law of nature, or scientific truth. You cannot patent *gravity*, but you *could* patent a process that uses gravity in a novel way. The U.S. Supreme Court is currently examining a patent case related to this issue, diagnosing B vitamin deficiencies by measuring something in the patient's blood.

---

[3]A patent file history contains all documentation relation to the *prosecution* (processing) of a patent application. This provides a detailed history of the entire life of a patent from its application to its issuance.

19.5 INFRINGEMENT

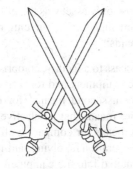

Inventor **A** has a patent. He – how sexist! – claims Infringer **B** is using it without obtaining a license to do so. Inventor **A** claims *infringement*. Infringer **B** claims:

1. What he is doing is different from what Inventor **A** has described in his patent; that is, Infringer **B** does not infringe; and

2. Inventor **A** should never have been granted a patent because someone else was the first to invent this invention; that is, Inventor **A**'s patent claims are not valid.

Crossed Swords (Courtesy TheColoringSpot.com)

A resolution of the dispute is needed. The questions to be answered to decide whether or not infringement has occurred include:

- Do the claims in both patents deal with an identical function? *and*
- Do the patents have the same or equivalent structures/acts?

The dispute is settled by the inventors without a duel in a civilized – albeit more costly – manner in courts, with lawyers doing the dueling.

If the filing date of Inventor **B**'s patent is *before* that of Inventor **A**'s patent *and* Inventor **B**'s patent is valid, there is no infringement. Even if the filing date of Inventor **B**'s (the party of the first part) patent is *after* the filing date of Inventor **A**'s patent (the party of the second part), Inventor **B** may still *not* be guilty of infringement, if it can be shown that

- The invention practiced by Inventor **B** does not *infringe* the claims of the earlier patent of Inventor **A**, or
- The earlier-filed patent of Inventor **A** is invalid because of the *prior art*.

Is that clear? That's why we need lawyers! Nevertheless, this brief patent background should guide us through a review of several specific cryptographic patents.

19.6 THE ROLE OF PATENTS IN CRYPTOGRAPHY

Cryptologia published *United States Cryptographic Patents: 1861–1981*, by Jack Levine, which lists several hundred U.S. patents relating to cryptography spanning two decades:

- #31,902 – Alfred E. Parks – April 2, 1861 ♠ "Telegraph Register".
- #4,308,556 – Hiroshi Osaka – December 29, 1981 ♠ "Television Video Signal Scrambling System".

19.7 U.S. PATENT 3,543,904 [CONSTABLE, 1970]

As described in Chapter 18, a successful ATM transaction involves two ingredients:

1. The account number read from the ATM banking card, and
2. The Personal Identification Number (PIN) entered at the ATM's keyboard.

In the 1980s, the National Cash Register Corporation (NCR) and Chubb Integrated Systems were involved in litigation regarding a claim of patent infringement.

Chubb had purchased Smith Industries Limited whose only asset was the '904 patent (Fig. 19.1). Chubb claimed that NCR's ATM system infringed on its invention of the protocol to validate an ATM-user. Clain 1 in the '904 reads:

1. Access-control equipment for selectively enabling access to a facility, comprising first means[4] for receiving a coded token presented to the equipment and for reading from the token[5] a plurality[6] of numbers encoded thereon, second means[7] for entering separately into the equipment a further number[8] third means that is selectively operable for enabling access to said facility, and fourth means for comparing effectively the numerical result of a predetermined arithmetical operation involving said-numbers read from the token, and the said further number entered into the equipment · · · and means to operate[9] said third means as aforesaid in dependence upon whether a predetermined correspondence exists[10] between said number result and said further number.

There were two trials: The first was to determine if infringement occurred, the second to determine monetary damages. If it can be shown that infringement was intentional, treble (3×) damages may be assessed.

United States Patent [11] 3,543,904

[72]	Inventors	**Geoffrey Ernest Patrick Constable** Cheltenham, England; **Graeme E. Cullen, Castle Douglas,** Scotland; **Richard Swarbrick, Glasgow,** Scotland
[21]	Appl. No.	**710,601**
[22]	Filed	**March 5, 1968**
[45]	Patented	**Dec. 1, 1970**
[73]	Assignee	**Smiths Industries Limited** London, England, a British Company
[32]	Priority	**March 6, 1967**
[33]		**Great Britain**
[31]		**No. 10537/67**

[54] **ACCESS-CONTROL EQUIPMENT AND ITEM-DISPENSING SYSTEMS INCLUDING SUCH EQUIPMENT** 26 Claims, 3 Drawing Figs.

[52] U.S. Cl. 194/4

[51] Int. Cl. G07f 1/06
[50] Field of Search 194/4; 221/2

[56] **References Cited**
UNITED STATES PATENTS

3,401,830	9/1968	Mathews	221/2
3,443,675	5/1969	Yamamoto et al.	194/4

Primary Examiner—Stanley Tollberg
Attorney—Hall, Pollock and Vande Sande

ABSTRACT: A money-dispensing system dispenses a pack of money in response to a bank customer's punched card and keyed entry of his personal identification number, only if that number equals the numerical result of summation without carry of numbers read from the card. Admission of a card to the equipment is barred unless it has a predetermined hole distribution along a leading edge, and dispenser operation is inhibited unless the entered card satisfies a magnetic authenticity check.

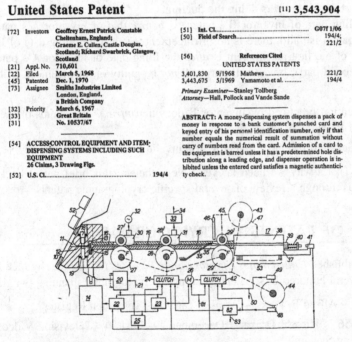

Figure 19.1 '904 patent.

[4]The term *means* in a patent refers to some device for performing some function.

[5]ATM card.

[6]*Plurality*, a multitude, state of being numerous; in the world of patent law, plurality usually just means more than one.

[7]Keyboard for PIN entry.

[8]The PIN.

[9]Dispense cash.

[10]The PIN corresponds to the ATM card number.

The trials were held in Washington, D.C., before Hon. James F. Davis, a retired Federal judge, both litigants agreeing to accept his decision. Several issues were contested; first, the meaning of the words *coded* (as in ASCII) and *encoded* (as in DES) in Claim 1 '904. Judge Davis opined that

- Coding indicated a *representational process* was involved when the PINOffset and ACCT were written on the ATM card;
- *Encoded* in Claim 1 '904 involved some sort of encipherment process;
- The PINOffset and Account_Number (ACCT) were interpreted as the "plurality of numbers" in Claim 1, '904.

The first trial found that NCR did infringe the patent held by Chubb integrated Systems; the second trial decided on a damage figure.

19.8 U.S. PATENT 4,200,770 [HELLMAN ET AL., 1977]

The *anticipation* requirement Section 35, U.S.C. § 102(b), requires that an application for a U.S. patent be filed within one year of *disclosure* of the invention. When Diffie and Hellman discovered public key cryptography, they presented their ideas at various meetings, including a conference in mid-June 1976 [Diffie and Hellman, 1976] more than a

United States Patent [19]

Hellman et al.

[11] **4,200,770**

[45] **Apr. 29, 1980**

[54] CRYPTOGRAPHIC APPARATUS AND METHOD

[75] Inventors: Martin E. Hellman, Stanford; Bailey W. Diffie, Berkeley; Ralph C. Merkle, Palo Alto, all of Calif.

[73] Assignee: Stanford University, Palo Alto, Calif.

[21] Appl. No.: 830,754

[22] Filed: Sep. 6, 1977

[51] Int. Cl.^{2} H04L 9/04
[52] U.S. Cl. .... 178/22; 340/149 R; 375/2; 455/26
[58] Field of Search .... 178/22; 340/149 R

[56] **References Cited**
PUBLICATIONS

"New Directions in Cryptography", Diffie et al., *IEEE Transactions on Information Theory*, vol. IT–22, No. 6, Nov. 1976.
Diffie & Hellman, Multi–User Cryptographic Techniques", *AFIPS Conference Proceedings*, vol. 45, pp. 109–112, Jun. 8, 1976.

Primary Examiner—Howard A. Birmiel
Attorney, Agent, or Firm—Flehr, Hohbach, Test

[57] **ABSTRACT**

A cryptographic system transmits a computationally secure cryptogram over an insecure communication channel without prearrangement of a cipher key. A secure cipher key is generated by the conversers from transformations of exchanged transformed signals. The conversers each possess a secret signal and exchange an initial transformation of the secret signal with the other converser. The received transformation of the other converser's secret signal is again transformed with the receiving converser's secret signal to generate a secure cipher key. The transformations use non-secret operations that are easily performed but extremely difficult to invert. It is infeasible for an eavesdropper to invert the initial transformation to obtain either conversers' secret signal, or duplicate the latter transformation to obtain the secure cipher key.

8 Claims, 6 Drawing Figures

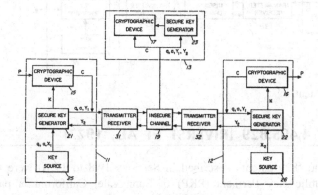

Figure 19.2 '770 patent.

year before the '770 patent application was filed. Whether a technical talk or conference constitutes disclosure in the sense of Section 35 U.S.C. §102(b) is a legal issue matter for litigation. As their invention was described at various public events, the validity of their patent was open to question.

19.9 U.S. PATENT 4,218,582 [HELLMAN AND MERKLE, 1977]

United States Patent [19]
Hellman et al.

[11]   **4,218,582**
[45]   **Aug. 19, 1980**

[54] **PUBLIC KEY CRYPTOGRAPHIC APPARATUS AND METHOD**

[75] Inventors: Martin E. Hellman, Stanford; Ralph C. Merkle, Palo Alto, both of Calif.

[73] Assignee: The Board of Trustees of the Leland Stanford Junior University, Stanford, Calif.

[21] Appl. No.: 839,939

[22] Filed: Oct. 6, 1977

[51] Int. Cl.² H04L 9/04
[52] U.S. Cl. 178/22; 364/900
[58] Field of Search 178/22

[56]   **References Cited**
       PUBLICATIONS

"New Directions in Cryptography," Diffie et al., *IEEE Transactions on Information Theory,* vol. II22, No. 6, Nov. 1976, pp. 644–654.
"A User Authentication Scheme not Requiring Secrecy in the Computer," Evans, Jr., et al., *Communications of the ACM,* Aug. 1974, vol. 17, No. 8, pp. 437–442.
"A High Security Log-In Procedure," Purdy, *Commu-* *nications of the ACM,* Aug. 1974, vol. 17, No. 8, pp. 442–445.
Diffie et al., "Multi-User Cryptographic Techniques," *AFIPS Conference Proceedings,* vol. 45, pp. 109–112, Jun. 8, 1976.

Primary Examiner—Howard A. Birmiel

[57]   **ABSTRACT**

A cryptographic system transmits a computationally secure cryptogram that is generated from a publicly known transformation of the message sent by the transmitter; the cryptogram is again transformed by the authorized receiver using a secret reciprocal transformation to reproduce the message sent. The authorized receiver's transformation is known only by the authorized receiver and is used to generate the transmitter's transformation that is made publicly known. The publicly known transformation uses operations that are easily performed but extremely difficult to invert. It is infeasible for an unauthorized receiver to invert the publicly known transformation or duplicate the authorized receiver's secret transformation to obtain the message sent.

17 Claims, 13 Drawing Figures

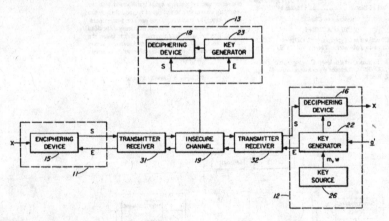

Figure 19.3   '582 patent.

19.10 U.S. PATENT 4,405,829 [RIVERST ET AL., 1977]

The '770, '582, and '829 patents described in Sections 19.8 to 19.10 were to be the motherlode for Public Key Partners (PKP) of Sunnyvale, California, a partnership between *RSA Data Security Incorporated* (RSADSI), now shorted to RSA and Caro-Kahn,

Incorporated, the parent corporation of Cylink. In [Fougner, 1999], PKP's licensing officer claimed that these patents

> *... cover all known methods of practicing the art of Public Key, including the variations collectively known as El Gamal.*

Oink, Oink, Oink!

... and if you exponentiate, you will pay, pay, pay!

United States Patent [19]

Rivest et al.

[11]   **4,405,829**

[45]   **Sep. 20, 1983**

[54] **CRYPTOGRAPHIC COMMUNICATIONS SYSTEM AND METHOD**

[75] Inventors: **Ronald L. Rivest**, Belmont; **Adi Shamir**, Cambridge; **Leonard M. Adleman**, Arlington, all of Mass.

[73] Assignee: **Massachusetts Institute of Technology**, Cambridge, Mass.

[21] Appl. No.: **860,586**

[22] Filed: **Dec. 14, 1977**

[51] **Int. Cl.³** H04K 1/00; H04I 9/04
[52] **U.S. Cl.** 178/22.1; 178/22.11
[58] **Field of Search** 178/22, 22.1, 22.11, 178/22.14, 22.15

[56]   **References Cited**

U.S. PATENT DOCUMENTS

3,657,476   4/1972   Aiken 178/22

OTHER PUBLICATIONS

"New Directions in Cryptography", Diffie et al., *IEEE Transactions on Information Theory*, vol. IT–22, No. 6, Nov. 1976, pp. 644–654.
"Theory of Numbers" Stewart, MacMillan Co., 1952, pp. 133–135.
"Diffie et al., Multi–User Cryptographic Techniques", AFIPS. Conference Proceedings, vol. 45, pp. 109–112, Jun. 8, 1976.

Primary Examiner—Sal Cangialosi
Attorney, Agent, or Firm—Arthur A. Smith, Jr.; Robert J. Horn, Jr.

[57]   **ABSTRACT**

A cryptographic communications system and method. The system includes a communications channel coupled to at least one terminal having an encoding device and to at least one terminal having a decoding device. A message-to-be-transferred is enciphered to ciphertext at the encoding terminal by first encoding the message as a number M in a predetermined set, and then raising that number to a first predetermined power (associated with the intended receiver) and finally computing the remainder, or residue, C, when the exponentiated number is divided by the product of two predetermined prime numbers (associated with the intended receiver). The residue C is the ciphertext. The ciphertext is deciphered to the original message at the decoding terminal in a similar manner by raising the ciphertext to a second predetermined power (associated with the intended receiver), and then computing the residue, M′, when the exponentiated ciphertext is divided by the product of the two predetermined prime numbers associated with the intended receiver. The residue M′ corresponds to the original encoded message M.

40 Claims, 7 Drawing Figures

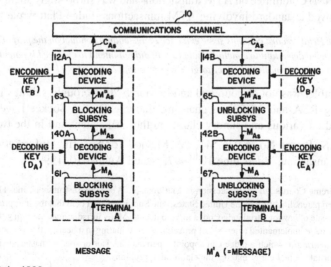

Figure 19.4 '829 patent.

Ultimately, the "partners" had a falling out, primarily because PKP was not able to receive royalties from their licensing of RSADSI products and after all … the Merkle–Hellman knapsack system seemed like an unlikely source of riches.

19.11   PKS/RSADSI LITIGATION

When the "partners" had a falling out, litigation was pursued. The matter ultimately reached the United States District Court for the Northern District of California.

A *Markman hearing*[11] was held in October 1996 before the Hon. Judge Spencer Williams. It consisted of tutorials on cryptography to provide the judge with an understanding of the technical issues. It was the position of PKP that Claims 1 to 6 of the '582 patient established their right to *all* public key cryptosystems. RSADSI advanced the view that the '582 claims were means plus function claims and that they were limited to the knapsack cryptosystem described in the specification. Often the courts will decide that a patent revealing a new technology should be given great latitude in its claims. The parties negotiated a settlement before the issue was resolved.

19.12   LEON STAMBLER

Leon Stambler is an engineer who had been employed at RCA Laboratories; he is retired now and lives in Parkland, Florida. Mr. Stambler is also a prolific inventor and has been issued many patents. Mr. Stambler sued Diebold Incorporated, NCR Corporation, and Manufacturers Hanover Trust claiming infringement of U.S. Patent No. 5,793,302: "A Method for Securing Information Relevant to a Transaction", filed November 12, 1996, issued August 11, 1998. Mr. Stambler claimed that the use of the PIN in ATM transactions by these defendants infringed the claims made in his '302 patent.

His suit was *not* successful; Hon. Judge Thomas C. Platt invoked the doctrine of *estoppel* in writing his opinion in the U.S. District Court for the Eastern District of New York. *Equitable estoppel* refers to a situation when a patent holder makes a misleading communication and subsequently a purported infringer relies on this to carry out his business practice. It appears that Mr. Stambler had been a member of an American National Standards Institutes (ANSI) Committee on ATM transactions and was surprisingly silent when the committee approved a standard involving ATM transactions. Judge Platt wrote that

> The [trial] record contains some evidence of misleading conduct on the part of the plaintiff that may have led defendant to conclude that plaintiff did not intend to enforce his patent. Silence alone is not sufficient affirmative conduct to give rise to estoppel.

Mr. Stambler was not discouraged and in March 2001 brought suit against various parties including RSA and VeriSign, charging that the Secure Socket Layer (SSL) protocol infringed on various and sundry claims in the '301 patent and in the two patents

- U.S. Patent No. 5,936,541, "A Method for Securing Information Relevant to a Transaction," filed June 10, 1997, issued August 10, 1999.

[11]The Supreme Court's landmark decision in Markman V. Westview Instruments, Inc. 116 S.Ct. 1384 (1996) transformed patent litigation in the United States. The Supreme Court held that the interpretation of patent claims is now an issue of law for a trial judge, not a jury, to decide. Many jurisdictions, including the Northern District of California, have implemented a new set of procedures, culminating in a hearing that is commonly referred to as a *Markman hearing* in which a judge can appoint a personal advisor or special master to either address technical concerns or take a first cut at making the claim interpretations.

- U.S. Patent No. 5,974,148, "A Method for Securing Information Relevant to a Transaction," filed May 13, 1997, issued October 26, 1999.

Mr. Stambler drafted new claims intended to encompass technologies commercialized by other inventors after the filing date of his patent!

Bruce Schneier refers to Stambler's '148 patent as a *submarine patent*, a patent published long after the original application was filed. Like a submarine, the patent remains unpublished for several years and then emerges – is granted and published. This practice is generally only possible under U.S. patent law, and to a very limited extent since the U.S. signed WTO's TRIPs agreements, making compulsory the publication of patent applications 18 months after their filing or priority date. Submarine patents are considered by many to be a procedural lache (a delay in enforcing one's rights, which may cause the rights to be lost). This practice is not new with Mr. Stambler; it was popularized by the Nevada inventor Jerome Lemelson, who holds more than 450 patents.

Mr. Stambler asked for damages of $20,000,000. A trial resulted in March 2003 in the courtroom of the Hon. Sue L. Robinson, United States District Court in Wilmington (Delaware). There were to be two segments in the trial; the first, to decide if RSA and Veri-Sign did infringe on one or more of the claims in the Stambler patents. The second segment – if needed – was to question whether or not *prior art* rendered the claims in these patents invalid. The second trial never took place as the jury decided that the practice of SSL did *not* infringe Mr. Stambler's patents. Why?

As described in Chapter 18, in the Secure Socket Layer (SSL), the Server (e.g., *amazon.com*) delivers its certificate to the Client (e.g., *konheim@ucsb.edu*) in the second phase of an SSL transaction. As the intent is to establish the validity of the Server's public key, the Server's certificate alone does not accomplish this. It must be accompanied by the certificate of the Certificate Authority (CA) that issued the Server's certificate. In the practice of the *real* SSL, the certificate of the CA (e.g., VeriSign), which issued the Server's certificate, resides in the Server's browser. The jury found that the real SSL did not infringe on the invention claimed by Mr. Stambler. The shareholders of RSA and VeriSign could once again sleep soundly.

REFERENCES

W. DIFFIE AND M. E. HELLMAN, "Multiuser Cryptographic Techniques," *National Computer Conference* (New York, NY), **45**, 1976.

R. B. FOUGNER, "Public Key Standards and Licenses", RFC 1170, January 1991.

M. E. HELLMAN AND R. C. MERKLE, U.S. Patent No. 4,218,582, "Public Key Cryptographic Apparatus and Method", Filed October 6, 1977; Issued August 19, 1980.

M. E. HELLMAN B. W. DIFFIE, AND R. C. MERKLE, U.S. Patent No. 4,200,770, "Cryptographic Apparatus and Method", Filed September 6, 1977; Issued April 29, 1980.

G. E. P. CONSTABLE, U.S. Patent No. 3,543,904, "Access-Control Equipment and Item-Dispensing Systems Including Such Equipment", Filed March 5, 1968; Issued December 1, 1970.

R. L. RIVEST, A. SHAMIR, AND M. ADLEMAN, U.S. Patent No. 4,405,829, "Cryptographic Communications System and Method", Filed December 14, 1977; Issued September 20, 1983.

U.S. Patent No. 4,218,582, "Public Key Cryptographic Apparatus and Method", Martin E. Hellman and Ralph C. Merkle; Filed, October 6, 1977; Issued August 19, 1980, United States Patent Office.

U.S. Patent No. 4,200,770, "Cryptographic Apparatus and Method", Martin E. Hellman, Bailey W. Diffie and Ralph C. Merkle; Filed, September 6, 1977; Issued April 29, 1980, United States Patent Office.

U.S. Patent No. 3,543,904, "Access-Control Equipment and Item-Dispensing Systems Including Such Equipment", Geoffrey Ernest Patrick Constable; Filed March 5, 1968; Issued December 1, 1970; United States Patent Office.

U.S. Patent No. 4,405,829, "Cryptographic Communications System and Method", Ronald L. Rivest, Adi Shamir and Leonard M. Adleman; Filed December 14, 1977; Issued September 20, 1983; United States Patent Office.

INDEX